D0953480

FEMINIST PERSPECTIVES ON EATING DISORDERS

Feminist Perspectives on Eating Disorders

Edited by
PATRICIA FALLON
MELANIE A. KATZMAN
SUSAN C. WOOLEY

THE GUILFORD PRESS
New York   London

© 1994 The Guilford Press

Chapter 5 © 1991 Naomi Wolf
Chapter 20 © 1994 Jean Kilbourne

Published in 1994 by The Guilford Press
A Division of Guilford Publications, Inc.
72 Spring Street, New York, NY 10012

All rights reserved

No part of this book may be reproduced, stored in a retrieval system, or transmitted, in any form or by any means, electronic, mechanical, photocopying, microfilming, recording, or otherwise, without written permission from the Publisher.

Printed in the United States of America

This book is printed on acid-free paper.

Last digit is print number: 9 8 7 6 5 4 3 2

Library of Congress Cataloging-in-Publication Data

Feminist perspectives on eating disorders / edited by Patricia Fallon,
   Melanie A. Katzman, Susan C. Wooley.
      p.   cm.
   Includes bibliographical references and index.
   ISBN 0-89862-180-1
   1. Eating disorders—Social aspects.   2. Feminist therapy.
3. Women—Psychology.   4. Body image.   5. Feminist criticism.
6. Fallon, Patricia.   7. Katzman, Melanie.   8. Wooley, Susan.
RC552.E18F46   1993
616.85'26'0082—dc20
                                                     93-23951
                                                        CIP

Contents

II. A PLACE FOR THE FEMALE BODY

III. TREATMENT ISSUES: A FEMINIST REANALYSIS

IV. RECONSTRUCTING THE FEMALE TEXT

V. POSSIBILITY

Knowing My Place

. . . the work . . . the life must have their origins in a
place of conviction for the poet. It is a known place, full
of meaning for the poet. What he is and does takes vitality
from the certainty of that place.

—John Haines

As a woman I have no country.
—Virginia Woolf

I am beginning to know my place:
my place is woman.

Making my maps as I go,
on foot, without benefit of compass
or clock, often on hands and knees
I am exploring the difficult
terrain, the once-green valleys
defoliated, the ancient mountains,
strip-mined, strip-mind.

I am becoming a regional writer
learning the secrets
of the neither regions:
womb/tomb
madonna/whore
woman/writer,

but to say the secrets in English,
Man/glish really makes me tongue-tied,

I am beginning to speak Broken English,
the speaking is breaking me open.
They will call me half-cracked
when they see the flames leaping
the fury tongues, fiery tongues.
This pentecost is costing me plenty
but it is worth the price,

it is a miracle without device
the miracle of taking place, making place
where I can speak/write/sing
without shame
my earliest, my beloved,
my Mother tongue.

MARY PIERCE BROSMER (1988)

Introduction

It is strange, really, that this book should be among the first collections of feminist writings on eating disorders,[1] and stranger still that it should serve as the occasion for many contributors to write their first explicitly feminist pieces. For although feminist perspectives have informed this field since its inception—commanding increasing attention in recent years—a list of published works with a feminist orientation could easily fit on the cocktail napkins used at conference receptions where women, hungry for such ideas, eagerly seek each other out.

One may speculate about the role of gender in many conditions, but in the case of eating disorders, where nearly all the sufferers are female, the importance of gender is beyond debate. However, the exact way in which gender predisposes women to eating disorders is the crucial mystery of our field. In the past 15 years, as bulimia nervosa has emerged from the shadows to become, along with anorexia nervosa, among the most publicized disorders of our time, theorists have been challenged to account for both their increasing prevalence and their power to symbolize widespread cultural concerns. To many, there was an obvious resonance between the acute anguish of eating disorder sufferers and the troubles of ordinary women. In an important sense, eating-disordered women had become the eyes and ears for a generation—repositories of unarticulated cultural information that fell just beyond our ability to define. Anorexic and bulimic women carried our deepest fears but expressed them in a bodily language—arguably, our "mother tongue"—from which we had grown remote. We would spend over a decade piecing together its grammar, syntax, and vocabulary.

Initial formulations of the sociocultural meaning of eating disorders were limited to the now-conventional observation that appearance norms had become increasingly oppressive. In less than two decades the acceptable female body size had been whittled down by one-third, and most women could no longer fit into it. Attempts to do so commanded more and more of their time, leading some theorists to speculate that weight norms had become a purposeful form of female oppression. Other observers asked what the new thin female body symbolized and came up with a fascinating array of answers. Many suggested that the pursuit of thinness was a form of "male impersonation," in which women cut their ties with the traditionally generous female body. Women who aspired to share with men the ability to influence culture had first to symbolically deny their "otherness," before a true place could be made for it. Still others found in the gaunt female body an association with other historical events and images, such as religious traditions of asceticism, earlier female maladies, escape from sexuality, and a return to childhood.

Therapists who worked with eating-disordered women became increasingly sensitive to the difficulties of wrestling with historically oppressive social roles now undergoing rapid change. Cast as lifelong caregivers in nearly every known society, women understandably feel unentitled to much that men take for granted. Our era's culminating demand that women give up nourishment and a large share of their bodies pushed many to an apparent point of no return. They did not know what to return to; depleted by the sacrifices exacted from them, they lacked the energy to do so even if they had known. Rehearsing her sterile dilemma with the sole props of food and a scale, an eating-disordered woman expressed her need through binges, her guilt through purges, and her will to succeed through starvation.

The new opportunities that the culture offered often proved unattainable or unendurable. Expectations of the good wife and mother diminished not at all, and may even have escalated, as women added to their lives the demands of careers. But time allotment was not the worst of it. Not only did a woman's dual roles make uncompromising claims on her time and energy, but they made seemingly irreconcilable demands to define who she was. Required at home to subjugate achievement and personal gain to relationships, she was encouraged in the workplace to transcend her "emotional nature" and just get the job done. No sooner had research by female scholars begun to discover and define women's gender-based skills, than women felt called upon to abandon them.

Together with other social change came the uncovering of high rates of sexual abuse among women in general, and eating-disordered women in particular. Sexual violation made women long to escape their bodies, trapping them in shame and silence. Gradually it became clear that women's roles as secret bearers constituted a powerful impediment to their voices, and encouraged metaphorical, bodily expressions of experience that were too dangerous to name. Expansion of roles had made it possible for many women to leave abusive domestic situations, and therefore to speak, but had also raised questions about the required degree of allegiance to a code of silence as a condition of success in predominantly male spheres. Could a woman who endangered men hope to survive in their world? Few women knew.

Eating disorders symbolize both the degree to which role demands have fractured female experience, and women's need to integrate parts of themselves into more powerful, whole persons who can make themselves heard. Multiple personality disorder—in which the development of distinct selves has proved necessary for psychic survival—appears likely to succeed eating disorders as the illness that rivets public attention, and understandably so. It provides a compelling metaphor for an age in which women's identities line up like frozen images in a trail behind them. Fragmentation of the self is perhaps an unavoidable consequence of the intergenerational discontinuity, impossibly conflicting role demands, and high rates of assault on the female body that are features of our age.

A FEMINIST VIEW

Eating-disordered women and their therapists have been grappling with these issues—and many more—for well over a decade now. A body of knowledge has evolved that has still to be fully set down. This volume is one step in that direction. We have the sense that this book probably could have been written by women whom we do not know or did not think to include—that the ideas recorded here are part of an intellectual and cultural shift in which female experience is given more credence. We would like to acknowledge the energy and ideas of the many women whose knowledge informs this work. If this book serves no other purpose, it will at least help like-minded people to find each other.

But just as there is a community of practitioners and scholars contributing from diverse areas of thought to further a contextual understanding of eating disorders, there has also been some undeniable antagonism to feminist thought. Some of the chapters in this book address schisms that have developed between feminist and more traditional views—schisms that will become clearer and perhaps more troublesome as feminist views are more clearly formulated, making comparison possible and necessary. This process may be labeled divisive by some, but we believe that it is rejuvenating and essential to growth of the field.

Our struggle as a field to acknowledge, name, and integrate female experience mirrors struggles in many other fields and in the larger culture. Growing pressures to admit feminist and other new streams of thought are not unique to our field. In an invited address to the Division of General Psychology of the American Psychological Association, Kenneth Gergen (1992) pointed to the emerging postmodern consensus that since truth is socially constructed, it is better served by inclusiveness and diversity. "The very idea of a 'mainstream psychology' is suspect," he said. "In effect there is no distinction to be made between psychological and cultural activity" (p. 14).

Since feminist models are in the process of emerging, it is neither possible nor desirable to define them with precision. Why build a fence around a garden of still-unknown shape? We can, however, say that in choosing pieces for this book, we considered a feminist view to contain one or more of the following elements:

1. *The concepts or methods described are based upon the psychology of women.* Most of the authors in this book have gone beyond "general" or "gender-free" psychology, knowing that it is not in fact gender-neutral, but establishes male development as a norm against which female development is viewed and usually found deficient. A recent examination of sexism in the psychology literature notes that only 10% of the studies surveyed hypothesized gender differences, and that in only 10% of studies employing a single-sex sample was a reason given (Gannon, Luchetta, Rhodes, Pardie, & Segrist, 1992). The authors noted that emphasis on gender as a focus of study is controversial even among feminists, and reiterated Wittig's (1985) argument that the debate is really about metatheoretical perspectives—scholarship versus advocacy, science versus humanism, objectivity versus subjectivity. We feel that a special case can be made for attention to gender differences in the study of eating disorders. There is an important and growing literature on the psychology of women; this work is especially relevant because of its focus on gender-specific changes in adolescence, which coincide with the period of greatest vulnerability to eating disorders.

2. *There is an explicit commitment to political and social equality for women.* This simple premise carries more implications for research and practice within an area than are usually immediately apparent. For example, when the members of the self-created "Women's Project" in family therapy (Walters, Carter, Papp, & Silverstein, 1988) undertook to examine the gender implications of practices within their field, they easily filled a decade with their task; meanwhile, many other women in the field undertook parallel examinations (e.g., Luepnitz, 1988; Goldner, 1985; McGoldrick, Anderson, & Walsh, 1988; Avis, 1985; Hare-Mustin, 1978; Bograd, 1984). By 1989, this work had resulted in the launching of the *Journal of Feminist Family Therapy.* The field was forever changed.

Gender assumptions are deeply embedded in all aspects of the practice of psychology, and in none more than in eating disorders. A commitment to political and social equality for women implies a critical reanalysis of theoretical assumptions with an eye to their proximal and remote influences on girls and women, and an equally critical appraisal of all aspects of practice. Some of the better-developed areas to date include the study of sociocultural appearance and behavior norms that are oppressive to women; analyses of the power structures of families; advocacy of the rights and needs of victims of physical and sexual abuse; and the intersection between psychotherapy and political consciousness raising and empowerment.

3. *There is a re-evaluation of therapy, based upon understanding of the needs of women patients and the potentially differing contributions of male and female therapists.* Many assumptions about therapy owe more than we usually acknowledge to the fact that the therapy tradition was largely shaped by male theorists using an androcentric model of development. Therapies conducted by and for women have often, though not always, moved away from the passive and neutral stance of traditional therapies; have generally been more interactive, capitalizing on the capacities of both patient and therapist; and have tended to put greater emphasis on women's interpersonal relationships as a focus of concern. None of these changes is unique to feminist therapy, and none is universally endorsed by feminists, but all are overarching trends.

Concern with the gender-appropriateness of specific therapies also increases attention to the gender implications of the way programs are staffed; the existence of gender hierarchies in treatment teams; and the impact of gender-stereotypic behaviors of male and female therapists. As thinking in this area matures, there is likely to be a shift—indeed, such a shift is already noticeable—from criticism of existing practices to increasingly intentional and creative uses of therapist gender.

ORGANIZATION OF THE BOOK

In planning this book, we were not overly concerned with definitions of feminism or with the final structure of the book. We encouraged writers we knew to have an interest in gender to write *something,* and we tried to find *someone* to write on topics that suggested themselves as we went along. Unlike most anthologies in the field, this one contains work by new authors as well as by many already known for their work in the area. We feel especially pleased that this book allows new voices to be heard and old ones to speak more freely on the topics of their choice.

The first section of the book, "A Gendered Disorder: Lessons from History," examines a number of historical and social issues plausibly related to eating disorders. We doubted that the subject of the sociocultural contributions to eating disorders had been exhausted; in fact, we suspected that the surface had barely been scratched. The chapters in this section more than justify that faith, expanding some lines of inquiry and opening up many new ones. The history of fashion, the history of male conceptual and artistic representations of the female body, the history and impact of appearance norms for women, and the history of predominantly female maladies are all examined for the light they shed on our current dilemma. Naomi Wolf's persuasive discussion of hunger as a phenomenon of backlash is also reprinted from her book *The Beauty Myth*.

The next section, "A Place for the Female Body," looks at the problems that having a body constitutes for the female patient and therapist—minor, we realize, when compared to the problems of not having one, but important nonetheless. One chapter weaves a compelling narrative of a female therapist's own multigenerational history of body image development. Another explores the problems and opportunities associated with therapist pregnancy. The last describes a feminist approach to treating body image disturbance, which was among the earliest feminist approaches within the field.

The third section, "Treatment Issues: A Feminist Reanalysis," looks at a number of old issues from a new point of view. Application of a feminist perspective changes the questions asked and leads to different conclusions on many subjects: sexual abuse and the controversy regarding its relevance to eating disorders; fatness, fitness, and health; the use of medications in eating disorder treatment; the role of hospitalization and suggestions for maximizing its benefits; the mother–daughter relationship, which has been so negatively depicted in our literature; and Twelve-Step programs, which have long been a controversial topic among feminist therapists.

The fourth section, "Reconstructing the Female Text," introduces some female voices not usually heard: the voices of adolescent girls pondering their bodies; the voice of the female therapist as she tries to define what is different—and right—about therapy done by a woman; and the diverse voices of women whose experiences have often been excluded by assumptions about the "modal" patient.

The final section, "Possibility," discusses the complexity of preventing a disorder mired in gender politics; of influencing "culture" through control of advertising images; of educational approaches to prevention; and of a thoughtfully defined feminist research agenda. These chapters pull together much that we know, while also calling attention to the current limits of knowledge.

ACKNOWLEDGMENTS

Editing this book was harder than we expected, and also more rewarding. We have had no other opportunity to read so much that is so original. It was gratifying to help get this material out of people's minds and hearts (and, as one author notes, the women's bathroom) and into the light of day. We learned some things about ourselves. For example, we supported one current theory about women by our relative lack of concern over failures to meet achievement deadlines, as well as our intense shame when some aspect of our work exposed a relationship problem in which one of us was implicated. We feel quite certain that we talked more than male coeditors of similar anthologies (racking up over 100 hours in conference calls), but cannot determine whether this reflects the greater difficulty of nudging such a work into existence or our boundless enjoyment of conversation. We saw two children born and another off to college, and still the book was lodged in the birth canal. We struggled with our desire to be free of the constraints of our training and our great difficulty in relinquishing old habits. "Loosen up," we invited our authors; then we complained about citations of nonoriginal sources and reversals of "and's" and "&'s". We fantasized at one point that the contributors had formed a support group to cope with our excessively "hands-on" approach and conflicting directives.

We thank the authors, who have taken many risks and shown their brilliance. We believe that readers will find many breaths of fresh air. We thank our female colleagues around the country for all we have learned from them. We thank our patients, who patiently taught us to do therapy; we now understand how they got that name. We thank our colleagues, some of whom helped us by editing our own chapters, and many of whom gracefully endured the extra responsibilities that at times resulted from our preoccupation with this book. We thank Zita Flannery, Wilma Shulman, Allyson Thompson, and Laura Kastner for their unflagging support. And we thank our husbands, Wayne Wooley, Dan Coleman, and Russell Makowsky, who were also extremely patient; wherever this book falls short, however, the blame should be laid squarely on them.

S.C.W.
P.F.
M.A.K.

NOTE

1. There have been several important anthologies on fatness and weight obsession: for example, *A Woman's Conflict: The Special Relationship between Women and Food* (Kaplan, 1980); *Shadow on a Tightrope: Writings by Women on Fat Oppression* (Schoenfielder & Weiser, 1983); and *Fat Oppression and Psychotherapy: A Feminist Perspective* (Brown & Rothblum, 1989). There is also at least one, *Fed Up and Hungry: Women, Oppression and Food* (Lawrence, 1987), on eating disorders. In addition, we are aware of some parallel efforts that will probably reach print at about the same time as this book.

REFERENCES

Avis, J. M. (1985). The politics of functional family therapy: A feminist critique. *Journal of Marital and Family Therapy, 11,* 127–138.

Bograd, M. (1984). Family systems approaches to wife battering: A feminist critique. *American Journal of Orthopsychiatry, 54,* 558–568.

Brown, L., & Rothblum, E. (Eds.). (1989). Fat oppression and psychotherapy: A feminist perspective [Special issue]. *Women and Therapy, 8*(3).

Gannon, L., Luchetta, T., Rhodes, K., Pardie, L., & Segrist, D. (1992). Sex bias in psychological research: Progress or complacency? *American Psychologist, 47*(3), 389–396.

Gergen, K. (1992). Psychology in the postmodern era. *The General Psychologist, 28*(3), 10–15.

Goldner, V. (1985). Feminism and family therapy. *Family Process, 24,* 31–47.

Hare-Mustin, R. C. (1978). A feminist approach to family therapy. *Family Process, 17,* 181–194.

Kaplan, J. R. (Ed.). (1980). *A woman's conflict: The special relationship between women and food.* Englewood Cliffs, NJ: Prentice-Hall.

Lawrence, M. (Ed.). (1987). *Fed up and hungry: Women, oppression and food.* New York: Peter Bedricks.

Luepnitz, D. A. (1988). *The family interpreted.* New York: Basic Books.

McGoldrick, M., Anderson, C., & Walsh, F. (Eds.). (1988). *Women in families: A framework for family therapy.* New York: Norton.

Schoenfielder, L., & Weiser, B. (1983). *Shadow on a tightrope: Writings by women on fat oppression.* Iowa City, IA: Ann Lute.

Walters, M., Carter, B., Papp, P., & Silverstein, O. (1988). *The invisible web: Gender patterns in family relationships.* New York: Guilford Press.

Wittig, M. A. (1985). Metatheoretical dilemmas in the psychology of gender. *American Psychologist, 40,* 800–811.

Contributors

BONITA BRIGMAN, PhD, Department of Family Therapy, Eating Disorders Program, Saint Albans Psychiatric Hospital, Radford, VA; private practice, Virginia Highland Health Associates, Radford, VA, and Blacksburg, VA

DEBORA BURGARD, PhD, former Director of Clinical Services, Woodside Women's Hospital, Redwood City, CA; staff psychologist, Counseling Center, Santa Clara University, Santa Clara, CA; private practice, Palo Alto, CA

MARJORIE CRAGO, PhD, Research Specialist, Health Services Section, Department of Family and Community Medicine, College of Medicine, University of Arizona, Tucson, AZ

ELIZABETH DEBOLD, MEd, Research Associate, Project on Women's Psychology and Girls' Development, Graduate School of Education, Harvard University, Cambridge, MA

PATRICIA FALLON, PhD, private practice, Seattle, WA; Clinical Faculty, Department of Psychology, University of Washington, Seattle, WA

MARCIA GERMAINE HUTCHINSON, EdD, private practice, Sherborn, MA

MELANIE A. KATZMAN, PhD, private practice, New York, NY; Clinical Faculty, Department of Psychiatry, New York Hospital–Cornell Medical Center, New York, NY

JEAN KILBOURNE, EdD, Visiting Scholar, Stone Center, Wellesley College, Wellesley, MA

PAT LYONS, RN, MA, Regional Health Education Consultant, Northern California Kaiser Permanente, Oakland, CA

JAMES E. MITCHELL, MD, Professor, Department of Psychiatry, University of Minnesota Medical School, Minneapolis, MN

DEBORAH PERLICK, PhD, Associate Professor, Department of Psychiatry, Cornell University Medical College, White Plains, NY; Director of Psychology, Outpatient Department, New York Hospital–Cornell Medical Center, White Plains, NY

LINDA PETERS, PhD, private practice, Seattle, WA

JUDITH RUSKAY RABINOR, PhD, Consultant, Eating Disorders Treatment Unit, Holliswood Hospital, Holliswood, NY; Supervisor, Center for the Study of Anorexia and Bulimia, New York, NY; private practice, Lido Beach, NY

NANCY C. RAYMOND, MD, Assistant Professor, Department of Psychiatry, University of Minnesota Medical School, Minneapolis, MN

ESTHER D. ROTHBLUM, PhD, Professor, Department of Psychology, University of Vermont, Burlington, VT

ROBERTA P. SEID, PhD, Lecturer, Program for the Study of Women and Men in Society, University of Southern California, Los Angeles, CA

ROBIN SESAN, PhD, Director, Brandywine Psychotherapy Center, Wilmington, DE

CATHERINE M. SHISSLAK, PhD, Associate Professor, Health Services Section, Department of Family and Community Medicine, University of Arizona, Tucson, AZ

BRETT SILVERSTEIN, PhD, Associate Professor, Department of Psychology, City College of New York, NY

CATHERINE STEINER-ADAIR, EdD, Faculty, The Family Institute of Cambridge, Watertown, MA; Research Associate, Project on Women's Psychology and Girls' Development, Graduate School of Education, Harvard University, Cambridge, MA; private practice, Lexington, MA

RUTH H. STRIEGEL-MOORE, PhD, Assistant Professor, Department of Psychology, Wesleyan University, Middletown, CT

BECKY THOMPSON, PhD, Assistant Professor, Department of Sociology and Center for Research on Women, Memphis State University, Memphis, TN

DEBORAH L. TOLMAN, EdD, Visiting Research Scholar, Center for Research on Women, Wellesley College, Wellesley, MA; Lecturer, Graduate School of Education, and Research Associate, Project on Women's Psychology and Girls' Development, Graduate School of Education, Harvard University, Cambridge, MA

KATHERINE VAN WORMER, MSSW, PhD, Associate Professor, Department of Social Work, University of Northern Iowa, Cedar Falls, IA

NAOMI WOLF, BA, Yale University, New Haven, CT; Rhodes Scholar, New College, Oxford University, Oxford, U.K.

O. WAYNE WOOLEY, PhD, Associate Professor of Psychology and Co-director, Eating Disorders Clinic, University of Cincinnati College of Medicine, Cincinnati, OH

SUSAN C. WOOLEY, PhD, Professor of Psychiatry and Co-director, Eating Disorders Clinic, University of Cincinnati College of Medicine, Cincinnati, OH

FEMINIST PERSPECTIVES ON EATING DISORDERS

I

A GENDERED DISORDER:
LESSONS FROM HISTORY

1

Too "Close to the Bone": The Historical Context for Women's Obsession with Slenderness

ROBERTA P. SEID

W HY HAVE AMERICANS, particularly American women, become fatphobic? Why and how have they come to behave as though the shape of their lives depends on the shape of their bodies? Why have they clung to these beliefs despite the toll they take on private lives, and especially despite their most extreme and dangerous manifestation, eating disorders? This chapter addresses these questions by placing the phenomenon in a broad historical context, with particular focus on fashion and the unique and dangerous twist it has taken in our era.

Although current explanations for our thinness mania are valuable, they often leave many questions unanswered. Feminists have often blamed fashion for oppressing and subordinating women, but fashion has rarely had the destructive effects we see today. Moreover, the fashion for thinness, which has prevailed only for the past 40 years or so, requires explanation itself. The eating disorders literature, often focused on individual psychopathology, has found neither a consistent etiological profile nor a universally accepted explanation for why eating disorders have swelled into a social disease. Nor does it explain why millions of women without clinical eating disorders mimic the behavior and mind set of affected women. Finally, a much weaker body of literature attributes the phenomenon to the mass media's influence. Although the

3

media's power to shape our perceptions cannot be underestimated, this explanation also begs the question. Why would the media necessarily promote slenderness?

A more comprehensive explanation emerges when we stand back and, employing a broad historical perspective, look at the underlying cultural beliefs that affect both genders. Our culture is swept up in a web of peculiar and distorted beliefs about beauty, health, virtue, eating, and appetite. We have elevated the pursuit of a lean, fat-free body into a new religion. It has a creed: "I eat right, watch my weight, and exercise." Indeed, anorexia nervosa could be called the paradigm of our age, for our creed encourages us all to adopt the behavior and attitudes of the anorexic. The difference is one of degree, not of kind. Like any religion worthy of the name, ours also has its damnation. Failure to follow the creed—and the corporeal stigmata of that failure, fatness and flabbiness—produce a hell on earth. The fat and flabby are damned to failure, regardless of professional and personal successes. Our religion also has its rewards, its salvation. In following the creed, one is guaranteed beauty, energy, health, and a long successful life. Followers are even promised self-transformation: The "thin person within," waiting to burst through the fat, is somehow a more exciting, sexy, competent, successful self. Virtue can be quantified by the numbers on the scale, the lean-to-fat ratio, clothing size, and body measurements. And, in a curious inversion of capitalist values, less is always better.

BODY IDEALS BEFORE THE 20TH CENTURY

The creed of thinness is composed of prejudices, and they have a history. A cursory review of Western civilization's aesthetic and health ideals indicates the novelty and arbitrariness of current beliefs. The female body has not altered for thousands of years; the range of body types in the past does not differ from the range we know today. What has changed is the body type (or types) regarded as ideal, as well as the effort put into meeting this ideal and the methods used to do so. Although styles of dress have tended to change at an ever-quickening tempo since the 12th century, body ideals have changed slowly. By looking at the visual evidence provided by paintings of dressed people and of the nude, we can see that never before have men or women desired a body so "close to the bone."

There have been, of course, other periods when slenderness was admired. During the 15th century, paintings of long-limbed ladies reverberated with the vaulting reaches of Gothic cathedrals. Sixteenth-century Mannerists in northern Europe painted elongated nudes, such as the nymphs in Cranach the Elder's *The Judgement of Paris*. More recently, the Romantic vogue for slenderness in the 1830s–1850s encouraged young ladies to strive for the tiny waist favored by fashion—an effort later immortalized in *Gone with the Wind* when Scarlett O'Hara's stays are tightened to achieve a 17-inch waist.[1]

Nonetheless, it would be misleading to assume that these eras resembled our own. Gothic and Mannerist nudes had not a bone or muscle showing; they were sweetly and fully fleshed. Women of the Romantic period may have wanted tiny waists, but they also wanted their shoulders, arms, calves, and bosoms ample, indicating an "amorous plenitude."[2] Indeed, thinness was considered ugly, a woman's misfortune. The French epicure J. A. Brillat-Savarin defined thinness as those of his epoch typically did—as "the condition of the individual whose muscular flesh, not being filled with fat, reveals the forms and angles of the bony structure." Thinness in women was, he observed, "a terrible misfortune. . . . The most painstaking toilette, the sublimest costume, cannot hide certain absences, or disguise certain angles."[3] Nor did the Romantic lady equate slenderness with health and energy as we do today; health was not part of her aesthetic ideal. Rather, slenderness signified delicacy and fragility, the qualities she sought.

Just a century ago, body ideals and ideas were the reverse of our own, underscoring the fact that there was no folk wisdom about the value of slenderness that science has recently confirmed. Indeed, the female ideal was Junoesque: tall, full-busted, full-figured, mature. Dimpled flesh—what we today shudderingly call "cellulite"—was considered desirable. Sinewy, "close to the bone" women "no bigger than a whipping post" suffered disdain, not those with amply fleshed curves properly distributed and disciplined only by the corset.[4] The undergarment industry even came to the aid of the slighted thin woman with inflatable rubber garments (replete with dimples) for her back, calves, shoulders, and hips. They may have provided meager comfort, for they could deflate at unexpected moments.[5]

Fat was seen as a "silken layer" that graced the frames of elegant ladies. It was regarded as "stored-up force," equated with reserves of energy and strength. Plumpness was deemed a sign of emotional well-being; it was identified with a good temperament, with a clean conscience, with temperate and disciplined habits, and above all with good health. Today, of course, we have totally inverted these associations.[6]

In the mid-19th century, the prolific writer Catherine Beecher described healthy weight. If you felt heavy and got on the scale (a rare experience in the 19th century), and weighed either heavy or light, you were in bad health. But if you felt light and weighed heavy, then you were in excellent health; weighing heavy was good. More importantly,

Beecher distinguished between feelings and actual weight—a distinction lost to many today, who determine how they feel by the numbers on the scale.[7]

DEVELOPMENT OF THE OBSESSION WITH THINNESS

The transformation of these values began at about the turn of the present century, when slenderness came into fashion. This occurred for a variety of reasons, among them the modernist aesthetic with its idealization of speed and motion, and its penchant for stripping things down to their essential forms. (Some called it the revenge of the thin who for so long had been slighted.) But "slim" is a relative term, and the women who boasted the new form would by contemporary standards be called overweight. In addition, in the first half of this century, the belief that plumpness signaled robust health remained strong.

The culture of slimming as we know it is really a post-World War II phenomenon.[8] Fashion continued to value a slender (if curving) form, and the health industry, finally convinced by insurance companies, launched massive campaigns to persuade Americans to lose weight. Key ideas that would take full force in subsequent decades began to emerge. Chief among these was "fatphobia," the conviction that animal fat of any kind—on the body, in the blood, on the plate—was dangerous. The perception developed that Americans were too fat and getting fatter; that they ate too much, ate the wrong foods, and were sedentary and therefore flabby. Americans' self-perception shifted to that of a diseased, unhealthy group, even though they enjoyed the best health and greatest longevity ever known in American society. These pronouncements did not abate, even though average life expectancy continued to improve. Most important was the growing fear that Americans were getting physically and *morally* soft. For at the heart of all the campaign literature was a moral concern about how Americans would react to postwar plenty and leisure—how they would handle modernization.

In subsequent decades, these ideas intensified. Weight loss techniques began to be seen as life-prolonging in and of themselves. The fitness ethic emerged from these beliefs and fueled obsession with exercise. But the new emphasis on fitness was just a variation on the theme of slenderness. The ideal remained a fat-free body. The "health food" craze played on the same dynamic, growing out of and then later helping to fuel and dignify diet obsessions. In addition, the standards of slenderness grew more extreme, both in charts of ideal weight and in fashion. The famous 1960s model Twiggy, at 5 feet 7 inches and 98 pounds, represented the boundary beyond which no ambulatory person could go; however, her image became one that women thereafter aspired to meet. Female beauty had come to be represented by a gawky, bare-boned adolescent. Simultaneously, definitions of "overweight" and "obesity" began to include normal-sized Americans.

More compelling, however, were the principles underlying fat-phobia, which turned it into a national obsession. The health industry embraced the questionable concept of "ideal weight"—the idea that the weight associated with optimum health and longevity could be determined by height. It was then decreed that everyone of the same height and bone structure should meet this ideal. But this injunction assumed that body weight and the ratios of fat to lean tissue were direct functions of exercise and eating habits. The obvious corollary was that everybody should reduce to ideal weight and that everybody could easily do so—if they exerted enough willpower. In short, these decrees blamed the victim: if you were fat, it was your fault. This is the most powerful and pernicious aspect of fatphobia; indeed, in modern America, being fat is as shameful as being dirty. We seem to believe that slenderness is as attainable as cleanliness, and as crucial to respectable grooming. We can easily embrace these ideas because they fit so well with America's self-help-oriented, democratic ideology. We can all be body aristocrats, we believe, if we just try hard enough. This set of beliefs fuels prejudices against fat and has allowed the thinness mania to spiral into a religion.

More and more evidence is emerging that discredits this whole ideology and shows that its premises are empirically flawed. The thinner are not necessarily healthier, nor are they more fit. Our fundamental beliefs—that people of the same height should have the same weight, and that people can exercise absolute control over their body weights—are also flawed. Numerous studies demonstrate that the majority of the "fat" cannot slim down permanently. The problem is not their lack of will-power, but the unreasonable expectation placed on them to weigh a certain amount. Animal breeders have long known that nature did not intend everyone to be the same size, but modern science seems to have temporarily forgotten.

Sadly, efforts to squeeze into the ideal size are often useless and destructive—not only because they can exacerbate the problem they are designed to cure, but because they trigger psychological, physiological, and behavioral consequences, including binge eating, food obsessions, and, in susceptible individuals, eating disorders. Even worse, dieters pay a price in sense of well-being, in health, and in the ability to lead rich and productive lives. The contemporary and historical literature on famine describes ennui, tension, irritability, preoccupation with food, loss of libido, and lassitude created by diets equivalent to those advised for weight loss. The United Nations World Health Organization has established a daily intake of 1000 calories as the border of semistarvation; modern diets often recommend less. The famine literature attributes these symptoms to hunger and undernourishment; the literature on overweight attributes them to lack of willpower or to psychopathology.

Laboring under perverse notions about food and appetite, we believe that permanent dieting and chronic hunger are healthy and energy-giving; we are convinced that food does not nourish, but rather kills. If we find ourselves eating with unbridled appetite, we believe that there is either something wrong with us or with the food itself, which must be "addictive." In truth, the well-nourished, not the undernourished, grow strong, healthy, and productive. Poor appetite is a sign of the depressed and the ill; indeed, women are often grateful for an illness—it makes dieting easier.

It is hard to resist the parallel between Victorian attributes toward sex and modern attitudes toward food. In the 19th century, the control of sexual instincts was the acme of virtue; sexual behavior was the yardstick of goodness. Today, eating habits and body weights have become the yardsticks of virtue, and food rules have become as dour and inhibitory as the sex rules of the 19th century. Perhaps cultures require some kind of instinctual control to feel that they qualify as "civilized."

WHY WOMEN MORE THAN MEN?

Given that this belief system pervades our culture, why does it affect women so much more than men? Why do more women than men suffer from eating disorders, obesity, and distorted body image? Why are women, not men, at war with their bodies? There are many reasons, some more obvious than others.

One reason is biological. Standards for males simply are not as extreme or as inimical to normal masculine body builds as are women's standards. Indeed, our female ideal violates the anthropomorphic reality of the average female body. The ideal female weight, represented by actresses, models, and Miss Americas, has progressively decreased to that of the thinnest 5–10% of American women. Consequently, 90–95% of American women feel that they don't "measure up."[9] Societies have never been kind to deviants, but in America a statistical deviation has been normalized, leading millions of women to believe that they are abnormal.

In addition, the taut, lean, muscled body—the "fit" form so many strive to achieve—is more like the body of a male than of a female. The goal is to suppress female secondary sexual characteristics, from dimpled flesh to plumpness in thighs, behinds, hips, and bosom. Women consequently are pitted in a war against their own biologies to meet the standard.

It is not just biology that confounds women. They strive to meet this unreasonable standard because it has become a moral imperative in our society, and because, despite a quarter-century of feminism, the quest for physical beauty remains deeply powerful. On even a practical level, women's self-image, their social and economic success, and even their survival can still be determined largely by their beauty and by the men it allows them to attract, while for men these are based largely on how they act and what they accomplish. Looks simply are of secondary importance for male success.

But the impulse toward beauty runs much deeper than the desire for social acceptance and success. Beauty and fashion are intertwined, and women try to meet unreasonable weight standards also because fashion—our system of dress—requires them to do so. Though many have castigated fashion as a shallow and frivolous vanity, it is propelled by profound impulses, which it shares with all dress systems. Dress and adornment are basic to all human cultures. Even the most primitive tribes find ways to decorate the body. The overwhelming importance of dress is underscored by the fact that from the moment we slip out of the womb to the moment of our deaths, we alter our natural appearance. How we choose to dress is a complex cultural phenomenon. Clothing and adornment are simultaneously a material object, a social signal, a ritual, and a form of art. Every facet of a society—from its economic base to its social structure, from its values about human beings and their bodies to its loftiest spiritual and aesthetic ideals—influences the forms and rules of dress. Each culture sets up its own rules, and in following them, people defer to and perpetuate fundamental social values and norms.

In obeying fashion's dictates, we are bowing to powerful constraints about self-presentation and about how others should interpret our attitudes, behavior, and identity. The enormous time and energy women (and men) devote to it is simply another of civilization's many demands and, possibly, pleasures. For in dressing, in following fashion, we are engaged in a game, a plastic art, a process whereby we partially create ourselves. We are involved in social and private play of the profoundest type—trying to transcend our uncivilized, animal state, to make ourselves human. Friedrich Nietzsche, in *The Birth of Tragedy,* argued that "We derive such dignity as we possess from our status as art works." Fun, fantasy, humor, artistic creativity, and our deepest aspirations exist in the dress constraints of everyday life.[10]

Fashion, the dress system of the West, has, however, taken a rather peculiar twist in recent decades—one that helps explain our body obsessions. Fashionable beauty is no longer about the clothes covering the body, but about the naked body itself. This has not been true before in the history of fashion. Fashion is, as we have seen, a plastic art. Although it would be foolhardy to describe the past as Edenic, it nonetheless is true that fashion has traditionally been a handmaiden to beauty. It allowed people to approach the reigning ideal by manipulating cosmetics and clothing—that is, by manipulating what they put *on* themselves, not what they *were* underneath those clothes, stays, girdles, and so forth.

By the late 20th century, however, women's bodies, which heretofore had never been exposed to the public eye, virtually became wholly exposed. With the introduction of the miniskirt and teeny tops, women's legs, thighs, and upper bodies were suddenly revealed, bereft of the aid of body-shaping undergarments. The fitness craze and the growing liberalization in censorship and in acceptable norms of nudity intensified the trend.

By the 1980s, even fashion magazines showed naked or leotarded bodies more than they showed clothing. The undressed body—the bare bones of being, celebrated as liberating and "natural"—had become the focus of fashion. No longer did a woman have the luxury of manipulating only what was outside her body, the "not me"; now she had to manipulate her self, the once private stretches of the body.

This new, "natural" look could not really be liberating, because fashion is antithetical (almost by definition) to nature, so stringent standards began being set for the now-exposed form. Suddenly, the average American woman became aware of flaws she never knew existed; pronouncements were made about how every private crevice of her anatomy was to look. Women consequently ran smack into a dilemma between the naked and the nude.

The art historian Sir Kenneth Clark argued that the nude is a form of art; the naked is merely the human body undressed, replete with all its flaws and blemishes. The naked becomes the nude through art, with the artist transforming that humble and flawed form into an ideal of beauty.[11] Yet today, bombarded by verbal and visual commercial images of the nude, women have been seduced into believing that they should—and could, with enough effort—have one of those perfect bodies. They expect the image reflected in their mirrors to look like the nude. It almost never does. And so they renew their battle against their recalcitrant bodies.

Changes in the structure of fashion contributed further to the battle: No authorities put brakes on the urge to meet the slender ideal. This, too, was new in fashion's history. Although there has always been considerable harmony among standards of feminine beauty, health, and the gestalt of an era, excesses of fashion were heretofore severely criticized by social authorities, including doctors, teachers, and clergy, parents, and, since the 19th century, feminists. The clergy and moralists, in particular, stressed that there were values more important than outward appearance; that the soul and one's deeds mattered, not fashion standards; that, in the words of the old adage, "Pretty is as pretty does." In the late 20th century—at least until alarm about eating disorders spread—all these authorities, especially physicians, seemed to agree that one could never be too thin. This unholy alliance between societal and fashion authorities allowed the vogue for thinness to go to extremes.

Even contemporary feminists have been slow to resist the slenderness fashion. They were initially seduced, perhaps, by its underlying message that biology is not destiny. Even more, the rhetoric of the slenderness ideal—that health is beauty and beauty health, and both are fit and thin—may have persuaded them. They applauded the fact that physical strength and health were now feminine ideals. It took a while for them to realize that what was sought, what had become ideal, was merely the *appearance* of health and vigor—and that dangerous means were being used to achieve it.

Despite the historical uniqueness of these developments, some rather cruel historical consistencies remain. More stringent bodily controls are still required of the female than of the male. Animal-like functions, such as belching, nose wiping, urinating, sweating, scratching, spitting, masturbating, farting, and even body odor, remain less permissible for women than for men. In the male subculture, unlike female subcultures, there is an acceptance of and a certain humor about these behaviors, which sometimes become the subject of good-natured contests. Men simply are permitted to be more comfortable about natural functions and to exhibit them to a greater extent in public. They do not compromise masculinity; rather, they often confirm it. Women, on the other hand, compromise their femininity if they do not control these behaviors. The same discrepancy applies to diet and body size: Women are expected to manage these even more stringently than men. Similarly, as long as control of appetite and body weight is regarded as virtuous, women must exercise this control more than men. Once again, women are expected to be the custodians and embodiments of virtue for the culture.

THINNESS AND OUR CULTURAL AND SPIRITUAL VALUES

What remains puzzling about this unique fashion for bare-boned skinniness is what it suggests about our aesthetic ideals—and, even more importantly, about our values, our gestalt. If we step back a moment and look at our ideal of beauty from a more distant perspective (perhaps that of a future historian or anthropologist), we can perhaps see how peculiar it is that we celebrate the living version of Giacometti sculptures, anorexics with barbells.

Future historians might conjecture that Americans had fallen in love with death, or at least with mortification of the flesh. They might speculate that terror of nuclear destruction had made fashion play with cadavers and turn them into images of beauty. Or they might argue that we had been so influenced by modern art, Bauhaus aesthetics, and contemporary steel architecture that our ideal human body also had come to consist only of the scaffolding that held it up and of the machinery that made it move. Or they might suggest that we had come to see technology, not human beings, as the prime force in history, and so had chosen to resemble our conquerors.

Alternatively, they might argue that our fascination with the unconscious, and our new awareness that scientific reality was concealed from us—that the universe was made up of particles we could not see and governed by laws that defied the logic of our senses—led us to strip the outer body of any meaning or significance and of any possible beauty. Or, more simply, they might conjecture that in an era of population density, it was more practical and economical to have skinny people. Thin people would need less room, so more of them could be squeezed into the spaces on mass transit and into workplaces, and they could live in smaller houses. It certainly also might be interpreted as democratic. No one had the right to take up more space than another or to command respect through the imposing grandeur of body size.

They might also conjecture that late 20th-century America had so confused its image of women that what looked female could no longer be considered beautiful. Even more, they might contend that we had dehumanized, not just masculinized, the human form. We had reduced it to its smallest, least imposing form. They might argue that we had come to idealize technology, and also (befitting our secular age) to distinguish humans from other animals and the civilized from the uncivilized not by the presence of consciousness, a soul, and a conscience, but by the suppression of animal fat. They might even suggest that we had become so terrified of what made us human—especially our passions and our vulnerability—that we didn't want our bodies to betray any softness, curves, or idiosyncrasies. Or they might think that we had suppressed tender flesh because we no longer saw human beings as sources of comfort and nurture.

From a purely aesthetic perspective, our fat-free beauties might come out no better. Indeed, even unprejudiced present-day observers may be taken aback. Faces are gaunt and angular; necks are steeples of bones. Unfleshed arms and legs, full of sharp angles, look gangly and disproportionately long. Indeed, dieted women look as though the life and color have been sucked out of them. Nor, for all the paeans to strength, do these scrawny, narrow women look strong or stable, or as if they have a stature to be reckoned with. Indeed, the lean body looks as repressed and controlled as the spirit that must have gotten it that way.

It is odd, too, that we have developed an erotic ideal that suppresses flesh and minimizes sexual characteristics. There is little to linger over, to explore, to discover. When the body has been efficiently reduced to a flat surface, it offers no softness, no warmth, no tenderness, no mysteries— qualities once integral to images of sexuality. Our erotic ideal has become as hard and unyielding, perhaps, as the love relationships that dominate social life.

In criticizing our new religion, I am not suggesting that we gorge wantonly or that we ignore our health and our physical appearance. This would be a surrender to the treacherous polarities that dominate our thinking: Our choices seem to be thinness or fatness, gluttony or stavation, vigorous exercise or lethargy, ascetic rituals or self-indulgence, youthfulness or old age, beauty or ugliness. I am suggesting that we recultivate our tastes and find a saner middle ground where our bodies can round out with more life, flesh, and health; where we can relish the fruits of our prosperity without self-punishment; and where we understand that the nourishment that is one of life's greatest pleasures is also one of its most basic necessities.

It would be a tragedy, after 25 years of the women's movement, if women did not rebel against this "religion" that threatens to sabotage their hard-won victories. Is the "liberated women," supposedly at ease in the boardroom, really consumed with self-loathing and obsessed with tallying calories, exercise, and the vital statistics of the body (weight, muscle-to-fat ratio, inches of breast, hip, and thigh)? Never measuring quite right, she may be as victimized by biology as her predecessors.

I am not suggesting, as many past and present feminists have, that we do away with beauty and fashion standards altogether. It would be a bleak world if we did not celebrate beauty and if we did not encourage the imagination and play involved in bedecking ourselves and molding our own images. The impulses toward adornment and self-beautification run deep in human culture and are connected to its noblest aspirations. Nor am I suggesting that fashion standards of the past were always benign. Each era has exacted its own price for beauty, though our era is unique in producing a standard based exclusively on the bare bones of being, which can be disastrous for human health, happiness, and productivity.

But I am urging that we dismantle this new religion, because it is misguided and destructive. It does not provide reasonable guidelines by which to live. Our bodies, our fitness, and our food should not be our paramount concerns. They have nothing to do with ethics, or relationships, or community responsibilities, or with the soul. They have nothing to say about the purpose of life, except that we should survive as well and as long and as beautifully as we can. They give us no purpose beyond ourselves. This is a religion appropriate only for a people whose ideals do not extend beyond their physical existence, and whose vision of the future and of the past is strangely empty. Surely Americans can produce a worthier creed.

In making the denial of hunger and its physical manifestations, thinness, into a primary virtue, our "religion" is unique among the major world religions. Although there is a long history of fasting for spiritual cleansing or purity, no religion has set it up as a virtue; indeed, most have condemned it. Buddha rejected fasting because he did not find it a way to enlightenment. Judaism prescribes only a few fast days a year. Otherwise, it proscribes such deprivation: According to the Talmud, people must be well nourished so they can do what is important in life—follow God's commandments and perform *mitzvot* (good deeds). The early fathers of the Christian Church, too, condemned fasting, and the Church exacted higher penances for the sin of not eating than it did for the sin of gluttony. The Muslims, even during their great fast of Ramadan, do not abstain from food. They are merely proscribed from eating during certain hours, and the other hours are given to feasting. In these religions, food has not been seen as a temptation put in humanity's path, but as vital for people to carry out their larger spiritual tasks.

It is one thing to follow a rigid dietary code and rituals of behavior in accordance with the laws of a God or gods we worship. The faithful are trying to fulfill God's or the gods' commandments, not only for their own salvation, but also to hasten the arrival of a more perfect world. It is quite another thing to follow rigid dietary and behavior codes only to improve our physical selves. Such actions are not part of a larger system of morals. They have no vision of a higher good or of a better future that their rituals might help create. This is a solipsistic religion in the narrowest and strictest sense, in that it is only about the bare bones of being. If avoiding fatness and possible disease is the main preoccupation of our lives, then what are we living for?

Our new religion bankrupts us. Historically unprecedented numbers of us are healthy—able to enjoy sex without fear of unwanted pregnancy, to go through childbirth without the once omnipresent threat of death, to treat once-fatal infectious diseases easily, and to alleviate the minor aches and pains that caused discomfort to our forebears (from toothaches to earaches to headaches to skin eruptions to upset stomachs). Advances in technology, medicine, and food production, wrought by painstaking human efforts, have given us a well-being virtually unknown in previous centuries. We should be grateful, but instead we hate our bodies because they bulge here or are flabby there or fail to respond to our most rigorous diets. Surely this is the worst form of hubris—to despise our bodies because they are not perfect. Our new religion neither puts checks on this kind of vanity nor underscores how trivial is the accomplishment of weight loss and of physical perfection. Instead, it seduces us into believing that this quest is the worthiest of human goals.

We must abandon our new religion because it trivializes human life itself. We must restore a humanistic vision in which self-improvement means cultivating the mind and enlarging the soul; developing generosity, humor, dignity, and humility; living more graciously with biology, aging, and death; living with our limitations. We need a concept of self-improvement that reminds us to learn from the past, to build on it, and to bequeath wisdom to future generations. We stand poised between a past for which we have lost respect and a future we must now struggle to envision.

NOTES

1. For a fuller discussion of past body ideals, see Roberta P. Seid, *Never Too Thin: Why Women Are at War with Their Bodies* (New York: Prentice-Hall Press, 1989), 37–81. The best sources for a general overview are Francois Boucher, *20,000 Years of Fashion: The History of Costume and Personal Adornment,* expanded edition (New York: Harry N. Abrams, 1987) and Kenneth Clark, *The Nude: A Study in Ideal Form* (Princeton, NJ: Princeton University Press, 1956).

2. See the excellent discussion of this ideal in Valerie Steele, *Fashion and Eroticism: Ideals of Feminine Beauty from the Victorian Era to the Jazz Age* (New York: Oxford University Press, 1985), 108–110.

3. Jean Anthelme Brillat-Savarin, *The Physiology of Taste or Meditations on Transcendental Gastronomy* (New York: Doubleday, 1926 [orig. 1826]), 172, 187.

4. Steele, 1985, 218–223; Hillel Schwartz, *Never Satisfied: A Cultural History of Diets, Fantasies, and Fat* (New York: Free Press, 1986), Illustration 5 (1857 cartoon from *Harper's Weekly*).

5. David Kunzle, "The Corset as Erotic Alchemy: From Rococo Galanterie to Montaut's Physiologies," in Thomas Hess and Linda Nochlin, eds., *Art News Annual,* vol. 38, *Woman as Sex Object: Erotic Art, 1730–1970* (1972); Steele, 1985, 128, 221.

6. Seid, 1989, 70–80.

7. Beecher's standards are quoted by Harvey Green, *Fit for America: Health–Fitness–Sport and American Society* (New York: Pantheon Books, 1986), 64.

8. For a fuller discussion with citations of sources, see Seid, 1989, Chapters 12 and 13.

9. Although exact figures on this subject remain elusive, many sources confirm this general trend. This percentage was suggested by Rita Freedman, *Beauty Bound* (Lexington, Mass.: Lexington Books, 1986), 149, but it is corroborated by other sources. I studied statistics of Miss America contenders with data for the earlier periods from Frank Deford, *There She Is: The Life and Times of Miss America* (New York: Viking Press, 1971) 313–316, and from Miss America Pageant Yearbooks, 1972–1983, and found a dramataic slenderizing trend. For more details, see Seid, 1989, Chapter 10. For a study of a similar development in the *Playboy* centerfolds, whose average weights dropped from 11% below the national average in 1970 to 17% below it in 1978, see Paul E. Garfinkel and David M. Garner, *Anorexia Nervosa: A Multidimensional Perspective* (New York: Brunner/Mazel, 1982), 108–109, and D. M. Garner, P. E. Garfinkel, D. Schwartz, and M. Thompson, "Cultural Expectations of Thinness in Women," *Psychological Reports* 47 (1980): 483–491. On the rise of an emaciated ideal in the ballet subculture, see L. M. Vincent, *Competing with the Sylph* (New York: Andrews & McNeel, 1979). Jennifer Brenner, professor of psychology at Brandeis University, and Dr. Joseph Cunningham recently reported the results of their study comparing the weights of New York fashion models and Brandeis students. "Female models are 9 percent taller and 16 percent thinner than average women," Brenner reported in an article by Lena Williams, "Girl's Self-Image Is Mother of the Woman," *New York Times* (National Edition), February 6, 1992, A1, A12.

10. Nietzsche's statement is quoted in Steele, 1985, 245. For a fuller theoretical discussion and bibliography on the role of dress and adornment in human culture, see Roberta P. Seid, *The Dissolution of Traditional Rural Culture in Nineteenth-Century France: A Study of the Bethmale Costume* (New York: Garland Press, 1987), 1–45.

11. Clark, 1956, 3–9.

2

. . . And Man Created "Woman": Representations of Women's Bodies in Western Culture

O. WAYNE WOOLEY

> *Are there women, really?*
> —Simone de Beauvoir,
> *The Second Sex*
> (1949/1989, p. xix)

FOR AS LONG AS I CAN REMEMBER, I have been intensely (at times obsessively, compulsively) interested in women's bodies, as bodies—as objects, but as the ultimate sacred objects. "Object" is too dead a word for what I experience. I recall a time from my Southern Baptist childhood when my cousin and I hid in the bushes to watch a woman put on her swimsuit—this was in the days when people still swam in creeks. I don't recall this being particularly sexual (not genital, at any rate); rather, it was "dirty," "bad." Knowing, but not knowing why, it was wrong to look at naked female bodies made them irresistible objects of curiosity.[1]

In adolescence, my interest became sexual. But before I learned all that was involved in sex, I envied those girls whose bodies were the source of my masturbatory images. There seemed to be an inherent, intimidating power that went with having such a body—a power that was every bit the equal of athletic prowess. I imagined that such a body would command more than unconditional love; it would impel awe. To have such a body was to be precious in and of oneself; it was to be without any sense of division between body and self. When I gazed at

17

certain girls, I longed to inspire that kind of awe and to feel precious and whole.

The following quote from Wendy Lesser's (1991) discussion of Edgar Degas's nudes expresses what I believe I felt before I learned what I was "supposed" to feel:

> There is an eroticism in Degas's bathers . . . but it is a kind of unselfconscious eroticism. . . . It is an eroticism of pure desire that has no hope or need of fulfillment and yet receives fulfillment through the eyes alone. It is . . . the desire of a small infant for its mother, or a mother for her small infant, at a phase when sexuality has not yet become conscious and gendered. . . . The feeling of connectedness that we have when looking at a Degas bather . . . lacks the violence and conflict of sex, the sense of opposition and opposition overcome that sex gives us. . . . Degas's nudes . . . represent the vanishing point toward which the best forms of erotic love strive to move: that imaginary place at which the other being is left alone in her self-contained privacy even as one identifies with her body to the point of feeling it as one's own. (pp. 79–80)

Without knowing how it happened, I eventually came to realize that it was my role as a "man" to be dominant, and that sexual access to women's bodies was the prize of dominance. For a long time, it was a source of great shame and anger for me that I was never able to assume that role; I did not and do not feel dominant. This sense of lack, this feeling of not being a man is reawakened in me when I see certain kinds of images of women's bodies. These images are, of course, ubiquitous. Like low-calorie food, they are there to be consumed without guilt or consequence; but like such food, they heighten rather than satisfy the craving they exploit. It is no surprise to me that these images are associated with and feed (and feed off) a feeling of hostility to women as a class. Sometimes I can't shake the feeling that something rightfully mine is being withheld from me; that something is being rubbed in my face; and that, somehow, the blame lies with women.

However, what I have said so far is not all there is to say about my relationships with women. The 20-plus years of my professional life as a clinical psychologist has been spent working with women who hate their bodies—women who feel "too fat," although most of them are not "fat." I have learned from these women that the very same images reminding me that I'm not a real "man" remind them that they aren't real "women." They feel they have failed at being beautiful, just as I feel I have failed at being dominant. They have allowed me to see that their body hatred registers, silently, voicelessly, in isolation, the hostility that our patriarchal culture feels for women. One of the participants in our program hated her body so much she cut the word "fat" on her abdomen—literally, scarlet letters of shame. Similar feelings have led millions of women to pay obesity surgeons and plastic surgeons to do much worse things to their bodies.

Because I care about my clients and want to understand them, I have examined the representations of women's bodies in our culture. Those objects, women's bodies, that are the source of much that men hold sacred (i.e., objects of fear, dread, awe, envy, hostility, art, beauty, even worship) are often despised by the women who actually inhabit them. In this chapter I will discuss my efforts to understand how this could be. These efforts have led me to question whether it is possible for women not to feel pathologically self-conscious—for them ever to feel comfortable with their bodies in a culture that is, on the one hand, flooded with idealized images of women's bodies; and, on the other hand, conditioned to see real (*really* real) women's bodies as being in need of change, repair, improvement, better "health."

I have found strong support for the conclusion that women's body hatred is "structural" (i.e., not accidental, but built into the system); that it is political; and that nothing short of a radical change—a revolution—will restore to women a sense of body ownership and safety. The feminist movement is and must be first and foremost a bodily movement.

One of my own efforts at understanding has been to conduct studies of body dissatisfaction among women and girls. These studies have shown that women are most dissatisfied with their bodies between the waist and the knees—the part of the body that is most sexual, that is the focus of the most obsessive media attention, that is the site of most cosmetic surgery and other size-reducing efforts and, that has been the target of most violent sexual attacks since the time of Jack the Ripper (Caputi, 1987). This dissatisfaction is greatest among the women who are targets of fashion ads: white women old enough to have some money to spend, and still young, powerless, and insecure enough to be manipulated by the criticisms implicit in fashion ads. Men, black women and girls, the very young and the very old, and nudists (including white female nudists) all feel more body satisfaction than the women in this target group. "[F]emale beauty is becoming an increasingly standardized quality throughout the world. A standard so strikingly white, Western and wealthy it is tempting to conclude there must be a conscious conspiracy afoot" (Chapkis, 1986, p. 37).

In this chapter I discuss the role of representations of women's bodies in gender politics. Because to represent is "to present clearly to the mind," representations include not only visual images such as paintings, drawings, sculpture, and photography, but also verbal descriptions of the form and function of female bodies. I look at the representations of women's bodies in three areas: the biology of sexual differences, the art of the Christian West, and women's magazines.

WOMAN AS BODY

The reproductive function of the female body is perhaps the paramount cultural and political fact. Fertile female bodies are the ultimate natural resource. The fate of the vast majority of individual women has been determined by their reproductive capacities.

Two pictures—one an untitled drawing by Fons Van Woerkom (Figure 2.1; Van Woerkom, 1973), the other a painting by René Magritte entitled *The Rape* (Figure 2.2; Haslam, 1978)—depict the plight of women in our culture. In Figure 2.1, a fetus and umbilical cord are a ball and chain, imprisoning and immobilizing a terrified woman. In the words of Sherry Ortner (1974), "It all begins . . . with the body and the natural procreative functions specific to woman alone" (p. 73). "It" refers to the ideological belief that women represent a lower order of beings, that they are "less transcendental of nature than men are" (p. 73). In Figure 2.2, *The Rape*, a woman's face is replaced by a headless, limbless female body. In the words of Ambrose Bierce (1911/1958), "Woman's

FIGURE 2.1. Fons Van Woerkom, untitled drawing, 1973.

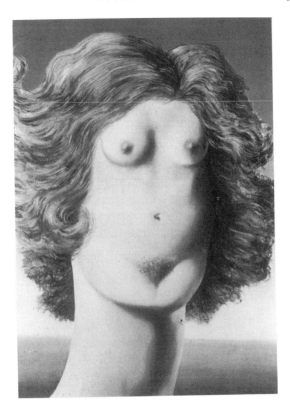

FIGURE 2.2. Rene Magritte, *The Rape,* 1934.

body is the woman."[2] People are identified by their faces; memory for faces is encoded in our brains. Magritte's painting suggests that a woman has no identity apart from her body.

Miriam Greenspan (1983) writes of woman as body:

> There is no running away from the problem . . . of Woman as Body: of suffering from an overexposure of physical visibility as a body combined with an impoverishment of genuine recognition as a person. As long as a woman is essentially defined by her body and as long as her body is appropriated by men, she will always have a problem of feminine identity. (p. 181)

PATRIARCHY

In order to fully understand the gender politics that are such an integral part of patriarchy,[3] it is necessary to understand what came before. The discovery and interpretation of early nonpatriarchal societies prove that civilization in general, and the making of symbols and images in particular, are possible in the absence of male domination. They show that patriarchy is cultural, not "natural," and that it was preceded by and can be replaced by something more egalitarian. But more than that, they suggest what it was that patriarchy was reacting to or against.

In the nature–worshipping societies of old Europe (Gimbutas, 1989), the capacity to give birth and to sustain life apparently made women's bodies sacred, and gave rise to the invention of goddesses (Eisler, 1988).[4] These goddess–worshipping cultures are evidenced by thousands of female figurines, such as the Venus of Willendorf (25,000 B.C.; Stone, 1976), the Venus of Lespuge (23,000 B.C.; Gimbutas, 1989), and the Venus of Laussel (19,000 B.C.; Sjoo & Mor, 1987).[5] What is striking to the 20-century eye about most of these figurines, which must be among the oldest of art objects,[6] is how fat they are.

Over a period of about 2500 years (Lerner, 1986, p. 8), culminating with the fall of Crete 3000 years ago (Eisler, 1988, p. 56), patriarchal cultures conquered, suppressed, and merged with these goddess-worshipping cultures.[7] The politics of this clash of cultures (and religions) is in many ways the politics of gender. When the dust had settled, women were subordinated to men; and their bodies became the legal property of their fathers and husbands, who were the agents of the patriarchal state. According to Gerda Lerner (1986), ancient law codes such as that of Hammurabi dictated that a man could use his wife and children as payment of debts. If one of his women (wife, daughter, or slave) was injured, raped, or otherwise damaged, he could demand as payment one of the women owned by the man who committed or was otherwise responsible for the act. "Two basic assumptions [underlie] these laws . . . : that male kin have the right of disposal over their female relatives and that a man's wife and children are part of his property to be disposed of as such" (Lerner, 1986, p. 90).[8]

These new power alignments based on gender became the model for slavery: "As subordination of women provided the conceptual model for the creation of slavery as an institution, so the patriarchal family provided the structural model" (Lerner, 1986, p. 89).[9] Camille Paglia (1990), vigorously defending and unashamedly in the thrall of patriarchy, over-states its case as well as any man could: "Men, bonding together, invented culture as a defense against female nature" (p. 9); "Male bonding and patriarchy were the recourse to which man was forced by his terrible sense of woman's power, her imperviousness, her archetypal confederacy with chthonian [infernal] nature" (p. 12).

The new archaeological findings (Gimbutas, 1989) suggest, however, that patriarchy, rather than creating a whole new order, seems to have stood the old order on its head. Good became evil. Earth goddesses were replaced by sky gods. Nature, life, body, and the senses were subordinated to spirit, death, mind, and ideas ("In the beginning was the Word"—John 1:1). Violence, which takes life (and which would almost appear to be patriarchy's main contribution to culture), became more valued than sex, which gives life (Girard, 1972).

Simone de Beauvoir (1949/1989) captures the essence of the new order:

> The warrior put his life in jeopardy to elevate the prestige of the . . . clan to which he belonged. And in this he proved dramatically that life is not the supreme value for man, but on the contrary that it should be made to serve ends more important than itself. The worst curse that was laid upon woman was that she should be excluded from these warlike forays. For it is not in giving life but in risking life that man is raised above the animal; that is why superiority has been accorded in humanity not to the sex that brings forth but to that which kills. (p. 64)

Creativity became something only males were capable of. Conception of a new human life was no longer viewed as a female capacity, but as a man's "having an idea in the female body" (Laqueur, 1990, p. 35). As Apollo says in the *Oresteia*:

> The mother is not the parent of the child
> Which is called hers. She is the nurse who tends the growth
> Of the young seed planted by its true parent, the male . . .
>   (quoted in Lerner, 1986, p. 205)

It is to this beginning that almost every aspect of gender politics can be traced. Ever since the triumph of patriarchy, men have controlled the means of representing women and their bodies. The overwhelming majority of priests, scribes, artists, writers, scientists, photographers, movie directors, and television producers have been male (Olsen, 1978).[10] This monopoly has precluded the development of a collective subjectivity among women and made them accomplices to their own oppression. Patriarchy's ceaseless war of words and images has kept women voluntarily chained to their bodies and robbed them of the potentially decisive political advantages they might have derived from their reproductive capacities. This war probably began with patriarchal interpretations of sexual differences.

THE BIOLOGY OF SEXUAL DIFFERENCES

> *The refusal to regard biology as a starting point is made not because biology belongs in the realm of nature but because, on the contrary, it belongs to culture.*
> —René Girard, *Violence and the Sacred* (1972, p. 227)

Women's bodies are the battleground on which the gender wars are waged, and biologists and physicians from Galen to Freud have been patriarchy's conquistadors. Forays into the dark continent have found nothing that would disconfirm and everything needed to justify ideologies of male domination. Thomas Laqueur (1990) writes: "The history of the representation of the anatomical differences between man and woman is . . . extraordinarily independent of the actual structures of these organs or of what was known about them. Ideology, not accuracy of observation, determined how they were seen and what differences would matter" (p. 88). Not only do "theories of sexual difference help to determine what scientists see and know but, more important, . . . the opposite is not the case. What scientists see and know at any given time does not circumscribe how sexual difference is understood or limit the aesthetics of its expression" (p. 142).

Laqueur (1990) labels all patriarchal theories of sexual difference as either "one-sex" or "two-sex" models. In the older one-sex paradigm, sexual differences were just the signs, not the basis, of gender. "Anatomy in the context of sexual difference was a representational strategy that illuminated a more stable extracorporeal reality. There existed many genders [i.e., levels of social, political, spiritual status], but only one adaptable sex" (p. 35). This "one adaptable sex" was male.

Aristotle's theory of representation, useful in understanding the one-sex concept, held that the artist should attempt "to render . . . *not the individual object* with its inevitable departure from the norm, *but its class or species.* . . . [Art] served the high intellectual purpose of revealing the generic norm. . . . Greek art . . . had at all times served the improvement of the human type. From the start it had set out to bridge the gap between the human and the divine by the creation of perfect human specimens" (Bernheimer, 1961, pp. 12–13; emphasis added). For the Greeks, the "generic norm," the "human type," and "perfect human specimens" were all male.

A prior assumption of the one-sex theory was that men were not simply superior to women because they had penises; rather, they had penises because they were more nearly perfect. The belief in the superiority of men was not based on sexual differences; rather, sexual differences were explained by assumed male superiority. The basic paradigm was this: "Man is to woman as God is to man. Men are higher on the Great Chain of Being than women." This certainty was reflected in the higher social and political standing of men and in the sexual differences between men and women.

According to the most influential one-sex theory, that of the Greek physician Galen (2nd century A.D.), women were imperfect men. Galen believed that "women . . . are but variations of the male form, the same but lower on the scale of being and perfection" (Laqueur, 1986, p. 5). Under this theory, women had penises but they were internal, rather than external like the male penis. The sex of the fetus was determined by the amount of heat *in utero*. Heat caused the penis to be extruded, creating a male child; if there was insufficient heat, the fetus was female. The male sex organs were a mirror image of (isomorphic with) those of females: The vagina and penis were the same, as were labia and foreskin, uterus and scrotum, ovaries and testicles. Finally, it was believed that at the point of orgasm women ejaculated a thick white fluid, similar to the seminal fluid of the male orgasm. Laqueur (1990, p. 66) quotes from Renaldus Columbus, the 16th-century "discoverer" of the clitoris: "If you rub it [the clitoris] vigorously with a penis, or touch it even with a little finger, semen swifter than air flies this way and that on account of the pleasure, even with them [women] unwilling." (The line between science and rape gets more than a bit blurred here.)

Books on anatomy illustrated this correspondence with schematic drawings of the male and female reproductive systems placed side by side. To the untutored eye they looked the same: It was impossible to say which was male and which female; pictures of vaginas looked like penises (e.g., see Figure 28 of Schiebinger, 1989). And that was the whole point.

Just as heat determined the sex of the fetus, it also explained why women were fatter than men. Londa Schiebinger (1989), quoting the 17th-century anatomist William Cowper, writes: "[T]he distinctive form of the female body does not derive from the shape of her bones but from 'the greater quantity of Fat placed under the skin of women.' Fat, of course, accumulates in the absence of heat" (p. 187).

In the world of the one-sex theory, sexual differences were secondary to teleological, political, and social distinctions. These latter were more fixed than the former; sex was determined more by gender than the other way around. It was believed that women could change into men. There were many stories of females sprouting penises when enough heat was generated by the hormones of puberty or by the friction associated with such physical activities as running or sexual intercourse. But men never became women, because "Nature tends always toward what is most perfect and not, on the contrary to perform in such a way that what is perfect should become imperfect" (Laqueur, 1990, p. 127; quoted from a 1605 work by Gaspard Bauhin).

By the middle of the 18th century, the two-sex model was well on its way to being established. Sexual differences went from being a sign of gender created by God to being its basis, the foundation from which all social and political arrangements between men and women naturally derived. As Laqueur (1990) states: "[T]he truths of biology . . . replaced divinely ordained hierarchies or immemorial customs as the basis for the creation and distribution of power in relations between men and women" (p. 193).

Women went from being imperfect versions of men to being totally different. "Women's bodies [, especially the] reproductive organs, come to bear an enormous new weight of meaning. Two sexes, in other words, were invented as a new foundation of gender" (Laqueur, 1990, p. 150). Scheibinger (1989) quotes Dr. J. J. Sachs (1830): "Sexual differences are not restricted merely to the organs of reproduction, but penetrate the entire organism. The entire life takes on a feminine or masculine character" (p. 189). Two examples illustrate how the scientific understanding of female anatomy and physiology was shaped by cultural imperatives, and how this "understanding" in turn came to have an impact on women's bodies. The main players in these dramas are the ovaries and the clitoris.

The Ovaries

Under the two-sex theory, the ovaries, formerly regarded as "male testicles," came to be seen altogether differently. A woman was said to exist "only through her ovaries" (Laquer, 1990, p. 149). Following the discovery in 1843 of spontaneous ovulation in dogs, menstruation in women was hypothesized (on the basis of the flimsiest of evidence) to be the equivalent of estrus in animals. In the scientific discourse that followed, female sexuality was compared to the behavior of animals in heat. Adam Raciborski, in an 1868 work on female reproductive physiology, wrote of madness or loss of socialization among dogs and cats in heat, and argued that such behavior demonstrated a relationship between menstruation and heat. So, just as the tranquility of the master–pet relationship was threatened by the heat, the socialization of women and the man–wife relationship were thought to be threatened by the menses. "Animal madness, in other words, acts as a sort of magnifying glass for what women experience during menstruation" (Laqueur, 1990, p. 218). Unbridled animal lust and passion were secretly found inside the bodies of women every month.

Walter Heape, an influential reproductive biologist and antifeminist, described menstruation in gruesome terms. He spoke of "a ragged wreck of tissue, torn glands, ruptured vessels, jagged edges of stroma . . . which it would seem hardly possible to heal . . . without the aid of surgical treatment" (Laquer, 1990, p. 221). Havelock Ellis wrote that "even in the healthiest woman a worm . . . unperceived, gnaws periodically at the roots of life" (Laqueur, 1990, p. 221). In men sexuality is "open, aggressive, unproblematic," but in women it is elusive, a "mocking mystery" (Laqueur, 1990, p. 226). Ehrenreich and English (1978) quote a Dr. Bliss: "[T]he influence of the ovaries over the mind is displayed in woman's artfulness and dissimulation" (p. 121).

"Facts" such as these and others just as bogus were, of course, used against women. It *could* have been argued, and was argued by feminists at the time, that women might be better suited than men to run things because they *had* to learn to control the tumultuous events going on in their bodies every month. But, instead, ominous statements such as this one by Walter Heape shaped opinion: "Male and Female are essentially different throughout . . . ; the accurate adjustment of society depends on proper observation of this fact" (Laqueur, 1990, p. 220).

In this climate of opinion, the idea that the surgical removal of healthy ovaries might make women more "womanly," more like the cultural ideal of what a "woman" should be, was bound to be advanced and acted upon. "The operation was judged successful if the woman was restored to a placid contentment with her domestic duties," wrote Ehrenreich and English (1978, p. 124). Since men and women were completely different, according to the two-sex theory, the idea of putting the male sexual apparatus under the knife as a way of socializing men was blocked out or defended against. The testicles remained sacrosanct.

The Clitoris

Even before its "discovery" by Renaldus Columbus in 1559, it was known (even by men) that the clitoris (yet another "female penis"), not the vagina, is the organ of sexual pleasure in females. Yet Freud concocted the notion that "mature," "healthy" female sexuality was achieved only by renouncing the clitoris in favor of the vagina; thus the vaginal orgasm was born and became the expected norm for all "women."

Laqueur (1990) raises the question of why Freud felt it necessary to invent such an obvious fiction. His answer is that Freud was under the same cultural and political influences that had made the two-sex theory necessary in the first place. Sander Gilman, in his essay "Male Stereotypes of Female Sexuality in *Fin-de-Siecle* Vienna" (1985), explicates the cultural context of Freud's "discoveries": "The seductive child and the degenerate lower-class female are both figments of the masculine imagination in turn-of-the-century Vienna, yet because they were articulated through works of art they became central metaphors for sexuality in Viennese society. They thus became the sexual fantasies, or nightmares, of an entire society" (p. 58). Gilman makes it clear that in the "masculine imagination" and men's "works of art," girls were more seductive than boys: The "seductiveness" of girls and the "degeneracy" of women were *natural,* and did not depend on either socialization or "seduction" (rape) by adult males, known to be a common occurrence at the time. For Freud, trained as a biological scientist, the migration of sexuality from the clitoris to the vagina explained the evolution of the ideally passionless (and unthreatening) Victorian upper-class "woman"; it justified pinning the blame for sexual abuse on its victims; and it relieved patriarchal society of blame for prostitution, a major social problem throughout Europe at the time. In Freud's own words:

> Prostitutes exploit the same polymorphous, that is, infantile, disposition for the purposes of their profession; and considering the immense number of women who are prostitutes or who must be supposed to have an aptitude for prostitution without becoming engaged in it, it becomes impossible not to recognize that this same disposition to perversions of every kind is a general and fundamental human characteristic. (quoted in Gilman, 1985, p. 39)[11]

In the rituals of heterosexuality—one of the most important requirements of patriarchy—the vagina was better suited to play the role of "opposite" to the penis. The clitoris's "easy responsiveness to touch makes it difficult to domesticate for reproductive, heterosexual intercourse" (Laqueur, 1990, p. 240). The vagina–penis opposition must have seemed more "natural," because men and women were "opposites," and so should their genitals be. The two-sex model required the suppression of similarities between men and women, and defined gender identity as the expression of supposed natural differences. So with the help of psychoanalysis, a bloodless clitoridectomy was performed: This newest version of the "female penis" was excised, and the passive, internal vagina was once again recruited to represent female sexuality, but without the potential perfectibility it had enjoyed in its former role as an internal penis.

The conclusion we can reach from these two biological fables is that it is acceptable to change the sexual functioning of women's bodies in such a way that they fit whatever version, representation, or ideal of feminine physique or psyche is fashionable in the patriarchal culture at the time. In both examples, "health" became an issue: It was thought that ovaries and the clitoris could potentially affect the physical and psychological health of women if some intervention (ovariectomy or psychoanalysis) were not made. In both instances, an organ believed to contribute to "excessive" female sexual pleasure was relinquished (with the aid of a doctor), so that the patient could avoid feeling like a failure as a "woman" and fulfill her role in the patriarchy as a good wife, mother, and procreator.

WOMEN'S BODIES IN THE ART
OF THE CHRISTIAN WEST

The Representation of Eve

The story of the creation of Adam and Eve and their fall from grace in the Garden of Eden has probably been the inspiration for more representations and images of women's bodies than any other source. This fable, as it has been interpreted by male religious leaders, contains all the elements of patriarchy's gender strategy. It discredits, devalues, and redefines symbols of prepatriarchal cultures. The serpent, who seduces Eve into eating the apple from the Tree of Knowledge, was once a positive symbol associated with the fertility goddess.[12] Now the story became the basis for defining women as inferior to men, because Eve is derived from Adam. By having her body come out of his, the story reverses the natural relationship, and makes man "the mother" of woman. In the Garden of Eden, the creative force, the source of life is not yet associated with woman. After the fall, procreation of the human race, once the inspiration of religious awe, becomes Eve's punishment. It carries no prestige, but is instead accomplished by that most disgusting of all necessary evils: sexual intercourse. Carnal knowledge (feminine creativity) becomes the very antithesis of spiritual knowledge (masculine creativity).

The story of Adam and Eve has been used to establish women's moral weakness, since the serpent approaches Eve rather than Adam. Margaret Miles (1989) writes, quoting Martin Luther: "Satan's cleverness was apparent in his attack on the 'weak part of human nature, Eve, not Adam. Because Satan sees that Adam is the more excellent, he does not assail him' " (p. 109).

The story has also been used as a justification for defining women's worth through procreation, for if woman is so evil, why does God create her in the first place? How can her creation be considered good? It does not do to suggest that Adam needs a helper to survive in a hostile world, because another man would be better. Nor can it be because Eve makes a good companion: "How much more agreeably could two male friends, rather than a man and a woman, enjoy companionship and conversation in a life shared together?" asks St. Augustine (Miles, 1989, p. 95). The only possible justification for Eve's creation is (in St. Ambrose's words): "[B]ecause the human race could not have been propagated from man alone" (Miles, 1989, p. 91). As Luther proclaimed, "[T]he entire female body was created for the purpose of nurturing children" (Miles, 1989, p. 111).

The story of Eve's fall from grace has been used as a warning against loving women too much. According to St. Augustine, Adam eats the forbidden fruit only because he loves Eve, not because he wants it. For Hildegard, abbess of a monastery at Bingen in the 12th-century and one of the few women of the church who ever commented on the story, the loss of the prelapsarian love and mutuality between Adam and Eve is the very essence of their punishment (Miles, 1989).

But most of all, the story associates Eve and thus all women with sin and death. As Lerner (1986) has written:

> To the question "Who brought sin and death into the world?" Genesis answers, "Woman, in her alliance with the snake, which stands for free female sexuality. . . ." [I]n the story of the Fall, woman and more specifically, female sexuality, became the symbol of human weakness and the source of evil. (p. 198)

Representations of Women and Death

Over the past several years, I have been collecting pictures in which women are associated with "Death." The women are usually naked, and "Death" is usually depicted as a corpse, a skeleton, or a skull. I have located more than 50 such drawings and paintings, extending from the early 1500s to the present. Figures 2.3, 2.4, and 2.5 present three pictures from the 16th-century; Figure 2.6 presents a picture from the late 19th century.

Most people in the 16th-century were illiterate, and pictures of Eve's naked body and of naked women in general were major propaganda tools by which the meaning of "woman" was disseminated. Pictures such as these appear to be the beginning of a new patriarchal language of images—a language easily adaptable to later secular traditions, such as erotic art, visual pornography, and the use of women's bodies to sell products.

In the drawing shown in Figure 2.3, *Death and the Maiden*, Hans Baldung (1484/5–1545), a Protestant German, shows Death presenting a naked woman to the viewer. According to Robert Melville (1973),

FIGURE 2.3. Hans Baldung, *Death and the Maiden*, 1515.

Baldung "is probably the originator of the theme of sexuality and death which so fascinated the Romantics, the Symbolists and the Surrealists" (p. 15). In an earlier woodcut (*The Fall*; Miles, 1989, p. 128) he depicted Adam offering Eve to the viewer; a later painting (*Eve, the Serpent, and Death*; Miles, 1989, p. 132) shows Eve with Death and the serpent but without Adam. Miles (1989) suggests that perhaps in this picture Death is Adam. I suggest that in *Death and the Maiden* Death represents the artist himself, offering his creation to the (male) viewer. It can be interpreted as a message from the grave: "Even though I'm dead (as you see me now), my creation lives on." This interpretation assumes that Baldung felt the ambivalence nearly all men feel toward female sexuality under patriarchy.

In the picture presented in Figure 2.4, *Death Surprising a Woman* by Agostino Veneziano de' Musi (1490–1540), a Catholic Italian (Olds, Williams, & Levin, 1976), the woman is looking at her back in a mirror

FIGURE 2.4. Agostino Veneziano de' Musi, *Death Surprising a Woman.*

as if to see if her wings are still there. One wing lies near her feet. William Levin says of the picture: "Here . . . is pictured a soul which, having dropped her wings, has fallen to earth and taken on human qualities and a female form" (Olds et al., 1976, p. 88). The Latin inscription can be translated as follows: "Made mortal, they must die."

Levin writes of *Death Seizing a Nude Woman*, by Hans Sibald Behan (1500–1550), a Protestant German (Figure 2.5): "[T]here is no suggestion of feminine purity, and Death . . . is obviously known to the woman in his grip. . . . Behan accentuates the woman's weakness to Satan's temptations and the role she plays as his early agent in her relationship with men" (Olds et al., 1976, p. 72). The Latin inscription can be translated thus: " Death destroys all human beauty."

Discussing the drawing by Norwegian expressionist Edvard Munch (1863–1944), shown in Figure 2.6, Jean Selz (1976) has attempted to define "the aspects of Munch's mental life that at a certain point are superimposed in his artistic creation":

FIGURE 2.5. Hans Sibald Behan, *Death Seizing a Nude Woman,* 1546.

On the one hand, woman is depicted as the instrument of man's destruction, and as having deadly power over him. On the other hand, the apparently very strong duality of his life instinct and his death instinct caused him to conceive a kind of successful union between Eros and Thanatos, expressed in an etching of 1894, *Maiden and Death,* in which we see a beautiful young female nude and a skeleton, in standing position, tenderly embracing. (p. 40)

In pictures like these, men are talking to men—using images of women's bodies as a language with which to describe, define, control, and exploit male sexuality. Erotic responses to women's bodies are something men have in common. According to Margaret Miles, 16th-century males would have found Baldung-Grien's images of Eve and of the "maiden" erotic: "They both represented and evoked male desire. That was the point of Baldung's new visual interpretation of the Fall: Eve's body, offered to the sixteenth-century male viewer, did not merely

FIGURE 2.6. Edvard Munch, *Death and the Maiden,* 1894.

symbolize but effectively reproduced the lust" (p. 136). Writing about Munch's *Maiden and Death* (Figure 2.6), Melville (1973) leaves little doubt about the erotic intent of the picture: "[T]he girl [*sic*] is seducing the skeleton; she presses luxuriously against his [*sic*] thigh bones, and covers the teeth in his [*sic*] skull with a kiss" (p. 204).

The official message of these pictures is that sex/lust is to be transcended.[13] However, the unofficial and more predominant message is that it is acceptable to hate, fear, and attack women's bodies. It is not surprising that the appearance of the pictures in Figures 2.3 through 2.5 coincided with the culmination of the great witch hunts of Europe. Baldung was one of the first artists to depict witches, and his naked witches look a lot like his Eves and maidens. "Baldung's work occurred at the same time that witch persecution was scapegoating large numbers of women, and in a geographical region in which more accused witches were burned than in all the rest of Europe put together" (Miles, 1989, p. 138).

Gimbutas (1989) brings out an important motive for the witch burnings: The Inquisition renewed patriarchy's ancient war against the goddess religions. The remnants of these religions formed the basis of whatever nonpatriarchal female culture there was in Europe at the time. The witch trials, says Gimbutas, were an attack on female collective subjectivity:

> The dethronement of this truly formidable goddess whose legacy was carried by wise women, prophetesses, and healers who were the best and bravest of the times, is marked by blood and is the greatest shame of the Christian Church. The witch hunt of the 15th–18th centuries is a most satanic event in European history in the name of Christ. The murder of women accused as witches escalated to more than eight million. (p. 319)

How did women react to the way they were represented? How did the ideology that made these gruesome pictures possible make women feel about themselves? It seems safe to say they did not make them feel good about themselves, but rather reinforced what they had already heard from priests and other representatives of the patriarchy, such as Tertullian: "You are the devil's gateway. . . . [T]he grace and beauty you enjoy naturally must be obliterated by concealment and negligence" (quoted in Armstrong, 1986, pp. 61–62).

The only record of what women thought, felt, and did that was condoned by the patriarchy comes from stories of female saints, virgins, martyrs, mystics, and ascetics. These women attempted to develop, within the narrow confines of Christianity, a subjectivity that transcended society's definition of "woman"—a religious self independent of sexuality and motherhood. In the face of culture's view that the female body was evil, dangerous, and despicable (and in what appears at first glance to be identification with the aggressor), they developed practices of bodily control that were even more ascetic than those of the male saints and mystics. They pushed the idea of "goodness" given to them by men to the extreme limit, almost to the point of caricature: They "became men."

If the female body was evil and the male spirit was good, then it was good to control or, better yet, to deny bodily needs. To succeed in this was to become like a man. Good men did not indulge in sexual activity. For women, who were believed to be naturally more dominated by lust, chastity—better still, perpetual virginity—was a requirement for would-be saints. As Miles (1989) has argued, "By renouncing sexual and reproductive activity, a woman could become the equal of a man, since it was precisely her sexual organs and reproductive functions that differentiated her from a man" (p. 66).

Many career virgins and female mystics dressed like men. Karen Armstrong tells of St. Margaret who, on her wedding day, renounced her husband's touch, cut her hair short, and began wearing men's clothes. She was such a good man that she became abbot of her own monastery. "Women plainly thought that male clothes would help them on their path to salvation which entailed becoming fully human and so male" (Armstrong, 1986, p. 147).

But these women may have been doing more than just imitating men. Caroline Walker Bynum (1985) has suggested that fasting had a special meaning for women. Her explanation hinges on the theological doctrine of the Incarnation and the meaning of Christ's choice to die on the cross, since, as God, he could have escaped this fate. Christ's suffering and death meant that God had taken a human (i.e., a physical, bodily) form. The Crucifixion symbolizes God's humanity and physicality. The Incarnation doctrine placed a positive value on Christ's physicality: If Christ assumed a physical form, it couldn't be all bad. According to Bynum, women were using their bodies in the only positive way available to them. It was as if they were saying, "You say we are nothing but our bodies, so we will use our bodies to develop a female religious self."

Denial of sexual needs may have also been used by female saints, ascetics, and mystics to develop a gender-specific religious subjectivity. Like the suffering of fasting, renunciation of normal sexuality may have been instrumental in getting closer to Christ. Karen Armstrong detects a strong element of eroticism in the stories of saintly suffering: "Since the very early days of the Church, virgins had been encouraged to imagine Christ as their lover in the privacy of their cells. Now [17th-century] women [were] using pain and suffering quite spontaneously to inflame that eroticism" (p. 206). Armstrong relates the story of St. Veronica Giuliani, who had a vision of Christ placing a crown of thorns on her head: "The excruciating pain of the thorns reduced Veronica to a state of orgasmic rapture. She wrote: 'I felt an agony of pain not only in my head but an ache which thrilled throughout my every limb, so that I was nigh swooning' " (p. 206).

It is hard to know how to interpret such stories. As Margaret Miles (1989) points out, male patriarchal authorities often determined the context in which these stories were told, and were not above using them for their own ideological ends.[14] If the church fathers encouraged the view that female asceticism was erotic, it may have been a way to control or contain their sexuality. It may be an example of what Miles calls "positive" images' being used to define what "good" female sexuality should be—something for women to imitate. "Positive images of women . . . play a very important role, even, or especially, in the most misogynist societies" (p. 130).

At the least, it would appear that these stories associate female sexuality with suffering. In this connection, a story told by Gloria Steinem (1991) is interesting: In simulating the first female orgasm ever filmed, the director of the movie *Ecstasy* plunged a large pin into the buttocks of the star, Hedy Lamarr, while the camera was focused on her face. In a similar vein, boys rated the faces of women displaying emotional distress—pain, fear—to be more sexually attractive than the same faces showing pleasure (Wolf, 1990).

WOMEN'S BODIES IN WOMEN'S MAGAZINES

The question of why the images of women's bodies in women's magazines became so thin at the time they did has never been fully answered. The whole blame cannot be put on the "war on obesity" declared and waged by the medical establishment, although it did prepare the ground for what followed by initiating a discourse on dieting. The argument that fat is unhealthy began in the 1950s, well before the pages of the fashion magazines became choked with pictures of emaciated models and words of "experts" on how to lose weight. The total number of articles listed under "diet" in the *Reader's Guide to Periodical Literature* actually *fell* by about one-half between 1955 and 1965. About 1965 the number skyrocketed, especially in women's fashion magazines, where over 70% of all diet articles after 1965 appeared (Wooley, 1993).

I suggest that the one-sex theory is making a comeback and that fat is now the predominant sign of gender (i.e., status). Fat may have become a more important sexual difference than genitalia. Fat is more "other" than femaleness per se. It has been a big part of the "otherness" of femaleness and what it has been made to symbolize. Fat is feminine, and like the concept of "feminine," it is thought to be "soft," "weak." Since girls are biologically programmed (as boys are not) to become fatter as they mature sexually into women, at puberty their body satisfaction plummets.

The early goddesses were fat and fecund, but with the overthrow of the goddess-worshiping cultures, fat became shameful and had to be concealed. Really "good" women (i.e., saints) starved it off their bodies. By the time the so-called sexual revolution had undressed "woman"—as the images of women's naked bodies metastasized from the peep shows of 42nd Street to the advertisements of Madison Avenue,[15] a move reminiscent of the migration of female sexual pleasure from the undomesticated clitoris to the more "womanly" vagina—*fat,* the sexual difference *par excellence,* the fat of women's buttocks, breasts, hips, abdomens, and thighs, could no longer be hidden.

Enormous changes in the technology by which images of women's bodies were produced and reproduced, reflecting the difference between camera art (i.e., photographs, film, TV) and traditional art (i.e., painting and drawings), help to explain why magazine images became so thin. Anne Hollander, in her book *Seeing through Clothes* (1978), has shown how paintings of nudes have been conditioned by clothes because such paintings always presuppose the clothed body. Up until some ill-defined point in history, there were relatively few images of naked female bodies to be seen in public; nude paintings were all there were, and there weren't many of them. On the other hand, there have always been many opportunities to see women wearing clothes. This is what the spectacle of fashion is all about; clothes have traditionally defined the erotic. As the fashions in clothes changed, the nude painting had to change with them in order to be perceived or responded to as erotic. Hollander (1978) says:

> Artistic idealizations purposely emphasize the erotic dimension, and they do so more successfully when they refer visually to the influence of fashion. . . . [P]erfect Classical or otherwise formal nudes, purporting to have only abstract and impersonal beauty, may sneakily be given a strong erotic cast by the simple means of slightly altering them to suit the current sense of the undressed body. . . . [Visual] details based on clothing make the nude look "realer" for its epoch and therefore sexier and more nude. . . . Neo-Classic statues at different epochs, all purporting to follow the originals, can be dated according to the dress of their own period and its influence even on incorruptible Greek perfection. (pp. 88–89)

> The erotic messages conveyed by fashion . . . are most acutely focused in the proportions of the female torso. It is the most significant field of fashionable alteration—and at the same time the one where the shape of fashion most readily appears to wear the authentic look of nature. The placement, size, and shape of the breasts, the set of the neck and shoulders, the relative girth and length of the rib cage, the depth and width of the pelvis and the exact disposition of its fleshy upholstery, front and back—all these, along with styles of posture both seated and upright, are continually shifting visually, according to the way clothes have been variously designed in history to help the female body look beautiful (and natural) *on their terms.* Nude art, unavoidably committed to Eros, accepts those terms. (p. 91, emphasis in original)

Hollander's analysis can be carried further by looking at the part played by photography in the social construction of the erotic. Benjamin (1969) argues that art changed in the "age of mechanical reproduction," marked by the introduction of the camera, first in photography and films and then in TV. Photography makes the implicit claim to be and is believed to be more "truthful" than drawings and paintings—indeed, to be "reality" itself (Kuhn, 1985).[16] There has been a geometrical increase in the number of images seen by the average person; this is as true of images of naked female bodies as it is of any other kind of image, if not more so. More people see more images of naked female bodies more often, and in an ever-increasing number of contexts, than ever before by a huge factor (Kuhn, 1985[17]; Wolf, 1990[18]). During the 1950s and 1960s, these images started becoming increasingly pornographic.

The increase in the number and influence of pornographic images (both in pornography "proper," and in the "legitimate" media such as advertisements, TV, and movies) is evidence, I believe, that pornography rather than fashion controls the meanings—the erotic connotations—of the images of women's bodies. Beer and car ads, *Sports Illustrated's* swimsuit issue, the intimate-apparel retailer Victoria's Secret (the heir to Frederick's of Hollywood), and many others use images whose power derives from pornography, especially readily available soft-core magazines like *Playboy*. This may be more than just another way that women's bodies have been appropriated; it may be bringing about decisive historical changes in the collective self-consciousness of women.

The Intensification of Women's Self-Consciousness

To understand fully how increased self-consciousness among women came about, it is important to understand the nature of the interactions among the actor or model, the camera, and the audience or viewer. Benjamin (1969) discusses this process with respect to the screen actor:

> The feeling of strangeness that overcomes the actor before the camera . . . is basically of the same kind as the estrangement felt before one's own image in the mirror. But now the reflected image has become separable, transportable. And where is it transported? Before the public. Never for a moment does the screen actor cease to be conscious of this fact. While facing the camera he [*sic*] knows that ultimately he will face the public, the consumers who constitute the market. This market, where he offers not only his labor but also his whole self, his heart and soul, is beyond his reach. (pp. 230–231)

As John Berger (1972) points out in a justly famous passage, women have long been in this kind of predicament. They have had to think of themselves as objects to be viewed, interpreted, and judged, like works of art:

> [A] woman's self [is] split into two. A woman must continually watch herself. She is almost continually accompanied by her own image of herself. . . . From earliest childhood she has been taught and persuaded to

survey herself continually. . . . The surveyor of woman in herself is male: the surveyed female. Thus she turns herself into an object—and most particularly an object of vision: a sight. (pp. 46–47)

Benjamin goes on to raise this question: "How does the cameraman compare with the painter?" (p. 233). To answer it, he uses an analogy involving a comparison of a surgeon who cuts his way into the patient's body and a magician (or "witch doctor") who practices the laying on of hands:

> Magician and surgeon compare to painter and cameraman. The painter maintains in his work a natural distance from reality, the cameraman penetrates deeply into its web. There is a tremendous difference between the pictures they obtain. That of the painter is a total one, that of the cameraman consists of multiple fragments which are assembled under a new law. Thus, for contemporary man [sic] the representation of reality by the film is incomparably more significant than that of the painter, since it offers, precisely because of the thoroughgoing permeation of reality with mechanical equipment, an aspect of reality which is free of all equipment. And that is what one is entitled to ask from a work of art. (pp. 233–234)[19]

Enter the Women's Movement

One effect of the women's movement is that women now spend more time in public and so are looked at more. Self-presentation has taken on an increased importance. What is presented (body plus clothes) is, by necessity, a statement and will be taken as such. Let us imagine a woman in a public situation—for example, a workplace. Let us assume that there is an "audience" of men, some of whom are her "superiors," which is to say they have power to make decisions affecting her interests. It is an audience not of her choosing. It is also an audience whose members believe it is their "birthright" to look at women's bodies. So far, none of this is particularly new; it would be more or less the same in the 1890s as it is in the 1990s. But this woman—unlike her predecessors—is aware that the gaze of men has been conditioned by movies and photographs, especially pornographic ones ("respectable" or otherwise). Her own eye has been trained by the same methods. She knows she is being judged by standards based, in large part, on pornography. These standards she knows at least as well as do the men who watch her. She has had to be constantly conscious of them, because her professional and personal fate may depend on how well she walks the line between "provocative" and "pretty."

Her "equipment" as a performer includes her clothes and her personality—what Berger (1972) calls her "exemplary treatment of herself [which] constitutes her presence [and which] regulates what is and is not 'permissible' within her presence" (pp. 46–47). But the gaze of the men in her audience is like Benjamin's (1969) camera, and the "reality" that it "gets at . . . free of all equipment" (p. 234) is the woman's own body. Deprived of her clothes and her personality, her body becomes the most important medium through which she can project her identity.

The habit of judging women's bodies has reached such a level of refinement that clothes might as well be invisible—so much so that the meaning of Hollander's (1978) title, *Seeing through Clothes,* can be seen to have shifted. Her original meaning was that artists, painting images of women's bodies, have been guided by the current fashion in clothes, so that it is "through" (i.e., by means or agency of) clothes that the artistic image of the body is "seen"—conceptualized, imagined, created. The new, more accurate, meaning of Hollander's title could be that we (both men and women) have been trained to the point that the tricks, the illusions, of fashion are no longer effective. Like Superman, we *are able to see through clothes, past them.* The clothes are discounted, or can be; their effect can be subtracted, nullified. A pretty accurate image of what a woman's body would look like undressed can be formed. This image is automatically compared to the abstract "ideal" images we carry in our heads, shaped by a steady diet of movies, magazine ads, and TV shows— a diet heavily flavored with pornography.

Little wonder that a woman dares not let her self-esteem and chances of success depend solely on her clothes and personality. The only thing she has to convey the message of how she wants to be treated, of what she wants people to think of her, is her body.

Why the Images Became Thin

Now to the question of why the images became thin. Naomi Wolf (1990) contends that women's magazines offer the closest thing women have ever had to a collective subjectivity:

> The images in women's magazines constitute the only cultural female experience which can begin to gesture at the breadth of solidarity possible among women, a solidarity as wide as half the race. It is a meager Esperanto, but in the absence of a better language of their own they must make do with one which is man-made and market-driven, and which hurts them. (p. 58)

The antifat sentiments of the magazines are fueled by women's culturally constructed embarrassment about their own naked bodies—an embarrassment heightened by the potent methods of the pornographic camera. Among the major elements of the aesthetics of pornography are the "fat" parts of the female body: buttocks, abdomen, hips, breast, and thighs. Kuhn (1985) writes about "a particular convention of photographic pornography, namely the fragmentation . . . of the human body":

> In pornography, photographs are often composed in such a way that a particular bodily part is greatly emphasized. . . . [A]n abstracted bodily part other than the face may be regarded as an expropriation of the subject's individuality. . . . But porn's attention to bits of bodies is never random. Pornography is preoccupied with what it regards as the signifiers of sexual difference and sexuality: genitals, breasts, buttocks. . . . [I]t is much more often the female body and its representation which receives this kind of treatment. (pp. 36–37)

The resumption of the feminist movement took place in the midst of a society flooded with pornographic representations of women's bodies. If women were going to be able to go out into the workplace, they needed representations of their bodies that could compete with, and "answer," the messages of pornography. They needed a new ideal body that they could carry in their minds—an ideal the attainment of which could hold at bay men's lust and leers.

The thinning of fashion magazine images is part of an attempt to change the meaning given the naked body by patriarchally condoned pornography. Patriarchy's attempt to reduce women to bodies has been met with a spiritualization of the representations of women's bodies—a removal of "excess" flesh,[20] reminiscent of the spiritualization attempted by medieval saints and ascetics, and for the same reasons. Karen Armstrong (1986) states:

> From the earliest days of the Church, although the overwhelming majority of women were married and dependent, Christianity kept before them the ideal of independent women who could liberate themselves from the shackles of their sex, free themselves of subjection to mere men and be fully equal to men. Later these women were the virgin saints. (p. 131)

A major difference between the church's early days and contemporary culture is the number and proportion of women who have adopted the ideal of "independence." This ideal has paved the way for the many diets that have accompanied the thin images in women's magazines. Women have been socialized to feel that they should suffer to attain an ideal, whether it be gender-specific "beauty" or the more general ideals of salvation, subjectivity, or autonomy. The fact that dieting and exercise are harder for women than they are for men thus *encourages* dieting and exercise rather than discourages them,[21] because "woman" should suffer more than "man": She has farther to go to reach perfection—a perfection that, because it is male-defined, still *looks* male. This is the legacy of the one-sex theory.[22]

So, once again, women are set against themselves, made to chase their own tails in a futile attempt to escape the trap patriarchy has made of their bodies. As Mary Wollstonecraft (1792/1971) wrote over 200 years ago:

> Why do [women] not discover, when, "in the noon of beauty's power," that they are treated like queens only to be deluded by hollow respect, till they are led to resign, or not assume, their natural prerogatives? Confined in cages like the feathered race, they have nothing to do but plume themselves, and stalk with mock majesty from perch to perch. (p. 73)

To summarize, the thinning of the magazine images began with two events: the geometric increase in pornography and the women's movement. The increase in pornography may have been independent of or may have been a reaction to the women's movement; it doesn't matter. What does matter is that women going into the work force needed representations or ideal images that could counter those of pornography. For reasons explained above, the counterimages had to involve primarily the body: Clothes had lost their power to enhance and protect body image. Given a long antifat tradition in the West—going all the way back to the overthrow of the goddess religions, continuing with the Christian traditions of asceticism, and culminating in the "war on obesity"—the direction of change was a foregone conclusion. The counterimages had to be thinner.

There was no alternative—at least not until a few years later, when musclebuilding became fashionable for women. Pornography had appropriated the "middle ground" in a double sense: the middle part of the female body (the hips, abdomen, buttocks, and breasts) and the middle-sized bodies. Bodies that were not too fat nor too thin—bodies of moderate, typical, or average size—had become, in the eyes of men *and* women, associated with the meanings given them by the pornographic camera.[23]

The magazines were in a position to respond to the need for images free of pornography's taint, and they did so in the only way they could. Adopting a one-sex strategy, they offered thin, then "toned," masculinized images of women's bodies; more and more (and increasingly stringent) diets; and even, in the wake of the failure of caloric restriction, other size-reducing, woman-diminishing methods, such as obesity surgery and liposuction.[24]

CONCLUSION: COLLECTIVE SUBJECTIVITY, REPRESENTATIONS, AND THE FUTURE

The fundamental fault of all the technologies of patriarchy that have had an impact on women's bodies (both surgical and representational) and the system that spawned them is this: the failure to recognize, to honor, to respect, and to make room for the subjectivity—the thoughts and feelings—of half the human race. The denial of collective subjectivity to women is a structural component of patriarchy. The effects of this failure permeate every phase of patriarchy, including its greatest achievement: science. The biological/physiological and increasingly surgical approach to obesity, to give one example, would have been abandoned years ago if the "warriors" against obesity had not held in contempt the women whose bodies they so futilely sought to change. Individual women have been forced to share this contempt, because the obesity "researchers," aided by the whole history of patriarchal representations of women, have convinced them that their failure to be "normal," "good," "beautiful" (i.e., thin) is their own fault. Their salvation can only be attained through suffering (i.e., starving, submission to surgery, and pointless physical labor), as Christianity has suggested to women for centuries. This strategy isolates individual women, destroying the possibility, if not the very idea, of the political power that comes from collective subjectivity.

Perhaps it is time for women to take a radically skeptical look at patriarchal science, especially the "health" sciences. What health professionals have done to women's bodies is every bit as violent as what sex criminals have done. I would wager that many more women have died from obesity treatments alone than have died from sex crimes. I would also wager that what the health industry ends up doing to women (and the women's movement) will make what the cosmetics and fashion industries have done pale in comparison.

It is becoming clear to many people that a megarevolution is needed in the way society is organized—a shift in paradigms as momentous as the advent of patriarchy. In the words of Gerda Lerner (1986):

> By making the term "man" subsume "woman" and arrogate to itself the representation of all of humanity, men have built a conceptual error of vast proportion into all of their thought. By taking the half for the whole, they have not only missed the essence of whatever they are describing, but they have distorted it in such a fashion that they cannot see it clearly. . . . The androcentric fallacy, which is built into all mental constructs of Western civilization, cannot be rectified by simply "adding women." What it demands for rectification is a radical restructuring of thought and analysis which once and for all accepts the fact that humanity consists in equal parts

of men and women and the experience, thought, and insights of both sexes must be represented in every symbolization that is made about human beings. (p. 220)

Patriarchy has reached its acme. It has made men into the perfect image of their God. Patriarchal culture, which institutionalized human violence and attributed it to a God of wrath, has finally delivered to man himself the ultimate patriarchal power: the power to end all human life.

There is a collective intuition that men have screwed up the world enough, and that if something isn't done about it very soon, the human race is doomed. In the words of Riane Eisler (1988):

> Today we stand at another potentially branching point [the first was the advent of patriarchy]. [It is] a time when the lethal power of the Blade— amplified a millionfold by megatons of nuclear warheads—threatens to put an end to all human culture. . . . The root of the problem lies in a social system in which the power of the Blade is idealized—in which both men and women are taught to equate true masculinity with violence and domi- nance and to see men who do not conform to this ideal as "too soft" or "effeminate." (p. xviii)

In the words of René Girard (1972):

> It seems increasingly clear that the pressure of violence or the insistence of truth . . . has forced modern man [*sic*] to come face to face with this same violence or truth. For the first time he [*sic*] is confronted with a perfectly straight-forward and even scientifically calculable choice between total destruction and the total renunciation of violence. (p. 240)

The subconscious awareness of what they have done to women— denying them humanity, a collective subjectivity—has haunted and still haunts men. It is a major source of "creative" guilt and dread. Kate Millett (1969), Camille Paglia (1990), and Wendy Lesser (1991) have all examined how male artists and writers have dealt with these effects— albeit from vastly different perspectives, ranging from worshipful awe (Paglia) to excoriating rage (Millett). Their conclusions are as wildly varying as the works and men they have analyzed. It is highly unlikely, however, that men will ever exorcise these demons without help from the "other half," or at least until women refuse to allow these demons to be palmed off as representative of women in general.

A big part of creating a female collective subjectivity will be gaining control of the process by which women are represented—by which the visual images of women are used to define "woman." In the words of Margaret Miles (1989):

> Women's collective self-representation in the public sphere ultimately has the task and responsibility of deciding both what is to be said about women as women and creating the imagery and language to say it.
>
> The task, no doubt, is enormous. But it is already launched. In courts of law, work places, churches, public media, and academic discourse, the process of achieving the conditions for women's collective self-representation has been going on for at least a century, and with gathering momentum for several decades. (p. 172)

Neither of the two predominant types of visual representations of "woman" is fully human. The "fat" pornographic images present (or represent) a female body without a mind, without subjectivity. The fashion models in women's magazines are meant to represent women with minds, to acknowledge and appeal to female subjectivity, but they have no bodies. Patriarchal culture still has not found an acceptable way to represent a whole woman; women remain far too frightening. An intelligent, strong-willed, full-bodied woman could, according to the ancient dogma of patriarchy, use her sexual powers to arouse the lust of man and thereby cloud his precious reason (lust and reason being his "essence") and manipulate him for her own unknown and unknowable end. She continues to be a terrifying prospect, representing the ultimate threat to patriarchy—the end of patriarchy, the void.

Like God, "man" is not represented, because men represent. Men are subjects; representations are objects created by subjects for other subjects. Man's representations are his way of creating, defining, and empowering himself, by casting out all that is not himself. He is shaped by what he disavows as much as by what he embraces; he is known by his works; his nature is inferred from his actions. As women define themselves by their actions and works, they disavow and free themselves of male representations, reclaiming their bodies and themselves as whole persons.

NOTES

1. Christensen (1990) asserts that male curiosity about women's bodies is "natural." It may be "natural," but "natural" is a cultural category, and this chapter is an attempt to examine the ideas of various thinkers who have treated it as such. The assertion that something is "natural" is no excuse for blocking needed social change; it is no reason not to begin to examine the possible effects on women's self-esteem of men's "natural" curiosity; and it should not prevent us from trying to understand the forces that shape it.

2. The whole piece from which this quotation comes, composed by Bierce's fictional poet "Jogo Tyree," foreshadows what is to be discussed later:

To men a man is but a mind. Who cares
What face he carries or what form he wears?
But woman's body is the woman. O,
Stay thou, my sweetheart, and do never go,
But heed the warning the sage hath said:
A woman absent is a woman dead.
(Bierce, 1911/1958; p. 9)

3. *"Patriarchy* . . . means the manifestation and institutionalization of male dominance over women and children in the family and the extension of male dominance over women in society in general. It implies that men hold power in all the important institutions of society and that women are deprived of access to such power. It does *not* imply that women are either totally powerless or totally deprived of rights, influence, and resources" (Lerner, 1986, p. 239).

4. "[A]long with the first awareness of self in relation to other humans, animals, and the rest of nature must have come awareness of the awesome mystery—of the fact that life emerges from the body of woman" (Eisler, 1988, p. 6).

5. "These statues of women . . . have been found [at] sites in areas as far apart as Spain, France, Germany, Austria, Czechoslovakia, and Russia. These sites and figures appear to span a period of at least ten thousand years" (Stone, 1976, p. 13).

6. Stone (1976, p. 15) quotes James Mellart: "Art makes its appearance in the form of animal carvings and statuettes of the supreme deity, the Mother Goddess."

7. Eisler (1988) writes: "The one thing they [the conquering patriarchal cultures] all had in common was a dominator model of social organization: a social system in which male dominance, male violence, and a generally hierarchic and authoritarian social structure was the norm. Another commonality was that, in contrast to the societies that laid the foundations for Western civilization [i.e., the prepatriarchal societies], the way they characteristically acquired material wealth was not by developing more effective technologies of production, but through ever more effective technologies of destruction" (p. 45). She continues: "The power to dominate and destroy through the sharp blade gradually supplants the view of power as the capacity to support and nurture life" (p. 53). Stone (1976, p. 66) quotes Giuseppi Sormani: "The Aryans [i.e., the patriarchal societies] came into contact with highly civilized and already ancient forms of settled society, in comparison with which they were barbarians."

8. Stone (1976), discussing ancient Hebrew laws, comments: "Perhaps the most shocking laws of all were those that declared that a woman was to be stoned or burned to death for losing her virginity before marriage . . . , and that, upon being the victim of rape, a single woman was forced to marry the rapist; if she was already betrothed or married she was stoned to death for having been raped" (p. 56).

9. Various comments by Lerner (1986) amplify this point: "The oppression of women antedates slavery and makes it possible" (p. 77); "[T]he rule of some men over men can be justified by ascribing to those men some of the same qualities ascribed to the female" (p. 209); "Class is not a separate construct from

gender; rather, class is expressed in genderic terms" (p. 213); "In its ultimate origin, 'difference' as a distinguishing mark between the conquered and the conquerors was based on the first clearly observable difference, that between the sexes" (p. 214).

10. Olsen (1978) says that in this century, only 1 of 12 writers have been women.

11. Girard (1972) takes issue with Freud on the issue of the source of forbidden impulses: "The incest wish, the patricide wish, do not belong to the child but spring from the mind of the adult. . . . The son is always the last to learn that what he desires is incest and patricide, and it is the hypocritical adults who undertake to enlighten him in this matter" (p. 175).

12. Lerner (1986) notes: "In the historical context of the times of the writing of Genesis, the snake was clearly associated with the fertility goddess and symbolically represented her. Thus, by God's command, the free and open sexuality of the fertility goddess was to be forbidden to fallen women. The way her sexuality was to find expresson was in motherhood. Her sexuality was so defined as to serve her motherly function, and it was limited to two conditions: she was to be subordinate to her husband, and she was to bring forth her children in pain" (p. 196). Gimbutas (1989) adds: "Worship of the nonpoisonous snake as a symbol of life energy, cyclic renewal, and immortality continued until the twentieth century. The hibernating and awakening snake [was] a metaphor of dying and reawakening nature and . . . an essential symbol of the immortality of life energy" (p. 319).

13. The idea that the masculine imagination must transcend the influence of transient female sexuality in order to create things of lasting cultural value is echoed in the following passage from Freud (quoted by Marcus, 1962, p. xxxix): "This very incapacity in the sexual instinct to yield to full satisfaction as soon as it submits to the first demands of culture becomes the source, however, of the grandest cultural achievements, which are brought to birth by ever greater sublimation of the components of the sexual instinct. For what motive would induce man [sic] to put his [sic] sexual energy to other uses if by any disposal of it he could obtain fully satisfying pleasure? He would never let go of this pleasure and would make no progress." These pictures of women and Death are in the service of the "demands of culture," it would seem.

14. "*The Martyrdom of Ss. Perpetua and Felicitas* is an unusually vivid example of the appropriation of a woman's writing as support for theological and ecclesiastical concerns her text does not acknowledge as her own" (Miles, 1989, p. 62).

15. Armstrong (1986) comments: "This new unsmiling sexiness [of present-day fashion models] is the traditional scowl that girls formerly wore only in pornographic photography, but which has now spread from the pages of *Playboy* out onto the billboards and into the Sunday color supplements" (p. 59).

16. Kuhn (1985) states: "One of the defining features of photography as against other forms of visual representation—painting and drawing, say—is its capacity to appear 'truthful.' Photography seems to record, rather than interpret, the piece of the world in front of the camera. A human artist may filter the 'real world' through her or his creative imagination, but the camera and lens are often

regarded simply as pieces of machinery which allows an image, a duplicate, of the world to be transferred onto film. A photograph stands as evidence that whatever is inside the frame of the image 'really' happened, was 'really' there: it is authentic, convincing, true. But photography actually involves as much artifice as does any other mode of visual representation" (p. 26).

17. Kuhn (1985) asserts: "Developments in techniques of mechanical reproduction of photographic images and consequently in the capacity to produce large quantities cheaply [footnote citing Benjamin, 1969] opened up limitless horizons for pornographers" (pp. 24–25).

18. Wolf (1990) adds: "[P]ornography [is] now the biggest media category. Worldwide, pornography generates an estimated $7 billion a year, more than the legitimate film and music industries combined. Pornographic films outnumber other films by three to one, grossing $365 million in the US alone, or $1 million a day" (p. 60).

19. The metaphor of the surgeon is especially apt in view of the earlier discussion of ovariectomy. Like biology, pornography has come to mean—via the technology of the camera, with its "surgical" technique and its "seeing is believing" propaganda—that women can be studied like any other "natural" object. Kuhn (1985) states: "The project of the softcore female pinup . . . promise[s] that femininity may be investigated, even understood, by scrutinizing its visible marks" (p. 38); "The spectator is addressed as if the quest for knowledge, pleasure, closure, were directed exclusively towards women and the feminine. . . . The feminine is constructed as the principal object of inquiry because the masculine is taken for granted as the place from which the spectator looks" (p. 34). In the same way that in the 19th-century male social behavior was never problematized and the male sexual organs never became the target of the surgeon's knife, male psychology and anatomy were pretty much off limits to the pornographer's camera as well. Kuhn (1985) finds it "hard to fathom why it is that both the sexual subjectivity which sets itself as the cultural norm (masculinity) and the sexual practice we are all meant to strive for (heterosexuality) are both in certain respects unrepresentable. Photographs of erect penises, for example, are usually confined to hardcore and to gay pornography, while representations of acts of heterosexual intercourse are also limited in availability. . . . The most widely available varieties of porn are preoccupied much more with the female than with the male body" (pp. 33–34).

20. Miles (1990) notes: "The association of excessive flesh with an inferior development of spirit or intelligence could be traced through centuries from Plato's general suggestion that any person with 'more flesh' was 'stupid and insensitive' to the more specific association of sin (or 'the flesh') with female flesh in medieval Christianity."

21. As Carole Spitzack (1990) says, "A *problematizing* of women's bodies mandates closer gazing and scrutiny, giving legitimacy to ever-greater discipline, to consuming attention to appearance" (p. 42, emphasis in original).

22. Susan Bordo (1990) makes similar observations. In the following passage from her "Reading the Slender Body," she first suggests that thinness may be a result of the fear of female sexuality (the goddess still survives!), and then discusses what it means from the viewpoint of women themselves: "[F]emale

hunger (as a code for female desire) is especially problematized during periods of disruption and change in established gender-relations and in the position of women. In such periods (of which our own is arguably one), nightmare images of . . . 'the consuming woman' theme proliferate in art and literature (images representing female desire unleashed [*Fatal Attraction*]), while dominant constructions of the female body become more sylphlike—unlike the body of a fully developed woman, more like that of an adolescent boy (images that might be called female desire unborn). . . . This shift, however, needs to be interpreted not only from the standpoint of male anxiety over women's desires . . . but also from the standpoint of the women who embrace the 'new look.' For them, it may have a different meaning; it may symbolize, not so much the containment of female desire, as its liberation from a domestic, reproductive destiny. The fact that the slender body can carry both the (seemingly contradictory) meanings is one reason . . . for its compelling attraction in periods of gender-change" (p. 103). Bordo does not emphasize, as I have done, the role pornographic images may have played in the new fashion for thin bodies.

   23. In trying to understand its meanings, it should be kept in mind that pornography—which first began to flourish in the 19th-century, when the two-sex theory was at its height—did what Greek and Christian art had not done (at least not at first; only as an afterthought, and/or not in a straightforward effort to create frankly erotic representations): It had as its project the creation of representations of an ideal female body different from the male body. As I have discussed, when these images began to seep, and then to flood, into the mainstream media because of the "sexual revolution," they met resistance; part of that resistance was the rise of the thin and (later) muscular ideals. Thin is a negative ideal—the female body is stripped of pornography's "well-placed" fat. Muscular is a positive ideal—muscles are masculine.

   24. These means of obtaining "beauty"—starving, exercising, and submitting to the surgeon's knife—dissipate, transform, and redirect the anger a woman feels toward the patriarchy back onto her body, and provide an ideology that allows her to experience her suffering as something spiritual, healthy, and good. And there are real rewards as well, such as jobs and sexual attention (granted, the latter is often a mixed blessing). Dieting and exercise have the further advantage of *appearing* to be "democratic" and "fair." The poorest woman can "afford" to starve and exercise. The "ugliest" woman can improve her looks by practicing these rituals. They *seem* to put power in the hands of individual women themselves.

REFERENCES

Armstrong, K. (1986). *The gospel according to woman: Christianity's creation of the sex war in the West.* Garden City, NY: Doubleday/Anchor.
Benjamin, W. (1969). *Illuminations.* New York: Schocken Books.
Berger, J. (1972). *Ways of seeing.* London: British Broadcasting Corporation.
Bernheimer, R. (1961). *The nature of representation: A phenomenological inquiry.* New York: New York University Press.

Bierce, A. (1958). *The devil's dictionary.* New York: Dover. (Original work published 1911)

Bordo, S. (1990). Reading the slender body. In M. Jacobus, E. F. Keller, & S. Shuttleworth (Eds.), *Body/politics: Women and the discourses of science.* New York: Routledge.

Bynum, C. W. (1985). Fast, feast, and flesh: The religious significance of food to medieval women. *Representations, 11,* 1–25.

Caputi, J. (1987). *The age of sex crime.* Bowling Green, OH: Bowling Green State Popular Press.

Chapkis, W. (1986). *Beauty secrets: Women and the politics of appearance.* Boston: South End Press.

Christensen, F. M. (1990). *Pornography: The other side.* New York: Praeger.

de Beauvoir, S. (1989). *The second sex* (H. M. Parshley, Trans.). New York: Vintage Books. (Original work published 1949)

Ehrenreich, B., & English, D. (1978). *For her own good: 150 years of the experts' advice to women.* Garden City, NY: Doubleday/Anchor.

Eisler, R. (1988). *The chalice and the blade.* San Francisco: Harper & Row.

Gilman, A. L. (1985). *Differences and pathology: Stereotypes of sexuality, race, and madness.* Ithaca, NY: Cornell University Press.

Gimbutas, M. (1989). *The language of the goddess.* London: Thames & Hudson.

Girard, R. (1972). *Violence and the sacred* (P. Gregory, Trans.). Baltimore: Johns Hopkins University Press.

Greenspan, M. (1983). *A new approach to women and therapy.* New York: Mc-Graw-Hill.

Haslam, M. (1978). *The real world of the surrealists.* New York: Galley Press.

Hollander, A. (1978). *Seeing through clothes.* New York: Viking Press.

Kuhn, A. (1985). *The power of the image: Essays on representation and sexuality.* London: Routledge & Kegan Paul.

Laqueur, T. (1986). Orgasm, generation, and the politics of reproductive biology. *Representations, 14,* 1–41.

Laqueur, T. (1990). *Making sex: Body and gender from the Greeks to Freud.* Cambridge, MA: Harvard University Press.

Lerner, G. (1986). *The creation of patriarchy.* New York: Oxford University Press.

Lesser, W. (1991). *His other half: Men looking at women through art.* Cambridge, MA: Harvard University Press.

Marcus, S. (1962). Introduction. In S. Freud, *Three essays on the theory of sexuality,* trans. J. Strachey. New York: Basic Books.

Miles, M. R. (1989). *Carnal knowing: Female nakedness and religious meaning in the Christian West.* New York: Vantage Books.

Melville, R. (1973). *Erotic art of the West.* New York: Putnam.

Millett, K. (1969). *Sexual politics.* New York: Ballantine Books.

Olds, C. C., Williams, R. G., & Levin, W. R. (1976). *Images of love and death in late medieval and Renaissance art.* Ann Arbor: University of Michigan Museum of Art. (Essays by Olds & Williams; catalogue by Levin)

Olsen, T. (1978). *Silences.* New York: Delta/Seymour Lawrence.

Ortner, S. B. (1974). Is female to male as nature is to culture? In M. Rosaldo & L. Lamphene (Eds.), *Women, culture and society.* Stanford, CA: Stanford University Press.

Paglia, C. (1990). *Sexual personae: Art and decadence from Nefertiti to Emily Dickinson*. New Haven, CT: Yale University Press.

Schiebinger, L. (1989). *The mind has no sex? Women in the original of modern science.* Cambridge, MA: Harvard University Press.

Selz, J. (1976). *Edvard Munch* (E. B. Hennessy, Trans.). New York: Crown.

Sjoo, M., & Mor, B. (1987). *The great cosmic mother: Rediscovering the religion of the earth*. San Francisco: Harper & Row.

Spitzack, C. (1990). *Confessing excess: Women and the politics of body reduction*. Albany: State University of New York Press.

Steinem, G. (1991, February). Women in the dark: Of goddesses, abuse, and dreams. *Ms.,* pp. 35–37.

Stone, M. (1976). *When God was a woman*. San Diego: Harcourt Brace Jovanovich/Harvest.

Van Woerkom, F. (1973). *Face to face: A collection of drawings and political cartoons*. New York: Knopf.

Wolf, N. (1990). *The beauty myth*. London: Chatto & Windus.

Wollstonecraft, M. (1971). *A vindication of the rights of women*. New York: Source Book Press. (Original work published 1792)

Wooley, O. W. (1993). Unpublished raw data.

3

"I'll Die for the Revolution but Don't Ask Me Not to Diet": Feminism and the Continuing Stigmatization of Obesity

ESTHER D. ROTHBLUM

> *Sometimes I think we've all gone crazy. Sometimes I feel like a feminist at a Right-to-Life conference, an atheist in Puritan New England, a socialist in the Reagan White House. Sometimes I fear that fat women have become our culture's last undefeated heretics, our greatest collective nightmare made all-too-solid flesh. I worry—despite our new ethos of sexual freedom—that female bodies are as terrifying and repulsive as ever, as greatly in need of purification and mortification. Certainly these days, when I hear people talking about temptation and sin, guilt and shame, I know they're referring to food rather than sex. . . . Everything, for women, boils down to body size.*
> —Carol Sternhell (1985, p. 62, emphasis added)

A FRIEND OF MINE was teaching an advanced seminar in women's studies. No matter what topic she covered, her students had a more radical analysis than she did. With one exception: When she discussed women's weight, the students did not believe that this had anything to do with feminism. These students' attitudes are reflected by feminists in general. Why haven't feminists focused on hatred of fat in our society? This chapter examines the social factors that influence women's feelings about their appearance and body size. Feminists have fought for women's rights in many arenas, including women's rights to

53

control their bodies. Women's body weight has yet to be included in this fight and is still under the influence of the mainstream media and the economy.

In a society that ranks people according to their financial value to society, a woman's appearance may be her most precious asset. To be female in the United States is to be acutely aware of one's appearance. Rubin (cited in Freeman, 1986) asked women to describe themselves, and found that most began by describing their appearance, even when they were highly successful in their professions. "Looksism," prejudice or discrimination based on appearance, has an adverse effect on all women who are not white, middle-class, heterosexual, young, thin, and able-bodied, as well as on many who are. Given the importance of physical appearance norms for women, it is vital that feminists consider all the ways in which women's appearance has been proscribed and controlled by social institutions.

Faludi (1991) and Wolf (1991) have argued that the feminist movement, rather than reducing the emphasis on women's appearance, has created a backlash that has heightened attention to women's bodies. The following sections examine the cult of appearance, with attention to the role played by feminism.

INTRODUCTION: FACTS ABOUT WEIGHT

"Obesity" is generally defined as a body weight 20% or more above stated ideals (U.S. Department of Health, Education and Welfare, 1979). Most people in the United States have seen these height and weight tables and know how much they "should" weigh. In fact, the tables were normed on a population of life insurance policy holders; are slanted toward affluent Caucasians of northern European descent residing on the East Coast; and are unrepresentative of people who do not fit this demographic profile. Furthermore, the tables were normed on young adults of both genders, whereas most women gain weight in middle age (see Bennett & Gurin, 1982, for a review of this literature). Regardless of actual weight, most females, especially adolescents, consider themselves "too fat." In contrast, the self-perceptions of men and adolescent boys are more closely related to their actual size (Tiggemann & Rothblum, 1988).

In Western society, it is universally believed that the "causes" of obesity are eating too much and exercising too little. It is, of course, true that with sufficient food restriction everyone loses weight, although women can survive starvation longer than men because of women's greater protective layers of body fat. But researchers have not found differences in the food intake of fat and thin people—even with methods that control for social desirability effects, such as the observation of fat and thin diners in cafeterias, or random home visits and examination of food available in fat and thin people's kitchens (see Wooley, Wooley, & Dyrenforth, 1979, for a review).

Weight differences appear to reflect differences in physiologically determined "set points" (Nisbett, 1972), which are unique for each individual. One person's set point may be 80 pounds, and that of another may be 350 pounds. Set point mechanisms counteract individual efforts to change weight through dieting; in fact, repeated dieting may result in a *higher* set point, as the body adjusts to this modern form of "famine" by storing more fat (Brownell, Greenwood, Stellar, & Shrager, 1986; Polivy & Herman, 1983). Set point notwithstanding, millions of women and girls in the United States diet. One recent survey found 63% of high school girls to be on diets (Rosen & Gross, 1987), compared with only 16.2% of boys. The longer the follow-up period, the more weight former dieters have regained, suggesting that it is virtually impossible to maintain weight losses for long periods of time (Bennett, 1986; Brownell & Jeffery, 1987; Garner & Wooley, 1991).

In Western society, it is strongly believed that it is unhealthy to be fat. The health care professions spend much time and money convincing the public that obesity is a health problem. In fact, research purporting to show a relationship between weight and various health risks is currently the subject of considerable controversy. For example, studies often fail to control for income and may suffer from a number of confounding variables, since in Western nations fat people are poorer than thin people. These studies compare the rich and poor on health risks, and poor people do not have the same access to health insurance and preventive care. Fat people diet more than thin people, and dieting itself can result in a number of health risks—including the very health risks often associated with obesity, such as hypertension, high cholesterol, and diabetes (Polivy & Herman, 1983). A recent article in the *New England Journal of Medicine* (Lissner et al., 1991) reported that people who dieted and regained weight had higher mortality rates than those who did not diet and stayed at the same (high) weight. In addition, fat people are subjected to stigmatization and discrimination, and the stress of such oppression can result in stress-related health problems.

THE STIGMA OF WEIGHT FOR WOMEN

Given the facts described above, why do women continue to diet, and why does the culture encourage them to do so? Obesity is highly stigmatized in Western society, particularly for women. Beginning in nursery school, children show a dislike of fatness, rating figure drawings of fat children more negatively than drawings of children with physical disabilities (Goodman, Richardson, Dornbusch, & Hastorf, 1963). This stigmatization continues in elementary school, adolescence, and adulthood, and involves the attribution of a number of negative social and academic/occupational qualities. It extends to attitudes held by professionals, including mental health professionals (Agell & Rothblum, 1991; Young & Powell, 1985), nutritionists (Maiman, Wang, Becker, Finlay, & Simonson, 1979), employers (Rothblum, Brand, Miller, & Oetjen, 1990), physicians (Maddox & Liederman, 1969), and even landlords (Karris, 1977).

Antifat prejudice is so acceptable in our society that Crandall (1991) has suggested that it is a better method for studying discrimination and prejudice than is racism or sexism, since the latter are influenced by social desirability factors. Furthermore, unlike skin color or gender, weight is thought to be under voluntary control, so that fat people are held responsible for their condition and for changing it (DeJong, 1980; Maddox, Back, & Liederman, 1968).

One consequence of antifat attitudes in the United States has been the downward economic mobility of fat people, especially women. The Midtown Manhattan Study (Moore, Stunkard, & Srole, 1962) found that 30% of women in the lowest socioeconomic group were obese, compared with only 4% in the highest-income group. The comparable figures for men were 33% and 22%, respectively—still different, but not as much as the figures for women. This study also found fatness in women to be associated with downward social mobility: Fat women tended to have lower incomes than their parents, whereas thin women had higher incomes than their parents.

Why are fat women poor and downwardly socially mobile? First, research has shown that thin women have a greater chance of being accepted by elite colleges, such as Ivy League and Seven Sisters colleges, than do fat women, even when their credentials (e.g., grades, SAT scores, IQ scores, extracurricular activities, parental income, health, and motivation to attend college) are identical (Canning & Mayer, 1966, 1967). Furthermore, when they do attend college, fat women are less likely to receive family financial support for attending college than are thin women; this remains true even when parents' education, income, race, family size, and number of children are factored out (Crandall, 1991). Education is an important prerequisite for success in most careers. Both of these studies found weight differences to have less impact for men.

Studies that have examined weight and employment have also

found discrimination against fat women. My colleagues and I (Rothblum et al., 1990) surveyed over 400 male and female members of a national association for fat persons about their employment; we found that the members had suffered considerable employment discrimination. Many had been turned down for jobs, denied promotions or raises, denied benefits, demoted, fired or pressured to resign, questioned about weight, or urged to lose weight. There was a positive correlation between weight and degree of discrimination. Furthermore, women experienced such employment discrimination at lower weights than did men. Weight was also correlated with more instances of victimization, such as discrimination during junior high, high school, or college, and lower self-confidence in work-related settings. Fat people more often indicated concealing their bodies (e.g., using the telephone rather than meeting in person) as a way of avoiding employment discrimination (Rothblum et al., 1990).

Other studies have focused on employers. Roe and Eickwort (1976) asked employers of women who were either current or former welfare recipients whether they would hire fat women, and about 16% responded that they would not. Furthermore, nearly half of these employers stated that obesity constituted a medical basis for denial of employment. We (Rothblum, Miller, & Garbutt, 1988) showed college students job resumés accompanied by photographs of either fat or thin women (matched for physical attractiveness) or written descriptions (not matched for physical attractiveness) of fat or thin women. No significant difference was found in response to photographs, but students who read resumés accompanied by written descriptions of fat women rated them lower on supervisory potential, self-discipline, professional appearance, personal hygiene, and ability to perform a physically strenuous job than did students who read the *identical* resumés when accompanied by descriptions of thin women. Larkin and Pines (1979) showed videotapes of either fat or thin men and women to college students. Students who saw videotapes of fat people were less likely to recommend that they be hired, and more likely to indicate that they themselves should be hired for a job, than did students who saw videotapes of thin people.

One way for women to achieve upward social mobility is to marry wealth, and it is likely that thin women marry wealthier men than do fat women. Research has indicated that men's status depends to a greater extent on the attractiveness of their female partners than on their own physical attractiveness (Berscheid & Walster, 1974). Since being fat is considered extremely unattractive in Western society (Tiggemann & Rothblum, 1988), fat women are probably less likely to marry "up."

Despite the documentation of educational and employment discrimination against fat women, it is still widely believed that poor people are fat because they do not know much about nutrition, because they cannot afford to exercise, because they are undereducated, or because they cannot afford healthy foods (see Rothblum, 1992, for a review). In short, most people believe that *poverty causes obesity,* when in fact research suggests that *obesity causes poverty.* The former theory holds fat people responsible for their condition, whereas the latter indicates that fat people are systematically denied economic success.

WOMEN'S APPEARANCE NORMS THROUGH HISTORY AND ACROSS CULTURES

As old paintings, photographs, and writings attest, female fashions in appearance and dress have changed dramatically across time and place; nevertheless, commonalities in norms can be found. Women have been expected to look and dress in ways that immobilize them. The constricting norms have been thought, by people of each time period, to be the invention of the women themselves. Without conformity to these norms, women have been considered ugly or immoral by men and blocked from marriage or otherwise functioning in society. Often, as noted by Brownmiller (1984), the fashion has been to extend and exaggerate the smallness of a feature that is naturally smaller in women to begin with (e.g., size of feet, body weight). The constricted body parts or articles of clothing have been considered highly erotic by men. And finally, in many instances the medical profession has endorsed a practice as health-promoting, while simultaneously treating large numbers of women for medical complications resulting from it. Three examples— foot binding, corsets, and genital mutilation—reflect the commonalities described above.

For a thousand years, the feet of young upper-class Chinese girls were bound in order to break and deform the bones of the feet and create 3-inch "lotus hooks." As adults, these women could not walk and had to be carried. Daly (1990) has described how Chinese men portrayed women as the inventors and supporters of this practice. Without conforming to this, upper-class women could not marry. Most importantly, the maimed feet were considered the height of erotica by men. Both Brownmiller (1984) and Daly (1990) have written about male sexual attraction to the "hobbled" women.

The corset was an article of clothing designed both to improve the appearance and to strengthen the torso of Western women. The corset applied between 20 and 80 pounds of pressure on the abdomen, caused difficulty breathing, and often led to fainting (Brownmiller, 1984). The medical profession endorsed the corset as improving women's weak waists and spines, when in fact it caused women's muscles to atrophy. As Brownmiller has pointed out, the corset and its relatives—bras, girdles, and garters—have remained items of erotica for men. It is probably no coincidence that the media focused on feminists in the 1960s and 1970s as "bra burners."

Throughout much of history, some women's genitals were cut off if they were too large (see Hosken, 1982, for a review). Female genital mutilation is still practiced in most central African nations today, affecting 60–90 million women (Lightfoot-Klein, 1989). In some nations of central Africa, the clitoris of a young girl is removed because it is thought to be a small penis, and thus the girl cannot be considered female until the clitoris is removed. In some nations (e.g., the Sudan, Egypt, and Djibouti), an even more drastic procedure is used to remove the clitoris, the labia minora, and the inner parts of the labia majora. The remaining skin is sewn shut, leaving only a hole the size of a matchstick for urination and menstruation. This procedure is done to provide a "chastity belt" for women until marriage (Lightfoot-Klein, 1989).

Most women in these nations are unaware that women in other parts of the world have not been "circumcised" in this way. The procedures are performed on young girls by female midwives, and are considered to be something that women do to one another. Some nations have made these practices illegal, yet their leaders complain that the practices continue because women want them. Women are not considered marriageable unless their genitals are mutilated in this way. Furthermore, women are told that their genitals are dangerous—that the clitoris can poison a man if it touches his penis during intercourse (Lightfoot-Klein, 1989). Women are also told that intact female genitals will cause voracious sexuality, bad odor, and complications during childbirth. In fact, the removal of genitals and the sewing together of the remaining skin cause odor as a result of menstrual and urinary retention, and lead to complications during childbirth. In urban areas, physicians and nurses (including missionaries) perform the operation, and there have been recent cases of European physicians' performing the operation on the daughters of African diplomats in Europe (Lightfoot-Klein, 1989).

These examples reflect important elements of social control of women's appearance. Under the guise of fashion—and fashion that was supposedly dictated by other women—women's behavior and appearance have been radically restricted. Wolf (1991) has also emphasized that what is important about women's beauty norms is that they affect *behavior* as much as appearance. Thus, women with bound feet cannot walk, and women with mutilated genitals cannot express their sexuality. The restrictions were often praised as healthy by the medical profession, even when they harmed women. At the same time, the changes in women's appearance made them appear less like men by accentuating what was already smaller in women's bodies (smaller feet, smaller waist, the clitoris as smaller than the penis), and this difference was eroticized by men. As Brownmiller (1984) has stated,

> Each device of beautification restricted [a woman's] freedom and weakened her strength; each provided a feminine obstacle course through which she endeavored to move with artificial grace. Each instrument of discomfort was believed by her to be a superior emblem of her privileged position and a moral requisite for correct behavior, and each ingenious constriction was sentimentalized by men as erotic in its own right, apart from the woman it was supposed to improve. (p. 33)

Society's strict appearance norms have had disadvantages for women (e.g., constriction of movement, health risks) and advantages for men (e.g., erotic enhancement, forced chastity of women).

WOMEN'S APPEARANCE NORMS TODAY

An angry fat woman
is a dangerous thing.
—Karen W. Stimson
(1991, p. 5)

In prehistoric times, goddess figures were both fat and pregnant, linking obesity with sexuality and fertility. In Victorian times, obesity in women was considered sexual, women's "silken layer" (Wolf, 1991, p. 192). In poor countries where large numbers of people die of malnutrition and infectious disease, thinness is not desired (Rothblum, 1990). Until the 20th century, women in the United States were considered beautiful if they had large breasts and large hips—symbols of reproductive ability (Ewen, 1988).

The positive view of body fat that prevailed for so much of history gave way in the 20th century in the United States to fat aversion. While the suffragists struggled to obtain new rights for women, the beauty ideal shifted to the thin and flat-chested "flappers." Hesse-Biber (1991) contends that the term "flapper" was also used by the media to ridicule the struggles of women by suggesting trivial, busy activity. After a period of return to traditional values, in the 1960s women renewed the struggle for political equality, and the famous fashion model Twiggy became the beauty ideal in the media. Since female models have continued to decrease in weight (Garner, Garfinkel, Schwarz, & Thompson, 1980), even Twiggy appears plump to us now! Wolf (1991) quoted a description of Twiggy that appeared in *Vogue*: "Twiggy is called Twiggy because she looks as though a strong gale wind would snap her in two and dash her to the ground" (p. 184). Thus, the fight for political and legal equality was accompanied by the media's portrayal of the ideal woman as weak and powerless. As Hesse-Biber (1991) has stated,

> Ironically, when women are demanding "more space" in terms of equality of opportunity, there is a cultural demand that they "should shrink." . . . Thinness may be considered a sign of conforming to a constricting feminine image, whereas greater weight may convey a strong, powerful image. (p. 178)

When women convey their power, men may be sexually drawn to female bodies that are childlike and helpless, rather than strong (Chernin, cited in Hesse-Biber, 1991).

Not surprisingly, given the historical precedents, the health care profession has enforced the social control of women's weight with gusto. Life insurance companies state that obesity shortens people's lives; the U.S. Surgeon General encourages weight reduction, ignoring the dangers of dieting and the limits imposed by set point. Being fat is equated with being ill. We take the relationship between obesity and illness so thoroughly for granted that it is difficult to conceive of fat, healthy women. Most females diet to improve their physical appearance and to increase their appeal, not to improve their health (Berman, 1975). This was evidenced in a study (Rodin, Silberstein, & Striegel-Moore, 1984) in which children with juvenile diabetes were asked whether they would prefer to remain diabetic and thin or to become healthy and obese. Most indicated that they would prefer the former. Furthermore, dieting has resulted in an epidemic of eating disorders among adolescent and young adult women. Nevertheless, medical texts and health professionals continue to promote dieting as healthy and obesity as dangerous.

In sum, the current obsession with women's weight is no different from the obsessional concerns in previous centuries and in other cultures. As Wolf (1991) has stated,

> A cultural fixation on female thinness is not an obsession about female beauty but an obsession about female obedience. . . . The nations seize with compulsive attention on this melodrama because women and men understand that it is not about cholesterol or heart rate or the disruption of a line of tailoring, but about how much social freedom women are going to get away with or concede. The media's convulsive analysis of the endless saga of female fat and the battle to vanquish it are actually bulletins of the sex war: what women are gaining or losing in it, and how fast. (p. 187)

INSTITUTIONS OF SOCIAL CONTROL: MAINTAINING STANDARDS OF WOMEN'S APPEARANCE

Why does society mandate oppressive and restrictive practices against women? A number of social institutions stand to gain from women's powerlessness and immobility. Two are examined here: the economy and the media.

The Economy

> *There are no ugly women, only lazy ones.*
> —Store window sign, Burlington, Vt.

The products and practices that maintain women's appearance are costly. The current market reflects a $33 billion per year diet industry, a $20 billion cosmetic industry, a $300 million cosmetic surgery industry, and a $7 billion pornography industry (Wolf, 1991). The economy would have much to lose if women stopped conforming to society's appearance norms, but the economic necessity of this spending is kept invisible. It is vital to the economy of beauty that women believe that they can enhance their attractiveness by purchasing products designed to change their hair, clothing, body shape, and weight. These methods of enhancing beauty usually involve abrupt departures from natural appearance. Women do not naturally have hairless armpits or red nails, for example. Women who engage in "makeovers" indicate that their motives are to be like others and to be liked by others; that is, they want to conform to social norms (Freeman, 1986).

In recent years, multinational companies have expanded the beauty industries worldwide, so that even poor nations are inundated with cosmetic and fashion products. Simultaneously, these companies have tried to market the products in similar ways, so that now it is possible to see the same products advertised in the same ways in all continents (Chapkis, 1986). Women's appearance itself has been labeled an economic asset. Wolf (1991, p. 20) cites expressions (e.g., "A woman looks like a million dollars," "She's a first-class beauty," "Her face is her fortune") that link feminine beauty with economic advancement. In a society in which men earn more than women in nearly every job category, the selling of bodies is a noteworthy exception. Female prostitutes and fashion models, for example, earn more than do men (Wolf, 1991). In sum, the economy has much to gain from women as consumers, and much to lose if women both understand and become part of the system.

The Media

Spend all you have for loveliness.
—Sara Teasdale, 1921 (quoted in Partnow, 1982, p.195)

The mass media barrage us with messages about attractiveness. Dermer and Thiel (1975) examined 150 women appearing in magazine advertisements, and found only one—advertising a mop—to be of average rather than high attractiveness. Downs and Harrison (1985) categorized over 4000 television commercials as related or unrelated to physical attractiveness. The authors found television to be "teeming with attractiveness-based messages" (p. 17). Specifically, viewers could expect to find a message about attractiveness "on every 2.1 personal care ads, 1.1 clothing ads, 0.5 weight reduction ads, 1.2 cosmetics ads, and 0.8 physical fitness ads. Overall, some form of attractiveness message was observed in one out of every 3.8 commercials" (p. 13). This study also found that the greatest proportion of attractiveness messages was delivered by female actors and male voiceovers. Thus, women symbolize the attractiveness of the product, while men give the authoritative message.

Media portrayals establish standards of attractiveness. *Charlie's Angels,* a television program popular in the 1970s that starred three extremely attractive women, was one benchmark. Kenrick and Gutierres (1980) wondered whether male college students watching *Charlie's Angels* would, in response to the implied standard, rate other women as less attractive. While *Charlie's Angels* aired, two male experimenters entered a dormitory room, and one said: "Listen, could I just interrupt you guys for 30 seconds? We're having a major philosophical dispute here and we need to do an informal survey to resolve the question. You see, we have a friend coming to town this week and we want to fix him up with a date, but we can't decide whether to fix him up with her or not, so we decided to conduct a survey" (p. 133). They then showed the students a photograph of a woman. Those students who had been interrupted while watching *Charlie's Angels* rated the woman's photograph as less attractive than did those students who saw the identical photograph but had been interrupted while watching another television program.

Of course, it could be argued that male college students who choose to watch television programs featuring beautiful women tend to have higher standards of attractiveness at all times. This occurred to the researchers too. Accordingly, they asked another group of male college students to come to an experimental session, and randomly assigned them to rate a photograph of a woman (the same used in the previous study) either with or without a magazine advertisement featuring a beautiful female model. Once again, the male students who first saw the magazine model rated the photograph of the woman more negatively than did those who did not see the magazine ad. Thus, media portrayals of beautiful women seem to raise male students' standards of attractiveness, so that the average woman no longer looks as good.

Umiker-Sebeok (1981) examined media portrayals of women over the lifespan. Describing the messages received by children, she states:

> Clothing, hair styles, nonverbal behavior, and size relationships combine to associate females with smallness, weakness, and subordination, that is, with characteristics of appeal rather than threat, passivity as opposed to aggressivity. . . . Boys, on the other hand, are more likely to be associated with threatening behavior, defense, strength, rationality, and leadership. These differences become more pronounced as the children become older. (pp. 212–213)

Adolescent girls are portrayed as innocent and childlike, still protected by their fathers but on the way to becoming sexual beings (Umiker-Sebeok, 1981). The adolescent girl is often shown as vulnerable, sexually alluring, and frantically outgoing. Portrayals of young adult women often show them doing nothing but displaying themselves. Male adults display ownership of women by towering over women or grasping them. The occasional middle-aged or elderly woman is shown as clumsy, plump, and comical, and nearly always engaged in domestic activity.

We have become so accustomed to images of attractive women in the media that sales pitches are not as persuasive if they lack female beauty. Loken and Howard-Pitney (1988) examined the effectiveness of cigarette advertisements with or without photographs of attractive female models, and found that female college students (whether or not they smoked) rated ads that used female models as more persuasive and attractive, but as less credible, than ads that showed only the product.

The media would have much to lose if women ceased to be influenced by its messages. Wolf (1991) indicated that in the late 1960s, women began spending less for clothing and fashion; sales of women's magazines in Great Britain decreased from 555.3 million in 1965 to 407.5 million copies in 1981. Advertisers, alarmed by this drop in their prime audience, changed their message so that the focus was on the body rather than on clothes. Steinem (1983) has described the power that the advertising media wield even over feminist magazines such as *Ms*.

PHYSICAL ATTRACTIVENESS:
WHAT IS BEAUTIFUL IS GOOD

> . . . *the beautiful seems right*
> *By force of beauty, and the feeble wrong*
> *Because of weakness.*
> —Elizabeth Barrett Browning, 1850
> (quoted in Partnow, 1982, p. 19)

It is important to examine exactly what messages institutions of social control want to convey about women's appearance. Feminist scholars and social psychology researchers have examined the importance of physical attractiveness in general, as well as its relationship to social, sexual, and occupational roles for women. Freeman (1986) has described how physical appearance is gender-linked. The word "beauty" refers specifically to physical characteristics and also suggests femininity. In contrast, the word "handsome" refers to behavior, such as strength and accomplishment, as well as to physical attractiveness. As Berger has stated (quoted in Schur, 1984, p. 66, emphasis added): "*Men act,* and *women appear.* Men look at women. Women watch themselves being looked at."

One of the most comprehensive analyses of physical attractiveness was conducted by Berscheid and Walster (1974). They coined the phrase "what is beautiful is good" (p. 169) to summarize the phenomenon in which people associate large numbers of positive characteristics with physical attractiveness. Thus, physically attractive women and men were rated as more kind, sensitive, sexually attractive and responsive, interesting, strong, modest, socially skilled, extraverted, nurturant, and exciting than were unattractive women and men. Furthermore, attractive women and men were rated as having more prestigious occupations, leading more fulfilling lives, having happier marriages, and being "masters of their own fate" to a greater degree (pp. 170–171). Although it is not clear whether most of these beliefs are true, there is some evidence that physically attractive women report having more sexual partners and say they have been in love more often than do less attractive women (Berscheid & Walster, 1974). Also, attractive people are less likely to be found guilty in jury trials than are unattractive people, and are given more favorable trial outcomes (Rodin et al., 1984).

Berscheid and Walster (1974) also examined specific attributes associated with attractiveness in the United States, such as height in men. Taller male college students were found to receive higher starting salaries after graduation. Recruiters stated a preference for taller male students. College students judged a man to be taller when he was described as successful than when the same man was described as less successful. And

Berscheid and Walster noted that in every presidential campaign in this century up to the time of their writing, the taller candidate was elected president. Only height was judged to be more important in males; all other body parts or characteristics were of greater concern in women. Women are more conscious of, and more desirous of changing, their weight, legs, hips, thighs, buttocks, waist, and overall appearance, than are men (Jackson, Sullivan, & Hymes, 1987).

Women in previous centuries were often considered to be asexual. Feminists such as Rowbotham (1973) have demonstrated the role of the media in creating the idea of romantic love and sexuality held by women today. Sexual pleasure and sexual relationships are portrayed as being so important that nothing can compensate for their lack. It is also suggested that women who fail to conform to society's norms will not attain these sexual and romantic heights. Men's status depends more on the attractiveness of their female partner than on their own attractiveness (Berscheid & Walster, 1974), suggesting that women will be concerned with their own attractiveness, whereas men will be concerned with the physical attractiveness of women.

In fact, men do spend a great deal of time looking at women. One research team (Rosenwasser, Adams, & Tansil, 1983) asked men and women to look at slides of men and women. The slides showed people clothed, in bathing suits, or nude. Unknown to the viewers, the slide projecter was connected to a computer that recorded how much time people spent gazing at each slide. Men spent more time gazing at all slides of women, and women spent the most time gazing at women who were clothed. No one spent much time gazing at slides of men.

One way of studying the effects of physical attractiveness on sexual appeal is to examine the "personals columns" of newspapers and magazines. Harrison and Saeed (1977) examined 800 such ads placed by heterosexual women and men to determine (1) what information people offered about themselves (which the researchers termed "revelations"); and (2) what information people required in return (which they termed "stipulations"). They found that women were more likely to seek partners who were older than themselves and to seek financial security, whereas men were more likely to seek partners who were younger than themselves and to seek attractiveness. Women offered attractiveness, and men offered financial security; furthermore, women sought sincerity, and men offered marriage. Thus, women offered what men sought, and vice versa. This study also found that both women and men who claimed they were attractive were more likely to seek good-looking partners. Women who claimed to be beautiful were more likely to seek financially secure partners and to ask for their photographs. The authors state:

Why was it that good-looking advertisers sought good-looking partners but rich advertisers did not seek rich partners? Perhaps it is useful to make a distinction between noncompensatory and compensatory social assets. An asset is noncompensatory if one partner's possession cannot make up for the other partner's lacking. Appearance is an example of a noncompensatory asset—no matter how good-looking one is, it won't make up for an ugly partner. An asset is compensatory if one person's surplus can make up for the other person's deficit. Money is an example: although it's always nice to have more money, a well-to-do person can compensate for a partner's poverty. (p. 263)

Franzoi and Herzog (1987) found that women's body esteem was related to sexual attractiveness, weight, and physical condition, whereas men's body esteem was related to physical attractiveness, upper-body strength, and physical condition. The authors concluded that these body concerns may be related to women's socialization to regard men as material providers, and men's socialization to regard women as sexual providers. Thus, women advertise their physical and sexual attractiveness in personals columns, and men advertise their financial and occupational attractiveness.

PHYSICAL APPEARANCE NORMS
AND FEMINISM

> *Wendy is a feminist. When I grow up, I am going to be just like her except I'll dress better.*
> —Eight-year old girl quoted in Chapkis (1986, p. 7)

Can feminists be attractive? The answer to this question demonstrates a fascinating relationship between social acceptance of a political movement and perceived attractiveness. When women first began to demand suffrage in the 19th century, the media focused on the ugly feminist. Wolf (1991) states: "Lucy Stone herself, whom supporters saw as 'a prototype of womanly grace . . . fresh and fair as the morning' was derided by detractors with 'the usual report' about Victorian feminists: 'a big masculine woman, wearing boots, smoking a cigar, swearing like a trooper' " (p. 18).

In 1975, Goldberg, Gottesdiener, and Abramson published a study in which female college students were first asked about their attitudes on "women's liberation" (about half were for it, half against) and then photographed. Next, female and male college students were asked to rate the photographs for physical attractiveness. The results indicated no relationship between the photographs' ratings and views on feminism. However, when the experimenters asked a different group of students to guess which of the women in the photographs supported "women's liberation," they found that both female and male college students rated the *unattractive* women in the photographs as feminists (p. 114).

Four years later attitudes had shifted (Johnson, Holborn, & Turcotte, 1979). Undergraduates were shown photographs of women and asked to predict which ones were supporters and which critics of the feminist movement, and which were active or passive supporters (p. 228). Both female and male students selected the more attractive women as *supporters* of the feminist movement! Female students (but not males) also selected more attractive women as more active participants in the movement (p. 229).

Men's attitudes about preferred physical characteristics in males have also been found to be related to attitudes toward women. Maier and Lavrakas (1984) asked male college students to rate male silhouettes (arms, upper trunk, lower trunk, and legs), and also gave them a questionnaire about attitudes toward women. They found that men who had negative attitudes toward women preferred a "tapering V" body. Women, in fact, did not seem to prefer a "tapering V" body in men as much as men did (pp. 425–426). The authors note: "If males have negative attitudes toward women (some of which may be related to a fear of femininity), one way to exercise control is by developing a strong body" (p. 431).

Over time, the negative stereotype of the ugly "women's libber" has changed. The studies reviewed here suggest the importance of attitude similarity in perceived attractiveness; as college students are increasingly endorsing feminist values, they are also viewing others with similar attitudes as attractive. This finding generalizes to other kinds of attitudes as well. Berscheid and Walster (1974) found that students who were placed in discussion groups rated group members who shared their viewpoints as more attractive than those who disagreed with them (p. 175).

What can account for the change in the public's view of the attractiveness of feminists? Feminists have argued that the media have cleverly brought images of the women's movement into product promotion. As Rowbotham (1973) has stated,

> . . . if a section of middle-class women manage to alter their position in society through agitation there is no reason why [advertisements] should not present these women with a spurious sense of liberation by inverting male-female roles in certain cases, and presenting men as commodities. (p. 423)

Women have feared the feminist movement precisely because of its
association in the mass media with ugliness and inattention to appearance. I have been amazed by the number of women who have told me
that they cannot be feminists because they like lace, and also the number
who have told me that they are feminists despite liking lace. Of all the
images available to women, it always seems to be lace that is mentioned.
Imagine my surprise when I saw the following in a local newspaper:

> I am a flexible feminist. That doesn't mean I do back flips in front of
> Planned Parenthood. It doesn't mean I am half-hearted about supporting
> the women's movement. It does mean that when I march on Washington
> in a prochoice demonstration, underneath my sloppy sweater and outsized
> overalls I may sport a set of lacy lingerie. (Older, 1991, p. 11)

What is conveyed by the image of lace, and what has it come to symbolize during the feminist movement? Lace is flimsy, vulnerable, sexy—the
epitome of feminine apparel. It is acceptable to be a feminist, but only if
one still appears feminine. It is the symbolism that is critical; no one can
see the lacy lingerie of the prochoice protester, but she knows it is there.
Women's refusal to wear appropriate clothing is more threatening to the
institutions of social control than any actions or words, however radical.

Wolf (1991) has presented convincing evidence that the more legal
and political rights women gain, the greater the backlash by institutions
of social control. She states:

> During the past decade, women breached the power structure; meanwhile,
> eating disorders rose exponentially and cosmetic surgery became the
> fastest-growing medical specialty. During the past five years, consumer
> spending doubled, pornography became the main media category, ahead
> of legitimate films and records combined, and thirty-three thousand
> American women told researchers that they would rather lose ten to fifteen
> pounds than achieve any other goal. More women have more money and
> power and scope and legal recognition than we have ever had before; but in
> terms of how we feel about ourselves *physically,* we may actually be worse
> off than our unliberated grandmothers. Recent research consistently shows
> that inside the majority of the West's controlled, attractive, successful
> working women, there is a secret "underlife" poisoning our freedom;
> infused with notions of beauty, it is a dark vein of self-hatred, physical
> obsessions, terror of aging, and dread of lost control. (p. 10)

Women who want to resist social norms often resist cosmetic
rituals, and may stop wearing makeup, allow hair to grow under their
arms or on their legs, and go without a bra. Freeman (1986) states: "[A]
woman who fails to play her proper part, even through a trivial act like

the omission of a bra, will soon be seen as a threat to the whole system" (p. 52). As noted earlier, it is not surprising that feminists were labeled "bra burners" even when the issues they advocated covered a wide range of sociopolitical topics. According to feminist historians (Brownmiller, 1984), feminists never burned bras; the image was probably created by the media to correspond to the burning of draft cards by men and, by comparison, to trivialize women's concerns. Men protested war, while women protested feminine clothing.

Feminists have adopted certain appearance norms to indicate group membership, one of which is refusal to shave body hair. As Brownmiller (1984) has argued, hair has been used throughout history to make political statements, and a hairless body has come to be a major component of femininity. Even short hair on women's heads has been considered an act of defiance. In 1915, Charlotte Perkins Gilman conceived of a futuristic society in which women were free from men and wore their hair short (Brownmiller, 1984). Basow (1991) asked over 200 women who were members of professional organizations why they did or did not shave body hair. Women who shaved did so to be feminine and attractive, and because it was the norm. Women who did not shave body hair frequently identified themselves as feminists and as lesbians.

SUMMARY: WOMEN'S APPEARANCE AS SOCIAL CONTROL

> *It is very little to me to have the right to vote, to own property, et cetera, if I may not keep my body, and its uses, in my absolute right.*
>
> —Lucy Stone, 1855 (quoted in Wolf, 1991, p. 11)

Mary Daly (1984) has examined strategies for changing women's rights in a patriarchal society, defining "plastic passions" as those that preoccupy and enervate women and result in feelings of disconnectedness. Daly states:

> The plastic passions, moreover, are endless in the sense that they cause those whom they infect/infest to feel deprived of purpose, end, final causality. Whereas genuine passions or e-motions move the woman experiencing them out of the fixed/framed state, plastic passions stop her dead. They function to hide the agents of her oppression/repression. (p. 201)

Daly's advice: Women need to collectively remember (a process she refers to as "metamemory," p. 357) other ways in which women have been oppressed in the past (e.g., foot binding, corsets) and express their outrage.

The feminist and social science literatures indicate that physical appearance has important consequences for women, who are looked at and objectified more than are men. Women's attractiveness has important consequences for their social and interpersonal success, and even for the success of the men in whose company they are seen. In this regard, the media perpetuate stereotypes about physical appearance and set norms for attractiveness. Women who are not Caucasian, heterosexual, able-bodied, and young are viewed as less desirable in U.S. society, and are also made invisible by their virtual absence in the media. Women are expected to invest enormous amounts of time and money in products and procedures (e.g., weight loss) intended to enhance their beauty.

Women's appearance norms are notable for the submissive status they indicate. Physical characteristics of dominance include increased size and use of space (such as height and weight; Frieze, Parsons, Johnson, Ruble, & Zellman, 1978, p. 322), yet women are expected to reduce weight and take up less space. In comparison to men's, women's clothing (e.g., short dresses, high heels) is more constricting, and permits less mobility and a smaller range of body postures. Although men are permitted and encouraged to stare at women, women's staring at men may be viewed as aggressive (Frieze et al., p. 331).

Schur's (1984) book *Labelling Women Deviant* describes the process by which women are objectified. Society's preoccupation with their looks is a major element. Women are portrayed as "depersonalized body parts" (e.g., breasts); their bodies are exploited (e.g., via pornography); they are treated as "decorative" objects, which are "collected" by men upon whom they confer status; and they are evaluated by narrow standards of conventional beauty. Consequently, women become preoccupied with their appearance, are obsessed with improving deficiencies, view themselves as objects, and respond to other women as competing objects (Schur, 1984, p. 33). It is important to emphasize that despite the research indicating marked benefits for attractive women, most women do not feel that they belong to this class. Schur states that the "definitions of female deviance are, in fact, so extensive that virtually every woman becomes a perceived offender of some kind" (1984, p. 37).

The importance of women's appearance norms is reflected in the fact that women have discarded gender roles on many fronts, but continue to worry about their looks, as reflected in the dieting epidemic. Rodin et al. (1984) argue that women's concerns with their appearance have not lessened as they have changed other traditional gender roles (p. 291). On the contrary, when women increase their rights, there is immediate retaliation by institutions of social control. The media have struggled to portray women who resist traditions as ugly; feminists and lesbians are women who don't shave their legs.

Women's appearance norms are not created by women, and they are not healthy for women. Rather, the norms profit men, define the erotic, pump money into the economy, and restrict women's power.

If, as women, we stopped responding to social control of appearance, we would reclaim a great deal of energy, sensation, insight, and time. As Freeman (1986) has stated, we would be able

> . . . to admit to feelings of hunger, satiation, lethargy, anxiety, exhaustion; to recognize the hyperactivity and insomnia caused by diet schemes; to observe awkward posture and loss of balance; to notice compulsive rituals of running to the mirror or climbing on the scale; to question the hours spent creaming, brushing, tweezing, outlining, examining, counting, covering, coloring, and agonizing over each inadequacy; to sense when pain is felt in connection with the daily cosmetic routine—soreness, stinging, aching, pinching, itching, burning, numbness. (p. 220)

To recognize the social control of women's appearance does not mean that we cannot act and look in ways that make us feel beautiful. We have long been made to feel guilty and immoral because we do not meet unattainable and debilitating standards of attractiveness. It is time to take control of our bodies. As we do so, we must tolerate differences, for other women may make other choices. Such a change would be radical, not trivial, as the media would have us believe. The institutions of social control, well aware of women's potential power, have much to lose when women discard restrictive and oppressive norms. The more rapidly women acquire freedom and power, the greater the backlash will be. We will hear that women "are going too far" (Wolf, 1991, p. 16), and will be presented with new modes of fashion that immobilize. The women's "movement" itself may be stalled by the constriction of individual women's "movements." A century ago, women were encouraged to be still, because activity would make them ill. In the intervening years, women's gains have required more sophisticated and subtle techniques to induce conformity.

ACKNOWLEDGMENTS

I would like to thank Beth Mintz for suggesting that the chapter focus on social control, and Pamela Brand, Clove, Carol Miller, Pamela Orosan, Sondra Solomon, Mary Willmuth, and Susan Wooley for their helpful suggestions.

REFERENCES

Agell, G., & Rothblum, E. D. (1991). Effects of clients' obesity and gender on the therapy judgments of psychologists. *Professional Psychology: Theory, Research and Practice, 22,* 223–229.

Basow, S. A. (1991). The hairless ideal: Women and their body hair. *Psychology of Women Quarterly, 15,* 83–96.

Bennett, G. A. (1986). Behavior therapy for obesity: A qualitative review of the effects of selected treatment characteristics on outcome. *Behavior Therapy, 17,* 554–562.

Bennett, W., & Gurin, J. (1982). *The dieter's dilemma.* New York: Basic Books.

Berman, E. M. (1975). Factors influencing motivations in dieting. *Journal of Nutrition Education, 7,* 155–159.

Berscheid, E., & Walster, E. (1974). Physical attractiveness. *Advances in Experimental Social Psychology, 18,* 157–215.

Brownell, K. D., Greenwood, M. R. C., Stellar, E., & Shrager, E. E. (1986). The effects of repeated cycles of weight loss and regain in rats. *Physiology and Behavior, 38,* 459–464.

Brownell, K. D., & Jeffery, R. W. (1987). Improving long-term weight loss: Pushing the limits of treatment. *Behavior Therapy, 18,* 353–374.

Brownmiller, S. (1984). *Femininity.* New York: Fawcett Columbine.

Canning, H., & Mayer, J. (1966). Obesity: Its possible effect on college acceptance. *New England Journal of Medicine, 275,* 1172–1174.

Canning, H., & Mayer, J. (1967). Obesity: An influence on high school performance. *American Journal of Clinical Nutrition, 20,* 352–354.

Chapkis, W. (1986). *Beauty secrets: Women and the politics of appearance.* Boston: South End Press.

Cohen, M. (1988). *The sisterhood: The true story of the women who changed the world.* New York: Simon & Schuster.

Crandall, C., & Biernat, M. (1990). The ideology of anti-fat attitudes. *Journal of Applied Social Psychology, 20,* 227–243.

Crandall, C. S. (1991). Do heavyweight children have a more difficult time paying for college? *Personality and Social Psychology Bulletin, 17,* 606–611.

Daly, M. (1984) *Pure lust: Elemental feminist philosophy.* Boston: Beacon Press.

Daly, M. (1990). *Gyn/ecology: The metaethics of radical feminism.* Boston: Beacon Press.

DeJong, W. (1980). The stigma of obesity: The consequences of naive assumptions concerning the causes of physical deviance. *Journal of Health and Social Behavior, 21,* 75–87.

Dermer, M., & Thiel, D. L. (1975). When beauty may fail. *Journal of Personality and Social Psychology, 31,* 1168–1176.

Downs, A. C., & Harrison, S. K. (1985). Embarrassing age spots or just plain ugly? Physical attractiveness stereotyping as an instrument of sexism on American television commercials. *Sex Roles, 13,* 9–19.

Ewen, S. (1988). *All consuming images: The politics of style in contemporary culture.* New York: Basic Books.

Faludi, S. (1991). *Backlash: The undeclared war against American women.* New York: Crown.

Franzoi, S. L., & Herzog, M. E. (1987). Judging physical attractiveness: What body aspects do we use? *Personality and Social Psychology Bulletin, 13,* 19–33.

Freeman, R. (1986). *Beauty bound: Why we pursue the myth in the mirror.* Lexington, MA: D. C. Heath.

Frieze, I. H., Parsons, J. E., Johnson, P. B., Ruble, D. N., & Zellman, G. L. (1978). *Women and sex roles: A social psychological perspective.* New York: Norton.

Garner, D. M., Garfinkel, P. E., Schwartz, D., & Thompson, M. (1980). Cultural expectations of thinness in women. *Psychological Reports, 47,* 483–491.

Garner, D. M., & Wooley, S. C. (1991). Confronting the failure of behavioral and dietary treatments for obesity. *Clinical Psychology Review, 11,* 729–780.

Goldberg, P. A., Gottesdiener, M., & Abramson, P. R. (1975). Another put-down of women?: Perceived attractiveness as a function of support for the feminist movement. *Journal of Personality and Social Psychology, 32,* 113–115.

Goodman, N., Richardson, S. A., Dornbusch, S. M., & Hastorf, A. H. (1963). Variant reactions to physical disabilities. *American Sociological Review, 28,* 429–435.

Harrison, A. A., & Saeed, L. (1977). Let's make a deal: An analysis of revelations and stipulations in lonely hearts advertisements. *Journal of Personality and Social Psychology, 35,* 257–264.

Hesse-Biber, S. (1991). Women, weight and eating disorders: A socio-cultural and political-economic analysis. *Women's Studies International Forum, 14,* 173–191.

Hosken, F. (1982). *The Hosken report: Genital and sexual mutilation of females.* Lexington, MA: International Network News.

Jackson, L. A., Sullivan, L. A., & Hymes, J. S. (1987). Gender, gender role, and physical appearance. *Journal of Psychology, 121,* 51–56.

Johnson, R. W., Holborn, S. W., & Turcotte, S. (1979). Perceived attractiveness as a function of active vs. passive support for the feminist movement. *Personality and Social Psychology Bulletin, 5,* 227–235.

Karris, L. (1977). Prejudice against obese renters. *Journal of Social Psychology, 101,* 159–160.

Kenrick, D. T., & Gutierres, S. E. (1980). Contrast effects and judgments of physical attractiveness: When beauty becomes a social problem. *Journal of Personality and Social Psychology, 38,* 131–140.

Larkin, J. C., & Pines, H. A. (1979). No fat persons need apply: Experimental studies of the overweight stereotype and hiring preference. *Sociology of Work and Occupations, 6,* 312–327.

Lightfoot-Klein, H. (1989). *Prisoners of ritual: An odyssey into female genital circumcision in Africa.* New York: Harrington Park Press.

Lissner, L., Odell, P. M., D'Agostino, R. B., Stokes, J., Kreger, B. E., Belanger, A. J., & Brownell, K. D. (1991). Variability of body weight and health outcomes in the Framingham population. *New England Journal of Medicine, 324,* 1839–1844.

Loken, B., & Howard-Pitney, B. (1988). Effectiveness of cigarette advertisements on women: An experimental study. *Journal of Applied Psychology, 73,* 378–382.

Maddox, G. L., Back, K., & Liederman, V. (1968). Overweight as social deviance and disability. *Journal of Health and Social Behavior, 9,* 287–298.

Maddox, G. L., & Liederman, V. (1969). Overweight as social desirability with medical implications. *Journal of Medical Education, 44,* 214–220.

Maier, R. A., & Lavrakas, P. J. (1984). Attitudes toward women, personality rigidity, and idealized physique preferences in males. *Sex Roles, 11,* 425–433.

Maiman, L. A., Wang, V. L., Becker, M. H., Finlay, J., & Simonson, M. (1979). Attitudes toward obesity and the obese among professionals. *Journal of the American Dietetic Association, 74,* 331–336.

Moore, M. E., Stunkard, A., & Srole, L. (1962). Obesity, social class, and mental illness. *Journal of the American Medical Association, 181,* 138–142.

Nisbett, R. E. (1972). Hunger, obesity, and the ventromedial hypothalamus. *Psychological Review, 79,* 433–453.

Older, A. (1991, March 7). Why I'm a flexible feminist. *Vermont Times,* p. 11.

Partnow, E. (1982). *The quotable woman: 1800–1981.* New York: Facts on File.

Polivy, J., & Herman, C. P. (1983). *Breaking the diet habit.* New York: Basic Books.

Rodin, J., Silberstein, L., & Striegel-Moore, R. (1984). Women and weight: A normative discontent. *Nebraska Symposium on Motivation, 32,* 267–307.

Roe, D. A., & Eickwort, K. R. (1976). Relationships between obesity and associated health factors with unemployment among low income women. *Journal of the American Medical Women's Association, 31,* 193–204.

Rosen, J. C., & Gross, J. (1987). Prevalence of weight reducing and weight gaining in adolescent girls and boys. *Health Psychology, 6,* 131–147.

Rosenwasser, S. M., Adams, V., & Tansil, K. (1983). Visual attention as a function of sex and apparel of stimulus object: Who looks at whom? *Social Behavior and Personality, 11,* 11–15.

Rothblum, E. D. (1990). Women and weight: Fad and fiction. *Journal of Psychology, 124,* 5–24.

Rothblum, E. D. (1992). The stigma of women's weight: Social and economic realities. *Feminism and Psychology, 2,* 61–73.

Rothblum, E. D., Brand, P. A., Miller, C. T., & Oetjen, H. (1990). The relationship between obesity, employment discrimination, and employment-related victimization. *Journal of Vocational Behavior, 37,* 251–266.

Rothblum, E. D., Miller, C. T., & Garbutt, B. (1988). Stereotypes of obese female job applicants. *International Journal of Eating Disorders, 7,* 277–283.

Rowbotham, S. (1973). *Imperialism and sexuality: Woman's consciousness, man's world.* Harmondsworth, England: Penguin Books.

Schur, E. M. (1984). *Labelling women deviant: Gender, stigma, and social control.* New York: Random House.

Steinem, G. (1983). *Outrageous acts and everyday rebellions.* New York: Holt, Rinehart & Winston.

Sternhell, C. (1985, April). We'll always be fat but fat can be fit. *Ms,* pp. 66, 68, 142–144, 146, 154.

Stimson, K. W. (1991). An angry fat woman is a dangerous thing. *Newsletter of the National Association to Advance Fat Acceptance,* No. 21, p. 5.

Tiggemann, M., & Rothblum, E. D. (1988). Gender differences in social consequences of perceived overweight in the United States and Australia. *Sex Roles, 18,* 75–86.

Umiker-Sebeok, J. (1981). The seven ages of woman: A view from American magazine advertisements. In C. Mayo & N. M. Henley (Eds.), *Gender and nonverbal behavior.* New York: Springer-Verlag.

U.S. Department of Health, Education and Welfare. (1979). *Obesity in America* (DHEW Publication No. NIH79-359). Washington, DC: U.S. Government Printing Office.

Wolf, N. (1991). *The beauty myth: How images of beauty are used against women.* New York: Morrow.

Wooley, S. C., Wooley, O. W., & Dyrenforth, S. (1979). Theoretical, practical, and social issues in behavioral treatments of obesity. *Journal of Applied Behavior Analysis, 12,* 3–25.

Young, L. M., & Powell, B. (1985). The effects of obesity on the clinical judgments of mental health professionals. *Journal of Health and Social Behavior, 26,* 233–246.

4

Faces of Female Discontent: Depression, Disordered Eating, and Changing Gender Roles

DEBORAH PERLICK
BRETT SILVERSTEIN

HROUGHOUT HISTORY, women who have striven to achieve intellectually, professionally, or politically have confronted massive barriers as a result of being female. We suggest that many such women have experienced ambivalent feelings regarding their gender, and that for centuries, women experiencing what we term "gender ambivalence" have developed a syndrome comprised of disordered eating, depression, anxiety, poor body image, menstrual dysfunction, somatic symptoms (e.g., headaches, breathing difficulties, or insomnia), and sexual indifference. Several descriptions of this syndrome have appeared in the medical literature over the centuries.

The Hippocratic texts of Greece (4th century B.C.) described a "disease of young women" (Lefkowitz & Fant, 1982; Littre, 1853) beginning at about the menarche, characterized by amenorrhea, wasting away, great hunger, vomiting, depression, suicidal ideation, anxiety, aches and pains, and breathing difficulties.

In the 17th through 19th centuries, a disorder known as "chlorosis" was commonly diagnosed among young women. Allbutt (1901) described chlorosis as a malady of women beginning in adolescence that appeared in most girls of the era. Symptoms included amenorrhea. appetite disturbance, depression, anxiety, headache, breathing difficulties, and insomnia, as well as disturbed body image: "Many young

women, as their frames develop, fall into a panic fear of obesity, and . . .
cut down on their food" (p. 485). Allbutt (1901, p. 485) also described
the alternation in chlorotic girls of anorexia and "excessive overeating
followed by vomiting." Another physician attributed the disordered
eating to the desire of the girls to give "graceful slenderness to the form"
(quoted in Loudon, 1984, p. 30).

The 19th-century disorder "neurasthenia" was characterized primarily by nervous exhaustion, but several reports indicate that young
females diagnosed as neurasthenic exhibited many symptoms characteristic of both chlorosis and the Hippocratic disease of young women. In
an article titled "Neurasthenia in Young Women," Deale and Adams
(1894) wrote that neurasthenia often afflicted women who were under
age 25, unmarried, and slender; symptoms of the disease included vomiting, nervous depression, headache, and insomnia. Physician George
Savage (1884) described a typical case of neurasthenia as follows:

> A woman, generally single, or in some way not in a condition for perform-
> ing her reproductive function . . . becomes bed-ridden, often refuses her
> food, or is capricious about it, taking strange things at odd times, or
> pretending to starve. . . . The body wastes, and the face has the thin,
> anxious look not unlike that represented by Rossetti in many of his pictures
> of women. (p. 90)

Hysteria was another common malady in the 19th and early 20th
centuries. Laycock (1840a) cited anorexia, bulimia, and lack of curva-
ceousness as common symptoms of hysteria. In their book *Studies on
Hysteria,* Breuer and Freud (1893–1895/1982) discussed hysteria as a
malady that appeared in women during adolescence, characterized by
menstrual irregularity, anorexia, chronic vomiting, depression, anxiety,
headache, difficulty breathing, and insomnia. Many of Freud's hysteric
patients exhibited symptoms of disordered eating. For example, in describing the case of Frau Emmy von N. (the woman with whom he
developed the technique of catharsis), Freud wrote:

> I called on her one day at lunch-time and surprised her in the act of
> throwing something wrapped up in paper into the garden, where it was
> caught by the children of the house-porter. In reply to my question, she
> admitted that it was her (dry) pudding, and that this went the same way
> every day. This led me to investigate what remained of the other courses
> and I found that there was more than half left on the plates. When I asked
> her why she ate so little she answered that she was not in the habit of eating
> more and that it would be bad for her if she did. . . . When on my next visit
> I ordered her some alkaline water and forbade her usual way of dealing
> with her pudding, she showed considerable agitation. . . . Next day the

nurse reported that she had eaten the whole of her helpings and had drunk a glass of the alkaline water. But I found Frau Emmy herself lying in a profoundly depressed state. . . . she said . . . "I've ruined my digestion, as always happens if I eat more or drink water, and I have to starve myself entirely for five days to a week before I can tolerate anything." . . . I assured her that . . . her pains were only due to the anxiety over eating. (Breuer & Freud, 1893–1895/1982, pp. 80–81)

Chlorosis, hysteria, "the disease of young women," and some cases of neurasthenia shared many characteristics. They afflicted young women at adolescence and involved many common symptoms, including disordered eating, depressed mood, anxiety, headache, breathing difficulties, sexual indifference, and amenorrhea. In addition, neurasthenic women were described as slender; chlorotic women were described as trying to be slender; and hysteric women were described as noncurvaceous. We believe that a syndrome characterized by these symptoms continues to afflict women in modern times to an extent that has not been fully recognized, because the syndrome has been subdivided into multiple diagnoses.

CONTEMPORARY EVIDENCE FOR THE EXISTENCE OF THE SYNDROME

Because of modern specialization, there is a separate literature dealing with each of the symptoms or disorders that make up the syndrome we have described above. Rarely do researchers refer to the patterns common to them. An examination of recent research done on disordered eating, depression, body image disorders, anxiety, headaches, intrinsic asthma (i.e., asthma not related to measurable allergies), insomnia, and sexual indifference indicates that they are more prevalent among females than among males (Ago, Sugita, Teshima, & Nakagawa, 1982; Cash & Pruzinsky, 1990; Kashani et al., 1987; Linet & Stewart, 1987; Price, Coates, Thoresen, & Grinstead, 1978; Nathan, 1986; Nolen-Hoeksema, 1990; Whitaker et al., 1990). They often coexist in the same people, and the relationship between the symptoms is stronger among females than among males (Dryman & Eaton, 1991; Frank, Carpenter, & Kupfer, 1988; Purtell, Robins, & Cohen, 1951; Richards, Casper, & Larson, 1990; Swartz, Blazer, Woodbury, George, & Landerman, 1986; Zetin, Sklansky, & Cramer, 1984). Finally, they increase dramatically among females but not males at adolescence (Allgood-Merton, Lewinsohn, & Hops, 1990; Richards et al., 1990; Verrulst, Prince, Vervururt-Pool, & de Jong, 1989). This is exactly the pattern described for these same symptoms in the discussions of the syndromes appearing in the medical literature of previous centuries. Because the modern psychiatric and psychological classification system used in the United States, the DSM-III-R (and the current draft of DSM-IV), does not describe this syndrome recognized under various names in previous centuries, we have termed it "the forgotten syndrome."

THE FORGOTTEN SYNDROME AND GENDER ROLE CHANGE

We have found several converging lines of evidence indicating that the forgotten syndrome is particularly likely to afflict women who strive to achieve in areas traditionally dominated by men and who come to feel limited by being female, particularly if their mothers were unable to achieve in these areas. First, disordered eating, depression, and headache all became prevalent among females during this century in the periods of changing female roles, when a larger proportion of women graduated from college than had done so during their mothers' generation. Under the names "chlorosis," "hysteria," and "neurasthenia," the syndrome was described as being prevalent among the first generation of females who attended college. Moreover, contemporary women who report distress regarding what they perceive as their mothers' limited lives and accomplishments are also likely to exhibit disordered eating combined with depression and with somatic symptoms. Second, comparisons of Freud's case descriptions of Viennese hysteric women at the turn of the century and Hilde Bruch's descriptions of American anorexic women in the 1970s indicate striking similarities between the two groups of women with regard to their own attitudes and those of their families toward female intellectual and professional achievement. Third, studies of the biographies of talented women from families in which the fathers were eminent but the mothers were not suggest much depression, disordered eating, and/or extreme thinness among these women.

Changes in Prevalence over Time

Temporal fluctuations in the prevalence among females of several of the symptoms of the forgotten syndrome follow a similar pattern, providing clues to its etiology. At the beginning of the 20th century, disordered eating among females did not appear to be common; however, it increased dramatically, reaching possible epidemic proportions in the 1920s, as evidenced in an emergency meeting of the American Medical Association called to discuss the health problems of anorexic female college students (Silverstein, Peterson, & Perdue, 1986). A retrospective study of the medical records of people living in Rochester, Minnesota between 1935 and 1984 demonstrated that the prevalence of anorexia was relatively high among females born between about 1916 and 1930, decreased among females born in the 1930s, and then rose precipitously once more among females born after World War II, leading people to think it was a new disease (Lucas, Beard, O'Fallon & Kurland, 1991). Gender differences in depression exhibited exactly the same pattern: They were small among people who reached adolescence during the 1910s and the 1940s, and large among people who reached adolescence during the other periods of the 20th century (Silverstein & Perlick, 1991). The same pattern applies to gender differences in the prevalence of "frequent, unexplained" headaches (Brewis, Poskanzer, Rolland, & Miller, 1966) and to thin standards of female beauty appearing in women's magazines (Silverstein, Peterson, & Perdue, 1986).

We believe that the forgotten syndrome afflicts many women during periods of change in female roles. Women born during the 1910s and 1920s, and after the 1930s, reached adolescence during periods when females graduated from college at a higher rate than had the females of their mothers' generation. Women born in the 20th century prior to 1910 and during the 1930s (particularly the early 1930s) reached adolescence during periods when females graduated from college at a lower rate than had the females of their mothers' generation (Silverstein & Perlick, 1991). Thus, disordered eating, depression, thin standards of female beauty, and headache characterized all generations of women reaching adolescence in periods when educational opportunities for women increased, but did not characterize either of the two cohorts of women reaching adolescence when educational opportunities remained stable or decreased.

In this context, it is of interest to note that in earlier centuries, medical authorities noted that chlorosis, neurasthenia, and hysteria appeared to be particularly common among young women who sought out greater educational opportunities. The observed relationship with education led authorities to misattribute these disorders to the stress placed upon the nervous systems of pubescent women attempting to "overeducate" themselves. "Mental strain" among young females seeking further education was considered to be implicated in the etiology of chlorosis (Allbutt, 1901; Simon, 1897), hysteria (Laycock, 1840b; Preston, 1897), and neurasthenia (Deale & Adams, 1894; Gosling, 1987). In discussing the causes of neurasthenia, Deale and Adams (1894) attributed the symptoms to "the natural nervous tendency" of a young girl or woman harassed by the ambitions of school life . . . or annoyed with household and family chores" (p. 191). One physician went so far as to cite neurasthenia as "a positive argument against higher education of women" (quoted in Gosling, 1987, p. 100). Breuer and Freud (1893–1895/1982, p. 240) noted that "adolescents who were later to become hysterical are for the most part lively, gifted and full of intellectual interests . . . They include girls who get out of bed at night so as secretly to carry on some study that their parents have forbidden from fear of their overworking" (p. 240). In an influential book on the supposed medical effects of higher education in the first generation of American college women, Clarke (1873) included the following symptoms: amenorrhea, digestive disturbance, thinness, depression, nervousness, headache, sleep disturbance, lack of sexuality, and hysteria. These similarities support the hypothesis that women who attempt to achieve academically (and probably professionally) in a context in which preceding generations of women have not so achieved may be more likely than other women to develop the forgotten syndrome.

Although additional research is needed to test this hypothesis fully, some preliminary evidence from contemporary studies links several of the symptoms with increased academic achievement among females compared to previous generations. High aspirations toward, or achievement of, academic and professional success among females have been found to be associated with bingeing and purgeing (Silverstein & Perdue, 1988; Silverstein, Carpman, Perlick, & Perdue, 1990), preferences for slimness (Beck, Ward-Hull, & McLear, 1976; Silverstein, Perdue, Peterson, Vogel, & Fantini, 1986), depression and suicide (Pitts, Schuller, Rich, & Pitts, 1979; Weiner et al., 1979), and inhibited sexual desire (Avery-Clark, 1986).

Increased achievement relative to previous generations has also been implicated by contemporary researchers in the development of disordered eating, depressed mood, and several somatic symptoms. Symptoms of disordered eating have been found to be frequent among college females who report that their mothers did not achieve academically or that their mothers were dissatisfied with their own career choices (Horend & Perdue, 1990; Silverstein, Perdue, Wolf, & Pizzolo, 1988; Wooley & Wooley, 1986). High school females who reported distress regarding what they perceived as the limited lives and achievements of their mothers were found to be much more likely than those who did not to exhibit combined symptoms of disordered eating, depressed mood, and frequent headaches, breathing difficulties, or insomnia (Silverstein, Perlick, Clauson, & McKoy, 1993). College females who reported similar distress regarding perceived maternal limitations were found to be over 20 times as likely as other women to exhibit combined symptoms of depressed mood and disordered eating, but no more likely than the other women to report just one of these two symptoms (Perdue,

Pizzolo, & Norman, 1991). These findings further link the forgotten syndrome to generational changes in female roles.

Childhood Experiences of Women Suffering from the Forgotten Syndrome: Freud's and Bruch's Cases

Our historical investigations of the past syndromes including symptoms of disordered eating have revealed similarities between the cases of women who suffered from these syndromes in earlier times and cases of contemporary women with eating disorders. In this section we describe striking similarities in descriptions made by two renowned clinicians, Sigmund Freud and Hilde Bruch, of women diagnosed with two disorders—hysteria and anorexia nervosa—who lived on different continents almost a century apart. We have chosen Hilde Bruch because she is probably the clinician who has exerted the greatest influence on contemporary views of anorexia nervosa. In her 1973 book *Eating Disorders,* she described the workings of anorexia nervosa, a disorder that had not yet received much attention. A few years later, she published a collection of case descriptions that remains the most complete and influential such collection (Bruch, 1978). The most famous cases of women suffering from hysteria appear in Breuer and Freud's (1893–1895/1982) *Studies on Hysteria,* and Freud's (1905/1963) *Dora: An Analysis of a Case of Hysteria.* Although debate continues over the utility of the contributions of psychoanalytic theory to female psychology, Freud's clinical vignettes are nonetheless regarded as keen and detailed observations. Rather than focus on the therapeutic issues discussed in these collections, here we use the observations made by Bruch and by Breuer and Freud as anecdotal data in order to demonstrate the striking similarities between Freud's descriptions of the childhood experiences of hysterics and Bruch's descriptions of the childhoods of women suffering from eating disorders, with regard to issues of gender and achievement in their families.

Bruch (1978, p. 52) described anorexics as "outstanding students," while Breuer and Freud (1893–1895/1982, p. 13) described hysterics as having "the clearest intellect . . . and highest critical power." Anna O., whose symptoms included anorexia, depression, and headache, was described as "markedly intelligent," possessing a "powerful intellect" and "bubbling over with intellectual vitality" (Breuer & Freud, 1893–1895/1982, pp. 21, 22). Emmy von N., whose anorexia has been described above, revealed "an unusual degree of education and intelligence" (Breuer & Freud, 1893–1895/1982, p. 49), and Dora, whose symptoms included anorexia as well as depression, headaches, and breathing difficulties, manifested "intellectual precocity" (Freud, 1905/1963, p. 34).

Although the marked intelligence of both Bruch's anorexics and Freud's hysterics was highly valued by their fathers, these fathers also associated intelligence with maleness. Bruch (1978) wrote, "It is significant that the fathers value their daughters for their intellectual brilliance . . ." (p. 24), and noted that "In [one] case the patient was convinced that not having a son had not been a problem for her father, that he took pride in his daughters, that he treated them intellectually as sons" (p. 25). The father of Elisabeth von R., the hysteric woman with whom Freud developed the technique of free association, "used to say that this daughter of his took the place of a son and a friend with whom he could exchange thoughts" (Breuer & Freud, 1893–1895/1982, p. 140). Dora's father "had been so proud of the early growth of her intelligence that he had made her his confidante while she was still a child" (Freud, 1905/ 1963, p. 74).

However, intelligence was not without costs to the women, leading some of Bruch's anorexics and some of Freud's hysterics to regret being female. Bruch (1978) wrote about the anorexics: "Though few express it openly, they had felt throughout their lives that being a female was an unjust disadvantage and they dreamed of doing well in areas considered more respectful and worthwhile because they were 'masculine' " (p. 55). Of Elisabeth von R., Freud wrote, "Although the girl's mind found intellectual stimulation from this relationship with her father, he did not fail to observe that her mental constitution was on that account departing from the ideal which people like to see realized in a girl" (Breuer & Freud, 1893–1895/1982, p. 140). Freud added that Elisabeth von R. "was greatly discontented with being a girl. She was full of ambitious plans. She wanted to study . . . and she was indignant at the idea of having to sacrifice her inclinations and her freedom of judgement by marriage" (Breuer & Freud, 1893–1895/1982, p. 140). She described her emotional state just prior to the onset of hysteria as the "despair of a lonely girl like her being able to . . . achieve anything. . . . Till then she had thought herself strong enough to be able to do without the help of a man; but she was now overcome by a sense of her weakness as a woman" (Breuer & Freud, 1893–1895/1982, p. 155). Remarkably similar was Freud's description of Dora's feelings when she first manifested her symptoms. Freud (1905/1963) reported her "declaration that she had been able to keep abreast with her brother up to the time of her illness, but that after that she had fallen behind him in her studies. It is as though she had been a boy up till that moment, and had then become girlish for the first time" (p. 101).

Anna O. was brighter than her brother, who was sent to the University of Vienna, which was closed to women. Because she was female, she remained at home "engaged in her household duties"

(Breuer & Freud, 1893–1895/1982, p. 22). According to Breuer, "This girl, who was bubbling over with intellectual vitality, led an extemely monotonous existence in her puritanically-minded family" (Breuer & Freud, 1893–1895/1982, p. 22). He added: "She possessed a powerful intellect which would have been capable of digesting solid mental pabulum and which stood in need of it—though without receiving it after she had left school" (Breuer & Freud, 1893–1895/1982, p. 21).

Anna, whose real name was Bertha Pappenheim, went on to a distinguished career as an influential social worker and leader of the Jewish women's movement. She wrote a play entitled *Women's Rights*, dealing with women's powerlessness and exploitation by men; she also translated into German Mary Wollstonecraft's *A Vindication of the Rights of Women,* which argued for equal educational opportunity. She saw women as "beasts of burden" to men (Hunter, 1983, p. 478) and thought of her lack of formal education as "defective spiritual nourishment" (Hunter, 1983, p. 470).

As a child, Dora had exhibited intellectual precocity, but at adolescence, she too was pressured by her parents to stay at home doing household chores. On her own, she attempted to obtain what further education she could, "attending lectures for women" and carrying on "more or less serious studies," even though her mother "was bent upon drawing her into taking a share in the work of the house" (Freud, 1905/1963, p. 38).

Breuer and Freud noticed these similarities. They described the "features which one meets with so frequently in hysterical people," including "giftedness," "ambition," and "the independence of . . . nature which went beyond the feminine ideal" (Breuer & Freud, 1893–1895/ 1982, p. 161).

Those anorexics and hysterics who did have brothers appear to have been very envious of their achievements. Bruch (1978) described one anorexic as remembering "her father's teasing as painful in his sarcastic remarks that she did not bring home as many prizes as her older brother had" (p. 33). About another anorexic, Bruch (1978) wrote: "Her whole life was an endless competition with an older brother. . . . Only what her brother did was counted as worthwhile" (p. 52). About Dora, Freud (1905/1963) wrote: "During the girl's earlier years, her only brother . . . had been the model which her ambitions had striven to follow" (p. 35). While Dora was being pressured to clean the house, her brother was given the education that allowed him to become a leader of the Austrian Socialist Party.

In light of later developments in psychoanalytic theory, it is interesting to note that in these early case studies Freud paid very little attention to the mothers of his patients. The only description of a mother of a hysteric that Freud (1905/1963) gave in any detail was that of Dora's mother:

> I never made her mother's acquaintance. From the accounts given me by the girl and her father I was led to imagine her as an uncultivated woman and above all as a foolish one, who had concentrated all her interests upon domestic affairs. . . . She presented the picture, in fact, of what might be called the "housewife's psychosis." She had no understanding for her children's more active interests, and was occupied all day long in cleaning the house. (p. 34)

As a result, Dora was on "very bad terms with" and "looked down on her mother" (Freud, 1905/1963, pp. 35, 38).

Bruch and Freud drew very similar conclusions (cast in remarkably similar language) about the familial interactions of their patients in regard to issues of female achievement, as well as the discontent experienced by these women regarding traditional gender roles. Both groups of patients were bright, high-achieving females who were valued as children for their intelligence, even though intelligence was not considered by their families or culture as a desirable feminine characteristic. Women in both groups who had brothers often felt envious of their brothers' achievements and resented the limitations placed upon themselves because they were female.

In an attempt to discover whether the similarities apparent in these case histories help to explain disordered eating among contemporary women, we asked hundreds of female college students to describe the achievement-related attitudes of their parents. We found that women who reported symptoms of disordered eating were more likely than other women to report that their fathers did not think that the women's mothers were intelligent, that their mothers were dissatisfied with their own career choices, and that their fathers considered a male to be the most intelligent of his children (Silverstein et al., 1988). We also found that disordered eating and depression were more often reported by women who believed that their mothers were limited by being female, who reported feeling guilty about living better lives than their mothers, and who sometimes minimized their own accomplishments so that their mothers would not feel badly about themselves (Silverstein et al., 1993).

Daughters of Eminent Men

To further explore the roles played by high-achieving fathers and by mothers unable to achieve academically and professionally, we have studied the lives of the daughters of high-achieving men. Our study began with the daughters of the men whose ideas we believe have had the greatest influence on modern thought: Sigmund Freud, Karl Marx, Charles Darwin, and Albert Einstein. As part of a related investigation of highly successful women, we studied two other daughters of eminent men: Indira Gandhi, daughter of the first prime minister of India, Jawaharlal Nehru (and later prime minister in her own right), and Queen Elizabeth I, daughter of King Henry VIII.

The evidence regarding disordered eating among these six daughters of eminent men is indirect but intriguing. Little is known about Margot Einstein, stepdaughter of Albert, save that she had an illness throughout her life that was never discussed. She was described in various biographies of her father as having an "extremely fragile appearance"; as looking "excessively slim," "too slender," and "strangely like her [emaciated] dying sister"; and as "frail," "very frail," and "as frail as ever" (Sayen, 1985, p. 130; Vallentin, 1954, pp. 140, 236, 294).

As with Einstein's stepdaughter, little is known of the symptoms exhibited by Charles Darwin's daughter Henrietta, except that she was a lifelong invalid described as having "ill health" as a profession. Her niece described her as very "frail" and having a "tiny form," and wrote of Henrietta's calling down to the kitchen to ask the cook to count the number of pits on her plate to ascertain whether she had eaten three or four prunes for lunch (Raverat, 1958, pp. 122, 123).

The exact details of the symptoms exhibited by Indira Gandhi have not yet reached print. Beginning at adolescence, she was chronically ill for at least the next 20 years. She was sent away to convalesce during her adolescent illness, at which time she was described as "thin," "delicate," "wiry," "almost ethereal," and the familiar "frail." Many letters written to and received from friends by her father refer to recent weight loss or gain. Mahatma Gandhi, during an imprisonment for rebellious activities, thought it important enough to send a telegram to Nehru (imprisoned elsewhere), saying that he had seen Indira "in possession of more flesh" (Masani, 1976, pp. 36, 54, 65).

At adolescence, Queen Elizabeth I suffered a "breakdown of the nervous system," lost her appetite, refused to eat, and lost much weight (Lukes, 1973, p. 64). She also began to experience recurrent headaches. She was later described as "quite melancholy" and as experiencing "episodes of hysteria"; was said to be a "very light eater," eating "smally or nothing"; and was described as "thin and emaciated," "fleshless," and the omnipresent "frail." A physician called in to examine her claimed that Elizabeth was so thin "that her bones may be counted" (Erickson, 1983, pp. 187, 252, 281).

At adolescence, Eleanore Marx, daughter of Karl, became ill. The depression that was to lead to her eventual suicide began. She was described by her mother as "emaciated" after she stopped eating. Her biographer concluded that she was anorexic. Her father wrote to his colleague Friedrich Engels that one of the features of women's ailments "in which hysteria plays a part was that one had to affect not to notice that the invalid lived on earthly sustenance" (Kapp, 1972, pp. 162, 183).

Like Indira Gandhi, Anna Freud was sent away to recuperate from a little-discussed illness during her adolescence. Her biographer wrote that it was "not physical" and that she felt "exhausted and stupid" (Young-Bruehl, 1988, p. 59). During her recuperation, she exchanged several letters with her father, who wrote encouraging her to gain weight. She often replied that she had put on some poundage. If the problems we are studying were less serious, we might derive some amusement from the correspondence between several of the great thinkers of the last two centuries—Sigmund and Anna Freud, Karl Marx and Friedrich Engels, and Jawaharlal Nehru and Mahatma Gandhi—devoted primarily to the weight of daughters. Anna Freud's biographer concluded that Anna was suffering from "a mild eating disturbance of the kind Freud associated with hysteria" (Young-Bruehl, 1988, p. 59).

The women we studied were talented. Margot Einstein was described as an accomplished artist who was afraid of exhibiting her work. Henrietta Darwin served as an editor not only of her father's work, but of that of his colleague T. H. Huxley. Eleanore Marx made a reputation as an essayist and translator of her father's works. And Anna Freud, Indira Gandhi, and Elizabeth I earned great fame in their own rights.

But the biographies of these women indicate that they realized that their lives and those of their mothers had been very limited by the fact that they were female. Eleanore Marx's mother wrote, in a letter from the same time that she was showing signs of depression, ". . . while the men are invigorated by the fight in the world outside, strengthened by coming face to face with the enemy . . . we sit at home and darn stockings. It does not banish care and the little day-to-day worries slowly but surely sap one's vitality" (Kapp, 1972, p. 41). Upon the birth of Eleanore, Karl Marx wrote to his friend Friedrich Engels that she was "unfortunately of the sexe par excellence. . . . had it been a male the matter would be more acceptable" (Kapp, 1972, p. 41). Indira Gandhi noted that her mother had suffered because she was female, and vowed not to suffer in the same way herself (Masani, 1976, pp. 20, 46).

Some of the women we studied were born into situations in which there were economic or political pressures to have male children. Henry VIII, Queen Elizabeth I's father, went through six wives (and executed Elizabeth's mother) in an attempt to beget a royal male heir. Thus, we might conclude that Elizabeth knew that her mother died because she was a female in a much less powerful position than her husband, and because Elizabeth herself was not a male. Elizabeth surely had powerful reasons for feeling ambivalent about her femaleness.

Freud's biographer, Peter Gay (1988, pp. 59, 60), wrote that Freud's wife, Martha, was the "complete bourgeoisie" with an "unremitting sense of her calling to domestic duty." Bearing six children in nine years, she led what Freud called a "tormented life" and was not his intellectual companion. Like Dora, Anna Freud was intellectually precocious, was described as her father's confidante, and was faced with a father who modeled success and a mother who modeled domesticity.

Thus, these six daughters of eminent men had several things in common. They were bright and talented; had fathers who were extremely successful in the arena of intellectual or political achievement, but mothers who were not; and began to suffer at adolescence from ailments involving extreme thinness, and in many cases depression and disordered eating. Thus, evidence from biographies, case descriptions, and the medical literature of past centuries; recent studies in psychology and medicine; and analyses of temporal fluctuations in the prevalence of specific disorders all point to a similar conclusion: Women who strive to achieve in areas traditionally dominated by men and who come to feel limited by being female may develop a syndrome involving disordered eating, depression, and other somatic and psychological symptoms, particularly if their mothers were unable to achieve in these areas.

GENDER AMBIVALENCE

We believe that the key to the development of the forgotten syndrome is feeling ambivalent about one's own gender. What seems to happen is this: Some women strive to achieve in the areas that are most respected in society but that have traditionally been available only to males. Many of these women find that their parents do not reward their efforts, believing that a woman's place is in the home or in traditionally female careers. At the same time, the women often see many advantages given to their brothers. Even women who have been encouraged as children to achieve may find when they reach adolescence that much of this encouragement disappears. As a result of this bias, many come to feel the limitations imposed by their gender.

This process of the development of gender ambivalence is particularly likely to occur if their basic sense of what it is to be female is negative. The development of this basic sense is greatly influenced by observing how their mothers feel about being female, by noting the treatment received by the mothers from their spouses and from the society at large, and by reacting both cognitively and emotionally to the respect (or, usually, lack of respect) accorded to the mothers.

During periods of great change in gender roles, large numbers of women aspire to achieve in highly respected areas traditionally reserved for males. However, even during these periods of liberation they realize that being female places them at a disadvantage in these areas, and that the traditional female roles of wife, mother, and homemaker remain relatively unrespected. They are thus faced with one of two problematic situations. If their mothers are also nontraditional, the daughters may identify with them, at the same time observing the great limitations placed upon the mothers because of their gender. If their mothers are traditional, the daughters may be socialized to devalue the roles played by the mothers and may confront difficulties in identifying with their mothers. In either case, their sense of self-worth as mature adult females suffers.

Because these processes afflict large numbers of females during periods of changing gender roles, the symptoms of the forgotten syndrome, including disordered eating, poor body image, depression, and somatic symptoms, become particularly prevalent during these periods. That, we believe, is why disordered eating and depression now appear to be so common among females.

One implication of our findings is that, as discussed in other chapters of this book, therapies for disordered eating, depression, and other symptoms of the syndrome must incorporate an understanding of the gender-related aspects of the disorders; therapists should attempt to help women to see why they may have become ambivalent about something so central as their gender, and to reduce that ambivalence. But as necessary as therapy is in order to help the thousands of women who now suffer from the forgotten syndrome, therapy alone is not enough. New preventative measures must also be developed, such as special classes in middle schools to ready young females for the adolescent transition to adulthood, targeted toward those who aspire to intellectual and professional achievement but who come from families in which the mothers were not able to achieve in these areas. Also important is the education of family physicians, school nurses, and psychologists to recognize that an adolescent girl who presents with headache, insomnia, amenorrhea, or other specific somatic and psychological symptoms may be suffering from a syndrome that is no longer recognized in diagnostic systems in current use. But the real "cure" for these problems lies in the elimination of gender bias. The forgotten syndrome will disappear only when women who desire to achieve in areas historically reserved for males are given equal encouragement and opportunity, and when traditionally "feminine" pursuits are accorded respect as well.

REFERENCES

Ago, Y., Sugita, M., Teshima, H., & Nakagawa, T. (1982). Specificity concepts in Japan. *Psychotherapy and Psychosomatics, 38,* 64–73.

Allbutt, T. C. (1901). Chlorosis. In T. C. Allbutt (Ed.), *A system of medicine by many authors* (Vol. 5, pp. 481-518) New York: Macmillan.

Allgood-Merton, B., Lewinsohn, P. M., & Hops, H. (1990). Sex differences and adolescent depression. *Journal of Abnormal Psychology, 99,* 55–63.

Avery-Clark, C. (1986). Sexual dysfunction and disorder patterns of working and nonworking wives. *Journal of Sex and Marital Therapy, 12*(2), 93–107.

Beck, S. B., Ward-Hull, C. I., & McLear, P. M. (1976). Variables related to women's somatic preferences of the male and female body. *Journal of Personality and Social Psychology, 34,* 1200–1210.

Breuer, J., & Freud, S. (1982). *Studies on hysteria.* New York: Penguin. (Original work published 1893–1895)

Brewis, M., Poskanzer, D. C., Rolland, C., & Miller, H. (1966). Neurological disease in an English city. *Acta Neurologica Scandinavica, 42*(Suppl. 24), 1–89.

Bruch, H. (1973). *Eating disorders.* New York: Basic Books.

Bruch, H. (1978). *The golden cage.* Cambridge, MA: Harvard University Press.

Cash, T. F., & Pruzinsky, T. (Eds.). (1990). *Body images: Development, deviance, and change.* New York: Guilford Press.

Clarke, E. (1873). *Sex in education: Or a fair chance for the girls.* Boston: J. R. Osgood.

Deale, H. B.. & Adams, S. S. (1894). Neurasthenia in young women. *American Journal of Obstetrics, 29,* 190–195.

Dryman, A., & Eaton, W.W. (1991). Affective symptoms associated with the onset of major depression in the community: Findings from the US National Institute of Mental Health Epidemiologic Catchment Area Program. *Acta Psychiatrica Scandinavica, 84,* 1–5.

Erickson, C. (1983). *The first Elizabeth.* New York: Summit.

Frank, E., Carpenter, L. L., & Kupfer, D. J. (1988). Sex differences in recurrent depression: Are there any that are significant? *American Journal of Psychiatry, 145,* 41–45.

Freud, S. (1963). *Dora: An analysis of a case of hysteria.* New York: Collier. (Original work published 1905)

Gay, P. (1988). *Freud: A life for our time.* Garden City, NY: Doubleday/Anchor.

Gosling, F. G. (1987). *Before Freud: Neurasthenia and the American medical community.* Urbana: University of Illinois Press.

Horend, I., & Perdue, L. (1990, August 10). *Bingeing, purgeing and developmental changes in parental concern for achievement.* Paper presented at the annual meeting of the American Psychological Association, Boston.

Hunter, D. (1983). Hysteria, psychoanalysis, and feminism: The case of Anna O. *Feminist Studies, 9,* 465–488.

Kapp, Y. (1972). *Eleanore Marx.* New York: Pantheon.

Kashani, J. H., Beck, N. C., Hoeper, E. W., Fallahi, C., Corcoran, C. M.,

McAllister, J. A., Rosenberg, T. K., & Reid, J. C. (1987) Psychiatric disorders in a community sample of adolescents. *American Journal of Psychiatry, 144,* 584–589.

Laycock, T. (1840a). *An essay on hysteria.* Philadelphia: Haswell, Barrington & Haswell.

Laycock, T. (1840b). *A treatise on the nervous diseases of women.* London: Longman, Orme, Brown, Green & Longmans.

Lefkowitz, M. R., & Fant, M.B. (1982). *Women's life in Greece and Rome.* Baltimore: Johns Hopkins University Press.

Linet, M. S., & Stewart, W. F. (1987). The epidemiology of migraine headache. In J. N. Blau (Ed.), *Migraine: Clinical and research aspects* (pp. 451–477). Baltimore: Johns Hopkins University Press.

Littre, E. (1853). *Oeuvres completes d'Hippocrate.* Paris: Baillière.

Loudon, I. (1984). The diseases called chlorosis. *Psychological Medicine, 4,* 27–36.

Lucas, A. R., Beard, M., O'Fallon, W. M., & Kurland, L. T. (1991). 50-year trends in the incidence of anorexia nervosa in Rochester, Minn.: A population-based study. *American Journal of Psychiatry, 148*(7), 917–922.

Lukes, M. M. (1973). *Gloriana: The years of Elizabeth I.* New York: Coward & McCann.

Masani, Z. (1976). *Indira Gandhi: A biography.* New York: Thomas Y. Crowell.

Nathan, S. G. (1986). The epidemiology of the DSM-III psychosexual dysfunctions. *Journal of Sex and Marital Therapy, 12,* 267–281.

Nolen-Hoeksema, S. (1990). *Sex differences in depression.* Stanford, CA: Stanford University Press.

Perdue, L., Pizzolo, C., & Norman, C. (1991, August 17). *Depressive mood and women's reports of low achieving, discontented mothers.* Paper presented at the annual meeting of the American Psychological Association, San Francisco.

Pitts, F. N., Schuller, A. B., Rich, C. L., & Pitts, A. F. (1979). Suicide among US women physicians. *American Journal of Psychiatry, 136,* 694–698.

Preston, G. J. (1897). *Hysteria and certain allied conditions.* Philadelphia: P. Blakiston.

Price, V. A., Coates, T. J., Thoresen, C. E., & Grinstead, O. A. (1978). Prevalence and correlates of poor sleep among adolescents. *American Journal of Diseases of Children, 132,* 583–586.

Purtell, J. J., Robins, E., & Cohen, M. E. (1951). Observations on clinical aspects of hysteria. *Journal of the American Medical Association, 146,* 902–909.

Raverat, G. M. D. (1958). *Period piece: A Cambridge childhood.* London: Faber & Faber.

Richards, M. H., Casper, R. C., & Larson, R. (1990). Weight and eating concerns among pre- and young adolescent boys and girls. *Journal of Adolescent Health Care, 11,* 203–209.

Savage, G.H. (1884). *Insanity and allied neuroses.* Philadelphia: Henry C. Lea.

Sayen, J. (1985). *Einstein in America.* New York: Crown.

Silverstein, B., Carpman, S., Perlick, D., & Perdue, L. (1990). Nontraditional sex role aspirations, gender identity conflict and disordered eating among college women. *Sex Roles, 23,* 687–695.

Silverstein, B., & Perdue, L. (1988). The relationship between role concerns, preferences for slimness and symptoms of eating problems among college women. *Sex Roles, 18*(1/2), 101–106.

Silverstein, B., Perdue, L., Peterson, B., Vogel, L., & Fantini, D.A. (1986). Possible causes of the thin standard of bodily attractiveness for women. *International Journal of Eating Disorders, 5*(5), 907–916.

Silverstein, B., Perdue, L., Wolf, C., & Pizzolo, C. (1988). Bingeing, purging and estimates of parental attitudes regarding female achievement. *Sex Roles, 19,* 723–733.

Silverstein, B., & Perlick, D. (1991). Gender differences in depression: Historical changes. *Acta Psychiatrica Scandinavica, 84,* 327–331.

Silverstein, B., Perlick, D., Clauson, J., & McKoy, E. (1993). Depression combined with somatic symptomatology among adolescent females who report concerns regarding maternal achievement. *Sex Roles, 28,* 637–653.

Silverstein, B., Peterson, B., & Perdue, L. (1986). Some correlates of the thin standard of bodily attractiveness in women. *International Journal of Eating Disorders, 5*(5), 895–905.

Simon, C. (1897). A study of chlorosis. *American Journal of Medical Science, 113,* 399–423.

Swartz, M., Blazer, D., Woodbury, M., George, L., & Landerman, R. (1986). Somatization disorder in a US Southern community: Use of a new procedure for analysis of medical classification. *Psychological Medicine, 16,* 595–609.

Vallentin, A. (1954). *The drama of Albert Einstein.* Garden City, NY: Doubleday.

Verrulst, F. C., Prince, J., Vervururt-Pool, C., & De Jong, J. (1989). Mental health in Dutch adolescents: Self-reported competencies and problems for ages 11–18. *Acta Psychiatrica Scandinavica,* (Suppl. 256).

Weiner, A., Marten, S., Wochnick, E., Davis, M.A., Fishman, R., & Clayton, P. J. (1979). Psychiatric disorders among professional women. *Archives of General Psychiatry, 36,* 169–173.

Whitaker, A., Johnson, J., Shaffer, D., Rapoport, J. L., Kalikow, K., Walsh, B. T., Davies, M., Braiman, S., & Dolinsky, A. (1990). Uncommon troubles in young people: Prevalence estimates of selected psychiatric disorders in a nonreferred adolescent population. *Archives of General Psychiatry, 47,* 487–496.

Wooley, S. C., & Wooley, O.W. (1986, October). Thinness mania. *American Health,* pp. 68–74.

Young-Bruehl, E. (1988). *Anna Freud.* New York: Summit.

Zetin, M., Sklansky, G. J., & Cramer, M. (1984). Sex differences in inpatients with major depression. *Journal of Clinical Psychiatry, 45*(6), 257–259.

5

Hunger

NAOMI WOLF

> *I saw the best minds of my generation*
> *destroyed by madness, starving . . .*
> —Allen Ginsberg, "Howl"

THERE IS A DISEASE SPREADING. It taps on the shoulder America's firstborn sons, its best and brightest. At its touch, they turn away from food. Their bones swell out from receding flesh. Shadows invade their faces. They walk slowly, with the effort of old men. A white spittle forms on their lips. They can swallow only pellets of bread, and a little thin milk. First tens, then hundreds, then thousands, until among the most affluent families, one young son in five is stricken. Many are hospitalized and die.

The boys of the ghetto die young, and America has lived with that. But these boys are the golden ones to whom the reins of the world are to be lightly tossed: the captain of the Princeton football team, the head of the Berkeley debating club, the editor of the *Harvard Crimson*. Then a quarter of the Dartmouth rugby team falls ill; then a third of the initiates of Yales' secret societies. The heirs, the cream, the fresh delegates to the nation's forum selectively waste away.

The American disease spreads eastward. It strikes young men at the Sorbonne, in London's Inns of Court, in the administration of The

Adapted from *The Beauty Myth: How Images of Beauty Are Used Against Women* by Naomi Wolf, 1991, New York: Morrow. Copyright 1991 by Naomi Wolf. Adapted by permission of the author and publisher.

Hague, in the Bourse, in the offices of *Die Zeit,* in the universities of Edinburgh and Tübingen and Salamanca.. They grow thin and still more thin. They can hardly speak aloud. They lose their libido, and can no longer make the effort to joke or argue. When they run or swim, they look appalling: buttocks collapsed, tailbones protruding, knees knocked together, ribs splayed in a shelf that stretches their papery skin. There is no medical reason.

The disease mutates again. Across America, it becomes apparent that for every well-born living skeleton there are at least three other young men, also bright lights, who do something just as strange. Once they have swallowed their steaks and Rhine wine, they hide away, thrust their fingers down their throats, and spew out all the nourishment in them. They wander back into Maury's or "21", shaking and pale. Eventually they arrange their lives so they can spend hours each day hunched over like that, their highly trained minds telescoped around two shameful holes: mouth, toilet; toilet, mouth.

Meanwhile, people are waiting for them to take up their places: assistantships at *The New York Times,* seats on the Stock Exchange, clerkships with federal judges. Speeches need to be written and briefs researched among the clangor of gavels and the whir of fax machines. What's happening to the fine young men, in their brush cuts and khaki trousers? It hurts to look at them. At the expense-account lunches, they hide their medallions of veal under lettuce leaves. Secretly they purge. They vomit after matriculation banquets and after tailgate parties at the game. The men's room in the Oyster Bar reeks with it.

How would America react to the mass self-immolation by hunger of its favorite sons? How would western Europe absorb the export of such a disease? One would expect an emergency response: crisis task forces convened in congressional hearing rooms, unscheduled alumni meetings, the best experts money can hire, cover stories in news magazines, a flurry of editorials, blame and counterblame, bulletins, warnings, symptoms, updates—an epidemic blazoned in boldface red. The sons of privilege *are* the future; the future is committing suicide.

Of course, this is actually happening right now, only with a gender difference. The institutions that shelter and promote these diseases are hibernating. The public conscience is fast asleep. Virginia Woolf, in *A Room of One's Own,* had a vision that someday young women would have access to the rich forbidden libraries of the men's colleges, their sunken lawns, their vellum, the claret light. She believed that would give young women a mental freedom that must have seemed all the sweeter from where she imagined it: the wrong side of the beadle's staff that had driven her away from the library because she was female.[1] Now young women have pushed past the staff that barred Woolf's way. Striding across the grassy quadrangles that she could only write about, they are halted by an immaterial barrier she did not foresee. Their minds are proving well able; their bodies self-destruct.

When she envisaged a future for young women in the universities, Woolf's prescience faltered only from insufficient cynicism. Without it one could hardly conceive of the modern solution of the recently all-male schools and colleges to the problem of women: They admitted their minds, and let their bodies go. Young women learned that they could not live inside those gates and also inside their bodies.

What happened? Why now? Until 75 years ago in the male artistic tradition of the West, women's natural amplitude was their beauty; representations of the female nude reveled in women's lush fertility. Various distributions of sexual fat were emphasized according to fashion—big, ripe bellies from the 15th to the 17th centuries, plump faces and shoulders in the early 19th, progressively generous dimpled buttocks and thighs until the 20th—but never, until women's emancipation entered law, this absolute negation of the female state that fashion historian Ann Hollander in *Seeing through Clothes* characterizes, from the point of view of any age but our own, as "the look of sickness, the look of poverty, and the look of nervous exhaustion."[2]

Dieting and thinness began to be female preoccupations when Western women received the vote around 1920; between 1918 and 1925, "the rapidity with which the new, linear form replaced the more curvaceous one is startling."[3] In the regressive 1950s, women's natural fullness could be briefly enjoyed once more, because their minds were occupied in domestic seclusion. But when women came *en masse* into male spheres, that pleasure had to be overridden by an urgent social expedient that would make women's bodies into the prisons that their homes no longer were. Women's advancement and gratification are being run underground, as reflected in a 1984 survey by *Glamour* in which respondents chose losing 10 to 15 pounds above success in work or in love as their most desired goal.[4]

Those 10 to 15 pounds, which have become a fulcrum, if these figures are indicative, of most Western women's sense of self, are the medium of what I call the One Stone Solution. One stone, the British measurement of 14 pounds, is roughly what stands between 50% of women who are not overweight but believe they are and their ideal selves. That one stone, once lost, puts these women well below the weight that is natural to them, and beautiful. But the body quickly restores itself, and the cycle of gain and loss begins, with its train of torment and its risk of disease, becoming a fixation of a woman's consciousness. The inevitable cycles of failure ensured by the One Stone Solution create and continually reinforce in women a uniquely modern neurosis. This great weight shift bestowed on women, just when they were free to begin to forget them, new versions of low self-esteem, loss of control, and sexual shame. It is a genuinely elegant fulfillment of a collective wish: Simply as a result of dropping the official weight one stone below most women's natural level, and redefining a woman's womanly shape as by definition "too fat," a wave of self-hatred swept over First World women; a reactionary psychology was perfected; and a major industry was born. It suavely countered the historical groundswell of female success with a mass conviction of female failure, a failure defined as implicit in womanhood itself.

The proof that the One Stone Solution is political lies in what women feel when they eat "too much": guilt. Why should guilt be the operative emotion, and female fat be a moral issue articulated with words like "good" and "bad?" If our culture's fixation on female fatness or thinness were about sex, it would be a private issue between a woman and her lover; if it were about health, it would be between a woman and herself.

But female fat is the subject of public passion, and women feel guilty about female fat, because we implicitly recognize that under the myth our bodies are not our own but society's, and that thinness is not a private aesthetic, but hunger a social concession exacted by the community. A cultural fixation on female thinness is not an obsession about female beauty, but an obsession about female obedience. Women's dieting has become a never-ending passion play given international coverage out of all proportion to the health risks associated with obesity, and using emotive language that does not figure even in discussions of alcohol or tobacco abuse. The nations seize with compulsive attention on this melodrama because women and men understand that it is not about cholesterol or heart rate or the disruption of a line of tailoring, but about how much social freedom women are going to get away with or concede. The media's convulsive analysis of the endless saga of female fat and the battle to vanquish it are actually bulletins of the sex war: what women are gaining or losing in it, and how fast. The great weight shift must be understood as one of the major historical developments of the century, a direct solution to the dangers posed by the women's movement and by economic and reproductive freedom. Women's advances had begun to give them high self-esteem, a sense of effectiveness, activity, courage, and clarity of mind. Prolonged and periodic caloric restriction is a means to take the teeth out of this revolution. The great weight shift and its One Stone Solution followed the rebirth of feminism so that women just reaching for power would become weak, preoccupied, and (as it evolved) mentally ill in useful ways and in astonishing proportions.

Women do not eat or starve within a public social order that has a material vested interest in their troubles with eating. Individual men don't spin out fashionable images (indeed, research keeps proving that they are warm to women's real shapes and unmoved by the Iron Maiden); multinational corporations do that. The many theories about women's food crises have stressed private psychology to the neglect of public policy, looking at women's shapes to see how they express a conflict about their society, rather than looking at how their society makes use of a manufactured conflict with women's shapes. Many other theories have focused on women's reaction to the thin ideal but have not asserted that the thin ideal, is proactive, a pre-emptive strike.

We need to re-examine all the terms again, then, in the light of a public agenda. What, first, is food? Certainly, within the context of the intimate family, food is love, and memory, and language. But in the public realm, food is status and honor.

Food is the primal symbol of social worth. Whom a society values, it feeds well. The piled plate, the choicest cut, say: "We think you're worth this much of the tribe's resources." Samoan women, who are held in high esteem, exaggerate how much they eat on feast days. Publicly apportioning food is about determining power relations, and sharing it is about cementing social equality: When men break bread together, or toast the queen, or slaughter for one another the fatted calf, they've become equals and then allies. The word "companion" comes from the Latin for "with" and "bread"—those who break bread together.

But under the beauty myth, now that all women's eating is a public issue, women's portions testify to and reinforce their sense of social inferiority. If women cannot eat the same food as men, they cannot experience equal status in the community. As long as women are asked to bring a self-denying mentality to the communal table, it will never be round, men and women seated together; it will remain the same traditional hierarchical dais, with a folding table for women at the foot.

As women, we do not feel entitled to enough food because we have been taught to go with less than we need since birth, in a tradition passed down through an endless line of mothers; the public role of "honored guest" is new to us, and the culture is telling us through the ideology of caloric restriction that we are not welcome finally to occupy it.

What, then, is fat? Fat is portrayed in the literature of the myth as expendable female filth—virtually cancerous matter, an inert or treacherous infiltration into the body of nauseating bulk waste. The demonic characterizations of a simple body substance do not arise from its physical properties but from old-fashioned misogyny, for above all fat is female; it is the medium and regulator of female sexual characteristics.

Fat is sexual in women; Victorians called it affectionately their "silken layer." The leanness of the modern ideal impairs female sexuality. One-fifth of women who exercise to shape their bodies have menstrual irregularities and diminished fertility. Hormonal imbalances promote ovarian and endometrial cancer and osteoporosis. Fat tissues store sex hormones, so low fat reserves are linked with weak estrogens and low levels of all the other important sex hormones, as well as with inactive ovaries. Rose E. Frisch in 1988 refers to the fatness of Stone Age fertility figures, saying that "this historical linking of fatness and fertility actually makes biological sense,"[5] since fat regulates reproduction. Underweight women double their risk of low-birthweight babies. Fat is not just fertility in women, but desire. To ask women to become unnaturally thin is to ask them to relinquish their sexuality.

What, finally, is dieting? "Dieting," and, in Great Britain, "slimming," are trivializing words for what is in fact self-inflicted semistarvation. In India, one of the poorest countries in the world, the very poorest women eat 1400 calories a day, or 600 more than a Western woman on the Hilton Head Diet.[6]

During the great famine that began in May 1940 during the German occupation of the Netherlands, the Dutch authorities maintained rations at between 600 and 1600 calories a day, or what they characterized as the level of semistarvation. At 600–1600 calories daily, the Dutch suffered semistarvation; the Diet Centers' diet is fixed at 1600 calories. When they had lost 25% of their body weight, the Dutch were given crisis food supplementation. The average healthy woman is trying to lose almost exactly as much.[7]

In the Lodz ghetto in 1941, besieged Jews were allotted starvation rations of 500–1200 calories a day. At Treblinka, 900 calories was scientifically determined to be the minimum necessary to sustain human functioning. At "the nation's top weight-loss clinics," where "patients" are treated for up to a year, the rations are the same.[8]

The psychological effects of self-inflicted semistarvation are identical to those of involuntary semistarvation, including irritability, poor concentration, anxiety, depression, apathy, lability of mood, fatigue, and social isolation. Authoritative evidence is mounting that eating disorders are caused mainly by dieting. Now, if female fat is sexuality and reproductive power; if food is honor; if dieting is semistarvation; if women have to lose 23% of their body weight to fit the Iron Maiden and chronic psychological disruption sets in at a body weight loss of 25%; if semistarvation is physically and psychologically debilitating, and female strength, sexuality, and self-respect pose the threats explored earlier against the vested interests of society; if women's journalism is sponsored by a $33 billion industry whose capital is made out of the political fear of women—then we can understand why the Iron Maiden is so thin. The thin "ideal" is not beautiful aesthetically; she is beautiful as a political solution.

Hunger makes women feel poor and think poor. A wealthy woman on a diet feels physically at the mercy of a scarcity economy; the rare woman who makes $100,000 a year has bodily income of 1000 calories a day. Hunger makes successful women feel like failures: An architect learns that her work crumbles; a politician who oversees a long-range vision is returned to the details, to add up every bite; a woman who can afford to travel can't "afford" rich foreign foods. It undermines each experience of control, economic security, and leadership that women have had only a generation to learn to enjoy. Those who were so recently freed to think beyond the basics are driven, with this psychology, back to the feminine mental yoke of economic dependence: fixation on getting sustenance and safety. Virginia Woolf believed that "one cannot think well, sleep well, love well if one has not dined well." "The lamp in the spine does not light on beef and prunes," she wrote, contrasting the dispiriting food of poverty, of the hard-pressed women's colleges with that of the rich men's colleges, the "soles sunk in a deep dish, over which the college cook has spread a counterpane of the whitest cream."[9] Now that some women at least have achieved the equivalent of £500 a year and a room of their own, it is back once more to 4 ounces of boiled beef and three unsweetened prunes, and the unlit lamp.

The anorexic may begin her journey defiant, but from the point of view of a male-dominated society, she ends up as the perfect woman. She is weak, sexless, and voiceless, and can only with difficulty focus on a world beyond her plate. The woman has been killed off in her. She is almost not there. Seeing her like this, unwomaned, it makes crystalline sense that a half-conscious but virulent mass movement of the imagination created the vital lie of skeletal female beauty. A future in which industrialized nations are peopled with anorexia-driven women is one of few conceivable that would save the current distribution of wealth and power from the claims made on it by women's struggle for equality.

For theorists of anorexia to focus on the individual woman, even within her family, misses the tactical heart of this struggle. Economic and political retaliation against female appetite is far stronger at this point than family dynamics. This can no longer be explained as a private issue. If suddenly 60–80% of college women can't eat, it's hard to believe that suddenly 60–80% of their families are dysfunctional in this particular way. There is a disease in the air; its cause was generated with intent; and young women are catching it.

Our culture gives a young woman only two dreams in which to imagine her body, like a coin with two faces: one pornographic, the other anorexic; the first for nighttime, the second for day—the one, supposedly, for men and the other for other women. She does not have the choice to refuse to toss it—not, yet, to demand a better dream. The anorexic body is sexually safer to inhabit than the pornographic.

At the same time, it works for male-dominated institutions by processing women smoothly, unwomaned, into positions closer to power. It is "trickling down" to women of all social classes from elitist schools and universities because that is where women are getting too close to authority. There, it is emblematic of how hunger checkmates power in any women's life: Hundreds of thousands of well-educated young women, living and studying at the fulcrum of cultural influence, are causing no trouble. The anorexic woman student, like the anti-Semitic Jew and the self-hating black, fits in. She is politically castrated, with exactly enough energy to do her schoolwork neatly and completely, and to run around the indoor track in eternal circles. She has no energy to get angry or get organized, to chase sex, to yell through a bullhorn, asking for money for night buses or for women's studies programs or wanting to know where all the women professors are. Administering a coed class half full of mentally anorexic women is an experience distinct from that of administering a class half full of healthy-confident young women. With the woman in these women canceled out, it is closer to the administration of young men only, which was how things were comfortably managed before. For women to stay at the official extreme of the weight spectrum requires 95% of us to infantilize or rigidify to some degree our mental lives.

DEAD EASY

It is dead easy to become an anorexic. When I was 12 I went to visit an older, voluptuous cousin. "I try," she said, to explain the deep-breathing exercises she did before bedtime, "to visualize my belly as something I can love and accept and live with." Still compact in a one-piece kid's body, I was alarmed to think that womanhood involved breaking apart into pieces that floated around, since my cousin seemed to be trying to hold herself together by a feat of concentration. It was not a comforting thought. The buds of my breasts hurt already. As she did her exercises, I leafed through a copy of *Cosmopolitan,* which had an article demonstrating to women how to undress and pose and move in bed with their partners so as to disguise their fatness.

My cousin looked me over. "Do you know how much you weigh?" No, I told her. "Why don't you just hop on the scale?" I could feel how much my cousin wished to inhabit a simple, slight 12-year-old body. That could only mean, I thought, that when I was a woman, I would want to get out of my own body into some little kid's.

A year later, while I was bending over the drinking fountain in the hall of my junior high school, Bobby Werner, whom I hardly knew, gave me a hard poke in the soft part of my stomach, just below the navel. It would be a decade before I would remember that he was the class fat boy.

That evening I let the juice of the lamb chop congeal on my plate. I could see viscous nodules of fat, a charred outer edge of yellow matter, cooling from liquid to solid, marked USDA CHOICE in edible blue dye. The center bone, serrated, had been cloven with a powerful rotary blade. I felt a new feeling, a nausea wicked with the pleasure of loathing. As I rose hungry from the table, a jet of self-righteousness lit up under my esophagus, intoxicating me. All night long I inhaled it.

The next day I passed the small notepad kept by the dishwasher. I knew what it said, though it was my mother's and private: "½ grpfruit. Blk. coff. 4 Wheat Thins. 1 Popsicle." A black scrawl: "binge." I wanted to tear it up. Some memoir.

I had no more patience for the trivial confessions of women. I could taste from my mouth that my body had entered ketosis, imbalanced electrolytes—good. The girl stood on the burning deck. I put the dishes in the sink with a crash of declaration.

At 13, I was taking in the caloric equivalent of the food energy available to the famine victims of the siege of Paris. I did my schoolwork diligently and kept quiet in the classroom. I was a wind-up obedience toy. Not a teacher or principal or guidance counselor confronted me with an objection to my evident deportation in stages from the land of the living.

There were many starving girls in my junior high school, and every one was a teacher's paragon. We were allowed to come and go, racking up gold stars, as our hair fell out in fistfuls and the pads flattened behind the sockets of our eyes. When our eyeballs moved, we felt the resistance. They allowed us to haul our bones around the swinging rope in gym class, where nothing but the force of an exhausted will stood between the ceiling, to which we clung with hands so wasted the jute seemed to abrade the cartilage itself, and the polished wooden floor 35 feet below.

An alien voice took mine over. I have never been so soft-spoken. It lost expression and timbre and sank to a monotone, a dull murmur the opposite of strident. My teachers approved of me. They saw nothing wrong with what I was doing, and I could swear they looked straight at me. My school had stopped dissecting alley cats, since it was considered inhumane. There was no interference in my self-directed science experiment: to find out just how little food could keep a human body alive.

The dreams I could muster were none of the adolescent visions that boys have, or free and healthy girls; no fantasies of sex or escape, rebellion or future success. All the space I had for dreaming was taken up by food. When I lay on my bed, in that posture of adolescent reverie, I could find no comfort. My bones pressed sharply into the mattress. My ribs were hooks and my spine a dull blade and my hunger a heavy shield, all I have to stave off the trivialities that would attach themselves like parasites to my body the minute it made a misstep into the world of women. My doctor put his hand on my stomach and said he could feel my spine. I turned an eye cold with loathing on women who evidently lacked the mettle to suffer as I was suffering.

I made a drawing: myself, small, small, curled in a sort of burrow, surrounded by nesting materials, with a store of nuts and raisins, protected. This smallness and hiddenness were what I craved at the time of life when Stephen Dedalus longed to burst like a meteor on the world. What did that drawing mean? It was not a longing to return to the womb, but to return to my body. I was not longing to be saved from the choices of the world, but from the obligations to enter into a combat in which I could only believe if I forgot all about myself, and submitted to starting again dumber, like someone hit hard on the back of the head.

Adolescent starvation was, for me, a prolonged reluctance to be born into womanhood if that meant assuming a station of beauty. Children resist being baffled with convention, and often see social madness in full dimensions. In seventh grade, we knew what was coming, and we all went berserk with cogent fear—not a normal craziness of adolescence, but panic at what unnaturally loomed. Like a life-sized game of Mother May I, we know that beauty was going to say, "Freeze," and wherever we were, that would be it.

Anorexia was the only way I could see to keep the dignity in my body that I had had as a kid, and that I would lose as a woman. It was the only choice that really looked like one: By refusing to put on a woman's body and receive a rating, I chose not to have all my future choices confined to little things, and not to have the choices made for me, on the basis of something meaningless to me, in the larger things. But as time went on, my choices grew smaller and smaller. Beef bouillon or hot water with lemon? The bouillon had 20 calories—I'd take the water. The lemon had four; I could live without it. Just.

Now, when I can bring myself to think of that time at all—another blackout, by beauty, of the cities of memory—my sadness can't shake off the rage that follows it close behind. To whom do I petition for that lost year? How many inches in height did I lose from having calcium withheld from my bones, their osteoblasts struggling without nourishment to multiply? How many years sooner will a brittle spine bend my neck down? In the Kafkaesque departments of this bureau of hunger, which charged me guilty for a crime no more specific than inhabiting a female body, what door do I knock upon? Who is obliged to make reparations to me for the thought abandoned, the energy never found, the explorations never considered? Who owes me for the year-long occupation of a mind at the time of its most urgent growth?

In our interpretation of the damages done by the beauty myth, it is not yet possible to lay blame anywhere but on oneself. I can say finally, for myself at least: At 13, to starve half to death? Not guilty. Not that child. There is certainly a charge of guilt to be made, long overdue. But it doesn't belong to me. It belongs somewhere, and to someone else.

The youngest victims, from earliest childhood, learn to starve and vomit from the overwhelmingly powerful message of our culture, which I found no amount of parental love and support strong enough to override. I knew my parents wanted me not to starve because they loved me, but their love contradicted the message of the larger world, which wanted me to starve in order to love me. It is the larger world's messages, young women know, to which they will have to listen if they are to leave their parents' protection. I kept a wetted finger up to the winds of that larger world: Too thin yet? I was asking it. What about now? No? Now?

The larger world never gives girls the message that their bodies are valuable simply because they are inside them. Until our culture tells young girls that they are welcome in any shape—that women are valuable to it with or without the excuse of "beauty"—girls will continue to starve. And institutional messages then reward young women's education in hunger. But when the lesson has been taken too dangerously to heart, they ignore the consequences, reinforcing the disease. Anorexics want to be saved, but they cannot trust individual counselors, family members, or friends; that is too uncertain. They are walking question marks challenging—pleading—with schools, universities, and the other mouthpieces that transmit what is culturally acceptable in women, to tell them unequivocally: "This is intolerable. This is unacceptable. We don't starve women here. We value women." By turning an indifferent eye to the ravages of the backlash among their young women, schools and universities are killing off America's daughters; and Europe is learning to do the same to its own.[10] You don't need to die to count as a casualty. An anorexic cannot properly be called alive. To be anorexic is to keep a close daily tally of a slow death—to be a member of the walking undead.

Since institutions are treating this epidemic as one of those embarrassing feminine things imported into the cloister like tampon dispensers or commoner's gowns worn over skirts, there is no formal mourning. Women students are kept from openly recognizing what they privately know is going on around them. They are not permitted to claim this epidemic as real, and deadly, and taking place beside and inside them. So they have to repress horrifying knowledge, or trivialize it, or blame the sufferer. Another one sickens. Another disappears. Another one bites the dust.

As women, we must claim anorexia as political damage done to us by a social order that considers our destruction insignificant because of what we are—less. We should identify it as Jews identify the death camps, as homosexuals identify AIDS: as a disgrace that is not our own, but that of an inhumane social order.

Anorexia is a prison camp. One-fifth of well-educated American young women are inmates. Susie Orbach compared anorexia to the hunger strikes of political prisoners, particularly the suffragists.[11] But the time for metaphors is behind us. To be anorexic or bulimic *is* to be a political prisoner.

THE THIRD WAVE: FROZEN IN MOTION

If we look at most young women's inert relationship to feminism, we can see that with anorexia and bulimia, the beauty myth is winning its offensive. Where are the women activists of the new generation, the fresh blood to infuse energy into second-wave burnout and exhaustion? Why are so many so quiet? On campuses, up to a fifth of them are so quiet because they are starving to death. Starving people are notorious for a lack of organizational enthusiasm. The same young women who would seem to be its heiresses are not taking up the banner of the women's movement, for perhaps no more profound reason than that many of them are too physically ill to do much more than cope with immediate personal demands. And on a mental level, the epidemic of eating disorders may affect women of this generation in such a way as to make feminism seem viscerally unconvincing: Being a woman is evidently nothing to be up in arms about; it makes you hungry, weak, and sick.

Beyond this are other succession problems generated by the myth. Young women inherited 20 years of the propagandizing caricature of the Ugly Feminist, so—"I'm feminine, not a feminist," says a college senior in a *Time* magazine report; "I picture a feminist as someone who is masculine and doesn't shave her legs." Too many young women do not realize that others pictured "a feminist" in that way so that they would be sure to respond as this one does. Others, alarmingly, blame the women's movement for the beauty backlash against it—"Kathryn," a 25-year-old quoted by Sylvia Ann Hewlett, describes a party at her law firm: "I often resent . . . the way women's liberation has increased the expectations of men." Twenty years ago, she complains, a young male lawyer would want to arrive with "a drop-dead clone" on his arm, whereas today he and his colleagues compete to escort the highest achiever—"the only catch was that these yuppie women had to look every bit as glamorous as the drop-dead blonds of the past."[12] Finally, the myth seeks to discourage all young women from identifying with earlier feminists— simply because these are older women. Men grant themselves tradition to hand down through the generations; women are permitted only fashion, which each season renders obsolete. Under that construct, the link between generations of women is weakened by definition: What came before is rarely held up for admiration as history or heritage, but derided by fashion's rigid rule as embarrassingly *démodé*.

To share a meal with a young woman of the present generation, you have to be prepared to witness signs of grave illness. You ignore her frantic scanning of the menu, the meticulous way she scrapes the sauce. If she drinks five glasses of water and sucks and chews the ice, you mustn't comment. You look away if she starts to ferret a breadstick into her pocket, and ignore her reckless agitation at the appearance of the pastry tray, her long shamefaced absence after the meal, before the coffee. "Are you okay?" "I'm *fine*." How dare you ask?

When you share the bill, you haven't shared a meal. The always renewed debate that young people of each generation take for granted, about how to change the world to suit their vision, is not going to be renewed for women over a table such as this. The pastry cart comes first; its gilt handles tower over you, blocking out the landscape. The world will have to wait. That's how it works.

There is no villain lurking by the cash register. No visible enemy has done this to you two; there's only your waiter, and the block-print tablecloths, the blackboard with the daily menu, the ice bucket full of melting cubes, the discreet hallway that leads to the bathroom with its sliding bolt. Evil, said Hannah Arendt, is banal. But the work is done anyway, and it looks as if it has been done by your own hands. You claim your coats and step outside and part ways, having talked nothing new whatever into life.

Young girls and women are seriously weakened by inheriting the general fallout of two decades of the beauty myth's backlash. But other factors compound these pressures on young women so intensely that the surprise is not how many do have eating disorders, but that any at all do not.

Girls and young women are also starving because the women's movement changed educational institutions and the workplace enough to make them admit women, but not yet enough to change the maleness of power itself. Women in "coeducational" schools and colleges are still isolated from one another, and admitted as men *manqué*. Women's studies are kept on the margins of the curriculum, and fewer than 5% of professors are women; the world view taught to young women is male. The pressure on them is to conform themselves to the masculine atmosphere. Separated from their mothers, young women on campus have few older role models who are not male; how can they learn how to love their bodies? The main images of women given them to admire and emulate are not of impressive, wise older women, but of girls their own age or younger, who are not respected for their minds. Physically, these universities are ordered for men or unwomaned women. They are overhung with oil portraits of men; engraved with the rolling names of men; designed—like the Yale Club in New York, which for 20 years after women were admitted had no women's changing room—for men. They are not lit for women who want to escape rape; at Yale, campus police maps showing the most dangerous street corners for rape were allegedly kept from the student body so as not to alarm parents. The colleges are only marginally concerned with the things that happen to women's bodies that do not happen to the bodies of the men. Women students sense this institutional wish that the problems of their female bodies would just fade away; responding, the bodies themselves fade away.

Added to this isolation and lack of recognition is the unprecedented level of expectation placed on ambitious young women. Older women, in some ways, explored the best of both gender roles: They grew up as women and fought their way into the masculine work force. They learned to affirm the values of women and master the work of men. They are doubly strong. Young women have been doubly weakened: Raised to compete like men in rigid male-model institutions, they must also maintain to the last detail an impeccable femininity. Gender roles, for this generation of women, did not harmonize so much as double: Young women today are expected to act like "real men" and look like "real women." Fathers transferred to daughters the expectations of achievement once reserved for sons; but the burden to be a beauty, inherited from the mothers, was not lightened in response.

Ceremonies of achievement play out this conflict: Meant to initiate young people into a new level of power or expertise, those ceremonies summon an unfeminine emotion—pride. But with each rite of passage through these institutions, payment is exacted from a young woman in the form of "beauty"; placating and flattering to men in power, it is required at these times as proof that she does not mean anything too serious by winning this diploma or this promotion. On the one hand, here again the powerful stress the beauty myth so as to neutralize the achievement of the women involved; on the other, women do homage to the myth at such moments in request for its protection, a talisman that will let them get to the next stage unpunished.

In the 1950s, domesticity was what mitigated these moments of achievement. As a Listerine ad put it: "What was the diploma compared to those precious sparkling rings Babs and Beth were wearing?" Today "beauty" does the same work: "Only fifteen days until Becky's graduation. I want her to be proud of me too. . . . Alba makes your diet a sweet success." In a Johnnie Walker ad, it takes two high-fashion models to muse that "he thinks it's fine for me to make more than he does." *The New York Times* cites a woman whose boyfriend gave her breast implants for completing her doctorate. A current trend in the United States is for graduating daughters to get breast implant surgery while boys get the traditional grand tour of Europe. Women are having breast surgery, liposuction, rhinoplasty, not only as rewards for attaining power—doctorates, inheritances, bat mitzvahs—they are also having these things, and being asked to have them, as antidotes for having attained this power.

This sacrificial impulse is religious, to propitiate the god before undertaking the next stage of a journey. And the gods are thirsty; they are asking to be propitiated. "Boys, that's all," said the administrator preparing Rhodes Scholarship interviewees (including myself) at Yale. "Girls, please stay a few moments for pointers on clothes, posture, and makeup." At the interview luncheon, when boys were asked, "How do you plan to save the world from itself?" a girl was asked, "How do you manage to keep your lovely figure?"

Achievement ceremonies are revealing about the need of the powerful to punish women through beauty, since the tension of having to repress alarm at female achievement is unusually formalized in them. Beauty myth insults tend to be blurted out at them like death jokes at a funeral. Memories of these achievement ceremonies are supposed to last like Polaroid snapshots that gel into permanent colors, souvenirs to keep of a hard race run; however, for girls and young women, the myth keeps those colors always liquid so that, with a word, they can be smeared into the uniform shades of mud.

At my college graduation, the commencement speaker, Dick Cavett—who had been a "brother" of the university president in an all-male secret society—was confronted by 2000 young female Yale graduates in mortarboards and academic gowns, and offered them this story: When he was at Yale there were no women. The women went to Vassar. There, they had nude photographs taken in gym class to check their posture. Some of the photos ended up in the pornography black market in New Haven. The punch line: The photos found no buyers.

Whether or not the slur was deliberate, it was still effective: We may have been Elis, but we would still not make pornography worth his buying. Today, 3000 men of the class of 1984 are sure they are graduates of that university, remembering commencements as they are meant to:

proudly. But many of the 2000 women, when they can think of that day at all, recall the feelings of the powerless: exclusion and shame and impotent, complicit silence. We could not make a scene, as it was our parents' great day for which they had traveled long distances; neither could they, out of the same concern for us.

The sun streamed through the rain, the microphone crackled, the mud churned; we sat still, all wrong, under our hot polyester gowns. The speaker had transposed us for a moment out of the gentle quadrangle, where we had been led to believe we were cherished, and into the tawdry district four blocks away where stolen photographs of our naked bodies would find no buyers. Waiting for the parchment that honored our minds, we were returned with reluctant confusion to our bodies, which we had just been told were worthless. Unable to sit still for the rest of the speeches unless we split our minds, being applauded, from our bodies, being derided, we did so. We wanted the honor; we deserved it. The honor and derision came at the same time from the same podium. We shifted in our seats.

We paid the price asked of us. With moments like that to live through, the unreal-sounding statistics of young women's eating diseases begin to come clear. A split like that makes one nauseous. The pride of 4 years' hard work and struggle was snatched back from us at the moment we reached for it, and returned to us fouled. There was a taste of someone else's bile in our mouths.

OFF THE ROAD

When women have the rare opportunity to listen to older women, the gap between the ages causes grave mistranslations. "This is what I say to get their attention," says Betty Friedan of her college audiences:

> "How many of you have ever worn a girdle?" And they laugh. Then I say . . . "It used to be that being a woman in the United States meant that . . . you encased your flesh in rigid plastic casing that made it difficult to breathe and difficult to move, but you weren't supposed to notice that. You didn't ask why you wore the girdle, and you weren't supposed to notice red welts on your belly when you took it off at night." And then I say, "How can I expect you to know what it felt like when you have never worn anything under your blue jeans except panty hose, or little bikinis?" That gets to them. Then I explain how far we've come, where we are now, and why they have to start saying, "I am a feminist."[13]

For many young women in Friedan's audience, the girdle is made of their own flesh. They can't take it off at night. The "little bikinis" have not brought this generation heedless bodily freedom; they have become props that superimpose upon the young women chic pseudosexual scenarios that place new limits on what they can think, how they can move, and what they can eat. The backlash does to young women's minds—so much more free, potentially, than any ever before—what corsets and girdles and gates on universities no longer can.

If a girl were to eat, she would have energy; but adolescence is arranged for the safe venting of masculine steam. From athletic events to sexual conquests to a moody walk in the woods, boys have outlets for that agitation of waiting to fly. But if a girl has her full measure of wanderlust, libido, and curiosity, she is in a bad way. With ample stores of sugar to set off the buzz for intellectual exploration, starch to convert into restlessness in her elongating legs, fat to fuel her sexual curiosity, and the fearlessness born from a lack of concern over where her next meal will come from—she will get in trouble.

What if she doesn't worry about her body and eats enough for all the growing she has to do? She might rip her stockings and slam-dance on a forged ID at a Pogues concert, and walk home barefoot, holding her shoes, alone at dawn; she might babysit in a battered-women's shelter one night a month; she might skateboard down Lombard Street with its seven hairpin turns, or fall in love with her best friend and do something about it, or lose herself for hours gazing into test tubes with her hair a mess, or climb a promontory with the girls and get drunk at the top, or sit down when the Pledge of Allegiance says stand, or hop a freight train, or take lovers without telling her last name, or run away to sea. She might revel in all the freedoms that seem so trivial to those who could take them for granted; she might dream seriously the dreams that seem so obvious to those who grew up with them really available. Who knows what she would do? Who knows what it would feel like?

NOTES

1. Virginia Woolf, *A Room of One's Own* (San Diego: Harcourt Brace Jovanovich, 1981); reprint of 1929 edition.

2. Ann Hollander, *Seeing through Clothes* (New York: Viking Penguin, 1988), p. 151.

3. Hollander, op. cit., p. 151.

4. Susan C. Wooley and O. Wayne Wooley, "Feeling Fat in a Thin Society," *Glamour* (February 1984).

5. Rose E. Frisch, "Fatness and Fertility," *Scientific American* (March 1988).

6. D. Taylor, A. Desari, T. Brekke, M. Shirazi, M. French, Z. Jie, J.

Tweedie, Nawal el Saadawi, G. Gree, E. Poniatowska, and A. Davis, *Women: A World Report* (Oxford, England: Oxford University Press, 1985).

7. M. Pyke, *Man and Food* (London: Penguin, 1970).

8. See Lucian Dobrischitski, ed., *The Chronicles of the Lodz Ghetto* (New Haven: Yale University Press, 1984). See also Jean-Francis Steiner, *Treblinka* (New York: New American Library, 1968).

9. Woolf, op. cit., p. 10.

10. The Intercollegiate Eating Disorders Conference, mentioned by Brumberg (J. J. Brumberg, *Fasting Girls: The Emergence of Anorexia Nervosa as a Modern Disease* [Cambridge, MA: Harvard University Press, 1988]), did draw many colleges' representatives. But according to women's centers in several Ivy League universities, eating diseases are not dealt with beyond self-help groups, and certainly not at an administrative level. The entire term's budget for the Yale University Women's Center is $600, up from $400 in 1984. "Diet-conscious female students report that fasting, weight control and binge eating are a normal part of life on American college campuses" (Brumberg, op. cit., p. 264, citing K. A. Halmi, J. R. Falk, and E. Schwartz, "Binge-Eating and Vomiting: A Survey of a College Population," *Psychological Medicine 11* [1981]: 697–706).

11. S. Orbach, *Hunger Strike: The Anorexic's Struggle as a Metaphor for Our Age* (London: Faber & Faber, 1986).

12. S. A. Hewlett, *A Lesser Life: The Myth of Women's Liberation in America* (New York: Warner, 1987).

13. Betty Friedan, "Friedan, Sadat," *Lear's* (May/June 1988).

II

A PLACE FOR THE FEMALE BODY

6

Four Generations of Women: Our Bodies and Lives

BONITA BRIGMAN

MY 41 YEARS OF LIFE have culminated in the story you are about to read. It is a story about me; my grandmother, Nora Lou; my mother, Hazeltine; and my twin daughters, Erin and Tara. It is my story—seen through my eyes. Using the personal to illustrate theory is a feminist tradition, as is making a woman the subject of her own life, no longer obscured by a central male character. During the past three years I have had dreams and images in which my mother insists that I share this story so that you might learn something from all of us. Warmly, I invite you into our lives.

MY GRANDMOTHER

My grandmother's name is Nora Lou. She died when I was 14 years old, but she affects my life to this day. Her influence washed down through my mother to me.

> At age 9, I skip onto the red cement porch and turn the knob of the side door to my grandmother's small brick house. I can see through the middle of the three windows in the door, and knock lightly as I push the door open to call "Hello." My younger sister, Beryl, follows with my mother. My mother's name is Hazeltine. Her mother named her, she does not like her name.

115

We step directly into my grandmother's kitchen. It is a large room with an old-fashioned white gas oven. The pungent smell of gas reminds me of the cozy warmth of my grandmother's home. I walk past the side cupboard that holds our favorite yellow cake, iced with chocolate that seeps down into the cake, making it gooey. I glance at Beryl with delight; we both know we will be poking crumbs onto our forks before we leave today. A bowl of fresh fruit adorns the kitchen table. This china fruit bowl is in my kitchen today. No one saved the cake recipe.

Nora Lou, sitting in the immaculate living room, rises to meet us in the doorway. I hug my grandmother around the neck and give her a kiss on the mouth, which is our family custom. I feel loved as she clutches my hand in hers. Her hands are wrinkled up like raw chicken skin, but they feel soft and strong to me. I stand aside to let my sister and mother greet her, as I look at Nora Lou to see if her eye is straight. This is a courtesy I learned years earlier, when Nora Lou had her eye removed on a false suspicion of cancer. The surgeon found no cancer and replaced her eye with a glass one. This glass eye fascinates and scares me, and we all check it often for straightness. If Nora Lou's right eye is gazing off to the side or upward to the ceiling, it is our job to tell her. Today, it needs no correction.

While I am checking the eye, I notice that my grandmother is now the same height as I am—can this be possible? I will be taller than she is. She is wearing a crisp blue cotton dress covered by a small-print apron, stockings secured above her calves with elastic bands, and sturdy black shoes with low heels. Her hair is black, short, and neat. My mother gives her home perms. She smells of the perfume that older women wear to church. She is 79 years old. And I know now, but never even thought then, that she is fat.

In retrospect, I have likened my grandmother's body size and shape to those of Aunt Bee on *The Andy Griffith Show*; Nora Lou, at 4 feet 11 inches, weighed about 210 pounds. Her fatness was of no consequence to me at age 9. Yet I do recall my curiosity on the few occasions when I saw her undress for bed.

It is a winter night and because my stepgrandfather is in the hospital, I am staying over. It is 10:00 and time for bed. We both enter the bedroom and begin to undress. This is simple for me—slipping out of my shoes, socks, pants, and shirt, and pulling my flannel nightgown over my head. I try not to stare at my grandmother, but I want to watch, so I do so out of the corner of my eye. This is what I see: She unties her apron and places it in a little laundry bag in the closet. She unbuttons the front of her print dress from top to bottom. Carefully taking the dress off, she folds it and places it in the laundry bag. Next, she takes off her stockings, then her slip, and then her corset, which she calls her "foundation garment." I am in my nightgown now, and jump onto the bed to face her for a better view. She unlaces the monstrous elastic that wraps around her body and slowly pulls it from her, leaving red marks on her skin. She tugs and squirms as she lowers it, stepping out and over as it drops to the floor. The garment can stand on its own, but she hangs it on the back of the bedroom door. It looks huge and ugly.

With the removal of this layer, my grandmother's body unfolds before my eyes. Especially her breasts. Her full breasts spread across her protruding stomach and fall to her belly button. It is a wondrous sight as her body is allowed to flow into its own form and shape, no longer constrained. In her yellow nightgown, she is even more round, and I like this. I feel safe and loved as I lay my curly head on the embroidered pillowcase to join her in sleep. The next morning I watch her pull the corset back on, stuffing her body back into its elastic cage. I decide right then that I don't like this garment—I like my grandmother's body much better without it.

I loved my grandmother and did not separate her from her body. To me, she was perfect just the way she was. I never heard her discuss her size, shape, or weight. And I don't know what she thought of that corset—it seemed like a ritual she took part in without question. I never heard her mention the words "diet," "fat," or "exercise." She remained active, tending a ¼-acre vegetable garden, preserving its harvest, washing clothes with a wringer washer, and attending the Primitive Baptist Church until she died at 82.

MY MOTHER

My mother, Hazeltine, was beautiful and intelligent. I heard these words used to describe her for as long as I can remember, but as a child I never thought of her this way. She looked like an ordinary mother. I loved her touch, especially when she played with my curls. Beauty was both my mother's power and her undoing. I learned that it happened in this way.

Hazeltine was born on February 13, 1919 to Nora Lou and George Cabell, 14 years after their first daughter, Dorothea. Hazeltine was a beautiful child, so Nora Lou clothed her in lace-trimmed bonnets and dresses, and had her photographed often. She made an impressive picture. Dorothea was jealous of her new sister, who "stole the show." Since Dorothea was entrenched in her closeness with Nora Lou, there was no room for Hazeltine. Hazeltine had to find another place to fit, and did so right next to her father, G.C., with whom she developed a mutual admiration. He displayed her beauty, and she idealized his power and presence. They were so close that she could not see herself without looking up into his eyes.

At a very young age Hazeltine was trained in the flirtation, manipulation, and beguiling power of beauty. As a teenager, she learned that her beauty attracted men, which was flattering and fun. At the same time she began pulling away from her parents. Frequent disagreements with Nora Lou strained her relationship with her father. Feeling lonely, Hazeltine found herself in the eyes of Leslie, who was 9 years her senior. She started dating him at age 15 and, to her parents' dismay, married him on November 28, 1935. With so much focus on her beauty, it is easy to forget that Hazeltine was also intelligent. She skipped several grades in school and graduated from high school at 16 in 1936. Unfortunately, her scholastic achievement went unrecognized. Her graduation was overshadowed by her 7-month pregnancy. She did not attend the ceremony.

Still, Hazeltine was joyful; she had created a new closeness with Leslie that felt almost as good as the one she had had with her father. But Hazeltine had no idea of what this marriage—based on beauty, eye gazing, and male power—was going to be like. By the time she was 18, she had given birth to a daughter, Merle, and a son, Jimmy. The grandchildren reconnected her to Nora Lou and G.C., whom she had missed terribly.

Hazeltine watched her marriage deteriorate over the next ten years, feeling powerless to prevent its decline. Leslie had a drinking problem and was prone to violent attacks on Hazeltine and her children. She was afraid of Leslie and tried fiercely to change his ways and protect her children. Leslie, in constant need of glory, had a long string of affairs, which he often flaunted before his wife. Hazeltine's beauty took a beating. While Leslie was striking blows to her body, her sense of self crumbled. One evening she packed Merle and Jimmy into the car and drove to her parents' home for safety. Her father would not let her stay: "You've made your bed, now lie in it," he said. Hazeltine was crushed. She chose to believe that this was Nora Lou speaking through G.C., yet she felt incredibly betrayed by both. Where could she look for help?

Hazeltine secured a good job at a large corporate textile plant. Her coworkers still describe her as "a beautiful woman" and "one of the best women supervisors." Her spirit and intelligence created this success. But her reflection in the eyes of men remained at the heart of her being. A coworker, Roy, became dazzled by her; paving the way to her divorce from Leslie in 1950, not long after the birth of her third child, Barry.

Roy adored Hazeltine—her beauty was working again. He begged her to marry him, and once again, she took a chance. Roy adopted her three children; they moved to a neighborhood in the suburbs; and Hazeltine continued to work outside the home. However, she never understood why Leslie had not found her worthy of fidelity and love, and she mourned this for many years.

Within the year she was pregnant, and at age 33 gave birth to me, Bonnie. During this time G.C. developed Parkinson's disease. He deteriorated right before her eyes—which meant that she was dissolving too. He died in 1952 when I was six months old. Hazeltine was lost; the first eyes in which she had seen herself were gone. She stared into space and fell into chronic depression.

This was when my mother first became ill. The doctors thought she had a brain tumor. She was hospitalized for months of tests and given a spinal tap that resulted in years of severe headaches, while revealing no evidence of a tumor. No one ever considered that she was depressed. Next, the family doctor entered—a new male sent to cure her. Of course, he never did. Instead, by writing endless prescriptions to relieve her pain, he ensured that she would never find her self—the one behind the beauty.

My father, Roy, became my mother's caregiver, which he did tirelessly. His love for Hazeltine was romantic, unrelenting, and his devotion to her needs fulfilled his own. For the first time in her life, Hazeltine began to question the power of romantic love to bring her into existence. Her naive trust in such power was broken after Leslie's beatings and her father's death. Still dazed, Hazeltine turned her sights away from men to meet the demands of social images: mothering, small-town expectations, and—as always—beauty.

The first step toward Hazeltine's realization of the 1950s dream was to quit her well-paid work at the textile plant, which she did after Beryl was born in 1954. My mother worked hard for our comfort, making "our house a home." She gave the best birthday celebrations, with cakes of her own design. At Thanksgiving, Mama presented a festive meal as we crowded into the dining room to enjoy the aroma of celery–onion dressing and the sight of pimento-clad potato salad, annually displayed in our potato salad bowl. Hazeltine's Christmas rituals reverberated throughout our home. We lined the front door with red foil and arranged "Frosty" amidst pine boughs and bright lights. We joyfully sang as we placed our silver-and-red star atop the tree. On less celebrated days, my mother would simply make us hot chocolate and cinnamon toast to warm us before we ventured to the school bus. In addition, for 15 years she cared for children in our home, to earn money while obeying the 1950s dictate that "A good mother stays home." She provided us with a wonderful life while she lost her connection to the public world. I am certain that Hazeltine's misplaced trust in domestic happiness contributed to the downward spiral of her sense of worth. But it took her years to admit that this lie had failed her.

At 38, Hazeltine was still a stunning woman, and she attended to her appearance in great detail. Meticulously, she dressed for church or special occasions, buying brocade suits, stylish hats, and expensive shoes. And at age 38, she became a grandmother. She was delighted with Mike's birth, forming a strong attachment to her grandson. Nevertheless, she did not want to be a "grandmother," and never allowed her grandchildren to use that word. From the ages of 40 to 50, my mother struggled with changing roles, a changing body, and aging. As her attempts at fulfillment failed, she became weary and sick.

Hazeltine's decline intensified with Nora Lou's failing health in 1963. Since her father's death 11 years before, Hazeltine had tried to win her mother's admiration. Dorothea had moved away, and Hazeltine became the dutiful daughter. Grandmother telephoned each morning to tell my mother her dreams, and then mother shared these with us. We visited Nora Lou often during these years. I thought all this was fun, but I didn't know how hard my mother was working to carve a niche for herself in her mother's heart.

Taking care of five children, two grandchildren, a husband, and a mother stricken with a stroke took its toll on my mother when I was 12 years old. In a life-or-death frenzy, she entered Duke University Hospital in 1964. She was treated for bromide poisoning resulting from a toxic dose of Nervine, a popular over-the-counter drug that was advertised to help housewives with the stress of daily life. It nearly killed my mother. She received good care, an antidepressant, and a referral to outpatient treatment. When she left the hospital, Hazeltine looked in the mirror and saw the woman she had become. At 45, the power of her beauty was gone, usurped by the young. Yet Hazeltine held onto this essential image of herself with all her strength.

My mother probably became bulimic in response to the weight gain brought on by her medication and her mother's death in 1966. We were all saddened by Nora Lou's death, but Hazeltine bereaved her mother. She could not bring her mother back, but she could stop her own weight gain, and did so by terminating her use of the antidepressant. Once again, she stared into space. For years I tried to reach her; my sisters and brothers did also, and Dad tried the hardest. She never saw how important she was to me or them. Gradually, we settled into a daily pattern, typical when I was 17.

Mother is in the kitchen preparing dinner, which is ready every evening at 5:00. Beryl and I come in from school, throwing our books on the stairs; we kiss Mama hello and chat about the boredom of school. When my father comes in, we sit down to dinner. Mother serves us, then attends to the parents picking up their children left in her care. When the children are out the door, Mama sits down, eats a few bites, smokes two cigarettes, and sips endlessly on Nescafé coffee. Mama asks Dad who he saw at work, and tells him about the events of her day.

After dinner, Beryl and I wash and dry the dishes, while watching *The Andy Griffith Show*. Mama makes a grocery list for Dad, who goes shopping at 6:00. Mama disappears to the bathroom for about half an hour. She always throws up because her stomach is upset or something she eats disagrees with her. She says she doesn't tolerate milk very well. She never seems bothered by this behavior, so neither are we. It is routine. Enemas are also routine.

As Beryl and I put away the pots and pans, Mama returns to the kitchen, getting a cup of coffee and a pack of melba toast. She chews on melba toast frequently. When Dad returns from the grocery, he hands her a box of bridge mix. She likes this candy a lot, but instead of eating it, she sucks the chocolate off and spits the middle into a napkin. Mother also keeps Ayds candy, a 1960s diet product, in her vanity drawer, eating them while drinking coffee and smoking Pall Mall cigarettes. And, from time to time, she gets into exercise regimens—the latest is to wear a white plastic top and pants so she can sweat while she cleans house.

Talking, I follow my mother to her bedroom and watch while she removes her makeup. She always does this before her bath. Then she undresses, taking off her slacks, her shell top, her briefs, and her padded bra. My mother's breasts are small and shrunken, so she wears a padded bra. Now, at age 49, she worries about wrinkles in her face. She has false teeth, which she has had since she was 25. She uses greasy cream on her face and neck. I don't like the smell of DuBarry cream, her favorite. She suggests I begin this nightly ritual. "No," I protest. "It's enough trouble for me to put on liquid makeup, mascara, and the brown eyeliner, that I can barely draw along my lids."

I am comfortable seeing my mother nude, and she seems comfortable too. She has had a hysterectomy, and a scar goes down the middle of her abdomen. As she turns her back to me, I see her squared-off buttocks. This is my mother getting ready for her bath. I love our talk and the casual comfort of being together; it fills me with content.

You might well imagine the next stage of our lives as my siblings and I began our final exit from home. This was a strain on all of us. I believe my brother Barry had the hardest time, since my mother had transplanted the last of her hopes and dreams into him. My move to California was met with silence and disdain. And my sister Beryl stepped into adulthood after 2 years of chaos during high school, ending 37 years of active mothering in Hazeltine's life.

I drive up to the one-floor apartment where my parents moved after selling our home last summer. Dad greets me, my husband Phil, and my daughters at the door. Waving us into the apartment, he whispers to let us know that my mother is asleep in the back room. We enter the small kitchen as Dad hangs his head in despair. He hardly knows what to say to me, so instead he opens the cabinet, showing me all the pills my mother takes. "I don't see why Dr. Irwin keeps giving her all this; look at all this Valium," he exclaims in confusion. I can see the anguish and fear in his face; he doesn't know what to do to reverse my mother's rapid race toward death.

I return to the dark living room and turn on *Sesame Street* so that my daughters are entertained. I notice the half-eaten pack of melba toast, an ashtray filled with cigarette butts, and the chocolate film on the glass next to my mother's usual seat. "What is this?" I ask. "She drinks Sego all the time. It's like Carnation Instant Breakfast, except this comes in cans, so it's easy to refrigerate," Dad replies softly. I feel queasy.

Around 7:00 my mother stirs, and my father gives me permission to go in to see her. My eyes have adjusted to the low light, even dimmer in her room. I haven't seen my mother for 2 years, and I tremble at the change in her as I blink to keep my tears inside. She is small and languid; she has dwindled from her sturdy size 12 to maybe 90 pounds. Her hair is stringy, gray, and unkempt. Her skin feels clammy as I sit on the bed to kiss her and wrap her in my arms. She is skin and bones. "Did you bring the babies?" she asks, as if all the apparent changes don't exist. "Yes. Do you want me to help you walk to the other room so you can see them?"

"No, I'm lucky to make it to the bathroom right now. I feel so sick, and Dr. Irwin is not helping. He doesn't know what to do with my blood pressure—they think I'm losing blood somehow," she reports in her raspy voice, between the coughs of emphysema.

I bring Erin and Tara in to visit, and my mother's eyes light up for a moment. She tires quickly, so the reunion is brief. When my mother asks to use the bathroom, Phil takes the girls back to watch TV.

I help Mama up from the bed, as she leans on my right shoulder. She is unsteady and slow. I get her to the sink, brushing aside the foil remnants of Ex-Lax packets, so she can hold onto the edge and lower herself to the toilet. I step back to close the door and notice the enema bag hanging from under her robe. My eyes dart to the wall beside the toilet to see if vomit stains spot the wallpaper, as they used to in our home. "Mother, are you still getting sick after you eat?" I ask. "Yes. And I still can't go to the bathroom right— nothing helps," she says with resignation . . . as if all this is the way it is supposed to be.

Mother was hospitalized repeatedly the following year. In January 1979, she suffered a stroke and entered the hospital for the last time. The stroke left her unable to speak, except with her eyes, which were sad and pleading. Beryl and I sat on her hospital bed trying to fill her with enough love to keep her alive. But within a few weeks, she gave up her external search for relief. Closing her eyes, she slept often. She died 1 month following her 60th birthday, weighing 67 pounds.

ME

I am my mother's daughter. There is no way I could escape the beliefs that influenced Hazeltine's life. I have worked hard to untangle myself from the patriarchal monsters that strangled the life from my mother. Yet I shyly admit that insecurity, beauty, and men have played far too crucial roles in my own life. This was how it began.

I was a pretty little girl with golden curls and bright blue eyes. When I was 3 my mother entered me in the "Little Miss Sunbeam" contest—a competition to select a child to be pictured on the wrapper of Sunbeam bread. Given my mother's history with beauty, thank goodness, I did not win. As a very young child, I loved to laugh, dance, and sing; I was playful, with a wildly fun imagination.

Over time, these parts of me began to fade. When my mother was unable to take care of me, my sister Merle, who was 17, provided hearty nurturance. Merle attended to me after the birth of my sister Beryl, when I was 2. When I was 4, Merle married Bob and moved nearby, but it wasn't the same as having her there in the house. I felt alone. Looking to find a place for myself, I saw my dad go to work each day; my mother caring for Beryl; and my brother Jim leaving for college. I had my brother Barry, age 9, who became my caregiver and my mother's support. My mother cherished and looked up to Barry, so I learned to do this too. The longer I looked to him for my specialness, the more the joyful part of me began to disappear—like glitter thrown into the air, then floating away.

For a while, I fit well with Barry—we had such adventures! But as we grew older, my being younger and a girl began to interfere with our closeness. I became a tomboy, ready to play with the boys when they let me. I felt a surge of importance whenever I was in my brother's presence. Association with him, even by name—"Barry's sister"—brought me into existence. However, at age 11, I noticed that being a tomboy didn't catch the attention of 16-year-old boys. This realization came one blue-gray afternoon in February, 1963.

The snow flurries around our faces and eyes as we pull our sleds, trudging up the steepest part of Cherokee Trail to meet Barry's friends. Barry and I share a sled, and after five rides off a ramp, the boys decide to make the ramp high enough to propel us all the way to Lake Lanier. Since we need more speed, I climb onto Barry's back this time, as he stretches out across the sled to navigate us into the fun and excitement of the afternoon. We are off! I am hanging on with all my might. I don't have a secure position, so holding onto Barry is my only grounding. I grab his collar as we round the widest curve before the silvery lake comes into view. The curve drives us far to the right, and as Barry slides the bar to move us left, he screams, "Roll off!" I am not quick enough. We smack into the curb just before it drops into the lake. I am thrown off, and Barry's wrist is caught between the curb and the sled.

I want to cry, but I am too frightened—catching my breath as I scramble to my feet. All the boys run to Barry. He is stunned, yet seems to be okay. They all check him for broken bones. Wes wraps his arm around Barry's shoulder to comfort him, but no one asks about me. I look down, surprised to see that my tartan wool slacks are ripped through the lining, gaping open to expose my leg from thigh to knee. I am so embarrassed that I quickly pull the flaps of wool together, wrapping my scarf around to cover my leg. My eyes scan to see if any of the boys see me scurrying to hide the part of me that is exposed.

The walk home is damp and chilly as the late afternoon fades to early evening. I am lagging behind, falling back to my place on the periphery. My leg stings with cold, so I furtively rub my hand inside the wool slit to warm my leg. When I pull my hand out it is covered with blood! I never looked past the tear in my slacks to see that the skin on my leg is shaven away in chunks across my thigh. Now I am confused—I want to call for help and hide at the very same time. [HELP!] I look up ahead. The boys have paid no attention to me as they walk off into their world, leaving me alone in mine. "If only I were less of a tomboy and more of a girl," I think to myself, "maybe they would be here with me." I do not realize that it is the girl in me that has learned so young to keep my needs silent and to live on the romantic hope that someone—someone *MALE*—will see.

My metamorphosis from tomboy to teenage girl was not easy. My body shape and weight were well within cultural norms—I was never chubby or fat. My breasts grew earlier than many of my peers', and I was self-conscious, slouching my shoulders whenever my mother wasn't telling me to stand up straight. I hated my hair; it was frizzy and unruly. And worse yet, when I was 12 the Beatles landed in the United States, ushering in straight, long hair. I didn't look pretty or sweet between the ages of 12 and 14. I wasn't popular and there was nothing in particular at which I excelled. Barry, on the other hand, was popular and successful. We spent less time together and he left for college when I was 13.

By age 16, I learned to position my body to accentuate rather than disguise my breasts, and my legs became a sexy extension of miniskirts. Leaving the tomboy behind, I practiced dancing before the full-length mirror on my closet door. I moved in for a closer view, modeling my smile for hours so I could project my most sweet and sincere self to males who looked my way. This attracted D. H., 4 years my senior, whom I dated throughout high school. During my freshman year in college, I met Phil. He had just returned from Vietnam. I was impressed with this 23-year-old, "worldly" man and ended my relationship with D. H. Phil and I dated for 2 years.

Dependent on Phil and desperate to break the powerful hold I felt my mother had on me, I left my parents' home amid intense conflict in July, 1972. I moved in with Phil, and we decided to marry in September. My mother did not speak to me the entire summer, feeling I had betrayed her by moving out, even though she had insisted I leave "her home." My father worked hard to reunite us before my mother finally consented to attend the wedding. It was a miserable sendoff to married life. A year later, at age 21, I got pregnant.

I open the window so I can hear and smell the stirring of early spring—chirping robins, the whir of a tractor plowing earthy clay, and the sweet fragrance of cherry blossoms. Sliding into the rocking chair, I pull up my blouse to look at my tummy as it continues to swell. Just under my right breast, my skin moves into a configuration of a misshapen ball. I try to figure out if this is my baby's foot, elbow, or hand. I gently lay my fingers over this lump to touch the moving child inside. Such delight!

I am sad and frustrated, and I have no one to talk to today. Early this morning, two obstetricians poked and pushed me so hard that I was afraid they would harm my baby. They were trying to decide if

I am having twins. Their conclusion was no. So they chastised me for overeating and pushing my weight up. I told them that I am eating no more than usual. They don't believe me. Tears dampen my cheek as I sit here, because I really want a chocolate–marshmallow ice cream cone today. I have not had any sweets in 3 weeks. I stare out the window, crying, because the doctors will not give me permission to eat normally and I can't stop gaining weight.

I lift my shirt again and look at my stomach. I have marbled runners flowing vertically down my abdomen. These stretch marks are ugly. To prevent permanent carvings in my skin, I rub my stomach with cocoa butter and Mother's Friend cream. I smell like a chocolate bar, and I see no evidence of relief. My friends tell me how pretty I look and pat my enormous abdomen. I smile, graciously accepting these compliments, yet I know that they do not see the red gouges winding through my skin. I stare at the most severe erosion—a solid ravine that runs from my navel out of sight to the underside of my belly. It is beginning to bleed, and I'm afraid that I might burst open. I rub my skin for comfort and let warm tears flow down my face. Abruptly, I hear Phil's car enter the driveway. Startled, I quickly stand, pull my blouse down, and grab a Kleenex to wipe away any hint of sadness from my face.

As my pregnancy advanced to change my body, Phil changed our lives. He joined the Air Force and in March, 1974 left for Officers' Training School. I returned to my parents' home for the last 3 months of my pregnancy. At 8 months, I learned that my ballooning size *was* indeed due to twins. In late May we rejoiced over the birth of our two daughters, Erin and Tara.

In July, we flew to Phil's first assignment in Sacramento, California. I was 22, had two five-week old girls and was 3,000 miles from family and friends. Depression slowly invaded every cell of my body, and when I looked at my shrunken stomach, I was disheartened by what I saw. My male obstetrician said the excess skin looked like "an accordion," or "a piece of elastic that stretches so far that it won't go back in place." I had to agree: it just sits there, puffed out, hanging loosely from where it fit before. It was difficult to adjust to this change in my body while I was fighting the depression that grew out of our move. Although I returned to my prepregnant weight, my body felt totally different. On August 14, 1974, I wrote in my diary: "To console myself, I come to you, diary— the only place I can come, now. I need friendship so badly. I'm so disgusted with myself! I'm so proud of these girls—they are *perfect!* I wish I were. I'm so sick of my body—I feel so ugly! Phil couldn't be proud of me and I hate that—I wish I was cute again!"

One day in the midst of depression and disgust with my body, I read Tom Robbins' book *Even Cowgirls Get the Blues,* and adopted his vision of stretch marks as the road map to motherhood. This gave me the patience to integrate my body changes into an overall sense of who I am—a woman who birthed healthy twin daughters. Choosing this perspective, I felt better about my body and myself.

I dealt better with my changing body than with the emotional distance that grew between me and Phil. He was brimming with happiness, devoutly busy with his career. A busy mother all day, I was lonely at night. I felt blessed when an assignment to North Carolina brought us closer to our Virginia home. Beryl, who had also joined the Air Force, was stationed at the same base, and I was thrilled that I would be reunited with my sister. However, I was unaware that another reunion would create the most painful turmoil of my life.

It is 2:00 and I am putting Erin and Tara down for an afternoon nap, tucking their yellow crocheted coverlets around them to keep away the autumn chill. I tilt my head and strain to hear who Phil is speaking with as he enters the kitchen. I walk down the long hall, eavesdropping to hear if this is a voice I know. I peek into our living room, just as Phil rises: "Bonnie, do you remember Rob? He was in my fraternity. I think you met him a few times." I vaguely remember him, recalling his rebellious nature and the fact that he is bald.

I smile and extend my hand to greet Rob with a warm hello. As I lift my head, our eyes lock in an attraction that I silently observe. I feel a surge that takes my breath away and notice my rapid heartbeat. Phil invites Rob and his wife, Nancy, to dinner next Friday evening.

Over a year's time, Rob and I share *Andy Griffith* reruns, the Beatles' *White Album,* and tomato seedlings. When we are alone, he talks of his attraction to me, and says he loves my frizzy hair. Soon he tells me he loves me. I want this closeness and romance, and I find it staring at me in Rob's intense hazel eyes that soften when he smiles at me. Before I know it, Rob separates from his wife; then, he tells Phil he loves me. My marriage shatters like glass: For a moment all the cracks are apparent, and then the pieces begin to fall, cutting us sharply with pain.

Phil and I tried for 4 more years to make our marriage work, yet we continued to drift apart. Rob attempted to reconcile with his wife, but I never learned what the outcome was. My mother died, sending me deeper into isolation and sadness. In the fall of 1982, Phil and I separated. He received orders to go to California, and Erin, Tara, and I moved to Virginia.

I was severely depressed and lost more weight than ever before in my adult life, dropping from 137 to 117 pounds, although I didn't notice until my friends started commenting on it. I became conscious of how thin I looked and I enjoyed it. I felt as if I had awakened to a different body. Unfortunately, my accordion abdomen looked much worse thin—without fat to puff them out there were more pleats of skin. Within 6 months, my depression lifted and my hunger returned. I began a fad diet to keep my weight suppressed. The diet consisted of one food a day with fruit, vegetables, and rice. This induced such diarrhea that I had to stop the regimen and devour Kaopectate. I tried this twice, with the same result. Soon I had my fill of dieting; I allowed my body to return to 140 pounds as I turned 31.

I didn't give my body much thought for several years, considering myself attractive. Instead, I focused on my unconsoled heart. I longed for romance and eye gazing, but the pain of my divorce prevented any closeness. I developed intense but distant relationships with several men, and vowed never to marry again. I knew that I was trapped inside a generational warp that I must straighten out to survive. Slowly, I stopped searching for myself in men's eyes. And over the years, the joy and boldness that had begun to wither when I was a girl returned.

It's a cold morning, a few days before Christmas 1991. I walk into my bathroom, discarding the nightshirt I wrinkled in my sleep. This Christmas is sad. My second husband, Joe, learned that his mother is terminally ill with cancer just before our wedding last August. My father diligently attends to his second wife, Lucile, who at age 80 is nearly bedridden with spinal degeneration. And Merle's husband, Bob, died suddenly of a heart attack last week. I flip on the lights. I catch a glimpse of myself in the mirror and turn frontward to reflect on the years that reveal themselves in my body.

At 39, I can no longer pretend to look younger than I am. I've made peace with my curly red hair, noticing only an occasional strand of gray. My face is often washed out and blotchy, from long, stressful hours of work. I'm trying to recall what I ate last night, because my skin feels tight on my face and my rings barely turn on my fingers; it must have been too salty. I lean over the washbasin to check my puffy eyelids, deciding to wear my glasses instead of contact lenses. I look older, showing the first lines of aging on my neck and a fullness beneath my cheekbones. My jutting jaw has more fat. I survey my mouth and break into a smile that exposes the origins of the wrinkles that curve around my lips. I release a deep sigh.

The front view of my body reveals my sturdy, full breasts that give me a healthy look. Just below, I see the 4-inch gallbladder scar which became a part of me when I was 24. I turn right to catch a side view of my stomach because sometimes I look pregnant when I breathe out. Today I don't protrude. My abdomen is still marbled from stretch marks, which now give a woven texture to otherwise smooth skin, and a heavy fold replaces the pleating of my younger years. I step back from the mirror and twist my waist to see my backside; I turn around and stretch to see my buttocks and thighs. I see more fat all over—my upper arms, my side ripples, my hips, and my thighs. I now weigh 174 pounds.

I have watched with curiosity as my body has expanded. Three years ago, I gained 15 pounds while taking a prescription allergy medication before I realized that it was the culprit. I wonder if the fat I see is what scared my mother into dieting, vomiting, and laxative use. I feel sad that she didn't make a different choice, but now I realize the difficulty of accepting my own body as it continues to grow larger. When I begin to feel "fat and ugly," I spend some time alone. I use this time to draw from the center of my "self," so that I move through the world with ease and confidence.

I smile and rub my tummy with affection. Joe knocks to enter so he can take a shower. I do not hide from him, and he sees that I am pensive about my body. "You are so pretty," he warmly announces as he touches my shoulders and leans downward to kiss me. And as I look up, I see Joe *and not myself* in his eyes.

MY DAUGHTERS

Erin Michelle and Tara Elizabeth are my 19-year-old daughters. Throughout their lives, I have loved them for themselves and celebrated them for being female. Ever since they were babies, I have told them that they are wonderful, smart girls with good, healthy bodies. As infants, I introduced them into our family ritual. It goes like this: Whenever you change a diaper, you softly massage the baby's legs, then stretch them downward, pulling them gently together at the ankles. And then you say, "You have such pretty legs!" So all the children in my family, including the boys, have grown up feeling proud of their legs, even though there is great variety among them. I have no idea how this ritual began, but I think Hazeltine started it.

Over the years, I have had fleeting worries about Erin's and Tara's bodies. I watched their chubby progression through puberty; feared that their high school peers might introduce dieting into their lives; and anxiously waited to see how much of themselves they might jeopardize for male attention. My most recent worry is this: how will they handle future changes in their bodies and what choices will they make? I trust that they, too, will successfully integrate such changes into an overall positive sense of themselves. I hope I'm right.

> I have a high four-poster bed. I love this bed. Its comfort invites my daughters to join me atop the blue-and-cream woven wool spread as we chat about our day. Tonight, after an especially tiring day, I lie staring at the ceiling when Erin knocks to see if I have any shampoo. "Yes," I answer as she scoots through my room with a towel clutched to cover her nude body. I glance at her thighs, waist, and breasts as she hurries by. I am struck by how much her body looks like my own at 19. I feel as if I have the right to stare because it's my body I'm looking at—reminiscing over the contour and shape that I recall as my own. It feels strange seeing my body in Erin's. Then I'm reminded that this is Erin's body and not mine; I shouldn't stare. She is uncomfortable when I stare. In exasperation, she cries "Mother!", which is her way to tell me to turn my eyes away. I smile and say, "It's okay for me to see your body; I'm your mother." But I respect her need for privacy, keeping my gaze fixed on her sparkling blue eyes.
> Her sister Tara roams into my bedroom, awaiting her turn in the shower and throws herself on my bed: "Ma, please rub my back." I turn over to massage her shoulders and ask, "How were classes today?" "Boring," she tells me in a slow, tired voice, closing her eyes as she continues to chat. "Ma, pull my hair," she insists. And I do. Since Tara was a baby with a head full of curls, I have played with her hair. Now I have to inch my fingers up under the nape of her neck to find the soft strands of hair not hardened by hairspray. I stretch the soft curls around to her ear. She smiles softly, nearly falling asleep.
> Relaxed, Tara announces that she will take a bath instead of a shower tonight. I sit on the bed listening to the two of them exchanging places in the bathroom. I recall that I haven't told them that Beryl called today. I jump off my bed and walk into the open doorway of their bath, saying, "I talked with Beryl. She wants Merle and us to come to the beach in August." Tara calls from the tub, "We start classes August 24. We'll have to go before that." I continue to talk casually, and as I walk into Tara's line of vision, she protests: "Mo-ther, I'm trying to take a bath." My view of her body is brief—a second replica of my own younger body. Again, I say, "It's no big deal if I see you take a bath," but it is a big deal to her, so I turn my head and walk out of view.

Both Erin and Tara frequently see me nude as I undress, shower, and dress; they seem perfectly comfortable with this. I am reminded of watching Nora Lou when I was 9 and Hazeltine when I was 17—this seemed so natural. I was comfortable pulling off my clothes at 9, yet I would have been uneasy if mother had watched me at 17. In fact, I don't recall ever undressing in front of my mother at that age—I would have claimed I was too modest. I feel sad as I realize that the babies I once held in my bursting belly are no longer mine to see and touch. At 19 their need for privacy prevails. Knowing this separation of mother and daughter is necessary makes it no less painful. Now, as I sit on the edge of my bed, I smile through glistening tears, envisioning the day when Erin and Tara, in the comfort of motherhood, share a bath with their young daughters.

CONCLUSION

My sense of myself springs from Nora Lou and Hazeltine and flows into Erin and Tara. It seems incomprehensible to me that I would have loved my grandmother more had she been smaller in size. It haunts me that my own mother lost herself to her body, allowing it to define her. And seeing my daughters grow into women is a poignant reminder of the transformations our bodies undergo in a lifetime. When I grieve for my younger body or fear for my future, I recall these images and thoughts. Sometimes out of despair and anger I cry until I reach the place in me that knows to celebrate the person I am. I do this until I know in my heart that to reject my body is to reject Nora Lou, Hazeltine, Merle, Beryl, Erin, and Tara, as well as myself. Reject them—how absurd! I love these women. I gather them around me until I am proud of who I am: safe, sane, secure. If you could see me, I would show you that my feelings of comfort and confidence are experienced in the middle of my chest as I spread my right hand in a flowing motion out of me toward you, saying, "This is me, the me I want you to know."

ACKNOWLEDGMENT

The author wishes to lovingly thank Pat Lyons whose unclothing uncloaked these memories.

7

When Reproductive and Productive Worlds Meet: Collision or Growth?

MELANIE A. KATZMAN

> *And the Lord God caused a deep sleep to fall upon the man and he slept; and he took one of his ribs, and closed up the flesh instead thereof;*
> *And the rib, which the Lord God had taken from man, made he a woman, and brought her unto the man.*
> —Genesis 2:21–22

THE FIRST ACT OF CREATION was God's; then flesh begat flesh as woman was formed from the body of man. Last in line for the privilege of reproduction was woman. Why did man surrender this holy right? Perhaps in the initial fits of pain he swore the process away, only to regret it later. The story of childbirth has been rewritten many times—regarded in the Bible as punishment for sin, diminished in importance, its sacrifice denied, and ultimately recast as illness by men who proclaimed themselves experts to regain control of a process they gave up long ago.

All human societies have rituals specific to birth. These beliefs and traditions vary widely: Some cultures regard childbirth as a natural, joyful part of daily life, while others focus on dirt and possible death. In the Judeo-Christian tradition, birth is unclean; Leviticus devotes a section to the purification of women after childbirth. Patriarchal American culture has taken the attitude that childbirth is an illness. In 1963, Atlee described the attitudes of his colleagues as follows:

This chapter is dedicated to Wyndam and Harper.

We obstetricians seem to think and act as if pregnancy and labor constitute a pathologic rather than a physiologic process. Our entire basic medical education is so obsessed with pathology that it is practically impossible for us to think of any woman who comes to us as other than sick. (p. 514)

More recently, in 1981, U.S. Public Health Advisor Paul Ahmed went even further: "Professional literature in the field of health care has tended to view pregnancy as a sickness—biologically, psychologically and sociologically" (Ahmed & Kolker, 1981).

Given the associations of pregnancy and childbirth with danger, pain, and illness, perhaps it is not surprising that issues surrounding therapist pregnancy have rarely been examined. Before 1966, the topic had never been addressed directly; only a single article had explored a related area, the analyst's miscarriage (Hannet, 1949). Since then, fewer than 30 articles and three books have specifically considered the topic of the pregnant therapist; only one article discusses the pregnant therapist's impact on eating-disordered women (Katzman, 1993).

Most of the available papers are theoretical (i.e., they describe and interpret client reactions). Of the six that are research-oriented, two rely on unstructured narratives (Lax, 1969; Schwartz, 1975); two use retrospective questionnaires to psychotherapists (Berman, 1975; Naparstek, 1976); and two include more rigorous prospective, structured interviews with psychotherapists and subsequent follow-ups (Fenster, 1983; Grossman, 1990).

Examining the social factors that discourage discourse in this area, Benedek (1973) suggests that pregnancy belongs to a taboo subject—sexuality. Barbanel (1980) discusses the common superstition that talking about pregnancy may result in an unwanted outcome. Naparstek (1976) suggests that the female therapist, in an effort to do it all, denies the impact of pregnancy on herself, her colleagues, and her clients, and consequently fails to explore its importance. Lax (1969, p. 371) argues that the therapist's need to maintain a "narcissistic masculine identification" and to avoid the "re-arousal of conflicts around femininity" contributes to the professional hush surrounding the topic.

However, the silence may have a practical basis. In many instances, especially in hospital or agency settings, the announcement of a pregnancy produces a shift in status after which the expectant woman is treated as a mother and not as a professional. The therapist's reluctance to focus on her pregnancy (or even to tell a client she is pregnant), coupled with the likelihood that the client will follow the rules of therapy and not ask the obvious but pointed personal question, can lead to collusion between client and therapist, with both acting as if they believe the stork brings babies.

Statistics indicate that increasing numbers of women choose careers in medicine (Braslow & Heins, 1981) and psychology (Adler, 1991; Ostertag & McNamara, 1991). Many become mothers and are confronted with the complex social, theoretical, and practical issues that arise during pregnancy. As more women combine professions with motherhood, the need to address issues raised by pregnancy becomes an important social reality. For a male therapist, the experience of becoming a parent can be shared or kept out of the clinical experience, as he chooses. The expectant female clinician cannot choose neutrality; she unavoidably must share a personal experience while performing in a professional role. If pride in empowering others through childbirth and mothering is to be fostered, we must address both the growth-promoting and unsettling aspects of pregnancy in our personal lives and in our work with clients.

Although pregnancy challenges therapists who work with any psychiatric population, a number of factors suggest that the physical and social consequences of childbearing are particularly salient issues for eating-disordered clients. First, the majority of eating-disordered clients are women. This is particularly significant, since Fenster, Phillips, and Rapoport (1986) report that female clients are more reactive than males to a therapist's pregnancy. Second, most of these clients are at the age when childbearing is a relevant personal issue. Third, many of the issues raised within a general psychiatric practice in response to pregnancy (i.e., envy, abandonment, loss, fertility, and sibling rivalry) are particularly difficult matters for the eating-disordered woman. For example, bulimics and their families are often unable to express and resolve anger, jealousy, grief, and loss (Root, Fallon, & Friedrich, 1986), and have difficulty with competition, femininity, and the demands of nurturing (Kearney-Cooke, 1989). Fourth, pregnancy induces dramatic bodily changes, the most obvious of which is weight gain. In a study of eating-disordered women anticipating pregnancy, 85% feared pregnancy's impact on their appearance (Lemberg & Phillips, 1989). Fifth, Wooley and Kearney-Cooke (1986) have suggested that, given the achievement orientation of many bulimic women, childbearing and its constraints for women in male-dominated society may result in conflict and depression. In fact, concerns about successfully balancing motherhood and career have been voiced by many anorexic and bulimic women who bear children (Lemberg & Phillips, 1989).

Several theorists have described the bulimic woman's struggle against a full, soft, womanly body in favor of a controlled, hard, and masculine one as symbolic of the conflict between caring for others and culturally valued independence and achievement (Steiner-Adair, 1986; Wooley & Wooley, 1985). The therapist's pregnancy brings into sharp relief the collision of these two worlds, as therapist and client confront the competing demands of the relational world in which the therapist nurtures and is cared for, and her professional world of socially validated strength. For the eating-disordered woman who is striving for a new construction of womanhood (Wooley & Kearney-Cooke, 1986), the therapist who has proven her worth in a man's world through academic achievement and financial success may become an even more imposing challenge as her growing body further establishes her worth in a woman's world as well. The spilling of a softer, "reproductive" world into the hard, "productive" world may evoke disdain or admiration, empathy or competition.

Given the importance of this issue for the eating-disordered woman, one wonders why it has been virtually ignored. As Striegel-Moore (1990; see also Chapter 22, this volume) points out, the field of eating disorders has not struggled with the meanings of pregnancy and motherhood for female identity, nor with the message expressed when "legions of girls aspire to a body ideal that renders fertility unlikely" (p. 443). This chapter reviews the research on pregnancy's effect on therapists and their clients, highlighting limitations in the available literature, as well as possibilities for therapeutic growth for both professionals and their female clients. Self-in-relation theory is reviewed, and case examples are discussed in an effort to illustrate how pregnancy can give birth to improved therapy relations.

REVIEW OF THE LITERATURE

The Therapist and Her Clients during Pregnancy

The literature on psychological aspects of pregnancy generally reflects society's bias toward pathologizing childbirth as discussed earlier, with pregnancy seen as a "hurdle to overcome" (Breen, 1977). However, some authors recognize pregnancy as a normal developmental phase involving alterations in roles, values, relationships, and physiology (Benedek, 1956; Bibring, Dwyer, Huntington, & Valenstein, 1961; Breen, 1977; Ballou, 1978; Entwisle & Doering, 1981; Pines, 1972)—changes that challenge old solutions and require new levels of intrapsychic equilibrium and organization (Breen, 1977).

Although the pregnant clinician may experience the same changes as other pregnant women, few articles address the added complexity of conducting therapy while pregnant (see Fenster et al., 1986, and Kleinplatz, 1992, for more thorough reviews). In general, a process of introversion, self-absorption, and withdrawal has been noted (Balsam,

1975; Barbanel, 1980; Baum & Herring, 1975; Paluszny & Poznanski, 1971; Rubin, 1980; Schwartz, 1975), along with a simultaneous, paradoxical increase in acuity and sensitivity toward clients (Barnabel, 1980; Nadelson, Notman, Arons, & Feldman, 1974).

Also common is a stance of "business as usual" (Baum & Herring, 1975; Benedek, 1973; Lax, 1969). This may reflect a denial of the therapist's heightened sense of vulnerability (Nadelson et al., 1974), or an effort to conform to the demands of our culture and clinical training to "stay professional" and "act like a man."

When Naparstek (1976) asked therapists to describe clients' responses, she found that most were surprised at the primitive, affect-laden responses of clients in all diagnostic categories. Berman (1975) found an increase in violent behavior, therapy termination, "inappropriate" sexual behavior, and unplanned pregnancy during the pregnancies of nine psychiatrists as compared to a 6-month control period.

Lax (1969) reported that male clients used denial and isolation, in contrast to female clients, who suffered a "profound transference storm" (p. 370). Positive reactions were not discussed in either the Berman (1975) or Lax (1969) study. Whether this was due to an absolute lack of positive reactions or to the authors' negative bias toward pregnancy is unclear. Case reports suggest that pregnancy intensified clients' dynamics and issues, but did not skew the treatment (Bender, 1975; Cole, 1980). Clients commonly feared that the therapist would die or be injured. In one of the few unequivocally positive reports, Kleinplatz (1992) described negligible or benign client reactions that transcended the nature of the clients' presenting problems. She attributed this to her existential–experiential model of therapy (which does not rely on the therapist–client relationship as a vehicle for change), as well as her early elimination of any ambiguity regarding the pregnancy and maternity leave.

Client difficulty in recognizing pregnancy and subsequent acting out were reported in most studies in which the therapist did not disclose her pregnancy early on. Barbanel (1980) found that clients were more comfortable assuming that the therapist was fat, was gaining weight because she was without a man, or was homosexual, than discussing the possibility that she might be pregnant.

Paluszny and Poznanski (1971), in describing reactions to a therapist's pregnancy, reported central themes of rejection, sibling rivalry, Oedipal strivings, and identification with the therapist. Nadelson et al. (1974) commented on the upsurge of feelings such as sexual conflict, abandonment fears, loss, sibling rivalry, and competition. Browning (1974), in one of the few reports on children, points to heightened denial, displacement, and fears of abandonment. There are no studies of adolescents' reactions.

The differences between group and individual responses to pregnancy were examined by Raphael-Leff (1980) and Breen (1977), who noted family themes and sexual curiosity in groups. In individual therapy, by contrast, feelings of exclusion, deprivation, competition, envy of the therapist's creativity, and impingement on therapy by the outside world were expressed.

The limited literature on the responses of supervisors and colleagues suggests that these interactions were conflictual for the therapist and staff (Butts & Cavenar, 1979) and that male supervisors attempted to minimize and deny the conflict (Benedek, 1973).

I conducted the only study to date of eating-disordered clients' responses to a therapist's pregnancy (Katzman, 1993). The themes of loss, sexuality, competition, abandonment, dependency, jealousy, and desire for children were similar to those in previous research on general psychiatric populations; in addition, reactions were intensified for clients who had longer histories with the therapist. Behaviors such as premature termination, changes in appearance, and "accidental" pregnancy were most common in women who *denied* the impact of the pregnancy. A notable number of clients also appropriately chose to discuss their own pregnancy or became pregnant during this time. Older, single, and childless women spoke the most about their reactions, which included conflict centering around career and family goals. The study suggests that articulating and processing a range of emotions may inoculate women against acting out and may attenuate premature termination—a process aided by early disclosure of the pregnancy. Many clients reported that identifying, expressing, and working through the very potent positive and negative feelings in a close relationship was valuable, as was developing the ability to hold powerful competing emotions about the same person.

Finally, this study reported the ways clients used the experience to explore feelings about fertility and maternity. In a 1-year follow-up questionnaire, many women said that the therapist's pregnancy had helped them identify desires, had provided a new role model, and had encouraged them to address the conflicts between professional and personal aspirations.

In reviewing the literature on pregnancy's impact on therapeutic relations, I was struck by the general negativity and the emphasis on description and practical management issues. Little attention was given to the impact of pregnancy on the life of the clinician or the female client. Although therapist pregnancy may induce negative emotions and destructive behaviors, the potential to make positive therapeutic use of these reactions is usually ignored. Pines described pregnancy as "a crisis point in the search for feminine identity . . . a point of no return" (1972,

p. 333). The potential excitement and challenge for clients and therapist have been lost. Women clients are described as reactive to their therapists' pregnancies, but no one seems interested in asking, "Why?"

The Absence of Female Voices
in the Pregnancy Literature

Freud (1931) saw pregnancy as gratification of a woman's basic wish and, as such, saw no evidence of its creating conflict. He described pregnancy as "a period of calm . . . reflecting inner peace emanating from the sense of fulfillment." Perhaps loyalty to Freud has led female therapists to believe that the *resolution* of ambivalence about mothering is crucial for women's sense of self (Ballou, 1978)—as if the questions and demands would ever go away!

The reassurance and relief achieved by linking one's fears to a community of women are denied in such an idealized view of fertility. Although Lax pioneered the discussion of a therapist's pregnancy, her classical recommendation "not [to] interact emotionally with patients concerning [the pregnancy]," since "the private life of the analyst should not impinge upon the patients" (1969, p. 371), denies young women the chance to explore concerns about pregnancy and motherhood with a person who can articulate the joys, strains, and decisions that childbearing involves. In her preface to *Critical Psychophysical Passages in the Life of A Woman* (1988), a book about the cycles of a woman's life (including menarche, pregnancy, and menopause), Offerman-Zuckerberg describes the turmoil she endured as she compromised her career to raise her children and postponed editing a book until they were grown. Though proud of her decision, she acknowledges the losses involved. But the body of the book ignores her experience, exploring the psychology of women without addressing the conflict between personal and professional worlds. As female therapists, what useful lessons do we deny young women by our resistance to discussing the conflicts we all share? The professional literature encourages not only the therapist but the client to remain silent. There are few recommendations that clients discuss the pregnancy's impact on them or that the therapist disclose the "secret."

In a study of 22 therapists, Fenster et al. (1986) report that the majority believed one should wait for the client to bring up the pregnancy rather than "prematurely impose the therapist's personal event," (p. 23). However, this view is not supported by research, which indicates that the therapist's early introduction of the topic allows for greater exploration of feelings (Katzman, 1993; Naparstek, 1976) and may decrease acting-out behavior (Kleinplatz, 1992). Naparstek (1976) asserts that it is *not* narcissistic to make the pregnancy real for patients—a view echoed by Benedek (1973) with respect to staff interactions. She cautions against the supervisory folklore that says, "Because you are pregnant you are going to become increasingly self-involved and more likely to feel that everything your patients do is a result of your pregnancy" (1973, p. 23).

How Pregnancy Can Birth Better Therapists

In the studies that asked about changes in therapeutic style as a result of pregnancy, clinicians reported that increased relatedness and shared humanity had the most powerful impact. Participants in Fenster's (1983) study judged themselves to be significantly more self-revealing than usual with their clients during pregnancy. This move toward greater mutuality, employing self-involving statements (i.e., direct expressions of therapists' feelings toward the clients) along with self-disclosure (i.e., therapists' discussion of past personal experiences), produced a genuine connection that was seen as unusually reparative. The clinicians in Fenster's study reported that pregnancy allowed for therapist and client to "meet each other more simply and directly [with] the possibility of caring and concern" (1983, p. 55). An increased sense of relatedness toward clients was also reported by Barbanel (1980) and Rubin (1980). In Grossman's (1990) study, therapists reported that pregnancy resulted in altered theories about what was curative in the therapeutic relationship, with the essential change centering around the therapist's "becoming more real" and using herself more in her work. Grossman interviewed therapists at a 3-year follow-up and found that the process of change "evolved not in a premeditated fashion, but rather from the discovery that being more present in a personal way not only was not damaging to patients but rather was beneficial for the majority of them" (1990, p. 73).

It is striking that both Fenster (1983) and Grossman (1990) are describing a spontaneous movement toward a self-in-relation perspective. Surrey (1991) describes how women's sense of self is formed in the context of important relationships, grows with the deepening of relational competence, and is healed through the development of mutual empathy. In this interactional model, as people share emotions, understanding, and regard, reciprocity leads to empowerment, self-knowledge, and self-esteem. Understanding is as essential to self-worth as being understood. Consequently, treatment progresses when new self-images are formed in the context of therapy that is recognized as a relationship. It is possible that the move toward "being more real" described by pregnant therapists contributes to a working through of important emotional issues, as well as to the development of reciprocity.

Steiner-Adair (1991) writes, "If the therapist is not present *as a real person*, she risks recreating the cultural image of perfection and social acceptability that requires the truth of one's feeling and beliefs to live underground" (p. 229, emphasis added). She describes how a mutual relationship, employing dialogue rather than mirroring, is crucial in the process of female identity formation. In this model, the self is defined through engagement with the therapist. This defining context is particularly salient for young women with eating disorders, who cannot be expected to reinhabit their bodies if there is no "I" or self who speaks directly from the body of the therapist. The therapist's pregnancy can be a way in which dialogue is facilitated in treatment.

Research on therapeutic efficacy in a general population supports this perspective. LeBerie and Sturnilo (1987) found that clients reported self-involving statements by the therapist as both positive and helpful. It appears that whatever the orientation of the therapist, her expanding womb may force her presence not only into the room but also into connection with her client, despite professional training that promotes maintaining distance. It is possible that the interaction that a therapist's pregnancy demands gives female clinicians permission to do in treatment what they might have been inclined to do naturally, before their professional training taught them to neutralize their emotional experience and label it "countertransference" (Wooley, 1991).

STRUGGLING TOGETHER: SOME CASE ILLUSTRATIONS

"I'm So Surprised; You Don't Look Any Different."

April, a 14-year-old anorexic, offered no comment on my pregnancy for 4 months. She had recently decided not to talk to her mother about her alcoholic father's abusive behavior, "for fear of upsetting her." She was again preoccupied with "fat thoughts." I asked her whether this might be related to concerns she was afraid of raising with me. "No," she said, complaining that I always "look for bad things." When I asked whether she had suspected I was pregnant, she said no. "Would you have told me if you suspected?" I asked, and she replied, "No, that wouldn't have been right." She then went on to ask detailed questions about what would happen to her while I was gone—all the while proclaiming, "This is great."

Brown (1989) and Steiner-Adair (1991) describe the "tyranny of kind and nice" that forces adolescent girls not to acknowledge the anger and conflicts that exist in the context of relations with others, but instead forces them to be "polite" and avoid "hurtful" treatment of others. In

April's case, I suspected that she was editing out her unkind thoughts toward me. My goal was to challenge her rule of niceness and to invite her to explore questions she had taught herself were off limits.

My hunch was confirmed in the following session, when she revealed that she had, in fact, noticed my weight gain. She had wondered, "How could you help me if you have a weight problem?" While I acknowledged that it is difficult to discuss a therapist's weight changes, I also asked how it would feel to "be so unsure of a person who was meant to help her." She described feeling frightened and alone. We went on to discuss how hurtful it was for her not to say what she thought or to let me respond to her fears. I suggested that her difficulty in trusting others might relate to the censorship she imposed on discussing "not nice topics," forcing her to pull away, questioning the motives that she had ascribed to others.

During this session, I maintained a focus on the value of April's views, both to me and to her care. I acknowledged that she might have many concerns about secrets that she had been taught to ignore, but reassured her that it was unlikely she would destroy anyone by confronting what she knew. I encouraged her to begin testing this out with me, since I believed she knew more than she said she did. I explained that gaining her trust was important to me, and when she shared her observations, I was impressed by how attuned she was to the details of human interactions. She relaxed and began to ask me many questions—not only about my pregnancy, but what I thought about her "selfish and angry feelings" toward the members of her family, all of whom expected her to be happy despite her father's abusive behavior and her mother's attempt to ignore it.

"This Is Stupid. I Have No Right to Cry."

Shortly after I told Karen (a 26-year-old bulimic) that I was pregnant, she asked, "What are the rules? I can't switch to talking about your life, but it is impacting on mine." Although she felt it was selfish to personalize my pregnancy, I assured her that a range of emotions are common and that I was interested in her reactions because she mattered to me. We discussed her mixed feelings about my pregnancy in detail that day.

One month later she spoke about feeling alone, admitting that she was isolating herself from others in anticipation of my leave. The following transcript captures the struggle that ensued as we challenged her assumption that to be close to or have an impact on others, a person needs to be just like them, to be the only one in their lives, and to say only what they want to hear. My goal was to support her independence while acknowledging her need for comfort and connection.

Karen: I see changes in your body and they say, "I have my own life"—don't you get it? I shouldn't feel this way. What is the client–doctor relationship? I'm too attached—I'm a fool—I think you're laughing.

Melanie: I'm not laughing. I'd be surprised if you didn't have feelings about my leave. If I didn't see you for months before our work was complete, I would miss you. I'm concerned about you, too. I know my leave will coincide with significant events in your life, and I wish I could be here to hear about them. Are you afraid your feelings are too one-sided?

K.: I'll lose control; this should be scientific.

M.: Why do you expect me not to care?

K.: (*In tears*) I'm so embarrassed.

M.: Do you feel this ashamed to relate your feelings to anyone else? Do you expect criticism?

K.: It's too painful, too embarrassing.

M.: To care so much?

K.: (*Nods*)

M.: Does anyone laugh?

K.: I just . . . I have no place in their lives. I love my parents and my stepdad more than they love me.

M.: How does it feel to be doing the loving?

K.: Foolish, embarrassing; it will always be this way.

M.: What do you think prompts these feelings?

K.: With my stepdad, going against his view—my opinion is always invalid. My natural father cares about my stepbrother's feelings and well-being, and it reminds me of all he didn't do for me when he was using drugs and married to my mom. With Mom—I used to be the most important thing to her.

M.: They all have other people in their lives now, and just like how your life with Mom started changing when she had your brother, are you afraid I will have no time for you once this baby is born?

K.: Yes, but I'm also so afraid you're angry now.

M.: Rather than fearing being selfish or getting me angry, how about trying not to isolate, to talk more with me so we can learn from this? I'm not laughing.

The following week, Karen said she was relieved after our last meeting. She had called her friends and told them that the summer might be a rough time for her. She also told me she had taken a pregnancy test 2 weeks earlier; she hadn't had sex, nor was her period late, but she had thought it would make us closer if somehow she too had a baby. We explored how her desire to connect with others was often reflected in mimicking their behaviors, as opposed to finding a common ground for mutual respect. In retrospect, she said that her desire to be pregnant seemed silly, since really we could talk without having the same life events.

Culling from both feminist and object relations theory, Anne Kearney-Cooke (1991) has developed a three-stage model of recovery from eating disorders. The middle phase of treatment is described as a testing of experiences with self and others. She suggests that the therapist respond empathetically both to the client's autonomous behavior and to her need for support and continued dependency. In Karen's case, I felt that encouraging her to express complex and conflicting feelings in a vacuum seemed cruel. To pretend that she had no effect on my life, or to edit out my concern, would have confirmed her assumption that you can't share "what you really feel" directly with another person and maintain that person's love or respect. Helping a client express feelings of dependency on a therapist who is about to go on leave, while affirming her ability to take care of herself, is a critical task at this time.

"The Only Working Woman I Know Who Got Pregnant Miscarried at the Airport Running between Meetings."

Jean Baker Miller (1991) describes the development of self as a complex process including "a quest for power over others and power over natural forces including one's own body" (p. 25). In Miller's definition, power is more closely associated with nurturance; sharing power doesn't diminish it.

During the last 5 minutes of a group meeting, May, a 28-year-old woman, asked whether I was pregnant. She related happiness when I confirmed that I was, and declared it "a group baby that everyone can watch grow." Later, in an individual session with me, she described her fear that any child of hers was "a disaster waiting to be born," affirmed again her happiness for me, and then described her former boss's miscarriage in the airport while attempting to "do it all." Her sessions continued to focus on issues of balancing career and relationship goals at a time when she had left her husband and her job, moved in with a new boyfriend, and started a different career. She continued to deny any reactions to my pregnancy, but she repeated the miscarriage story four times, each time changing the month of the loss to correspond with my continuing pregnancy. She then asked for a break from all therapy for "financial reasons."

For May, being competent and respected was equivalent to being in control of her feelings and others. Her reluctance to address her reactions toward me mirrored her difficulty in being vulnerable with anyone. The view that one should maintain a strong facade and retain control was heavily reinforced in her achievement-oriented family. Although she was intellectually aware that successful leaders are not invulnerable, her open competition with me intensified as she repeatedly challenged my authority in what appeared to be a desire to find my Achilles heel. I made a greater effort to relate to her my questions and concerns about her progress, the group, and my time off, in an effort to counter her view that I was infallible, that all this was easy, and that people get respect only when they have all the answers. She responded by questioning whether she needed to leave me or increase the frequency of sessions. Her attempt to control all contact with me, the group members, and her friends was leaving her more confused. Despite her confident and challenging demeanor, she was at a loss as to who she had become, given the many changes in her life. I again inquired about her anger toward me, and she acknowledged competition with me and my readiness to have a child.

In a rare display of tears, she discussed how she had equated pregnancy with loss. May saw her mother as giving up her own life for her children. She saw her boss choose to give up mothering for a career after her miscarriage. She had no role models of integration and feared that "time was running out" before she could "get her life together to have a child." She also wondered how I would manage her care during the time I was gone and after I returned.

Fenster (1983) describes the relief clients experience when a brief description of plans for combining career and motherhood is shared (i.e., child care arrangements and possible changes in work responsibilities). This assures clients that the therapist will be available, is a good mother, and can serve as a model of power and nurturance who can negotiate responsibilities of home and work. I followed this suggestion with May and found her quite interested and relaxed. I then asked her whether she wanted to continue trying to push me out of her life—or perhaps, instead of resenting me for what I had, to learn how I got the things she wanted. My goal was to defuse her power struggle with me, affirm that competition is real, and work toward a collaborative way of relating that allowed her to experiment with being powerful without being invulnerable.

In each of these examples, my pregnancy allowed clients to explore their assumptions about closeness in a relationship. For some, closeness required being nice to, or the same as, the other person, with anger being the expected response to independent feelings. For others, closeness required vulnerability. Renegotiating the roles people played in their lives was critical, whether it meant recognizing that in close relationships one person is seldom the sole recipient of attention, or realizing that growth and change presented new options for all parties, including the clients. Although the case examples above involved an adolescent and two young adults, as women clients get older the issues spurred by a therapist's pregnancy may shift from a focus on mother/family and niceness themes to concerns about body image and the increasingly loud ticking of one's biological clock. As my research (Katzman, 1993) indicated, older women without children may be most vocal about their concerns—fears that generally center around career compromises and their own options or abilities to mother.

POWER AND NURTURANCE

For reparative work to be accomplished, the client must be encouraged to speak truthfully of her reactions to the therapist's pregnancy. This requires giving the client permission to experiment with being the less-than-perfect child or woman. Similarly, the therapist, in her effort to share her feelings, must recognize that she cannot always be a perfect mother to her client. Grossman (1990) captures this dilemma clearly:

> In our culture, motherhood has become idealized such that mothers are seen as devoted exclusively to nurturing and caring for their babies (Leifer, 1980), as the only one who can meet the needs of a baby (Chodorow & Contratto, 1982), and as not having a life independent of her child. This societal ideal is applicable to the role of therapists as well as mothers. Thus, therapists, who also are products of our culture, struggle with trying to be the ideal mother to both [their] clients and new baby. (p. 77)

In fact, Fenster et al. (1986) indicates that "there are times when the therapist as a new mother feels she is doing the same job everywhere" (p. 118).

Therapists, like other professionals, aspire to a sense of power in their work; yet they find themselves in a job in which success is defined by their ability to nurture. The boundary between these demands often gets blurred, and a therapist may become depleted as a result. The difficulties women experience in their efforts to satisfy yearnings for power and nurturance are highlighted by McClelland's (1979) findings that females tend to define "power" as having the strength to care for and give to others, while men define "power" as control over others. Grossman (1990) argues that a distinction between the two is critical and asserts that "nurturance" is synonymous with caring for another, whereas "power" is the capacity to produce an effect on others. This includes "individuals, institutions and social systems" (Grossman, 1990, p. 61).

This difference in definition becomes critical in examining pregnant therapists' work with clients. Upon returning to work after having children, the therapists in Grossman's (1990) study viewed their clients' demands as less benign and more noxious than before. This resulted in increased limit setting on potentially abusive behavior, increased expectations of their clients, and attempts to differentiate between nurturing a client and a baby. One of the most consistent reactions of pregnant therapists in Grossman's study was the wish to see clients as less infantile and more adult. This change in therapists' attitudes frequently had positive consequences for clients, who felt more empowered and received greater support for independence (Grossman, 1990).

However, in contrast to pregnant therapists, who are devoted to making sure that clients' needs will be taken care of before maternity leave, returning therapists as new mothers may grow to resent clients' criticism about not getting enough. They may, as a result restrict exploration of neediness and abandonment issues. Increasing the treatment team (i.e., referring clients to additional resources, such as biofeedback, couples treatment, family therapy, or group therapy) can provide not only an expanded concept of nurturance, but a supportive community as well. Both therapist and client are empowered when nurturing connections are understood to mean more than dependency for the client and a drain for the clinician.

The value of redefining closeness is consistent with the finding that clients returning after the therapist's maternity leave credited the identification of dependency on the therapist and the development of ways to care for themselves with increasing their insight into the role of nurturance in an intimate relationship (Katzman, 1993). In this study, women were given the choice to join a group, see a covering therapist, or take a "therapeutic holiday" during the break. Women who saw a covering therapist realized that people other than the therapist could be fulfilling. In fact, by "tasting" the nourishment available in different relationships, the women upon their return had the basis to compare what they liked in different therapeutic contacts, and used this opportunity to identify and ask for changes. Those who opted for a therapeutic holiday also reported very positive consequences, as they felt more empowered by their independence and ability to continue growth and change. A number of the "vacationers" returned to therapy with an altered view: No longer were they "sick people" needing to be cured, but capable individuals employing additional resources for guidance. As a result, change, so often feared and avoided, was reassessed as providing positive opportunities and not simply as a loss of control.

When therapy resumed, most of the women I studied (Katzman, 1993) expressed a sense of closeness to the therapist as a result of having "shared" her pregnancy. This closeness led to additional questions about the ways in which the therapist would integrate her personal and professional life. Clients wanted a model for success and power that would validate motherhood as well. Although a therapist cannot be expected to achieve a full resolution of every dilemma involved in combining career and motherhood, her willingness to share the struggle validates women's anxiety and may allow them to articulate their frustration with prevailing images of successful women.

THE POWER IN SHARED RESPONSIBILITY

Therapists, as professionals, also have an opportunity to grow through life events such as pregnancy; however, like clients, they also need permission to question their desires and goals and to look to role models for guidance. The current literature provides few insights and guidelines.

For many expectant therapists, the redefinition of personal and professional identities is a central task prior to and after childbirth (Fenster et al., 1986; Grossman, 1990). The entrance to motherhood may result in surrendering an institutional affiliation while building a private practice and beginning a family. Motherhood may also result in decreased time or desire to write, to conduct research, or to travel for consultations and conventions. The demands of a growing family may also prompt a woman to say no to flattering offers she worked hard to obtain, such as TV and radio appearances, membership on advisory boards, or guest lecturing. Changes in the amount and type of these professional activities may be experienced as a loss of prestige and legitimacy as a professional. This can have a negative impact on clients and on the clinician herself if the therapist overfunctions in an effort to affirm her worth. Conversely, examining one's professional "obligations" can have a positive effect, as the therapist evaluates those activities that are most satisfying for her and eliminates extraneous commitments.

An early and realistic assessment of client and therapist needs can ameliorate some of this tension. Discussing the pregnancy with clients by the fourth or fifth month not only allows for greater emotional exploration; it also places the burden of exposing an obvious, but mutually unaddressed, secret on the therapist and not on clients who may have great difficulty discussing issues that may be perceived as off limits. Allowing clients to decide when they will cease care (or transfer to a covering therapist) also provides a sense of control and involvement in an inevitable separation.

Discussing plans for coverage not only assures the clients of continuing care; it encourages the therapist to examine and include additional treatment resources. This can reduce the anxiety associated with being responsible for others at a time when one's own life is becoming less predictable. Establishing a projected date for termination (preferably at least several weeks prior to the birth) provides clients reassuring predictability in the absence of control, while allowing the therapist some time to energize herself and shift focus prior to the birth.

Having clients meet covering therapists about 1 month prior to the leave asserts the reality of the situation for everyone involved, and allows for discussion with the therapist of issues that might otherwise arise once she is gone and later interfere with a return to treatment. It is empowering for clients to see that extending one's emotional community is not an act of disloyalty.

In addition, scheduling an appointment before the therapist goes on leave for after her return offers reassurance, as does offering involvement in a time-limited group during the leave. My clients found the support and shared experience of a group comforting; for some, the ambivalence about working with another therapist was lessened in this modality. Women who chose group rather than individual therapy during the break found the balance between a constant support and the freedom to "experiment" on their own liberating. Covering therapists found the option of sharing a difficult case with a group therapist very appealing as well. Moreover, as a therapist with a group practice, I found that being able to provide this option was a comforting extension of my work in my absence.

From the time the topic is introduced until the last session before the break, the baby becomes a presence in the therapy room, whether discussed or not, and its birth has an impact on clients. Not notifying the clients of the child's arrival negates this involvement and prevents the assurance that the therapist has "survived." Sending an announcement continues and respects the connections built during this period.

By accepting, understanding, and using her pregnancy, the therapist can incorporate treatment goals with maternity. Rather than viewing the pregnancy as a time of emotional upheaval to be endured, with the goal being a return to prepregnancy equilibrium, a therapist can treat her pregnancy as an opportunity to strengthen bonds, explore new terrains, and regroup at a healthier level. The story of childbirth needs to be rewritten yet again, but this time by women. By writing, researching, and discussing the power of pregnancy, female therapists can begin to reverse the pathologizing of this unique ability and restore it to a venerated status.

REFERENCES

Adler, T. (1991, October). Will feminization spell decline for the field? *APA Monitor,* p. 12.

Ahmed, P., & Kolker, A. (1981). Coping with medical issues. In P. Ahmed (Ed.), *Pregnancy, childbirth and parenthood.* New York: Elsevier.

Atlee, H. B. (1963). Fall of the queen of heaven. *Obstetrics and Gynecology, 21,* 514.

Ballou, J. (1978). *The psychology of pregnancy.* Lexington, MA: Lexington Books.

Balsam, R. (1975). The pregnant therapist. In R. Balsam (Ed.), *On becoming a psychotherapist.* Boston: Little, Brown.

Barbanel, L. (1980). The therapist's pregnancy. In B. L. Blum (Ed.), *Psychological aspects of pregnancy, birthing, and bonding,* (pp. 232–246). New York: Human Sciences Press.

Baum, E., & Herring, C. (1975). The pregnant psychotherapist in training. *American Journal of Psychiatry, 132,* 419–423.

Bender, E. (1975). *The pregnant therapist: Outpatient setting.* Unpublished manuscript.

Benedek, E. P. (1973). The fourth world of the pregnant therapist. *Journal of the American Psychoanalytic Association, 4,* 365–368.

Berman, E. (1975). Acting out as a response to the psychiatrist's pregnancy. *Journal of the American Medical Women's Association, 30,* 456–458.

Bibring, G., Dwyer, T., Huntington, D., & Valenstein, A. (1961). A study of the psychological process in pregnancy and of the earliest mother–child relationship. *Psychoanalytic Study of the Child, 16,* 9–72.

Braslow, J. B., & Heins, M. (1981). Women and medical education: A decade of change. *New England Journal of Medicine, 304,* 1129.

Breen, D. (1977). Some of the differences between group and individual therapy in connection with the therapist's pregnancy. *International Journal of Group Psychotherapy, 27,* 499–506.

Brown, L. (1989). *Narratives of relationship: The development of a care voice in girls ages 7 to 16* (Monograph No. 8). Cambridge, MA: Harvard University, The Study Center.

Browning, D. (1974). Patient's reactions to their therapist's pregnancy. *Journal of the American Academy of Child Psychiatry, 13,* 468–482.

Butts, N., & Cavenar, J. (1979). Colleagues' responses to the pregnant psychiatric resident. *American Journal of Psychiatry, 136,* 1587–1589.

Chodorow, N., & Contratto, S. (1982). The fantasy of the perfect mother. In B. Thorne (Ed.), *Rethinking the family* (pp. 54–75). New York: Longman.

Cole, D. (1980). Therapeutic issues arising from the pregnancy of the therapist. *Psychotherapy: Theory, Research, and Practice, 17,* 210–213.

Entwisle, D., & Doering, S. (1981). *The first birth: A family turning point.* Baltimore: Johns Hopkins University Press.

Fenster, S. (1983). Intrusion in the analytic space: The pregnancy of the psychoanalytic therapist. *Dissertations Abstracts International* (University Microfilms No. 83–17, 555)

Fenster, S., Phillips, S., & Rapoport, E. (1986). *The therapist's pregnancy: Intrusion in the analytic space.* Hillsdale, NJ: Analytic Press.

Freud, S. (1931). Female sexuality. *Standard Edition, 21,* 221–243.

Grossman, H. (1990). The pregnant therapist: Professional and personal worlds intertwine. In H. Grossman & N. Chester (Eds.), *The experience and meaning of work in women's lives* (pp. 57–81). Hillsdale, NJ: Erlbaum.

Hannet, F. (1946). Transference reactions to an event in the life of the analyst. *Psychoanalytic Review, 36,* 69–81.

Katzman, M. A. (1993). The pregnant therapist and the eating-disordered woman: The challenge of fertility. *Eating Disorders: The Journal of Treatment and Prevention, 1,* 17–30.

Kearney-Cooke, A. (1989). Reclaiming the body: Using guided imagery in the treatment of body image disturbances among bulimic women. In L. M. Hornyak & E. K. Baker (Eds.), *Experiential therapies for eating disorders* (pp. 11–33). New York: Guilford Press.

Kearney-Cooke, A. (1991). The role of the therapist in the treatment of eating disorders: A feminist psychodynamic approach. In C. L. Johnson (Ed.), *Psychodynamic treatment of anorexia nervosa and bulimia* (pp. 295–318). New York: Guilford Press.

Kleinplatz, P. J. (1992). The pregnant clinical psychologist: Issues, impressions and observations. *Women and Therapy, 12*(1–2), 21–37.

LeBerie, G., & Sturnilo, F. (1987, August). *Effects of self-involving statements on the counseling relationship.* Paper presented at the annual meeting of the American Psychological Association, New York.

Lax, R. F. (1969). Some considerations about transference and counter transference manifestations evoked by the analyst's pregnancy. *International Journal of Psycho-Analysis, 50,* 363–372.

Leifer, M. (1980). *Psychological effect of motherhood: A study of first pregnancy.* New York: Praeger.

Lemberg, R., & Phillips, J. (1989). The impact of pregnancy on anorexia nervosa and bulimia. *International Journal of Eating Disorders, 8,* 285–296.

McClelland, D. (1979). *Power: The inner experience.* New York: Irvington Press.

Miller, J. B. (1991). The development of women's sense of self. In J. V. Jordan, A. G. Kaplan, J. B. Miller, I. P. Stiver, & J. L. Surrey (Eds.), *Women's growth in connection: Writings from the Stone Center* (pp. 11–26). New York: Guilford Press.

Nadelson, C., Notman, M., Arons, E., & Feldman, J. (1974). The pregnant therapist. *American Journal of Psychiatry, 131,* 1107–1111.

Naparstek, B. (1976). Treatment guidelines for the pregnant therapist. *Psychiatric Opinion, 13,* 20–25.

Offerman-Zuckerberg, J. (Ed.). (1988). *Critical psychophysical passages in the life of a woman: A psychodynamic perspective.* New York: Plenum Press.

Ostertag, P. A., & McNamara, J. R. (1991). Feminization of psychology: The changing sex ratio and its implications for the profession. *Psychology of Women Quarterly, 15,* 349–370.

Paluszny, M., & Poznanski, E. (1971). Reactions of patients during the pregnancy of the psychotherapist. *Child Psychiatry and Human Development, 4,* 266–274.

Pines, D. (1972). Pregnancy and motherhood: Interaction between fantasy and reality. *British Journal of Medical Psychology, 45,* 333–343.

Raphael-Leff, J. (1980). Psychotherapy with pregnant women. In B. L. Blum (Ed.), *Psychological aspects of pregnancy, birthing and bonding* (pp. 174–203). New York: Human Sciences Press.

Root, M., Fallon, P., & Friedrich, W. (1986). *Bulimia: A systems approach to treatment.* New York: Norton.

Rubin, C. (1980). Notes from a pregnant therapist. *Social Work, 25,* 210–214.

Schwartz, M. (1975, January). Casework implications of a worker's pregnancy. *Social Casework,* pp. 27–34.

Steiner-Adair, C. (1986). The body politic: Normal female adolescent development and development of eating disorders. *Journal of the American Academy of Psychoanalysis, 1,* 95–114.

Steiner-Adair, C. (1991). New maps of development, new models of therapy: The psychology of women and the treatment of eating disorders. In C. L. Johnson (Ed.), *Psychodynamic treatment of anorexia nervosa and bulimia* (pp. 225–244). New York: Guilford Press.

Striegel-Moore, R. (1990). *Towards a feminist research agenda in the psychological research of eating disorders.* Paper presented at the 4th International Conference of Eating Disorders, New York.

Surrey, J. L. (1991). The "self in relation": A theory of women's development. In J. V. Jordan, A. G. Kaplan, J. B. Miller, I. P. Stiver, & J. L. Surrey (Eds.), *Women's growth in connection: Writings from the Stone Center* (pp. 31–36). New York: Guilford Press.

Wooley, S. C. (1991). Uses of countertransference in the treatment of eating disorders: A gender perspective. In C. L. Johnson (Ed.), *Psychodynamic treatment of anorexia nervosa and bulimia* (pp. 245–294). New York: Guilford Press.

Wooley, S. C., & Kearney-Cooke, A. (1986). Intensive treatment of bulimia and body image disturbance. In K. Brownell & J. Foreyt (Eds.), *Handbook of eating disorders* (pp. 476–502). New York: Basic Books.

Wooley, S. C., & Wooley, O. W. (1985). Intensive outpatient and residential treatment of bulimia. In D. M. Garner & P. E. Garfinkel (Eds.), *Handbook of psychotherapy for anorexia nervosa and bulimia* (pp. 391–430). New York: Guilford Press.

8

Imagining Ourselves Whole: A Feminist Approach to Treating Body Image Disorders

MARCIA GERMAINE HUTCHINSON

WOMEN AND BODY IMAGE

THE RELATIONSHIP TO OUR BODIES is the first relationship we have and the foundation of our selves. Yet it is an uneasy relationship for most people in Western society, especially women. As women we battle with our bodies, attributing to them the power to define our lives, blaming them for everything that goes wrong. We split our bodies off from our selves and turn them into objects that we disown, deny, haul around as burdens, and find wanting. We live in a culture where it is normal for us to feel that we should be thinner, prettier, firmer, younger, and in all ways better. We deprive our bodies of food and drag them to the gym to whip them into shape. We dedicate our time, energy, and obsessive attention—in short, our lives—to trying to "fix" our bodies and make them "right." We do everything except live in them.

Our troubled relationship to our bodies spills over into troubled relationships to our selves and is central to the current epidemic of disordered eating, low self-esteem, depression, and self-contempt. There can be no true healing of an eating disorder without attention to the disordered relationship between self and body—the negative body image.

The relationship between the self and the body not only underpins women's disordered relationship to food, but is also the keystone of their identity. It is an issue that involves the intersection of mind, body, and culture. A feminist approach to the treatment of disordered eating must deal with negative body image as a destructive adaptation, shared by most women, to a culture that is sick. For us as women to become whole, we must see clearly the toxicity of patriarchal culture as it impinges unrelentingly on our lives, and take political action against it. But while we wait for the culture to change, we must also heal our psyches, releasing the effects of centuries of brainwashing and becoming impermeable to the continuing onslaught. We must take back our bodies as homes, not as enemies, or as commodities.

Although the majority of women I have treated for body image disorders also suffer from a disordered relationship to food, my focus has not been on eating disorders, but on treating negative body image with a therapeutic group process (Hutchinson, 1985; Sankowsky [Hutchinson], 1981). I work to return to my clients and readers the birthright to feel at home in the bodies they have—even if those bodies fail to conform to external or internalized standards of appearance.

Everything about our socialization as females in a patriarchal culture leads us to value our selves in terms of our bodies—as objects of love, as childbearers, as nurturers, and as ornaments for men. Powerful messages echo our early and deeply embedded learning that for a woman, a successful life means to please, to be in relationship, to be chosen, to belong. Our success or failure in accomplishing these prescriptions is determined by the appearance of our bodies.

Body image is the image of the body that a person sees with the mind's eye; it is the image of the body that allows a person to know about emotions, sensations, bodily needs, and appetites, and to negotiate the physical environment; it is the image of the body that a person hears about as she listens to her inner speech. I use the term "body image" in a broad way to describe the psychological space where body, mind, and culture come together—the space that encompasses our thoughts, feelings, perceptions, attitudes, values, and judgments about the bodies we have.

Body image, a product of the imagination, is not to be confused with the actual physical body or with the image that the body projects to an outside observer. The term "body image" is an unfortunate one because it echoes this confusion. Raised with the images of the mass media, we are members of a society that, in general, confuses image with reality. Although "body image" describes an internal and subjective sense a person has of her own body, the term easily jumps from the subjective to the objective.

Translation from the physical body to the body image that represents it is a complex process, prone to distortion. Most of us live with body images shaped and distorted by attitudes about being women in a society that devalues everything female. The distortion comes from many sources: the ways our parents and family related to our bodies when we were growing up; traumatic life experiences that have become "frozen" into our body images; the body role modeling we have had; the acceptance or rejection of our bodies we have felt from family, peers, and important others; and the ways we have perceived our bodies to fit or not to fit the cultural image. Values, which in the past were shaped at a community level and transmitted slowly from parent to child, have now been replaced by media versions of the world.

The meteoric speed with which values are made and changed by television is unprecedented in history, reaching all social levels and all geographic corners. These images are carefully regulated by big business. It is estimated that the average American spends 30 hours per week watching television (over one-quarter of all waking hours), and 110 hours per year reading magazines (Pratkanis & Aronson, 1991, p. 3). Both on TV and in magazines, we are exposed to images of women who are anorexic, surgically altered, and airbrushed or computer-altered. These are not real women. The campaign persists because it works. We see the images and "buy" the need to measure up. Our economy is based on setting up this tension in us so that we consume. It is the American way. The war against fat and the natural fleshiness of the female body continues to escalate. It is a war against nature.

Woman is seen as mistress of the dark, mysterious, and powerful realm of the flesh; her body is associated with instinct, irrationality, unpredictability, sensuality, uncleanliness, and evil. Because woman has been seen as essential but feared, she has been controlled, as has her body, by being objectified and placed under restraints. The continued objectification of women's bodies by society and by women themselves sustains the disembodiment and disempowerment that are central aspects of the female experience. The realm of the feminine—body, nature, emotion, intuition, cooperation, affiliation, and community—finds little room in a patriarchal/capitalistic system where the power, giftedness, values, and contributions of women go unacknowledged. The voices and power of women—fully realized women who do not imitate men—would provoke a major disruption of the status quo if loosed on the social order.

The obsessive and destructive relationship that most women have with their bodies is an internalization of society's relationship to women's bodies—simultaneously one of contempt and worship. Some women battle to bring the hated antagonists in line with cultural requirements, attempting to sculpt and perfect their bodies as a prelude to worship. But obsession with the body is not the same as embodiment. We can be disembodied while being excruciatingly obsessed. Body hatred and body narcissism both treat the body as if it were an object separate from the self.

DISEMBODIMENT AND ITS CONSEQUENCES

In our disembodiment, we are numb to our bodies, repressing so much bodily experience that our bodies feel alien to us. We repress dimensions of our experience that frighten us or make us vulnerable—pain, sexuality, hunger, anger, and even excitement and pleasure. Eventually we obliterate the experience of our somatic selves, removing our bodies from our self-images. We deny their existence or importance. If pleasure in our bodies was punished when we were children, then we may functionally amputate the source of the pleasure from our selves rather than live in continuing fear of punishment. If, on the other hand, our bodies were the victims of physical or psychic violation, we may dissociate from them, writing them out of our experience of our selves.

Repression of body experience is often manifested as an armoring of the muscles, forming particular chronic holding patterns or tensions that give us our characteristic posture, expression, gait, and style of movement. Armoring deadens us, creating a hole in our experience. We feel disconnected from ourselves, trapped in flesh that is alien. Armored and unembodied, we are able to endure the boredom, pain, stress, overstimulation, and violence of conventional lifestyles. Often the functional amputation of our bodies is incomplete; the feared excitement, deadness, pain or pleasure breaks through, and we anesthetize or excite ourselves through compulsive behavior or substance abuse.

To be embodied is to experience the body as the center of existence—not as focus, but as a reference point for being in the world. It is to feel alive, to perceive bodily states as they change from pleasure to pain, from hunger to satiety, from energy to fatigue, from vitality and excitement to calm and tranquility. Everything we think, feel, or do registers in our bodies through subtle changes in the musculature and bodily functions. There is no emotion without motion, however small: a change in pulse or body temperature, a restriction of the breathing, a tensing of the musculature. Body awareness helps us perceive changes that signal emotional shifts; intuition is also based on awareness of the subtle, felt shifts in our bodies.

TREATING NEGATIVE BODY IMAGE

After years of struggle with my own body (which would not conform to the societal requirement for thinness), and with a resulting negative body image, my doctoral project was an opportunity to focus on ways of treating negative body image in women, including myself. I was struck by the dearth of approaches to help women accept their bodies as they were, and the plethora of programs directed at changing the body—none of which had ever worked for me.

In 1978 there was nothing that suggested that I was allowed to accept myself. Everything available said, "Change your body and it will change your life"; try as I might, however, I could not change my body. When it finally occurred to me that it was not my body but my body image that needed to change, I found little in the literature to help me with that task.

Although Freud (1923/1961) placed body image—or "body ego," as he referred to it—in a key role in his theoretical system, most of the initial scientific and clinical interest in the phenomenon of body image focused on the neurological and perceptual aspects of pathological body image distortions. These ranged from gross distortions produced by organic brain damage, phantom limb phenomena, psychosis, sleep, and orgasm to those produced under artificially altered conditions (e.g., hypnosis, shock treatment, mind-altering drugs, and distorting lenses). Body image proved to be vulnerable to radical change from both internal and external agency (Sankowsky, 1981, p. 31).

Much of the psychological literature about body image deals with the relationship between body image and other dimensions of the self and the life experience; the body and the body image are viewed as a frame of reference for being in the world. There has been relatively little scholarly attention to the study of feelings about the body or "body cathexis" (Fisher & Cleveland, 1972), and even less to its special role in the lives of women (Jourard & Secord, 1955a, 1955b).

Finding a paucity of attention to the treatment of a negative body cathexis (Sankowsky, 1981), I realized that I would have to figure out how to change my body image on my own. Systematic and recorded treatment approaches for changing body image are still relatively sparse, and range from the psychodynamic (Krueger, 1989) to the feminist/ experiential (Sankowsky, 1981; Hutchinson, 1985; Wooley & Kearney-Cooke, 1986; Kearney-Cooke, 1989, 1991) to the cognitive–behavioral (Cash & Pruzinsky, 1990; Thompson, 1990; Freedman, 1989). The scientific literature is dominated by the cognitive–behavioral camp. Briefly, proponents of this approach view body image disturbances as the results of cognitive errors (irrational thoughts and unrealistic expectations) that lead to emotional and behavioral responses (e.g., depression and dieting). Behavioral techniques are used to correct faulty underlying belief structures. In my experience, I have found cognitive–behavioral techniques to be useful in an adjunctive capacity with clients who have mild body image issues. With few exceptions (Freedman, 1989), they fail to address deep resistance to change, in cases where body image is entrenched in the identity and continually reinforced by social values.

I confine this chapter to a description of my own work in this area. I developed a treatment that was tested on a group of 15 women, whose responses were compared to 15 matched subjects in a waiting-list control group. Volunteers responded to a flyer advertising a group for women who disliked their bodies. The group was composed of women of average weight who were not clinically eating-disordered. Of the 114 women I interviewed, all but 5 reported a disordered relationship to food and weight. The experimental group participated in a 7-week group process and were also given audiotaped exercises to do as homework. The results of the treatment were dramatically positive. Quantitative measures indicated statistically significant improvement in both body image and self-image. Interviews and questionnaires at posttest supported these findings (Sankowsky, 1981), while an additional questionnaire administered as a 6-month follow-up measure revealed that changes were maintained or deepened for most subjects.

The therapy, which has evolved in the intervening years, now consists of 12 weekly group meetings lasting 2½ hours each, limited to a maximum of 10 women; weekend workshops are conducted with larger groups. The method continues to be based primarily on experiential exercises. Interactive guided imagery is employed in conjunction with journal processing, group sharing, movement, and expressive media. Having led hundreds of women through this process since the original treatment study, I continue to find that this approach significantly affects women's relationship to their bodies, and by extension their relationship to their selves.

IMAGERY AS A CLINICAL TOOL

Guided imagery is used as the major clinical tool, for several reasons:

1. Body image is itself an image, and controlled imaging is an appropriate tool for entering the realm where the subjective experience of the body can be accessed and altered. Since image is the language of the unconscious and of feelings, the focused use of imagery is also appropriate for accessing primary-process material and affective memories.

2. Working with imagery is a soft and respectful, albeit powerful, therapeutic approach. The subtle, nonintrusive, and often symbolic character of imagery does not trigger defenses or resistance, but often evokes profound revelations. Images are very efficient. A single image can symbolize and arouse an entire constellation of meanings, which can then be explored.

3. Imagery is the language of the inner self. Working with one's inner imagery is a way of coming into deep contact with the self. Inherent in imaginal work is the understanding that the internal world is valuable and worth noticing. Paying attention to one's own image making brings to the foreground one's internal integrity, sense of meaning, and sense of selfhood. Lack of a solid sense of self is a frequent characteristic of women with eating disorders. Mapping the landscape of the self—feelings, images, memories, thoughts, inner voices, sensations, and intuitions—is an antidote to feelings of emptiness. A more substantial sense of self is essential for taking a stand counter to what the culture holds valuable.

4. Work with imagery takes place in a deeply relaxed state of altered consciousness, which is in itself healing. New mental patterns can be created, and deep emotional healing can occur.

5. Finally, extensive work with imagery conveys the power of the imagination in shaping reality, and shows each woman her ability to gain access to and control her cognitive maps (such as body image) that are presently manifested in destructive attitudes, moods, and compulsive behavior patterns.

Working in a respectful relationship to a person's imagery as a significant part of the total personality is a key to psychic reconstruction. Deeply repressed material can be brought to the surface and worked through on a symbolic level under the guidance of the therapist.

TREATMENT OBJECTIVES

Making peace with our bodies almost always involves identifying the obstacles to positive feelings: the ways we have internalized the treatment and judgments of our significant others; the body shame that we have taken on from family role models; the tyranny of the internalized, ideal bodies that we keep alive through negative self-talk. The treatment intervention has several broad objectives: relieving isolation; heightening awareness of body issues; exploring the roots of body issues; exploring blockages and resistance to change; and re-embodiment.

Relieving Isolation

Working in a group format is essential to relieving the sense of isolation that most women feel with their body struggles. In spite of the pervasiveness of negative body image in this country, it is remarkable that most women feel that they are the only ones who truly hate their bodies or have body defects (real or perceived). It is common for women to complain about weight and discuss diets, but rare for them to speak authentically with others about the painful events in their body histories. Deep feelings about their bodies remain shrouded for most women. Even when they are a core issue, they are rarely shared with therapists of many years.

Although treatment takes place in a group, I do not view it as group therapy. The group serves primarily as a source of support rather than as an interpersonal laboratory. The original research was designed to factor out the effects of my leadership and of the group, so that I could measure the effect of the imaginal intervention itself. I led the exercises, but did not facilitate the processing of any material that was elicited. After each exercise, participants processed their own material through journals with focusing questions. With the exception of introductions, and conversation before group sessions, there was no group interaction at all.

In current groups, I still entrust the major processing to journal work, remaining available to facilitate when a client encounters a blind spot or intense feeling that needs working through. The group sharing that follows each exercise provides opportunities to place individual issues in a larger shared context, and to have individual pain and discoveries witnessed. In hearing each other's stories, participants can glimpse the tragic proportions of this self-torture extrapolated to the greater society of women . Awareness of waste often arouses anger at the system that drives body hatred—an anger I encourage as fuel for political challenge. Group members often say how important it is to see that attractive women (i.e., all other members of the group) also struggle with their bodies, and that physical attractiveness confers no immunity against body obsession. This realization reinforces the premise that their attitudes are what need to be changed, not their physical bodies.

Heightening Awareness of Body Issues

Although the entire process maintains a tenacious focus on body issues over many weeks, the first two sessions help define the terrain. Exercises in sensory awareness reveal size distortions, indicate where emotions are held in the body, and show how body tension patterns reflect and affect experience. This is done on a visual level through mirror exercises performed in the imagination; on an auditory level by listening to and identifying negative body/self-talk; and on a symbolic level by exploring images and metaphors that represent issues to be overcome and directions for change.

Exploring the Roots of Body Issues

I operate from the assumption that negative body image has been learned, and can therefore be unlearned and replaced with new learning. This phase of the treatment spans several weeks; it involves uncovering and peeling away attitudes that have been internalized in the course of development, and placing them in the larger sociocultural context. Personal history is explored through experiential exercises designed to expose and work through the sources of faulty learning and injury to the body image. Included in this section are exercises involving age regression; imaginal investigation of family role modeling and interactions with parents and significant others; and rewriting of key psychohistorical events. The awareness and insights that these exercises often evoke tend to be visceral rather than intellectual. They articulate the injuries and begin a process of differentiation from the sources of faulty learning. In an age regression, one of my subjects had the following realization:

> Looking at my mother closely I realize how I didn't look at her closely. I like her body (a first time realization). Part of liking her body engenders in me feelings that my body's not good enough. I wish she would reach out to me—I wish she could like herself—maybe like me. She is distant. I had a sudden flash of my mother washing me in the tub—with a sense of dislike on her part—moving my hand away from my vulva. Feeling like my body was a thing—and not a good thing—to her. I also felt that my chunkiness, physical slowness was awful compared to her slimness and agility. . . . I feel . . . her ridicule of my body. . . . I feel much of my life I've continued to treat my bodyself the way she has treated me. (Sankowsky, 1981, pp. 128–129)

The following is a transcript of an exercise, "Rewriting History," that is designed not only to identify personal historical experiences that contributed to faulty learning about the body/self, but also to afford an opportunity to heal old wounds that live on in a negative body image.

Rewriting History

1. Sit comfortably, close your eyes, and relax by paying attention to your breathing (relaxation induction).

2. Imagine that you are in a comfortable room with a soft, cushy couch. Sit down on the couch and make yourself comfortable. . . .

3. You will notice, as you look over to your right, that near you is a side table on which there is a photo album. Pick up the photo album and place it on your lap. . . . Notice that it is the photo album that documents your life. . . .

4. Somewhere in the past you made a decision to adopt a negative body image. There was a time—even if it was brief—when your body image was "clean" and clear of negativity. A time before you learned that there was something wrong with the way you look or the way you are. A time before you *learned* to devalue your body.

The way you are in relation to your body is something that has been learned, and is something that can be unlearned. The decisions you make about yourself as a result of this learning shape your attitudes about yourself and about life, and also shape your behavior.

It's important to go back into your history to ferret out the decisions you made at earlier times—decisions about your body and its acceptability. Maybe there was one major decision. More likely there were many small decisions. (For some of you the decision that your body was not OK came very early when, as an infant or toddler, you learned from the way your mother and father touched or looked at you; for others the lessons were learned later, through teasing, criticism, abuse, over-involvement, or neglect—either from family or peers; still others of you learned lessons when your body collided with religious, or educational, or media expectations in the world around you.) The events of your life have left psychic scars that mar your relationship with your body today. I'm going to lead you back in time in search of one experience where you learned to feel negatively about your body, so that you have another chance to write your body history so that the outcome is more positive for you.

5. In your present relationship with your body, what is the nature of the negative feelings you feel? (Shame, contempt, inadequacy, a sense of misfitting, what? . . .)

6. Flip through your photo album, looking for a photo of you at a time in the past when negativity had already crept into your relationship with your body. . . . Find a photograph that captures a time that was particularly painful and shaming for you. Perhaps it was when you actually learned to feel bad about your body. . . . Take some time to do this now. . . .

Step into the photo that you have chosen. Actually identify with this younger you. . . . *Feel* what it is like to be in this younger version of you. . . . *Be aware* of the feelings you have about your body. . . . *Experience* the world that you were living in. . .

7. *Scan* that time of your life in search of a single incident that was damaging to your feelings about your body/self or of a type of situation that happened frequently to you. . . . When you find an appropriate memory image, mentally place it in your nondominant hand, which will now serve as the repository for this old negative memory. . . . As we go along, when you need to bring up the feelings of this memory, all you will have to do is to squeeze this hand and this memory will come back to you.

8. In a moment you will squeeze your hand and bring the memory into focus. You will let the adult *observing you* stand off to the side as if you were watching a movie. . . . You are about to watch a scene in which the younger you received a clear negative message about yourself that has shaped the way you relate to your body. . . .

9. Now squeeze your hand and *watch* calmly as the memory image unfolds, letting there be some objective distance between you and the memory scene that unfolds. . . .

As you watch the movie, notice how old you were . . . where you are . . . what you are wearing . . . who is there with you. . . . What is happening? . . . Who says what to whom? . . . How is the younger you reacting? . . . Watch carefully now as the details of the memory image unfold, so that you can grasp all the important details. . . .

10. One at a time, identify with and enter into the experience of the other significant players in the scene. . . . Experience how they see it. . . . Try to find out as much as you can about those aspects of the situation that the younger you did not and could not understand at that time. . . .

11. As the adult you, reflect on the negative messages the younger you is receiving here. . . . What are the self-defeating lessons the younger you is taking in from this incident? . . . In this scene you are learning to make a particular decision about your body/self or about yourself in relation to the world. What is the decision you are making? . . .

12. Let yourself become aware of the feelings that the younger you is experiencing deep inside as a result of this experience. . . .

Let yourself get in touch with the feelings that you as an adult are having right now for the younger you. . . . Allow your heart to reach out to the younger you. . . . *(long pause)* . . . How can you reach out physically to your child? . . . Can you touch or hold or hug her? . . . Can you hold her lovingly in your gaze? . . . Move into the memory image, and make some contact so that the younger you feels that you are really there with her for her support. . . . Do it now, as vividly as you can, using as many of your imaginal senses as you can summon to the experience. . . . *(long pause)*

13. You were younger then. You are older and wiser now, and have many more resources available to you than you did then when this happened—a whole arsenal of resources. You have lived more years, have more skills, and have more maturity and wisdom that you didn't have then—you have a wealth of responses and perspectives now that you didn't have then.

14. Is there some new way that you can help the younger you to see, think, or feel about this incident, so that the outcome of this scene might have been different? . . . So that your relationship to your body might have turned out differently? . . .

If you could have had any attitude or response *then* that you are capable of *now*, what would it be? . . . Would you have needed to trust yourself more? . . . to understand why people act the way they do? . . . to be more assertive? . . . less sensitive? . . . Did you need permission to express your feelings more? . . . to reach out for support? . . . to walk away? . . . to see the humor in it? . . . to be more forgiving? . . .

15. When you are clear about the new resource you want to introduce to this memory image, think about a recent time you exercised this quality or skill or response? It doesn't have to be in relation to your body; it can be in any area of your life. . . . Find a really good example of a time when you manifested it. . . . (If you can't find a real example, make one up, but make it vivid and lifelike.) . . .

Take some time to experience this recent memory image as vividly as you can. Feel what you felt. See what you saw. Hear what you heard. Engage as many of your imaginal senses as you can. . . . Now transfer all of the positive feelings of exercising this resource into your dominant hand, and imagine the feelings concentrating into a palpable ball of energy that you can see, and feel in your hand. . . . Give it a color.

16. You know what the younger you needs to know and needs to hear from you right now. . . . Focus on the ball of color in your dominant hand. . . . Take her dominant hand in your dominant hand, and let these positive feelings transfer from your hand to her hand. . . . As you do, take some time now to communicate this warm wisdom to her, so that she can respond differently and turn the situation around. . . .

17. Now squeeze your nondominant hand—the repository of the old negative memory image—and switch back into the past to the negative memory. . . . Really feel those feelings. . . . Imagine the feelings as a palpable ball of negative energy that you can see and feel in your hand. . . . Give it a color.

18. Now slowly shift your attention back and forth between the two images, by alternately squeezing your right and left hands, bringing up the feelings and memories of each scene as you do. . . .

19. Hold both hands in front of you, becoming very aware of the two different-colored energy balls in your hands. . . .

In a moment you are going to rewrite your history, by replaying your original childhood scene but with a difference—by introducing your new resource into it, so that this scene becomes a model for dealing with situations like it . . . in a way that leaves the younger you feeling good. . . .

20. Clasp both hands together, and as the two balls of color merge, experience the original scene—*be in it*—again, as it plays out in a totally different and positive manner.

21. When the scene is completed, put both hands down.

22. Now imagine a situation in the near future where you can exercise your redecision that you are OK—where you can behave in a new and satisfying way because of your new attitude.

Exploring Blockages and Resistance to Change

Changing body image is not easy. Although body struggles are painful and limiting, the resistance to letting them go can be very powerful. I continue to be astounded by the tenacity with which most women hold on to destructive programming. One exercise explores negative body image issues as a form of imprisonment in which we limit ourselves with our beliefs about our bodies. Participants are asked to identify the way their self-limitation feels, and to represent their felt experience with an image or metaphor of entrapment. Exploring the trap symbolically reveals many things: aspects of the self that have been repressed or inhibited, the inhibitory forces (internal and external), the barriers to freedom, and the secondary gains of imprisonment. In the end, participants are asked to attempt an imaginal escape from their prison, thereby exploring on a metaphorical level the route to freedom.

Another exercise, which usually takes three or four sessions, is designed to heighten awareness of negative self-talk by embodying it in the form of inner saboteurs—subpersonalities that operate self-destructively out of the field of awareness. These saboteurs serve a defensive function, but one that is outdated and has destructive consequences of its own. Participants choose three from a menu of saboteurs: Critic/Perfectionist, Rebel, Overprotector, Pleaser, Victim, and Pusher/Driver. Working with the negative inner voices of saboteurs provides an opportunity to explore cognitive errors in very concrete form—to reduce vague and global inner noise to manageable inner "characters" with whom one can talk and negotiate. Participants process their imaginal experience through journal questions, drawing, and group sharing. In large groups, it is fruitful to process with other participants, grouped according to saboteur.

The ultimate objectives of working with resistance are to identify the functions that the defenses serve, to expose secondary gains, and to find more functional ways of addressing these needs. As one woman described her experience with her version of the Overprotector:

> The other part of myself that I meet with is "the Crusher"—who tries to squash me, hold me in, tone me down. She paces the floor, throws up her hands, rants about danger and not knowing what will happen, the need to be careful, to hide. I rub her back and tell her that I hear her concerns . . . but I will not go back to that old way . . . that I want more pleasure and joy in my life. But I hear the need for safety and together we can work out

other ways to meet it. I decide that I can embrace the fear and be at peace with it. I can say "no" to other people and new experiences if I wish without a *good reason*. I can hide occasionally as a resting place. I tell "the Crusher" that she can depend on me . . . and though she is wary, I think she'll take a chance. (Sankowsky, 1981, p. 135)

In explorations of resistance, some issues frequently come up. Many of us assume that it is only by hating our bodies that we keep control over them. To like our bodies is to lose control and get fat. Negative body attitudes are frequently used as an excuse not to express ourselves, protecting against both success and failure. If we were to like our selves and our bodies, we fear that we would have *no choice* but to be sexual, powerful, successful, and so on, all of which involve some degree of risk. Body issues are also used to stake boundaries and say "no."

As women, we seek connection over separation. We experience our body negativity as a requirement for membership in the "club" of female gender. We fear that if we feel pride in ourselves, we will experience isolation, envy, or the negative judgment of our peers, threatening the loss of that membership. Our perceived body imperfections humanize us and and act as a leveling agent that gives us permission to succeed in other areas of our lives that are not so central to the female identity in this culture.

Finally, there is fear of the vacuum that would be left if negative body attitudes were eliminated. Many of us have built our identities around the struggle between our selves and bodies. Letting go of negative body attitudes threatens the very foundation of how we see ourselves and construct our lives.

Re-Embodiment

Central to negative body image is a dissociation between self and body, in which the body becomes an object to criticize, torture, starve, and perfect. To heal this split, there must be re-embodiment work that directly engages the physical body. Movement, primarily the Feldenkrais Method of neuromuscular re-education, reconnects us with our bodies (Feldenkrais, 1977; Zemach-Bersin & Reese, 1990). In work with groups, I use only *Awareness through Movement* (Feldenkrais, 1977)—verbally guided group movements. The method also has a hands-on form, "Functional Integration," used in individual lessons with a private teacher. In the absence of a trained teacher, there are many excellent taped series available to the public (see the list of resources following the References section).

The Feldenkrais Method is a unique psychophysical approach that uses movement exercises to retrain the nervous system, enhancing body image and promoting embodiment. It was developed by Moshe Feldenkrais, a physicist, judo expert, and Renaissance man who applied his biomechanical genius to developing thousands of mindful and gentle sequences that pose unusual and challenging movement problems, which can only be solved from inside by connecting with one's subjective body experience. Some lessons recapitulate early developmental movements (rolling over, rocking, and crawling), and thus connect some individuals to early body memories. Other lessons involve relearning how to perform ordinary functional movements (lying to sitting, sitting to standing, walking), in order to enhance ease and grace in daily movements. Some lessons are simply opportunities to become attuned to one's body.

Although almost any body-oriented work is helpful, Feldenkrais movement is especially well suited to reintroducing women to their disowned bodies in a nonjudgmental way. Feldenkrais exercises hone body awareness exquisitely, providing participants with a means to feel grounded in their bodies and to develop respect for the integrity of their bodies. In contrast to many movement approaches based on imitation of "correct" form, Feldenkrais movements instead lead participants through a process of internal discovery of what is correct, based on their bodies' unique design. Participants experience harmonious cooperation between body parts, as well as a sense of lightness and grace, regardless of their size, shape, or level of functioning.

CONCLUSION

Making peace with our bodies involves several accomplishments: holding clearly in mind the image of mental and physical health that we wish for ourselves; refusing to allow ourselves to be tyrannized by the idealized cultural images of women; clearing away the social and emotional debris that obstructs a clear vision of the beauty of our selves; establishing measures of success that have nothing to do with thinness or body perfection; ending the compulsive style of starvation, chronic restraint, and dieting and bingeing; and relearning how to eat in a nurturing and pleasurable way. In sum, we must stop harming, deforming, and starving our female bodies, and begin instead to celebrate them.

Instead of helping our female clients change their bodies so they can feel good about themselves, we must help them feel good about themselves and their bodies *first*. It is important that the drive for change come from true self-caring, and not from the self-contempt and desperation that usually fuel our efforts at "self-improvement."

Transforming our body images requires both inner and outer work. Imagery challenges the inner part, but we must collectively challenge the myths that dominate our culture (Wolf, 1991). Our new eyes must begin to conceptualize beauty norms that are more flexible—that can expand to embrace women of many shapes, sizes, ages, colors, and ethnicities: some gloriously curvaceous, others mighty and muscular, a few pencil-slim.

Together we must demand the responsible use of the power that the media manipulators use for profit at our expense. We must exercise the power of the purse, write letters, boycott products, and refuse to "buy" images that keep us from accepting ourselves as we are. This is a political issue, and for many women healing cannot occur without political involvement. On a daily level, we can refuse to participate in conversations about dieting. Instead, we can share with women friends the pain that comes from our body shame, bringing it out from the realm of private agony and into that of collective pain. We can stop announcing the numbers on the scale, and stop complimenting other women for their conformity to the media's ideal. Instead, we must pay attention to and reward the evidence of our humanity.

So what does it mean to have a healthy body image? As we embrace a new notion of beauty, we will enjoy our bodies, their roundness, curves, lines, and planes—and their unique idiosyncrasies. We will revel in our bodies' strength and femaleness. We will eat in a way that nourishes us, and that honors the signals and needs of our bodies. We will exercise in order to increase energy and manage stress rather than to shrink size. We will explore physical movement in order to feel more fully alive and embodied. We will dress comfortably in colors and fashions that enhance our unique endowments, and will avoid clothing that binds or confines us. We will feel and be beautiful because we know, enjoy, and accept ourselves as we are now. We will choose to be who we are rather than conform to a contrived formula for feminine beauty. As we reclaim our right to self-definition, creating our own standards for health and beauty, we will enjoy the most beautiful state of all.

As women, we are fighting against our flesh when we should be fighting for a livable environment, equal rights, and world peace. The state of our relationship to nature and to our planetary home mirrors the relationship we have to our bodily homes: Both the earth and our bodies are seen as something to be controlled, mastered, exploited. The duality between maleness/mind and femaleness/body permeates every aspect of our culture and our values. This split hurts all of us—women and men alike. At this fragile time in our history, it is critically important for women, men, and society to reconnect with values that are called "feminine"—nurturance, compassion, a sense of relationship and context, and a vision of the impact of our behaviors on future generations. If we could honor these qualities, and the female bodies that often contain them, we could go a long way toward creating and sustaining a peaceful world.

REFERENCES

Cash, T. F., & Pruzinsky, T. (Eds.). (1990). *Body images: Development, deviance, and change*. New York: Guilford Press.

Feldenkrais, M. (1977). *Awareness through movement: Health exercises for personal growth*. New York: Harper & Row.

Fisher, S., & Cleveland, S. E. (1972). *Body image and personality*. New York: Dover.

Freedman, R. (1989). *Body love*. New York: Harper & Row.

Freud, S. (1961). *The ego and the id*. London: Hogarth Press. (Originally published 1923)

Hutchinson, M. G. (1985). *Transforming body image: Learning to love the body you have*. Freedom, CA: Crossing Press.

Jourard, S., & Secord, P. F. (1955a). Body-cathexis and the ideal female figure. *Journal of Abnormal and Social Psychology, 50*, 243–246.

Jourard, S., & Secord, P. F. (1955b). Body-cathexis and personality. *British Journal of Psychology, 46*, 130–138.

Kearney-Cooke, A. (1989). Reclaiming the body: Using guided imagery in the treatment of body image disturbance among bulimic women. In L. M. Hornyak & E. K. Baker (Eds.), *Experiential therapies for eating disorders*. New York: Guilford Press.

Kearney-Cooke, A. (1991). The role of the therapist in the treatment of eating disorders: A feminist psychodynamic approach. In C. L. Johnson (Ed.), *Psychodynamic treatment of* New York: Guilford Press.

Krueger, D. (1989). *Body self and psychological self*. New York: Brunner/Mazel.

Pratkanis, A., & Aronson, E. (1991). *Age of propaganda: The everyday use and abuse of persuasion*. New York: W. H. Freeman.

Sankowsky, M. H. [Hutchinson, M. G.] (1981). *The effect of a treatment based on the use of guided visuo-kinesthetic imagery on the alteration of negative body-cathexis in women*. Unpublished doctoral dissertation, Boston University.

Thompson, J. K. (1990). *Body image disturbance: Assessment and treatment*. Elmsford, NY: Pergamon Press.

Wolf, N. (1991). *The beauty myth: How images of beauty are used against women*. New York: Morrow.

Wooley, S. C., & Kearney-Cooke, A. (1986). Intensive treatment of bulimia and body-image disturbance. In K. D. Brownell & J. P. Foreyt (Eds.), *Handbook of eating disorders: Physiology, psychology, and treatment of obesity, anorexia, and bulimia*. New York: Basic Books.

Zemach-Bersin, D., & Reese, M. (1990). *Relaxercise*. San Francisco: Harper.

Feldenkrais Method Resources

International Practitioner Directory: The Feldenkrais Guild, 524 Ellsworth St. P.O. Box 489, Albany, OR 97321-0143.

Books and movement tapes: Feldenkrais Resources, P.O. Box 2067, Berkeley, CA 94702.

III

TREATMENT ISSUES:
A FEMINIST REANALYSIS

9

Sexual Abuse and Eating Disorders: The Concealed Debate

SUSAN C. WOOLEY

N O ISSUE HAS SO THREATENED to divide our field as the largely concealed debate on the importance of sexual abuse in understanding and treating eating disorders. A gender effect, in which predominantly female patients more often disclose histories of abuse to female than to male therapists, has caused men and women to work from increasingly divergent experience bases; this has created differences in perspective that we have yet to reconcile. That the unmasking of sexual abuse has different emotional meanings for women and men only furthers the division, for beneath the explicit content of debate lie layers of meaning, saturated with the history of gender politics.

More than other fields, the eating disorders field seems arrested in the effort to integrate new findings on sexual abuse—to make an adequate place for them in theory and treatment models. We seem locked in a discourse that, despite shifting players and locales, has become perseverative. It is difficult to document the debate, because it has taken place less in journals, books, and meeting rooms than in convention corridors, hotel rooms, private meetings, and anonymous manuscript reviews. Although there is a public component of the debate, it is largely ritualistic and symbolic, signaling more than it actually reveals. Over the years I have formed an impression of this debate. I have become convinced that our failure to reach consensus, or even to bring the issues into open discussion, has encouraged a destructive polarization that grows larger as it covertly informs professional alliances and distorts the meaning of discussions of even intrinsically neutral topics.

It is difficult to define membership in the debate, since any formula ignores important exceptions. Although the division falls primarily along gender lines, a number of dichotomies are involved. These include research versus clinical orientation; a reliance on medical versus sociocultural models of disease; technical versus humanistic therapy approaches; and apolitical versus feminist analysis. One side of the debate is anchored by male researchers for whom eating disorders represent a medical subspecialty; the other side is anchored by female clinicians for whom eating disorders represent a topic in the psychology of women. These designations locate many people in intermediate positions, and indeed I think there does exist a middle ground; however, it is notably silent, as though its members wish to avoid being caught in the crossfire. Although I speak hereafter of men's and women's views, I do so in the recognition that this is an oversimplification.

Debate usually implies approximately equally involved groups of participants. In a perhaps predictable expression of parallel process, this debate is asymmetrical. Although its issues gnaw at both women and men, men's emotional involvement is generally less. Women feel identified with the victims whose interests they advocate, and, like the victims, they carry strong feelings rarely expressed to those regarded (correctly or incorrectly) as adversaries. Some men may be unaware that they have been targeted as opponents in a battle that they barely know exists. Identification with largely male abuse perpetrators can encourage men toward denial and avowed ignorance.

To name this growing division is to risk being accused of creating it. But it is not going to go away, and, like any family secret, it becomes more pathogenic the longer it is ignored. It is time to confront the division, so that we can prevent further destructive polarization, both for the sake of our individual patients and because our actions have a broad import. History is giving our field a second chance to respond to the unmasking of sexual abuse. The first response, by Freud and others of his generation, spawned a construction of the human psyche that was distorted by the exclusion of critical data; this construction continues to inform an entire culture. Our generation has the power to influence not only the way in which particular illnesses are defined, but the understanding of gender that we bequeath to our children. The psychology of women is being persuasively reformulated in many quarters. It would be ironic if our field, which deals with clearly gender-linked and culture-bound phenomena, should fail to contribute to this transformative cultural undertaking.

In this chapter, the explicit and implicit content of the debate is examined, followed by an attempt to clarify some of the issues, to suggest possible areas of agreement, and to explore the larger cultural meanings of our acts. The social embeddedness of theory and epistemology in social science makes even empiricism a form of social action. I regard our field's struggle as a largely inevitable mirroring of a broader struggle to shift the narrative center of the story known as humanity, in order to accommodate the perspective of women.

THE TERMS OF DEBATE

The debate as it is now constituted—sometimes explicit, more often (as the chapter title indicates) covert—centers around the following themes. Female therapists believe that they know more about sexual abuse than most men, because patients have confided in them more and because, as women, many have shared certain features of their patients' experience. Female therapists also believe that they are more concerned about abuse. They perceive their male colleagues as having been, in turn, uninterested, incredulous, and (more recently) fixated upon a line of research whose real purpose seems to be only to discredit women's hypotheses. They note that discussions of abuse by women at major conferences were long consigned to small workshop sessions rarely attended by men; however, when the subject could no longer be ignored, women were replaced at the podium by men, effectively dictating the kind of attention the topic received. Recent major talks have reflected what many women now regard as the sole and obsessive focus of male colleagues: the comparative prevalence of sexual abuse in different groups. This topic has been discussed to the continuing exclusion of such others as the therapeutic conditions required for disclosure, treatment for the sequelae of abuse, and the cultural implications of these discoveries. Women have experienced these events as a replication of social powerlessness, and have become increasingly disaffected from the mainstream of the field. Growing interest in feminist writings and conferences expresses many women's sense that their interests are not understood or addressed by men.

For their part, men perceive women as having abandoned the scientific method in their fervor to call attention to abuse. They question the accuracy of prevalence rates based on patients' self-reports without confirmatory data. They believe that women have concluded prematurely and capriciously that sexual victimization causes eating disorders; they cite the absence of evidence that rates of abuse among eating-disordered women differ from rates observed in other clinical populations or even in normal controls. They hear in women's passionate concern with abuse an implicit accusation that men are to blame for eating disorders and are thus unlikely to be part of the solution. Along with some women, they fear the popularization of this subject encourages patients to invent or overemphasize abuse histories, and are concerned that a seemingly endless list of common or equivocal symptoms and signs passes for evidence that abuse has occurred. Some fear a recreation of the climate of McCarthyism, in which innocent men and their families are destroyed by unfounded accusations stemming from unscientific appraisals of abuse reports. Men are baffled and dismayed when attempts to respond to women's concerns by "studying" abuse are dismissed as insensitive and sexist.

Sexual abuse is one of the most loaded issues our society will ever have to face, largely because it is tied to the history of gender roles. Although girls and women do perpetrate sexual abuse, the great majority of perpetrators are male; although boys and men are victimized, the majority of victims are female (Finkelhor, 1984). To women, male power is the fundamental substrate from which sexual abuse grows and in which its existence has historically been tolerated and concealed. That this is an overgeneralization should not blind us to its massive core of truth: Had women wielded greater physical, economic, and political power, there would almost certainly have been less sexual abuse. Discussion of sexual abuse quickly puts women in touch with a lifetime of inchoate rage over social inequities of which sexual abuse is but an emblem—enormously important in its own right, but of a piece with the cultural milieu in which it has flourished.

Understandably, men feel threatened by this rage and are usually quick to distance themselves from abusers—a response that, rather than calming women, often angers them further. Women do not want men to cordon off and deny the abusers in themselves, either individually or collectively; they know that until men explore this part of themselves, abuse will continue. Furthermore, all of us will be denied the chance to understand the crucial features of male psychology that encourage abuse, and will be hindered in the necessary collaborative work of changing the way we parent and revising the cultural models of manhood offered to boys. Instead, women hope that more men will follow the lead of a courageous few, performing a self-examination similar to that performed by women, who have been unable to ignore their similarities to the women they treat (see S. Wooley, Chapter 16, this volume).

As lifelong victims of abuses of power, both large and small, women may be better able than men to contain the paradox of the good–bad male. Women understand, perhaps better than men, the constraints of male upbringing that encourage men to seize what is too shameful to request; to confuse sexuality and intimacy; and to make dominance an essential component of male identity. Women do not want to see more people hurt, but most stand poised to work at the side of men committed to altering destructive and sometimes deadly gender socialization processes. Until men understand this, there can be no real dialogue, because men dare not use the essential tools of introspection and empathy; they are forced instead to deny, project, and disavow the feelings they need most to explore.

Perhaps we can approach the issue of abuse anew. We will be debating numbers for years to come, but there are many important points on which we could agree.

CLINICAL OBSERVATIONS ARE A VALID SOURCE OF DATA

The first reports on sexual abuse and eating disorders were based on case descriptions and observations from clinical series. The findings were, by and large, dismissed because they were not drawn from controlled studies. Yet many of the seminal writings in the field were tallies of the self-reported behaviors and experiences of patients in treatment series (e.g., Kay & Leigh, 1954; King, 1963; Crisp, 1965, 1967; Ziegler & Sours, 1968; Theander, 1970; Halmi, 1974; Morgan & Russell, 1975; Kalucy, Crisp, & Harding, 1977; Russell, 1979; Casper, Eckert, Halmi, Goldberg, & Davis, 1980; Pyle, Mitchell, & Eckert, 1981; Mitchell, Pyle, & Eckert, 1981; Garfinkel & Garner, 1982; Lacey, 1982; Fairburn, 1984).

We were made familiar with most of the key phenomena of eating disorders through such data bases. It is how we learned about the core symptoms: the drive for thinness (Ziegler & Sours, 1968; Bruch, 1973; Crisp, 1967; Theander, 1970); the denial of hunger and the concealment of low food intake (Kay & Leigh, 1954; Mayer, 1963; Crisp, 1965, 1967; Bruch, 1970); the secret rituals of bingeing and vomiting (Russell, 1979; Palmer, 1979; Mitchell et al., 1981); and the extraordinary bouts of exercise (Gull, 1874/1964; Mayer, 1963; Crisp, 1967; Halmi, 1974; Garfinkel & Garner, 1982). It is how we learned the phenomenology of eating disorders: the euphoria that accompanies restriction (Lasegue, 1873/1964; King, 1963; Dally, 1969; Bruch, 1973); the dreaded "bloat" that follows eating (Crisp, 1965; Morgan & Russell, 1975; Garfinkel & Garner, 1982); the preoccupation with food (Crisp, 1965; Beumont, George, & Smart, 1976; Russell, 1979; Garfinkel & Garner, 1982); and the fantasied layers of body fat (Mayer, 1963; Bruch, 1973).

Such series also introduced us to symptoms that sometimes accompany eating disorders: disturbed moods (King, 1963; Theander, 1970; Halmi, 1974; Russell, 1979; Casper et al., 1980; Lacey, 1982; Fairburn,

1984); alcohol and drug use (Crisp, 1967; Lacey, 1982; Pyle et al., 1981; Lacey, 1982); stealing (Crisp, Hsu, & Harding, 1980; Casper et al., 1980; Wooley & Wooley, 1981; Pyle et al., 1981; Garfinkel & Garner, 1982); promiscuity (Crisp, 1967; Beumont et al., 1976; Lacey, 1982); and self-mutilation (Rosenthal, Rinzler, Wallsh, & Klausner, 1972; Russell, 1979; Garfinkel & Garner, 1982), to name but a few. Similarly, we gained strong impressions of important psychodynamic (Crisp, 1965; Bruch, 1973; Selvini Palazzoli, 1974; Bram, Eger, & Halmi, 1992), familial (Dally, 1969; Bruch, 1973; Sours, 1974; Selvini Palazzoli, 1974; Morgan & Russell, 1975; Kalucy et al., 1977; Minuchin, Rosman, & Baker, 1978; Root, Fallon, & Friedrich, 1986), and cultural (Halmi, 1974; Boskind-Lodahl, 1976; Bruch, 1978; Wooley & Wooley, 1980; Schwartz, Thompson, & Johnson, 1982; Garner, Garfinkel, Schwartz, & Thompson, 1980) influences in the development of eating disorders. Family typologies still in use today grew out of informal clinical observations, as did our picture of the cultural mandates for appearance and behavior with which eating-disordered women complied.

We did not label such reports unscientific because they did not involve comparisons with control groups. Nor did we demand, as we often have in the case of sexual abuse, independent evidence that patients' reports were true—that they had in fact binged and purged, stolen things, or injured themselves. Distressing as these discoveries were, they were consistent with prevailing cultural and psychological models of female psychopathology.

It is true that many of these reports were later followed up with controlled research. New ways to measure more precisely such symptoms as body dissatisfaction/striving for thinness (e.g., Secord & Jourard, 1953; Garner, Olmsted, & Polivy, 1983; Cooper, Taylor, Cooper, & Fairburn, 1987; Wooley & Roll, 1991); cognitive distortions (e.g., Phelan, 1987); and disturbed attitudes toward eating (e.g., Herman & Polivy, 1975; Garner & Garfinkel, 1979) made it possible to describe clinical populations more carefully. Reported features of eating disorders, such as poor impulse control and mood disturbances, were tested in controlled studies (Cooper & Fairburn, 1986; Bunnell, Shenker, Nussbaum, Jacobson, & Cooper, 1990; Elmore & Castro, 1990; Leon, Carroll, Chernyk, & Finn, 1985; Steere, Butler, & Cooper, 1990). The proposed effects of disturbed family functioning were examined (Kog & Vandereycken, 1985; Johnson & Flach, 1985; Strober & Humphrey, 1987; Humphrey, 1988, 1989; Waller, Slade, & Calam, 1990; Blouin, Zuro, & Blouin, 1990; Dolan, Lieberman, Evans, & Lacey, 1990). Numerous surveys compared the prevalence of disturbed eating behaviors and attitudes in clinical populations and in normal controls (see Johnson & Connors, 1987, for a review).

However, we understandably regarded much of this work as the mop-up: the validation of knowledge that was already well accepted by clinicians, for whom the consistency of observations had painted a convincing if "unproven" picture. Therapies were developed and advocated well in advance of such work. To give but one of many possible examples, the rationale for cognitive–behavioral theapy advanced by Garner and Bemis (1982) and Garfinkel and Garner (1982) in their influential early works consisted of two published reports describing four patients (Crisp & Fransella, 1972; Ben-Tovim, Hunter, & Crisp, 1977), their own informal observations, and an extrapolation of Bruch's (1973, 1977, 1978) clinical theories.

Why then were reports of sexual abuse in up to 60% of patients in series from reputable centers so slow to find their way into the field's specialized books and journals and into the body of accepted clinical knowledge? Why were female clinicians' presentations of such data so often met with hostile demands for proof that reports of abuse were accurate? These clinicians did not remember such questions being asked—and certainly not with such an emotional charge—about reports of vomiting, shoplifting, or maternal neglect and interference. Why was the importance of abuse said to depend on evidence that it was unique to eating-disordered women? After all, eating disorders themselves were widely held to represent a point on a continuum (Loeb, 1964; Nylander, 1971; Fries, 1977; Wooley & Wooley, 1980; Button & Whitehouse, 1981; Thompson, Berg, & Shatford, 1987; Prather & Williamson, 1988), and the drive for thinness—the core defining symptom—was said to be a "normative discontent" (e.g., Orbach, 1978; Wooley, Wooley, & Dyrenforth, 1979; Rodin, Silberstein, & Striegel-Moore, 1984).

One reason why reports of sexual abuse received such a chilly reception was that these reports were coming from only half of the professional population—females. To men, who had founded the field, this information had to come as an embarrassment and a shock. Understandably, it was held suspect. In their lauded 1982 volume, ably summarizing the state of the art, Garfinkel and Garner listed 17 predisposing, 5 precipitating, and 11 maintaining factors for eating disorders. Sexual abuse did not appear on any of these lists or anywhere else in the book, just as it did not appear in other analyses of that time period or in many that followed in subsequent years. Dominant thinking on the relationship between sexuality and anorexia nervosa in the early 1980s is reflected in the following quotation from Garfinkel and Garner (1982):

> Patients with anorexia nervosa lose all interest in sex. . . . When sexual experiences do occur they are usually not enjoyed. . . . Crisp (1970) has postulated that the central psychopathology underlying the "weight pho-

bia" relates to a basic avoidance of psychosexual maturity. . . . As Selvini
Palazzoli (1974) has observed, it is an oversimplificaton to insist that the
anorexic merely wants to revert to childhood. Rather she wishes to become an autonomous adult in a distorted sense—by rejecting those apsects
of the feminine body which, to her, signify potential problems. (pp. 8–9)

The relationship between sexuality and bulimia nervosa was described
by these authors as follows:

> Bulimic patients are sexually active but usually feel misused and are unable
> to enjoy sex. They often report that a feeling of being out of control
> sexually exacerbates the bulimia. As in their eating and other areas of
> self-control, they do not know "in-betweens" in sexual behavior. Moreov-
> er their moods are labile and they frequently feel out of control. They
> behave in harmful impulsive ways: For example, 19% of our bulimic
> patients had previously attempted suicide and 12% were involved in steal-
> ing. . . . We found that 7% . . . had previously engaged in self-mutilation.
> Several authors have also observed the association of self-mutilation, parti-
> cularly genital self-mutilation, with disturbances in eating. (p. 50)

In another section, Garfinkel and Garner cited the following perplexing
findings regarding bulimics:

> Crisp (1967) had observed previously that this group "rushed into one
> relationship after another . . . in the mistaken belief that they would then
> feel secure and wanted" (p. 128). He noted that their sexual relationships
> were frequently characterized by fellatio and that this was followed by
> vomiting. (p. 47)

In the same year that Garner and Garfinkel's (1982) book was
published, two other uncontrolled studies reported that a sexual challenge was the commonest precipitant of anorexia (Abraham & Beumont,
1982) and of bulimia (Lacey, 1982). In the first, all anorexic patients were
said to conform to one of four subtypes of sexual abnormality: avoidance, developmental retardation, passivity, or compulsive sexual behavior. In the second study, bulimics were divided into two major
subtypes: neurotics, characterized by failed sexual relationships and anger, usually toward a male partner or "men in general"; and a per-
sonality-disordered group prone to substance abuse, promiscuity, and in
some cases prostitution, of whom Lacey wrote:

> The humiliation or devaluation of the sexual partner seems to be part of a
> desperate attempt to deny feelings of dependence. So interrelated [are]
> bulimia and sexual activity in the minds of such patients that they may use

intercourse or masturbation as a means of thwarting a bulimic attack or, alternatively, gorging to sedation may be used to lower heightened sexual drive. (p. 64)

Without debating the scientific foundation of these many assertions, one would have imagined that adherents of these views would have found, in the discovery of sexual abuse histories in up to 60% of eating-disordered patients, a strikingly apt explanatory hypothesis regarding the disordered sexuality described above. Certainly the consistency with which female clinicians began to report their results should have lent such data the same provisional credibility accorded to dozens of prior clinical reports.

By 1989, when the first controlled studies appeared, eating disorders and sexual abuse had been linked in at least 17 published reports of cases or patient series (Oppenheimer, Howells, Palmer, & Chaloner, 1985; Wooley & Kearney-Cooke, 1986; Wooley & Wooley, 1986; Root et al., 1986; Wooley & Lewis, 1987; Sloan & Leichner, 1986; Schechter, Schwartz, & Greenfield, 1987; Goldfarb, 1987; Grace, Emans, & Woods, 1988; Kearney-Cooke, 1988b; Lucido & Abramson, 1988; Pyle, Perse, Mitchell, Saunders, & Skoog, 1988; Powers, Coovert, & Brightwell, 1988; McFarlane, McFarlane, & Gilchrest, 1988; Root & Fallon, 1988) and in countless presentations by women (our own staff alone gave more than 40), with no sign of assimilation into mainstream theorizing. Successive influential anthologies (Garner & Garfinkel, 1984; Brownell & Foreyt, 1986; and Johnson, 1991) reflected little integration of these findings. The first contained no discussion of abuse; the second, one (Wooley & Kearney-Cooke, 1986); and the third, three (Wooley, 1991; Humphrey, 1991; Kearney-Cooke, 1991), all by female authors. The words "sexual abuse" appeared in only three additional sentences in the remainder of these three books. In a curious reversal of the usual sequence, the first article on sexual abuse to be accepted for publication in the *International Journal of Eating Disorders* was entitled "Eating Disorders and Sexual Abuse: Lack of Confirmation for a Clinical Hypothesis" (Finn, Hartman, Liam, & Lawson, 1986).

Women who described treatment of sexual abuse at national conferences noticed that men often attacked the data, suggesting that reports were fabricated by patients, inflated by female therapists, and in any case irrelevant because sexual abuse was endemic. Women, burned by these hostile reactions and by frequent rejections of papers on their discoveries, became increasingly defensive about both their own and their female patients' credibility. They began to perceive men as the enemy of an undeniable truth: that sexual abuse figured prominently in the lives of many women with eating disorders, and often dominated the clinical picture as the gradual retrieval of traumatic memories led to panic attacks, confusion, disorganization, worsening of eating, and an array of self-destructive symptoms. By the time women might have been sharing the relief of seeing patients complete their terrifying passages, exorcised of their demons, they felt that no one cared. It began to seem that men *preferred* to think of eating disorders as the result of defective mothering, which remained the focus of most theoretical discussions.

In an influential volume, Johnson and Connors (1987) divided both anorexic and bulimic patients into "borderline" and "false-self" subtypes, to create four major groups. Although it has since been well documented that the vast majority of borderline patients have histories of sexual abuse (Herman, Perry, & van der Kolk, 1989; Zanarini, Gunderson, Marino, Schwartz, & Frankenburg, 1989; Westen, Rudolph, Misle, Ruffins, & Block, 1990; Brown & Anderson, 1991; Ogata, Silk, & Goodrich, 1992), these authors either found no evidence of abuse or considered it unimportant, instead identifying four subtypes of pathogenic mothering to account completely for the psychopathology of the borderline and false-self groups: benevolent and malevolent maternal intrusion, and benevolent and malevolent maternal neglect. Although sexual abuse was mentioned twice in this book, each time in a case history, only a single sentence on a small subgroup of "neurotic" patients suggested that the authors regarded abuse as an etiological factor in eating disorders: "Pursuit of thinness among this group often revolves around identity and achievement issues or it can be seen as a more transitory adaptation to trauma" (Johnson & Connors, 1987, p. 122).

And yet passages from this book evoke the spectre of abuse as hauntingly as those in Garfinkel and Garner's (1982) work. Of restricting borderlines, Johnson and Connors (1987) wrote:

> [These patients] are similar to paranoid state patients who develop elaborate defenses to protect themselves from a perceived threat. . . . Fat becomes a concrete symbol of a *feared feeling of hostile invasion and control*. It then becomes a paranoid object that has many distortions associated with it, including an attribution of volition (fat *has a mind of its own, goes where it is unwanted, will take over*. . . .) (pp. 106–107, emphasis added)

> [M]others of [anorexic] patients are domineering, intrusive, overprotective . . . and often *respond to the child according to their own needs rather than those of the child*. (p. 99, emphasis added)

Fathers received not a single mention in this scenario, nor in the discussion of bulimic borderline patients, in which the case to indict the mother became exceptionally strained:

[M]others of bulimic patients have been described as passive, rejecting, and disengaged. . . . It is important to emphasize that they usually are not blatantly neglectful caretakers; on the contrary, superficially they *appear to adequately attend to their child's primary needs.* The underinvolvement [is] more subtly manifested as a type of emotional unavailability. (pp. 100–101, emphasis added)

These patients often internalize the emotional unavailability . . . as evidence that they are *unlovable, worthless and deserving of punishment.* They will then *mutilate themselves in an effort to punish themselves,* with the body once again becoming a concrete representation of self. Interpersonally, they are *repeatedly involved in sadomasochistic relationships.* (p. 110, emphasis added)

The false-self adaptations described by Johnson and Connors also raise the possibility of abuse, emphasizing, as they do, parentification and ambivalence about dependency and/or intimacy. Anorexics in this category were described as "parent-pleasers" who "learn to freely accommodate themselves to others because they would be lost if the relationship were disrupted" (p. 115). Bulimics within the same group were said to have made "a unique adaptation to the maternal disengagement . . . by affecting a pseudomature adaptation," and by "prematurely taking responsibility for their own and often others' self regulation" (p. 119).[1]

Almost 10 years after female clinicians began describing the effects of sexual abuse on many of their eating–disordered patients, there is still resistance to including abuse among recognized risk factors or otherwise according it importance. Pope and Hudson's (1992) widely quoted but selective review seemed intent upon disproving an association between sexual abuse and eating disorders, dismissing five studies for failure to meet poorly defined inclusion criteria and ignoring others. The authors discredited studies supporting the sexual abuse hypothesis for a variety of curious reasons: that a control group selected for absence of psychiatric history of the subjects and their first-degree relatives was "supernormal"; that student controls probably enjoyed an immunity to sexual abuse; that reported abuse occurring after age 17 "likely . . . began after the onset of the eating disorder" (p. 456); that "only the broadest definition of sexual abuse revealed a significant difference" (p. 458); and that a reported 9% rate of abuse in a control group was implausibly low. They argued, however, that in a patient series that detected only a 7% rate of abuse it was unlikely that cases were missed, since, in subsequent psychotherapy with female therapists, no further cases came to light. Such a finding might, under different assumptions, have suggested that the 3-hour interviews—all performed by one male examiner who inquired into sexual abuse at the end—had effectively suppressed the disclosure of abuse.

Pope and Hudson (1992) concluded that the negative findings of their search were "even more impressive" in light of factors alleged to create a bias in the direction of positive results (p. 461). These included unconscious encouragement of abuse reports in patients by biased interviewers, and a tendency for patients exposed to the sexual abuse hypothesis to exaggerate or fabricate abuse in an "effort after meaning" (p. 461). Arguing in one paragraph that accurate reports of abuse depend on the existence of a sustained trusting relationship, and in the next paragraph that credible results require interviewers to be "blind," they effectively acknowledged the impossibility of proving to their satisfaction a link between sexual abuse and eating disorders—since both conditions obviously cannot be met at once. In the last paragraph, the authors suggested, "These conclusions should not be interpreted to mean that childhood sexual abuse is an unimportant issue in the therapy of bulimic patients" (p. 462); readers who *did* believe in its importance understood that they were being thrown a bone. Nowhere in the authors' numerous published works have they addressed the treatment of sexual abuse.

The discovery of the possible role of sexual abuse in the etiology and maintenance of eating disorders was not received as a welcome new avenue for understanding and helping affected women. It was received as a disruptive invasion of a well-ordered territory. Many women felt this and learned to talk about abuse only among themselves. In what might be considered a characteristically female response, growing out of the collective female experience, many gave up on communicating what they knew and retreated. But resentment was growing, and in many private conversations, men's words (or omissions) on this topic were carefully noted.

The hidden rift lent new meanings to previously innocuous works, as women therapists found their own sleep disrupted, their own minds invaded by intrusive thoughts in the "vicarious traumatization" (McCann & Pearlman, 1990) or "contact victimization" (Courtois, 1988) syndrome. Fairburn's (1984) suggestions, for example, took on a repressive tone to ears sensitized to the requirements for abuse disclosure. A chapter section entitled "Establishing a Sound Therapeutic Relationship" consisted of only two sentences, quoted below in their entirety:

> Considerable effort should be devoted to the establishment of an effective working relationship. However, while genuine interest and concern in the patient and her problems is important, the therapist should be capable of being firm and authoritative, particularly when discussing homework assignments. (p. 168)

The extraordinary anguish of abuse victims seemed more than trivialized by some of Fairburn's advice:

> Having taught the patient the principles of problem solving (and a didactic manner is perfectly appropriate), the therapist should ask the patient to practice problem solving as often as possible. . . . *She should be told that problem solving can be applied to any day-to-day difficulty, including mood disturbance.* . . . Many patients find that they can elevate their mood by listening to certain pieces of music, taking exercise, having a bath or shower, or changing into attractive clothes. (pp. 177–178, emphasis added)

And Fairburn's cautions against the possible dangers of exposure to feminist writings operated as an inadvertent allusion to well-known feminist texts on the history of patriarchal control in medicine.

> A minority of patients become particularly interested in the influence of sociocultural factors. They may be recommended books as *Fat Is a Feminist Issue* (Orbach, 1978) and *Womansize* (Chernin, 1983). However, they should be advised against following the advice contained in these books without first discussing the matter with the therapist. (p. 183)

Perhaps women would look back more charitably if attitudes had really changed in the intervening years. But they haven't. In the first keynote address on sexual abuse at the National Conference on Eating Disorders, Fairburn (1992) unveiled a new study of the comparative prevalence of abuse, concluding with regret that time did not permit discussion of the implications. Of approximately 400 presentations given at this conference over a period of 10 years, only 8 (or about 2%) have been devoted to sexual abuse. The first five of these were given by women (Kearney-Cooke, 1988a, 1991; McClintock, 1988; Powers, 1990; Boch, 1990). The last three, in 1992, all had a male as the sole or first-named presenter (Fairburn, 1992; Pyle, 1992; Johnson & Zerbe, 1992); however, the issues addressed in the last two offered some reason for encouragement.

The biennial International Conference on Eating Disorders has a similar history of inattention to abuse. There were no workshop or plenary presentations on sexual abuse from 1984 to 1990.[2] In 1990, 2 out of 144 scientific papers (Wonderlich, Donaldson, Staton, & Leach, 1990; Holyoak & Abramson, 1990), 1 out of 19 workshops (Enoch, Herman, & Walsh, 1990) and none of the 18 plenary talks concerned abuse. In 1992, the count was 1 of 144 scientific papers (Adler & Prendergast, 1992), 2 of 21 workshops (Weisberg & Herzog, 1992; Zerbe, 1992), and 1 of 19 plenary talks—not surprisingly, a prevalence study presented by a male-headed group (Wonderlich et al., 1992). But in 1990 and 1992 many female plenary speakers, though not invited to speak on sexual abuse, tried nonetheless, raising it as an issue in about half of the talks that they gave.

Many attendees of the 1992 International Conference experienced a particularly bewildering disappointment. In a plenary case presentation extraordinary for its eloquence and feeling, Strober (1992) described his treatment of an adolescent girl whose behavior cried out for investigation into possible abuse: sex with more than 50 partners in a year; participation in such sadomasochistic acts as penetration with a loaded revolver; and genital self-mutilation triggered by a fantasy of sexual contact with her dying mother. If sexual abuse is not the only way these acts can be explained (and, indeed, a coherent and humanistic alternative was offered), clearly it must be seriously considered. Failure by the presenter and first male discussant even to raise the possibility of abuse seemed all but designed to provoke women—an interpretation that gained credence when the single female discussant (Steiner-Adair, 1992) reported that she had asked about abuse in a preparatory phone conversation and had been told by the presenter that it was likely. At the same conference, only the sole female (myself—Wooley, 1992b) on a five-member plenary panel entitled, "How Are We Doing? Restrospective/Perspective," discussed sexual abuse with respect to either the history of the field or its anticipated future.

"Brain trust"-type consensus conferences appear to have fared no better. DeAngelis's (1990) report of a Kent State Applied Psychology Center conference on individual, familial, and sociocultural aspects of bulimia, attended by 11 experts, contains no mention of sexual abuse. The forum concept of the conference was reportedly developed because the center's director had observed, "What's really stimulating at conferences is the 5 minutes between sessions." They were apparently less successful in capturing the discourse of women than of men. Similarly, a 1991 Seattle conference bringing together a large group of invited experts from North America included only one paper on sexual abuse—a review of prevalence studies (de Groot, 1991). Finally, in an isolated but noteworthy paper, British researcher Derek Scott (1987) reviewed the role of psychosexual factors in the causation of eating disorders. Abuse was not mentioned at all; despite conflicting data, he reached this strange conclusion: "Having examined various notions concerning psychosexual factors playing causative roles in the etiology of eating disorders, it may be concluded that the majority of these are 'red herrings,' at least insofar as females are concerned" (p. 211).

The clinical observations of women and the small number of men who have worked in this area need to be taken seriously, as does their decade of experience in treating abuse. It is not men's fault that female patients have concealed abuse from them, but it is not the fault of female therapists either—and even less the fault of their patients. We should recall that abuse was concealed from therapists of both genders for almost a century after Freud recanted his early views. But men *are* at fault in holding up a double standard for science: Observations made by them have been taken for fact, while reports of female clinicians have been dismissed as fabrication, gullibility, or gossip. Patients are the hostages in this war of the sexes. Men owe women an apology. When women get it, they should accept it and move on.

THE DEBATE ABOUT CAUSALITY IS SPECIOUS

The major argument used to define much that women have asserted about abuse as unscientific and irrelevant is that abuse has not been proven to cause eating disorders—a claim that, in fact, female clinicians and researchers have generally been careful not to make (e.g., see Root & Fallon, 1988; Kearney-Cooke, 1988b). This argument is based in turn on the claim that sexual abuse has not been shown to be more common among eating-disordered women than among women with other psychological disorders or among women in the general population. As already noted, the same criticism might be applied to many proposed etiological factors; more to the point, however, these arguments do not stand the test of logic. The fact that sexual abuse is as or more likely to result in chemical dependency, depression, or borderline symptoms no more proves that it does not cause eating disorders than the fact that smoking causes heart arrhythmias and bronchitis proves that it does not cause lung cancer.

In dealing with causes that produce a given effect in only some instances, it is customary to speak of "risk factors." This does not mean that a particular variable is not a cause, as most of us understand this word; it only means that at the levels in question it is not a sufficient cause, and that it may not be a necessary one. In most instances, it suggests that there are mediating factors that elude us. Smoking presumably produces lung cancer in some but not all smokers because the impact of smoking is blocked in some individuals (e.g., by a genetic or other immunity); additive (e.g., with other lung irritants or carcinogens); dose-dependent in ways that have escaped measurement (e.g., depth of inhalation); or obscured (e.g., by death from other causes before lung cancer develops or is detected). But the relationship is real. Whatever language we use, smoking can apparently produce lung cancer through a series of understandable physical influences on physical processes. In the same way, it appears that sexual abuse often (though not always) produces an eating disorder through a series of comparably well-understood psychological influences on psychological processes. Recent evidence further suggests that abuse may also lastingly alter certain neurotransmitter systems (van der Kolk, 1988), which, as Wonderlich et al. (1992) have noted, are known to be involved in the regulation of eating behavior.

Even a demonstration that the incidence of abuse in eating-disordered women did not differ from the incidence in the general population would not *prove* that abuse does not cause eating disorders; it would simply eliminate one avenue of proof that it does. Again, to consider an analogy, the hypothetical finding that the frequency of automobile accidents was the same in the general population as in a sample of drivers killed in fatal crashes would not prove that the accidents didn't kill those who died in them. Obviously there would be crucial differences between the fatal and nonfatal crashes, but at first glance these might be difficult to identify. Speed of the vehicles, point of impact, configuration and composition of the colliding objects, the use of seat belts or air bags, time to rescue, and the quality of ensuing medical care would all be relevant to predicting mortality.

In fact, the best comparative studies do suggest that there are higher rates of abuse in psychiatric than in nonpsychiatric populations (Mullens, Romans-Clarkson, Walton, & Herbison, 1988; Burnam et al., 1988; Steiger & Zanko, 1990; Fairburn, 1992; see also Brown & Finkelhor, 1986; Courtois, 1988; Briere & Zaidi, 1989; and Herman, 1992, for reviews). But figures obtained for both groups vary so widely that they are hard to interpret—a fact that reflects both the emergent nature of definitions of sexual abuse and the extreme difficulties of measurement.

Given our current state of knowledge, a finding of small or nonexistent differences between rates of abuse in clinical and control populations is virtually meaningless as evidence that abuse is not damaging. Not everyone in the nonpsychiatric population is healthy. Entry into treatment is influenced by dozens of factors, many of which are only tangentially (if at all) relevant to an individual's condition—for example, the availability of therapy, financial resources, and the acceptance of psychotherapy within an individual's subculture. Some factors related to severity of damage from abuse are probably also responsible for treatment avoidance: for example, threats by the abuse perpetrator, risk of devastating repercussions within an unstable family, diminished social circumstances, and fear of disabling distress. Although he had predicted higher rates of abuse in a clinical than in a community sample of women with bulimia nervosa, Fairburn (1992) found that the reverse was true; he attributed the result to shame-induced treatment avoidance by many abused women.

We have only begun to acquire the kind of data that would allow us to scale the severity of abuse (i.e., to quantify the "dose") or to identify such possible mediating factors as these: the age and level of psychosexual development at which abuse began and at which it ended; the age at which it was disclosed and the initial and later responses to disclosure; the availability of general social support; the degree of continuing threat from the original abuser; the overlap of conditioned aversive stimuli with stimuli in the individual's current life; sexual arousal and response during abuse; the fear of or fact of pregnancy following abuse; conditionability and temperament of the victim; fear associated with detection; ego state in which abuse occurred (e.g., degree of wakefulness); degree of associated intimidation and violence; degree of predictability in the pattern of abuse; healing or resensitization in later sexual experiences; concurrent physical or emotional abuse; concurrent physical or emotional neglect; the meanings ascribed to abuse within the family, microculture, and subculture; and opportunities for symbolic reworking outside formal therapy.

The data that do exist suggest both the complexity of the involved phenomena and the importance of specificity with respect to the characterization of abuse, the measurement of consequences, and the identification of mediating factors. Thus, for example, some studies have found that extrafamilial abuse bears a special relationship to the diagnosis of bulimia (Beckman & Burns, 1990; Gregory-Bills, 1990; Miller, 1991). Several studies have suggested that sexual abuse is more predictive of bulimic than of anorexic symptoms (Bailey & Gibbons, 1989; Steiger & Zanko, 1990; Wonderlich et al., 1992; Waller, 1992a, 1992b), and of purging than of starving among anorexics who are affected (Waller, Halek, & Crisp, 1993). Waller (1992a) found that within an abused subsample of bulimic women, early abuse was strongly related to the frequency of bingeing; intrafamilial abuse was predictive of both bingeing and vomiting. Calam and Slade (1989) found that three abuse variables—perpetration by a family member, use of force, and occurrence of intercourse—each related to distinctive outcome variables. Other mediating factors that have been found to affect the relationship between sexual abuse and eating disturbance, defined in various ways, have included an initial reaction of fear or shock and a negative retrospective evaluation (Abramson & Lucido, 1991); parental unreliability (Smolak, Levine, & Sullins, 1990); and the presence of post-traumatic symptoms, perceived vulnerability, and social isolation (Wonderlich et al., 1992). One frequently overlooked mediating factor that appears to be particularly important is childhood physical abuse (Pyle, 1992; Wonderlich et al., 1992).

Also of interest are hypothesized mediating factors that have, in at least some studies, proven irrelevant. These include self-esteem and perceived family function (Waller, 1992a); history of rape as opposed to childhood sexual abuse (Bailey & Gibbons, 1989); and concurrent diagnosis of borderline personality disorder (Wonderlich et al., 1992). In some investigations, even variables widely assumed to be important—such as the age, frequency, and duration of abuse and the inclusion of intercourse—have failed to emerge as predictors of eating disturbance (Wonderlich et al., 1992), highlighting the difficulties in achieving consensus. Studies such as those by Wonderlich and colleagues and by Waller and colleagues most nearly approximate the level of sophistication that will be required to specify the effects of abuse.

And yet many problems remain. The findings cited above are but a single snapshot of a moving target, which will be obsolete before it reaches print. Many basic methodological questions are still unresolved. For example, Fairburn (1992) has argued that the interview technique most effective in uncovering abuse is the "funnel" method, which progresses from general to specific questions; Miller (1991) had argued for the greater accuracy of the "inverted-funnel" method, used by Russell (1986). Fairburn (1992) contended that interviews result in the highest rates of abuse disclosure, while at the same conference Pyle (1992) reported finding that anonymous questionnaires elicit higher rates of abuse than interviews. Although some progress has been achieved—for example, the identification of bulimic symptoms as the most responsive dependent variable—the detection and scaling of abuse remain highly problematic, and the study of mediating variables is in its infancy.

In addition to the fact that sexual abuse is a nonspecific cause, the fact that sexual abuse is a *non-necessary* cause of eating disorders has also been used to minimize its importance. Emphasizing that his own finding that 30% of bulimic women had been sexually abused meant that 70% had *not been* abused, and that the "common equation of eating disorders with sexual abuse" is therefore in error, Fairburn (1992) apparently attacked a straw man, for I can find no one who has claimed that *all* eating disorders are caused by abuse. However, such an argument is sometimes believed to imply that abuse is never *really* causal. Though such an argument is illogical (not all lung cancer is preceded by smoking), the concept of a non-necessary cause is one that frequently confuses people who believe it, on that account, to be less potent than other causes.

But the truth is that we really have *no idea* how many eating-disordered patients have been abused. The silencing of victims is the core phenomenon of abuse—a virtual prerequisite for its occurrence and the source of many of the most destructive sequelae, since victims must rely on primitive and often incapacitating defenses to accomplish the related psychological tasks of repression and concealment. One of the few clear findings of the past decade is the extremely long delay that may precede disclosure even among patients in intensive therapy (Herman & Schatzow, 1987; Palmer, Oppenheimer, Dignon, Chaloner, & Howells, 1990; Miller, 1991). Our own experience is illustrative. Most patients treated in our intensive residential program (Wooley & Wooley, 1984; Wooley & Kearney-Cooke, 1986) have had extensive prior therapy, yet many first disclosed their abuse to us. Five years ago, Kearney-Cooke (1988b) reported a combined incidence of molestation, incest, and rape of 59% in a patient series. A number of the unaffected 41% have since recalled and/or disclosed abuse. Miller (1991) found that 33% of patients/subjects who acknowledged abuse in her interview study had denied it throughout 5 weeks of hospitalization at a center highly sensitized to its importance and experienced in abuse treatment. Therapists in the same study underestimated the number of cases. *No one* knows the actual incidence of abuse in any population defined in any way, and underestimation in cross-sectional studies is virtually unavoidable.

Interestingly, critics of the scientific standing of abuse reports usually express a concern with over- rather than underestimation, despite the lack of evidence for the former and the abundant evidence for the latter—an inescapable problem in the early stages of quantifying a variable that can be expressed over a time span of more than 50 years. The only possible basis for suspecting overestimation is a belief in patient or therapist fabrication. This suspicion holds sexual abuse to a test not customarily applied to clinical data. In individual instances it *should* be held to a higher test, since reports of abuse, unlike other reports in patients' histories, criminally implicate other people. But this is an entirely separate criterion related to ethical and legal, rather than scientific, standards. Tremendous confusion results when this legal standard is selectively applied to the validity of scientific and clinical data.

The relentless questioning of the veracity of abuse reports reflects an unwillingness to see male behavior as the cause of female illness. It is arguably the same unwillingness that led Freud to recant his initial views on the role of abuse in mental illness, and to recast women's complaints of abuse as longings for it. Such self-serving motivation is by no means a relic of our past. It recently accounted for the dismissal of Anita Hill's persuasive complaints and the acceptance of the improbable argument that Clarence Thomas, who was undergoing a job interview—the outcome of which would affect the nation for decades to come—should be given the criminal defendant's right to a presumption of innocence

(Wooley, 1992a). This same culturally induced distortion accounted for the bewildering absence of sanction or peer censure of Denver psychiatrist Jason Richter, and the ostracism and financial boycott of Martha Gay, a female psychiatrist who encouraged her patient to seek remedies for Richter's uncontested sexual misconduct (Zaretsky, 1991).

Testing the *overall* accuracy of reports of abuse is difficult but not impossible, and a few investigators have described such efforts. In one study, Herman and Schatzow (1987) found independent comfirmation for 74% and indirect support for 9% of reported incest memories in a clinical series; none were found to be fantasies. In general, such research requires us to trust the reports of clinicians—something critics seem disinclined to do. For example, nearly all the female patients in our program who have alleged abuse by family members have confronted the alleged perpetrators during family therapy. In only a small handful of instances did the family members fail to confirm the complaint. In only one case could it be said that the charge was unequivocally denied; in all other failures to confirm, the alleged perpetrators either failed to respond directly or claimed that they didn't remember, sometimes adding that if they had behaved as described, they were sorry. Clinical series in which incest allegations are followed up in family therapy are the simplest and possibly the most accurate way to assess the validity of such reports. Reports of rape can be assessed with some degree of success by interviewing family and friends of the victims and by searching police, court, and medical records.

But such studies are as fraught with peril as the attempts of past researchers to compare the IQs of racial groups. It is reasonable to ask whether the information that might be gleaned warrants the risk of inflaming sensitivities during a period of cultural turmoil. The "rediscovery" of abuse is a cultural as well as a scientific event, and our role as professionals includes the encouragement of a constructive social response. Studies that repeatedly challenge patients' veracity invite destructive polarization.

From a clinical standpoint, I believe that report verification research is unnecessary. Based on the small number of even anecdotal reports of disconfirmation—by professionals who are either proponents *or* critics of abuse theories—there is no more reason to disbelieve adult patients' reports of abuse than to disbelieve other features of their histories. Simulation of the physical and emotional responses that typically accompany disclosure, including an array of involuntary behaviors, requires consummate acting skill. No doubt there are occasional delusions and fabrications, and we sometimes mistake the false for the real—probably in about the same frequency that we mistake factitious for real physical illness. But the well-known existence of the factitious–illness syndrome has not caused us to deny, treat with hostile suspicion, or ignore the treatment needs of the mass of patients with legitimate disease. The possibility of fabrication should not cause us to ignore the needs of patients claiming abuse.

Though some innocent persons may be falsely charged with abuse, the same problems attach to robbery, assault, mugging, and other crimes whose prosecution depends largely on identification by victims. To be sure, therapists must be careful not to overstep their bounds by making irresponsible charges against alleged perpetrators. Without confirmatory physical evidence, they cannot properly testify that any contested abuse report is undeniably true. Such a conclusion, in its strongest form, simply falls outside the ability to know; no symptom pattern *proves* that abuse has occurred. In cases that reach the courts, defendants have legal representation to make such limits of knowledge abundantly clear.

Therapists must walk a fine line, giving enough credence to memory fragments and suggestive symptoms that patients receive the support required for recall and disclosure, while avoiding definitive pronouncements about what must have happened and by whom it was done. To guard against the very real risks of damaging therapeutic error, time spent debating the precise rates of sexual abuse might better be spent in exploring the powerful countertransference feelings that such scenarios evoke (McCann & Pearlman, 1990; Briere, 1989; Chu, 1988; Courtois, 1988; Abney, Yang, & Paulson, 1992; Johnson & Zerbe, 1992; van der Kolk, 1987) and the dynamics of patients' and therapists' conflicting wishes to protect and to indict possible abusers (Wooley, 1991). Berliner and Loftes (1992) offer a balanced and useful discussion of these issues in which they attempt to reconcile their differing interests as frequent advocates of victims and of the accused.

SEXUAL ABUSE CAN BE AN IMPORTANT MAINTAINING FACTOR

Whether sexual abuse has caused eating disorders in specific individuals or groups is not the sole or major determinant of the emphasis it should receive in treatment. The variables maintaining illness frequently differ from those that caused it. Although most scientists would readily agree with this point, it is in constant danger of being forgotten. Contemporary analyses (Pope & Hudson, 1992; Fairburn, 1992) increasingly emphasize the importance of excluding from the data base and subsequent analysis instances of abuse that occurred after the first eating disorder symptoms appeared. Even if one's interest is restricted to antecedent etiological factors, such an approach may be unwise, since later abuse may in fact be a marker of earlier, as yet repressed or undisclosed childhood sexual abuse (van der Kolk, 1989). Certainly the recurrent finding (Folsom, Krahn, Canum, Gold, & Silk, 1989; Calam & Slade, 1989; Beckman & Burns, 1990; Gregory-Bills, 1990) that bulimic women have unusually high rates of sexual assault in late adolescence and early adulthood begs for explanation.

A purist pursuit of antecedent etiological as opposed to exacerbating and maintaining factors seems to put an agenda of intellectual clarity above concern for patients whose interest lies in comprehensive and effective treatment. Pyle's (1992) research on abuse and treatment outcome is a welcome exception to the dominant focus on etiology. In fact, etiological factors that play no current role in an illness are irrelevant, apart from their role in the patient's construction of a coherent and heuristic self-narrative. It is hard to see how even a prevention agenda is served by narrowly focused etiological research. Whether or not sexual abuse causes (or maintains) eating disorders would hardly be decisive with respect to a social commitment to its eradication.

How much importance should therapists attach to sexual abuse as a possible maintaining factor? To perseverate on an unimportant instance of abuse, to the exclusion of more critical issues, is a therapeutic error like any other. But we are coming out of a century—perhaps more accurately, out of millennia—in which we have ignored and even sanctioned sexual abuse. We should err in the direction of overattention until we learn to weigh its importance with the same skill used to weigh other contributing factors. Therapists who have now amassed a decade or more of concentrated experience have come a long way from the early shocks of recognition, and can assess with increasing accuracy the role played by the sequelae of abuse in maintaining eating disorders. Therapists without such an experience base should make liberal use of consultation.

If we continue to do abuse prevalence studies, we should at least vary these studies to ask not only whether abuse is associated with the occurrence of eating disorders, but whether it is associated with the intractability of symptoms. Suggestions that abuse is related to symptom severity have already been discussed. It seems a reasonable hypothesis that abuse histories are associated with treatment failure, especially (but not solely) when the abuse has not been addressed. There already exists some evidence for this point of view (Pyle, 1992). Studies showing poorer treatment results among patients with borderline personality disorder (Johnson, Tobin, & Dennis, 1990) and certain other forms of comorbidity speak to this point because of the strong association between these disorders and abuse. Rothschild, Fagan, Woodall, and Andersen (1991) recently reported that even after being weight-restored women with eating disorders severe enough to require hospitalization scored below the first percentile on sexual functioning and satisfaction when compared to normal controls. Although the authors do not mention abuse, it appears that this study may have captured a sample whose abuse history led to failure of outpatient therapy. Similarly, Leon, Lucas, Ferdinand, Mangelsdorf, and Colligan (1987) found that initial negativity toward sexuality predicted poor psychological status at outcome, influencing patients' measures of body image, personality, and social skills.

It is apparent that many abuse victims contend with excruciating dysphoria that does not lift in response to music, baths, or "changing into attractive clothes" (Fairburn, 1984, p. 178). Failure to diagnose their underlying problem and the prescription of such balms may worsen their symptoms and create a lasting distrust of therapy. The "successive-hurdles" model of therapy, in which failures of one method are passed on to the next, fails to take account of the damage that a therapy that trivializes suffering can cause. If we could show that therapies that ignore sexual abuse fail to cure its victims (or some subset), and may even adversely affect long-term prognosis, we would be taught the importance of accurate early diagnosis.

THE NEED TO SCREEN FOR AND TREAT ABUSE IS BEYOND DEBATE

Even under the unlikely condition that it were to be determined beyond all doubt that abuse neither causes nor contributes to the maintenance of eating disorders, we would still have the same task: to find ways to encourage abuse disclosure and to treat its consequences. Eating disorders bring many young women into treatment. Now that we know that sexual abuse is a common experience within this group, we are obliged to look for its presence in much the same way that pediatricians are obliged to test for lead poisoning in children living in high-risk areas. It is simply unconscionable to perform detailed psychological examinations of symptomatic young people without screening for a known pathogen of such importance. And once it is discovered, we are obliged to act. At the very least, we are required by law and professional ethics to consider the risk of continuing or new abuse of minors currently in the care of alleged abuse perpetrators, and, in accordance with prevailing statutes, to report such possibilities for further investigation. We are further obliged, I believe, to explore in some detail and with the benefit of expertise the probable extent and damages of the abuse, and to suggest treatment options.

Therapists who have little or no experience with abuse—especially male therapists, for whom elicitation and discussion are inherently more difficult—should collaborate with experienced, preferably female, therapists to assist in the assessments and to bring them up to a greater level of skill. Sometimes abuse victims withhold the disclosure of abuse from even very knowledgeable and sympathetic male therapists because of their gender. For this reason, male therapists should routinely tell female patients that if at any point in their treatment there is something they cannot tell a man, arrangements will be made for them to talk to a woman. Similarly, female therapists should offer to make a male therapist available to men. This issue of selective disclosure has generally escaped mention in discussions of therapist gender (e.g., Zunio, Agoos, & Davis, 1991).

Refusal by men who are inexperienced in the diagnosis and treatment of abuse to involve better-qualified female therapists in the evaluation or treatment of female patients is arguably a failure of professional standards. With the unmasking of high rates of sexual abuse, we are in a period of rapid flux—even crisis—in our understanding and treatment of emotional distress. Most of us, male and female, were trained to practice in ways that utterly failed to elicit abuse disclosure. Our theories are flawed by failure to appreciate the role of abuse as a cause of psychological distress. Accidental differences among us—our gender, the populations in which we have specialized, and the settings in which we have worked—have created in a mere decade enormous disparities of experience in treating abuse. We should set about correcting these in a spirit of cooperation on behalf of our patients, and for our own benefit as well.

Therapists who lack skills should take advantage of conferences and workshops devoted specifically to abuse. Diagnosis and treatment of abuse should be made regular topics in eating disorder conferences; they should be given, for example, at least as much attention as such popular subjects as affective disorders, personality disorders, and pharmacotherapy. In addition to indigenous but often overlooked resources, we should invite to our conferences authorities on abuse who do not specialize in eating disorders. Although we in eating disorders remain mired in confusion, the sexual abuse field is a sophisticated and rapidly maturing one, built on a foundation of high-quality empirical research. Keeping abreast of this work will require sustained effort. Perhaps it is time to consider the development of brief, intensive training programs at a few centers. It is awkward to find ourselves in this spot, but worse to deny it. Few of us—including women—know as much about abuse as we should.

WE STILL HAVE MUCH TO LEARN

Fifteen years ago, few therapists had knowingly treated a patient who had been sexually abused. Although many otherwise excellent therapists still have not treated abuse, others have spent much of the past 10 years immersed in the problem. Those of us who did so were required, in the absence of data, to make educated guesses about how to proceed and have worked in the intervening years to refine the approach we chose. Many of us now hold strong opinions about how treatment should be done. But none of us really knows what works best. We cannot know; there has been barely time to conceptualize the problems and develop experimental treatment techniques. Only now are the opinions and findings of those working in the area being made known. Already many differences in opinion have emerged, and there will be many more.

The difficulty of abuse work has necessitated passionate commitment; dispassionate analysis will not be easy. We must try to hold our theories with a loose grip as we undertake comparative studies, searching not only for the most effective methods but for criteria that will enable us to match patient to technique. Perhaps we can put our fatigue to good use, acknowledging that we need the chance to stand back: to get fresh perspectives from colleagues; to discuss the debilitating stress some courses of treatment impose on both patients and therapists; to admit what we are still unable to do. We have amassed a vast collective experience as we have worked—usually in relative isolation, as individuals or as groups. But the findings of a decade of hands-on work have yet to be fully gleaned.

Pressing questions include how best to assess whether patients have been abused; whether retrieval of memories is essential to cure and how retrieval can be assisted; whether or for whom catharsis is valuable or essential; the unique contributions of such techniques as hypnosis, guided imagery, art therapy, and psychodramatic enactment; whether, when, and how to confront abuse perpetrators; how to work with other members of the family when abuse is intrafamilial; the indications for individual, group, and family therapy; the optimal pacing of treatment; how to manage treatments involving ambiguous memories, particularly when these implicate family members; how best to help sexually dysfunctional abuse victims and their partners; how to alleviate the acute anguish and resulting self-destructive behaviors of survivors; whether contact with other survivors is important; the order in which best to address interrelated problems of sexual abuse, eating disorders, substance abuse, and/or other demanding symptoms; and the natural history of treated and untreated abuse-related post-traumatic stress responses.

The impact of abuse work on therapists is also an important area for study (see Chapter 16, this volume). It is apparent that this work is unusually stressful, because of both the inherent impact of the material and the frequency of crises. These difficulties call upon us to consider new structures for our practices, which can provide us with emotional and practical supports that are rarely needed in other kinds of work.

THE ISSUE EXTENDS BEYOND THE TERMS OF THE CURRENT DEBATE

Judith Herman, perhaps the nation's most eminent authority on child sexual abuse, writes in her far-reaching book *Trauma and Recovery* (1992):

> The study of psychological trauma has repeatedly led into realms of the unthinkable and foundered on fundamental questions of belief. . . . Advances in the field occur only when they are supported by a political movement powerful enough to legitimate an alliance between investigators and patients and to counteract the ordinary social processes of silencing and denial. In the absence of strong political movements for human rights, the active process of bearing witness inevitably gives way to the active process of forgetting. Repression, dissociation, and denial are phenomena of social as well as individual consciousness. (pp. 7–9)

Our perseveration as a field on prevalence studies of sexual abuse carries a number of metamessages it is time for us to consider. It suggests that we remain more interested in mapping female pain then in alleviating it, and that we are unprepared to face the cultural embeddedness of eating disorders beyond the trivial acknowledgment of oppressive appearance norms (see Vandereycken & Hoek, 1993).

Women's lifelong marginal status positions them to perceive, if not always to articulate easily, aspects of female experience not captured by our current science. The overwhelming importance and meaning of sexual abuse constitute only one example, but it is an extremely important example, because it reveals the limitations of our methods of discovery and proof. A science of seismology incapable of detecting an earthquake would be rejected as a failed paradigm. It seems an open question whether the science of psychology in general, or the field of eating disorders in particular, has a paradigm so flawed that it cannot encompass the influence of gender inequities on the subjects it studies, or whether there is simply a profound cultural resistance to data generated within the paradigm. As we struggle to answer this question, we will be challenging more than the understanding and treatment of eating disorders. We will be confronting a failure that signals critical weaknesses in inclusiveness, communication, and flexibility within our field. One thing is clear: We have grown too remote from the most persuasive data bases.

In an invited address to the American Psychological Association's Division of General Psychology, Kenneth Gergen (1992) examined psychology's 100-year history and the broad intellectual shift in which modernist views of the Enlightenment are giving way to postmodernism, with its rejection of the simplistic notion of scientific progression toward unitary truth, and its emphasis on the relativistic and constructed nature of reality. Stressing the oppressiveness of models that have invested a small elite with an exclusive claim on truth, Gergen argued that psychology's blind faith in empiricism is misplaced and implies that knowledge, a product of transactions, is as rich or as impoverished as the breadth of participation in the discourse:

> To speak . . . of the "material world" and "causal relations" is not to describe what there is, but to participate in a textual genre—to draw from the immense repository of sayings that constitute a particular cultural tradition. . . . Social constructivist writings . . . single out various aspects of the taken-for-granted world . . . and attempt to demonstrate their socially constructed character. They attempt to show, in Bateson's terms, that, "The map is not the territory." . . . They sensitize us to our participation in constituting our world, thus emphasizing our potential for communally organized change. (p. 13)

Sexual abuse is not so much "discovered" as socially constructed. Sex between children and adults, and the imposition of nonconsensual sex on adult women, have probably been present for more of human history than not (Rush, 1980; Demause, 1991; Kahn, 1991). They have at many points received full cultural and legal endorsement. Harsh criticisms of female scholars for failure to provide precise definitions of sexual abuse ignore the emergent nature of the concept. Destructive boundary violations that occur within a lifetime of contact between parent and child, for example, are not likely to be easily or fully captured by a simple physical definition. Without clear legal, scientific, or historical precedents on which to base such definitions, we rightly struggle to grasp what forms of sexual activity are destructive to women's and children's emotional health and to label these as abuse. The potential objection that such a process makes it impossible, for example, to demonstrate that abuse is harmless only illustrates the ways in which an intellectual tradition drawn from logical positivism can impede rather than advance the acquisition of socially useful knowledge.

Of course, this raises the question of *whom* such knowledge is useful for; it brings into focus the diverging interests of men, considered for a moment as one political bloc, and women, considered as another. The conceptualization of abuse and gender inequality, and the social change resulting from this process, limit males' historical power. Contemporary men are powerfully conditioned to resist the relinquishment of power, whether or not, in some far-reaching sense, it is really in their "best interests" to do so. Not all men think that it is. Many leaders in the men's movement feel that men must help one another heal from the wounds that lead to sexual violence (Keen, 1991). Brooks (1990), in an examination of sexual misconduct by therapists, finds a welcome opportunity to explore problems in male gender socialization that limit men's capacity for communication and intimacy. Brennan (1992), writing in the pro-feminist male-directed periodical *Ending Men's Violence Newsletter,* argues that, "Men must also claim responsibility for social change. . . . Every time . . . we simply ignore that women are sold to us like commodities, we taken another step closer to dehumanizing and marginalizing women" (pp. 9–10). O. W. Wooley (Chapter 2, this volume) considers the contribution of male artistic and intellectual traditions to the problems of contemporary women, and concludes: "The subconscious awareness of what they have done to women—denying them humanity, a collective subjectivity—has haunted and still haunts men. It is a major source of . . . guilt and dread" (p. 45).

As Kenneth Pope (1989) has argued, our culture has had "a persistent and pervasive difficulty in addressing effectively—or, in many cases, even recognizing as a problem—phenomena in which a disproportionate percentage of women are victimized." In an interesting examination of violence in animals and humans, Lore and Schultz (1993) argue that both "are easily capable of inhibiting their use of violence in predictable ways in response to seemingly minor changes in their social environment" (p. 24), but that Americans' traditional emphasis on personal freedoms and individual rights stands in the way. Clearly these are predominantly male prerogatives. But it is difficult to assess what "men want," since there has been so little meaningful public dialogue. There is reason to hope that, with greater exposure of problems, we are entering a period of accelerated social change.

There has been a great hue and cry against the "popularization" of psychological issues and their discussion in self-help books and the mass media (e.g., Tavris, 1993). Many professionals are made acutely uncomfortable by this trend. And yet it is precisely from such a cultural dialogue that we can hope to detect and define important phenomena and to construct a reality reflective of more than the experience of educated white males. As Gergen (1992) put it, illustrating that he has himself been influenced by women's views: "If we are to retain viability as a discipline, if we are to add significantly to the cultural dialogue, we must be listeners as well as speakers. . . . In relational listening, we stand to be changed, expanded or transformed" (pp. 1–4).

Though Tavris, in her withering criticism of "the incest-survivor machine," tried to exempt Judith Herman from the charge of pandering to a gullible public, Herman (1993), in a letter to the editor, declined the favor. She said, "I wish to affirm my solidarity with the grass-roots women in the incest-survivor movement: the social workers, popular authors and victim advocates for whom Ms. Tavris displays such contempt" (p. 3). As Diana Russell (1986) noted, the attention now being paid to sexual abuse is an achievement not of the health professions, but of abuse survivors and feminist activists within the professions. Though Tavris (1993b) faults such laypeople for "the excesses of the recovery movement" (p. 27), there would be no movement at all without them.

Tavris's article coincides roughly with the establishment of "Forgotten Memory Syndrome" (FMS), a national organization formed to help those "falsely accused" of abuse (Wasserman, 1992). FMS boasts a number of scientists on its board making claims far more extravagant than those it attacks. Dr. Ralph Underwager, for example, asserts that body memories are "a completely false and erroneous concept"; that "there is no evidence to support the repression of events that occur repeatedly over time"; and that he can determine innocence by a failure of the accused to fit the "profile" of an abuser (quoted in Wasserman, 1992, p. 18). It is not surprising that there should be a backlash against women's gradual acquisition of greater power over their bodies. But Underwager gets more nearly to the heart of the matter when, singling out *The Courage to Heal* (Bass & Davis, 1988) as a "political statement that preaches anger and revenge," he wails that the book "turns the basis of Western Civilization [i.e., logic] [*sic*] on its ear" and could cause us "all to return to living in caves" (quoted in Wasserman, 1992, p. 18).

Perhaps the delineation of abuse *does* stand civilization on its ear; certainly it challenges the "logic" of our culture, including its social sciences. Although it is not a step back to living in caves, it *is* potentially transformative, and should be understood as a cultural event that cannot be conceptualized in the same way as the study of such other "risk factors" as a familial history of affective disorder or genetic predisposition to a culturally unacceptable body shape. Rape, incest, sexual harassment, and wife beating, along with such other "phenomena" as employment discrimination and gender differences, are not entities that are discovered, like elements, but are emerging constructs—definitions that cut the old pie in a way so different that it may no longer be correct to call it a pie. The Thomas–Hill hearings (Wooley, 1992a), the William

Kennedy Smith and Mike Tyson trials, and Hillary Rodham Clinton's redefinition of the role of "First Lady" are all cultural events with the power to change forever what certain events mean.

We must all decide what our role in this process of cultural transformation will be: whether we will ignore it, oppose it, or participate in it. I deeply hope that the men in my field will choose to become passionate—yes, even *emotional*—participants. It will be said that this chapter is emotional. I hope so. This is no time to be moribund unless we want to be buried, along with the tools of our trade. Although awareness of the widespread existence of sexual abuse could, of course, be suppressed again, as it has been in the past, women will eventually abandon treatments that do not meet their real needs.

I think I speak for most female therapists in saying that women do not want to exclude male therapists from the treatment of abuse; on the contrary, we greatly need the help of men who are willing to become emotionally and intellectually involved. It is extremely hard work—harder than anything most of us have ever done. It is because so many of us have been working so hard, and because we come together with such overwhelming needs for support and revitalization, that we are so stunned when—instead of finding these—we find skepticism that the problems almost bringing us to our knees even exist. No one who has been meaningfully engaged in abuse treatment can doubt its importance or the moral mandate to assist sexual abuse victims.

With so much to do, we must give careful thought to our priorities. Our first order of business is not, it seems to me, to determine the precise rates of abuse in various populations or even the precise weighting of abuse as an etiological or maintaining factor in eating disorders; instead, it is to decide how to respond as a profession to a moment thousands of years in the making. We are confronted—indeed, inundated—with a profoundly painful aspect of the human condition, affecting more lives than any of us imagined. It is an enormous responsibility. It is also an opportunity to interrupt perhaps the major preventable cause of mental illness, exceeded only by poverty and racial inequality as a socially caused form of human suffering. We need to take good care of one another because the work is hard, because it is essential, and because it requires us all.

NOTES

1. In fairness it should be noted that both Johnson and Connors have since made valuable contributions to the study of sexual abuse (Johnson & Zerbe, 1992; Connors & Morse, 1993).

2. The conference organizers were unable to provide a history of scientific papers for the years 1984–1988.

REFERENCES

Abney, V. D., Yang, J. A., & Paulson, M. J. (1992). Transference and counter-transference issues unique to long-term group psychotherapy of adult women molested as children. *Journal of Interpersonal Violence, 7*(4), 559–569.

Abraham, S. F., & Beumont, P. J. (1982). Varieties of psychosexual experience in patients with anorexia nervosa. *International Journal of Eating Disorders, 1*(3), 10–19.

Abramson, E. A., & Lucido, G. M. (1991). Childhood sexual experience and bulimia. *Addictive Behaviors, 16*(6), 529–532.

Adler, L., & Prendergast, P. (1992, April 24–26). *Eating disorder patients with a history of sexual abuse.* Paper presented at the Fifth International Conference on Eating Disorders, New York.

Bailey, C. A., & Gibbons, S. J. (1989). Physical victimization and bulimic-like symptoms: Is there a relationship? *Deviant Behavior, 10*(4), 335–352.

Bass, E. B., & Davis, L. (1988). *The courage to heal: A guide for women survivors of child sexual abuse.* New York: Harper & Row.

Beckman, K. A., & Burns, G. L. (1990). Relation of sexual abuse and bulimia in college women. *International Journal of Eating Disorders, 9,* 487–492.

Ben-Tovim, D. I., Hunter, M., & Crisp, A. H. (1977). Discrimination and evaluation of shape and size in anorexia nervosa: An exploratory study. *Research Communications in Psychology, Psychiatry and Behavior, 2,* 241–257.

Berliner, L., & Loftes, E. (1992). Sexual abuse accusations: Desperately seeking reconciliation. *Journal of Interpersonal Violence, 7*(4), 570–578.

Beumont, P. J. V., George, G. C. W., & Smart, D. E. (1976). "Dieters" and "vomiters and purgers" in anorexia nervosa. *Psychological Medicine, 6*(4), 617–622.

Blouin, A. G., Zuro, C., & Blouin, J. H. (1990). Family environment in bulimia nervosa: The role of depression. *International Journal of Eating Disorders, 9*(6), 649–658.

Boch, L. P. (1990, October 7–9). *Tolerating countertransferences during treatment of sexually abused women with anorexia or bulimia.* Small group workshop presented at the Ninth National Conference on Eating Disorders, Columbus, OH.

Boskind-Lodahl, M. (1976). Cinderella's stepsisters: A feminist perspective on anorexia nervosa and bulimia. *Signs: Journal of Women in Culture and Society, 2,* 342–356.

Bram, S., Eger, D., & Halmi, K. (1982). Anorexia nervosa and personality type: A preliminary report. *International Journal of Eating Disorders, 2*(1), 67–74.

Brennan, T. (1992). Hush Puppies joins a dangerous trend. *Ending Men's Violence Newsletter, 8*(1), 9–10.

Briere, J. (1989). *Therapy for adults molested as children: Beyond survival.* New York: Springer.

Briere, J., & Zaidi, L. Y. (1989). Sexual abuse histories and sequelae in female psychiatric emergency room patients. *American Journal of Psychiatry, 146,* 1602–1606.

Brooks, G. R. (1990). The inexpressive male and vulnerability to therapist–patient sexual exploitation. *Psychotherapy, 27*(3), 344–349.

Brown, A., & Finkelhor, D. (1986). Impact of child sexual abuse: A review of the literature. *Psychological Bulletin, 99,* 66–77.

Brown, G. R., & Anderson, B. (1991). Psychiatric morbidity in adult inpatients with childhood histories of sexual and physical abuse. *American Journal of Psychiatry, 148*(1), 55–61.

Brownell, K., & Foreyt, J. (Eds.). (1986). *Handbook of eating disorders: Physiology, psychology, and treatment of obesity, anorexia, and bulimia.* New York: Basic Books.

Bruch, H. (1970). Instinct and interpersonal experience. *Comprehensive Psychiatry, 11*(6), 495–506.

Bruch, H. (1973). *Eating disorders.* New York: Basic Books.

Bruch, H. (1977). Psychological antecedents of anorexia nervosa. In R. Vigersky (Ed.), *Anorexia nervosa.* New York: Raven Press.

Bruch, H. (1978). *The Golden cage.* Cambridge, MA: Harvard University Press.

Bunnell, D. W., Shenker, I. R., Nussbaum, M. P., Jacobson, M. S., & Cooper, P. (1990). Subclinical versus formal eating disorders: Differentiating psychological features. *International Journal of Eating Disorders, 9*(3), 357–362.

Burnam, M. A., Stein, J. A., Golding, J. M., Siegel, J., Sorenson, S. B., Forsythe, A. B., & Telles, C. A. (1988). Sexual assault and mental disorders in a community population. *Journal of Consulting and Clinical Psychology, 56*(6), 843–850.

Button, E. J., & Whitehouse, A. (1981). Subclinical anorexia nervosa. *Psychological Medicine, 11,* 509–516.

Calam, R., & Slade, P. (1989). Sexual experience and eating problems in female undergraduates. *International Journal of Eating Disorders, 8,* 391–397.

Casper, R. C., Eckert, E. D., Halmi, K. A., Goldberg, S. C., & Davis, J. M. (1980). Bulimia: Its incidence and clinical importance in patients with anorexia nervosa. *Archives of General Psychiatry, 37*(9), 1030–1035.

Chu, J. A. (1988). Ten traps for therapists in the treatment of trauma survivors. *Dissociation, 1*(4), 24–32.

Chernin, K. (1983). *Womansize: The tyranny of slenderness.* London: The Women's Press. (Published in the United States as *The obsession: Reflections on the tyranny of slenderness.*)

Connors, M. E., & Morse, W. (1993). Sexual abuse and eating disorders: A review. *International Journal of Eating Disorders, 13*(1), 1–11.

Cooper, P. J., & Fairburn, G. C. (1986). The depressive symptoms of bulimia nervosa. *British Journal of Psychiatry, 148,* 268–274.

Cooper, P. J., Taylor, M. J., Cooper, Z., & Fairburn, C. (1987). The development and validation of the Body Shape Questionnaire. *International Journal of Eating Disorders, 6*(4), 485–494.

Courtois, C. (1988). *Healing the incest wound: Adult survivors in therapy.* New York: Norton.

Crisp, A. H. (1965). Clinical and therapeutic aspects of anorexia nervosa: Study of 30 cases. *Journal of Psychosomatic Research, 9,* 67–78.

Crisp, A. H. (1967). The possible significance of some behavioral correlates of weight and carbohydrate intake. *Journal of Psychosomatic Research, 11,* 117–131.

Crisp, A. H. (1970). Premorbid factors in adult disorders of weight with particular reference to primary anorexia nervosa (weight phobia). *Journal of Psychosomatic Research, 14,* 1–22.

Crisp, A. H., & Fransella, K. (1972). Conceptual changes during recovery from anorexia nervosa. *British Journal of Medical Psychology, 45,* 395–405.

Crisp, A. H., Harding, B., & McGuiness, E. (1974). Anorexia nervosa: Psychoneurotic characteristics of parents: Relationship to prognosis. A quantitative study. *Journal of Psychosomatic Research, 18*(3), 167–173.

Crisp, A. H., Hsu, L. K. G., & Harding, B. (1980). The starving hoarder and the voracious spender: Stealing in anorexia nervosa. *Journal of Psychosomatic Research, 24,* 225–231.

Crisp, A. H., Palmer, R. L., & Kalucy, R. S. (1976). How common is anorexia nervosa? A prevalence study. *British Journal of Psychiatry, 128,* 549–554.

Dally, P. J. (1969). *Anorexia nervosa.* New York: Grune & Stratton.

DeAngelis, T. (1990, December). Who is susceptible to bulimia, and why? *APA Monitor,* p. 8.

de Groot, J. (1991, December 5–8). *Correlation between eating disorders and prior sexual abuse: Theory, evidence and future directions.* Paper presented at the North American Scientific Symposium on Eating Disorders in Adolescence, Seattle.

Demause, L. (1991). The universality of incest. *Journal of Psychohistory, 19*(2), 191–214.

Dolan, B. M., Lieberman, S., Evans, C., & Lacey, J. H. (1990). Family features associated with normal weight bulimia. *International Journal of Eating Disorders, 9*(6), 639–647.

Elmore, D. K., & Castro, J. M. (1990). Self-rated moods and hunger in relation to spontaneous eating behavior in bulimics, recovered bulimics and normals. *International Journal of Eating Disorders, 9*(2), 179–190.

Enoch, J., Herman, C., & Walsh, S. (1990, April 27–29). *Sexual abuse and eating disorders.* Workshop presented at the Fourth International Conference on Eating Disorders, New York.

Fairburn, C. G. (1984). Cognitive–behavioral treatment for bulimia. In D. M. Garner & P. E. Garfinkel (Eds.), *Handbook of psychotherapy for anorexia nervosa and bulimia.* New York: Guilford Press.

Fairburn, C. G. (1992, October 25–27). *Sexual abuse and eating disorders.* Paper presented at the Eleventh National Conference on Eating Disorders, Columbus, OH.

Finkelhor, D. (1984). *Child sexual abuse: New theory and research.* New York: Free Press.

Finn, S. E., Hartman, M., Leon, G. R., Lawson, L. (1986). Eating disorders and sexual abuse: Lack of confirmation for a clinical hypothesis. *International Journal of Eating Disorders, 5,* 1051–1060.

Folsom, V. L., Krahn, D. D., Canum, K. K., Gold, L., & Silk, K. R. (1989). Sex abuse: Role in eating disorders. In *New research program and abstracts: 142nd*

Annual Meeting of the American Psychiatric Association. Washington, DC: American Psychiatric Association.

Fries, H. (1977). Studies on secondary amenorrhea, anorectic behavior, and body image perception: Importance for the early recognition of anorexia nervosa. In R. Vigersky (Ed.), *Anorexia nervosa.* New York: Raven Press.

Gannon, L., Luchetta, T., Rhodes, K., Pardie, L., & Segrist, D. (1992). Sex bias in psychological research. *American Psychologist, 47*(3), 389–396.

Garfinkel, P. E., & Garner, D. M. (1982). *Anorexia nervosa: A multidimensional perspective.* New York: Brunner/Mazel.

Garner, D. M., & Bemis, K. M. (1982). A cognitive–behavioral approach to anorexia nervosa. *Cognitive Therapy and Research, 6,* 1–27.

Garner, D. M., & Garfinkel, P. E. (1979). The Eating Attitudes Test: An index of the symptoms of anorexia nervosa. *Psychological Medicine, 9,* 273–279.

Garner, D. M., & Garfinkel, P. E. (Eds.). (1985). *Handbook of psychotherapy for anorexia nervosa and bulimia.* New York: Guilford Press.

Garner, D. M., Garfinkel, P. E., Schwartz, D., & Thompson, M. (1980). Cultural expectation of thinness in women. *Psychological Reports, 47,* 483–491.

Garner, D. M., Olmsted, M. P., & Polivy, J. (1983). Development and validation of a multidimensional eating disorder inventory for anorexia nervosa and bulimia. *International Journal of Eating Disorders, 2,* 15–34.

Gergen, K. (1992). Psychology in the postmodern era. *The General Psychologist, 28*(3), 10–14.

Goldfarb, L. (1987). Sexual abuse antecedent to anorexia nervosa, bulimia and compulsive overeating: Three case reports. *International Journal of Eating Disorders, 6*(5), 675–680.

Grace, E., Emans, S. J., & Woods, E. R. (1988). Eating disorders: Sequelae of sexual abuse. *Behavioral Pediatrics, 21,* 161A.

Gregory-Bills, T. (1990). *Eating disorders and their correlates in earlier episodes of incest.* Unpublished doctoral dissertation, University of Houston.

Gull, W. W. (1964). Anorexia nervosa. In R. M. Kaufman & M. Heiman (Eds.), *Evolution of psychosomatic concepts. Anorexia nervosa: A paradigm.* New York: International Universities Press. (Original work published 1874)

Halmi, K. A. (1974). Anorexia nervosa: Demographic and clinical features in 94 cases. *Psychosomatic Medicine, 36*(1), 18–25.

Herman, C. P., & Polivy, J. (1975). Anxiety, restraint and eating behavior. *Journal of Personality, 84,* 666–672.

Herman, J. L. (1992). *Trauma and recovery.* New York: Basic Books.

Herman, J. L., (1993, February 14). Letter to the editor. *New York Times Book Review,* p. #3.

Herman, J. L. & Perry, J. C., & van der Kolk, B. A. (1989). Childhood trauma in borderline personality disorder. *American Journal of Psychiatry, 146*(4), 490–495.

Herman, J. L., & Schatzow, E. (1987). Recovery and verification of memories of childhood sexual trauma. *Psychoanalytic Psychology, 4,* 1–14.

Holyoak, T., & Abramson, E. E. (1990, April 27–29). *Restraint, anxiety, depression and childhood sexual experience as predictors of bulimia nervosa.* Paper presented at the Fourth International Conference on Eating Disorders, New York.

Humphrey, L. L. (1988). Relationships within subtypes of anorexic, bulimic and normal families. *Journal of the American Academy of Child and Adolescent Psychiatry, 27*(5), 544–551.

Humphrey, L. L. (1989). Observed family interactions among subtypes of eating disorders using structural analysis of social behavior. *Journal of Consulting and Clinical Psychology, 57*(2), 206–214.

Humphrey, L. L. (1991). Object relations and the family system: An integrative approach to understanding and treating eating disorders. In C. L. Johnson (Ed.), *Psychodynamic treatment of anorexia nervosa and bulimia.* New York: Guilford Press.

Johnson, C. L. (Ed.). (1991). *Psychodynamic treatment of anorexia nervosa and Bulimia.* New York: Guilford Press.

Johnson, C. L., & Connors, M. E. (1987). *The etiology and treatment of bulimia nervosa: A biopsychosocial perspective.* New York: Basic Books.

Johnson, C. L., & Flach, A. (1985). Family characteristics of 105 patients with bulimia. *American Journal of Psychiatry, 142*(11), 1321–1324.

Johnson, C. L., Tobin, D. L., & Dennis, A. (1990). Difference in treatment outcome between borderline and non-borderline bulimics at one-year follow-up. *International Journal of Eating Disorders, 9*(6), 617–627.

Johnson, C. L., & Zerbe, K. (1992, October 25–27). *Transference and countertransference issues of sexual assault and eating disorders.* Track workshop presented at the Eleventh National Conference on Eating Disorders, Columbus, OH.

Kahn, B. (1991). The sexual molestation of children: Historical perspectives. *Journal of Psychohistory, 19*(2), 101–213.

Kalucy, R. S., Crisp, A. H., & Harding, B. (1977). A study of 56 families with anorexia nervosa. *British Journal of Medical Psychology, 50*(4), 381–395.

Kay, D. W. K., & Leigh, D. (1954). Natural history, treatment and prognosis of anorexia nervosa based on study of 38 patients. *Journal of Mental Science, 100,* 411–431.

Kearney-Cooke, A. (1988a, October 5–7). *Clinical considerations in the treatment of sexual abuse among eating disordered patients.* Track workshop presented at the Seventh National Conference on Eating Disorders, Columbus, OH.

Kearney-Cooke, A. (1988b). Group treatment of sexual abuse among women with eating disorders. *Women and Therapy, 7*(1), 5–21.

Kearney-Cooke, A. (1991). The role of the therapist in the treatment of eating disorders: A feminist psychodynamic approach. In C. L. Johnson (Ed.), *Psychodynamic treatment of anorexia nervosa and bulimia.* New York: Guilford Press.

Kearney-Cooke, A. (1991). *Treating eating disorders and sexual abuse.* Track workshop presented at the Tenth National Conference on Eating Disorders, Columbus, OH.

Keen, S. (1991). *Fire in the belly: On being a man.* New York: Bantam.

King, A. (1963). Primary and secondary anorexia nervosa syndromes. *British Journal of Psychiatry, 109*(1), 470–479.

Kog, E., & Vandereycken, W. (1985). Family characteristics of anorexia nervosa and bulimia: A review of the research literature. *Clinical Psychology Review, 5,* 159–180.

Lacey, J. H. (1982). The bulimic syndrome at normal body weight: Reflections on pathogenesis and clinical features. *International Journal of Eating Disorders, 2*(1), 59–66.

Lesegue, C. (1964). De l'anorexie hysterique. In R. M. Kaufman & M. Heiman (Eds.), *Evolution of psychosomatic concepts. Anorexia nervosa: A paradigm.* New York: International Universities Press. (Original work published 1873)

Leon, G. K., Carroll, K., Chernyk, B., & Finn, S. (1985). Binge eating and associated habit patterns within college student and identified bulimic populations. *International Journal of Eating Disorders, 4*(1), 43–57.

Leon, G. R., Lucas, A. R., Ferdinand, R. F., Mangelsdorf, C., & Colligan, R. C. (1987). Attitudes about sexuality and other psychological characteristics as predictors of follow-up status in anorexia nervosa. *International Journal of Eating Disorders, 6*(4), 477–484.

Loeb, L. (1964). The clinical course of anorexia nervosa. *Psychosomatics, 5,* 345–347.

Lore, R. K., & Schultz, L. A. (1993). Control of human aggression: A comparative perspective. *American Psychologist, 48*(1), 16–25.

Lucido, G., & Abramson, E. E. (1988). Adverse childhood sexual experiences and bulimia. In *Abstracts of Third International Conference on Eating Disorders.* New York: Montefiore Medical Center.

Mayer, J. (1963). Anorexia nervosa. *Postgraduate Medicine, 34,* 529–534.

McCann, L., & Pearlman, L. A. (1990). Vicarious traumatization: A framework for understanding the psychological effects of working with victims. *Journal of Traumatic Stress, 3*(1), 131–149.

McClintock, J. (1988, October 5–7). *Unwanted sexual experiences, sexual relationship satisfaction and eating disorders.* Small group workshop presented at the Seventh National Conference on Eating Disorders, Columbus, OH.

McFarlane, A., McFarlane, C., & Gilchrist, P. (1988). Post-traumatic bulimia and anorexia nervosa. *International Journal of Eating Disorders, 7*(5), 705–708.

Miller, C. (1991, November 15–17). *The prevalence of chilhood sexual abuse among women with eating disorders.* Paper presented at the Renfrew Foundation Conference, Philadelphia.

Minuchin, S., Rosman, B. L., & Baker, L. (1978). *Psychosomatic families: Anorexia nervosa in context.* Cambridge, MA: Harvard University Press.

Mitchell, J. E., Pyle, R. L., & Eckert, E. D. (1981). Frequency and duration of binge-eating episodes in patients with bulimia. *American Journal of Psychiatry, 138*(6), 835–836.

Morgan, H. G., & Russell, G. F. M. (1975). Value of family background and clinical features as predictors of long-term outcome in anorexia nervosa: Four year follow-up study of 41 patients. *Psychological Medicine, 5,* 355–371.

Mullens, P. E., Romans-Clarkson, S. E., Walton, V. A., & Herbison, G. P.

(1988). Impact of sexual and physical abuse on women's mental health. *Lancet, i*(8590), 841–845.

Nylander, I. (1971). The feeling of being fat and dieting in a school population: An epidemiologic interview investigation. *Acta Sociomedica Scandinavica, 3,* 17–26.

Ogata, S. N., Silk, K. R., & Goodrich, S. (1990). Childhood sexual and physical abuse in adult patients with borderline personality disorder. *American Journal of Psychiatry, 147*(8), 1008–1013.

Oppenheimer, R., Howells, K., Palmer, R. L., & Chaloner, D. A. (1985). Adverse sexual experience in childhood and clinical eating disorders: A preliminary description. *Journal of Psychiatric Research, 19*(2–3), 357–361.

Orbach, S. (1978). *Fat is a feminist issue.* London: Paddington Press.

Palmer, R. L. (1979). The dietary chaos syndrome: A useful new term? *British Journal of Medical Psychology, 52,* 187–190.

Palmer, R. L., Oppenheimer, R., Dignon, A., Chaloner, D. A., & Howells, K. (1990). Childhood sexual experiences with adults reported by women with eating disorders: An extended series. *British Journal of Psychiatry, 156,* 699–703.

Phelan, P. W. (1987). Cognitive correlates of bulimia: The Bulimic Thoughts Questionnaire. *International Journal of Eating Disorders, 6*(5), 593–607.

Pope, H. G., & Hudson, J. I. (1992). Is childhood sexual abuse a risk factor for bulimia nervosa? *American Journal of Psychiatry, 149*(4), 455–463.

Pope, K. S. (1989). Therapists who become sexually intimate with a patient: Classification, dynamics, recidivism, and rehabilitation. *Independent Practitioner, 9,* 33–41.

Powers, P. (1990, October 7–9). *Sexual abuse, character pathology and eating disorders.* Track workshop presented at the Ninth National Conference on Eating Disorders, Columbus, OH.

Powers, P., Coovert, D., & Brightwell, D. (1988). Sexual abuse history in three eating disorders. In *New research program and abstracts: 141st Annual Meeting of the American Psychiatric Association.* Washington, DC: American Psychiatric Association.

Prather, R. C., & Williamson, D. A. (1988). Psychopathology associated with bulimia, binge-eating and obesity. *International Journal of Eating Disorders, 7*(2), 177–184.

Pyle, R. L. (1992, October 25–27). *Physical and sexual abuse in bulimia nervosa.* Track workshop presented at the Eleventh National Conference on Eating Disorders, Columbus, OH.

Pyle, R. L., Mitchell, J. E., & Eckert, E. D. (1981). Bulimia: A report of 34 cases. *Journal of Clinical Psychiatry, 42*(2), 60–64.

Pyle, R. L., Perse, T., Mitchell, J. E., Saunders, P., & Skoog, K. (1988). Abuse in women with bulimia nervosa. In *New Research Program and Abstracts: 141st Annual Meeting of the American Psychiatric Association.* Washington, DC: American Psychiatric Association.

Rodin, J., Silberstein, L., & Streigel-Moore, R. (1984). Women and weight: A normative discontent. In *Nebraska Symposium on Motivation* (Vol.). Lincoln: University of Nebraska Press.

Root, M. P. P., & Fallon, P. (1988). The incidence of victimization experiences in a bulimic sample. *Journal of Interpersonal Violence, 3*(2), 161–173.

Root, M. P. P., Fallon, P., & Friedrich, W. N. (1986). *Bulimia: A systems approach to treatment.* New York: Norton.

Rosenthal, R. J., Rinzler, C., Wallsh, R., & Klausner, E. (1972). Wrist-cutting syndrome: The meaning of a gesture. *American Journal of Psychiatry, 11,* 1363–1368.

Rothschild, B. S., Fagan, P. J., Woodall, C., & Andersen, A. E. (1991). Sexual functioning of female eating-disordered patients. *International Journal of Eating Disorders, 10*(4), 389–394.

Rush, F. (1980). *The best kept secret: Sexual abuse of children.* Englewood Cliffs, NJ: Prentice-Hall.

Russell, G. F. M. (1979). Bulimia nervosa: An ominous variant of anorexia nervosa. *Psychological Medicine, 9,* 429–448.

Russell, D. E. H. (1986). *The secret trauma: Incest in the lives of girls and women.* New York: Basic Books.

Schechter, J. O., Schwartz, H. P., & Greenfield, D. G. (1987). Sexual assault and anorexia nervosa. *International Journal of Eating Disorders, 6,* 313–316.

Schwartz, D. M., Thompson, M. G., & Johnson, C. L. (1987). Anorexia nervosa and bulimia: The sociocultural context. *International Journal of Eating Disorders, 1*(20), 20–36.

Scott, D. W. (1987). The involvement of psychosexual factors in the causation of eating disorders: Time for a reappraisal. *International Journal of Eating Disorders, 6*(2), 199–213.

Secord, P. F., & Jourard, S. M. (1953). The appraisal of body-cathexis: Body-cathexis and the self. *Journal of Consulting Psychology, 17,* 343–347.

Selvini Palazzoli, M. P. (1974). *Self-starvation.* London: Chaucer.

Sloan, G., & Leichner, P. (1986). Is there a relationship between sexual abuse or incest and eating disorders? *Canadian Journal of Psychiatry, 31,* 656–660.

Smolak, K., Levine, M., & Sullins, E. (1990). Are child sexual experiences related to eating-disordered attitudes and behaviors in a college sample? *International Journal of Eating Disorders, 9,* 167–170.

Sours, J. A. (1974). The anorexia nervosa syndrome. *International Journal of Psycho-Analysis, 55,* 567–579.

Steere, J., Butler, G., & Cooper, P. J. (1990). The anxiety symptoms of bulimia nervosa: A comparative study. *International Journal of Eating Disorders, 9*(3), 293–301.

Steiger, H., & Zanko, M. (1990). Sexual traumata among eating-disordered, psychiatric, and normal female groups. *Journal of Interpersonal Violence, 5*(1), 74–86.

Steiner-Adair, C. (1992, April 24–26). *Discussion of clinical case presentation.* Paper presented at the Fifth International Conference on Eating Disorders, New York.

Strober, M. (1992, April 24–26). *The difficult patient: Clinical case presentation.*

Paper presented at the Fifth International Conference on Eating Disorders, New York.

Strober, M., & Humphrey, L. (1987). Familial contributions to the etiology and course of anorexia nervosa and bulimia. *Journal of Consulting and Clinical Psychology, 55,* 654–659.

Tavris, C. (1993a, January 3). Beware the incest-survivor machine. *New York Times Book Review,* pp 1, 16, 17.

Tavris, C. (1993b, February 23). [Letter to the editor.] *New York Times Book Review,* p. 27.

Theander, S. (1970). Anorexia nervosa: A psychiatric investigation of 94 female cases. *Acta Psychiatrica Scandinavica,* (Suppl.), 1–190.

Thompson, D. A., Berg, K. M., & Shatford, L. A. (1987). The heterogeneity of bulimic symptomatology: Cognitive and behavioral dimensions. *International Journal of Eating Disorders, 6*(2), 215–234.

van der Kolk, B. A. (1987). The role of the group in the origin and resolution of the trauma response. In B. A. van der Kolk (Ed.), *Psychological trauma.* Washington, DC: American Psychiatric Press.

van der Kolk, B. A. (1988). The trauma spectrum: The interaction of biological and social events in the genesis of the trauma response. *Journal of Traumatic Stress, 1,* 283–290.

van der Kolk, B. A. (1989). The compulsion to repeat the trauma: Re-enactment, revictimization and machochism. *Psychiatric Clinics of North America, 12*(2), 389–411.

Vandereycken, W., & Hoek, H. W. (1993). Are eating disorders culture-bound syndromes? In K. A. Halmi (Ed.), *Psychobiology and treatment of anorexia nervosa and bulimia nervosa.* Washington, DC: American Psychiatric Press.

Waller, G. (1992a). Sexual abuse and bulimic symptoms in eating disorders: Do family interaction and self-esteem explain the links? *International Journal of Eating Disorders, 12*(3), 235–248.

Waller, G. (1992b). Sexual abuse and the severity of bulimic symptomatology. *British Journal of Psychiatry, 161,* 90–93.

Waller, G., Halek, C., & Crisp. A. H. (1993). *Sexual abuse as a factor in anorexia nervosa: Evidence from two separate case series.* Manuscript submitted for publication.

Waller, G., Slade, P., & Calam, R. (1990). Family adaptability and cohesion: Relation to eating attitudes and disorders. *International Journal of Eating Disorders, 9*(2), 225–228.

Wasserman, C. (1992, November 18–20). FMS: The backlash against survivors. *Sojourner: The Women's Forum,* pp. 18–20.

Weisberg, L., & Herzog, D. B. (1992, April 24–26). *Sexual abuse in eating disorders: Evaluation and treatment.* Workshop presented at the Fifth International Conference on Eating Disorders, New York.

Westen, D., Ludolph, P., Misle, B., Ruffins, S., & Block, M. J. (1990). Physical and sexual abuse in adolescent girls with borderline personality disorder. *American Journal of Orthopsychiatry, 60*(1), 55–60.

Wonderlich, S. A., Donaldson, M. A., Staton, R. D., & Leach, L. R. (1990,

April 27–29). *Eating and personality disorder symptoms in incest victims*. Paper presented at the Fourth International Conference on Eating Disorders, New York.

Wonderlich, S. A., Donaldson, M. A., Staton, R. D., Carson, D., Gertz, L., & Johnson, M. (1992, April 24–26). *Eating disturbance in incest victims: A controlled study*. Paper presented at the Fifth International Conference on Eating Disorders, New York.

Wooley, O. W., & Roll, S. (1991). The Color-a-Person body dissatisfaction test: Stability, internal consistency, validity, and factor structure. *Journal of Personality Assessment, 56*(3), 395–413.

Wooley, O. W., Wooley, S. C., & Dyrenforth, S. R. (1979). Obesity and women II: A neglected feminist topic. *Women's Studies International Quarterly, 2*, 81–92.

Wooley, S. C. (1991). Uses of countertransference in the treatment of eating disorders: A gender perspective. In C. L. Johnson (Ed.), *Psychodynamic treatment of anorexia nervosa and bulimia*. New York: Guilford Press.

Wooley, S. C. (1992a). Anita Hill, Clarence Thomas and the enforcement of female silence. *Women and Therapy, 12*(4), 3–23.

Wooley, S. C. (1992b, April 24–26). Contribution to *How are we doing? Retrospective/perspective*. Plenary Session III presented at the Fifth International Conference on Eating Disorders, New York.

Wooley, S. C., & Kearney-Cooke, A. (1986). Intensive treatment of bulimia and body image disturbance. In K. Brownell & J. Foreyt (Eds.), *Handbook of eating disorders: Physiology, psychology and treatment of obesity, anorexia, and bulimia*. New York: Basic Books.

Wooley, S. C., & Lewis, K. G. (1987). Multi-family therapy within an intensive treatment program for bulimia. In J. C. Hansen & J. E. Harkaway (Eds.), *Eating disorders*. Rockville, MD: Aspen Publishers. (The Family Therapy Collections, Aspen Series)

Wooley, S. C., & Wooley, O. W. (1980). Eating disorders: Obesity and anorexia nervosa. In A. M. Brodsky and R. T. Hare-Mustin (Eds.), *Women and psychotherapy: An assessment of research and practice*. New York: Guilford Press.

Wooley, S. C., & Wooley, O. W. (1981). Eating as substance abuse. In N. Mello (Ed.), *Advances in substance abuse* (Vol. 2). Greenwich, CT: JAI Press.

Wooley, S. C., & Wooley, O. W. (1984). Intensive residential and outpatient treatment of bulimia. In D. M. Garner & P. E. Garfinkel (Eds.), *Handbook of psychotherapy for anorexia nervosa and bulimia*. New York: Guilford Press.

Wooley, S. C., & Wooley, O. W. (1986). Ambitious bulimics: Thinness mania. *American Health, 5*(8), 68–74.

Zanarini, M. C., Gunderson, J. G., Marino, M. F., Schwartz, E. O., & Frankenburg, F. R. (1989). Childhood experience of borderline patients. *Comprehensive Psychiatry, 30*(1), 18–25.

Zaretsky (producer). (1991, November 12). *My doctor, my love*. Boston: WGBH-TV.

Zerbe, K. J. (1992, April 24–26). *An integration of feminist, object relations, and self-psychological perspectives in the treatment of eating disorders*. Workshop presented at the Fifth International Conference on Eating Disorders, New York.

Ziegler, R., & Sours, J. (1968). A naturalistic study of patients with anorexia nervosa admitted to a university medical center. *Comprehensive Psychiatry, 9*(6), 644–651.

Zunio, N., Agoos, E., & Davis, W. N. (1991). The impact of therapist gender on the treatment of bulimic women. *International Journal of Eating Disorders, 10*(3), 253–263.

10

Alternatives in Obesity Treatment: Focusing on Health for Fat Women

DEBORA BURGARD
PAT LYONS

> *My grandmother died not long ago at the age of 85.*
> *They put "obesity" as the cause of death on her death*
> *certificate. Just how old does a fat person have to get*
> *before they are able to die of old age?*
> —Fat Lip Readers' Theatre, San Francisco, CA

MANY FAT PEOPLE, particularly women, live well into healthy old age. There are no medical or psychological problems that only fat people develop. The critical experiences fat people share are social prejudice and relentless pressure to lose weight. The widespread presumption that fatness is always pathological, a result of compulsive eating, fuels the belief that treatment must alter eating behavior with weight loss as the outcome—a belief rarely questioned by health professionals or those seeking their help. But these assumptions actually impede the development of compassionate, clinically effective care. The two of us—a psychologist specializing in eating and dieting disorders, and a nurse/health education consultant specializing in health care access and delivery, respectively—work to help women be as healthy as they can, whatever their size. We focus on health and self-acceptance, not weight loss. We discuss our approach in this chapter.

Any woman can enhance her physical and mental health by engaging in pleasurable physical activity, eating hearty and nutritious food, building support networks of family and friends, and learning to cope more effectively with conflict and social prejudice. Developing a positive partnership with health care providers can make all the difference in attaining long-term success. All people deserve access to high-quality medical and psychological services, based on science, not myth, and delivered with respect and compassion uncompromised by prejudice. But the stigmatization of fat people creates significant barriers to obtaining such care. This is the problem that must be addressed.

We are in a period of paradigm strain. Traditional weight loss treatment has failed abysmally, with 90–98% of those in every form of treatment regaining weight within 2–5 years (Willard, 1991; Greenwood, 1991; Garner & Wooley, 1991; National Institutes of Health [NIH], 1992). Standard treatment has aimed to modify eating behavior; however, research has shown that fat people as a group eat no differently from thin people (Rodin, 1980), although because of social pressure many fat people have probably dieted repeatedly. Dieters may become "restrained eaters," unable to eat naturally (Herman & Polivy, 1984). This often results in weight cycling, which appears to increase health risks (Brownell, 1988; Lissner et al., 1991; Wing, 1992). What is often ignored is that body weight is highly determined by genetic factors (Stunkard, 1986; Greenwood, 1991). The body employs a variety of physiological mechanisms to resist weight change and stay at "set point" (Bennett & Gurin, 1982). Given these facts, it is no wonder that some have for many years questioned whether obesity should be treated at all (Wooley & Wooley, 1984).

The panel of experts assembled to review over 1000 research papers for the 1992 NIH Technology Assessment Conference on Voluntary Weight Loss and Control came to some startling conclusions, considering that in 1984 they called obesity a "killer disease"—a statement that fueled a national wave of dieting mania. The 1992 panel (1) conceded the failure of traditional treatment; (2) warned the public against participating in commercial weight loss programs that are unable to produce scientific long-term participation rates and efficacy data; and (3) recommended that "a focus on approaches that can produce health benefits independently of weight loss may be the best way to improve the physical and psychological health of Americans seeking to lose weight" (NIH, 1992, p. 947). Although commercial programs and some scientists will dispute the recommendations of the panel and continue to promote weight loss, the panel's recommendations are nonetheless a long-overdue call to action for those concerned about practice ethics.

Continuing to view weight as the problem and weight loss as the solution is not helping fat people. We must step back and ask: What is problematic about being fat? Health professional and client must both reassess whether the client's problems consist of medical or mobility problems related to weight, internal conflicts about weight and body image, futile struggles with dieting and eating, social isolation or poor relationships, or the myriad other issues that arise for people of all sizes. If the client were thin, what questions would the health professional ask? What treatment would be offered?

Shifting from a weight loss model to one based on health entails a fundamental transition, which cannot be achieved by a simplistic juggling of therapeutic techniques. Shifting the focus from weight and dieting to enhancement of quality of life and health is radically different from the "before-and-after" school of personal transformation. Improving health is a lifelong proposition; there is no quick fix. Health professionals must create a safe, nurturing environment, free of fat bias, in which women can examine issues. Medical care is a common entry point for fat women seeking assistance; too often they find criticism instead of compassion. Barriers to respectful care must be removed if we are ever to see change in practice models.

THE CONSEQUENCES OF FAT PREJUDICE IN THE DELIVERY OF MEDICAL CARE

There is great resistance to the idea that fat people can be healthy just as they are, and may simply need routine medical care on occasion. Obesity is traditionally viewed both as a medical problem in its own right and as a risk factor in the development of several other conditions. Although epidemiologists have found that the medical risks of obesity have been greatly exaggerated (Ernsberger & Haskew, 1987), the assumption of pathology persists.

The words "do no harm" are fundamental to medical care, but for fat people this promise is broken again and again. Millions of healthy fat people are denied health insurance solely because of their weight; those who seek care may encounter insults, humiliation, or verbal abuse from physicians (Rothblum, Brand, Miller, & Oetjen, 1989). When a physician, who is expected to provide expertise and offer comfort, offers criticism instead, it can be emotionally devastating—even life-threatening.

An attitude of "Lose 50 pounds and call me in the morning" often substitutes for a sound treatment plan. Whether they are seeking care for pink eye, a sprained ankle, a stiff neck, or a gynecological problem, fat women receive weight loss lectures. One woman told us that she went to get glasses and was admonished for her weight! This kind of experience would be laughable if it weren't for the tragic consequences that can occur when fat people avoid or delay obtaining needed medical care.

A woman who had recently had a mastectomy reported that despite her apparent risk for cancer, she would not undergo routine Pap smears because she had been so humiliated in the past by a physician who said she was too fat for a proper exam. A physician told us of a 60-pound abdominal tumor that was overlooked because the thought of palpating a very fat abdomen was abhorrent to the examining physician. Recent newspaper reports of the discovery of a 180-pound ovarian cyst and a 303-pound abdominal tumor—both found in obese women—raise questions, since the growths had been present for years. Did fear of humiliation keep the women from seeking care? Did a fat-phobic physician fail to do a proper exam? The only early symptoms of ovarian cancer are bloating and persistent backaches; how many women with these complaints have been told to solve their problems by losing weight? How many women avoid care because they are sent to a freight scale to be weighed when the office scale doesn't go over 300 pounds?

As large women can attest, these incidents occur daily in the richest, most medically sophisticated country in the world. There is simply no excuse. People cannot be shamed into better health. To our knowledge, there has been no research on the effect of fat bias in medical care on the health of fat people; nor have any medical malpractice claims been based specifically on fat discrimination. But that time may not be far off. Lawsuits brought by over 500 Nutri/System clients charged failure to warn clientele of the greatly increased risk following rapid weight loss of gallstones requiring surgery. Lawsuits get attention, but do not automatically make care more accessible; often they have the opposite effect. For example, the dramatic rise in obstetric-related malpractice claims has reduced the numbers of obstetric practitioners and access to pregnancy-related care. In order for access to improve, consumers must take action on many fronts.

Just as women's health activists have had to fight for equal access and respectful medical care on the basis of gender, fat people are finally standing up for themselves and refusing to accept mistreatment. Women have told us that they have written to individual doctors or group health providers to voice complaints about negative staff attitudes or being automatically put on diets. They have pointed out that they pay the same rates for care as smaller people, and therefore equipment—gowns, blood pressure cuffs, wheelchairs, etc.—should come in sizes to fit their large bodies. The courage it takes to complain is worth it. It helps women put the problem where it should be—in the legitimate arena of quality of care and patient satisfaction—rather than continue to blame themselves and their bodies by remaining silent. It also puts providers on notice that "business (or bias) as usual" will no longer be tolerated.

A way for fat women to begin speaking up for themselves in a low-risk situation is to "just say no" to being weighed. A simple exercise pairs women to play the role of nurse and then patient, practicing ways to say no. Women are amazed that they *can* choose not to be weighed; just as in any medical treatment, the power of consent rests with the individual receiving care. Good medical care is not something that is "done" to people.

There are times when being weighed is a necessary part of medical treatment—for example, prenatal care, the monitoring of medications such as diuretics, or the treatment of wasting diseases. But usually it is just part of the routine. In our weight-conscious society, everyone may dislike it, but for a fat woman the weigh-in can be a barrier to obtaining timely care. It takes courage to challenge medical care providers, but women tell us they have been surprised by the willingness of some doctors to listen and redirect the focus of care appropriately. Some have found a sensitive response a litmus test of their doctor's credibility.

Educating physicians and other medical staff members about fat prejudice is fundamental to improving health care. As the AIDS epidemic has shown, attitude change by health professionals toward the population served is critical to providing appropriate and compassionate care. Health care professionals can reduce the stigmatization of fat by modeling respectful attitudes. Medicine put the pressure on fat people to become smaller; it is time to take it off.

GUIDELINES FOR CLINICAL PRACTICE

- *Establish a respectful clinical environment.* Reinforcing self-respect, without inducing guilt or shame, is fundamental to a positive health encounter. Environmental requirements include equipment that accommodates people of all sizes (e.g., chairs, gowns, exam tables, blood pressure cuffs, adaptors for scales to weigh people over 300 pounds), as well as privacy during required weighing. Automatic weigh-ins should be eliminated; when weighing is clinically indicated, it should be done only with the patient's consent. Patients should be asked whether they want to know the weight.
- *Allow people to explain fully why they are seeking help.* On average, a physician only listens to a patient for 18 seconds before starting to ask questions (Beckman & Frankel, 1984). Although physicians see this as a way to save time and focus visits, allowing patients to finish their explanation permits a more complete history and decreases the likelihood of the "doorknob" question—a problem voiced just as a physician is leaving the room, which often turns out to be the real point of the visit. Attentive listening is also more therapeutic for the patient. A woman in a focus group said:

My doctor actually puts her pencil down, looks at me, and listens. It's amazing, but just being heard makes me feel better. I hate feeling rushed to say what's wrong and then being given advice or some treatment before I even finish saying what's bothering me.

- *Treat people for their presenting problems.* Unsolicited advice about weight loss, particularly in the context of a visit for a totally unrelated issue, only embarrasses or angers people, making them reluctant to seek timely preventive care or treatment. Prescribing weight loss is not harmless. If these people could lose weight permanently, they probably would have already done so. Physicians should consider what treatment would be suggested for a thin person with the same presenting problem and offer it.
- *Discuss diet, weight, and lifestyle with sensitivity, but in a matter-of-fact way.* Sound nutrition, not dieting, is basic to good health. If nutrition is discussed, physicians and other health care personnel should let fat people know that they are not being singled out for this advice because of their size. Anyone can benefit from ample consumption of fruits, vegetables, and fiber and from minimal intake of foods high in saturated fat. Since nutrition education can be heard as "Lose weight," it must be clear that these issues are discussed with everyone.

Attaining a stable weight is a legitimate health goal. There are people with whom weight must be discussed in light of overall health concerns or weight fluctuations. Weight cycling and disordered eating endanger health. Weight cycling is usually associated with repeated dieting; the recommendation not to diet may be one of the best suggestions a physician can give. A thorough history should be taken with attention to family history, dieting history, weight fluctuations, and fat distribution, as well as changes in eating or exercise patterns or increased stress. Frustration with fat patients, particularly if it has escalated into suppressed anger or disgust, calls for referral to a provider with more compassion and respect.

WHEN A FAT WOMAN HAS A MEDICAL PROBLEM

There is a growing trend to help healthy women stop obsessing about their weight and come to terms with their size. But what about those fat women with illness or a positive family history of illness associated with fatness (e.g., cardiovascular disease, adult-onset diabetes, or hypertension), or with a condition that is aggravated by higher body weight (e.g., arthritis or back problems)? This is the most difficult issue to surmount in convincing physicians to "lighten up" on weight loss for fat patients. They feel obligated to prescribe weight loss, even though most would concede that they rarely achieve this result. A fat person represents the failure to find a "cure"; a person with serious medical problems presents a daunting case that a doctor cannot "fix." Patients with cardiovascular disease, diabetes, and hypertension may be spending hundreds of dollars a month on medications and undergoing frequent hospitalizations, with little hope of improvement in the foreseeable future. Although it seems that weight loss would help in theory, in practice it is not a viable solution.

What is reasonable to do? Even for people faced with medical problems, dieting is not the answer. Dieters almost inevitably regain weight, and may end up fatter than if they had not dieted in the first place; they can have more problems with hypertension and heart disease as a result of weight cycling; they regain weight in the abdomen, producing a pattern of body fat distribution associated with greater health risks. New federal public health consensus guidelines advise increased physical activity and a focus on health, not weight (Greenwood, 1991; Willard, 1991; Goodrich & Foreyt, 1991; Wood, Stefanick, Williams, & Haskell, 1991).

Fat individuals should not be denied medication or other treatment because physicians think they "should" be able to lose weight. Chronic medical conditions can be improved by moderate, sustained lifestyle changes without great reduction in weight (Goldstein, 1992). This requires that the patient accept responsibility for making the behavioral changes. Change is most effective when made in small steps that can be maintained. But lifestyle change may require improved self-esteem; people must believe they are "worth it." If quality of life is not addressed, people will rightly ask, "Why add years to a life full of misery?" We must help to find answers that make change feel worthwhile, remembering that our role is to facilitate rather than to dictate the healing process.

We believe that the most overlooked but most powerful lifestyle change is to become more physically active.

PLEASURABLE PHYSICAL ACTIVITY

> Not to have confidence in one's body is to lose confidence in oneself. . . . It is precisely the female athletes, who being positively interested in their own game, feel themselves least handicapped. . . . Let [women] swim, climb mountain peaks . . . take risks, go out for adventure and they will not feel before the world timidity.
>
> —Simone de Beauvoir (1952)

Much attention has been paid to women's preoccupation with thinness, relationships with food, and body image conflicts (Allon, 1982; Chernin,

1981; Seid, 1989). Much less attention has been given to the importance of sport, dance, and movement for women and girls. This is surprising, since feeling confident and comfortable in one's body is fundamental to health, self-confidence, and self-esteem. Perhaps playing and dancing do not seem as serious as developing political awareness or insight. But discussions of weight and women's health can no longer afford to ignore the role of activity. We must become much more skilled in helping women overcome barriers to being active and "more at home" in their own skin.

Regular aerobic exercise improves the function of virtually every body system—cardiovascular, respiratory, nervous, endocrine, musculoskeletal, and immune—and can often improve medical conditions (e.g., hypertension, diabetes and arthritis) without weight loss. It reduces stress, increases self-confidence, and improves mood. It can also improve body image and self-esteem; this is particularly important for women steeped in the stereotype of feminine frailty (Allen, 1972; Bennett & Gurin, 1982; Blair & Kohl, 1989; Bouchard, Shephard, Stephens, Sutton, & McPherson, 1990; Neiman, 1990; Melpomene Institute Staff and Researchers, 1990; Moore, 1988). It is the most tangible way for women to shift the view of their bodies from objects to instruments. Sport and dance offer ways for women to challenge themselves or simply to let go and have fun. None of these benefits are based on the size of the participants.

Although advice to "just do it" may sell athletic shoes, it is not helpful to a woman who has been ridiculed for being fat and has spent her life on the sidelines. She must overcome internal and external barriers to begin activity (Lyons & Burgard, 1990; Packer, 1989). In the standard weight loss paradigm, fat people exercise to lose weight. Fitness books are filled with graphs and charts of the calorie-burning potential of every possible activity; activities that "do the most good" (i.e., burn the most calories) are encouraged. Pleasure is rarely mentioned.

It is no surprise, then, that many people view exercise as punishment—a bitter pill that must be swallowed for "the sin of being fat." As data on the ineffectiveness of dieting have been more widely disseminated, professionals are now adopting an evangelistic tone about exercise, the new "cure" for obesity. This approach is the "exercise diet," which is as doomed as its predecessors to failure in realizing long-term weight loss. The idea that exercise could be an end in itself is unfamiliar to many. But pleasurable activity can last a lifetime, helping women improve and maintain their health along the way.

Large women can discover pleasure in movement when they feel safe enough to begin. Although issues related to pace and impact on the body do need to be considered when recommending safe activity to fat people (Lyons & Burgard, 1990), the critical point is to help women to focus on their strengths and help them become experts on their own bodies in motion. We must create more opportunities for safe, fun, noncompetitive exercise, such as renting a pool for private swim sessions or establishing dance/exercise classes taught by large instructors. These opportunities help women see large bodies, including their own, as capable of strength, vitality, and beauty. There is simply no substitute for this kind of experience.

Physical activity is a key ingredient in improving the health of fat women—physical movement can stimulate movement on other issues as well—and we discuss a movement group that was part of a treatment program in a later section. But, first, what about food and eating?

FAT WOMEN AND FOOD

If fat people eat no differently from thin people, and body size is primarily determined by genetics, we should abandon the focus on eating behavior. Women of all sizes may develop eating disorders, but clinicians should ask themselves whether they are equally likely to ask about this (and to believe their clients) regardless of the clients' body size. In addition, because most fat women have dieted, some will need assistance in "detox'ing" from this destructive practice. Unfortunately, the psychological and physical sequelae of dieting have only recently begun to be taken seriously.

Both clinician and client may be confused about what "normal" eating really is. As Ellyn Satter (1987), a dietician and therapist, sees it,

> Normal eating is being able to eat when you are hungry and continue eating until you are satisfied. . . . It is leaving some cookies on the plate because you know you can have some again tomorrow, or it is eating more now because they taste so wonderful when they are fresh. Normal eating is overeating at times: feeling stuffed and uncomfortable. It is also undereating at times and wishing you had more. Normal eating is trusting your body to make up for your mistakes in eating. Normal eating takes up some of your time and attention, but keeps its place as only one important area of your life. In short, normal eating is flexible. It varies in response to your emotions, your schedule, your hunger, and your proximity to food. (p. 69)

Therapists need to be sensitive to the sometimes subtle differences between disordered eating behavior resulting from dieting and similar behavior resulting from emotional conflicts. Defining the problem and working on solutions can be very different, depending on this formulation. Most fat women have been taught that conflicts about being thin are leading to their "eating problems," but many are victims of an iatrogenic process: The "solution" of dieting has caused problems with eating that were nonexistent before the diet.

One example of this is the "feast and famine" pattern common to dieters, as well as to people with more profound conflicts about food. Dieting encourages "all-or-none" thinking: Some foods are "acceptable/legal/healthy" and others are "bad/forbidden/dangerous"; and the dieter is "good" or "bad," depending on how she's eating. She often feels that she cannot trust her body to regulate itself when it comes to food, or even that her body has betrayed her. True disorders of appetite are rare in humans, but many people experience confusion about the source of their desire to eat. Dieting teaches the dieter to disregard her body's hunger and satiety cues, and instead to make eating decisions based on the diet's prescriptions for when, what, and how much. The ideology of any diet thus reinforces the split between the dieter's mind and her body, and asks her to distrust her body, which is seen as the source of sabotage.

Many women need only to be reintroduced to their physical hunger and given permission to eat in accord with those cues. Roth (1984), Hirschmann and Munter (1988), Kano (1985), and Ciliska (1990) have written excellent guides that reject "self-discipline" in favor of a relaxed and trusting relationship with one's appetites. They challenge the notion of self-deprivation, and emphasize the legitimacy (and even necessity) of learning how to give to oneself *more*.

Reluctance to stop dieting may come from many sources. Dieting can be very reinforcing, because in the short run, when effort and enthusiasm are the highest, it does result in weight loss. The dieter may assume that only when she becomes disgruntled and tired does the weight loss slow, and thus may conclude that ambivalence causes the regain of weight. The idea is seductive that if she could just feel clear enough or strong enough she could do it.

Many dieters also feel that they will be better accepted if they are trying to lose weight. The misconception that people are fat because they are lazy, greedy, or the like requires fat people to appear to be actively making the effort to be thin.

Dieting is also reinforced by fantasies. The dream of being thin usually has important meanings: being "together," invulnerable, happy, and confident. Sometimes this is experienced as a desirable but "false" (socially compliant) persona. Sometimes there is a fear that thinness will cause a woman to feel too attractive, too successful; she may be afraid of becoming the focus of envy or jealousy, or may fear that weight loss will remove checks on sexuality, competitiveness, hostility, and self-absorption. Rather than being viewed as clues about why a client "stays fat," these themes can reveal drives and conflicts she feels in the present, which she is trying to work through by changing her body size. Finally, investment in dieting and a fantasied future allows some clients to remain disengaged from life in the present, with its conflicts, imperfection, and unpredictability.

To give up dieting is to give up the dream of being in control over one's body—a desire so strong that watching the numbers go down on the scale can become an addiction. The desire for such control may stem from the wish to be less vulnerable to being shamed and humiliated about being fat. In addition, women who internalize the external oppression and feel their bodies are to blame may wish to punish the bodies they feel have betrayed them; dieting can be penance for the sin of being fat.

There is an almost seamless web of assumptions that a fat woman's body is out of control and cannot be trusted. Although this is a cultural message for all women, the "proof" of a fat body reinforces this. What Satter (1987) describes as the trust that one's body will "make up for your mistakes in eating" is hard-won, particularly for fat women. In fact, fat bodies seem to regulate themselves as precisely as thin bodies; they just do so around a higher set point. Normal human bodies, including fat ones, can be trusted to adjust (i.e., *not* to change weight in response) to transitory changes in how we eat.

Returning to a more natural way of eating can raise significant conflicts relating to self-acceptance. How we feed ourselves is one way to express self-hatred or self-love. To the extent that fat women internalize the cultural message of being undeserving, they find it difficult to respond to their own needs.

SELF-ACCEPTANCE AS A GOAL

> *I know so many people who want to be "perfect" and [think that] when they are "perfect" then they will love themselves. They think that if they accept themselves as they are they'll never change. . . . I suspect the whole thing is backwards, i.e., if you are truly self-accepting, weight is not an issue. If you are not self-accepting, you'll find lots of things to be unhappy about and weight is likely to be one of them.*
> —Respondent quoted in Burgard (1991, p. 88)

When health care professionals acknowledge the failure of "treatment" to reduce body weight permanently, interventions shift to promoting a healthy life, and self-acceptance becomes the goal. This shift can be difficult for both a health care professional and a client. On the one hand, the client is usually convinced that her body size is unacceptable. On the other hand, she may be angry that the culture has imposed that "unacceptability" on her. The health care provider may feel asked to take a stand on the client's acceptability. Instead, the client should be given information about the poor prospects for weight loss, and the alternative possibility of self-acceptance.

Research on 100 women weighing over 200 pounds, many of whom are involved with the size acceptance movement (Burgard, 1991), found that a majority felt self-accepting and that this self-acceptance was unrelated to how fat they were. Interestingly, dieters scored significantly lower than nondieters on measures of self-esteem and feelings of self-control. Self-esteem was related to perceiving oneself as having self-control, but in a surprising way. A respondent described the dieting process:

> When I am dieting I usually feel wonderful, sexy, alive, and full of hope. Then I stop due to some emotional catastrophe. I start to eat the bad things again. I stop exercising. I get depressed and eat more. Then I start to despise myself for yet again letting myself falter. I despise myself for not being able to say no to sweets, for not sticking with an exercise regimen. Pretty soon it's too late. The double chin is back, the tone in my muscles is gone, and all those months of dieting are for naught. I get resigned to being a failure. . . . Thank goodness for my cat! (quoted in Burgard, 1991, p. 96)

Believing that one should be able to diet, but experiencing repeated failure, engenders an overall sense of ineffectiveness. Respondents who believed that body weight was not really something they could choose felt more in control of other areas of their lives, and had higher self-esteem.

The fat women surveyed in this study have much to teach therapists who are working with a more troubled population. Instead of basing our views of all fat people on the clients who come to us for help, we can look to the experience and strengths of healthy fat people for information about how to help our clients.

Psychotherapy may be helpful for fat women who need more than information and assistance in overcoming the legacy of dieting or the barriers to physical activity. Clients should be assessed as individuals. Although fat people may have common experiences based on their shared status, the therapist must try not to re-enact the traumatizing experience of viewing a patient only in terms of body size. Group psychotherapy is a valuable adjunct to individual psychotherapy, especially when interpersonal functioning or social isolation is a problem. The group provides an opportunity for members to make social connections, discover common experiences, make positive identifications with other large women, and share coping skills.

ISSUES IN A PSYCHOTHERAPY GROUP
FOR FAT WOMEN

One of us (Burgard) designed and ran a time-limited (10-week) psychotherapy program. Participants met twice a week for 90 minutes. A
discussion group was held on one evening, and movement therapy on
the other, both with the explicit objective of fostering self-esteem and
self-acceptance. The goals of the program were for participants to learn
about the physiological dynamics of body weight, normalize eating,
experience pleasurable physical activity, explore common experiences as
fat women, identify external sources of stigma, replace "compliance"
with "entitlement" to good health, increase the ability to label and
tolerate emotions, increase the acceptance of feeling "needy," risk greater
self-assertion in relationships, learn "self-defense" against shaming experiences, examine personal meanings of body size, and identify and
change patterns of self-deprivation. The group was limited to large
women who were seeking outpatient psychotherapy.

Weight loss was explicitly *not* a goal of the group. It was assumed
that each person's healthiest weight was, by definition, whatever she
achieved when working toward the goals stated above. Since many of
the goals are long-term, a particular "healthy weight" was not identified;
instead, the focus was kept on concerns that could be addressed directly
in the present.

Initial Themes

The women who came to the group came with various objectives. Many
felt discouraged about repeated weight loss failures, but were not sure
what to do for themselves in lieu of dieting. Several expressed concerns
that their eating behavior seemed "out of control." Most of the women
expressed a general sense of depression, low self-esteem, and unhappi-
ness in relationships.

The ambivalence many group members felt about identifying themselves as fat women, and being in a group with other fat women, was
one of the first issues to arise. Many women had never had a friend who
was fat, and talked about avoiding other fat women in an effort to
minimize their awareness of their body size or the pain they expected to
confront in identifying with others. They talked about reactions they
expected to occur if they simply walked down the street as a group of fat
women, and their desire to avoid being targets for public humiliation.
On the other hand, it was common for a woman to feel validated and
relieved that others had often felt and thought the same way, and as time
went on, the association with walking down the street as a group began
to shift to a sense of power and solidarity.

Feelings about the Group Leaders

A useful part of the group experience was exploring members' feelings about the leaders. There were two leaders for the discussion group and two leaders for the movement group, and differences in their degree of fatness were meaningful to the group. For example, the thinner leader of the discussion group was seen as more knowledgeable and authoritative. Members tended to direct informational questions, requests, and reactions about the group rules to her. They talked about identifying more strongly with the fatter leader, seeing her as a role model in dress and personal presentation, and asking her more personal questions. However, her authority in the group was also questioned more, and members expressed more worries about whether her silences were expressions of sadness. This exploration provided the opportunity to see "internalized oppression" at work, and allowed group members to notice how their views of other fat women affected their own self-esteem.

For some members, exploring the division of responsibility between the leaders and the members was useful. The initial sense of euphoria and hopefulness about the group gave way to anger and disappointment when it became clearer that there would be no "before-and-after" transformations. As the women uncovered some hidden expectations of being "fixed" by the leaders, anger about past treatment relationships emerged. Members repeatedly confronted the leaders with the question of "what to *do* about it" once they identified feeling a certain way. Many women experienced a great deal of anguish in facing the need to care for themselves—to read their own needs accurately and attempt to meet them. Wishes that the leaders would give what earlier caregivers had failed to give began to emerge. Some of the members went on to realize that the opportunity to relive their childhoods "the right way this time" was over, and recognized that the task of developing their own internal caregivers would be a lifelong, challenging process. Others continued to expect some sort of compensation for their past deprivations.

Themes about Identity

Being the target of a stereotype figured prominently in the group's explorations. The women examined their responses to being seen in terms of being fat, rather than being perceived in terms of their individuality. Many spoke about organizing their lives to disprove the "fat woman" stereotype and the cost of being vigilant about never appearing sloppy, lazy, overbearing, or hungry. It was sometimes confusing for a woman to experience these states even fleetingly, as people normally do, because of fears that they confirmed the worst cultural beliefs about her as a fat woman. The women noted that because they were reacting so precisely against it, the stereotype was determining their behavior and feelings as surely as if they followed it to the letter.

Reacting against the stereotype had certain results. Not allowing themselves to be overbearing or angry had prevented some women from seeing themselves as victims of discrimination, and distanced them from other fat women; it inhibited taking action. Trying not to appear lazy, greedy, or hungry also worked against their acknowledging and responding to their own needs for rest, play, even letting go of control at times. Furthermore, it inhibited their making demands in relationships or relinquishing a caretaking role. Many women found their identification with the nurturing, understanding maternal role to be a compromise: not representative of the more autonomous or aggressive sides of themselves, but the one positive part of the "fat woman" stereotype.

Some members of the group spoke about their exhaustion and anger at having to tolerate being a walking symbol, always serving as the screen for other people's projections—feeling pitied, shamed, used as a symbol of other women's fears, or used as a symbol of others' fantasies about their sexuality or appetites. A common reaction was a feeling of wanting to hide or be less visible; this resulted in an inhibition of normal self-expression, especially in terms of clothing, physicality, and sexuality. Being darker, drabber, quieter, smaller was self-protective, and the women's new awareness of the wish to express themselves often felt dangerous.

Most of the women felt less conflicted about their intellectual competence, and felt that others could acknowledge these strengths. This sometimes made the women vulnerable to overwork, taking on excessive amounts of responsibility, and so on; the idea of not having to earn acceptability through their performance was foreign.

Ambivalence about Movement

The exercises were usually gentle, playful explorations to increase body awareness, such as feeling grounded, moving through space, and creating gestures to express feelings. Each session included a warm-up exercise, higher-intensity dancing to music, a cool-down and relaxation phase, and a discussion about how members felt about the movement.

The movement classes were powerful for the group members, who had sometimes retreated from an awareness of their bodies to "living above the chin." These experiences were thus a source of both pleasure and pain.

Several members were pleasantly surprised to note their physical strength and competence, and felt exuberant about the freedom to play. Many women noticed a progressive increase in their ability to move through their daily lives with greater stamina. In a subtle way, they observed a sense of "reoccupying" their bodies and of feeling more grounded.

The experience also forced some members to become aware of losses in their mobility over the years, which sometimes prompted anger and grief. These women began to sort out the results of aging and inactivity from those of body size as they saw each other's capabilities, and their own increasing strength and agility.

Dancing as a group brought back sometimes painful memories of childhood, especially of being chosen or not (to dance, or to play on a team). For some women, becoming more aware of their bodies made them more aware of past physical or sexual abuse. This could be initially frightening, but also offered the possibility of working through the trauma.

As they experienced their bodies more directly, the women began erasing the line separating their heads from their bodies, and instead focused on how to draw lines in other spheres—for example, setting limits in relationships, or replying to abusive comments about their weight. One group member challenged her physician's insistence that she embark on a liquid-protein diet, citing her past experiences that dieting in attempts to achieve quick weight loss had made her fatter. Several other members brought up ways in which they were experimenting with saying no to children or partners, albeit with some trepidation. It seemed as if they were redrawing boundaries to include their bodies, to be aware of their physical selves, and to strengthen their defenses against external exploitation.

Tolerating Feelings

Focusing on feelings was an all-important and often difficult endeavor. Participants found various ways to avoid feelings, the most popular of which was to obsess about dieting and weight. Often, members avoided attempting psychotherapeutic exercises designed to increase awareness of feelings between group meetings, and experienced this as "not doing the homework." They could then become involved in concerns about complying or rebelling against the presumed authority of the leaders, which was in itself another sort of distraction. The leaders questioned the use by adult women of self-descriptions as "good girls" and "bad girls"; they asked the group members to focus on their own choices to do the exercises or avoid feelings, and on whether they felt served by these choices.

There was much discussion about the members' anxiety at relinquishing their normal methods of distraction, and sometimes anger at the group leaders for not rescuing them. As some group members experimented with expressing these feelings, they began seeing how dangerous they perceived them to be. Some people were able just to let themselves experience the present and discover that no one died as a result, which was quite relieving. Other group members were not ready to experiment with this and remained more committed to their inhibitions.

Working It Through

> I'm tired of being Sisyphus and rolling the weight loss boulder up the hill over and over. I'm accepting my body as having been the innocent victim of society's torment. I want to love it, not hate it.
> —Respondent quoted in Burgard (1991, p. 98)

It was the process of relearning normal eating, and learning to ask themselves the simple question, "Am I hungry? What am I hungry for?," that often led to examining and labeling other feelings and needs that no amount of food (or dieting!) would address. For many group members, the belief that they needed to impose their willpower on their out-of-control appetites shifted to the more accurate comprehension of how deprived they routinely were, and how giving themselves more, not less, of what they need could lead to health.

CONCLUSION

The relationship of weight to health is highly complex and will remain so until every past assumption is questioned. Our hope in this discussion has been to shine a light down a different path and to ask new questions, for when we look for health rather than assuming pathology, our perspective shifts. Healthy fat women have always existed. Now that they are being asked, they are providing us with visions of how women of all sizes might embrace the fullness of life in the present.

REFERENCES

Allen, D. (1972). Self-concept and the female participant. In *Women and sport: A national research conference* (Penn State HPER Research Series, No. 2). University Park: Pennsylvania State University.

Allon, N. (1982). The stigma of overweight in everyday life. In G. Bray (Ed.), *Obesity in perspective* (DHEW Publication No. NIH 75–708, pp. 83–102). Washington, DC: U.S. Government Printing Office.

Beckman, H., & Frankel, R. (1984). The effect of physician behavior on the collection of data. *Annals of Internal Medicine, 101:* 692–96.

Bennett, W., & Gurin, J. (1982). *The dieter's dilemma.* New York: Basic Books.

Blair, S., & Kohl, M. W. (1989). Physical fitness and all-cause mortality: A prospective study on healthy men and women. *Journal of the American Medical Association, 262*(17), 2395–2401.

Bouchard, C., Shephard, R., Stephens, T., Sutton, J., & McPherson, B. (1990). *Exercise, fitness, and health: A consensus of current knowledge.* Champaign, IL: Human Kinetics Books.

Burgard, D. (1991). *Correlates of self-esteem, perceived self-control, body size acceptance and intention to lose weight in women over 200 pounds.* Unpublished doctoral dissertation, Wright Institute, Berkeley, CA.

Chernin, K. (1981). *The obsession: Reflections on the tyranny of slenderness.* New York: Harper & Row.

Ciliska, D. (1990). *Beyond dieting: Psychoeducational interventions for chronically obese women, a non-dieting approach.* New York: Brunner/Mazel.

de Beauvoir, S. (1952). *The second sex.* New York: Knopf.

Ernsberger, P., & Haskew, P. (1987). *Rethinking obesity.* New York: Human Sciences Press.

Garner, D. M., & Wooley, S. C. (1991). Confronting the failure of behavioral and dietary treatments for obesity. *Clinical Psychology Review, 11,* 729–780.

Goldstein, D. (1992). Beneficial health effects of modest weight loss. *International Journal of Obesity, 16,* 397–415.

Goodrich, G., & Foreyt, J. (1991). Why treatments of obesity don't last. *Journal of the American Dietetic Association, 91,* 1243–1247.

Greenwood, M. R. C. (1991). *Obesity as a public health challenge: Federal consensus.* Keynote address presented at Obesity Update: Assessment and Treatment of the Patient with Medically Significant Obesity, University of California at Davis School of Medicine.

Herman, P., & Polivy, J. (1984). A boundary model for the regulation of eating. In A. J. Stunkard & E. Stellar (Eds.), *Eating and its disorders* (pp. 141–156). New York: Raven Press.

Hirschmann, J., & Munter, C. (1988). *Overcoming overeating.* Reading, MA: Addison-Wesley.

Kano, S. (1985). *Making peace with food.* Danbury, CT: Amity.

Lissner, L., Odell, P., D'Agostino, R., Stokes, J., Kreger, B., Belanger, A., & Brownell, K. (1991). Variability of body weight and health outcomes in the Framingham population. *New England Journal of Medicine, 324,* 1839–1844.

Lyons, P., & Burgard, D. (1990). *Great shape: The first fitness guide for large women.* Palo Alto, CA: Bull.

Melpomene Institute Staff and Researchers. (1990). *The bodywise woman.* New York: Prentice Hall Press.

Moore, J. (1988). *Energy need, nutrient intake, fitness, body composition and health risk factors in women with childhood and adult-onset obesity before and after a 9-month nutrition education and walking program.* Unpublished doctoral dissertation, Oregon State University.

National Institute of Health (NIH), Technology Assessment Conference Panel. (1992). Methods for voluntary weight loss and control. *Annals of Internal Medicine, 116*(11), 942–949.

Neiman, D. (1990). *Fitness and sports medicine: An introduction.* Palo Alto, CA: Bull.

Packer, J. (1989). The role of stigmatization in fat people's avoidance of physical exercise. In L. Brown, & E. D. Rothblum (Eds.), *Overcoming fear of fat.* Binghamton, NY: Harrington Park Press.

Rodin, J. (1980). The externality theory today. In A. J. Stunkard (Ed.), *Obesity* (pp. 226–239). Philadelphia: W. B. Saunders.

Roth, G. (1984). *Breaking free from compulsive eating.* Indianapolis: Bobbs-Merrill.

Rothblum, E. D., Brand, P., Miller, C., & Oetjen, H. (1989). Results of the NAAFA survey on employment discrimination: Part II. *NAAFA Newsletter, 17*(2), 4–6.

Satter, E. (1987). *How to get your kid to eat—but not too much.* Palo Alto, CA: Bull.

Seid, R. (1989). *Never too thin: Why women are at war with their bodies.* New York: Prentice Hall.

Stunkard, A. J. (1986). An adoption study of human obesity. *New England Journal of Medicine, 314,* 193–198.

Willard, M. (1991). Obesity: Types and treatments. *American Family Physician, 43,* 2099–2108.

Wing, R. (1992). Weight cycling in humans: A review of the literature. *Annals of Behavioral Medicine, 14*(2), 113–119.

Wood, P., Stefanick, M., Williams, P., & Haskell, W. (1991). The effects on plasma lipoproteins of a prudent weight-reducing diet, with or without exercise, in overweight men and women. *New England Journal of Medicine, 325,* 461–466.

Wooley, S. C., & Wooley, O. W. (1984). Should obesity be treated at all? In A. J. Stunkard & E. Stellar (Eds.), *Eating and its disorders* (pp. 185–192). New York: Raven Press.

11

A Collaborative Approach to the Use of Medication

NANCY C. RAYMOND
JAMES E. MITCHELL
PATRICIA FALLON
MELANIE A. KATZMAN

A COLLABORATIVE APPROACH to the use of medication in the treatment of any condition requires attention both to the efficacy and limitations of the drug and to the quality of the communication among the patient, the physician, and others involved in the patient's care. Research studies have documented the usefulness of various medications in suppressing some symptoms of patients with eating disorders. However, a careful reading of the literature also indicates that medications alone have limitations in the treatment of these disorders.

The interplay among prescription, prescriber, and patient is a salient issue in the pharmacological treatment of eating disorders, since the medical model with which most physicians are familiar is one in which the authority of the physician, when used inappropriately, can overpower or silence the receiver's wishes and concerns. For women who have difficulty questioning authority and asking for what they want, the incorporation of medication into treatment needs to be handled with care. This requires a realistic appraisal of the drug's potential usefulness, as well as the system in which it will be monitored.

This chapter begins with a review of recent studies designed to evaluate the short- and long-term efficacy of various medications in the treatment of eating disorders. Data on response rates to various medications in controlled studies are presented. This empirically based section is followed by a more clinical discussion of the therapeutic issues that arise in collaborative decision making about the use of medication. This section includes clinical treatment recommendations based on research data and clinical experience.

REVIEW OF THE LITERATURE ON PHARMACOLOGICAL TREATMENT

Anorexia Nervosa Literature

The literature on the pharmacological treatment of eating disorders is fairly succinct, particularly for anorexia nervosa, for which the number of controlled trials is quite modest. The initial treatment intervention usually involves many components, including nutritional management, medical stabilization, psychotherapy, and milieu therapy; this makes it particularly difficult for researchers to sort out and control for the various elements. Also, anorexia nervosa is a fairly rare condition, and patients with anorexia nervosa are frequently uncooperative with research.

Antidepressants were among the first agents used for anorexia nervosa, based on the observation that many patients appear depressed at intake, and some continue to experience depressive episodes even when normal weight is restored (Halmi et al., 1991). In addition, data suggest that a family loading exists for affective disorders in the first-degree relatives of anorexia nervosa patients. However, one well-controlled study suggests that higher rates of depression in family members are restricted to the relatives of those anorexic patients who are themselves depressed (Strober, Lampert, Morrel, Burroughs, & Jacobs, 1990).

Despite a wealth of anecdotal reports, only three placebo-controlled, double-blind studies have been published. The first, by Lacey and Crisp (1980), was a small study using clomipramine at a dosage of 50 mg/day, a conservative dose; this was reasonable, given the minimal experience with medication therapy for anorexia nervosa at that time. In retrospect, however, the dosage was probably subtherapeutic, and this may have contributed to the lack of significant findings. The other two studies, by Biederman et al. (1985) and by Halmi, Eckert, LaDu, and Cohen (1986), both used amitriptyline. The latter study also used another active substance, cyproheptadine. The Biederman et al. (1985) study, which used a smaller sample size and lower mean serum dosage, found no effect. The Halmi et al. (1986) study, using a higher dosage of amitriptyline and a larger sample, demonstrated greater "treatment efficacy" (a variable having to do with the rapidity with which patients reached their target weight). However, the advantage for the active drug was not dramatic. Two open-label studies of maintenance rather than acute treatment (Kaye, Weltzin, Hsu, & Bulik, 1991; E. D. Eckert, personal communication, 1992), both using the serotonin reuptake inhibitor fluoxetine hydrochloride, have found an apparent advantage for this drug. However, these findings need to be replicated in placebo-controlled trials.

Cyproheptadine was originally proposed as a possible treatment for anorexia nervosa, based on the observations that cyproheptadine stimulated appetite and weight gain in individuals with allergies. Two studies (Vigersky & Loriaux, 1977; Goldberg, Halmi, Eckert, Casper, & Davis, 1979) found no significant effect, although the latter identified a subgroup of patients that might be more responsive. The amitriptyline study by Halmi et al. (1986) also included a cyproheptadine cell, as noted above; these authors found a significant effect of cyproheptadine at high dosages, usually 32 mg/day, on treatment efficacy and depression. Although the results were statistically significant, clinically they were not dramatic. Restricting anorexics appeared to benefit from cyproheptadine, whereas bulimic anorexic patients were unaffected and some patients actually had a worsening of symptoms—a finding that indicates possible differences in the pathophysiology of these two subgroups of patients.

Lithium was studied in an inpatient setting and was found to have a slight advantage over placebo at weeks 3 and 4 in producing weight gain. However, the authors were not enthusiastic about the results and discussed at some length the problems in using lithium in this population (Gross et al., 1981). Although neuroleptics were widely used to treat anorexia in the 1950s and 1960s, two controlled trials of antipsychotic drugs—one using pimozide (Vandereycken & Pierloot, 1982) and one using sulpiride (Vandereycken, 1984)—failed to find a statistical superiority for active drug over placebo. Clonidine, an alpha$_2$-adrenergic agonist, was also studied (Casper, Schlemmer, & Javaid, 1987), because this class of medications had been reported to increase food consumption. However, in trials in inpatient anorexic women, the medication did not significantly increase their food intake.

Bulimia Nervosa Literature

Most of the literature on pharmacotherapy for bulimia nervosa has focused on the use of antidepressant drugs. Several other types of drugs (e.g., opioid antagonist and antiepileptic drugs) have been tried, some with interesting results. The findings of these studies are presented because the possibility of their use in the treatment of bulimia nervosa may be raised from time to time. However, none of these other drugs can currently be recommended for clinical usage, given either the paucity of data, the lack of efficacy, or the potential side-effects.

Antidepressant Treatment

Pope and Hudson (1982) and Walsh et al. (1988) were the first to recommend antidepressants for bulimia. They noted that bulimic patients were often depressed, and hypothesized that improvement in their depression might improve their eating behavior. Following these initial open-label trials, 14 placebo-controlled trials have appeared in the literature, and one other multicenter trial of fluoxetine remains unpublished. These data are summarized in Table 11.1. Also of interest are three studies that have compared the efficacy of cognitive–behavioral therapy and medications (Mitchell et al., 1990; Agras et al., 1992; Fichter et al., 1991); these are discussed later.

Nearly all classes of antidepressants have been studied including tricyclics (imipramine, amitriptyline, and desipramine), monoamine oxidase inhibitors (phenelzine and isocarboxazid), a selective serotonin reuptake inhibitor (fluoxetine hydrochloride), and several atypical antidepressants (mianserin, bupropion, and trazodone). A few of the studies have employed a crossover design, in which the subject is first given either active drug or placebo and then switched after a fixed interval to the other treatment for the same number of weeks. Most have used a parallel design, in which each individual subject receives either active drug or placebo for the same number of weeks. Many of these studies were rather short in duration, most lasting only 6–8 eight weeks. Exceptions include a study by Agras, Dorian, Kirkely, Arnow, and Bachman (1987), the Fluoxetine Bulimia Nervosa Collaborative (FBNC) Study (FBNC Study Group, 1992), an as-yet-unpublished fluoxetine treatment study (Dista Pharmaceuticals, 1993), and a recent study by Agras et al. (1992), all of which are of longer duration. Many of these studies have had small sample sizes, with approximately 40 or fewer subjects in each group completing the trial.

When one examines the percentage of reduction in binge-eating frequency from pre- to posttreatment in the antidepressant studies listed in Table 11.1, the results are impressive. All but two studies found significantly greater reduction in binge eating and/or purging on active medication, with most studies reporting fairly dramatic reductions in binge-eating frequency, ranging from 31% to 91%. The mean reduction in binge-eating frequency was 63%. Placebo response rates varied from an increase of 21% to a decrease of 52%, with a mean reduction in

TABLE 11.1. Controlled Pharmacotherapy Studies of Bulimia Nervosa

Study	Drug/dosage	Design	Duration	n at start	% completing treatment	% reduction pre to post BE	V	% abstinent last week
Pope et al., 1983	Imipramine (200 mg)	Parallel	6 wk	D = 11	82%	70%		0%
				P = 11	91%	0%		0%
Sabine et al., 1983	Mianserin (60 mg)	Parallel	8 wk	D = 20	70%			
				P = 30	73%			
Mitchell & Groat, 1984	Amitriptyline (150 mg)	Parallel	8 wk	D = 21	76%	72%	78%	19%
				D = 17	94%	52%	53%	19%
Hughes et al., 1986	Desipramine (200 mg)	Parallel	6 wk	D = 10	79%	91%		68%
				P = 12	75%	−19%		0%
Agras et al., 1987	Imipramine (mean = 176 mg, max = 300 mg)	Parallel	16 wk	D = 10	100%	72%	72%	30%
				P = 12	83%	43%	35%	10%
Barlow et al., 1988	Desipramine (150 mg)	Crossover	6 wk	47	51%			4%
Blouin et al., 1988	Desipramine (150 mg)	Crossover	6 wk	36	61%		45%	
	Fenfluramine (60 mg)						43%	
Horne et al., 1988	Bupropion (225–450 mg)	Parallel	8 wk	D = 55	68%	67%		
				P = 26	46%	2%		
Kennedy et al., 1988	Isocarboxazid (60 mg)	Crossover	6 wk	29	2%			
Pope et al., 1989	Trazadone (400–650 mg)	Parallel	6 wk	D = 23	87%	31%		10%
				P = 23	96%	−21%		0%
Walsh et al., 1988	Phenelzine (60–80 mg)	Parallel	8 wk	D = 31	74%	64%		35%
				P = 31	88%	5%		4%
Mitchell, Pyle, et al., 1989	CBT group + placebo	Parallel		34	85%	89%		45%
	CBT group + imipramine			52	75%	92%		56%
	Imipramine			54	67%	49%		10%
	Placebo					3%		
Agras et al., 1991	Desipramine—16 wk	Parallel		12			33%[a]	
	Desipramine—24 wk			12				42%
	CBT + desipramine—16 wk			12		83%		
	CBT + desipramine—24 wk			12			64%[a]	70%
	CBT (individual)			12		48%		55%

(cont.)

[a]Assessed at 16 weeks.

TABLE 11.1. (cont.)

Study	Drug/dosage	Design	Dura-tion	n at start	% com-pleting treat-ment	% reduction pre to post BE	% reduction pre to post V	% abstinent last week
Fichter et al., 1991	Fluoxetine + BT (individual)	Parallel		20	100%	47%		
	Placebo + BT (individual)			20	100%	25%		
Freeman et al., in press	Fluoxetine (60 mg)	Parallel	6 wk	D = 20	70%	51%		
				P = 20	90%	17%		
Walsh et al., 1991	Desipramine (200–300 mg)	Parallel	8 wk	D = 40	80%	47%		12.5%
				P = 38	84%	–7%		7.9%
FBNC Study Group, 1992	Fluoxetine (60 mg)	Parallel	8 wk	D = 128	70%	67%	56%	
	Fluoxetine (20 mg)			D = 127	77%	45	29%	
				P = 127	62%	33%	5%	

Note. BE, binge eating; V, vomiting; D, active drug; P, placebo; CBT, cognitive–behavioral therapy; BT, behavior therapy.

binge-eating frequency of 11%. However, the number of subjects actually free of binge-eating symptoms at the end of treatment is quite disappointing: only one study found remission rates greater than 35%. This low remission rate is problematic, because recent evidence indicates that abstinence from bingeing and purging is a good predictor of long-term recovery (Maddocks, Kaplan, Blake, Langdon, & Piran, 1992). The study by Hughes, Wells, Cunningham, and Illstrup (1986), which found a remission rate of 91%, is clearly not representative of the majority of the treatment studies. Overall, one must conclude that antidepressants suppress but usually do not eliminate binge eating and vomiting; this appears to be true regardless of whether the patient has affective symptoms. Most studies also show that among patients with significant affective symptoms, these symptoms also respond to antidepressants.

Available follow-up studies (Pyle et al., 1990; Walsh, Hadigan, Devlin, Gladis, & Roose, 1991; Pope, Hudson, Jeans, & Yurgelun-Todd, 1985) show that it is difficult to maintain patients successfully on antidepressants. Many patients require multiple dose adjustments or trials of multiple medications. In the best maintenance study conducted to date, many subjects initially considered to have had a successful medication trial (50% reduction in binge eating) relapsed within the next 6 months on medication continuation (Walsh et al., 1991).

Three treatment studies have compared the efficacy of antidepressants, cognitive–behavioral therapy, and combined treatment. Mitchell et al. (1990) found that treatment with cognitive–behavioral therapy was superior to treatment with imipramine alone. Adding imipramine to cognitive–behavioral therapy did not improve outcome with regard to bulimic symptoms (binge eating and purging), but did decrease depressive symptoms to a greater degree. Agras et al. (1992) reported a complicated study that compared desipramine given alone for 16 or 24 weeks, combined cognitive–behavioral therapy and desipramine given for either 16 or 24 weeks, and cognitive–behavioral therapy alone. In general, the study indicated that combined treatment given for a longer period of time yielded a greater improvement in bulimic symptoms. Fichter et al. (1991) reported yet another study of combined treatment, in which inpatients received fluoxetine while undergoing behavior therapy. Behavior therapy alone was quite effective in changing eating behavior, and no additional improvement was seen with the addition of fluoxetine.

Other Medication Trials

Opioid antagonists and antiepileptic drugs have also been tried in the treatment of bulimia nervosa. Opioid antagonist drugs were employed in an attempt to suppress binge eating in bulimia nervosa, since opioid antagonists have been shown to reduce stress-induced feeding in animals. Jonas and Gold (1986) first reported an open-label trial of naltrexone, an orally active narcotic antagonist; they found that it suppressed binge eating. Two later studies replicated the findings among bulimia nervosa subjects, some of whom were receiving antidepressants (Jonas & Gold, 1986–1987, 1988). The dosages used by Jonas and Gold (1986–1987) were generally higher than recommended by the package label, up to 300 mg (a dosage that was later found to be associated with hepatotoxicity). In one study, they demonstrated that response to a moderate dose of naltrexone (50 mg) had no effect, while the higher dose (300 mg) did. Mitchell, Christenson, et al. (1989) and Igoin-Apfelbaum and Apfelbaum (1987) both reported double-blind, placebo-controlled trials at the more usual dosages of 50 mg/day and 120 mg/day, respectively, without effect. In summary, opioid antagonists may have some value; however, this has not been demonstrated in placebo-controlled, double-blind trials, and the dosages required to produce therapeutic effect are of considerable concern.

Some early reports suggested that binge eating might be responsive to the antiepileptic drug phenytoin (Green & Rau, 1974, 1977). However a subsequent placebo-controlled trial was confounded by a crossover design (Wermuth, Davis, Hollister, & Stunkard, 1977), and subsequent attempts to use newer antiepileptics have been for the most part un-successful (Kaplan, Garfinkel, Darby, & Garner, 1983).

Lithium carbonate, a mood-stabilizing drug used in the treatment of manic–depressive disorder, has also been suggested as a treatment for bulimia nervosa. Following initial reports of success using lithium car-bonate, a placebo-controlled trial failed to find evidence for a significant advantage over placebo (Hsu, Clement, Santhuse, & Ju, 1991). Fenflur-amine, a serotonergic agonist, has been considered for the treatment of bulimia nervosa, since serotonin is thought to decrease hunger. Initial reports have indicated some limited success with this medication (Blouin et al., 1988).

THE COLLABORATIVE APPROACH: ISSUES AND TREATMENT RECOMMENDATIONS

This section describes the issues that arise when pharmacotherapy and psychotherapy are integrated in a way that respects the power of the patient and reflects a realistic appraisal of what medications can add to treatment. In particular, this section highlights the importance of attend-ing to the relationships among patient, physician, and other treatment team members. Specific clinical treatment recommendations will also be provided, based on the literature review provided above and our own clinical experiences with the various medications.

When to Refer a Patient for Medical Consultation

Involving the Patient in Decision Making

The possibility that a patient might benefit from medication may be apparent during the initial phase of treatment, or medication use may become a realistic alternative during later stages of recovery. For some-one who has restored her weight to a healthy range or whose binge eating and purging have diminished, the introduction of medication can be presented as an additional resource.

The decision by a therapist to refer a patient for a medication evaluation needs to be handled with care. The patient may interpret the referral to a physician as a means to "get rid" of her. She may think that the therapist is frustrated or angry with her, especially if the reasons for the referral have not been clearly explained. Framing the decision as a collaborative one sets the stage for healthy interactions. Exploring this option requires educating the patient about the medication, as well as about the logistics of adding another dimension of care. These logistics include (1) how the patient will pay for the doctor's visits and medication; (2) whether she has the time for additional appointments, and (3) how the care by multiple providers will be coordinated.

The referral process may take some time after the initial suggestion, as the patient may need time to express her concerns in regard to rejection or not being "good enough," and to state her preferences for either a female or a male psychiatrist. By providing several possibilities for a referral, the therapist may promote a woman's sense of choice. However, if a clear single choice is most appropriate, this can be offered.

The woman's questions and concerns need to be answered directly and taken seriously in a nonauthoritarian way. When making the referral, the therapist should stress to the woman that this is an evaluation for medication, thus allowing for the possibility that drugs may not be prescribed. An evaluation by another professional can serve several purposes. In a positive collaboration, it allows another clinician to evaluate the progress of therapy, confirm the diagnosis, and provide feedback about the therapy process. Sometimes the patient will tell the physician something she has not told the therapist (e.g., use of alcohol, suicidal ideation, transference feelings), which is important information for the therapist. If there has been a clear agreement between the caregivers not to keep secrets, this can be helpful in facilitating recovery.

Choosing a Medical Consultant

The therapist can set the stage for collaborative work by suggesting a physician whom she or he respects and feels comfortable working with. It often helps to discuss the case with the physician before the patient's visit. The therapist needs to attend carefully to the way the physician interacts with her or him, as this may often mirror the way in which the physician will interact with the referred patient. It is important to choose a physician who communicates an understanding of the eating disorder and who is comfortable discussing the emotional and nutritional problems the woman is facing. It is also useful to adopt a nonjudgmental manner so that the patient can feel comfortable expressing shame, anger, and other feelings. To prescribe a drug without knowing the woman's circumstances invites passivity, noncompliance, or misuse. It is also irresponsible on the part of the caregivers and may discourage the patient from seeking the care she needs.

In most instances the prescribing doctor will be a psychiatrist, but in some cases (e.g., when a psychiatric consultant is not available or when the patient is a very young girl), the family doctor, pediatrician, or internist may be the best choice if this physician has an established relationship with the patient.

In cases where there is a choice between a male and a female psychiatrist, either option has potential positive and negative effects. Having a female therapist and a male psychopharmacologist (or vice versa) can create a comforting "family," especially if appropriate communication and respect are modeled. However, the introduction of a male doctor when the therapist is female may precipitate issues centering around power, authority, and control. When the team consists of two women, there is the opportunity to model healthy cooperation between strong women, as opposed to the competition that is sometimes experienced in female relationships.

The Use of Medication

When and What to Prescribe for Anorexia Nervosa

Given the dearth of adequate research, there is little evidence to support a prominent role for pharmacotherapy in the treatment of anorexia nervosa. However, many clinicians find that medications can be a useful adjunct to other types of therapy.

Emaciation can itself result in depressive symptoms, and weight gain often alleviates these symptoms. In the absence of severe depressive or obsessive compulsive symptoms, nutritional rehabilitation and psychotherapy are usually used without concurrent medications. If the patient does not seem to be responding well to these approaches, medications can be added. However, if severe depressive or obsessive compulsive symptoms make other treatment difficult, an antidepressant can be prescribed during the initial phase of treatment. Typically, fluoxetine hydrochloride is tried first; the dosage is rapidly increased from 20 to 40 or 60 mg, if the patient does not have side effects. Given the anorexic effects of fluoxetine hydrochloride, one might be concerned that it would cause additional weight loss; however, in practice this does not seem to occur. Observed benefits of fluoxetine include decreased depressive symptoms and decreased obsessional thinking about food and weight, especially when used at dosages of 40 to 80 mg/day (a range frequently used in obsessive compulsive disorder).

Tricyclic antidepressants are agents to consider for patients who do not respond to fluoxetine. The less anticholinergic, less sedating antidepressants, such as desipramine or nortriptyline, are often used first. Clomipramine is also a useful drug in patients with obsessional symptoms, although its sedative and anticholinergic side effects can be problematic.

Despite some suggestions in the literature that cyproheptadine or amitriptyline may be useful in inducing weight gain, the results of clinical trials suggest modest benefit, and must be balanced against the risks of side effects. Both are seldom used clinically in the treatment of anorexia nervosa. Clonidine is not used clinically to treat this disorder. There is no clinical indication for the use of antipsychotic drugs such as pimozide or sulpiride in the treatment of anorexia nervosa, unless there is a concurrent psychotic disorder.

Medications, especially the newer agents such as the selective serotonin reuptake inhibitors, may be helpful in preventing relapse and maintaining weight once nutritional rehabilitation has been completed. Exactly how this use should be integrated into an ongoing treatment program remains unclear. It may be helpful to use these agents for depressive and obsessional symptoms during the weight maintenance phase of treatment. Research is needed to test the effectiveness of this approach.

When and What to Prescribe for Bulimia Nervosa

Given the evidence for the effectiveness of psychotherapy in treating bulimia nervosa, this approach along with nutrition education is often the initial intervention. However, in patients with incapacitating depression, patients with depression that predates the eating disorder, or patients who do not respond well to psychotherapy, medication can be used. Given the low abstinence rate in subjects treated with medication alone, we do not recommend medication as the primary mode of therapy for patients with bulimia nervosa.

Serotonin reuptake inhibitors (e.g., fluoxetine hydrochloride) are currently the first choice for the treatment of bulimia nervosa. One study (FBNC Study Group, 1992) found that 60 mg was superior to 20 mg, with subjects reporting improvement in mood, decreased binge eating and purging, and decreased obsessional thinking about food and weight. There are few data available on the recently released drug sertraline, but it is a logical alternative treatment in patients who find the side effects of fluoxetine particularly bothersome.

Tricyclic antidepressants, particularly desipramine, are an alternative for patients who do not respond to fluoxetine. Because of its anti-obsessional quality, clomipramine is also a reasonable alternative, particularly if there is a strong obsessional component present. However, because of the higher incidence of anticholinergic and sedative side effects with clomipramine, studies of the use of this drug in bulimia have not been carried out. Bupropion is contraindicated in this population, because of the high incidence of seizures in bulimic patients taking this medication. The monoamine oxidase inhibitors are difficult to use in this population because of their side effect profile, as well as the dietary restrictions required to prevent hypertensive crises. Trazodone has significant sedative side effects at the dosages required for treatment, and therefore it is not chosen as a first-line medication.

The opioid antagonists, antiepileptic drugs, and lithium are not recommended for the treatment of bulimia nervosa. As noted earlier, opioid antagonists have potential liver toxicity at dosages that may be effective. Because of the lack of strong evidence supporting its use, fenfluramine is seldom used. There is not good evidence for the efficacy of antiepileptic drugs or lithium in the treatment of bulimia nervosa.

Collaborative Decision Making and Informed Consent

Although the physician may or may not decide that medication is indicated, the woman ultimately makes the final decision and is accountable for using it appropriately. If she is involved in the decision-making process, a choice not to take medication can be viewed as positive rather than resistant.

One of the aspects of this process of using medications is that there can be transference both to the caregivers and to the medication itself. When medications are prescribed, the woman may view the medication as the "magic pill" that is going to solve her problems and resolve her eating disorder. Thus she may feel that she no longer needs to be concerned about attempting to alter her behavior or about being actively engaged in the therapeutic process. Alternatively, she may see medication as evidence that there is something "really wrong" with her, and may feel hopeless about her ability to change her thoughts, feelings, and behavior. Clearly, the way in which the medication is presented is crucial in determining not only the outcome of the medication trial but perhaps also the success of therapy. The woman may find it helpful to adopt the attitude that the medication will assist her in gaining control of her eating behavior and will enable her to be more successful as she participates in therapy.

Encouraging a woman to take responsibility for the choice allows her to take responsibility for the gains made during treatment. The patient is less likely to relapse after the medications are discontinued if she realizes that she is responsible for her improvement (with the assistance of medications) than if she attributes all of the improvement to the medication alone.

It is best to be direct with patients about the extent and limits of our knowledge about medications. We know, for example, that they improve mood in some patients but that they also help some people who do not have a disturbed affect. We know that they help suppress binge eating to some extent in some patients, whether or not they meet the criteria for bulimia nervosa. We also know that the drugs may change metabolism slightly. For example, the tricyclics decrease resting energy expenditure, and the serotonin reuptake inhibitors increase it.

Side effects need to be described in detail. Information such as when to call the physician or discontinue the medication needs to be reviewed, and the patient should be encouraged to ask as many specific questions as needed. It is also important to inform the patient about how soon the therapeutic effect is likely to be apparent, what the optimal dosage of the medication is likely to be, and how long the medication trial will last without a response before the possibility of discontinuing it will be discussed. Most patients are used to taking analgesics for headaches or antibiotics for 10 days for an infection. The notion of taking a medication that does not cause an immediate response or needs to be taken for months at a time may be anathema to patients who have not previously taken this type of medication. Patients should be informed that the available studies suggest that those who discontinue the medication without other therapeutic intervention may relapse; therefore, the treatment will remain primarily psychological in focus. Although it might seem that such a stance would make the medication less "powerful," it shifts the power and responsibility to the patient.

When Not to Prescribe

As with the use of any medication for any disorder, there are certain instances in which medication use for eating disorders must be approached with caution. Women who are trying to conceive, are pregnant, or are lactating are generally not good candidates for medications. Appropriate medication selection is important in patients at risk for suicide; fluoxetine and sertraline are far less likely than tricyclics to be lethal in overdose. Given the data suggesting that a substantial number of women with eating disorders also drink and use illicit drugs to excess (Mitchell, Specker, & de Zwaan, 1991), it is critical that a detailed history in this area be obtained. The inappropriate use of alcohol or illicit drugs may be a contraindication for medication use. Telling a patient that she must decide not to drink or use drugs if she takes medication is a useful way of confronting her use of these substances. In such instances, it is particularly important that the team work together to provide clear information about substance abuse to the patient.

Although the introduction of medicine sometime brings with it certain expectations for an effortless cure, the studies described above indicate that medication may not always be indicated and that its impact when used alone may be modest. As a result, medication may best be described as a useful tool that can augment changes in affect and eating behavior when used in conjunction with psychotherapy.

In some cases, the decision will be made not to prescribe any medication. This also can be a powerful intervention, and the implications can be used to guide the direction of treatment. Because starvation can be an underlying mechanism of depression and may prompt binge eating, the physician may decide not to prescribe medication until the patient has gained some weight. Telling the patient that the best medication for her is food may provide powerful feedback. Some patients may find eating so anxiety-provoking that they actually wish for a medication to cure the eating disorder, rather than face the fact that they need to eat more and perhaps gain weight in order to recover.

If the decision is made not to prescribe, it is best for the therapist treating the patient to learn this directly from the physician, so that she or he can discuss the decision with the patient appropriately. It is also important that the physician, in recommending or not recommending medication, not undermine the credibility of the therapist involved with the patient. Sometimes the final recommendation to the patient should be left open until the two care providers have had a chance to confer.

The Decision to Discontinue Medication

A 6-week trial of each medication is usually recommended before switching to a different drug, adding a potentiating drug, or abandoning the use of medication. There is some evidence in the literature that if the first medication trial fails, the use of an alternative medicine may work. One study (Mitchell, Pyle, et al., 1989) found that 50% (5 of 10) subjects initially treated unsuccessfully with imipramine were able to attain complete remission of bulimic symptoms when tried on other tricyclics or monamine oxidase inhibitors.

If a medication is successful, it is suggested that the patient take it for at least 6 months. Before discontinuing the medication, the entire treatment team should confer. This allows for an assessment of the patient's current stress level and any pending changes in treatment. The chances of relapse are higher if the patient is ending therapy or making some other major life change. Since the therapist may have more information about events than the physician, or greater insight into factors affecting whether to continue or stop the medication, the physician will want to confer with the therapist before suggesting that the woman discontinue the medication. Successful discontinuation of the medication will be influenced by the patient's attitude toward the medication. If the patient sees the medication as the "answer" to her problems and she improves during the course of treatment, she may be prone to relapse. However, if she believes that the medication is an adjunct to other treatment, and if she is encouraged to believe that she is the one responsible for changes in her behavior, she is more likely to maintain her improvement.

The caregivers also need to be sensitive to the patient's feelings about the unsuccessful use of medications. She may experience a renewed sense of despair, worry, and depression if she had high hopes for a complete recovery on medication. Providers can offer interpretations that are affirming rather than negative. If the woman has been informed about the potential limitations of medications then the failure of an individual medication can be attributed to the medicine itself. The patient can be complimented for the courage she displays by being willing to explore all options available to assist her in her recovery. Medication failure becomes an opportunity to discuss other medications or psychotherapeutic interventions that can be tried. Predicting the desire to give up or drop out of treatment, and discussing this during the process, can at times circumvent its occurrence.

The Collaborative Approach as a Healthy Example of Family Dynamics

Although different types of theoretical approaches can be used with eating-disordered patients, almost all acknowledge the importance of the therapeutic relationship. Many affected women come from families in which there are power imbalances, triangulation, over- or underprotection, and poor parental communication (Root, Fallon, & Friedrich, 1986). Since issues of confidentiality, splitting, and trust are heightened with the addition of more caretakers, there is the potential to replicate dysfunctional family interactions when both a therapist and a physician are involved in the care of a patient.

Alternatively, the team can model the advantages of a healthy, well-functioning system if care providers respect each other and demonstrate this to the patient. They must communicate that each professional plays an important part in the recovery process. In order to avoid splitting, the physician needs to be aware that if the patient is raising questions with her or him about the appropriateness of the therapy, the physician can listen and encourage an honest discussion between the therapist and patient; the same is true for the therapist if the patient raises questions in therapy about the appropriateness of the medical treatment. The keeping of secrets must not be tolerated by the team. This open atmosphere of communication can be demonstrated to the patient by holding three-way conference calls or by having a session in which both the therapist and physician are present.

In most cases, the patient who lives with her family is encouraged to discuss her use of medication with the family. Where appropriate, family members may be included in the decision process so as not to undermine the treatment. When medication is given to a woman who is in family therapy, its use has to be framed carefully, so that family members do not see the prescription as validating a patient's illness and thereby undermining the therapist's effort to encourage the family to see how the disturbed family system has contributed to the patient's symptoms (Sargent, 1986).

Another possible family parallel can occur if the treatment team struggles to control medication intake in the way a family tries to control food intake. The patient may seem overtly compliant, but may not take the medication out of fear of weight gain or anger at one or the other of the caregivers. The therapist can become the one "checking up on her," much as her parents check on her restricting, binge eating, or vomiting behaviors. Helping the patient identify what she would have the most difficulty disclosing to the therapist or to the physician can open discussion of these issues.

There are a number of ways in which dysfunctional family patterns can be repeated in the typical scenario of a female therapist and a male physician treating a young female patient. The male physician can be viewed as the more powerful but unreachable father, while the female therapist may be experienced as a warm and communicative but ineffective mother who needs the father to come in to solve the daughter's problems. The patient may feel that the female therapist with whom she has a close working relationship cannot really "help," and that she is being referred to the male doctor to get the problem "fixed." A similar dynamic may be experienced even if both the therapist and the physician are female, because of the real or perceived differences in power between the two.

Given the high numbers of women with eating disorders who have a history of physical and/or sexual abuse by family members and people outside the family (some have even been abused by past therapists or physicians), it is important to recognize the way in which this affects the triad and the therapeutic relationship. A woman who has been abused often presents in therapy as a passive, compliant individual who may experience depression and a feeling of being out of control of her body. She may not ask many questions, as she is not used to being asked for opinions. If either caregiver is a man, she may have particular difficulty in a relationship with a male whom she perceives as having power over her. It is up to the caregivers to be sensitive to these issues and to discuss them with the woman. Acknowledgment of the pain and long-term consequences of abuse, and of its potential impact on the therapeutic relationship, is another way to avoid replication of dysfunctional family experiences. Finally, a woman who has been abused is often numb to her feelings, and some of the side effects of medications may heighten or obscure the intensity of her feelings. The drugs may also recreate familiar feelings of being out of control of her body, and thus activate memories of sexual abuse.

SUMMARY

The collaborative use of medication requires attending not only to the choice of medication but to the manner in which it is introduced, the collective efforts of the team, and the strengths of the patient. Compliance with a medication regimen is reconceptualized as the choice of the patient and the recognition of her control over her recovery. Collaborative use of medication requires that as caregivers we recognize the impact of our language, involve patients in our decisions, and evaluate the way we invoke our authority. This includes opportunities for the patients to say what they want and how they feel and to negotiate these needs and feelings in the context of healthy therapeutic relationships.

REFERENCES

Agras, W. S., Dorian, B., Kirkely, B. G., Arnow, B., & Bachman, J. (1987). Imipramine in the treatment of bulimia: A double-blind controlled study. *International Journal of Eating Disorders, 6,* 29–38.

Agras, W. S., Rossiter, E. M., Arnow, B., Schneider, J. A., Telch, C. F., Raeburn, S. D., Bruce, B., Perl, M., & Koran, L. M. (1992). Pharmacologic and cognitive–behavioral treatment for bulimia nervosa: A controlled comparison. *American Journal of Psychiatry, 149,* 82–87.

Barlow, J., Blouin, J., Blouin, A., & Perez, E. (1988). Treatment of bulimia with desipramine: A double-blind crossover study. *Canadian Journal of Psychiatry, 33,* 129–133.

Biederman, J., Herzog, D. B., Rivinus, T. M., Harper, G. P., Ferber, R. A., Rosenbaum, J. F., Harmatz, J. S., Tondorf, R., Orsulak, P. J., & Schildkraut, J. J. (1985). Amitriptyline in the treatment of anorexia nervosa: A double-blind, placebo-controlled study. *Journal of Clinical Psychopharmacology, 5,* 10–16.

Blouin, A. G., Blouin, J. H., Perez, E. L., Bushnik, T., Zuro, C., & Mulder, E. (1988). Treatment of bulimia with fenfluramine and desipramine. *Journal of Clinical Psychopharmacology, 8,* 261–269.

Casper, R. C., Schlemmer, R. F., & Javaid, J. I. (1987). A placebo-controlled crossover study of oral clonidine in acute anorexia nervosa. *Psychiatric Research, 20,* 249–260.

Dista Pharmaceuticals. (1993). Unpublished raw data.

Fichter, M. M., Leibl, K., Rief, W., Brunner, E., Schmidt-Auberger, S., & Engel, R. R. (1991). Fluoxetine versus placebo: A double-blind study with bulimic inpatients undergoing intensive psychotherapy. *Pharmacopsychiatry, 24*, 1–7.

Fluoxetine Bulimia Nervosa Collaborative (FNBC) Study Group. (1992). Fluoxetine in the treatment of bulimia nervosa. *Archives of General Psychiatry, 49*, 139–147.

Freeman, C. P. L., Davies, F., & Morris, J., (in press). A double-blind controlled trial of fluoxetine versus placebo for bulimia nervosa. *British Journal of Psychiatry*.

Goldberg, S. C., Halmi, K. A., Eckert, E. D., Casper, R. C., & Davis, J. M. (1979). Cyproheptadine in anorexia nervosa. *British Journal of Psychiatry, 134*, 67–70.

Green, R. S., & Rau, J. H. (1974). Treatment of compulsive eating disturbances with anticonvulsant medication. *American Journal of Psychiatry, 131*, 428–432.

Green, R. S., & Rau, J. H. (1977). The use of diphenylhydantoin in compulsive eating disorders: Further studies. In R. A. Vigersky (Ed.), *Anorexia nervosa* (pp. 377–382). New York: Raven Press.

Gross, H. A., Ebert, M. H., Faden, V. B., Goldberg, S. C., Nee, L., & Kaye, W. H. (1981). A double-blind controlled trial of lithium carbonate in primary anorexia nervosa. *Journal of Clinical Psychopharmacology, 1*, 376–381.

Halmi, K. A., Eckert, E., LaDu, T. J., & Cohen, J. (1986). Anorexia nervosa: Treatment efficacy of cyproheptadine and amitriptyline. *Archives of General Psychiatry, 43*, 177–181.

Halmi, K. A., Eckert, E. D., Marchi, P., Salperganaro, V., Apple, R., & Cohen, J. (1991). Comorbidity of psychiatric diagnosis in anorexia nervosa. *Archives of General Psychiatry, 48*, 712–718.

Horne, R. L., Ferguson, J. M., Pope, H. G., Hudson, J. I., Lineberry, C. G., Ascher, J., & Cato, A. (1988). Treatment of bulimia with bupropion: A multicenter controlled trial. *Journal of Clinical Psychiatry, 49*, 262–266.

Hsu, L. K. G., Clement, L., Santhuse, R., & Ju, E. S. Y. (1991). Treatment of bulimia nervosa with lithium carbonate: A controlled study. *Journal of Nervous and Mental Disease, 179*, 351–355.

Hughes, P. L., Wells, L. A., Cunningham, C. J., & Illstrup, D. M. (1986). Treating bulimia with desipramine. *Archives of General Psychiatry, 43*, 182–186.

Igoin-Apfelbaum, L., & Apfelbaum, M. (1987). Naltrexone and bulimic symptoms. *Lancet, ii*, 1087–1088.

Jonas, J. M., & Gold, M. S. (1986). Naltrexone reverses bulimia symptoms. *Lancet, i*, 807.

Jonas, J. M., & Gold, M.S. (1986–1987). Treatment of antidepressant-resistant bulimia with naltrexone. *International Journal of Psychiatry in Medicine, 16*, 305–309.

Jonas, J. M., & Gold, M. D. (1988). The use of opiate antagonists in treating bulimia: A study of low-dose versus high-dose naltrexone. *Psychiatry Research, 24*, 195–199.

Kaplan, A. S., Garfinkel, P. E., Darby, P. L., & Garner, D. M. (1983). Carbamazepine in the treatment of bulimia. *American Journal of Psychiatry, 140,* 1225–1226.

Kaye, W. H., Weltzin, T. E., Hsu, L. K. G., & Bulik, C. M. (1991). An open trial of fluoxetine in patients with anorexia nervosa. *Journal of Clinical Psychiatry, 52,* 464–471.

Kennedy, S. H., Piran, N., Warsh, J. J., Prendergrast, P., Mainprize, E., Whynot, C., & Garfinkel, P. E. (1988). A trial of isocarboxazid in the treatment of bulimia nervosa. *Journal of Clinical Psychopharmacology, 8,* 391–396.

Lacey, J. H., & Crisp, A. H. (1980). Hunger, food intake and weight: The impact of clomipramine on a refeeding anorexia nervosa population. *Postgraduate Medical Journal, 56,* 79–85.

Maddocks, S. E., Kaplan, A. S., Blake, D., Langdon, L., & Piran, N. (1992). Two year follow-up of bulimia nervosa: The importance of abstinence as the criterion of outcome. *International Journal of Eating Disorders, 12,* 133–141.

Mitchell, J. E., Christenson, G., Jennings, J., Huber, M., Thomas, B., Pomeroy, C., & Morley, J. (1989). A placebo-controlled, double-blind crossover study of naltrexone hydrochloride in outpatients with normal weight bulimia. *Journal of Clinical Psychopharmacology, 9,* 94–97.

Mitchell, J. E., & Groat, R. (1984). A placebo-controlled, double-blind trial of amitriptyline in bulimia. *Journal of Clinical Psychopharmacology, 4,* 186–193.

Mitchell, J. E., Pyle, R. L., Eckert, E. D., Hatsukami, D., Pomeroy, C., & Zimmerman, R. (1989). Response to alternative antidepressants in imipramine nonresponders with bulimia nervosa. *Journal of Clinical Psychopharmacology, 9,* 291–293.

Mitchell, J. E., Pyle, R. L., Eckert, E. D., Hatsukami, D., Pomeroy, C., & Zimmerman, R. (1990). A comparison study of antidepressants and structured intensive group psychotherapy in the treatment of bulimia nervosa. *Archives of General Psychiatry, 47,* 149–157.

Mitchell, J. E., Specker, S. M., & de Zwaan, M. (1991). Comorbidity and medical complications of bulimia nervosa. *Journal of Clinical Psychiatry, 52,* 13–20.

Pope, H. G., & Hudson, J. I. (1982). Treatment of bulimia with antidepressants. *Psychopharmacology, 78,* 176–179.

Pope, H. G., Hudson, J. I., Jeans, J. M., & Yurgelun-Todd, D. (1983). Bulimia treated with imipramine: A placebo-controlled, double-blind study. *American Journal of Psychiatry, 140,* 554–558.

Pope, H. G., Hudson, J. I., Jeans, J., & Yurgelun-Todd, D. (1985). Antidepressant treatment of bulimia: A two-year follow-up study. *Journal of Clinical Psychopharmacology, 5,* 320–327.

Pope, H. G., Keck, P. E., McElroy, S. L., & Hudson, J. I. (1989). A placebo-controlled study of trazodone in bulimia nervosa. *Journal of Clinical Psychopharmacology, 9,* 254–259.

Pyle, R. L., Mitchell, J. E., Eckert, E. D., Hatsukami, D., Pomeroy, C., & Zimmerman, R. (1990). Maintenance treatment and 6-month outcome for bulimic patients who respond to initial treatment. *American Journal of Psychiatry, 147,* 871–875.

Root, M., Fallon, P., & Friedrich, W. (1986). *Bulimia: A systems approach to treatment.* New York: Norton.

Sabine, E. J., Yonace, A., Farrington, A. J., Barratt, K. H., & Wakeling, A. (1983). Bulimia nervosa: A placebo controlled double-blind therapeutic trial of mianserin. *British Journal of Clinical Pharmacology, 15,* 195S–202S.

Sargent, J. (1986). Psychopharmacology and family therapy: Is there a role for drugs in family treatment? *The Family Therapy Networker, 10,* 17–19.

Strober, M., Lampert, C., Morrel, W., Burroughs, J., & Jacobs, C. (1990). A controlled family study of anorexia nervosa: Evidence of familial aggression and lack of shared transmission with affective disorders. *International Journal of Eating Disorders, 9,* 239–253.

Vandereycken, W. (1984). Neuroleptics in the short-term treatment of anorexia nervosa: A double-blind placebo-controlled study with sulpiride. *British Journal of Psychiatry, 144,* 288–292.

Vandereycken, W., & Pierloot, R. (1982). Pimozide combined with behavior therapy in the short-term treatment of anorexia nervosa: A double-blind placebo-controlled cross-over study. *Acta Psychiatrica Scandinavica, 66,* 445–450.

Vigersky, R. A., & Loriaux, D. L. (1977). The effect of cyproheptadine in anorexia nervosa: A double-blind trial. In R. A. Vigersky (Ed.), *Anorexia nervosa* (pp. 349–356). New York: Raven Press.

Walsh, B. T., Gladis, M., Roose, S. P., Stewart, J. W., Stetner, F., & Glassman, A. H. (1988). Phenelzine vs. placebo in 50 patients with bulimia. *Archives of General Psychiatry, 45,* 471–475.

Walsh, B. T., Hadigan, C. M., Devlin, M. J., Gladis, M., & Roose, S. P. (1991). Long-term outcome of antidepressant treatment for bulimia nervosa. *American Journal of Psychiatry, 148,* 1206–1212.

Wermuth, B. M., Davis, K. L., Hollister, L. E., & Stunkard, A. J. (1977). Phenytoin treatment of the binge-eating syndrome. *American Journal of Psychiatry, 134,* 1249–1253.

12

Feminist Inpatient Treatment for Eating Disorders: An Oxymoron?

ROBIN SESAN

THE DECISION TO RECOMMEND inpatient treatment for eating-disordered clients is a difficult one for many mental health professionals. It becomes an even more complicated and conflictual decision for feminist therapists, who are concerned about the oppressive nature of inpatient settings, which all too often replicate destructive patriarchical patterns (Chesler, 1972; Greenspan, 1983). Hospitalization engenders frightening images of disempowerment and failure for both the client and her therapist, because the need for inpatient care may be seen as a consequence of unsuccessful therapy. In addition, both client and therapist may be faced with issues of loss and separation as a result of the hospitalization.

Approximately 9000 patients are hospitalized annually in our country for the treatment of anorexia nervosa, bulimia nervosa, and related disorders (Travis, 1988). Over the past several years the roles of dual diagnoses, substance abuse, and childhood sexual abuse in the etiology of serious eating disorders have become more evident; as a result, treatment decisions are becoming increasingly complicated (Hatsukami, Eckert, Mitchell, & Pyle, 1984; Hiller & Zaugid, 1989; Root & Fallon, 1988; Wonderlich, Swift, Slotnick, & Goodman, 1990). There appears to be a trend toward both long- and short-term hospital treatment for women with eating disorders who are dually diagnosed (Fornari, Katz, Halmi, & Marcus, 1990; Johnson & Connors, 1987; Johnson, Tobin, & Dennis,

1990; Marcus & Katz, 1990). However, data on the effectiveness of this type of treatment for comorbidity are inconclusive (Gartner, Marcus, Halmi, & Loranger, 1989; Herzog, Hamburg, & Bratman, 1987; Steinhausen & Glanville, 1983; Wamboldt, Kaslow, Swift, & Ritholz, 1987). Inpatient facilities may be relying on dual diagnosis of eating-disordered clients to assure both admission to a unit and continued insurance reimbursement. As therapists, we need to be particularly aware of the potential for diagnostic misuses when referring eating-disordered clients for inpatient treatment, and vigilant about protecting the best interests of our clients. With the recent proliferation of specialized eating disorder treatment units within traditional hospital and psychiatric inpatient settings, there is an increased opportunity to use hospitalization as part of the long-term treatment process for some women with eating disorders (Anderson, 1985).

This chapter explores inpatient treatment of eating disorders from a feminist perspective. A brief historical overview on hospital treatment of eating disorders is presented, along with a discussion of newly emerging inpatient and residential treatment programs. Factors entering into the decision to recommend hospital treatment to a client are discussed, and inpatient treatment models are critiqued according to feminist therapy principles. Because inpatient treatment may be a necessary component in the overall recovery for some women with eating disorders, theory on the psychology of women is applied to inpatient treatment models to present a more feminist approach to inpatient care. If women are to be hospitalized for the treatment of eating disorders, it is essential that we apply what we know about the psychology of women and feminist therapy in order to create healthy, nonoppressive environments in which real healing can occur.

A BRIEF HISTORICAL PERSPECTIVE

Prior to 1975, hospitalization for a patient with an eating disorder was seen as a treatment of "last resort" (Bruch, 1973). The majority of patients hospitalized were diagnosed with anorexia nervosa, and the sole purpose of the hospitalization was to help the patients gain weight. The decision to hospitalize a patient with an eating disorder was viewed as a life-saving measure, similar to the hospitalization of a suicidal patient. Thus, treatment interventions were medically based, including nutritional (Crisp, 1965). electroconvulsive (Bernstein, 1964), and pharmacological (Dally & Sargant, 1966) therapies. In addition, forced feeding of patients by nasogastric tube (Wall, 1959) or hyperalimentation (Maloney & Farrell, 1980) was often used to achieve the goal of weight gain. Since anorexia nervosa was viewed as a medical disorder, hospitalization for these patients did not address the underlying psychological and sociocultural issues (George, Weiss, Gwirtsman, & Blazer, 1987). Typically, patients "complied" with procedures to gain weight while in the hospital, only to lose the weight once released, often precipitating rehospitalization. Bruch (1974) cautioned against this focus on weight gain in treating anorexia nervosa, because the other, more substantial psychological and emotional issues went unheard.

There has been a gradual shift in inpatient treatment for eating-disordered patients since the mid-1970s. This shift has reflected a growing awareness of the coexistence of medical and psychological factors in the etiology of eating disorders. Beginning in the mid-1970s, eating-disordered patients were increasingly admitted to psychiatric rather than to medical units. Although a strong emphasis on weight gain remained, treatment on a psychiatric service allowed for attention to psychological issues within the therapeutic milieu (Gunderson, 1978; George et al., 1987; Vandereycken, 1985). The use of behavior modification, along with modified bed rest and high-calorie supplements to achieve weight restoration, replaced forced feedings. Supportive counseling was offered to patients to help prevent relapse following discharge (Garfinkel & Garner, 1982; Garfinkel, Garner, & Kennedy, 1985).

Over the last 10 years, hospital-based and residential programs focused exclusively on the treatment of eating disorders have emerged. Patients with a wide range of eating disorders, including anorexia nervosa, bulimia nervosa, and binge eating, are now treated in inpatient facilities. The newer programs define themselves as multidimensional and hold hope for moving beyond traditional medical models of treatment. The majority of these programs tend to integrate behavioral management of eating disorder symptomatology with a range of individual, group, and family therapy options. They acknowledge a sociocultural context for the development of eating disorders, and many include as part of intensive treatment a focus on body image, women's issues, and assertiveness training (Andersen, Morse, & Santmyer, 1985; Levendusky & Dooley, 1985; Roth, 1986).

Nonetheless, the majority of programs continue to focus on weight gain, weight stabilization, and normalization of eating behaviors as primary goals, with only secondary attention paid to underlying psychological distress. Most programs rely heavily on cognitive–behavioral approaches to control eating disorder symptomatology, including the use of cognitive therapy and behavioral contracts for weight gain prior to the onset of insight-oriented treatment (Levendusky & Dooley, 1985; Roth, 1986). These programs do not appear to use cognitive–behavioral therapy to help women understand how their thought processes may be inhibiting the emotional expression necessary for healing and coping. Both Bruch (1974, 1982) and later Wooley (1990) cautioned clinicians about the exclusive use of cognitive–behavioral interventions in treating women with eating disorders. Wooley stated that cognitive–behavioral therapy alone does not heal; when it is applied to control eating disorder symptoms, it may be teaching women to suppress emotions, encouraging the restriction of affect that is at the heart of the problem. She stressed the need for application of theory and research on women's unique psychology in the development of eating disorder treatment paradigms.

THE DECISION TO HOSPITALIZE

Although inpatient treatment options for clients with eating disorders have improved over the years, the decision to recommend hospitalization remains a difficult one. Clinicians need to be aware of the different gradations of care available for women with eating disorders, in order to provide treatment within the least restrictive environment. Gradations of care, ranging from least to most restrictive, include the following: (1) self-help and support groups (Enright, Butterfield, & Berkowitz, 1985); (2) psychoeducational treatment (Connors, Johnson, & Stuckey, 1984; Davis, Olmsted, & Rockert, 1990; Weiss, Katzman, & Wolchik, 1986); (3) outpatient individual and/or group therapy (Johnson & Connors, 1987; Johnson, 1991); (4) outpatient intensive treatment programs (Mitchell et al., 1985; Wooley & Kearney-Cooke, 1986; Wooley & Wooley, 1985); (5) day treatment programs (Piran & Kaplan, 1990); (6) residential treatment programs (Wooley & Wooley, 1985); and (7) traditional hospital-based programs (Andersen et al., 1984; Halmi, 1984; Levendusky & Dooley, 1985; Roth, 1986). It is generally recommended that clients be treated on an outpatient basis prior to referral for inpatient care. In fact, many inpatient programs will only admit clients who have had a course of outpatient psychotherapy. Johnson and Connors (1987) have stated that it is preferable to work with both bulimic and anorexic clients on "mastering self-regulatory and life management problems" (p. 197) in real-life settings, rather than in artificially controlled hospital environments.

The decision to intensify the treatment by recommending a more structured environment is based on observation of progress or lack thereof. In addition, more structured environments are often recommended for clients who (1) present a significant medical or suicidal risk; (2) are self-mutilating; (3) cannot sustain an adequate level of self-care; (4) do not have family or significant others to provide an adequate psychological environment to support recovery; (5) are dually diagnosed; or (6) need help interrupting a binge–purge cycle that has become out of control (Garfinkel & Garner, 1982; Johnson & Connors, 1987). Furthermore, the containing environment of an inpatient setting may be an essential piece in the recovery process for women with both eating disorders and dissociative disorders that are the result of childhood sexual abuse (Bloom, 1991; Herman, 1992).

A FEMINIST CRITIQUE OF CURRENT INPATIENT TREATMENT MODELS

A feminist analysis of current inpatient treatment models first requires identification of the guiding principles of feminist therapy. In this section, several general principles of feminist therapy are outlined (e.g., Butler, 1985; Gilbert, 1980; Lerman, 1986; Travis, 1988); they are then used to critique current models of inpatient care for their congruence with a feminist treatment perspective.

A Sociocultural Perspective

1. Feminist therapy recognizes that many of the problems women bring into therapy, including eating disorders, depression, low self-esteem, and feelings of powerlessness, are the results of sexism and oppression of women within our culture.

2. Feminist therapy helps clients explore the inherent contradictions in prescribed social roles, and encourages change rather than adaptation to these roles.

3. Feminist therapy recognizes that the idealization of masculine qualities and the devaluation of feminine qualities within our culture create conflicts for women. A feminist therapist values clients' attainment of autonomy and need for connection. Feminist therapy helps women to value their strengths in typically devalued areas.

4. Feminist therapists are sensitive to the fact that a high percentage of women have experienced victimization as children or adults, recognize that victimization of girls and women is the result of oppression, and use this knowledge in the evaluation and treatment of disorders of high prevalence among women.

The majority of current inpatient treatment programs acknowledge a sociocultural component in the etiology of eating disorders. As a result, most programs include women's issues groups, where patients are encouraged to explore the costs and consequences of living within narrow role prescriptions. Women in treatment are helped to explore their overidentification with caretaking roles, their needs to please and seek approval from others, and their identification with the cultural ideal of slenderness as factors in their body hatred and drive for thinness. Furthermore, the majority of inpatient programs now include sexual abuse treatment within their prescribed protocols.

Although sociocultural issues are addressed in treatment, the very nature of most inpatient treatment settings may be perpetuating a pattern of oppression by rigidly controlling women's behaviors and actions and inadvertently "silencing" them once again (Kearney-Cooke, 1991). Orbach (1986) has suggested that women with eating disorders display internal conflicts of autonomy versus accommodation, denial versus desire, and the wish for invisibility versus the drive to be seen. These conflicts are expressed in self-starvation and in bingeing and purging behaviors. Most inpatient programs, in their attempt to control eating disorder symptomatology, may be preventing women from expressing themselves in the only way they know how.

For example, the model of treatment in most inpatient settings has been one of deprivation. Women have been denied access to bathrooms (Halmi, 1985; Roth, 1986), have been on meal plans that either restrict or "force-feed" (Levendusky & Dooley, 1985; Marcus & Katz, 1990), have been restricted from participating in certain activities if their weight is too low (Garfinkel & Garner, 1982), and have been denied "privileges" if their behavior is not within the prescribed rules (Levendusky & Dooley, 1985). Although many women benefit from the structure of an inpatient setting, the restrictive nature of most settings reinforces deprivation as a norm.

In addition to the more traditional hospital programs, which use behavioral management techniques to control women's behavior, newly emerging "food addiction" inpatient programs based on an abstinence model of recovery impose another type of deprivation (Vandereycken, 1990). These programs deprive women of white flour, refined sugars, wheat, and a number of other food substances, based on an unproven theory that women with eating disorders are "addicted" to these foods. For women, whose eating has been out of control for many years, such a model provides short-term relief, but eventually replicates a familiar pattern of depriving themselves of needs, wants, and desires.

Furthermore, the restrictive nature of setting goal weights, monitoring meal plans for calorie content, and limiting or requiring exercise within most inpatient programs tends to parallel our culture's objectification of "woman as body," thereby defining women's bodies for them rather than facilitating self-definition (Greenspan, 1983; Kearney-Cooke, 1991). The majority of women with eating disorders have unquestioningly adopted the cultural norm of thinness as valuable, and attribute many desirable masculine qualities to being thin (Streigel-

Moore, Silberstein, & Rodin, 1986). Women with bulimia have been described as both overidentifying with the female role and metaphorically embodying the conflict of meeting female expectations while excelling in a male-valued manner (Boskind-Lodahl, 1976; Steiner-Adair, 1986; Wooley & Kearney-Cooke, 1986). Women with anorexia have been characterized as rejecting the feminine in pursuit of the masculine (Barnett, 1986). Orbach (1985) has suggested that the anorexic's stance is one of rebellion against domination. By taking control of her body, the woman with anorexia nervosa is not participating in society's objectification of her.

By narrowly defining the acceptable form for a woman's body, current inpatient programs collude with oppressive standards for thinness. Women with eating disorders are often dissociated from their bodies (Goldner, Cockhill, & Bakan, 1990). They need opportunities to feel fullness and hunger, and the attending feelings of emptiness, deprivation, and satiety. They need to learn that they have value as women and that their presence in the world is important. All women, but especially those with eating disorders, need to have the opportunity to define themselves and their bodies in whatever shape or form they may come (Wooley & Wooley, 1985; Kearney-Cooke, 1991).

Feminist therapists take issue with deprivation models of treatment, suggesting that these models often lead to a false sense of control and effectiveness, similar to the ways women feel when they are dieting and purging. Inpatient programs that do not restrict behaviors or activities allow women the opportunity to experiment with feelings of fullness and deprivation. Replacing a deprivation model with a fullness model, in which women can learn to feel comfortable being seen and heard, leads to important changes as opposed to continued adaptation to damaging cultural norms and prescriptions (Surrey, 1991; Kearney-Cooke, 1991).

The Therapy Relationship

1. Feminist therapy strives to minimize the power differential between therapist and client. A psychoeducational model is used, with clients as learners and therapists as consultants/teachers. The cooperative nature of the therapy relationship is stressed, and this helps to demystify the therapy relationship.

2. Feminist therapists are constantly exploring their values and biases concerning women and confront their tendencies to maintain the status quo.

Most hospital settings are hierarchical and male-dominated, resulting in significant power differentials between patients and staff and among staff members themselves (Greenspan, 1983). Women are increasingly choosing to pursue medical degrees (Braslow & Heins, 1981); more than half of the doctoral students in psychology are women (Adler, 1991; Ostertag & McNamara, 1991); and more women than men choose to specialize in the treatment of eating disorders. Nonetheless, the majority of inpatient and residential programs for eating disorders are headed by men, trained in traditionally male models of therapy.

Most inpatient programs use a team approach. Examination of the hierarchy of these teams often reveals that a male physician, psychiatrist, or psychologist is the treatment team leader, and that other team members are typically women nurses, social workers, psychologists, or counselors who have lower status on the team and within the treatment facility. This hierarchy, with a man as the expert in a position of power and women in subordinate positions, is similar to current patriarchical conditions (Bloom, 1991; Chodorow, 1978; Luepnitz, 1988; Miller, 1976). On many units, the treatment team leader or medical director provides only a weekly hour of psychotherapy or a medication check and is often absent from daily activities; the female staff members tend to patients' day-to-day emotional crises and needs. Power differences between men and women are replicated as female patients are exposed to patterns of oppression similar to those they have observed and experienced outside of the "therapeutic" milieu.

The balancing of power within the inpatient setting should allow for more egalitarian therapy relationships. However, it is rare to find egalitarian relationships between staff and patients on most inpatient units. Team leaders, case managers, and therapists are often in positions of power and control over their patients as they attempt to help them manage eating disorder symptoms. Closed treatment team meetings, charts, and records further mystify the therapy relationship and deny patients the opportunity to engage in a discussion of their progress, setbacks, strengths, and weaknesses. The therapists continue to be seen as the experts, minimizing the patients' self-expertise. A feminist treatment model that includes patients' attending treatment team meetings, and reading and making entries in their charts, helps promote an atmosphere of trust, equality, and openness between staff and patients.

A therapist's specific knowledge about eating disorders also contributes to a power differential between therapist and patient. The majority of inpatient programs provide a range of treatments, but few, if any, actually educate the patients about their eating disorders. Many facilities provide this type of education and support to family members but not to patients. Incorporating a seminar on eating disorders for patients (Sesan, 1988) is a further aid in balancing power, demystifying therapy, and encouraging patients to assume greater responsibility for their eating disorders and resulting recovery.

Social Action/Social Change

1. Feminist therapists acknowledge that therapy is not the only cure and encourage clients to pursue all avenues for help, including self-help and social action. An underlying belief of feminist therapy is that personal change can be effected through political change (Steiner-Adair, 1991b).

2. Feminist therapy rejects the notion that the source of psychological distress is solely internal. Rather, psychological problems are viewed within a social context, with an emphasis in therapy on sociocultural and systemic approaches to change.

Although the majority of inpatient programs described in the literature recognize inpatient treatment as one step in a lengthy treatment process, no such program has addressed social action as a component in treatment. It can be highly empowering for an eating-disordered patient who has felt ineffective all her life to challenge the very social structure that contributes to her eating disorder. For example, patients can be encouraged to find a magazine ad or a business venture that they believe perpetuates the cultural idealization of slenderness and to write a letter expressing their concern, asking that the ad be withdrawn, or even suggesting an alternative ad (Sesan, 1988). Similarly, patients within the inpatient system can be asked to evaluate the system in terms of male domination, oppression, and replication of patriarchy, and to share their perceptions and suggested changes with the hospital administrator. Patients are learning important coping skills in this process that will be transferable to their aftercare environments.

On a broader scale, the structure of insurance coverage for eating disorder treatment parallels our patriarchical system by forcing decisions on clients that may not be in their best interests. In an ideal world, the decision to hospitalize an eating-disordered client would be made by examining both the history of her eating disorder and her therapy, treating her in the least restrictive environment, and collaborating with her in making decisions regarding the best intensive treatment options available. Unfortunately, a good deal of treatment is managed and dictated by insurance practices in our country, and decisions are often made without taking individual client needs into consideration. For example, Kaye, Enright, and Lesser (1988) found that a majority of women seeking insurance coverage for inpatient care of an eating disorder were offered only short-term treatment, were refused reimbursement, were reimbursed only for certain types of treatments, or were prematurely discharged because of limits in their insurance coverage. Furthermore, some insurance companies did not reimburse for "pre-existing" conditions. For example, if a client had had prior outpatient therapy, she would not be covered for inpatient care. Other insurance companies did not reimburse for disorders involving "self-injury" (including self-induced vomiting), or would not admit a patient because her weight was not "low enough." On the other hand, there are insurance companies that only reimburse for hospitalization, thus limiting a client's access to outpatient care and choice in selecting a less restrictive intensive outpatient option. As a form of social action, Kaye et al. (1988) have suggested that clinicians need to educate insurance companies about effective treatment options for women with eating disorders and the cost-effectiveness of providing long-term treatment. They urged the clients they surveyed to lobby third-party payers for better benefits and the option of choice in their care.

TOWARD MORE FEMINIST INPATIENT TREATMENT ENVIRONMENTS

Research on the psychology of women with eating disorders (Steiner-Adair, 1991a; Steiner-Adair, Fallon, Striegel-Moore, & Wooley, 1990; Surrey, 1991) can help guide the development of new models for inpatient care. Although many inpatient treatment programs for eating disorders integrate a feminist etiological perspective into treatment protocols, few base individual treatment plans and overall operation of the unit on an underlying philosophy that reflects women's psychological and emotional development. Integration of self-in-relation theory (Stiver, 1991; Surrey, 1983), a morality of connection and care (Gilligan, 1982), and an understanding of women's unique ways of learning (Belenky, Clinchy, Goldberger, & Tarule, 1988) can help to create more feminist inpatient treatment environments.

Self-in-Relation Theory

Eating disorders do not develop in isolation or without a cultural context that supports women's desire for thinness, comfort with restriction and deprivation, and fears of asserting themselves in a public domain. Furthermore, the valuing of separation and independence and the devaluing of connection and dependence within our culture create a "crisis of connection" for some female adolescents and adults (Gilligan, 1982; Steiner-Adair, 1986, 1991a). Young women in Western culture are being asked to forgo connections with others in order to develop their identities, whereas it is more natural for women to develop a sense of self within the context of relationships (Gilligan, 1982; Kaplan, 1986; Miller,

1986). Those women most at risk for developing eating disorders are those who have most internalized these sociocultural and interpersonal prescriptions (Streigel-Moore et al., 1986).

Eating disorders and their attendant symptomatology at times help young women to maintain connections with family and friends, as seen in the example of a college sophomore whose bulimic symptoms required her to return home after a brief period of separation. On the other hand, the shame associated with the eating disorder symptoms helps women avoid connections or separate from relationships in which they feel trapped, unseen, or uncared for, without having to assert such independence or autonomy to do so. In either situation, women with eating-disorder symptoms attempt to meet their relational needs while adhering to cultural demands for thinness and prescribed sex roles of passivity, indirect expression of needs, and difficulty with independence and autonomy. Both paths represent compromise solutions, with many costs for the individual woman and for the family and friends who care about her.

Most inpatient programs provide a predominantly female community for patients, with an emphasis on group therapy. Thus a feminist component is potentially built into inpatient treatment. The building of intimate connections as a treatment goal has healing effects on women (Fedele & Harrington, 1990). Participation in a therapeutic women's community provides an opportunity to work on mother–daughter issues and issues of envy and competition (Beattie, 1988), thus enabling women to learn to value their strengths and develop greater self-definition (Burden & Gottlieb, 1987). Although many women benefit from involvement in a women's community, feminist treatment also recognizes the need to involve family and friends in the recovery process. Using family therapy sessions and multifamily treatment groups to explore the context in which the eating disorder developed helps all family members, including the "identified patient," to heal past wounds and change destructive relational patterns (Root, Fallon, & Friedrich, 1986; Wooley & Lewis, 1989). A woman is freer to choose wellness when she trusts that she can maintain important interpersonal connections and be valued for her relational as well as her agentic qualities.

Feminist inpatient treatment environments value and foster "safe" connections and facilitate interdependence as opposed to fostering isolation and competition. For example, in more traditional inpatient programs, modified bed rest to help with weight gain and room restrictions for rule violations create isolating environments for patients. Often women who continue to binge and purge in the inpatient setting are denied privileges and social contact with others. Competition is fostered among residents when they are asked to report on one another for rule infractions.

Women who continue to be symptomatic on an inpatient unit are often expressing longing for or fears of connection with others (Steiner-Adair, 1991a). When symptom expression is prevented, these women may not be able to share themselves with others. Instead of imposing increased isolation for the symptomatic patient, feminist treatment environments would enhance opportunities for connection and provide avenues for exploring the impact of connections and disconnections in women's lives (Miller, 1988). For example, if a woman on an inpatient unit continues to starve herself, a feminist stance may be to provide her with increased opportunities for connection, rather than imposing bed rest and isolation. She can be paired with a "buddy" or offered more intensive therapy contact. Increased opportunities for family therapy can be provided to help heal and strengthen damaged intergenerational connections (Lerner, 1985; Root et al., 1986). Furthermore, within the context of intensive group therapy, women can be helped to explore the isolating nature of their symptoms and encouraged to make choices leading to connection rather than to isolation.

In current inpatient programs, there is little opportunity for women to break through their shame and isolation. By providing a safe, containing, nurturing environment in which symptoms are accepted and their functional nature understood, a feminist inpatient treatment can help women move beyond the deprivation and the socialization that have silenced them. Women can be encouraged to reach out to others prior to a binge, not necessarily to prevent the symptom, but as a way to be supported and to experience connection during a binge and eventual purge. As an example of "accepting the symptom" (Orbach, 1985), Wooley (1990) described the experience of two bulimic women in an outpatient intensive treatment program embracing as one vomited and the other one comforted her. This is a vision of connection, of women breaking through shame and isolation as they voice their pain to one another.

The freedom of being in a women's community can also facilitate the working through of past sexual abuse. Women with eating disorders who have been sexually abused constitute a substantial subgroup (Miller, 1990; Root & Fallon, 1988). An inpatient setting can be a safe environment for the disclosing and working through of victimization histories only when women believe that they will not be revictimized upon disclosure (Bloom, 1991; Herman, 1992). Feminist inpatient treatment provides groups for survivors of sexual abuse (Courtois, 1988), as well as art therapy and other expressive therapies for the uncovering and working through of incest and sexual abuse histories (Rice, Hardenbergh, & Hornyak, 1989; Stark, Aronow, & McGeehan, 1989).

Feminist inpatient treatment also makes use of expressive therapies to treat body image disturbances. The multidisciplinary setting of an inpatient unit makes it especially suited for intensive body image treatment, taking the focus away from stringent symptom management and appearance. Several programs note success in treating eating disorders through intensive body image work, as opposed to a focus on symptom reduction. Body image therapy groups help women become more aware of distorted body images, messages received about their bodies from family members and culture, bodily sensations, and bodily traumas (Hutchinson, 1985; Wooley & Kearney-Cooke, 1986; Wooley & Wooley, 1990). Inpatient programs with an intensive body image focus are more congruent with a feminist philosphy of treatment. Programs such as these encourage women to define their own bodies, convey a valuing for women's presence, recognize the impact of culture and victimization on the development of body image, and help women feel more comfortable with their power.

A Morality of Connection and Care

Gilligan's (1982) research on women's moral decision making suggested that women base their moral judgments on context, rather than on abstract rules of right and wrong. Yet the day-to-day workings of many inpatient units seem to be based on a morality of rights and wrongs, a male morality of justice. As a result, women are punished for breaking rules when they are making decisions for themselves and others that are based on a morality of care and efforts not to hurt others.

Inpatient treatment programs can support women's moral development and growth by clarifying that their decisions and choices are based on an overfocus on the needs of others and an underfocus on themselves. Patients can be helped to explore the costs and consequences of consistently choosing other-care over self-care, and guided in moving toward a more integrated focus on self and other. An environment that operates according to abstract rules of rights and wrongs cannot help women understand their decisions within a context of connection and care. Thus, they cannot learn about themselves within the inpatient setting or in the outside world. A more feminist inpatient unit would be characterized by cooperation as opposed to competition, and by decision making based on circumstances and context rather than on abstract criteria (Bloom, 1991).

Women's Ways of Knowing

The work of Belenky et al. (1988) on women's learning styles is also applicable to therapy for women with eating disorders and the development of more feminist inpatient treatment programs. Belenky and her colleagues have identified a variety of unique ways in which women learn and receive knowledge about the world and about themselves. Many women with eating disorders enter treatment as "received knowers," looking to the voices of others to know and define themselves. The process of therapy and recovery from eating disorders can help women move from positions of received knowers to those of "constructed knowers." Constructed knowers are able to integrate knowledge from others, internal self-knowledge, knowledge from feelings, and knowledge from thinking.

Both Belenky and her colleagues (1988) and Steiner-Adair (1991a) have discussed the need for interactive models in education and therapy with women. The model of "connected teaching" described by Belenky and her colleagues is a model in which students gain knowledge within the context of a relationship. They have described education as a dialogue in "assisting the students in giving birth to their own ideas, in making their knowledge explicit and elaborating on it" (p. 217). Steiner-Adair (1991a) has similarly described an interactive therapy model for women with eating disorders. She suggests that therapy needs to be a dialogue, a two-way interactive process rather than a mirroring. A connected teaching model applied to therapy helps to demystify the therapy relationship while clients learn important information about themselves. Therapists can teach women to be themselves and remain connected by modeling "real-self" as opposed to "false-self" relationships (Lerner, 1985).

A feminist model for inpatient treatment would incorporate the values of connected teaching by advocating for a less male-dominated hierarchical structure, encouraging a more nurturing paternal presence (Luepnitz, 1988), and using consensus decision making within the inpatient setting (Belenky et al., 1988; Bloom, 1991). The presence of a male-dominated hierarchy does not necessarily make an inpatient program nonfeminist. If those in power recognize that the inpatient environment can replicate a pattern of oppression that contributes to the development of eating disorders (Chernin, 1981; Orbach, 1978), essential therapeutic work can ensue. Patients in community meetings can be supported in their challenges to male authority, helped to understand their fears of not pleasing those in power, and helped to explore conflicts of dependence and independence within male–female relationships (Greenspan, 1983).

A feminist model of inpatient care is based on open engagement among patients, therapists, and other staff members. Incorporating an interactive therapy model into inpatient environments helps clients rely less on the authority of others as they define themselves. Shifting from an autocratic to an interactive model of inpatient care depends on the leadership of the unit (Bloom, 1991). Such a shift can occur only if there are women staff members openly modeling challenges to the hierarchy, and if those in power are willing to relinquish some control for the common good of the women's community. Typically, the medical director has the power to set the tone of the inpatient setting, and either creates an environment in which real selves are valued or one in which patients and staff alike are forced into false-self stances. In order for treatment team members to model real relationships, the medical director needs to be comfortable with sharing power, cooperative decision making, and creating an environment conducive to nurturing, training, and protection for patients and staff (Ruddick, 1980; Bloom, 1991). It is within such an environment that healing from eating disorders is most likely to occur.

CONCLUDING REMARKS

Although it is not possible for inpatient settings to be entirely feminist, these ideas may stimulate discussion among staff members on inpatient units and may challenge treatment providers and medical directors to explore both the feminist and nonfeminist components of their programs. Feminist elements are regular parts of many inpatient treatment programs; however, as highlighted above, many programs are clearly nonfeminist in that they treat eating disorders within male-dominated systems based on male models of development and male hierarchies, thereby replicating destructive patterns of oppression for women.

Feminist therapists have power to effect change within inpatient settings. This is a call to social action! The majority of clinicians treating women with eating disorders are women. Thus it is often women who are referring clients to inpatient treatment programs. As female clinicians, we can increase our power and effect change by applying a feminist analysis when evaluating programs in our communities, and subsequently by referring clients to inpatient programs congruent with a feminist philosophy of treatment. We can also provide feedback and education to medical directors and hospital administrators concerning our decision to refer or not to refer. Furthermore, we can educate our clients about their options and encourage them, as consumers of inpatient care, to evaluate programs critically and to make their choices accordingly. All of us—therapists and clients alike—will feel more empowered and less dominated if we channel our power toward individual choices and work toward effecting changes in the larger social system.

REFERENCES

Adler, T. (1991, October). Will feminization spell decline for field?. *APA Monitor*, p. 12.

Andersen, A. E., Morse, C. L., & Santmyer, K. S. (1985). Inpatient treatment for anorexia nervosa. In D. M. Garner & P. E. Garfinkel (Eds.), *Handbook of psychotherapy for anorexia nervosa and bulimia* (pp. 311–343). New York: Guilford Press.

Anderson, H. J. (1985, October). Hospitals' eating disorders units fill empty beds with paying patients. *Modern Healthcare*, pp. 62–66.

Barnett, L. R. (1986). Bulimarexia as a symptom of sex-role strain in professional women. *Psychotherapy, 23,* 311–315.

Beattie, H. J. (1988). Eating disorders and the mother–daughter relationship. *International Journal of Eating Disorders, 7,* 453–460.

Belenky, M. F., Clinchy, B. M., Goldberger, N. R., & Tarule, J. M. (1988). *Women's ways of knowing: The development of self, voice and mind.* New York: Basic Books.

Bernstein, I. C. (1964). Anorexia nervosa successfully treated with electroshock therapy and subsequently followed by pregnancy. *American Journal of Psychiatry, 120,* 1023–1025.

Bloom, S. L. (1991). *The sanctuary model: A trauma-based approach to inpatient care.* Unpublished manuscript.

Boskind-Lodahl, M. (1976). Cinderella's stepsisters: A feminist perspective of anorexia nervosa and bulimia. *Signs: Journal of Women in Culture and Society, 2,* 342–356.

Braslow, J. B., & Heins, M. (1981). Women and medical education: A decade of change. *New England Journal of Medicine, 304,* 1129.

Bruch, H. (1973). *Eating disorders.* New York: Basic Books.

Bruch, H. (1974). The perils of behavior modification in treatment of anorexia nervosa. *Journal of the American Medical Association, 230,* 1419–1422.

Bruch, H. (1982). Anorexia nervosa: Therapy and theory. *American Journal of Psychiatry, 139,* 1531–1538.

Burden, D. S., & Gottlieb, N. (1987). Women's socialization and feminist groups. In C. M. Brody (Ed.), *Women's therapy groups: Paradigms of feminist treatment* (pp. 24–39). New York: Springer.

Butler, M. (1985). Guidelines for feminist therapy. In L. B. Rosewater & L. E. A. Walker (Eds.), *Handbook of feminist therapy* (pp. 32–38). New York: Springer.

Chernin, K. (1981). *The obsession: Reflections on the tyranny of slenderness.* New York: Harper & Row.

Chesler, P. (1972). *Women and madness.* Garden City, NY: Doubleday.

Chodorow, N. (1978). *The reproduction of mothering.* Berkeley: University of California Press.

Connors, M. E., Johnson, C. L., & Stuckey, M. K. (1984). Treatment of bulimia with brief psychoeducational group therapy. *American Journal of Psychiatry, 141,* 1512–1516.

Courtois, C. A. (1988). *Healing the incest wound*. New York: Norton.

Crisp, A. H. (1965). Clinical and therapeutic aspects of anorexia nervosa: A study of thirty cases. *Journal of Psychosomatic Research, 9,* 67–78.

Dally, P. J., & Sargant, W. (1966). Treatment and outcome of anorexia nervosa. *British Medical Journal, ii,* 793–795.

Davis, R., Olmsted, M. P., & Rockert, W. (1990, April). *Brief psychoeducational group treatment for bulimia: II Clinical significance and prediction of change.* Paper presented at the Fourth International Conference on Eating Disorders, New York.

Enright, A. B., Butterfield, P., & Berkowitz, B. (1985). Self-help and support groups in the management of eating disorders. In D. M. Garner & P. E. Garfinkel (Eds.), *Handbook of psychotherapy for anorexia nervosa and bulimia* (pp. 491–512). New York: Guilford Press.

Fedele, N. M., & Harrington, E. A. (1990). *Women's groups: How connections heal.* (Work in Progress No. 47; available from the Stone Center for Developmental Services and Studies, Wellesley College, Wellesley, MA)

Fornari, V., Katz, J. L., Halmi, K. A., & Marcus, R. (1990, April). *Co-morbidity in eating disorder patients: Treatment implications.* Workshop presented at the Fourth International Conference on Eating Disorders, New York.

Garfinkel, P. E., & Garner, D. M. (1982). *Anorexia nervosa: A multidimensional perspective.* New York: Brunner/Mazel.

Garfinkel, P. E., Garner, D. M., & Kennedy, S. (1985). Special problems of inpatient management. In D. M. Garner & P. E. Garfinkel (Eds.), *Handbook of psychotherapy for anorexia nervosa and bulimia* (pp. 344–359). New York: Guilford Press.

Gartner, A. F., Marcus, R. N., Halmi, K., & Loranger, A. W. (1989). DSM-IIIR personality disorders in patients with eating disorders. *American Journal of Psychiatry, 146,* 1585–1591.

George, D. T., Weiss, S. R., Gwirtsman, H. E. & Blazer, D. (1987). Hospital treatment of anorexia nervosa: A 25 year retrospective study from 1958–1982. *International Journal of Eating Disorders, 6,* 321–330.

Gilbert, L. A. (1980). Feminist therapy. In A. M. Brodsky & R. T. Hare-Mustin (Eds.), *Women and psychotherapy* (pp. 245–265). New York: Guilford Press.

Gilligan, C. (1982). *In a different voice.* Cambridge, MA: Harvard University Press.

Goldner, E. M., Cockhill, L. A., & Bakan, R. (1990, April). *Dissociative experience and eating disorders: A psychometric investigation.* Paper presented at the Fourth International Conference on Eating Disorders, New York.

Greenspan, M. (1983). *A new approach to women and therapy.* New York: McGraw-Hill.

Gunderson, J. G. (1978). Defining the therapeutic processes in psychiatric milieus. *Psychiatry, 41,* 327–335.

Halmi, K. A. (1985). Behavioral management for anorexia nervosa. In D. M. Garner & P. E. Garfinkel (Eds.), *Handbook of psychotherapy for anorexia nervosa and bulimia* (pp. 147–159). New York: Guilford Press.

Hatsukami, D., Eckert, E., Mitchell, J., & Pyle, R. (1984). Affective disorder and substance abuse in women with bulimia. *Psychological Medicine, 14,* 701–704.

Herman, J. L. (1992). *Trauma and recovery.* New York: Basic Books.

Herzog, D. B., Hamburg, P., & Bratman, A. (1987). Psychotherapy and eating disorders: An affirmative view. *International Journal of Eating Disorders, 6,* 545–550.

Hiller, W., & Zaugid, M. (1989). Comorbidity of eating disorders in comparison with mood disorders. *Annals of the New York Academy of Sciences, 575,* 532–534.

Hutchinson, M. G. (1985). *Transforming body image: Learning to love the body you have.* New York: Crossing Press.

Johnson, C. L. (Ed.). (1991). *Psychodynamic treatment of anorexia nervosa and bulimia.* New York: Guilford Press.

Johnson, C. L., & Connors, M. (1987). *The etiology and treatment of bulimia nervosa: A biopsychosocial perspective.* New York: Basic Books.

Johnson, C. L., Tobin, D. L., & Dennis, A. (1990). Differences in treatment outcome between borderline and nonborderline bulimics at one-year follow-up. *International Journal of Eating Disorders, 9,* 617–622.

Kaplan, A. G. (1986). The "self-in-relation": Implications for women and depression. *Psychotherapy, 23,* 234–242.

Kaye, W. H., Enright, A. B., & Lesser, S. (1988). Characteristics of eating disorders programs and common problems with third-party providers. *International Journal of Eating Disorders, 7,* 573–579.

Kearney-Cooke, A. (1991). The role of the therapist in the treatment of eating disorders: A feminist psychodynamic approach. In C. L. Johnson (Ed.), *Psychodynamic treatment of anorexia nervosa and bulimia* (pp. 295–318). New York: Guilford Press.

Lerman, H. (1986, August). *Women in context: Contributions of feminist therapy.* Workshop presented at the 84th Annual Convention of the American Psychological Association, Washington, D.C.

Lerner, H. G. (1985). *The dance of anger.* New York: Harper & Row.

Levendusky, P. G., & Dooley, C. P. (1985). An inpatient model for the treatment of anorexia nervosa. In S. W. Emmett (Ed.), *Theory and treatment of anorexia nervosa and bulimia* (pp. 211–233). New York: Brunner/Mazel.

Luepnitz, D. A. (1988). *The family interpreted: Feminist theory in clinical practice.* New York: Basic Books.

Maloney, M. J., & Farrell, M. K. (1980). Treatment of severe weight loss in anorexia nervosa with hyperalimentation and psychotherapy. *American Journal of Psychiatry, 137,* 310–314.

Marcus, R. N., & Katz, J. L. (1990). Inpatient care of the substance-abusing patient with a concomitant eating disorder. *Hospital and Community Psychiatry, 41,* 59–63.

Miller, J. B. (1976). *Toward a new psychology of women.* Boston: Beacon Press.

Miller, J. B. (1986). *What do we mean by relationships?* (Work in Progress No. 22; available from the Stone Center for Developmental Services and Studies, Wellesley College, Wellesley, MA)

Miller, J. B. (1988). *Connections, disconnections and violations.* (Work in Progress No. 33; available from the Stone Center for Developmental Services and Studies, Wellesley College, Wellesley, MA)

Miller, K. J. (1990). *Childhood sexual abuse as a factor in eating disorders in women: Prevalence and symptom severity.* Unpublished doctoral dissertation, Temple University.

Mitchell, J. E., Hatsukami, D., Goff, G., Pyle, R. L., Eckert, E. D., & Davis, L. E. (1985). Intensive outpatient group treatment for bulimia. In D. M. Garner & P. E. Garfinkel (Eds.), *Handbook of psychotherapy for anorexia nervosa and bulimia* (pp. 240–256). New York: Guilford Press.

Orbach, S. (1978). *Fat is a feminist issue.* New York: Berkeley Books.

Orbach, S. (1985). Accepting the symptom: A feminist psychoanalytic treatment of anorexia nervosa. In D. M. Garner & P. E. Garfinkel (Eds.), *Handbook of psychotherapy for anorexia nervosa and bulimia* (pp. 83–104). New York: Guilford Press.

Orbach, S. (1986). *Hungerstrike: The anorexic's struggle as a metaphor for our age.* New York: Basic Books.

Ostertag, P. A., & McNamara, J. R. (1991). Feminization of psychology: The changing sex ratio and its implications for the profession. *Psychology of Women Quarterly, 15,* 349–370.

Piran, N., & Kaplan, A. S. (Eds.). (1990). *A day hospital group treatment program for anorexia nervosa and bulimia nervosa.* New York: Brunner/Mazel.

Rice, J. B., Hardenbergh, M., & Hornyak, L. M. (1989). Disturbed body image in anorexia nervosa: Dance/movement therapy interventions. In L. M. Hornyak & E. K. Baker (Eds.), *Experiential therapies for eating disorders* (pp. 252–278). New York: Guilford Press.

Root, M. P. P., & Fallon, P. (1988). The incidence of victimization experiences in a bulimic sample. *Journal of Interpersonal Violence, 3,* 161–173.

Root, M. P. P., Fallon, P., & Friedrich, W. (1986). *Bulimia: A systems approach to treatment.* New York: Norton.

Roth, D. (1986). Treatment of the hospitalized eating disordered patient, *Occupational Therapy in Mental Health, 6,* 67–87.

Ruddick, S. (1980). Maternal thinking. *Feminist Studies, 6,* 342–367.

Sesan, R. (1988, March). *Eating disorders 101: Prevention and treatment of eating disorders through a university seminar.* Workshop presented at the annual convention of the Association of Women in Psychology, Rockville, MD.

Stark, A., Aronow, S., & McGeehan, T. (1989). Dance/movement therapy with bulimic patients. In L. M. Hornyak & E. K. Baker (Eds.), *Experiential therapies for eating disorders* (pp. 121–143). New York: Guilford Press.

Steiner-Adair, C. (1986). The body politic: Normal female adolescent development and the development of eating disorders. *Journal of the American Academy of Psychoanalysis, 14,* 95–114.

Steiner-Adair, C. (1991a). New maps of development, new models of therapy: The psychology of women and the treatment of eating disorders. In C. L. Johnson (Ed.), *Psychodynamic treatment of anorexia nervosa and bulimia* (pp. 225–244). New York: The Guilford Press.

Steiner-Adair, K. (1991b, November). *Generations of silence: Women's struggles with resistance*. Paper presented at the Renfrew Foundation Conference on Intergenerational Issues of Women with Eating Disorders, Philadelphia.

Steiner-Adair, C., Fallon, P., Striegel-Moore, R., & Wooley, S. C. (1990, April). *Psychology of women and the treatment of eating disorders*. Plenary Session II presented at the Fourth International Conference on Eating Disorders, New York.

Steinhausen, H. C., & Glanville, K. (1983). A long-term follow-up of adolescent anorexia nervosa. *Acta Psychiatrica Scandinavica, 68,* 1–10.

Stiver, I. P. (1991). The meaning of care: Reframing treatment models. In J. V. Jordan, A. G. Kaplan, J. B. Miller, I. P. Stiver, & J. L. Surrey (Eds.), *Women's growth in connection: Writings from the Stone Center* (pp. 250–267). New York: Guilford Press.

Striegel-Moore, R. H., Silberstein, L. L., & Rodin, J. (1986). Toward an understanding of risk factors for bulimia. *American Psychologist, 41,* 246–263.

Surrey, J. (1983). *The relational self in women: Clinical implications.* (Work in Progress No. 13; available from the Stone Center for Developmental Services and Studies, Wellesley College, Wellesley, MA)

Surrey, J. L. (1991). Eating patterns as a reflection of women's development. In J. V. Jordan, A. G. Kaplan, J. B. Miller, I. P. Stiver, & J. L. Surrey (Eds.), *Women's growth in connection: Writings from the Stone Center* (pp. 237–249). New York: Guilford Press.

Travis, C. B. (1988). *Women and health psychology.* Hillsdale, NJ: Erlbaum.

Vandereycken, W. (1985). Inpatient treatment of anorexia nervosa: Some research guided changes. *Journal of Psychiatric Research, 19,* 413–422.

Vandereycken, W. (1990). The addiction model in eating disorders: Some critical remarks and a selected bibliography. *International Journal of Eating Disorders, 9,* 95–101.

Wall, J. H. (1959). Diagnosis, treatment and results in anorexia nervosa. *American Journal of Psychiatry, 115,* 997–1001.

Wamboldt, F. S., Kaslow, N. J., Swift, W. J., & Ritholz, M. (1987). Short-term course of depressive symptoms in patients with eating disorders. *American Journal of Psychiatry, 144,* 362–364.

Weiss, L., Katzman, M., & Wolchick, S. (1986). *Treating bulimia: A psychoeducational approach.* Elmsford, NY: Pergamon Press.

Wonderlich, S. A., Swift, W. J., Slotnick, H. B., & Goodman, S. (1990). DSM-IIIR personality disorders in eating disorder subtypes. *International Journal of Eating Disorders, 9,* 607–616.

Wooley, S. C. (1990, April). Contribution to *Psychology of women and the treatment of eating disorders*. Plenary Session II presented at the Fourth International Conference on Eating Disorders, New York.

Wooley, S. C., & Kearney-Cooke, A. (1986). Intensive treatment of bulimia and body image disturbances. In K. D. Brownell & J. P. Foreyt (Eds.), *Handbook of eating disorders* (pp. 476–502). New York: Basic Books.

Wooley, S. C., & Lewis, K. G. (1989). The missing woman: Intensive family-oriented treatment of bulimia. *Journal of Feminist Family Therapy, 1,* 61–83.

Wooley, S. C., & Wooley, O. W. (1980). Eating disorders: Obesity and anorexia. In A. M. Brodsky & R. T. Hares Mustin (Eds.), *Women and psychotherapy* (pp. 135–158). New York: Guilford Press.

Wooley, S. C., & Wooley, O. W. (1985). Intensive outpatient and residential treatment for bulimia. In D. M. Garner & P. E. Garfinkel (Eds.), *Handbook of psychotherapy for anorexia nervosa and bulimia* (pp. 391–430). New York: Guilford Press.

Wooley, O. W., & Wooley, S. C. (1990). *Intensive treatment program for bulimia: Outcome data.* Unpublished manuscript.

13

Mothers, Daughters, and Eating Disorders: Honoring the Mother–Daughter Relationship

JUDITH RUSKAY RABINOR

> *Every mother contains her daughter in herself and every daughter her mother, and every woman extends backwards into her mother and forwards into her daughter.*
> —C.G. Jung, *The Archetypes of the Collective Unconscious* (1959, p. 189)

THEORISTS FROM A WIDE VARIETY of orientations agree that early interactions with caretakers become the foundations for beliefs, attitudes, and expectations about the self. When the primary caretaker is the mother (still the most prevalent child-rearing situation), it is in the mother–child relationship that the self is born (Jordan & Surrey, 1986; Kohut, 1971; Mitchell, 1988; Surrey, 1985; Winnicott, 1971). As a result, the profound psychological influence mothers have on their daughters has been generally unquestioned (Caron, 1991; Chernin, 1985; Surrey, 1985).

Unfortunately, observations that honor the positive connection inherent in the mother–daughter relationship are for the most part absent from the psychological literature. Research and clinical writing tend to emphasize psychopathology rather than healthy development. Since Freud, psychoanalysts, developmental psychologists, and family therapists have concluded that when a child has problems, the mother is at fault (see Bassoff, 1991; Caplan, 1986; Luepnitz, 1988; and Segunda,

1990, for extensive reviews); this bias is reflected in the popular as well as in the professional press. The eating disorders literature has carried on this unfortunate tradition. When a woman develops an eating disorder, poor mothering is often cited as a critical etiological factor (Bruch, 1978; Geist, 1985; Johnson & Connors, 1987; Selvini Palazzoli, 1978; Pike & Rodin, 1991). The true multidetermined nature of these disorders, which results from a delicate interplay among intrapsychic, familial, and cultural factors, is thereby ignored.

The issue of mother-blaming is particularly relevant to the treatment of eating disorders. Eating disorders arise out of the profound issues of gender identity and relational bonding that characterize the mother–daughter relationship (Benjamin, 1988; Chernin, 1985; Gilligan, 1982; Surrey, 1985). Devaluing the mother and imposing unrealistic standards for mothering can cause confusion and despair in the daughter's own journey through womanhood. This process leads her to devalue herself, limiting her ability to relate to others, to love, and to grow.

In this chapter I examine the impact of mother-blaming on eating disorder treatment and illustrate how these conditions actually reflect problems in the family and culture rather than simply problems in the mother–daughter relationship. I then suggest an alternative perspective that is multidetermined and mother-affirming. Finally, I present specific clinical interventions that honor and heal the mother–daughter relationship, restoring its rightful status as a source of strength and growth.

THE SOCIAL CONTEXT
OF MOTHER-BLAMING

Investigating nine major mental health journals published between 1970 and 1982, Caplan (1986) concluded: "In the 125 articles, mothers were blamed for 72 different kinds of problems in their offspring, ranging from bedwetting to schizophrenia, from inability to deal with color blindness to aggressive behavior, from learning problems to 'homicidal transsexualism' " (p. 47). A follow-up study, which examined 100 cases reported in four leading family therapy journals from 1978 to 1987 found that the focus on mother-blaming had increased. "Mothers just could not get it right," the report concluded (Wylie, 1989, p. 44).

Although mainstream theories of disordered eating stress a multideterminied etiology, investigators rarely give more than lip service to cultural factors and the impact of fathers. Retrospective reconstructions of the early mother–child relationship commonly focus on maternal pathology. Even when fathers are abusive, passive, or emotionally absent, usually the impact of their neglect is unexamined, whereas maternal behavior is further scrutinized. Examinations of "parenting" are often, in reality, condemnations of mothering.

Innumerable contradictory maternal behaviors have been identified as contributing to disordered eating. For example, Beattie (1988) cites "hostile dependent conflicts" and "ambivalent struggles for autonomy" (p. 455) as such precursors. Such destructive mother–daughter dynamics have been found to result from a wide variety of maternal behaviors. For example, mothers of anorexic and bulimic daughters have been described as symbiotic, intrusive, enmeshed, and controlling (Minuchin, Rosman, & Baker, 1978; Rampling, 1980), as well as nonresponsive, withdrawn, distracted, and aloof (Lerner, 1991; Selvini Palazzoli, 1978). In reviewing these inconsistent findings regarding the mother–daughter relationship, Frankenburg (1984) concludes: "The anorectic's relationship with her mother has been described as a mixture of dependence, resentment, envy, jealousy and spitefulness" (p. 28).

Just as innumerable patterns of poor mothering have been identified as related to disordered eating, many different developmental stages have been reported to be critical points at which pathological mothering might result in disordered eating. The early feeding situation, various phases of the separation/individuation process, and adolescence have been the focus of several investigators (Beattie, 1988; Charone, 1982; Hall & Brown, 1983; Tustin, 1959). In sum, when a woman develops an eating disorder, poor mothering is often understood as the critical etiological factor.

Conceptualizations that acknowlege sociocultural factors yet focus on pathological mothering fail to expand our understanding of either the etiology or the treatment of disordered eating, and often produce therapeutic interventions that damage the mother–daughter relationship. For example, therapists are often advised to "explain" maternal psychopathology to eating-disordered clients (see Geist, 1985), whereas explanations of the impact of fathers and of patriarchal values are not mentioned. Clinical formulations and interventions that aim to understand and "fix" mothers while ignoring fathers are implicitly mother-blaming (Beattie, 1988; Bruch, 1978; Ehrensing & Weitzman, 1970; Geist, 1985; Hall & Brown, 1983; Selvini Palazzoli, 1978; Pike & Rodin, 1991; Rampling, 1980; Zunino, Agoos, & Davis, 1991).

The deleterious consequences of such a blanket denunciation of mothering have been identified and investigated by a number of feminist scholars and social critics (Bassoff, 1991; Caplan, 1986; Hare-Mustin, 1978; Hare-Mustin & Broderick, 1979; Segunda, 1990; Silverstein, 1991; Smith, 1991) and are particularly salient for the eating-disordered female.

First, the overemphasis on the mothers' role ultimately undervalues the influence of fathers. Hochschild (1989), Lerner (1988), Luepnitz (1988), Maine (1991), and Silverstein (1991) all suggest that clinicians often do not recognize paternal disengagement to be as powerful a determinant as maternal overinvolvement in child development. Second, even when a father is implicated in child abuse, incest, and/or battering (all risk factors for a daughter developing an eating disorder), responsibility is often insidiously shifted to the mother, whose ignorance of the situation becomes the new focus of blame (Caplan, 1986; Root & Fallon, 1989; Herman, 1981; Marecek & Hare-Mustin, 1991). In disregarding the devastating impact of paternal neglect or abuse, clinicians also disregard the powerful healing effects of a positive father–daughter relationship, and thus do not avail themselves of this potential resource.

The typical family, with an overinvolved mother and an underinvolved father, is a reflection of patriarchal culture. Referring to centuries of gender-specific arrangements that have given rise to economic dependence and inequality, sexual violence, and emotional and physical subordination of females (all precursors of eating disorders), Jean Baker Miller (1976) has argued, "It is easier to blame mothers than to comprehend the entire system that has restricted women." As transmitters of the culture, mothers *and* fathers cannot avoid communicating the sexist/patriarchal realities of female powerlessness to their children.

Eating-disordered women cite familial and cultural values as causes of their obsessions with appearance, dieting, and thinness. In treatment, they frequently recall their mothers' having been disparaged and shamed by others (often their husbands, the women's fathers) for gaining weight and being heavy, or praised for losing weight and being slim. In either case, they often report a familial overemphasis on appearance. Mothers who feel negative about their own bodies are often blamed for communicating their body image dissatisfaction to their daughters, who internalize the powerlessness and self-deprecation they have observed.

Blaming mothers for this obsession with slimness distracts attention from the negative impact of patriarchal culture on women (Freedman, 1988; Rothblum, Chapter 3, this volume; Seid, Chapter 1, this volume; Wolf, 1991; Wooley & Wooley, 1984). Despite a growing consciousness of the ill effects of dieting, the vast majority of women of all ages and backgrounds continue to diet and to judge their own bodies harshly (see Rothblum, Chapter 3, this volume). Most women focus on dieting and improving their appearances in order to feel powerful in a world that denies them true power. Mothers who diet need to be understood in their cultural milieu, rather than admonished for exhibiting personal inadequacies.

Blaming mothers also minimizes the culture's effect on the mother–

daughter relationship (Benjamin, 1988; Chodorow, 1978; Luepnitz, 1988). For a daughter to remain at odds with her mother is to be at odds with the female body they share, and to be at odds with her body is to be vulnerable to developing an eating disorder (Kearney-Cooke, 1989). By simply attributing her eating disorder to deficits in the mothering relationship, a daughter learns little about her own development, her mother, or the function of her illness. She is ill prepared to overcome cultural obstacles, both those filtered through her mother and those affecting her directly. To emphasize maternal pathology without helping the daughter understand the cultural and environmental circumstances of her own as well as her mother's life devalues the mother inappropriately.

Hancock (1989) suggests that what daughters really want is to transform, not sever, their relationships with their mothers. Creating a meaningful sense of connectedness and genuine intimacy with their mothers is one of the final goals of development, a hallmark of psychological growth (Hancock, 1989; Caplan, 1986; Segunda, 1990; Surrey, 1985; Wooley, 1991). My own experience with eating-disordered clients and their mothers bears this out. Influenced by popular mother-blaming messages, eating-disordered daughters often *do* wonder whether their mothers caused their eating disorders. Simultaneously, mothers are often guilt-ridden and upset about their failure to be "good enough" (Winnicott, 1971), a concept that has perhaps contributed to mother-blaming. These feelings of blame and guilt produce and reinforce feelings of helplessness and powerlessness in mother and daughter alike, impairing the ability to grow. Most eating-disordered daughters and their mothers want to repair their relationship with each other. Healing this relationship is an essential step in recovery.

FROM MOTHER-BLAMING TO MOTHER-AFFIRMING: CLINICAL INTERVENTIONS

Although traditional theories often suggest that pathology is passed from mother to daughter, a feminist reformulation suggests a different dynamic. Motivated by a desire to remain connected to their mothers, daughters remain unconsciously loyal to their mothers' values and lifestyles. What daughters learn from our patriarchal culture, transmitted predominantly by their mothers, is that their bodies are their most powerful tools. A mother-blaming perspective fails to account for the social context in which a woman's appearance is often the most obvious or the only socially condoned form of power openly afforded her. In perfecting her body by dieting, the eating-disordered daughter mirrors her mothers'attempts to be powerful (Wooley & Wooley, 1984; Young-Eisendrath & Wiedemann, 1987). It is a mark of female resilience that in the face of no access to real power, mothers do train their daughters to have access to the only power that exists: body power. A positive reframing of dieting—from competition to loyalty and connection—can affirm the strength of the mother–daughter bond.

When a therapist highlights how a mother has developed strengths and obtained power despite adverse cultural conditions, maternal vitality is respected. Helping an eating-disordered woman see the positive function of her disordered eating serves to build self-esteem rather than to reinforce a negative, destructive female identity shared by mother and daughter. Finally, helping the daughter develop alternative ways of feeling genuinely powerful in relationships—with her self, her therapist, a group, her family, and finally in the larger world—facilitates healing.

Although any treatment that ignores mother-blaming is compromised, strategies that heal the mother–daughter relationship are most useful when integrated into a multifocused treatment approach (see Garner & Garfinkel, 1985; Johnson & Connors, 1987; Root, Fallon, & Friedrich, 1986; and Weiss, Katzman, & Wolchik, 1985, 1986, for comprehensive, multifaceted treatment approaches). Although individual psychotherapy forms the cornerstone of my work with eating-disordered clients, additional treatment modalities are useful at different stages of treatment. Family sessions offer a unique opportunity to address mother-blaming and heal family relationships.

A series of such sessions proved invaluable for Marcy, a 22-year-old who had been bulimic for 8 years. After spending many months in individual sessions identifying how feelings of ineffectiveness and powerlessness manifested themselves in dieting, exercising, and disordered eating, the therapist initiated a family session where Marcy was encouraged to express her feelings of anger and frustration directly to her parents. Sadly, Marcy recalled the impact of her mother's focus on how she *looked* rather than how she *felt*. "Didn't you know that dragging me from diet doctor to diet doctor—beginning at age 9—would make me feel fat and hideous?" she wept, recounting feelings of failure and shame, and the development of her bulimia.

Her mother responded first by apologizing, and second by explaining herself to her daughter. Still suffering from the consequences of being overweight herself as a child, Mrs. Stephans *had* encouraged Marcy's dieting, unknowingly contributing to her eating disorder. "I didn't want you to have my horrible fate of being the fattest girl in the class," explained mother to daughter. The therapist had an opportunity to underscore how expectations of thinness had affected both mother and daughter in the past and continued to influence them in the present. In listening to her daughter's pain and apologizing for her own behavior, Mrs. Stephans had the opportunity to transform herself into a more empathic mother in the present. As Marcy came to recognize her mother's positive motivation in encouraging her to diet, she was freed to think of herself as acceptable and loved rather than "fat and hideous." When mother and daughter were encouraged to talk about their unhappy childhoods, each extended empathy for the other, contributing to a deepened capacity for relating.

Many clients are reluctant to acknowledge their mothers' pain, fearing that if they feel sorry for their mothers, they will no longer have the right to their own injured feelings (Bassoff, 1991). The therapist's role in such a case is to acknowledge that developing compassion for one's mother does not preclude feeling angry and/or sad at one's legitimate hurts. By inviting a daughter to listen to her mother's struggles, the therapist has the opportunity to help the daughter better understand her mother—a necessary step in the healing process. Marcy came to realize that her mother's goal in encouraging her daughter's dieting was to assist her daughter in achieving what she herself desired and was unable to achieve: recognition and power.

Several sessions examined other ways in which this mother and daughter might achieve power and recognition in their current lives (e.g., in work, in interpersonal relationships, etc.). The therapist continually highlighted how each therapy session itself offered the opportunity to set and achieve goals by relating more honestly and openly. By struggling together and suppporting each other's growth in the present, both Marcy and her mother developed a deep appreciation of the genuine power that is developed through emotional connectedness. In this way, the therapist created a reparative experience by helping mother and daughter restructure their relationship as one where each could develop empathy and compassion for the other, instead of reinforcing guilt and blame.

Interspersed with several mother–daughter sessions occurring over a period of months, a series of father–daughter sessions offered Marcy the opportunity to heal her relationship with her father. As her father's story emerged, Marcy's understanding of his behavior expanded. In attempting to prevent his family from suffering the economic deprivation that had marked *his* childhood, Mr. Stephans worked two jobs, inadvertently creating a different but equally serious problem. Both daughter and father came to see how his attempt to be a devoted husband and father had unintentionally backfired and made him into an overworked, unavailable parent and spouse.

"I never knew much about those battles about the diet doctors! I wish I could have helped the two of you when you needed me," Mr. Stephans acknowledged apologetically to his wife and daughter. His recounting memories of his own childhood, marked by emotional as well as economic deprivation, permitted Marcy to develop compassion for her father and allowed the two to become closer.

Such sessions allowed Marcy to see both her mother's and father's strengths and weaknesses, and gain insight as to how both parents' journey toward identity was limited and shaped by cultural pressures. The therapist normalized paternal workaholism and maternal preoccupation with attractiveness as reflecting each parent's individual history and cultural gender norms, rather than as indicating pathology. Working actively to support Marcy in acknowledging her parents' pain as well as to express her own pain and anger, the therapist supported Marcy's reconnection to her parents—a prerequisite to being able to interact in a more intimate way with others (Zimmerman, 1991).

Just as many women are reluctant to acknowledge their parents' pain, they often fear expressing their own anger and love. When therapists are catalysts in both processes, a deeper level of connection and intimacy can be achieved. Achieving a more intimate relationship with both parents—one that involves expressing genuine emotions, including anger, frustration, and love—will enable a daughter to reach out to others in a healthier way (Benjamin, 1988; Chodorow, 1978; Jack, 1991; Jordan & Surrey, 1986; Surrey, 1985).

In family therapy, it is often not only the daughter, but also the mother who needs permission to find a new identity. As the daughter faces the opportunities and challenges that adolescence and adulthood bring, the mother can benefit from engaging in her own corresponding new experiences. In the past, mothers received little support for their own development. Such support can be given in mother–daughter sessions or, if appropriate and/or available, in the mother's individual therapy. The therapist (or therapists) supports *both* the daughter and mother in assuming new roles by helping the mother redefine her role as her daughter matures. Such a shift makes the mother a more empowered role model for her daughter, one who celebrates her own vitality and growth.

Group therapy as an adjunctive modality is also useful in addressing the issue of mother-blaming. For example, Nancy, a 29-year-old anorexic, described feeling pressured in her family to be "perfect." She acknowledged how inadequate she felt while whe was growing up, and how losing weight initially was a simple solution to being the perfect daughter. With group support, Nancy explored her feelings of anger at her parents. In response to Nancy, Esther, a 40-year-old compulsive eater, turned to the group and said:

> In hearing Nancy, I'm thinking about my daughter Sara, and what kind of mother I was. I wonder if she knows that I just wanted her to be the terrific person I know she is, or whether she felt pressured by me the way Nancy feels her parents pressured her.

Through the process of identification, the group members offered one another the opportunity to gain empathy for the circumstances of their own lives. In hearing Nancy's story, for instance, Esther reflected upon the impact her own behavior might have had on her daughter. By witnessing Nancy's struggle, she developed empathy and compassion for her daughter; in telling her own story, she developed forgiveness for herself. Correspondingly, impressed with Esther's self-awareness, Nancy was able to wonder about the validity of her own assumptions that had kept her stuck for many years. "I always felt that I wasn't good enough for them . . . that I was a disappointment," she said sadly. "I've blamed them all these years. Maybe they didn't know the hurt they caused me. Maybe they didn't even mean it the way I took it."

"Imperfect though she may be, my mother is my best friend," is a comment I have heard literally hundreds of times from eating-disordered women. Such comments have made me aware of the importance of helping clients express and get beyond their feelings of anger and blame. In addition to individual, group, and family treatment, I have conducted intensive workshops to explore and transform the mother–daughter relationship. A description of such a workshop follows.

MOTHERS AND DAUGHTERS: A HEALING WORKSHOP

I am JoEllen, daughter of Meg.
I was welcomed to womanhood by Meg, Happy and Smiling.

I am Marnie, daughter of Rita.
I was welcomed to womanhood by Rita, Angry at the World.

I am Suzanne, daughter of Mary Beth.
I was welcomed to womanhood by Mary Beth, Dislocated.

Thirty eating-disordered women are sitting on the floor in a circle, introducing themselves to one another. They have just participated in an exercise in guided imagery, in which each particpant has been asked to imagine browsing though a photograph album and selecting a photograph of her mother that has something important to tell her. The purpose of the imagery is to deepen participants' awareness of how their body image development is interwoven with their relationship with their mothers by focusing questions on three areas: how their mothers felt about their own bodies; how their mothers felt about their daughters' bodies, and how their mothers' feelings about their own and their daughters' bodies affected their daughters' body image.

After each participant has meditated on the photograph she has selected, the therapist announces:

Your mother is the most important woman you will ever know.
Your mother welcomed you to the world.
Your mother welcomed you to the world of womanhood.

The therapist then instructs each participant to select a frame and a title for her photograph, and asks:

What does the frame you chose for this picture tell you about your mother? What does the title you selected tell you about your mother and about how she felt about her body? How did her feelings about her body influence her feelings about your body?

Next, the therapist opens the group discussion by introducing herself using the language and the title from her own guided imagery, and requests that participants do likewise.

I am Judy, daughter of Peggy.
I was welcomed to the world by Peggy, Queen of the Hop.

In defining herself as a daughter, she elevates that status; in emphasizing her connection to her mother, she highlights the mother–daughter lineage (one rarely celebrated). As the introductions continue, the repetitive phrases build to a rhythmic chant and create a ceremonial atmosphere, reminiscent of ancient rituals.

Throughout history, ceremonies and rituals have been used to celebrate important passages, transitions, and relationships in life. In general, women's lives have been underritualized (Imber-Black, Roberts, & Whiting, 1988; Laird, 1991). Existing rituals, such as baby and bridal showers, celebrate women's strengths as childbearers and wives—roles where they invisibly support and guide the well-being of others, rather than their own growth and development. The ritualistic aspect of this all-female workshop honors the interconnectedness that women cherish and that is devalued in our culture. Guided imagery offers participants the opportunity to go inward and heal themselves by accessing forgotten memories. Group processing offers the opportunity to deepen connections with others (Kearney-Cooke, 1989; Wooley & Kearney-Cooke, 1986).

In response to this imagery, participants are often able to experience the powerful impact of their mothers. One participant called me after a workshop to say that she had gone home and called her mother.

I didn't realize how much I meant to her. But there was something about seeing her face as she stood there at the stove that reminded me of how hard her life was, and how what she really wanted for me was to have a good life. To her, having a good life meant I should find a husband to provide me with security. What she believed was that being attractive, and in particular being thin, would help me catch a man.

Therapists are powerful healing agents who exert enormous force in helping clients construct stories that explain their own behavior (Laird, 1991; Rampage, 1991). The stories that a client constructs about her eating disorder and about her family are determined in part by a therapist's questions and guidelines. In instructing each participant in this workshop to think of her mother as "the most important woman you will ever know," and as a "welcomer to womanhood," the therapist creates an atmosphere of reverence and respect for mothering and for the mother–daughter relationship. The therapist's choice of language plants what the Plain Tree Indians called a "seed thought"—a thought that liberates the mind and enlivens the imagination (Buffalo, 1990). Such language encourages participants to think about their mothers and their lives in a new way, opening the door for creativity and healing.

Ultimately a daughter inherits the attitudes, beliefs, roles, and struggles of her mother. Generations of mothers have struggled with feelings about their lives that have been communicated to their daughters in body and self-image issues. This workshop provides an opportunity for daughters' multifaceted connections with their mothers to be explored. The imagery stimulates the expression of feelings of disappointment, rage, shame and suffering—the "chains of female misery" (Bassoff, 1991, p. 165) that are passed down from mother to daughter, and live on in the present generation in the symptoms of anorexia and bulimia. Simultaneously, voices attest to the positive qualities mothers pass on to daughters: love, care, and attachment. As the participants recall the positive impact of their mothers, strong emotions are voiced, and a powerful connection develops among the women present. In recapturing maternal strengths and shortcomings, this ceremonial group experience affirms a yearning for connectedness in the present as well as in the past, as the mother–daughter relationship is celebrated and honored.

A NEW CONNECTION

> We are taught to believe that pent-up hostility is dangerous, yet the real tragedy is pent-up love. . . . The release of pent up love and respect for our mothers brings the added gift of love and respect for ourselves.
>
> —Caplan (1986, p. 35).

Steiner-Adair (1991a) reminds us that "a lot of attention is paid to helping women with eating disorders express their anger, especially at their mothers" (p. 240). Although the expression of anger is both necessary and healing, what I have discovered is that it is not the inability to express anger that limits growth, but the inability to express love and caring. Offering daughters an opportunity to affirm the positives as well as the negatives of this prototypical relationship will have a profound impact on the daughters' quest for interpersonal intimacy—the hallmark of healthy development (Jack, 1991; Steiner-Adair, 1991b; Surrey, 1985).

As this chapter has outlined, mother-blaming, besides being misdirected, weakens the connection between mothers and daughters and limits the daughters' ability to grow. In blaming her mother, a daughter blames herself, circumscribes her affective responses, and remains crippled in her ability to develop satisfying relationships with people. In its proper context, however, the mother–daughter connection can be viewed quite differently. As Bassoff (1991) notes,

> Knowing how our grandmothers and mothers were hurt cannot undo or excuse the hurt they may have caused us—but it can provide explanations for their inadequacies. Instead of seeing their maternal failings as personal defects, we can try to understand them as outgrowths of a society that stunted women . . . we can look on them as victims of their times. (p. 165)

By identifying, expressing, and letting go of her anger at her mother, the eating-disordered woman breaks the chain of misery that might otherwise have bound her not only to her mother, but to her future daughters. Understanding and identifying with the difficulties her mother has faced can enable the daughter to move beyond blame. As she becomes capable of transforming her relationship with her mother, she becomes capable of developing more satisfying relationships with other people as well. Through the process of actively healing her relationship with her mother, she expands her own capacity to develop healing connections with others—ultimately a source of strength, growth, and power.

ACKNOWLEDGMENT

I would like to thank Melanie Katzman for her extensive editorial input and support in the preparation of this chapter.

REFERENCES

Bassoff, E. (1991). *Mothering ourselves*. New York: Dutton.
Beattie, H. J. (1988). Eating disorders and the mother–daughter relationship. *International Journal of Eating Disorders, 7*, 453–460.
Benjamin, J. (1988). *The bonds of love*. New York: Pantheon.
Bruch, H. (1978). *The golden cage*. Cambridge, MA: Harvard University Press.
Buffalo, Y. (1990). Seeds of thought, arrows of change: Native storytelling as metaphor. In T. Laidlaw, C. Malmo, & Associates (Eds.), *Healing voices*. San Francisco: Jossey-Bass.
Caplan, P. J. (1986). *Don't blame mother: Mending the mother–daughter relationship*. New York: Harper & Row.

Caron, A. F. (1991). *Don't stop loving me: A reassuring guide for mothers of adolescent daughters.* New York: Holt.

Charone, J. (1982). Eating disorders: Their genesis in the mother–infant relationship. *International Journal of Eating Disorders, 4,* 15–43.

Chernin, K. (1985). *The hungry self: Women, eating and identity.* New York: Time Books.

Chodorow, N. (1978). *The reproduction of mothering.* Berkeley: University of California Press.

Ehrensing, R., & Weitzman, E. (1970). The mother–daughter relationship in anorexia nervosa. *Psychosomatic Medicine, 32,* 201–208.

Frankenburg, F. R. (1984). Female therapists in the management of anorexia nervosa. *International Journal of Eating Disorders, 3*(4), 25–33.

Freedman, R. (1988). *Bodylove: Learning to like our looks—and ourselves.* New York: Harper & Row.

Garner, D. M., & Garfinkel, P. E. (Eds.). (1985). *Handbook for psychotherapy of anorexia nervosa and bulimia.* New York: Guilford Press.

Geist, R. A. (1985). Therapeutic dilemmas in the treatment of anorexia nervosa: A self psychological perspective. In S. W. Emmett (Ed.), *Theory and treatment of anorexia and bulimia.* New York: Brunner/Mazel.

Gilligan, C. (1982). *In a different voice: Psychological theory and women's development.* Cambridge, MA: Harvard University Press.

Hall, A., & Brown, L. B. (1983). A comparison of the attitudes of young anorexia nervosa patients and non-patients with their mothers. *British Journal of Medical Psychology, 56,* 39–48.

Hancock, E. (1989). *The girl within.* New York: Dutton.

Hare-Mustin, R. T. (1978). A feminist approach to family therapy. *Family Process, 17,* 181–94.

Hare-Mustin, R. T., & Broderick, P. C. (1979). The myth of motherhood: A study of attitudes towards motherhood. *Psychology of Women Quarterly, 4,* 114–128.

Herman, J. L. (1981). *Father–daughter incest.* Cambridge, MA: Harvard University Press.

Hochschild, A. (1989). *The second shift.* New York: Viking.

Imber-Black, E., Roberts, J., & Whiting, R. (Eds.). (1988). *Rituals in families and family therapy.* New York: Norton.

Jack, D. C. (1991). *Silencing the self: Women and depression.* Cambridge, MA: Harvard University Press.

Johnson, C. L., & Connors, M. (1987). *The etiology and treatment of bulimia nervosa: A biopsychosocial perspective.* New York: Basic Books.

Jordan, J. V., & Surrey, J. L. (1986). The self in relation: Empathy and the mother–daughter relationship. In T. Bernard & D. W. Canton (Eds.), *The psychology of today's woman: New psychoanalytic visions.* Hillsdale, NJ: Analytic Press.

Jung, C., G. (1959). *The collected works of C. G. Jung: Vol. 9, Part 1. The archetypes in the collective unconscious* (R. F. C. Hull, Trans.). Princeton, NJ: Princeton University Press.

Kearney-Cooke, A. (1989). Reclaiming the body: Using guided imagery in the treatment of body image disturbances among bulimic women. In L. M. Hornyak & E. K. Baker (Eds.), *Experiential therapies for eating disorders.* New York: Guilford Press.

Kohut, H. (1971). *The analysis of the self.* New York: International Universities Press.

Laird, J. (1991). Enactments of power through ritual. In T. J. Goodrich (Ed.), *Women and power.* New York: Norton.

Lerner, H. G. (1988). *Women in therapy.* New York: Haworth Press.

Lerner, H. (1991). Masochism in subclinical eating disorders. In C. L. Johnson (Ed.), *Psychodynamic treatment of anorexia nervosa and bulimia.* New York: Guilford Press.

Luepnitz, D. A. (1988). *The family interpreted: Feminist theory in clinical practice.* New York: Basic Books.

Marecek, J., & Hare-Mustin, R. T. (1991). A short history of the future: Feminism and clinical psychology. *Psychology of Women Quarterly, 15,* 521–536.

Maine, M. (1991). *Father hunger.* Carlsbad, CA: Gurze Books.

Miller, J. B. (1976). *Towards a new psychology of women.* Boston: Beacon Press.

Minuchin, S., Rosman, B. L., & Baker, L. (1978). *Psychosomatic families. Anorexia nervosa in context.* Cambridge, MA: Harvard University Press.

Mitchell, S. (1988). *Relational concepts in psychoanalysis.* Cambridge, MA: Harvard University Press.

Pike, K.M., & Rodin, J. (1991). Mothers, daughters and eating disorders. *Journal of Abnormal Psychology, 100,* 198–204.

Rampling, D. (1980). Abnormal mothering in the genesis of anorexia nervosa, *Journal of Nervous and Mental Disease, 168,* 501–504.

Rampage, C. (1991). Personal authority and women's self stories. In T. J. Goodrich (Ed.), *Women and power.* New York: Norton.

Root, M., & Fallon, P. (1989). Treating the victimized bulimic. *Journal of Interpersonal Violence, 4*(1), 90–100.

Root, M., Fallon, P., & Friedrich, W. (1986). *Bulimia: A systems approach to treatment.* New York: Norton.

Segunda, V. (1990). *When you and your mother can't be friends.* New York: Bantam.

Selvini Palazzoli, M. (1978). *Self-starvation.* New York: Jason Aronson.

Silverstein, L. B. (1991). Transforming the debate about childcare and maternal employment. *American Psychologist, 46,* 1025–1032.

Smith, J.M. (1991, June 10). Mothers: Tired of taking the rap. *New York Times Magazine,*

Steiner-Adair, C. (1991a). New maps of development, new models of therapy: The psychotherapy of women and the treatment of eating disorders. In C. L. Johnson (Ed.), *Psychodynamic treatment of anorexia nervosa and bulimia.* New York: Guilford Press.

Steiner-Adair, C. (1991b). When the body speaks: Girls, eating disorders and psychotherapy. *Women and Therapy, 11,* 253–267.

Surrey, J. (1985). *Self-in-relation: A theory of women's development.* Wellesley, MA: Stone Center for Developmental Studies, Wellesley College.

Tustin, F. (1959). Anorexia nervosa in an adolescent girl. *British Journal of Medical Psychology 55,* 567–576.

Weiss, L., Katzman, M., & Wolchik, S. (1985). *Controlling bulimia: A psychoeducational approach.* Elmsford, NY: Pergamon Press.

Weiss, L., Katzman, M., & Wolchik, S. (1986). *You can't have your cake and eat it too: A program for controlling bulimia.* Saratoga, CA: R & E.

Winnicott, D. W. (1971). *Playing and reality.* New York: Basic Books.

Wolf, N. (1991). *The beauty myth: How images of beauty are used against women.* New York: Morrow.

Wooley, S. C. (1991). Uses of countertransference in the treatment of eating disorders: A gender perspective. In C. L. Johnson (Ed.), *Psychodynamic treatment of anorexia nervosa and bulimia.* New York: Guilford Press.

Wooley, O. W., & Wooley, S.C. (1984). The Beverly Hills eating disorder: The mass marketing of anorexia nervosa. *International Journal of Eating Disorders, 1,* 57–60.

Wooley, S. C., & Kearney-Cooke, A. (1986). Intensive treatment of bulimia and body image disturbance. In K. Brownell & J. Foreyt (Eds.), *Handbook of eating disorders.* New York: Basic Books.

Wylie, M. S. (1989). The mother knot. *Networker, 13,* 42–52.

Young-Eisendrath, P., & Wiedemann, F. L. (1987). *Female authority: Empowering women through psychotherapy.* New York: Guilford Press.

Zimmerman, J. K. (1991). Crossing the desert alone: An etiological model of female adolescent suicidality. *Woman and Therapy, 11,* 223–241.

Zunino, N., Agoos, E., & Davis, W. N. (1991). The impact of therapist gender on the treatment of bulimic women. *International Journal of Eating Disorders, 10*(3), 253–263.

14

"Hi, I'm Jane; I'm a Compulsive Overeater"

KATHERINE VAN WORMER

THE OVEREATERS ANONYMOUS (OA) PROGRAM is attended by tens of thousands of women each year, yet it fails to meet the needs of many participants—in particular, those of women suffering from eating disorders. A journey into the world of the Twelve-Step groups may provide insight into why women who are desperate to find relief from low self-esteem, disturbed body image, and depression relinquish control of their eating and thoughts to an ideology that leaves them feeling powerless, contemptuous of their bodies, and prone to failure. There is little academic discussion of the practice and principles of OA, but much criticism by therapists and former OA members. This chapter provides a conceptual critique of the Twelve-Step program on which OA and most addiction treatments are based, and examines, from a feminist perspective, beliefs embedded in the concepts of disease, powerlessness, codependency, and abstinence. Examination of the origins of the Twelve-Step concepts finds their roots in a scheme designed to help white middle-class male alcoholics of the 1930s maintain sobriety. These concepts are challenged with respect to their suitability for the treatment of women.

TRACING THE DEVELOPMENT OF TWELVE-STEP GROUPS

Robertson (1989), in an affectionate but honest rendering of history, records the origins of the patriarchy that was Alcoholics Anonymous

(AA). In 1935, two severely alcoholic men—Dr. Bob, an Akron, Ohio surgeon, and Bill W., a stockbroker from New York—came together. Both were considered "hopeless" drunks, but they found strength in the dynamic energy that flows between two people in a common search for solace. Dr. Bob and Bill W. learned that together they could accomplish what each could not accomplish alone. An entire social movement sprang from the momentum of these two pioneers.

AA originated as an organization for men helping men. Conventional and at times dogmatic, Dr. Bob consistently opposed the admission of women to AA (Robertson, 1989). Bill W., a compulsive womanizer with an incredible ego, scandalized AA with his numerous affairs (Bill B., 1981; Robertson, 1989), but he immortalized its dogma through his prolific writings. His *Alcoholics Anonymous,* known as the "The Big Book," is one of the best-sellers of all times. "The Big Book," along with the Twelve Steps and Twelve Traditions of AA, has been adopted by—but not *adapted* to—the needs of OA. As *Overeaters Anonymous* (OA, 1980), the official handbook, explains: "The recovery program is identical with that of Alcoholics Anonymous. We use AA's Twelve Steps and Twelve Traditions, changing only the words 'alcohol' and 'alcoholic' to 'food' and 'compulsive overeater' " (p. 2).

The first OA meeting was led in 1960 by a woman, known today only as Rozanne. After attending Gamblers Anonymous, Rozanne was inspired to start a group for women with eating problems. She and several other women attended open AA meetings to master the concepts. By 1980 OA had grown to a membership of 100,000 in over 24 countries (OA, 1980). Rozanne set out originally to modify the steps and program:

> The first thing I decided was just that those AA stages were very poorly written. I felt that Bill W., who with Dr. Bob had founded AA, was only a stockbroker, and, after all, I was a professional writer. Besides, I believed that I was not so weak that I had to turn my life and my will over to the care of any God, whether he existed or not. (OA, 1980, p. 12)

Rozanne "bristled at the thought of surrender and spiritual awakening." However, Jim W., the founder of Gamblers Anonymous, then steered her to an AA meeting. As a result, OA was created from the "rib" of AA, and the steps and teachings of AA—so effective for male alcoholics working on issues of power and undue pride—were borrowed intact for women whose eating disorders (and other substance abuse) were associated with self-hatred and low self-esteem.

Today OA remains a rapidly growing international self-help group for women and men who believe they have lost control over their eating. OA operates free of charge; it is long-term, cohesive, and built on a predictable, unifying framework. Compulsive overeating is regarded as a progressive illness that can be arrested but not cured. It works, say OA members, because it recognizes the problem for what it is—a disease (Koontz, 1988).

A MALE-ORIENTED PROGRAM

Sonia Johnson (1989) faults AA and other Twelve-Step recovery groups for keeping *male* reality the norm to which women must conform. To Johnson, AA is simply another male institution with the inevitable "self-abasing, powerless, external focus, and ultimate rejection of responsibility inherent in male religion and politics" (1989, p. 131). Johnson also faults women who are so brainwashed by patriarchal values that they espouse a near-religious fundamentalism. These women, she asserts, have internalized oppression, self-hatred, and the "slave mind." That the founders of OA failed to heed the female voice and to remold the stages and the program in women's own image may indicate such oppression.

Jean Kirkpatrick's objection to AA is more personal than political. Kirkpatrick (1990) relates her decision to give up on AA as follows:

> The meetings were a big aggravation. The men were set in their ways and ideas, they dominated the meetings, their stories were often lurid and contained an ego element of bragging, their descriptions of women were very often chauvinistic . . . and their constantly calling me a "gal" began to grate on my nerves. (p. 108)

THE BASIC CONCEPTS OF THE TWELVE-STEP APPROACH

A typical introductory speech by an alcoholism counselor describing the basic concepts of AA would probably include the following:

> Alcoholism is a disease. It is primary, chronic, progressive, and if undetected, fatal. There is no cure for addiction, but the disease can be arrested. What is alcoholism? Alcoholism is characterized by a lack of control, a powerlessness, over the substance alcohol. The alcoholic, unlike others, can never drink moderately but must abstain from alcohol each day, one day at a time. Recovery comes through lifetime membership in AA and through following the principles of the Twelve Steps. The alcoholic is always recovering but never recovered. This is why at the start of the AA meeting, the member always says, "Hi, I'm John; I'm an alcoholic."

The basic concepts of AA presented above can be summed up as follows: (1) disease progression, (2) powerlessness of the affected individual, (3) the clear-cut dichotomy between the alcoholic and nonalcoholic (or the addict and the nonaddict), (4) abstinence, and (5) the lifetime use of a self-label. All of these concepts form the basis for the Twelve-Step approach to eating disorders.

With slight modifications, the Twelve Steps of AA are utilized by OA. They are presented in Table 14.1.

ANALYSIS OF THE CONCEPTS

Overeating as a Disease

According to preliminary reports, the upcoming fourth edition of the *Diagnostic and Statistical Manual of Mental Disorders* (published by the

TABLE 14.1. The Twelve Steps of AA

1. We admitted we were powerless over [food]—that our lives had become unmanageable.
2. Came to believe that a Power greater than ourselves could restore us to sanity.
3. Made a decision to turn our will and our lives over to the care of God *as we understood Him.*
4. Made a searching and fearless moral inventory of ourselves.
5. Admitted to God, to ourselves and to another human being the exact nature of our wrongs.
6. Were entirely ready to have God remove all these defects of character.
7. Humbly asked Him to remove our shortcomings.
8. Made a list of all persons we had harmed, and became willing to make amends to them all.
9. Made direct amends to such people wherever possible, except when to do so would injure them or others.
10. Continued to take personal inventory and when we were wrong, promptly admitted it.
11. Sought through prayer and meditation to improve our conscious contact with God *as we understood Him,* praying only for knowledge of his will for us and the power to carry that out.
12. Having had a spiritual awakening as the result of these steps, we tried to carry this message to [compulsive overeaters] and to practice these principles in all our affairs.

Note. The Twelve Steps are reprinted with permission of Alcoholics Anonymous (AA) World Services. Copyright 1939, 1955, 1976 by AA World Services, Inc.

American Psychiatric Association) will incorporate a new diagnostic category for people who binge: binge eating disorder (Hohenshil, 1992). As a result of insurance reimbursement requirements there has been considerable pressure from the eating disorders treatment industry to include this group. Compulsive overeating according to OA (1980), is a disease like alcoholism—a disease of the mind, body, and spirit. Like alcoholism, it is a *progressive* illness:

> If you are really a compulsive overeater, the symptoms will grow worse. Within our ranks are those who were recovering but tried once again to control food by their own devices, with consequent return to serious overeating and, in many cases, massive weight gain. . . . The chances are that your symptoms will eventually reach those of late-stage compulsive overeating. (OA, 1980, p. 5)

Women who are told they have a disease that will only get worse may be unduly alarmed, as may their families. And women who are forced to assume a negative label—"Hi, I'm Jane; I'm a compulsive overeater"—are at risk for lowered self-esteem. The philosophy of bringing the male alcoholic "down to earth" may be absolutely detrimental to the woman (or man) needing a psychological boost. The sickness conceptualization is enunciated by Bill B. (1981) in *Compulsive Overeater,* a book widely read in OA circles:

> When we talk about relationships, the first thing we compulsive overeaters or alcoholics do is to acknowledge that we are *sick* people. That's why we are banded together in this Program.
> Ours is a threefold illness. First, we are physically sick—obviously, since most of us are fat. Second, we are emotionally sick. People who don't have emotional problems don't eat the way we eat and don't live the kind of lives we live. Most important of all, we are spiritually sick. (p. 247)

A questionnaire frequently used to define "compulsive overeating" and lure respondents to OA suggests that anyone who answers yes to three of the items may be a compulsive overeater. Among questions included are the following:

- Do you eat when you're not hungry?
- Do you go on eating binges for no apparent reason?
- Do you give too much time and thought to food?
- Have you tried to diet for a week (or more), only to fall short of your goal?
- Do you resent the advice of others who tell you to "use a little willpower" to stop overeating?
- Do you eat to escape from worries or troubles?

This widely circulated questionnaire is often seen in popular magazines (Koontz, 1988). Not surprisingly, when I administered the test to a large class of predominantly female social work students, the majority answered in the affirmative to at least three questions.

The label "compulsive overeating" or "eating disorder" is applied loosely and in harmful ways. Those who are overweight (or too thin) are likely targets. At a family treatment center in eastern Iowa with which I am familiar, a mother and daughter on the nontreatment staff were ordered to attend OA to work on their "problems." They both resigned, reportedly in a state of "denial." To bandy labels about in this manner is a serious disservice and constitutes discriminatory treatment.

Reckless use of the "eating disorder" label can also restrain women from needed political action; since problems are internalized, their external and political dimensions are obscured. OA and other Twelve-Step groups, argues Johnson (1989), brainwash women into patriarchal oppression. Viewing addiction as the problem, rather than as a symptom of societal pathology, holds women back from examining the political nature of the difficulty. Wolf (1991) explores the crippling aspects of "the beauty myth" and the concomitant "cult of thinness" into which women are inculcated at an early age. Images of female beauty operate as a political weapon impeding women's advancement.

Powerlessness, Surrender, and Humility

Among the Twelve Steps, the admission of "powerlessness" is the most significant and controversial. This step, explains Kasl (1990, p. 30), was intended to lessen the denial and inflated egos of alcoholic men. For women, Kasl suggests an alternative wording: "We admitted we were out of control with _____ and have the power to heal by taking charge of our lives and stop being dependent on others for our self-esteem and security" (see Table 14.3, below).

To teach people that they are powerless over a substance is to promote passivity detrimental to "finding the tools of liberation" (Johnson, 1989). As Johnson emphasizes, the Twelve Steps contain a "thoroughgoing negativity," ascribing to people powerlessness, unmanageability, and insanity. Bill B.'s (1981) remarks bear this out:

> It is not the "fat" that brought us here—but the insanity of our compulsiveness. The only difference between our insanity and craziness of people who are locked away is in how much time we spend being insane and how antisocial our behavior is. (p. 283)

Closely tied to the concept of powerlessness is the concept of "surrender." "The more total our surrender," instructs OA (1980, p. 3), "the more fully realized our freedom from food obsession. . . . It follows that if we had no power of our own, we needed a power outside ourselves to help us recover."

Step 2 describes turning over one's life to God—"as we understood Him." Johnson (1989, p. 136) lambasts the text for its male God and "maleficent presence." To Kasl (1990), the passive turn to God evokes images of women passively submitting their lives to male doctors, teachers, and ministers.

"Humility" is a crucial theme of Step 7 ("Humbly asked Him to remove our shortcomings"), and implicit in the remaining ones. Women in treatment would do better to focus on pride than on humility—pride in themselves and their survival skills. Yet a popular Hazelden publication promotes the self-abasing logic: "Self was most important to me, and egoism was my downfall. When I fell off my high horse and hit bottom, I had nowhere to go but to something outside of myself." (Food for Thought, 1980, p. 24).

Women in OA, like recovering alcoholics in AA, must make amends to persons they have wronged—a ritual far more appropriate to a history of alcoholism than to one of disordered eating. Far from being on "a high horse," women with eating disorders typically experience low self-esteem, poor body image, and depression; many have been victimized.

Dichotomizing

> *Will I abstain or will I overeat? For us, there is nothing in between.*
>
> —*Food for Thought* (1980, p. 20)

The Twelve-Step self-help groups are sometimes criticized for their all-or-nothing logic: Either one is an addict or one is not (Peele & Brodsky, 1991; van Wormer, 1988). Bill B. (1981) states, "The Twelve Step Program cannot be worked selectively. You either work it in total—all the steps—or you don't work it at all." The "program" demands absolute faith, absolute surrender, absolute abstinence.

Abstinence

In order for OA to parallel AA, the notion of "abstinence" had to be adopted. The alcoholic cannot drink moderately because of powerlessness over alcohol, so must abstain (Royce, 1989). The "food addict," therefore, also has to abstain. But from what?

In OA, abstinence may refer to overeating, bingeing, eating between meals, or eating particular substances such as sugar and white flour (which are erroneously believed to trigger binge eating). Bill B. (1981) equates OA's "abstinence" with AA's "sobriety." This is, in fact, a common though confusing usage of the term throughout OA literature. Garner (1986) contrasts the absolutist demands for abstinence by OA with the *normalizing* of food intake, and argues that OA's simplistic approach may exacerbate feelings of unworthiness in women whose weight loss does not meet current cultural standards. Indeed, thinness and abstinence seem to be taken as more convincing evidence of recovery than is moderation, flexibility, or independent thinking.

OA (1980) depicts a woman's progress in these terms:

> Back in the thirties I wore a size 18 dress. With diet pills, I managed to go down to an 11. Now, through OA, I have been maintaining a weight loss of about 40 pounds for four and a half years and now I wear a size 3 dress. (p. 63)

Similarly, Bill B. (1981, p. 275) announces in bold letters: **"Thinness will not make you well. But wellness will make you thin."**

Thinness is further equated with happiness in the following excerpt from another OA publication (OA, 1982, p. 311): "She kept right on coming back, parlaying that single step into a size 3 dress, a 110 pound body and a brand new life." As Bemis (1985) notes, an abstinence model for treatment of bulimia requires all bingeing and vomiting behavior to be eliminated as a precondition for therapy, paralleling the AA principle that the alcoholic in treatment must abstain from alcohol. Nonabstinence models, in contrast, advocate a more gradual reduction in bingeing episodes; furthermore, dichotomous thinking is discouraged.

A certain rigidity pervades treatment centers with Twelve-Step programs. For bulimic females, the effort to enforce abstinence may become unacceptably intrusive. Bathroom privacy may be violated in order to prevent purging of food, and food may be kept under lock and key. The lack of privacy mirrors the powerlessness and lack of control experienced by chemically dependent clients. In contrast, family therapy techniques based on feminist theory utilize interventions aimed at reversing such intrusive actions on the part of parents, and strive to rebalance power in the family (Root, Fallon, & Friedrich, 1986).

Codependency

According to Connors (1992), many bulimics fit the description of codependency because they put others' needs before their own. "Codependency" is a label indiscriminately used to describe a woman who reacts in socially prescribed ways. Although nurturance, sensitivity to others, and loyalty are pathologized in the Twelve-Step model, these characteristics are not inherently negative. Codependency has been medicalized into a diagnosable, treatable illness that exists independently of marriage to or a relationship with a chemically dependent person. Expanded, developed, and popularized beyond its original meaning, today codependency is generally accepted in alcoholism treatment circles—not as a disease paralleling that of the alcoholic family member, but as a disease in its own right (see van Wormer, 1989).

Not to be codependent, one must subscribe to a male model of inexpressiveness, instrumentality, and competitiveness. Old feminine ideals, including women's identification with mothering and relational concerns, are devalued in a society that values competition and narcissistic self-sufficiency (Haaken, 1990). Culturally engendered attributes are thus redefined as personal pathology.

ALTERNATIVE STEPS

Kirkpatrick (1990) has founded an alternative self-help organization, Women for Sobriety, which in the words of Sonia Johnson (1989) "keeps what is good about AA and dumps the rest." A Women-for-Healthy-Eating group would perhaps want to consider Kirkpatrick's proposed Thirteen Steps (see Table 14.2), but many of them still contain a subtle injunction to deny feelings and please others. Steps 2, 3, 9, and 11 are especially worrisome. Steps 2 and 3 deny the validity and usefulness of negative emotions. For women with histories of physical and sexual abuse, long-suppressed emotions such as anger and rage need to come to the forefront. The "happiness habit" may prevent such women from getting help or support. Step 9, "The past is gone forever," is a denial of the important role of the past—of our culture and history. To the survivor of rape or incest, this step is a slap in the face. Step 11, Enthusiasm is my daily exercise," would seem to play into the stereotyping of women as always smiling and effervescent.

To address women's special needs and affirm women in their own inner resources, Kasl (1992) has devised her own list of Sixteen Steps (see Table 14.3). Although somewhat unwieldy in their length, these steps are positive, oriented to strengths and politically relevant.

CONCLUSION AND IMPLICATIONS
FOR TREATMENT

When disorders such as codependency or anorexia/bulimia are defined, the conceptualization often utilizes an analogy model (Vandereycken,

TABLE 14.2. The Thirteen Steps of Women for Sobriety

1. I have a drinking problem that once had me.
2. Negative emotions destroy only myself.
3. Happiness is a habit I can develop.
4. Problems bother me only to the degree that I permit them in.
5. I am what I think.
6. Life can be ordinary or it can be great.
7. Love can change the course of my world.
8. The fundamental object of life is emotional and spiritual growth.
9. The past is gone forever.
10. All love given returns two-fold.
11. Enthusiasm is my daily exercise.
12. I am a competent woman and have much to give others.
13. I am responsible for myself and my sisters.

Note. From Kirkpatrick (1990). Copyright 1990 by Jean Kirkpatrick. Reprinted by permission.

1990). The addictions framework is commonly employed for eating disorders. Thus, in terminology borrowed from work with white male alcoholics, one speaks of bingeing, abstinence, disease, and the program of the Twelve Steps, worked "one day at a time." Addictions workers, often trained as alcoholism counselors, simply transfer the tools of treatment from problems with alcohol to problems with food. Many eating disorders clinics look to AA and OA for guidance.

On the positive side, OA, which is 95% female, is a rapidly growing organization made up largely of concerned women helping women. In OA, many members find peace of mind and acceptance of the *whole* person. OA shows the person whose eating is out of balance that she (or he) is not alone.

Many experts, however, favor a cognitive–behavioral approach in which the client is taught a form of "controlled" eating that is anathema to the Twelve-Step program. Women with eating disorders need self-help groups that are truly helpful, such as Kirkpatrick's (1990) Women for Sobriety. Despite the reservations about this group noted earlier, one of its great strengths is that women are encouraged to value themselves more—to develop self-esteem and self-confidence. Instead of saying, "I'm Jane; I'm an alcoholic," each member introduces herself by saying, "My name is Jane, and I am a competent woman." We must reconsider the unfounded assumptions passed down from Twelve-Step groups and institute major revisions.

TABLE 14.3. Sixteen Steps for Recovery and Empowerment

1. We admit we are out of control with _____, yet have the power to take charge of our lives and stop being dependent on substances or other people for our self-esteem and security.

2. We come to believe that God/Goddess/Universe/Great Spirit/Higher Power awakens the healing wisdom within us when we open ourselves to that power.

3. We make a decision to become our authentic selves and trust in the healing power of the truth.

4. We examine our beliefs, addictions, and dependent behavior in the context of living in a hierarchal, patriarchal culture.

5. We share with another person and the Universe all those things inside of us for which we feel shame and guilt.

6. We appreciate and develop our strengths, talents, and intelligence, remembering not to hide these qualities to protect others' egos.

7. We become willing to let go of shame, guilt and any behavior or thoughts that prevent us from loving ourselves and others.

8. We make a list of people we have harmed and people who have harmed us, and take steps to clear out negative energy by making amends and sharing our grievances in a respectful way.

9. We express love and gratitude to others and increasingly appreciate the wonder of life and the blessings we do have.

10. We learn to trust our reality and daily affirm that we see what we see, we know what we know and we feel what we feel. We increasingly become willing to speak truth to power.

11. We promptly admit to mistakes and make amends when appropriate, but we do not say we are sorry for things we have not done and we do not cover up, analyze, or take responsibility for the shortcomings of others.

12. We seek out situations, jobs, and people that affirm our intelligence, perceptions, and self-worth and avoid situations or people who are hurtful, harmful, or demeaning to us.

13. We take steps to heal our physical bodies, organize our lives, reduce stress, and have fun.

14. We seek to find our inward calling, and develop the will and wisdom to follow it.

15. We accept the ups and downs of life as natural events that can be used as lessons for our growth.

16. We grow in awareness that we are sacred beings, interrelated with all living things and we contribute to restoring peace and balance on the planet.

Note. From Kasl (1992). Copyright 1992 by Charlotte Kasl. Readers are free to make copies of these steps as long as credit is given to Charlotte Kasl. Reprinted by permission.

REFERENCES

B., Bill. (1981). *Compulsive overeater*. Minneapolis: Compcare Publications.

Bemis, K. M. (1985). "Abstinence" and "nonabstinence" models for the treatment of bulimia. *International Journal of Eating Disorders, 4*(4), 407–437.

Connors, M. (1992). Bulimia: Interdisciplinary team practice from a normative and developmental perspective. In E. Freeman, *The addiction process: Effective social work approaches* (pp. 192–303). New York: Longman.

Food for Thought. (1980). Center City, MN: Hazelden.

Garner, D. (1986). Problems with the Overeaters Anonymous model in the treatment of bulimia. *NAAS Newsletter, 13*(12), 1–2.

Haaken, J. (1990). A critical analysis of the co-dependence construct. *Psychiatry, 53*, 396–405.

Hohenshil, T. (1992). DSM-IV progress report. *Journal of Counseling Development, 71*, 249–251.

Johnson, S. (1989). *Wildfire: Igniting the she-volution*. Albuquerque, NM: Wildfire Books.

Kasl, C. D. (1992). *Many roads, one journey: Moving beyond the Twelve Steps*. New York: HarperCollins.

Kirkpatrick, J. (1990). *Turnabout: New help for the woman alcoholic*. New York: Bantam Books.

Koontz, K. (1988, February). Women who love food too much. *Health*, pp. 40–42.

Overeaters Anonymous (OA). (1980). *Overeaters Anonymous*. Torrance, CA: Author.

Overeaters Anonymous (OA). (1982). *For today*. Torrance, CA: Author.

Peele, S., & Brodsky, A. (1991). *The truth about addiction and recovery*. New York: Simon & Schuster.

Robertson, N. (1989). *Getting better: Inside Alcoholics Anonymous*. New York: Fawcett Crest.

Root, M. P., Fallon, P., & Friedrich, W. (1986). *Bulimia: A systems approach to treatment*. New York: Norton.

Royce, J. (1989). *Alcohol problems and alcoholism*. New York: Macmillan.

Vandereycken, W. (1990). The addiction model in eating disorders: Some critical remarks and a selected bibliography. *International Journal of Eating Disorders, 9*(1), 95–101.

van Wormer, K. (1988). All or nothing thinking: A cognitive approach. *Federal Probation*, pp. 28–33.

van Wormer, K. (1989). Codependency: Implications for women and therapy. *Women and Therapy, 8*(4), 51–63.

Wolf, N. (1991). *The beauty myth*. New York: Morrow.

IV

RECONSTRUCTING THE FEMALE TEXT

15

Conflicts of Body and Image: Female Adolescents, Desire, and the No-Body Body

DEBORAH L. TOLMAN
ELIZABETH DEBOLD

BODIES AND IMAGES

THE TWO WORDS in the term "body image" hold the tension of a split prevalent in Western culture between experiences of body and conventions of mind. These two words are in conflict. Consider the differences between "body" and "image." What does it mean to have a body? Imagine a sudden sound. The body responds with an alertness—who comes? Or imagine other physical responses to other situations: pounding feet and heart, breath rasping in and out of an aching chest, side stitched in pain, gooseflesh crawling down arms, a tight knot of anger in the gut, the queasy certainty that another person is lying, heaviness in the heart, the wetness and panting of passion, the gnawing of hunger, the feeling of lightheadedness, the delicious sensation of a hand grazing the neck, the unmistakable scent of a loved one. Living in a body means feeling hunger and desire (for food, for sex), satiation and frustration, pleasure and pain. And what, then, is an image? An image is created when someone is looking. It is what is formed on the retina when something is looked at. An image is flat, has no feelings, is silent. An image can have no appetite, no hunger, no desire, and no power of its own. An image creates a "no-body body," nobody's body, because we exist not in images that reflect others' desires but in desiring bodies.

302 RECONSTRUCTING THE FEMALE TEXT

In a recent study of adolescent health (Tetlin, 1990), 64% of girls in a Minnesota statewide survey reported having a negative body image. Even more disturbing, researchers have observed a consistently strong relationship between girls' negative body images—their worry and displeasure with how their bodies look—and signs of psychological distress (Allgood-Merton, Lewinsohn, & Hops, 1990; Brown, Cash, & Lewis, 1989; Fabian & Thompson, 1989; Freedman, 1984; Leon, Lucas, Colligan, Ferdinande, & Kamp, 1985; Rierdan, Koff, & Stubbs, 1987, 1989): Girls who have negative body images are more likely to suffer from depression, to have eating disorders, and to consider killing themselves. The pervasiveness of negative body images among adolescent girls may be understood in part as girls' attempt to live within the safety of an ideal image that looms large in the culture, rather than in the vulnerability and vitality of their female bodies.

The image of the desirable woman is posed as the model of success. She is a painfully familiar sight, appearing before us in the mass media and reflected in the expectations of others. There are few women who have not negotiated some relationship with her (see also Faust, 1983; Ussher, 1989). Current expectations of beauty are reflected in the images of women models, who by their omnipresence become unrealistic models for the way all women's bodies should be. These women are, on average, 5 feet 9 inches tall, and weigh less than the lowest weight considered healthy for their height (Rodin, 1992). Moreover, models today are expected to have ample breasts—nearly a physical impossibility, given their lack of body fat. Whatever their racial or ethnic origins, these models have patrician Anglo features (hooks, 1992). Perversely, the image of the desirable woman is the woman with no desire, with big breasts but barely a body to speak of. The allure and impossibility of living as this image haunts us in the same way that the nameless Sleeping Beauty of the childhood bedtime story does. We know the homage that is paid her. Women try to live within her impossible confines, because she holds the power to attract men's desire and to garner the protection of a man in a sexually violent world. However, the illusion of protection by one's man is absurd, given the pervasiveness of sexual violence against women, and the fact that the perpetrators of this violence are frequently the very men who are supposed to provide this "protection" (Kelly, 1988; Levy, 1991). The Mephistophelian bargain that this image offers women is this: by sacrificing knowledge of our bodily appetites and passionate feelings, we will be kept safe from rape, poverty, and loneliness. It is in adolescence that girls are faced with this offer and must negotiate a bargain for themselves.

The Mephistophelian bargain that girls negotiate is struck within the context of a political and social reality that establishes norms for feminine behavior and appearance that deny girls and women active desire. The girls we discuss in this chapter are, with one exception, "normal"; that is, they are not diagnosed as "eating-disordered." Yet what is "normal" and what is "disordered" for girls growing up in a culture that paradoxically cultivates denial of desire as life-affirming? Rather than resorting to traditional psychoanalytic explanations of a repressive unconscious, we find more helpful the Foucaultian analysis presented by Susan Bordo (1989): Within a sociopolitical context where the "hallucination [of a thin ideal] grows ever more influential and pervasive because of . . . conscious market manipulation" (Wolf, 1991, p. 19), we need "an analysis of power 'from below'" in order "to confront the mechanisms by which the subject becomes enmeshed, at times, into collusion with forces that sustain her own oppression" (Bordo, 1989, p. 15). As Bordo states, the "realm of femininity" is constituted through "the seemingly willing acceptance of various norms and practices" by girls and women (1989, p. 15). However, "willing" is a provocative term. By "willing," Bordo is referring to the ways in which girls exercise the power that has been made available to them—exhibiting the "power of weakness" (Goldner, 1985, p. 44), an internalization of mechanisms of their own oppression. Joining Bordo, we concur that "we desperately need an effective *political* discourse about the female body" (Bordo, 1989, p. 15, emphasis in original) that will make possible a critical perspective, a conscious understanding of how the power that seems to reside within this image is in fact illusory and oppressive. Girls' and women's power lies not in the knowledge of how to live as this desireless image, but in the knowledge that begins with a connection to their own embodied desires.

Our "normal" girls have been drawn from two longitudinal studies of adolescent girls' psychological development that were conducted by the Harvard Project on the Psychology of Women and the Development of Girls.[1] One study involves girls ages 6–17 attending a private girls' school in Cleveland, Ohio. All of these girls are educationally privileged; most are white and middle class.[2] The second study focuses on girls interviewed in the 8th, 9th and 10th grades in an urban public school in the northeast, who are considered by standard predictors to be at risk for early pregnancy and school dropout; these girls are primarily though not exclusively of color and are economically disadvantaged.[3]

Using a semistructured clinical interview, we ask girls about their experiences with conflict and with various relationships in their lives. Our method of analysis entails listening for and interpreting the different ways that girls give voice to their experience of themselves in relationships. We listen to the voices of girls as authorities on their own experience (Brown et al., 1988; Brown, Debold, Tappan, & Gilligan, 1991). While we read these interview texts, we attend to and explore our experiences as women as we listen to what these girls say and do not say. This feminist approach to qualitative data analysis (Brown & Gilligan, 1990) draws on the work of feminist literary critics who outline the strategy of "resistant reading." Feminist resistant reading demands that the reader bring her knowledge of women's oppression to a narrative, so as to raise questions about what may be known yet not explicitly stated by the narrator (e.g., Fetterley, 1978). As we read texts of interviews with these girls, we notice images of the desirable woman appearing spontaneously and clearly through their words, although we do not ask explicitly about such images. By listening with care to adolescent girls, we are beginning to understand how, in the course of adolescence, many girls seem to arrive at an impasse between the appetites in their bodies and the no-body image.

SEEING/BEING AN IMAGE

We have heard girls recognize the power of the image by acknowledging that she represents who they would like to become. Blaine is a ninth-grader in the third year of the private school study. She is asked, for the third year in a row, to describe herself to herself. Blaine finds this question puzzling, although she has answered it in previous years: "Myself to myself? What do you mean, like physical appearance or . . .?" Blaine is coming to know herself as "like physical appearance," how she appears to others. Blaine says that she has changed, and is asked by her interviewer, "So what has led to this change in the way that you see yourself?" She answers:

> I don't know. My appearance has changed a lot, like my physical appearance, like I am taller and thinner than I used to be. I don't know—I am all around better-looking than I used to be, so I guess when you are being better-looking than you used to be, you feel a little better than you used to feel.

Blaine links feeling better about herself with "being better-looking." Throughout the years of the study, Blaine, a willowy, blue-eyed blonde, will try to look better and better by becoming thinner and thinner and blonder and blonder. By 10th grade, she is under psychiatric care for anorexia, and struggles to understand why she's being told that she is "perfectionistic" when "I'm not perfect."

Irene, a seventh-grader in the same school, doesn't like to say positive things about herself:

> It's just that I don't like being—I don't like to sound that I think good of myself, 'cause I really don't. I don't see how people, like,

they say, "Oh, [you have] such a good personality and [are] so nice." And I'm like, "No, look at my nose, look at my legs, no."

To Irene, thinking "good" of herself is linked with her "nose" and "legs" rather than with her "good personality." Later in her interview, she says that what would make her happy is "Right now, like, being skinny."

Blaine and Irene seem to know and to see themselves refracted in the mirror of the desirable woman. They are conscious that being "taller and thinner" or having a certain nose is what makes them think "good of [themselves]." These girls also tell us that they know who is holding up the mirror that reflects the image of the woman they want to become. In 11th grade, Blaine says:

> I look put together on the weekends and everything, but in school, why should I bother to try? In school, it's a bad attitude, but hey, I don't want to, it is no reason for me to look good for a bunch of girls.

Melinda, another student at the school, adds:

> It would be a lot different if there were [boys at the school] because with the boys, we would—we wouldn't be ourselves at all, we wouldn't come to school without looking as good as we can. And here we just come to school and no one cares what anyone else looks like.

Girls do not simply live in their bodies but become aware of how their bodies appear in the eyes of boys. Melinda recognizes that, in a school where boys look, "[we] wouldn't be ourselves at all." By seeing their own bodies as images in boys' eyes, they begin to observe rather than to experience their own bodies; their bodies become Other to themselves (de Beauvoir, 1949/1961).

REPUTATION: LIVING AS THE IMAGE

Looking at themselves as if outside the flesh and feelings of their bodies, many of the girls have, as early as ninth grade, set aside the possibility of sexual pleasure to live within an image instead of in their flesh. A recent survey by the Centers for Disease Control found that by ninth grade, 40% of girls in the United States have had sexual intercourse (Nazario, 1992). As Pamela, a ninth-grade Hispanic girl in the urban public school study, explains: "For now, I'd say definitely no [to having sex], because I don't want my husband to be like, 'You are already leftovers,' you know, so I would want to be—I want to wear white when I get married, so . . ." Pamela protects her future and her image of herself as a bride in white by "definitely [saying] 'no' " to sex in order not to be seen as "leftovers." She thus responds to the unspoken dictates of a world shaped by future husbands, rather than by her own sexual desire and feelings. Sophia, another ninth-grader in the urban public school, describes wrestling for her reputation with a boy who "wanted to go up my shirt": "Like I don't have the reputation of being like the easy one around or anything, and I don't know where he got the idea from that. So . . ." Sophia doesn't speak of feelings in her body—perhaps feelings of arousal or anger; rather, she names and seems to know the image of herself that her behavior may project.[4]

Yet sometimes, as Marita, a 10th grade Hispanic girl, explains, though a girl can try to live bound within the image, others (girls as well as boys) have the power to frame how she is seen. Marita describes being tricked by a boy into appearing to have a feeling body:

> He grabbed me and said no, "I've got to talk to you." And he comes over and kisses me. . . . I had lipstick on, so my lipstick had gone away. I did not kiss him at all . . . and I walked away. . . . Then suddenly when I left, the crowd was right there, of boys . . . so I'm walking up putting on lipstick and everybody was like looking at me with a different view, no more the same smiley faces, just like that. And I'm like, "What's going on?" and I was like, "Everybody, I hope you didn't think that we kissed because we didn't." . . . It was so bad, I felt like I was dying. . . . And they would even look at me different. To this day, there are probably some boys that don't talk to me any more, girls either. And everybody was so against me, people didn't believe me that nuthin' happened. He's the one who just came on, I didn't do anything.

Because she appeared to display desire, Marita found that everybody "was . . . looking at me different." The power of this gaze made her feel "like I was dying." Marita's protest—"I hope you didn't think that we kissed"—suggests that she had been trying to live within the limits of the desired but desireless image. The loss of her image through the appearance of transgression resulted in her loss of voice, of "respect," and of relationship:

> Most of those kids that I used to say hi to, like the boys, I won't go up and say, "Hi, how are you, how was your day?" I'm like, "Hi," and that's it. Because when I pass by them in the hall, they're like, "Oh, she has a nice behind, oh, you got a nice behind," and they start whistling to you, you know, sometimes I see the boys and I take the other way. . . . By myself is when I feel better.

Marita feels uncomfortable in her body under the looks, whistles, and comments of the boys. While boys manipulate her image, girls collaborate in her punishment by acting as police—agents of social control dedicated to keeping all girls, and thus themselves, in line (Lees, 1986, 1987; Cowie & Lees, 1987). Marita has found that boys "started losing respect towards me," and, unable to speak out against this inaccurate perception, her solution to the problem is to "take the other way." Isolated and confused, she tells her interviewer that "when I leave this school, I don't leave happy. I don't. I don't know, I just don't feel happy." Aligning with the cultural message that her presumed behavior was out of line, she finds herself depressed, unhappy.

The expectations of others define life within the confines of this image. These girls "think good of [themselves]" for being "taller and thinner," for "looking as good as [they] can." Careful of their images, they watch themselves even as they are watched. They guard their reputations—so that they can wear white, so that boys don't whistle, so that girls will remain their friends. They do not have the power to control the situation outright or to determine how they will be seen by controlling themselves. Power lies with the men who "look at [them] different" and with other girls and women who will not "talk to [them] any more," leaving them isolated and vulnerable to violation.

NO-ING AND NOT KNOWING APPETITE

Living watched, desired, judged, these girls negotiate uneasy compromises between an ideal image that has no appetites and the feelings of the flesh in which they inescapably live. What do girls do about embodied hungers that threaten to undermine the image they have learned they need to maintain? We find that girls employ several strategies to try to maintain an impossible balance between embodied passion and supposed safety through the protection of men.

The awareness that the desired image is thin creates conflicts for some girls when their bodies cry for food. Victoria, a tall, blonde seventh-grader at the girls' school, is asked to tell about a moral conflict she has experienced. She describes a "conflict of whether I wanted the calories of two [pastries], or I should only have one." The conflict, she sums up, was "whether or not I wanted the calories or to be good." When asked what "good" means, she says, " 'Good' means not to have too many calories, or you'll be fat like I am."[5] Victoria is not the least bit fat, yet she grabs her leg and says with disgust, "Look at this flab, geez!" When her interviewer suggests that she's pointing to muscle, she complains, "It is fat. . . . I looked in the mirror, it is really nasty-looking." Victoria finds herself in a moral conflict over whether to resist this image by acting on her desire for the pleasure of the pastry, or to be "good" and thin.

Maude, a Jamaican–American 10th-grader in the urban school, is a heavy-set girl, about 20 pounds overweight by dominant white cultural standards. She says:

> The only thing I don't like about myself outside of school is that I eat too much. . . . I eat too much. . . . Yeah, I don't eat, like when I'm going to school. I don't eat breakfast, I don't have lunch. I go home and I pig out.

When her interviewer, who is also black and full-bodied, asks her what it is about "pigging out" that makes her feel bad, she replies:

> Because I put on weight. I don't like my—my size. . . . I try to cut down on what I eat, but it doesn't work. It's only one meal a day, but I don't know. Just I wish I didn't eat that much, especially on weekends. Everyone goes shopping and the house is full of food and you get so tempted."

Maude wishes to fit her body into the image of thinness, which creates conflict with the culture of her family. Maude, in fact, may be appropriately full-bodied by the norms of Jamaican culture (Gardine, 1991). However, she is attempting to sever herself from her hunger by confining her food intake to "only one meal a day" in a Jamaican household in which women eat to satisfy hunger and to give themselves pleasure. Maude is hungry yet disavows this hunger; she does not know why she "pigs out," why she "get[s] so tempted." She seems to be pulled out of connection with her own culture by the powerful attraction of the desirable woman who looms before her in the dominant white culture (Root, 1990; Dornbusch et al., 1984).

Victoria and Maude feel the conflicting desires to eat and to fit the image. Anorexic girls, who zealously pursue a life lived as the image of thin perfection, acknowledge neither hunger for food nor hunger for sex. The cessation of the experience of bodily desire "is their ultimate goal" (Bordo, 1988, p. 93). Although we have not heard any girl speak spontaneously of having no appetite for food, when we have asked girls about their appetite for sex, some of them spontaneously profess not to have sexual appetites.[6] The norms of reputation and conventions of speaking to adults may elicit this response, but what strikes us is the vociferousness of their denial. "I really never had those feelings about anybody, making a decision whether to have sex or not," says Prudence, a black 10th-grade girl of West Indian descent. Her interviewer asks, "You've never had those feelings?" Her reply is emphatically "No." Blanca, a Portuguese 10th-grader, when asked about her sexual feelings, answers the question in terms of her thoughts rather than her feelings: "I try not to think about that much. I don't really think about that much. I have other things to think about." These girls, living within the image of the desireless woman, have no sexual feelings to speak of, living out of connection with their bodies.[7]

DESIRE CONVERTED

Other girls also speak of their lack of sexual appetite; furthermore, they find the expression of sexual desire disgusting. Later in her interview, Victoria speaks of a time when she was at a party with friends who were "going over to their boy friends to have a little extra entertainment" meaning, as she explains, "bedtime play." She, however, "wasn't going to do it." In fact, as she says later, "I don't care if he is God himself"; she would still be uninterested. When asked why her friends "do it," Victoria explains, "They're sluts" and "I don't know, they're nasty." Not only does Victoria say that she does not have these feelings, but she finds it "disgusting" that her friends do. Physical disgust, acting as a form of aversion therapy, keeps her appetite unknown to her and keeps her friends in line.

Judy, an eighth-grader at the private school, speaks about a friend whose sexual appetite disqualifies her from living as this desireless image: "She has no morals or values about—I mean not sex, but how—I mean everyone goes out with guys now, but she, like, goes farther than most people would. And she's sort of proud of it, too." When Judy's friend "goes farther than most people would" by being sexually curious, it "ruins what I think of her." By exhibiting knowledge and experience and experience of her sexual appetite, her friend seems threatening to Judy, whose response is to think that her friend "has no morals." Not only does Judy decide that she can no longer be friends with the girl, but she feels physical disgust:

> I think that's so disgusting. . . . It sort of makes me feel sick. It's like it is really gross. . . . That just made me, if I had done something like that, I would feel like total dirt and totally worthless, and she's so proud of it. I just—I can't know how she did that. No one else would ever do that, because they don't—that's not romantic, that's just plain disgusting.

Sophia remembers her encounter with the boy who wanted to touch her breasts: "But it was like—I don't know, I just felt weird, because he just, like, went up my shirt and I just felt like—I don't know, kind of, like, disgusting or something, it felt like that, kind of like dirty and all this stuff." The image does not embody desire, and since girls must negotiate strong bodily feelings, disgust can be understood as a conversion of desire. Their response to female sexual appetite is a corresponding bodily feeling of revulsion—"it . . . makes me sick"—a protestation of purity through which, as we suggest, it is virtually impossible to feel desire.

RESISTING IMAGES

Not all the girls who have spoken to us deny or are disgusted by sexual feelings. A few of the girls in the urban school, when asked about sexual decisions they have made, speak about a knowledge of their bodily feelings. Stella neither denies her sexual feelings nor covers them over with disgust. She pays careful attention to her own desire as her way of knowing what she will do. Stella explains how she will know when she will want "to go further" with a boy:

> When it was supposed to be. I think it would just come natural. I don't think he would decide—well, I think both persons should agree on it, and I think it is the right thing to do. You shouldn't just do it. . . . I would rather wait until we both would be on it. Probably I wouldn't think in my head, "I agree with this, doing this." It would just come. . . . I don't know, you would be kissing and then it just goes on. I know if it is not supposed to be that way, I usually stop. . . . You shouldn't be doing it if you don't feel right about it. That's the way I would be.

Stella is an African-American girl for whom the image of the desirable woman is doubly impossible. The desirable woman who pervades the dominant culture is not only desireless but white. Stella is bombarded with this image through her education and through the mass media. Black girls, and other girls of color, may negotiate a variety of relationships with this image of the desirable woman that is uniquely impossible and oppressive for them, ranging from a complete rejection of themselves to a complete rejection of the image. Stella's strategy is to resist an image that does not represent her. In the ninth grade, she states explicitly that she is aware of embodying her own image: "I like to be different. I think that's more better. . . . You get a lot more attention that way than seeing everybody dressing the same—looking the same, come on, it's boring." This adolescent girl, whose miniskirt reveals flesh on bones and who will "walk down the hall and shake my booty," is connected to her body and its appetites. By knowing her feelings, Stella knows what she wants and what she wants to do. She thus holds her power in a situation where many girls, without regard for or even knowledge of their own embodied wishes, are pressured into doing what boys want to do. She describes how she made the decision to kiss her boyfriend:

> I wasn't going to get myself into something I didn't want to be in, so kissing sounds like, you know, no big deal, but feelings go along with that, too. Feelings of whether or not you want to get to know the guy and be with him or learn to love him or anything, and I don't know. I wasn't going to just kiss him to be friends with him, or kiss him because of the fact that he wanted me to kiss him, or anything like that. Because I wanted to, you know.

In a social world in which a majority of adolescent girls have had sexual intercourse by age 18 (Hofferth & Hayes, 1987), the care that Stella takes in deciding whether and when to kiss her boyfriend is noticeable, as is her ability to be an agent of her own experience: It is *her* "decision to kiss her boyfriend." Stella, who at 16 does not report having sexual intercourse, appears to be able to gauge her sexual activities by her own bodily knowledge—by feeling her own sexual wishes and pleasures. Stella is thus engaging in an act of resistance. Trying to embody a desirable but desireless image of femininity makes adolescent girls vulnerable to being controlled by boys' desire. When Stella resists the image of the desirable woman by relying on her own desires and pleasure as a guide, she may be less likely to have sexual intercourse and more likely to seek the pleasures of mutual masturbation and cunnilingus (see Hite, 1976; Thompson, 1990; Tolman, 1990a, 1990b), at a time when unplanned pregnancy and AIDS threaten her and other adolescent girls.

MOTHERS JOINING WITH DAUGHTERS

How can girls know their own hungers and live both fully and responsibly in their bodies? A clue may come from Stella. Stella's mother voices concern that Stella may be pressured into risking pregnancy. Stella and her mother talk about her mother's concerns. Stella tells the interviewer that she assures her mother, "I'm not stupid, I know what I'm doing." Instead of covering over the reality of Stella's sexuality with the image of the desireless and desirable woman, her mother is willing to listen to Stella voice her embodied desire and the care she takes in sexual relationships. Anita, another African-American girl, explains in her first interview in the eighth grade how her mother encourages her to pay attention to her own sexual feelings and to respond to them responsibly:

Well, she would say to me, "Anita, you know the consequences for it. If you do decide to do it, be protected and make sure he goes to the doctor, he has no disease. I don't want no kid with no disease," and then she will say, "Anita, I always thought that you had a mind of your own and I want you to use it," and she said, "I want you to use it right." She says, "Don't be stupid and do things that you don't want to do," and then she says, "If you do decide to do it," she said, "do it because you want to do it, don't do it because he wants you to do it." That's what she will say to me.

Stella and Anita know the feelings in their bodies. Although both are aware of being looked at and desired, neither has accepted their reflection in the eyes of others as a way of life. Both girls also speak of how their mothers acknowledge their daughters' embodied feelings. Black feminist scholars (Williams, 1989; Hill Collins, 1989; Dill, 1979; King, 1988) have described how black women teach their daughters the survival skill of knowing and taking care of their own wants and needs. We wonder whether these women may be guiding their daughters along the contours of their bodily knowledge—knowledge that is truly laced with both pleasure and danger.

CONCLUSION

Girls are vulnerable, whether they live in the impossible confines of an image or in the fullness of their flesh. Living as images with their feelings flattened and appetites unknown, they are at psychological risk. Freud (1895/1955) observed that not knowing one's bodily hungers does not make them go away, but only sends them deeper into the psyche to return in a more monstrous form. Alice Miller (1981) has observed that depression can be the result of not being "free to experience . . . enjoyment of [our] own bodies" (p. 46). The protection offered women at the cost of appetite is dubious when nearly 2.5 million women a year are victims of violent crime, such as assault and rape, and are far more likely than men to be attacked by someone with whom they are intimate (Lewin, 1991).

Living fully in a young woman's body can be physically dangerous in a world where women are threatened by the ever-present dangers of violence against women, unwanted pregnancy, AIDS, and social ostracism and denigration. However, we suggest that it is psychologically healthier for girls to resist the dissociation from their bodies demanded by the image of the desirable woman, through staying connected to their bodily hungers. In the world as we know it, neither solution—body or image—ensures the health and safety of girls.

As we acknowledge the reality of danger in the lives and bodies of girls and women, we remember also the adage that knowledge is power, and that the knowledge that girls and women hold in their bodies is a source of power that the image of the desirable woman obscures. We suggest that adolescent girls need encouragement to stay connected to the desire and hunger in their bodies, so that they can have the knowledge of what they want, the force of passion, and the courage, as Annie Rogers (1993) has called it, "to speak one's mind with all of one's heart" (p. 271). The research of the Harvard Project suggests that as adolescent girls begin to struggle with problems of relationship—to themselves, to others, to their social world—they turn to women for guidance (Gilligan, 1990; Gilligan, Rogers, & Tolman, 1991; Rogers, 1993). To resist the disconnections from bodily desire and hunger that the dominant culture promotes through this image, girls need the example, the support, critical perspectives, and the company of adult women (see Gilligan, 1990)—mothers, therapists, teachers.

Yet we ourselves, as women living in the shadow of the image, know how difficult it can be to resist. These voices of adolescent girls often sound extraordinarily familiar; they articulate choices and compromises that we adult women know only too well. When we take seriously the problem of the body in female adolescence, we often hear our own struggles, as adult women with our bodies, echoed. We, too, are implicated in this dilemma in the ways we embody and enforce "normality" for ourselves and for girls. Listening to girls has the potential to lead us into greater awareness of the sociopolitical contours of our relationships with our bodies. It is one thing to become cognizant of how we are constrained and constrain ourselves within the confines of this image, and yet another to move beyond these confines and be happy. Can we even imagine ourselves with the power to resist this impossible image of the desirable woman and her false protection? We have no clear-cut solution. We suggest a beginning: that women and girls—mothers with daughters, girls with their teachers, young women with their therapists—begin a dialogue about their bodies, their feelings of desire, and the ways in which female desire is often seen as so problematic and disruptive. As Carolyn Heilbrun (1988), in her call for a renewed practice of feminist consciousness raising, says, "To put it simply, we must begin to tell the truth, in groups, to one another" (p. 45). Our hunch is that if and when women and girls "tell the truth" of their struggles for the power of their own desires, then we will create new knowledge that embodies more powerful ways of being "feminine" in the world.

NOTES

1. The Harvard Project is a feminist research collaborative located at the Graduate School of Education, Harvard University, whose members currently include Lyn Mikel Brown, Elizabeth Debold, Carol Gilligan, Annie Rogers, Mark Tappan, Jill Taylor, Deborah L. Tolman, and Janie Ward.

2. Lyn Brown, Carol Gilligan, and Annie Rogers have written extensively about the girls from this study (Brown, 1989, 1991; Gilligan, 1990, 1991; Gilligan, Brown, & Rogers, 1990; see also Debold, 1990; Debold & Brown, 1991).

3. For other analyses from this study, see Gilligan, Taylor, Tolman, Sullivan, and Pleasants (1991), Taylor (1991), Taylor and Tolman (1992), Tolman (1990a, 1991).

4. According to research on adolescent girls' experiences of sexual desire (Tolman, 1992b), girls are able to articulate desire in varying degrees. Among girls in an urban school much like Sophia's, the girls who speak most clearly about their physical sexual desire make conscious choices about how they respond to these feelings in their bodies, while girls who are confused about their own sexual desire are not able to know what they want and have difficulty deciding what to do in sexual situations.

5. Judith Rodin observes that "getting in shape has become the new moral imperative—an alluring substitute for altruism and good work, a desire to look good replacing the desire to be good" (1992, p. 56).

6. The girls in the private school study have not been asked specifically to speak about sexual experiences, and we have found no spontaneous references to explicit sexual feelings (or the *lack of them*) in the private school interviews. Tolman (1990b, 1991) has suggested that, unless asked directly to speak about sex, girls will not raise the subject of their own volition—a politically astute stance in a culture that silences female sexuality (Vance, 1984; Snitow, Stansell, & Thompson, 1983).

7. See Tolman (1990b) for a more in-depth analysis of sexual subjectivity in this sample.

REFERENCES

Allgood-Merton, B., Lewinsohn, P., & Hops, H. (1990). Sex differences and adolescent depression. *Journal of Abnormal Psychology, 99*(1), 55–63.

Bordo, S. (1988). Anorexia nervosa: Psychopathology as the crystallization of culture. In I. Diamond & L. Quinby (Eds.), *Feminism and Foucault: Reflections on resistance* (pp. 87–118). Boston: Northeastern University Press.

Bordo, S. (1989). The body and the reproduction of feminity: A feminist appropriation of Foucault. In A. Jaggar & S. Bordo (Eds.), *Gender/body/knowledge: Feminist reconstructions of being and knowing* (pp. 13–33). New Brunswick, NJ: Rutgers University Press.

Brown, L. (1989). *Narratives of relationship: The development of a care voice in girls ages 7 to 16* (Monograph No. 8). Cambridge, MA: Harvard Project on the Psychology of Women and the Development of Girls.

Brown, L. (1992). Telling a girl's life: Self-authorization as a form of resistance. In C. Gilligan, A. Rogers, & D. Tolman (Eds.), *Women, girls and psychotherapy: Reframing resistance* (pp. 71–86). New York: Haworth Press.

Brown, L., Argyris, O., Attanucci, J., Bardidge, B., Gilligan, C., Johnston, D. K., Miller, B., Osborne, R., Tappan, M., Ward, J., Wiggins, G., & Wilcox, P. (1988). *A guide to reading narratives of conflict and choice for self and relational voice* (Monograph No. 1). Cambridge, MA: Project on the Psychology of Women and The Development of Girls, Harvard Graduate School of Education.

Brown, L., Debold, E., Tappan, M., & Gilligan, C. (1991). Reading narratives of conflict and choice for self and moral voice. In W. Kurtines & J. Gewurtz, Eds., *Handbook of moral behavior and development: Theory, research, and application.* Hillsdale, NJ: Erlbaum.

Brown, T., Cash, T., & Lewis, R. (1989). Body image disturbances in adolescent female binge-purgers: A brief report of a national survey in the U.S.A. *Journal of Child Psychology and Psychiatry and Allied Disciplines, 30*(4), 605–613.

Cowie, C., & Lees, S. (1987). Slags or drags. In *Feminist Review* (Ed.), *Sexuality: A reader.* London: Virago.

de Beauvoir, S. (1961). *The second sex.* (H. M. Parshley, Trans.) New York: Bantam Books. (Original work published 1949)

Debold, E. (1990, November). *The flesh becomes word.* Paper presented at the Association for Women in Psychology, Western Massachusetts and Vermont Region, Conference on "Diversity in Ways of Knowing," Brattleboro, VT.

Debold, E., & Brown, L. (1991, March 8). *Losing the body of knowledge: Conflicts between passion and reason in the intellectual development of adolescent girls.* Paper presented at the annual meeting of the Association for Women in Psychology, Hartford, CT.

Dill, B. (1979). The dialectics of black womanhood. *Signs, 4*(3), Spring, 543–555.

Dornbusch, S., et al. (1984). Sexual maturation, social class and the desire to be thin among adolescent females. *Journal of Developmental and Behavioral Pediatrics, 5*(6), 308–314.

Fabian, L., & Thompson, J. (1989). Body image and eating disturbance in young females. *International Journal of Eating Disorders, 8*(1), 63–74.

Faust, M. (1983). Alternative constructions of adolescent growth. In J. Brooks-Gunn & A. Petersen (Eds.), *Girls at puberty: Biological and psychosocial perspectives.* (pp. 105–125). New York: Plenum Press.

Fetterley, J. (1978). *The resisting reader: A feminist approach to American fiction.* Bloomington: Indiana University Press.

Freedman, R. (1984). Reflections on beauty as it relates to health in adolescent females. *Women and Health, 9*(2–3), 29–45.

Freud, S. (1955). The case of Fraulein Elisabeth von R. In J. Strachey (Ed. and Trans.), *The standard edition of the complete psychological works of Sigmund Freud* (Vol. 2). London: Hogarth Press. (Original work published 1895)

Gardine, J. (1991). *Will we succeed?: Black mothers and daughters negotiating a doubling of difference.* Unpublished manuscript, Harvard University.

Gilligan, C. (1990). Joining the resistance: Psychology, politics, girls and women. *Michigan Quarterly Review, 29*(4), 501–536.

Gilligan, C. (1991). Women's psychological development: Implications for psychotherapy. In C. Gilligan, A. Rogers, & D. Tolman (Eds.), *Women, girls and psychotherapy: Reframing resistance* (pp. 5–32). New York: Haworth Press.

Gilligan, C., Brown, L., & Rogers, A. (1990). Psyche embedded: A place for body, relationships, and culture in personality theory. In A. Rabin et al. (Eds.), *Studying persons and lives* (pp. 86–147). New York: Springer.

Gilligan, C., Rogers, A., & Noel, N. (1992, February). *Cartography of a lost time: Women, girls and relationships.* Paper presented to the Lilly Foundation, Indianapolis, IN.

Gilligan, C., Rogers, A., & Tolman, D. (Eds.). (1991). *Women, girls and psychotherapy: Reframing resistance.* New York: Haworth Press.

Gilligan, C., Taylor, J., Tolman, D., Sullivan, A., & Pleasants, P. (1991). *The relational worlds of a group of urban adolescent girls considered at-risk.* Final report to the Boston Foundation.

Goldner, V. (1985). Feminism and family therapy, *Family Process: 24,* 31–47.

Heilbrun, C. (1988). *Writing a woman's life.* New York: Ballantine.

Hill Collins, P. (1989). The social construction of black feminist thought. *Signs, 14*(4), 745–773.

Hite, S. (1976). *The Hite report.* New York: Dell.

Hofferth, S., & Hayes, C. (Eds.). (1987). *Risking the future: Vol. 2. Adolescent sexuality, pregnancy and childrearing.* Washington, DC: National Academy Press.

hooks, b. (1992). *Black looks.* Boston: South End.

Kelly, L. (1988). *Surviving sexual violence.* Minneapolis: University of Minnesota Press.

King, D. (1988). Multiple jeopardy, multiple consciousness: The context of a black feminist ideology. *Signs, 14*(1), 42–72.

Lees, S. (1986). *Losing out: Sexuality and adolescent girls.* London: Hutchinson.

Lees, S. (1987). Sexuality, reputation, morality and the social control of girls: A British study. In *Aspects of school culture and the social control of girls* (European University Institute, Working Paper No. 87/301, 1–20). Badia Fiesolana: San Domenico, Florence.

Leon, G., Lucas, A., Colligan, R., Ferdinande, R., & Kamp, J. (1985). Sexual, body image, and personality attitudes in anorexia nervosa. *Journal of Abnormal Child Psychology, 13*(2), 245–257.

Levy, B. (1991). *Dating violence: Young women in danger.* Seattle, WA: Seal Press.

Lewin, T. (1991, January 17). Women found to be frequent victims of assaults by intimates. *New York Times.*

Miller, A. (1981). *The drama of the gifted child.* New York: Basic Books.

Nazario, S. (1992, February 20). Schools teach the virtues of virginity. *Wall Street Journal,* p. B1.

Rierdan, J., Koff, E., & Stubbs, M. (1987). Depressive symptomatology and body image in adolescent girls. *Journal of Early Adolescence, 7*(2), 205–216.

Rierdan, J., Koff, E., & Stubbs, M. (1989). A longitudinal analysis of body image as a predictor of the onset and persistence of adolescent girls' depression. *Journal of Early Adolescence, 9*(4), 454–466.

Rodin, J. (1992, January/February). Body Mania: Insights of body image. *Psychology Today, 25*(1), 56–61.

Rogers, A. (1993). The development of courage in girls and women. *Harvard Educational Review, 63*(3), 265–295.

Root, M. (1990). Disordered eating in women of color. *Sex Roles, 22*(7–8), 525–536.

Snitow, A., Stansell, C., & Thompson, S. (1983). *Powers of desire: The politics of sexuality.* New York: Monthly Review Press.

Taylor, J. (1991, August). Breaking the structured silence: Asking questions about race. In C. Gilligan (Chair), *Resisting silence: Women listening to girls.* Symposium conducted at the annual meeting of the American Psychological Association, San Francisco.

Taylor, J., & Tolman, D. (1992, May). *Relational contours of race and racism: Voices of women and girls in research relationships.* Paper presented at the meeting of the Jean Piaget Society, Montreal.

Tetlin, P. (1990). *Reflections of risk: Growing up female in Minnesota.* Minneapolis: Minnesota Women's Fund.

Thompson, S. (1990). Putting a big thing in a little hole: Teenage girls' accounts of sexual initiation. *Journal of Sex Research, 27*(3), 341–361.

Tolman, D. (1990a). *Just say no to what?: A preliminary analysis of female adolescent sexual subjectivity in sexual decisionmaking narratives.* Paper presented at the meeting of the American Orthopsychiatric Association, Miami.

Tolman, D. (1990b). *Discourses of adolescent girls' sexual desire in developmental psychology and feminist scholarship.* Unpublished manuscript, Harvard University.

Tolman, D. (1991). Adolescent girls, women and sexuality: Discerning dilemmas of desire. In C. Gilligan, A. Rogers, & D. Tolman (Eds.). *Women, girls and psychotherapy: Reframing resistance* (pp. 55–70) New York: Haworth Press.

Tolman, D. (1992). *Voicing the body: A psychological study of adolescent girls' sexual desire.* Unpublished doctoral dissertation, Harvard University.

Vance, C. (Ed.). (1984). *Pleasure and danger: Exploring female sexuality.* Boston: Routledge & Kegan Paul.

Ussher, J. (1989). *The psychology of the female body.* London: Routledge & Kegan Paul.

Williams, P. (1989). On being the object of property. *Signs, 14*(1), 5–24.

Wolf, N. (1991). *The beauty myth: How images of beauty are used against women.* New York: Morrow.

16

The Female Therapist as Outlaw

SUSAN C. WOOLEY

SUBLIMINAL DREAD

GEORGE AND I ARE TALKING *on the phone when he notices two psychiatrists on* Nightline *discussing the scandal surrounding Boston therapist Margaret Bean-Bayog. Quickly I hang up and turn on my TV. It has a recalcitrant remote control that goes willingly only to certain channels; ABC is not one. I get as close as I can, then advance one channel at a time. I find two men practicing damage control for the profession. They are careful not to condemn Bean-Bayog, whose case has not been heard. They are noncommittal about her notes describing sexual fantasies about her young male patient—a Harvard medical student who, after termination from a therapy beset by crises, committed suicide. His family blames Bean-Bayog.*

The psychiatrists emphasize the importance of boundaries. One lists the warning signs of boundary violations: sessions that run over the allotted time, meetings outside the office, dual relationships (for example, getting financial advice from one's patient), and, of course, touch. He warns about the dangers of therapists who hug their patients. Well, the other says, you can't make hard and fast rules; the point is that the therapist should be willing to discuss these things. This is a confusing distinction; the point gets lost. A feeling of vague dread pours over me as I imagine former patients and their families warned by these serious men that touch marks a breach of ethics.

Although it is well known that male therapists are far more likely than female ones to engage in sexual misconduct with patients, the allegations of misconduct by Bean-Bayog were the first to command widespread media attention, highlighting a paradoxical vulnerability of female therapists. In a profession divided in two by gender, women are disadvantaged by their disproportionately small power to define—a disadvantage handicapping them in most professions. If there is a distinctly female way of doing therapy, it remains undescribed and "outside the law." Women are further made vulnerable by their relative innocence, their record of good conduct inviting attack at the very points where men feel most embattled—namely, around the boundaries that have proved so troublesome both to those who have stepped over the line and those who strain at the boundaries in dreams and fantasies. With the continued unmasking of sexual abuse threatening to indict an entire generation of men, and men's dominance in the field challenged by a growing preference on the part of female patients for female therapists, women will be closely watched. In important ways, they are unprepared.

> *I imagine myself before a court of law, asked if my therapy includes "unusual practices"; if I touch my patients, and if so, how often and in what way; if I ask their permission and if they would feel free to say no. But isn't it true, they ask, that in a case described in one of your own papers, you gauged a patient's progress by her ability to tolerate touch she initially refused? Yes, yes, I say, but let me explain. Please do, a voice purrs, I'm sure we would all like to hear. I look around at the dark suits, the piles of documents, the leather attaché cases; like an animal blinded by a headlight, I freeze. It is useless. I cannot explain—not the way I'm feeling, not to the people in this room.*

Women, as therapists and as human beings, know much more than we have put into words. This is dangerous in ways to which we seem blind. Socialized for centuries to believe that safety lies in silence, we still do not fully grasp our vulnerability outside the home, where men write the rules. As therapists, teachers, physicians, and public officials, we have carved out niches in the shape of women, creating new forms while ignoring the lack of fit with the old. As long as we remained insignificant, this carried little risk. But as we grow—in numbers or in influence—our failure to rewrite rules as we reshape practice can come to haunt us. Once a haven for women, silence must now be recognized as a danger.

> *I think of the women whose true story is told in the Dutch film A Question of Silence. Late one afternoon a housewife enters a small*

clothing boutique, takes a blouse from a rack, and stuffs it in her bag. Immediately the manager is at her side, leisurely intoning his words with unctuous sadism. Two other women—strangers to each other and to the first—turn to look. They are the only others in the store. Their eyes meet; silently they converge and bludgeon the man to death; then, without a word, they go their separate ways.

The film details the transformation of the female psychiatrist appointed by the court to examine the women and find them insane. "They are quite sane," she tells a stunned courtroom. The movie builds to a single punch line in a contextual joke. The psychiatrist explains what brought each woman to this point; they are familiar stories about gender. "But this has nothing to do with men and women," the judge proclaims. "It could just as easily have been a female clerk killed by three men." One of the defendants begins to laugh and another follows—then the third—then the psychiatrist. Soon every woman in the courtroom begins to laugh, and when I saw the movie, every woman in the theatre did the same.

Female knowledge, flawlessly communicated and intuitively acted upon, carries danger, as this film suggests. The heady excitement produced by its invocation of an international female language and an implicit female code of honor reminds us of the latent power in women's covert understanding. We know some things so well that no words are needed. But the excitement of recognizing our commonality tempts us to forget that we live in male contexts and are answerable to male law. This was not a problem so long as we did not openly rebel, so long as we remained invisible. Many of our most fundamental values and sensibilities are at variance with the way things are "supposed" to be—definitions we have lived around and failed to challenge.

Anxiously I return to a mental screening of therapy, culling from their contexts the excerpts that will condemn me. I see my hand reach out to the terrified girl who sits across from me; see her shudder and recoil. I see myself holding women as they sob, burying their faces in my neck, streaking my clothes with tears, mucus, and mascara. I see myself helping them to pound chairs, to scream their silenced screams. I hear the crashing at the door, the analyst with a trash can raised above his head, screaming, "I can make noise, too!" I recall the memos about our "noise," the suggestion that we do emotional work only at night or relocate our clinic in the tunnels.

I see the feelings on my face. Angry—fighting to bring them back to life. Crying. Laughing. Arguing with my cotherapist. Explaining that a re-enactment of a childhood scene has revived so much pain for me that for a moment I can barely speak. I watch as I challenge

the young woman whose anger sticks in her throat to arm-wrestle;
catch a body in midair as a woman flees the room; buy food so a
woman can binge in a group; ask the woman whose memories make
her vomit to stay with us, vomiting in a wastebasket in the room.

I think of my records, none of which begin, "23-year-old single
Caucasian female presents with 9-year history of abnormal eating
behavior and unipolar depression." There is no age of menarche, no
mental status exam. In their place are mounds of things sculpted,
written, and drawn; videotapes; genograms; lists of siblings explain-
ing what to expect from each; descriptions of abuse; ideas for
exercises; here and there a dream (hers or mine). And letters, piles of
letters.

"Is it proper to pretend you are a patient's mother?" the Nightline
interviewer asks. It sounds bad. I remember the countless dramas
where I have played someone's mother. "If your therapist says, 'I
love you,' you should be worried," one psychiatrist says, this time
with no equivocation. I have said this and meant it, moved to love
by faces shining with tears, ablaze with feeling. Sometimes, when
saying good-bye, they say, "I love you," and I answer, "I love you,
too." Sometimes I end a call with "Love ya!", like a girl's entry in a
yearbook. Often my letters are signed, "Love, Susan." And some-
times I have simply said, "I feel great love for you; I always will."

My knowledge of the female patients who have been so important
in my life has long been informed by touch as well as words: by the
coldness of their hands, the pounding of their hearts; by the sub-
stance of their bodies—frail and bony, supple and strong, or full and
yielding; by their tears, shakes, chills, and sweats; and by their
muscles—rigid as a fist or limp with relief and exhaustion. If I close
my eyes, I can see, feel, and hear them.

Most female therapists have an assortment of fears related to the way
they have quietly, often secretly, diverged from the dictates of their training
and the official version of psychotherapy. Perhaps men carry such fears, too.
Perhaps none of us feel such congruence with established views that the
discourse of our field envelops us like a well-loved blanket. But the experience of deviance comes in more and less severe forms. In a world designed
by men *for* men, we should not be surprised that men feel more at home. As
Broverman, Broverman, Clarkson, Rosenkrantz, and Vogel (1970) pointed
out many years ago, our image of a mentally healthy person overlaps
flawlessly with a mentally healthy male, while a mentally healthy woman is
. . . well, a woman. Different. Less.

Nightline ends abruptly, another victim of the clock. No one is
satisfied. The attempt to define a boundary that respects all worthy

schools of therapy has failed. After all, these ambassadors don't want to ignite thousands of malpractice suits for the American Psychiatric Association to defend. Reminded that not everyone is like them, they still have no idea what others are like, what variation should be permitted. They would doubtless be surprised to learn that their methods seem as strange to me as mine to them.

THE WOMEN'S CHANNEL

As long as I can remember, a sense of difference has been central to my experience. Parallel streams of consciousness have been for me, as they are for many women, a way of life. One station plays male discourse in which I am an attentive, if estranged, participant. My lines are learned, as is my body language and figures of speech that are foreign to my own experience. On this frequency I portray a person who, if the truth be known, I don't really understand. I don't know, for example, whether he—for the prototype is always male—is as calm as he appears, as impartial, as impervious to what others think.

At 15, my daughter suddenly began to speak in the idioms of a dozen or more imaginary characters, including a Valley girl, a Chicago housewife, a middle-aged woman from New Jersey, a belligerent Italian teenager from Brooklyn, an upper- and a lower-class English girl, an East Indian woman, and a generic "foreign" man. At first I thought this was the result of a decade of comedy TV. Then I realized she was just doing the psychological work of a teenage girl: learning to impersonate others. I remembered that one year in grade school she had sat down daily to turn out carefully rendered line drawings of girls, detailing their hairstyles, clothes, glasses, freckles, brows, noses, mouths, eyes, and ears. Each picture was captioned with name, age, address, list of interests, and school attended. The work of describing distinct identities begun in childhood was, I now saw, being continued in adolescence by learning to step into them.

My own mind has only two stations: the regular approved male version of the universe, Channel A, and the women's channel, Channel B—outlaw, secret, undefined. (My daughter, growing up in a multicultural age, has many.) The women's channel plays alongside the male network in my mind, though I have tried for most of my life to ignore it, as though it were static impeding reception of Channel A. My private channel has always scared me, for it seems to contradict much on Channel A and to broadcast threatening information. There is the disrespect for "the law"—the law, for example, that what 200 patients tell you is less valid than a paper-and-pencil survey at a mall; the law of therapist neutrality; the law that science is value-free. Then, too, there are the wayward longings for intimacy; the impulse to laugh hysterically at the "part-units" described by Masterson; surprise that therapists are afraid of feelings; obsession with color and smells. And dancers, choreographed in my head, their moving limbs leaving slowly fading images. We all conceive what we need.

> *Since early childhood, my daughter has associated each letter of the alphabet with a person. She knows the sex of each, what each is wearing, and what each is like. Some are friends and some are not; they do different things. Every number is a color, and all numbers above 9 are color combinations. Her private channel, more elaborated than mine, imbues even the stark worlds of letters and numbers with relational meanings and vivid hues.*

Since Channel B has no accepted laws, to think about its programs I had to think for myself. I noticed that I was simple-minded, and also that I was sometimes right. I had been a therapist for years before I learned how to use Channel B, listening to ideas that I never thought were ideas at all but only unruly mood states. Naturally, I first shared the news on Channel B with women only, and even then with trepidation. Later, I discovered that some programs interested men too. Gradually, the struggle to silence B in order to make out A was reversed. Now I strained to mute A in order to hear B's softer words, make out its more impressionistic graphics. By age 50, I relied on the women's channel for nearly all matters of importance. It is a frequency I share with many women, whose private broadcasts make them, too, feel like outlaws. Some, who learned early in life to attend to Channel B, have vast and precocious talents. But for most of us, knowing what we know has been a slow process. Sometimes listening to other women taught us to listen to ourselves.

Little of the information on the women's channel is organized or published. To be sure, we have encountered barriers, but the greatest barriers lie within ourselves. Unwilling to know ourselves and to make ourselves known, we have allowed our knowledge to be subsumed by male knowledge, to go unnamed and uncredentialed. As a result, we are often cut off from other women and made to feel inferior and illicit. Nowhere do we draw more on the private parts of ourselves than in doing psychotherapy, and no sooner do we overcome the feeling of being impostors than we begin to feel like outlaws.

It is often said that if every gay person in the country were to stand up at once, prejudice against homosexuality would be ended, since it would be immediately recognized that what we feared is as familiar and loved as our brothers, sisters, cousins, children, and friends. Similarly, women, who number half of the population and more than half of all psychotherapists, could in a day redefine therapy, making public room at last for their methods and their meanings. We need to do this, for the cost of silence is vulnerability to being criminalized: Activities we know to be as safe as cooking a meal, defined at best as eccentricity, and at worst as misconduct.

THE FEMALE CONTEXT

In the first year after my daughter was born, I struggled desperately to find a balance between my old and new responsibilities. I never did, but I eventually got used to the feeling. The precariousness of my adjustment was symbolized for me, as it is for many working mothers, by the depth of my dependence on my housekeeper—an ebullient Appalachian woman with the strength of an Amazon. Her sudden departure when my daughter was a year old, and my inability to find a replacement, plunged me into despair. It was a uniquely female malady, but I nonetheless imagined that a male therapist who was respected in the community could help me. At least I hoped so.

It was the dead of winter, and his only available time was 7:00 A.M. Under the best of circumstances, I would have found a 7:00 appointment brutal; with darkness, snow, a baby, and a job, it was all but impossible. I made it to three sessions on time, waiting eagerly for the moment when my therapist would start talking to me—when he would do something to help. On my fourth appointment, I arrived 6 minutes late. And so it was that his first and last intervention was to wonder aloud what it might mean that I had chosen to miss part of my session. With a sickening jolt of recognition, I realized that we had not a thought or feeling in common. Although I had learned about his world, he would never understand mine. To stay in this therapy could only heighten my sense of being a stranger in a foreign land.

Context is all. To women, for whom the events in therapy resemble the events in their kitchens, overobjectification of human suffering can make identification with the field impossible. We see in many theories posturing that seems at best absurd, and at worst collusive and oppressive. How seriously can we take the search for biochemical abnormalities to explain feelings that most women have every day? How do we respond—after the years during which we have watched sexually traumatized women cower, pale, and shake—to male researchers' new interest in discovering whether there is any link between sexual abuse and eating disorders (see Chapter 9, this volume)? It is the wrong question; now we must watch the wrong answers roll in, and listen politely as these answers are endlessly debated. The simple truth is that women tell female therapists things they don't tell men, but our testimony as female therapists is given little credence. Certain things that men grope to explain do not, from our perspective, need explanation. We understand them already; we just don't know how to explain them to men.

Women are not opposed to science, but a science that has failed during decades of study to uncover what nearly all female therapists have learned cannot fail to make them doubt its objectivity. Women do not reject the scientific foundation of the field, but many take it with a grain of salt, noticing that wherever "science" takes place—studies planned, grants reviewed, data collected and reported—there is a replication of the gender roles and behaviors that are at the heart of patients' pain. It is as though toxicologists were serving poison at their conventions; the irony is not lost. Science cannot answer questions that it doesn't ask. Social prejudice can overwhelm fact, as it has in the neighboring field of obesity, where arguments to keep women on diets have outlasted decades of evidence that diets don't work.

MY PATIENT, MYSELF

In the satiric novel *The House of God* (Shem, 1978), the chief resident, "The Fat Man," teaches the fundamentals of survival to his new recruits. Among the basic rules: "The patient is the one with the disease." Adding to our sense of disenfranchisement as female therapists is our inevitable identification with our women patients. As we treat women who are diminished, disempowered, and struggling to find a voice, we see ourselves. As we treat women aligned with a culture that rejects their bodies and makes their worth dependent on the approval of men, we see ourselves. As we see women resentfully sacrificing their lives—shying away from challenge, avoiding conflict, protecting men from emotional pain—we see ourselves. We see ourselves as girls, adolescents, students, mothers, therapists, and wives, and ourselves as we relate to our own profession. For many of us, the price of entry into our fields was the mastery of the pathogenic female role.

> *During my first week in graduate school, a senior professor held a party for the entering students at his home. None of us knew one another yet, and the mood was tense. Close to midnight some of us*

caught an astonishing sight: Our host, standing beside the food table, reached out and struck a female student across the face. The observers froze; the woman quietly fled the room, never to be seen by us again. There was a brief pause, in which those whose backs had been turned to the scene stared quizzically at the faces of the witnesses. Then, just as quickly, the conversation was resumed as though nothing had happened at all. The incident was never explained, and more astonishing still—to anyone still capable of astonishment—we never discussed it among ourselves. The memory quickly began to take on the dreamlike quality of the closing moments of Bonnie and Clyde.

To know what we had seen would have severed us from our dreams. And besides, in 1964 it didn't seem all that strange. Only months before, in interviews at medical schools where only 1% of those admitted were women, I had gamely tried to answer such questions as "How long have you worn your hair that way?"; "How did you choose that style?"; "Can you cook?"; and "How long do you usually date a man before you have sex?" I was very grateful to have been let into graduate school. In subsequent weeks, months, and years, we would watch 80% of the women in our entering class leave—of their own accord or driven. Drunken faculty members would hang on female graduate students at parties every Saturday night, and we would be told by the department chairman that if we wanted to succeed in our fields we should not marry. My master's advisor would explain to me the reasons it was necessary to have quotas on women. And we breathed not a word about the distinguished male scholar who lectured at night to a completely empty room.

How could we believe in the mythical boundary between ourselves and the women who sat with us in therapy rooms? Our very presence in those rooms depended on our acquiescence to the things that had made them "sick." Behind each patient's depression, anxiety, sexual dysfunction, or eating disorder, we began to grasp her dilemma as a victim of incest, as an impoverished single parent, or as a battered wife. Much of this understanding came not from the psychotherapeutic tradition but from feminism. Women (some professionals, many not) had begun taking matters into their own hands as they saw that law enforcement, the courts, social programs, and psychotherapy had all failed them. This recognition was possible because in the women who had been set apart and pathologized—as masochistic, provocative, borderline, frigid, or just plain bitchy—other woman saw their common history of socialization in a culture that has only begun to be embarrassed to use these terms to describe women.

For men, separated by gender from the vast majority of their patients, identification could be avoided and paternal benevolence felt instead. But for women, the authority of the role proved hollow, and we learned to offer authenticity in its place. "I am really very much like you," we said truthfully, as together we began to grow. This fluidity of role and boundary allowed our understanding to transcend the sterile forms of diagnostic nosology, capturing the crucial dynamics of the cultural contexts that we and our patients shared, and creating—with women in other fields—new social and legal structures to assist where therapy could not go. The consciousness raising of the women's movement fused the helper and the helped as women struggled to define common problems, to develop a social agenda to address them, and to grasp their own contributions to their plight.

No comparable self-examination has been undertaken by men, who have (until the recent past) seen little reason to change, and who have been protected from self-knowledge by social conventions in which men do not probe one another's feelings and women probe only gently, protecting men from emotional distress. Nor has psychotherapy been for men the wellspring of self-understanding it has been for women. It will not become such until men renounce their usual preference for female patients and begin, as some pathfinders have done, to specialize in the treatment of men. Men, if they are to understand themselves, must become immersed in the dynamics of incest, rape, domestic violence, estrangement, addiction to power, and fear of and contempt for women. They must realize, as women have, that the most deviant of their gender are but extensions of themselves.

The fledgling men's movement reflects a recognition by men that they must learn to relate meaningfully to one another, give up their sole reliance on women for emotional support, acknowledge their needs for their fathers, and learn to father their sons. The new movement invites and challenges men to feel their longing and their grief. But it lacks the crucial element of contextual analysis that was so central to the women's movement. Women convened in their own kitchens; their children came in and out; the clock ticked off the hours till dinner was due on the table and their husbands would come home. These were ample reminders of the role demands of women's lives and the realities of their relationships.

Sequestered in the woods, their feelings stirred by drumbeats, men have chosen to explore themselves within a mythic fantasy of manhood that, however inspiring, denies rather than highlights the real context of their lives. Gathered in groups of 500–600, their actions stimulated by a charismatic leader, they achieve a sense of communal power that can conceal the ways in which the male interaction style isolates men from one another and estranges them even from people they love. Attempts to meet at work might reveal the ritualized quality of their interactions; meetings in their homes might better underscore how often they are strangers who have not picked out a single item in a room, do not know how to use the stove, and do not know the schedules of their children or their wives.

Men must often feel like outlaws in their homes, just as women feel like outlaws in their professions: captured in a system governed by unspoken rules in which they have had no hand, in the service of goals with which they cannot identify. For many women govern their homes as tightly as men govern the workplace. I find it curious to think that in this sense, men and women have much in common and can appreciate the history of resentment that causes each stubbornly and usually unconsciously to refuse to make a place in their gendered territory for the other, even when this means going it alone.

BACK ALLEYS, DARK STREETS

Claire's mother stands beside her dignified husband in uncomfortable shoes and a suit that demands perfect posture as Claire's hands begin to claw the air. When Claire was born deaf, the doctor told her mother there was no risk in another pregnancy; but, incredibly, her second daughter was deaf too. I'm supposed to say "hearing-impaired," but I don't understand why: "Impairment" suggests diminution, not absence. Claire's mother says "hearing-impaired." She did everything she thought she should, sending Claire to the best schools to learn lip reading and speech.

Gingerly we suggest, as we have before to Claire, that learning to sign might decrease her isolation. Suddenly Claire cowers in fear and begins to moan. Chris translates for the rest of us Claire's unusually contorted words, and as the tale unfolds, we see that Claire has been returned to the past—to a classroom in 1965, where her attempts to use her hands even to point cause the teacher to strike her knuckles with a wooden stick. No! No! Claire screams, writhing, pressing her fists to her chest, folding her body around them, and finally rolling on the floor.

"My God!" I say out loud as tears flood my eyes, wetting the hands I raise for a moment to cover my face. I am crying, I think with surprise. How long has it been? How long have I sat, eyes bone-dry, listening to the now-familiar tales of horror, finally to learn in this unforeseen moment that I still have the capacity for shock?

"How can she play tapes of such emotional scenes and show so

*little feeling?" a conference attendee wrote last year in an evaluation
of my talk. Yes, how? I asked. How much of me is dead? How
much now wakes only to symbols of an innocent past: the Wedding
March, a band in a parade, a summer camp brochure describing
songs sung at sunset with herons overhead?*

A prominent theme in literature and film is the impact on the hunter of
the hunted. The magnetism between dark and light and their frequent
exchange of identities are cultural preoccupations illustrated in Hugo's
(1862/1951) *Les Miserables,* in which the cruel jailer, Javert, represents
evil, while his prisoner, Jean Valjean, represents good. After decades
spent in chase, Javert is transformed by the example of Valjean's life;
unable to reconcile his 40-year obsession with his current feelings, he
jumps from a bridge to his death.

Usually the story goes the other way: Evil proves more persuasive
than good. The idealist—studied across time or (since we all know this
story now) captured during moral collapse—becomes indistinguishable
from the object of his chase. Forced, in order to keep pace with the
criminal mind, to think like a criminal, and made more desperate by a
record of relentless failure, the hero becomes one with the damned.

Several truths are operating here that may be relevant to female
therapists, who have, for a decade or so, been absorbing the horrible
secrets of our culture: the crimes, not of the streets but of bedrooms and
sometimes of secret cults—more frightening because we were not prepared for what we were to learn. Therapists, whether they wanted to or
not, have been forced to become the Serpicos of white-pajama crime.
Exposure to this previously little-known underbelly of our collective life
has been deeply sickening; moreover, as Steiner-Adair (Chapter 19, this
volume) notes, therapists have nowhere to talk about it. Like the cop
whose obsession with the novel texts of crime gradually separates him
from others—set apart by constant study of what others cannot see—
many therapists have been through a process of transformation they have
yet to comprehend.

This process began many years ago with the first shock of discovery
and the incredulity left in its wake. I still remember a call from a patient I
saw in the 1970s—the first case in which I was led to the discovery of
abuse. A woman of remarkable integrity, this patient appeared to be in
flight from a truth too horrible to know. Our first year together was
spent patching up a life damaged by her vulnerability to fear and the
abrupt and peculiar acts that accompany terror. Later she began to sift
her past. Puzzled, she described an image she had recalled: her teddy
bear, slit from waist to throat, its stuffing hanging out. Then she telephoned in the night; she had been compelled, she said in a horrified

voice, to put the stuffed animals she had collected high on a shelf because she had found herself, with no memory of what had come before, standing over them with a knife.

In years to come, I would hear ever greater numbers of patients describe the memories of ever more repellent crimes: the knock on the door of the rapist who came often with a group of his friends, taking turns with their victim, who entered a dreamlike trance; the father who took his young daughter to the swimming hole, where he and his companions stuffed her vagina with stones, then took turns diving and pulling them out; the uncle who pushed the raped and battered body of his 9-year-old niece out of the car and drove home; the cheerleader whose coach took her to his house, tethered her limbs to the bedposts, raped her first with a knife, sodomized her, forced her to perform fellatio, and then raped her again, and again, and again; the Annapolis midshipman, star of her entering class, raped by four upperclassmen, who carved the word "NAVY" on her chest and threatened her with death if she told; the girl forced by her father, a leader in a cult, to watch the murder and dismemberment of a baby, and then to eat the body parts.

These atrocities make the crimes of the drug lords, which in our popular lore make strong men lose their minds, pale in comparison. And the stories of abuse come in at an ever-quickening pace, as though hearing them had changed the listeners' faces, inviting those who arrived later to tell their stories too. No doubt our faces are changed—and our voices and our insides. I live in a different world than I did 10 years ago. And like the cop who looks at edgy men gathered and gets the scent of crime, I go to a park and see families, watch men as they pour from a church, or look around the room in meetings and know that much is not as it seems. I have learned too often that men I didn't like—especially when there was nothing to account for my feeling—carried the secret of sexual abuse; small presentiments now make me squirm.

Living with such knowledge is bound to take its toll, and a heightening of the outlaw experience is certainly a part of the damage. Knowledge of such abuse sets us apart from society, binding us not only to the victims but to the perpetrators of these crimes—for it is they who share our knowledge, they to whom we are permitted to speak. In many cases, working with perpetrators of abuse has removed the once-secure dividing line between the good and the bad. Not only can abuse be found anywhere; the perpetrators, like the victims, are not always all that different from us. Even the inherent difficulties in empathizing with primarily male offenders whose socialization was so different from our own is transcended in bittersweet awareness of our shared humanity.

Ten years into work with the abused, many therapists have had their fill, but they don't always know that this is the case. What they know are an exhaustion that doesn't improve with rest, a resentment in search of a cause, and subtle but growing injuries to self-esteem. Puncture wounds to the barriers between the unspeakable and the self are weakening them. But at a time when therapists, reeling from intimate contact with the underside of everyday life, are most in need of support, time to reflect, and better ways to take care of themselves, they do not find a grateful society; instead, they find even greater restrictions on what they do and a social vote of no confidence. The proliferation of "case managers" in the era of managed care suggests that therapists do not manage well on their own—that, in fact, left to their own devices, they can be expected to offer inefficient and unnecessary treatment at society's expense. When we leave sessions with our patients, sickened by what we have heard, only to spend the few minutes before the next patient trying to persuade a stranger on a phone that our treatment is proper and necessary, we feel angered, devalued, and humiliated. There is little in the current climate to offset this, save the little we can give each other; with so many of us depleted and silent, it is simply not enough.

> *I like to think of Harriet Tubman [Susan Griffin's poem begins].*
> *Harriet Tubman who carried a revolver/ [I recoil for a moment,*
> *then read on] who had a scar on her head from a rock thrown/ by a*
> *slave-master (because she talked back) and who/ was never caught*
> *and who/ had no use for the law/ when the law was wrong/ who*
> *defied the law. I like/ to think of her/ I like to think of her especially/*
> *when I think of the problem of/ feeding children.*
> *. . . And then sometimes [her poem says] I think of the president/*
> *and other men/ men who practice the law,/ who revere the law/*
> *who make the law/ and operate through/ and feed themselves/ at the*
> *expense of/ starving children/ because of the law/ men who sit in*
> *paneled offices/ and think about vacations and tell women/ whose*
> *care it is/ to feed children/ not to be hysterical/ not to be hysterical as*
> *in the word/ hysterikos, the Greek for/ womb suffering.*
> *. . . I am tired wanting them to think/ about right and wrong/ I*
> *want them to fear/ I want them to feel fear now (Griffin, 1976, pp.*
> *10–12).*
> *[Yes, that's what I want, too. No, I don't. Yes, I do. Which is*
> *crazier: to feel hatred? compassion? or nothing at all? What differ-*
> *ence does it make? I will not be allowed to pick my madness from a*
> *menu.]*

In a strange way, we can identify with the Serpico cop, clothes rumpled and eyes feverish with an obsession with justice that becomes,

332 RECONSTRUCTING THE FEMALE TEXT

in the end, an obsession with revenge. Unable often to identify or confront the perpetrators of abuse, forced to choose daily between ignoring our patients' needs or playing fast and loose with the rules that govern payment for care (or, like the cops, doing more and more "off duty"), we feel thwarted and compromised. Often the lack of response to our patients' plight brings us face to face with the same incredulity or indifference that they, as victims, have encountered. We can no longer relate to the "reasonable" men in suits with MBAs in addition to or instead of doctorates, small calculators in their pockets where their beepers used to be, speaking of the abuses of therapists and their allegedly excessive piece of the gross national pie. And when at our professional conferences we try to talk, often we fare even worse; the validity of our diagnoses is challenged, the scientific basis of our observations impugned.

Faced with what feels like the ruthlessness of both managed care systems and perpetrators of abuse, we are drawn, like Serpico, like the fallen Kurtz in Conrad's (1902/1976) *Heart of Darkness,* to become ruthless ourselves. The increasing frequency of charges that therapists trump up cases of sexual abuse, in the process destroying innocent people's lives, must be seen for what it is—part of an inevitable collective will to shut psychotherapy down and put an end to its horrible disclosures, protecting some individuals from personal harm and the rest from their cherished sense of community, the "kinder and gentler" world of soporific dreams. But we need to remain aware ourselves that there is an inherent risk of adopting the tactics of our adversaries, and that in our desperate need to be heard, we may overlook rights to due process, demanding blood for blood.

The feminist exploration of our culture's hidden crimes must not be distorted into a quest for vengeance, with excessive punishment of the occasional perpetrator who gets "nailed." No, we must ask for what we need—support, understanding, renewal, and a life for ourselves. Because the next task ahead is even harder than the last. Like Marlowe, we must go in after Kurtz, facing "the horror! the horror!" We must enter the world of perpetrators and come out with the depth of understanding necessary to tell us what to do: how to raise sons and to redefine manhood so that men do not abuse. And we shall have to answer the same questions about the rarer but nonetheless important population of female abuse perpetrators, fingering the demons that we carry unknowingly in ourselves. We must hope and perhaps demand that men join in this search, for our intuitive grasp is circumscribed by our gender; besides, we will never last working alone. Nothing could go farther to heal our sense of being outlaws than to have more men beside us, working the same dark streets.

THE BORDERLAND

The speaker is a well-known man who says that he wants to take a risk and present some controversial case material. He was trained, he explains, in the classical psychodynamic tradition, but experience has taught him that in treating bulimia we should err in the direction of being human. He describes a treatment lasting many years—but for its length, an ordinary story. I don't see where he is going. At last we hear the punch line: In the third year of treatment, on one occasion, he hugged his female patient.

The rest of his talk attempts to place this act in some theoretical context while completing what has become, for me, a bewildering shaggy dog story. No doubt this is a discussion that men need to have, but the room is filled with women. The therapy will, the speaker believes, take about 10 years. Carefully, he addresses the problem of sexualizing the therapeutic relationship; he emphasizes the necessity of talking about this as a protection against acting out unexamined impulses. He moves on to other caveats and safeguards.

Squirming in my chair, I look furtively around to see if I can read other women's expressions. Their faces are in order, betraying nothing; they clap briskly when he is done. Finally I clap, too, but I am thoroughly confused. Surely these women aren't clapping because they have been introduced to a new idea?

Are they clapping because a man has tortuously given them permission to be what they already are? Are they afraid to break rank, knowing that any discussion of this talk might require them to reveal their real selves—a potentially dangerous move among strangers? Once again men's words have made me feel painfully alone, even in the company of women. For one awful moment, I feel like the only person in the world tuned to Channel B.

Boundary issues for female therapists are, by and large, different from those for men. Men, more idealized in the culture, are more idealized in their roles as therapists. Self-disclosure, especially of weakness, can produce an abrupt and disturbing de-idealization, since a man who shows these parts of himself violates a gender norm. Exposure of vulnerability by male therapists is a powerful intervention that can be put to good use but that requires caution. Patients may feel embarrassment and pity. Or such behavior may be experienced as seductive, since it is often associated with intimate romantic or sexual relationships. Patients' loyalty conflicts may be heightened as well, because the therapist has broken a family rule as well as a cultural one.

Touch by male therapists is also more dangerous, so that even in settings where female therapists routinely touch patients, most men hold back. Male therapists' attitudes about touch often operate as self-fulfilling prophecies: The man who avoids touch because it can be sexualized in essence sexualizes it by treating it differently from a woman's touch. Once the stage has been set in this way, the only safe touch is perfunctory and ritualized—a brief hug to celebrate a piece of work or to say good-bye. I have occasionally encountered male therapists who feel no confusion between sexual and nonsexual touch. By touching patients from the outset in the same way and for the same reasons that female therapists do, they establish their touch as neutral. However, there is no middle ground here; a man who is uncertain about touch must err on the side of none.

Male therapists are confronted with a dilemma if they try to encourage emotional expression in female patients, since masculinity is defined through the absence of emotion. Women's emotion evokes vague chivalrous impulses in men, requiring them to pretend not to notice, to give the woman something to make her feel better, or to become her protector and take on her foes. The man who resists these impulses still has the problem of what to do. There is something incongruous about encouraging a woman to sob and then sitting and looking at her; expressions of feeling at a certain level of intensity call for comforting. The withholding of response subtly discourages the behavior. Without therapist engagement, the therapist becomes a voyeur to the patient's pain.

In short, male therapists are hard-pressed to behave in ways that are not traditionally masculine, and this usually leads to bans on therapist self-disclosure, touch, and displays of strong emotion by either therapist or patient. Even discussion of these issues may be banned, and preoccupation with other boundary issues (punctuality, payment of bills, consistency in appointments) may be discussed instead. Obviously, some male therapists may be predisposed to be very critical of female therapists who do things differently; they may be unaware that the experienced sense of taboo comes not from real requirements for successful psychotherapy, but culture-based gender mandates.

For us as female therapists, these behaviors—self-disclosure, touch, emotionality—are far less conflictual and more easily integrated into therapy. They do not compromise our boundaries, because that is not where our boundaries are drawn; that is where men's boundaries are drawn. The conventions and metaphors of Channel A do not get to the heart of the matter on Channel B. We do not deny the need for boundaries, but we understand them differently. Our vulnerabilities gather in other places, around departures from female gender socialization.

Women therapists, like mothers, may have trouble with saying no, with putting a reasonable limit on their effort, or with resisting implicit demands for care and instead spurring the patient to do more work. They may overnurture, invoking a loyalty not unlike women's loyalty to their mothers, and thus making it difficult for their patients to be different, critical, or angry. Careful management of these boundaries by female therapists can help female patients learn to deal with anger in the situations where it is most often needed and the most difficult to express: in close relationships with people who have good intentions. Such situations paralyze women who are afraid to hurt one another and who feel unentitled to negative feelings, sometimes leading to the painful severing of these relationships.

We need new metaphors for boundaries that capture the challenges for us as female therapists, working at what is for *us* the crucial edge. These new metaphors would move us away from images of barriers or walls between people, and would instead help us to understand a critical boundary—one fundamental to parenting, teaching, and therapy—which, oddly, has no name. It is the strip of fertile space between release and containment, between reactivity and rest, between momentum and retreat.

> *The boundary is the rope around the ring that—far from dampening the match—propels the combatants back to the center, providing opposition to centrifugal force, emphasizing the ritual element of the struggle and its symbolic import. It reminds the contenders that their engagement is dictated, defined, agreed upon; it also separates them from outside intrusion that would obscure the outcome of their match.*
>
> *The boundary is the parent's watchful eye that, by intruding as little as possible, gives the toddler the sense that the whole world is hers to explore, while having in mind a clear distinction, ready to be enforced at any moment, between what is safe and what is not— how high to jump, how loud to shout, how fast to run. To the child, this watchful eye is both invisible and deeply felt; it invites freedom of movement by imparting a sense of safety.*
>
> *The boundary is the beaker in which acid and base are swirled, bringing up a foam that rises nearly to the top before it settles down. The beaker keeps its contents in contact with each other so that they can interact, but is itself unharmed by them; it has an integrity that will outlast any ingredient that goes into it, any experiment that is done.*

We need our own models of therapy—ones that legitimize what we do well while alerting us to potential problems. Intuition has its limits; not everything we need to know is found on Channel B. We need

insights into issues now obscured by the soft light. We need to discover
the extent to which female consensus is an illusion. But with one eye
always over our shoulders, we can hardly look closely at ourselves. We
will never know what we know until we make the public world safe for
discussion. Outlaws, after all, are not noted for self-appraisal.

LEGALIZING OURSELVES

*We are in the second day of this conference, billed as a gathering of
all the eminent North American scientists in eating disorders. Slides
(hundreds by now, maybe thousands) have posted the counts of
virtually everything that can be named and measured—with the
usual exceptions of sexual abuse, role constraints, powerlessness,
enforced silence. Men come and go from the podium, poised and
confident. Women listen attentively, reserving their thoughts for
the women's bathroom.*

*Outside this room in which we tell everything but the story, the
story plays on. The television broadcasts the William Kennedy
Smith trial for rape of a woman whose face is dissolved into a
computer-generated blur. I look out the window (an unusual luxury
in a conference room) and have the fantasy of casting a giant rope,
cordoning off a circle a mile in diameter around us. As a group, we
walk out of the hotel and enter kitchens, living rooms, bedrooms,
workrooms, and boardrooms. Passing unnoticed by the people in
them, we stand together and watch the story of gender. We see it
portrayed in hundreds of ordinary scenes—scenes that we see every
day, but that familiarity has rendered invisible.*

*It is raining outside. In my fantasy we come back at the end of the
day, wet and tired but fully educated in the simple truths that for
some reason seem forever to elude us. We take off our shoes, put up
our feet, order a beer—maybe we even light up a cigarette, for this is
my fantasy and cigarettes do not kill and we have not yet defined
every simple pleasure out of political correctness. And for the first
time, we really begin to talk.*

This shouldn't be so hard. We should be making gender work *for* us
rather than *against* us. As men and women working to treat a disorder
embedded in gender, we should be using our differing histories to
explore together the core of male and female experience in our culture,
secure in the knowledge that there is room for all of us.

Women's attempts to articulate oppressive social forces is not—as I
believe it is sometimes heard—the first step in a process destined to

exclude men from a role in the treatment of women. On the contrary, the implication of gender socialization in the etiology of eating disorders constitutes the strongest possible argument for males and females working together. Our patients need correctives to familial and cultural teachings; probably nothing we do in therapy is more important than what our actions say about gender. Probably nothing is more helpful to female patients than to see female therapists be bold; to see male therapists be tender; to see male and female therapists articulating their differing perspectives and engaging in lively conflict that they successfully resolve. One very simple truth about therapy is that it succeeds when it allows something different to happen. When we behave true to form in stale gender roles, we hardly create novelty; when we step out of them, we provide a breath of fresh air. Cross-gender behavior is powerful; it is probably the most accessible source of power we have. This fact should encourage us to stretch for ways to work in teams as often as we can and to consider the gender role implications of all that we do.

But real teamwork is predicated on equality. Because our accepted models provide a better fit for males, female therapists who are judged by those models will always be found wanting in "the right stuff." As long as women tacitly permit themselves to be viewed in terms of relative deficiencies, they cannot model, with or without men, an escape from pathogenic gender roles. Greater use of female mentors and supervisors is essential if we are to affirm and nurture skills and sensibilities that might otherwise be labeled "deviant" and driven underground.

Perhaps women have work to do by themselves before they can constructively engage with men. Perhaps there is a need for women's conferences, journals, and books for the same reason that we need women's colleges: to provide a safe place in which women can give one another their undivided attention, painstakingly articulating female knowledge so that we have models to place beside the male ones; so that we define ourselves affirmatively, not as footnote, aberration, omission, and anomaly. We must begin to talk, saying what we really feel, risking exposure. We have lifetimes of undigested, unassimilated experience to be unpacked, catalogued, and crafted into theory, providing the foundation from which to later speak to men. The only way to stop being outlaws is to become lawmakers, at last trusting our own experience.

REFERENCES

Broverman, I. K., Broverman, D. M., Clarkson, F. E., Rosenkrantz, P. S., & Vogel, S. R. (1970). Sex-role stereotypes and clinical judgements of mental health. *Journal of Counseling and Clinical Psychology, 34,* 1–7.

Conrad, J. (1976). *Heart of darkness*. New York: Penguin. (Original work published 1902)

Griffin, S. (1976). I like to think of Harriet Tubman. In *Like the iris of an eye*. New York: Harper & Row.

Hugo, V. (1951). *Les miserables*. New York: French & European. (Original work published 1862)

Shem, S. (1978). *The house of God*. New York: Dell

17

The Journey of Recovery: Dimensions of Change

LINDA PETERS
PATRICIA FALLON

T O ME RECOVERY WAS much more than stopping the bingeing and purging. It was a whole change in lifestyle—a greater sense of myself as an individual, new relationships, and different ways of relating. I also have a feeling of purpose and direction in my life, where before I was just drifting along.

Although clinicians recognize that recovery from bulimia is not a static state (Root, 1990), few studies have documented the complex process of change (Maine, 1985). Since DSM-III introduced the diagnosis of bulimia nervosa (American Psychiatric Association, 1980), research has focused on the etiology and treatment of bulimia.

Studies of eating-disordered women have been primarily studies of treatment outcome that employ behavioral parameters; "they focus on what the person does rather than what she feels or who she is" (Herzog, Hamberg, & Brotman, 1987, p. 546). The emphasis of treatment outcome studies has been on the quantification of predetermined factors assumed to be pertinent to the alleviation of bulimia and anorexia. The variables measured, while allowing for specific comparisons, have left no place for recovered women to instruct us about the process of change, nor has it allowed for the discovery of curative factors beyond the experimenters' assumptions.

Streigel-Moore (Chapter 22, this volume) argues that a feminist approach to research recognizes a broader spectrum of methods, including interviews that permit "a more collaborative relationship with the research participants" (p. 441). Such an interactive stance expands our knowledge of the phenomena under investigation and allows for a more textured analysis. This is particularly important in the field of eating disorders, where the overt disturbance may reflect complex problems in families, relationships, and society (Root, Fallon, & Friedrich, 1986). Although feminist theories of bulimia acknowledge the complexity of the disorder and the meanings that symptoms have for women, few studies have amplified the voice of eating-disordered women and allowed them to teach *us* what is involved in the process of recovery.

This chapter is based on an interview study of women clients who were recovering and recovered from bulimia (Peters, 1990); its purposes were to further our understanding of the complexity of change and the process of recovery, and to give women the opportunity to describe what had been healing for them. This study, in which the women themselves were viewed as experts, was an attempt to bridge the gap between clinical case studies (which may be relevant to only a few) and empirical studies (which often omit significant interpersonal and nonquantifiable information). We were interested in how the women defined recovery, including internal shifts and changes in their interpersonal relationships.

DESCRIPTION OF THE STUDY

The study utilized a semistructured, dialogue method of interviewing, which examined circumstances and relationships at the onset of the bulimia, treatment experiences, life changes, and the individual meanings of bulimia. Based on an unpublished pilot study, categories were identified by the interviewer so that data could be tagged according to their content, sorted by the computer, and then analyzed for themes and patterns in the women's accounts of their experiences. The categories included such headings as awareness of affect, thoughts about food and eating, dieting behavior, feelings about body, openness to treatment, feelings of shame, feelings of connection, social skills, differentiation from family, certainty about future, powerlessness, abuse, and so forth. The interviews were transcribed and coded according to the category system; Ethnograph, a computer program designed to sort text, was then used to group the data by categories for all interviews. This facilitated the inductive process of generating grounded theory (Glaser & Straus, 1967) by means of examining the data for common and divergent themes and patterns.

Thirty women were interviewed in the study; they were recruited through therapist referral and word of mouth. For purposes of contrast and comparison, the women were selected to represent varying lengths and types of treatment. Volunteers had to have previously met DSM-III-R (American Psychiatric Association, 1987) diagnostic criteria for bulimia nervosa, and to identify themselves as recovered or in the process of recovery.

At the time of the interview, the women's ages ranged from 19 to 46 years, with an average age of 29 years. The age of onset ranged from 10 to 28 years. Of the 30 women, 26 had received some type of treatment for their bulimia, 2 had become asymptomatic without treatment, and 2 had not yet begun treatment. Thirteen were symptomatic at the time of the interview, although 11 of these felt that they had achieved partial recovery despite their remaining symptoms; the other 17 were asymptomatic. The average length of time without bulimic symptoms for the 17 asymptomatic subjects was 1 year, 3 months. Each woman was interviewed for 90 minutes to 2 hours and was encouraged to elaborate on her treatment experiences and what recovery meant to her. The personal accounts gathered from these courageous and candid women illuminate the process of recovery and highlight important dimensions of the change process.

Rather than emphasizing the treatment modality or setting when talking about their recovery from bulimia, the women described general psychological and social changes in their lives. What emerged from the data analysis were three continua: "denial to reality," "alienation to connection," and "passivity to personal power" (Peters, 1990). Within these broad categories, the women talked about changes in thoughts, body image, food and eating behaviors, social relationships, the ways that they dealt with feelings, goals for the future, and attitudes toward the cultural standards mandating "acceptable" weight and shape. Although the women began at different starting points and had not made equal gains, the interviews revealed that recovery had involved movement along all of these dimensions.

DENIAL TO REALITY

My whole life was a lie. . . . I was so afraid that people would find out what I was really like.

This quote reflects a starting point in the transition from distortion and concealment to what became a reconstruction of reality. Not only did the women talk about how their eating disorder misrepresented reality to others; they acknowledged that lying to themselves and minimizing their symptoms had served to perpetuate the bulimia. One woman noted, "The lie I had was that I was getting away with it. It wasn't that bad. The way I thought things were wasn't the way they were." Dishonesty with self was projected to the outside world as well. One woman said, "Everyone thought I was such a happy person because I was smiling and energetic and acted like I didn't have a care in the world, but what no one saw was what I was like when the stage lights went out." Another woman reflected this shift by saying, "Things that matter to me now are a lot more about how I feel inside . . ."

From Solution to Problem

Coming to view bulimia as a *problem* rather than a *solution* was described by one woman as "stripping away the first layer of denial." This was critical to getting better and took from months to years for individual women.

For some of the women, the definition coincided with naming the binge–purge cycle what it was: "bulimia." For others, naming the behavior and defining it as a problem were separate events. One woman talked about knowing for years that what she had was an identified eating disorder but denying that it was a problem. Another remembered, "I was just shocked when [the doctor] told me that what I was doing . . . was an eating disorder. I thought it was OK before that." A number of the women also talked about how friends and family contributed to their denial by minimizing or ignoring their behavior. One woman said, "My parents knew for a long time what I was doing, and they would sometimes say stuff about stopping or whatever, but what I really got was that it was more important to be thin." For many of the women, the act of seeking treatment was an acknowledgment of a problem; others, however, spoke of feeling ambivalent about being in treatment and holding tenaciously to the perceived "benefits" of the bulimic behaviors.

Awareness and Acceptance of Affective States

On the denial end of the continuum, a blunted awareness of feelings, an inability to label or articulate feelings, and elaborate defenses against intense affect were described. One woman said, "It [bulimia] means denial to me. It means not coping with things. It's just like drugs. . . . I equate bulimia with the drugs I used." In this state, food became the focal point; emotions were translated into impulses to eat and were confused with bodily needs. One woman described starting therapy and her fears of dealing with emotions:

I got to a point with my therapist where I would get lots of anxiety and I wasn't able to cry because I was so shut down—it was like a wall. And all this time my bulimia was starting to get worse because I was eating instead of feeling.

Anger was a particularly difficult feeling. Not only did the women report trouble identifying their anger; they were often confused as to what to do once it was labeled. As one said,

I'm sure that a lot of times I did feel really angry. But I think I couldn't acknowledge it, at least partly because I felt trapped to do anything differently than I already was. It was threatening to me that I might have to rock the boat—it was easier to just keep bingeing.

One woman talked about how she made the link between her growing ability to accept and articulate her feelings and her bulimic behaviors:

I noticed that when I talked about stuff with my therapist, I didn't have to puke about it as much. Learning that tool seemed to help a lot. . . . I really connected and was aware of how I ate because I simply wasn't willing to feel. . . . It was about all of the sadness and how difficult life had been, and so once I became aware of that it was the beginning of recovery.

Dysfunctional Beliefs and Styles of Thinking

For many of the women, awareness of dysfunctional thinking was useful in modifying and restructuring the beliefs that had previously sustained their bulimic behaviors. Changes resulted in more flexible and constructive approaches to food and to other parts of their lives. Several women talked about their understanding of the interrelationship among negative self-talk, self-esteem, and moods. The belief that being thin would make them happy and lovable was a common theme that underwent revision. One woman remembered coming to the realization that "It was no wonder I never got to my ideal weight. I don't think I could have dealt with the reality that I still didn't have good relationships."

Several women discussed the value of being flexible and tolerant of ambiguity. One woman talked about how her less rigid approach to food had helped her deal with day-to-day variation in her intake:

I finally figured out that a couple of extra bites wasn't going to make me gain 5 pounds, and I realized that one time I might eat more and the next day I might eat less, so it all balances out.

Relationship to Food: From Bulimia to "Eating Normally"

Fundamental changes were also described in the beliefs related to food and eating. These modifications were recognizable in dieting and restricting practices, in food choices, and in bingeing and purging. Several of the women referred to this process as "learning to eat normally." One woman talked about learning that going long periods without eating was "giving up her power of choice," because it was then inevitable that she would overeat. Another talked about "reversing the restrictions" and "getting over the fear of certain foods" that she had previously associated with bingeing. Learning to tolerate feelings of "fullness," or "holding a binge" rather than purging, was reported.

Most of the women reported that they had given up dieting. One woman said, "I just will never diet again. . . . I guess I'm angry too at feeling like I had to do that to be acceptable as a woman. How you see me is how I'm going to be."

Body Image

Beginning with severe self-criticism and body image distortion, bulimic women in recovery talked about learning to evaluate their size and shape more realistically and becoming more accepting of their bodies. This was one of the most difficult areas to change, since it was necessary to reconcile their "imperfect" bodies with omnipresent reminders of what is valued by the culture. Even the women who had been asymptomatic the longest continued to struggle with this dichotomy. One said,

> Even though I want to like my body and feel accepting of the way I look, and I do most of the time, I'm still vulnerable to the external pressure when I'm feeling bad about myself—that's when the magazine covers with the beautiful women and the latest diets grab my attention.

Consistent with the notion that women in Western cultures frequently translate their distress into dissatisfaction with their bodies, several women recognized that these thoughts needed to be "decoded" and that they were actually unhappy about their lives.

> I try not to focus on appearance, because I know when it comes up that something else is wrong. Like right now, when I'm tired and stressed, I don't like to look at myself because I feel fat. "Fat" does not mean obese; fat means . . . not OK.

For many of the women, there was a return to the "normative discontent" (Rodin, Silberstein, & Streigel-Moore, 1985) prevalent among women in this culture. They were unable to feel comfortable with what they defined as overweight: "Most of the time I feel OK, but I still have a great aversion to ever being fat. Some things die real hard."

In summary, the denial-to-reality continuum involves a reciprocal relationship between honesty and recovery. As these women were able to be more honest, they rejected cultural "realities," replacing them with ones of their own making. They reported that as they let go of denial, they had more energy to take charge of their feelings, thoughts, and eating. What those around them saw was a progression from silent, compliant seekers of approval to articulate and sometimes angry women.

ALIENATION TO CONNECTION

When I was spending all my time and money bingeing and purging, I never went out, I didn't date; I was just this loner type of person. My idea of a good weekend was to close the drapes and bake and eat and throw up. Of course no one at work knew that this was what I was doing, but this is the way I dealt with my stress. I would have never thought to call a friend to talk about my frustrations and loneliness. I never believed I could make relationships work.

The second continuum, alienation to connection, describes the shift from the isolation that accompanies bulimia to an experience of connection with other people. The subjective experience of feeling "connected" was not just a matter of being with friends. In fact, some talked about their "private" exclusion before recovery of people with whom they were ostensibly involved. One woman said that even when she was with her friends, she was emotionally absent; she was thinking about what she was going to eat when she got home or how much she'd already eaten that day. The feeling of connection was contingent on women's willingness to be more direct and risk having their true selves be seen.

Secrecy

Fears of discovery and embarrassment made social contact too risky for many of the women. In this way, shame about bulimia contributed to its perpetuation. One woman explained, "In the beginning, I felt like it was a really bad thing and that no one should ever know I was bulimic." Another said, "It was more like a total disgust. I didn't like myself. I thought, 'I don't know how I got into this,' and I was real embarrassed to tell anyone about it." Feeling "different" or "weird" was another way that shame was articulated. Several women talked about how their feelings of inferiority extended to reluctance to tell their therapists about their bulimic behaviors. One said, "Uh, well, I think I wanted his approval. I told him maybe about 6 months after I started . . ."

Some parents contributed to the plight of their daughters with criticism, lecturing, and admonishments. The women's response to this was often to go back into hiding, "making it look good," when in fact nothing had changed. In other cases, the families' initial reaction was one of intense concern, which precipitated a flurry of activity to rescue the women. However, the families often became impatient with the demands of recovery and exasperated by what was perceived to be slow or absent progress. Often the bulimia then went underground again, and the women returned to hopelessness, secrecy, and shame.

Disclosure of Bulimia

Telling someone about the bulimia was often the first step in a progression from private experience to connection with another. Although living with the secret was often oppressive, it usually took a concerted gathering of courage to speak openly for the first time. One woman spoke about how she had wanted to talk long before she actually did:

> I think that the most frustrating thing was not being able to talk to anybody. No one wanted to talk and I probably wanted to all that time, I guess. I mean it was really hard. I had to have a big crisis or something that made me finally talk about it, but I probably all that time really wanted to.

Many of the women found it less threatening to tell a professional than a family member or friend. Sometimes a woman practiced telling with the therapist before she risked feared reactions from people with whom she had more history. Some used a therapy group as a place to share the secret. For other women, the sequence was reversed: A family member or a friend seemed safer than a stranger.

Assertive Social Interactions

For many of the women, recovery involved the development of new skills. This frequently meant breaking out of the mold of being a silent, compliant, "good girl," and becoming a direct, articulate, and assertive woman.

Women who came from families in which privacy, personal rights, and feelings were not respected did not know how to negotiate satisfactory interactions. The outgrowths of their negative past were distrust of the intentions of others, and difficulty determining appropriate expectations for friends. One woman described the model of relationships provided by her family as follows:

> Lots of family secrets. . . . Always undercurrents, nobody said what they meant. And I grew up that way. I grew up listening and then trying to figure out exactly what it was that they were saying. It has really screwed up other relationships, because I was trying to figure out these people who weren't at all like my family, and I'm trying to decode and there is nothing to decode. I couldn't hear a straight message. That really put up a wall for me, not being able to trust people in relationships.

Assertiveness contributed greatly to confidence in relationships. As one woman said, "Being more direct with people has helped. It changes my perception of people and it changes their interaction with me, so I don't always end up being stepped on." Talking about the future, one woman summarized the challenge:

> I think probably it will involve taking risks in social situations and experiencing what being in social situations feels like. I've really been avoiding social situations like the plague. I felt that people wouldn't accept me because of the way I look. So I want to try . . . new ways of relating to people so I am accepted. Learning what cues I give off that tell people that I'm not acceptable—that have nothing to do with the way I look.

Sexual Relationships and Sexual Identity

Making adjustments in relationships to men and sexual identity was another prominent aspect of development in the interpersonal dimension. For some, this meant leaving dysfunctional relationships; for others, it meant developing relationships with men; for still others, it meant acknowledging lesbian identities. This was a particularly difficult area for women who had been sexually and physically abused. Experiences of exploitation had left them with immense confusion about their sexuality. Some used their bodies as a means of getting male approval and affection. Several talked about their propensity for attracting men and repeating earlier abusive patterns; they described difficulty relating to men who treated them well. One woman said, "I didn't know how to handle a nice guy, so I ended up leaving him." Frequently anger and distrust were expressed by avoiding relationships with men altogether. Many women talked about difficulty in making commitments. They were often attracted to "safe" men who were unavailable:

I've had one serious relationship in my life, and that was about 3 or 4 years ago. And it was ideal because it was a long-distance relationship. . . . He flew out and stayed with me for a week . . . so it wasn't a normal relationship because we saw each other infrequently, and when we did see each other it was really exciting and fun, but it wasn't normal, like day in and day out . . . and he started talking about marriage and I, ah . . . I couldn't see how that was going to happen.

Another woman spoke of the strides she had made in this area:

I'm real committed to the relationship I have with Dave. [Interviewer: So is that a change?] Yes, very much a change. We've been together, very stable for 2½ years, and we're taking steps toward marriage by living together.

Another theme in relationships with men was a shift from childlike dependence to feeling more self-reliant and capable. One woman said, "I thought I'd die without him. It has felt much better to know I can be with him or not be with him, and like he's not the only one choosing. It's my choice too." Another woman put it this way:

It was more like a parent–child relationship. I was very dependent on him and felt like I had to do what he wanted because I couldn't make it without him. And the relationship I'm in now, I feel very good about it and I don't feel dependent on him . . . and even though I love him, I'm determined that nothing is going to overwhelm me or destroy me.

Differentiating from Family Members

Differentiation from the family of origin was often a central area in which changes were made. For many of the women, their roles as caretakers of other family members made separate identities difficult. Determining their own course based on their own wants was often complicated by guilt and fear of disappointing their parents. Defining themselves and defending their goals were often significant in the recovery process. One woman explained how changes that increased her control over her life were threatening to her family:

The way I deal with my family is different, and they perceive me as different. . . . I think my family views me as the "old one" and the "new one"—and I'm not sure they are really happy with the "new one." I'm more assertive and I'm not acting the way they are used to, which is unhealthy. I'm not at all as influenced and manipulated by what my family thinks about what I am doing. I certainly am influenced; I can't pretend that I don't care. But I know if something is important to me and they don't approve, I'm still going to do it. It's an indication to me that I am doing OK.

Frequently self-differentiation involved greater appreciation and acceptance of the limits of their parents. One woman spoke of her alcoholic mother:

I've learned some new tools for myself to help in dealing with her. . . . It's real difficult to love her and, like, have a lot of interaction with her. So it's not what I'd like it to be, but I've definitely learned that accepting her makes it a lot easier. She's got circumstances in her life that are miserable and terrible, and she's done the best that she can, and she's just recognizing that. And there are times when I still feel like "This sucks. Why can't she hear what I'm saying?" So it's just difficult.

Another family issue was modifying relationships with fathers— expecting and demanding respectful and nonabusive treatment. One woman described dealing with her father's holiday drinking scenes:

Before I went over to my father's house on Christmas, I walked over in the morning and told him my limits. I just decided to do it. Part of my therapy for myself. I'm really glad I did it. [Interviewer: What did you say?] If I go over there and he has been drinking, I will leave. If he starts drinking while I'm there, I'll leave, and if he abuses anybody in the family, I'll leave. [Interviewer: How did he take that?] At first he was kind of angry about it. He said, "Well, it's good that you have those limits, but what I do in my house is my business." "Yeah," I said, "but what *I* do is *my* business."

PASSIVITY TO PERSONAL POWER

At some point, I decided I didn't want to find myself an old lady and look back on my life and see that it had been about weight and food and that's all. And up to that point, I felt like that was all my life had been about, and I mean I feel like I've only started living for 4 years. That was a real important awareness.

The themes of "feeling lost," "drifting through life," "waiting for something to change," and "not knowing what I wanted to be" were prominent experiences of the bulimic period. Discontent with the powerlessness over future direction provided motivation for "learning how to take control of my life and actually doing it. And being powerful."

Resistance to Readiness

Beginning from positions of passivity and powerlessness, many women had made bulimia their pseudosolution to gaining control. As one woman said, "[Weight] was something I could control, and I needed that focus because I didn't feel like I could control the rest of my life." This function of bulimia was often very difficult to relinquish, and some of the women held tenaciously to what was described as "doing it my way":

> I wanted to stop because of what it was doing to my life. But to me, at that time, it was more important to stay thin and keep bingeing and purging than to risk gaining weight. It was worth it even though it made my life miserable, and I would have continued to binge and purge if I knew I'd get fat.

Beginning to assume personal power was described by several women as "readiness to change," and included several ingredients constituting an existential shift. "Readiness," for one thing, meant increased commitment to recovery. Initiating treatment, changing therapists, attending groups, or participating more fully in ongoing treatment were some of the actions that signaled readiness to change. Unsuccessful treatment heightened frustration and in some circumstances contributed to women's taking a more active role. One woman described what it meant to be ready to recover:

> By the time I went to see [my therapist], I was so fed up with it. I mean, I thought this could just go on the rest of my life. I was just ready to get better. And I think I was ready before but just didn't have the right push to do it. Because I think anybody that spent as much money as I did—I could have a Mercedes for the money that I've put into therapy. After 4 years of failure in therapy, there was something that wasn't being investigated. I began with a new therapist who pushed and pushed about my denial of abuse. She finally said that the only way my symptoms made sense was in the context of a history of abuse. I finally cried and cried and told her what I never told anyone before. My father molested me for years, but I tried to tell myself it wasn't a part of the eating disorder. It takes a real commitment to want to get better. It takes trust in a person. Without her intense caring and willingness to struggle through it with me, I'd still be puking my father into the toilet.

The exasperation and disengagement of family members sometimes became a catalyst for taking more control. One woman talked about how she had expected her mother to help her get treatment. When she did not, she found more strength to obtain the treatment herself:

> I told my mom that I needed help, and she said something that really spurred me on. She didn't care. . . . And she just was, like, "Well if you're going to get help, then just go get help, but I can't be of any support to you." . . . And you know if she would have said, "Oh, I'll help you" and done nothing, I would have probably waited for her to do something, and it would have just prolonged everything else . . .

Perspectives on the Cultural Standards: From Compliance to Outrage

Closely aligned with changes in body image and eating were attitudinal changes about the cultural standards for female weight and shape. The continuum ranged from a point of complete acceptance and arduous compliance to one of questioning and overt anger at what was seen as a sexist "bill of goods." One of the women said, "I think in our society it is pretty important to be thin. You don't see many successful people with fat hanging on them." In contrast, another woman talked about how eating disorders keep women less capable:

> I think it is kind of a way to keep [women] powerless that they collaborate in. If you are so hungry because you are not getting enough food [that] you can't think straight, you can't make decisions and you can't be physically powerful. It is the same thing with being bulimic, like, it just takes up your whole life and you really can't do anything else.

Several women spoke of outrage at media messages pertaining to women and food. On the one hand, women are promised comfort and stress reduction through food; on the other, they are sold diets as a means to a happier, fuller life. One said that dealing with these messages was an integral part of her recovery, and listed ways in which she lived out new values for herself:

> Gradually deciding that I don't buy the cultural ideal for being thin . . . like if you look historically, women haven't always been expected to be 5 feet 10 inches and 115 pounds. And looking at other women and thinking, "Do I think they are ugly? Am I ugly just because I don't look like that? No." And one thing that has really helped me out a lot is that at one time I'd read *Vogue* and stuff, and I stopped reading those magazines because they are too stupid. It's

like I really don't think about it as much when I'm not confronted all the time with some skinny 17-year-old.

Moving Beyond the Victim Stance

In connection with launching themselves and taking responsibility, women described a shift from feeling like victims of their circumstances to feeling like competent and powerful adults. One woman talked specifically about how becoming more powerful had contributed to her recovery:

> What helped me not be bulimic? I think being powerful. Taking charge of my life; not being the victim; not letting someone else put me down. So hard to explain. It's like if something upsets me, I think about things that I could do. If Jack is trying to manipulate me, I walk out the door. That was a real big thing. I felt powerful doing that. It was the only way that I could not be the victim. It took me a long time to realize it, but I did walk out the door. I learned that—I think I was ready to hear it, but my therapist was the one who asked me, "How can you be more powerful; how can you try?"

With a new direction, there was a clear shift in priorities. One woman said, "Now I'm dealing with what I am going to do with my life. Job, career—it's very much more important to me than what I weigh." Another woman said:

> One of the important things that happened in group was that one night we were talking about powerful women that we admired, and I realized that my models had changed. Now I look to smart, powerful women who can speak out and make a contribution—not just look nice and be attractive to some man.

CONCLUSION

As in generations past, disturbances of appetite and the use of the body as a means of self-expression are symbolic of women's personal and cultural oppression. Women who have recovered from bulimia are essential sources of information for clinicians and researchers who hope to understand and treat eating disorders successfully. As the collective voices of these women emerged, it became clear that recovery is a multi-dimensional process and involves a progression of changes in relationship to self, body, family, and culture.

Feminist therapy for bulimia acknowledges the complexity of the disorder and the individual meanings that bulimic behaviors have for women. Feminist therapy fosters genuine connections, which are recreated outside the therapeutic setting. Furthermore, as therapists refuse to collude in denial, family secrets, and cultural oppression of women, they model the expression of feelings and provide an opportunity to challenge the patriarchal mandates for women. An essential component of treatment described by the women was talking about physical, sexual, and emotional abuse to others who listened and honored the pain and anger. Without this experience, the eating disorder numbed and contained the pain, as well as adding an additional burden of shame. As the women began to talk about their pain and to feel understood, they were able to be more empathic with the experience of others. This reciprocity between individuals, both within and outside of therapy, resulted in their feeling connected and was the foundation for personal development and recovery.

What the interviews reveal is that bulimia is a disorder of denial, disconnection, and disempowerment. Understanding recovery as a personal awakening to secrets, alienation, and powerlessness provides researchers with a keyhole through which to view the forces behind the development of eating disorders. Furthermore, the three dimensions of change described lay the foundation for future research on the movement along the continua during recovery.

Recovery in the most fundamental sense is a process of human development and identity formation. Beyond the alleviation of bulimic behaviors, feminist treatment promotes the development of autonomy and of a proactive stance toward life that is internally mediated and socially connected.

REFERENCES

American Psychiatric Association. (1980). *Diagnostic and statistical manual of mental disorders* (3rd ed.). Washington, DC: Author.

American Psychiatric Association. (1987). *Diagnostic and statistical manual of mental disorders* (3rd ed., rev.). Washington, DC: Author.

Glaser, B., & Straus, A. (1967). *The discovery of grounded theory*. Chicago: Aldine.

Herzog, D. B., Hamberg, P., & Brotman, A. W. (1987). Commentary: Psychotherapy and eating disorders: An affirmative view. *International Journal of Eating Disorders, 6*(4), 545–550.

Maine, M. D. (1985). An existential exploration of the forces contributing to, sustaining, and ameliorating anorexia nervosa: The recovered patient's view (Doctoral dissertation, Saybrook Institute). *Dissertation Abstracts International, 46B,* 2071 (University Microfilms No. 85-17,642).

Peters, L. M. (1990). Recovery from bulimia: The woman's view (Doctoral dissertation, University of Washington). *Dissertation Abstracts International, 51B,* 5586 (University Microfilms No. 91-09,819).

Rodin, J., Silberstein, L., & Streigel-Moore, R. (1985). Women and weight: A normative discontent. In T. B. Sonderegger (Ed.), *Nebraska Symposium on Motivation: Vol. 32. Psychology and gender* (pp. 267–307). Lincoln: University of Nebraska Press.

Root, M. P. P. (1990). Recovery and relapse in former bulimics. *Psychotherapy, 27*(3), 397–403.

Root, M. P. P., Fallon, P., & Friedrich, W. N. (1986). *Bulimia: A systems approach to treatment.* New York: Norton.

18

Food, Bodies, and Growing Up Female: Childhood Lessons about Culture, Race, and Class

BECKY THOMPSON

I N THE LAST FIFTEEN YEARS, feminist researchers have breathed new life into the field of eating problems through their examination of how eating problems are influenced by gender inequality.[1] However, one challenge now facing researchers and health professionals is the creation of theoretical frameworks that account for eating problems not only among those assumed to develop them—white, middle- and upper-class heterosexual women—but also among groups of women traditionally absent from the normative epidemiological portrait. The recent literature on eating problems among African-American, Latina, Asian-American, and Native American women, working-class women, and lesbians casts doubt on the accuracy of this profile.[2] Taken as a whole, these studies suggest that this profile reflects which particular populations of women have been studied, rather than actual prevalence. Racial stereotyping and mainstream health professionals' lack of familiarity with ethnic diversity may have also obscured attention to women of color (Root, 1990; Thompson, 1991).[3]

Portions of this chapter are adapted from " 'A Way Outa No Way': Eating Problems among African-American, Latina and White Women" by Becky Thompson, 1992, *Gender and Society, 6*(4), 546–561. Copyright 1992 by Sage Publications, Inc. Adapted by permission.

This chapter focuses on socialization processes among African-American, Latina, and white women who have eating problems; it examines the messages they receive about eating, bodies, and appetites. This attention reveals race- and class-specific assertions about female socialization embedded in the feminist analysis, and the negative consequences that ensue when gender inequality is privileged over other systems of oppression. A multiracial focus illuminates crucial clues about how eating problems may begin as ways in which women cope not only with sexism, but also with racism, classism, sexual abuse, heterosexism, and poverty. This theoretical shift also permits an understanding of the economic, political, social, educational, and cultural resources women need in order to change their relationship to food and their bodies.

METHODOLOGY

In order to explore eating problems among African-American, Latina, and white women, I conducted 18 life history interviews and administered detailed questionnaires.[4] For this analysis, I constructed a purposive sample in which only certain women qualified. I sought women who identified themselves as having eating problems, two-thirds of whom were women of color and two-thirds of whom were lesbians, in order to keep both groups at the center of my theoretical focus. The sample included five African-American women, five Latinas, and eight white women; all of the white women and four of the women of color were lesbians (see Table 18.1). Five women were Jewish, eight were Catholic, and five were Protestant. Three women grew up outside the United States. The women represented various class backgrounds and ranged in age from 19 to 46 years (with a median age of 33.5 years).

The majority of the women reported having a combination of eating problems, and the particular types often changed during their life-spans.[5] The specific constellation of eating problems among the women did not vary with race, class, sexuality, or nationality. Two-thirds reported having eating problems for more than half their lives, and the weight fluctuation among the women varied from 16 to 160 pounds, with an average fluctuation of 74 pounds. The average age of onset was 11 years.

The second criterion for inclusion in the study was that the women considered themselves to be recovering from their eating problems. This criterion was based on the assumption that they might have more perspective and insight than those whose difficulties were at their peak.

TABLE 18.1. Demographics of Women Interviewed

Name	Race	Sexual preference	Age	Eating problems
Julie	White	Lesbian	23	Anorexia, dieting, bulimia, comp. eating
Ruthie	Latina, Puerto Rican	Lesbian	34	Bulimia, dieting, comp. eating
Laura	Latina, Puerto Rican	Lesbian	34	Comp. eating, dieting
Stephanie	White	Lesbian	19	Comp. eating, dieting
Gilda	White	Lesbian	21	Comp. eating, dieting
Elsa	Latina, Argentinian	Heterosexual	46	Comp. eating, dieting, anorexia
Julianna	Latina, Dominican	Heterosexual	24	Anorexia, bulimia, comp. eating
Jackie	White	Lesbian	28	Bulimia, dieting, comp. eating
Yolanda	African-American	Heterosexual	33	Comp. eating
Joselyn	African-American	Heterosexual	35	Comp. eating, dieting, bulimia
Rosalee	African-American	Heterosexual	36	Comp. eating, dieting
Carolyn	African-American	Heterosexual	31	Comp. eating, dieting
Sarah	White	Lesbian	21	Comp. eating, dieting, bulimia
Dawn	White	Lesbian	29	Bulimia, anorexia
Martha	White	Lesbian	37	Comp. eating, dieting
Vera	Latina, Puerto Rican	Lesbian	43	Comp. eating, dieting
Antonia	White	Lesbian	36	Comp. eating
Nicole	African-American	Lesbian	41	Comp. eating, dieting, bulimia

Note. From Thompson (1991). Copyright 1991 by Becky Thompson. Reprinted by permission.

CONTRIBUTIONS AND LIMITS
OF FEMINIST THEORY

Of the three theoretical models of eating problems—biomedical, psychological, and feminist—the feminist model has most effectively shown
how eating problems are rooted in systematic and pervasive attempts to
control women's appetites and body sizes. A feminist analysis explains
why the vast majority of people with eating problems are women; how
male-controlled institutions support dieting and discrimination against
fat people; and how dieting causes physiological stress, which makes
women susceptible to anorexia and bulimia (Chernin, 1981; Millman,
1980; Polivy & Herman, 1983; Schoenfielder & Wieser 1983). Some
feminists also question the term "disorder," particularly because dissatisfaction with weight and size is normative for women (Brown, 1987;
Rodin, Silberstein, & Striegel-Moore, 1985). Feminists assert that sexism
inevitably orchestrates human relations both within and outside the
family. By establishing this principle, feminists rescue eating problems
from the realm of individual pathology through showing how the disturbances are rooted in the current social and historical context.

The feminist framework is limited, however, by race- and class-
specific assertions about female socialization; the privileging of sexism
over other oppressions; and overreliance upon the culture-of-thinness
model to explain eating problems. Boskind-Lodahl (1976) links anorexia
and bulimia to women's exaggerated attempts to please others and rely
upon men for acceptance. Orbach (1985) argues that women's insecuri-
ties about their bodies are embedded in the construction of femininity, in
which women are taught not to initiate, be autonomous, or have needs.
Other theorists link eating problems to gender socialization, in which
women are taught to be passive and compliant (Boskind-White & White,
1983; Bruch, 1973).

These explanations about gender socialization may accurately describe what middle- and upper-class white Protestant women are taught.
However, this socialization does not apply to many African-American
and Jewish women, who are often encouraged to be assertive, self-
directed, and active both publicly and within their families. In addition,
many lesbian, single, divorced, and widowed women do not rely upon
men for economic support. This engenders an independence that varies
markedly from the gender behavior typically attributed to women with
eating problems.

The notion that eating problems have been on the rise partly because
of women's increased work outside of the home is also a race- and
class-specific assertion. Root, Fallon, and Friedrich (1986) argue that
bulimia is partly a response to diametrically opposed expectations wom-

en have confronted during the last two decades as more women have entered the labor force. These theorists reason that girls have been socialized to be passive and sacrifice themselves for others within their families, but that they also must be intelligent, assertive, and achievement-oriented in the public realm (p. 26). It is true that more middle- and upper-class, heterosexual, white women are struggling with contradictory gender expectations as they juggle work in paid and unpaid spheres. However, these complex expectations are not new for working- and middle-class African-American and Latina women, lesbians, and single mothers: They were working in the paid and unpaid labor market long before the 1970s ushered in the two-career family for middle- and upper-class white people (Cole, 1986; Espin, 1986). If the multiple and competing demands that result from being wives, lovers, mothers, and employees cause eating problems, then it may be that women who have been performing these feats all along used food to cope before anorexia and bulimia gained national attention.

Kim Chernin (1981) argues that the institutional imperative toward thinness is a backlash against women's increasing economic power and visibility in the public and private sphere. During the last 20 years, working-class women have not gained economic power; they have lost it. The presumed link between the backlash and augmented economic power is race- and class-specific; it renders invisible anorexia and bulimia among working-class women.

Ranking patriarchy, as a system of injustices, over other oppressions also limits the current feminist framework. This exclusionary practice is mirrored in much other feminist scholarship.[6] Feminists reject explanations about preoccupation with weight that ignore gender and the current historical context. Yet neither the traditional nor the feminist conceptualization considers that starvation may be a response to growing up as a lesbian amid heterosexist domination. Compulsory heterosexuality is a largely invisible but enormously powerful force that dictates what is considered acceptable female sexuality (Rich, 1986). With a few recent exceptions (Brown, 1987; Striegel-Moore, Tucker, & Hsu, 1990; Thompson, 1992), compulsory heterosexuality and lesbian identity are invisible as analytical categories in feminist research on eating problems; this makes it hard to see the possible implication of heterosexism in a young lesbian's eating patterns. This absence makes it difficult to gauge the influence of compulsory heterosexuality on heterosexual women's ideas about appetites and size as well.

Feminists also privilege sexism over other oppressions by attributing problematic family dynamics to patriarchy while ignoring the role of racism and religious discrimination. For example, a thin girl may diet because her mother taught her to accept the strictures that await her in womanhood (Orbach, 1985), but a parent's actions may be motivated by other social forces as well. Jewish or African-American parents who cannot protect their daughters from anti-Semitism or racism may encourage thinness to protect them from the further discrimination directed against fat people. An African-American or Latino/Latina parent who meddles with a daughter's food—telling her not to eat and then feeding her—can confuse her as she learns to feed herself. Yet these actions may also reflect a cultural tradition of nurturing through food. When a Puerto Rican mother feeds her 5-year-old daughter a food supplement to gain weight, then ridicules her when she gains weight in adolescence, pressures of assimilation may account for the mother's change of heart. Doing justice to the social context in which difficulties with food arise requires an integrated analysis —one that accounts for the intersecting influence of gender, race, sexuality, nationality, and class.

This expansive analysis also complicates the feminist reliance upon the culture-of-thinness model to explain the rise in eating problems. According to this model, thinness is a culturally, socially, and economically enforced requirement for female beauty. Revealing how institutions support thinness illuminates a critical way in which beauty is socially constructed. However, what constitutes beauty also reflects imperatives about age, color, and sexuality. For example, the often-cited study by Garner, Garfinkel, Schwartz, and Thompson (1980) documents the emergence of an imperative toward thinness by showing a marked decrease in the weights of centerfold models in *Playboy* and Miss America Pageant winners from 1959 to 1978. This study quantifies the relationship between the social emphasis on thinness and the increase in eating problems. However, what is *not* said about the women in *Playboy* and Miss America Pageant winners is also revealing: Historically, they have been almost exclusively white, young, and heterosexual. A more comprehensive analysis would also elucidate "tyranny" based on the glorification of white, young, heterosexual, and able-bodied people.

The tendency of white theorists to focus on the drive for thinness as the primary sociocultural force responsible for eating problems is one example of a schism between the agendas of many white feminists and feminists of color. Narrowing this schism requires a scrutiny of the power of racism and classism as they inform standards of appearance. The resilience of the stereotype of the fat black "mammy" shows the futility and damage of considering standards of beauty as separate from issues of race and racism.

Proponents of the culture-of-thinness model usually assume that poor women and women of color are less exposed to this culture than white middle-class women, but the concept of "exposure" needs to be re-evaluated. Weight and size norms do vary culturally. Growing up in an African-American rural community may partially protect some girls from believing that they must be thin to be pretty. However, few children escape exposure to television and advertising. Media permeation of even the most remote areas of the country makes it unlikely that any ethnic or racial group is unaware of the premium placed on dieting and thinness.

GROWING UP FEMALE: THE INFLUENCE OF RACE AND CLASS

An inclusive feminist theory benefits from a nuanced understanding of the lessons girls receive about their bodies and eating. Generalizations about gender socialization are either inadequate or inaccurate when applied across race and class. This reality, and the fact that eating problems do in fact occur among women of color and/or working-class women, raises important questions: What are African-American, white, and Latina girls taught as children about their racial, gender, and cultural identities, and in which ways are these lessons the filters through which girls learn about food and appetites? How might childhood experiences of girls of varying racial, class, and ethnic backgrounds make them vulnerable to eating problems? How might this information explain how and why girls and women use food to cope with trauma?

Understanding socialization and its influence on eating problems requires looking at both public and private contexts, since what some women of color learn in their families contradicts what they learn at school and in their communities. Furthermore, warnings about weight and appetite received by African-American women are often laced with race-biased ideas about skin color and hair texture. Stresses caused by assimilation and class changes may also shape what women of color learn as they grow up.

Latinas and Community Life

It is impossible to say that there is a single ethic about dieting and body size among Latinas, partly because of significant ethnic, racial, and socioeconomic heterogeneity. Among the Latina women I interviewed, one was raised by German governesses in an upper class family in Argentina; another was cared for by her grandmother in a middle-class family in the Dominican Republic; the other three were women of Puerto Rican descent who grew up in the United States and were from working- or middle-class backgrounds. The degree of assimilation among these women varied markedly, depending on whether or not

Spanish was their first language, their degree of contact with other Latinas, and the extent to which they themselves identified as Latinas.[7]

Among the Latinas, what was learned about weight and size was partly influenced by nationality. The woman who grew up in a small town in the Dominican Republic was taught:

> People don't think that fat is bad. You don't undermine fat people. You just don't. . . . The picture of a woman is not a woman who has a perfect body that you see on TV. A woman is beautiful because she is a virgin or because she is dedicated to her husband or because she takes care of her kids; because she works at home and does all the things that her husband and family want her to do. But not because she is skinny or fat.

According to this woman, thinness was not valued among any class of people in the Dominican Republic. By contrast, the woman raised in an upper-class family in Argentina said that a woman's weight was the primary criterion of her worth. She described her father's concern with diets and exercise, which he enforced on his wife and daughters, as "oppressive and Nazi-like." She explained, however, that judgments about weight varied with class and degree of urbanization:

> . . . The only people who see being fat as a positive thing in Argentina are the very poor or the very rural people, who still consider it a sign of wealth or health. But as soon as people move to the bigger cities, and are exposed to the magazines and the media, dieting and figures become incredibly important.

None of the Puerto Rican women benefited from the acceptance of women of size that the Dominican woman celebrated. Laura lived in Puerto Rico for 4 years as a child. As she remembered it, "Latina women were almost expected to be more overweight. Latin women living in Puerto Rico were not uncomfortable with extra weight. To them it wasn't extra. It wasn't an issue." However, Laura's exposure to this acceptance did not help her appreciate her own chunky body. Her family's disdain for fat people was more influential than the beliefs of Puerto Rican people on the island. The fact that her father was British and that her mother liked to "hang out with wealthy white women" undermined Laura's ability to adopt the values of the Puerto Rican community, including its acceptance of varying sizes among women. Although, to different extents, all three women were exposed to Puerto Rican culture and community, none learned to value variations in size among women.

African-American Girls and Community Life

There is also diversity among African-American girls with regard to messages about dieting and body size. Two African-American women reported that diversity in female body size was accepted in their communities. Rosalee grew up in a rural black community in Arkansas, where, as she described it, "home-grown and healthy" was the norm. She remembered that her uncles and other men liked a "healthy woman," meaning, as they used to say, "They didn't want a neck bone. They liked a picnic ham." Issues of weight did not determine beauty to the extent that skin color and hair did. Unlike most of the other women, Rosalee did not think about dieting until she was a teenager. "There were times when we hardly had food anyway, so we tended to slim down during those times. And then, you know, when the money was rolling in and everything was there, we celebrated. We ate and ate and ate."

Describing the ethic of eating when poverty is a constant threat, Rosalee explained, "When you are talking about being on a farm, dieting just isn't a household word, to tell you the absolute truth." This ethic did not stop Rosalee from bingeing at age 4, when she was sexually abused and witnessed battery. A cultural emphasis on thinness simply wasn't the primary factor. Carolyn, a middle-class woman who grew up in an urban area, remembered that her African-American friends considered African-American women of varying weights to be desirable and beautiful. By contrast, among white people she knew, the only women considered pretty were petite. When judging white girls' appearances, both the white and African-American men preferred the petite girls.

Women who, as girls, attended schools in which there were only a few African-American students remembered thinness as dominant. By contrast, women who went to racially mixed or predominantly African-American schools saw more acceptance of both fat and thin women. This suggests that one hazard for black students attending overwhelmingly white schools is exposure to cultural values—including a rigid emphasis on thinness—that they might not have encountered in predominantly African-American contexts.

The two African-American women who attended private, predominantly white schools were sent by parents who hoped that this education would open opportunities unavailable in public schools. As a consequence, however, they endured isolation from other African-American children. The parents discouraged them from socializing with neighborhood African-American children, who in turn labeled the girls arrogant, thus furthering their isolation. Both were also teased by neighborhood black children for being chubby and light-skinned. At school, they were ridiculed by white students for being fat and were excluded in subtle and overt ways. The racism of administrators and teachers robbed the girls of the attention and dignity they deserved. Joselyn remembered that at one school, "Sister Margaret Anna told me that, basically, what a black person could aspire to at that time was to Christianize the cannibals in Africa." This experience illustrates injuries of racism coupled with religious intolerance. Neither girl had a public context in which her racial identity was validated. As Nicole said, "By second or third grade, I was saying I wished I was white because kids at school made fun of me. I remember in second or third grade getting on the bus and a kid called me a brown cow." As both women were growing up, their weight and race were used to ostracize them.

African-American and Latina Girls and Their Families

Among the 10 African-Americans and Latinas, most were pressured to be thin by at least one and often all of their family members. For some, these pressures were particularly virulent because they were laced with racism. The African-American woman who grew up in Arkansas received contradictory messages about weight and size from her family. Like most African-Americans in her community, Rosalee's mother thought thin women were sickly, and took her young daughters to the doctor because they weren't gaining enough weight. But her father told her she "had better not turn out fat like her mother." Rosalee and her mother bore the brunt of his disdain, as he routinely told them that African-American women were usually fatter and less beautiful than white women. Rosalee recalled:

> I can remember fantasizing that "I wish I was white." You know, it seemed to be the thing to be if you were going to be anything. You know, they were considered beautiful. That was reinforced a lot by my father, who happened to have a strong liking for white women. Once he left the South, and he got in the army and traveled around and had more freedom, he became very fond of them. In fact, he is married to one now. He just went really overboard. I found myself wanting to be like that.

Although unfamiliar with dieting as a child, she feared weight gain and her father's judgments. At puberty, she began dieting. Because of her father's sexism and internalized racism—which was fueled by his exposure to white culture—Rosalee was subjected to overwhelmingly contradictory messages about beauty and weight.

Some of the Latina and African-American girls' relatives used the girls' bodies as territories to project their own frustrations and racial prejudices. Joselyn, an African-American woman, remembered her white grandmother telling her she would never be as pretty as her cousins because they were lighter-skinned. Her grandmother often humiliated her, making fun of her body while she was naked and telling her she was fat. As a young child Joselyn began to think that although she couldn't change her color, she could at least try to be thin. When Joselyn was young, her grandmother was the only family member who objected to her weight. However, as the family's class standing began to change, her father also began encouraging Joselyn and her mother to be thin. When the family was working-class, serving big meals, having chubby children, and keeping plenty of food in the house were signs that the family was doing well. But as the family became upwardly mobile, Joselyn's father began insisting that Joselyn be thin: "When my father's business began to bloom and my father was interacting more with white businessmen and seeing how they did business, suddenly thin became important. If you were a truly well-to-do family, then your family was slim and elegant."

Her grandmother's racism and her father's determined fight to be middle-class converged, and Joselyn's body became the playing field for their conflicts. While Joselyn was pressured to diet, her father still served her large portions and bought her and the neighborhood children treats. These contradictory messages confused her: "I could never see myself. I was always just like ashes thrown up in the air. Just no shape at all." Like many women, Joselyn was told she was fat from an early age, even though she was not. And, like many women, Joselyn was put on diet pills and diets before puberty; this began a cycle of dieting and compulsive eating, which eventually evolved into bulimia.

Another African-American woman also linked contradictory messages about food to her parents' internalized racism. As Nicole explained it, her mother operated under the "house nigger mentality," in which she saw herself and her family as separate from and better than other African-American people. Her father also believed this, saying that being part Cherokee made him different. Nicole attended private schools and a "very white Anglican upper-class church" in which she was one of a few black children. According to Nicole, both parents "passed on their internalized racism in terms of judgments around hair or skin color or how a person talks or what is correct or proper."

Their commandments about food and body size were played out in powerful ways. Nicole's father was from a poor, working-class, rural, Southern family, whereas her mother was from a "petit bourgeois" family, only one of three African-American households in a small New Hampshire town. While Nicole's father liked the fact that she was "solid," her mother restricted her food intake to ensure that she would grow up thin. Like Joselyn, Nicole was taught that eating a lot was a dangerous but integral part of the family tradition:

> When I was growing up, I thought that breakfast was a four- or five-course meal, the way you might think dinner is. I thought that breakfast involved fruit and maybe even juice and cereal, and then the main course of breakfast, which was eggs and bacon and toast. On Sundays we had fancy breakfasts like fish and hominy grits and corn bread and muffins. So breakfast had at least three courses. That is how we ate. Dinner was mostly meat and potatoes and vegetables and dessert and bread. Then my father would cajole my mother into making dessert. There were lots of rewards that all had to do with food, like going to Howard Johnson's or Dunkin' Donuts.

Nicole's mother put her on a diet when she was 3 and tortured her about her weight. Nicole became terrified of going to the doctor because she was weighed and lectured about her weight. Yet, after each appointment, her mother bought her a powdered jelly donut. When her father shopped, he bought Nicole treats that her mother snatched and hid, accusing him of trying to make Nicole fat. In her mother's view, Nicole's weight and curly hair kept her from being perfect; her body became the contested territory onto which her parents' pain was projected.

The same confusion about body size and class expectations troubled two Puerto Rican women. Vera attributed her eating problems in part to the stress of assimilation as her family moved from poverty to the working class. When Vera was 3, she was so thin that a doctor prescribed appetite stimulants. However, by the time she was 8, her mother compared her to other girls who stayed on diets or were thin.

Ruthie, another Puerto Rican woman, also linked changes in the family ethic about size and eating to pressures of assimilation. In keeping with Puerto Rican tradition, her mother considered chubby children a sign of health and well-being. Ruthie said that according to Puerto Rican culture, "If you are skinny, you are dying. What is wrong with you?" When Ruthie was 10 to 12 years old, her mother made her take "Weight On," a food supplement, and iron pills to make her hungry. But when she became a teenager her mother's attitude changed. Ruthie recalled,

> When I was little, it was not okay to be skinny. But then, at a certain age, it was not okay to be fat. She would say, "Your sister would look great in a bikini and you wouldn't." . . . Being thin had become something she valued. It was a roller coaster.

Ruthie attributed this change to her mother's assimilation with Anglo standards, a change she tried to enforce on Ruthie's eating and body size.

These diverse experiences highlight the risk of generalizing about class and thinness among women of color, and call into question the notion that African-American and Latina women as groups are less exposed to or influenced by a cultural emphasis on thinness than are white women. Those African-American and Latina women who saw acceptance of different sizes in public contexts did not escape pressure to be thin within their families. Although growing up in a rural area and/or attending predominantly black schools did protect two of the African-American girls from pressures to diet, traumas they faced in childhood nevertheless resulted in eating problems. For the women of color whose parents had internalized racism, the emphasis on thinness was particularly intense; this suggests that women of color may, under certain circumstances, be more rather than less vulnerable than white women to eating problems.

White Girls in Their Families and Communities

Diversity among the white women with respect to ethnicity, religion, and nationality made it difficult to generalize about their socialization. With the exception of a Sephardic Jewish woman who grew up outside the United States, none of the white women escaped an emphasis on dieting and thinness. However, ethnic and religious identity did influence their eating patterns. In addition, anti-Semitism and ethnic prejudice shaped the way some of the girls interpreted strictures about weight and eating. Like most of the women of color, the white girls had little access to contexts in which women of differing sizes were valued and were encouraged to diet.

All of the American Jewish women were taught that they needed to be thin. Although none were fat children, all had parents who were afraid they would become fat, and so took what they saw as precautions. Two Jewish women who went to predominantly Protestant schools said that belonging to a religious minority exacerbated pressures about body size. Both felt like outsiders because they were Jewish, and their Protestant classmates perceived them as talking, dressing, and looking different from the Protestant children. Both girls were called names and excluded from friendship groups. As was the case for many Latinas and African-American women, the discrimination Jewish children experienced was most overt when they were in the minority. One woman learned that some of her Protestant classmates thought that Jewish people had horns. The Sephardic Jewish woman remembered that when she began to attend school in the United States, other children spat on her and called her a "kike." She said, "It was the craziest thing I have ever experienced. I hadn't experienced it from people I was told we were at war with [in North Africa]. If anything, the Arab women and mothers were more supportive. Would take us in."[8] Children called her father the "Tasmanian devil" and made fun of her accent.

The girls coped with this discrimination by minimizing the ways they felt different or inferior to others, including trying to hide their body sizes. Sarah explained, "In the school I attended where I was only one of a handful of Jewish kids, I never felt like I fit in. I didn't have the right clothes, I didn't look the right way. I didn't come from the right family." As early as age 11, Sarah began "having the feeling that I had to lose weight or that something wasn't right." Although she wasn't fat, in her mind she was.

Only Gilda—who was Sephardic and lived in North Africa and France before settling in the United States—was exposed to a whole-hearted acceptance of food by at least one parent. For Gilda's father, who was raised in North Africa, family meals were a celebrated and central aspect of maintaining North African and Jewish culture:

> First of all, food and Friday night and Shabbos. Friday night for my father is a very important time. . . . We have a traditional [North African] meal with vegetables and different salads and [North African] spices. The whole flavor, the whole mood of the evening is not American at all. On holidays, Passover, we read the Haggadah in French, Arabic, Hebrew, and English. By page 30, you are ready to die of hunger and exhaustion.

Eating together as a family was a central aspect of this tradition. Gilda's mother, by contrast, was always on a diet, although she was never fat. Gilda's father became angry with Gilda when, during adolescence, she refused to eat with the family or keep kosher meals. Her mother, meanwhile, emphasized the importance of dieting. Amid these clashing attitudes and cultural changes caused by assimilation, Gilda grew up with contradictory messages about weight standards and eating.

Of the three white women raised in Christian contexts, two believed that being thin was crucial for females. Dawn, a middle-class white woman from a strict Catholic family, was taught from a young age that "a woman's worth was in her size." For Antonia, an Italian-American woman, ideas about eating and weight were deeply affected by her ethnic identity. Like some of the Jewish women and women of color, Antonia felt like an outsider at school, a status that was compounded by feeling overweight. At school she learned that she had to look and act like "WASPs," which required having straight blonde hair and being passive and quiet. She remembered, "I used to get called loud. I talked a lot. Very active. And I was very aggressive. I used to wrestle with the boys a lot. I stood out from other people."

Because Antonia was fat, other children often humiliated her. She remembered being called "taters" (a big potato) by one of the boys. In high school, she attended a prom fund raiser, called a "slave auction," where girls were auctioned off. "When it was my turn," she explained, "no one was bidding. To this day, . . . I can't even really remember the actual sequence of events. It was just the most humiliating thing in my life." By the time Antonia was 11, her mother put her on a diet—an act that Antonia would unsuccessfully repeat many times during her adolescence.

POVERTY AND HETEROSEXISM

A multiracial focus reveals the limits of assigning eating problems primarily to gender socialization. The women I interviewed did link anorexia and bulimia to gender inequality; however, they also cited a host of other injustices—emotional and physical abuse, racism, poverty, heterosexism, and acculturation. Although what constitutes "trauma" is often associated with specific events, it may also result from an accumulation of injuries caused by what Harriette McAdoo (1986) has termed the "mundane extreme environment" of racism (p. 188).[9] McAdoo argues that to grasp racism requires us to identify not only single, extraordinary interactions, but also the daily realities of life in a racist society.

The women I interviewed linked not one but multiple traumas to their eating problems. Their experiences demonstrate the extent to which eating problems begin as logical responses to these injustices, particularly given the lack of other available options. Lessons about race, religion, culture, and ethnicity inform women's responses to these traumas, including their reasons for bingeing, purging, or dieting.[10]

Poverty

Poverty can increase vulnerability to eating problems. Yolanda, a black Cape Verdean mother, began overeating when she was 27. After leaving an abusive husband in her early 20s, she had been forced to go on welfare. As a single mother with small children and few financial resources, she supported her family on $539 a month. Yolanda began bingeing in the evenings after putting her children to bed. Eating was something that calmed her, helped her deal with loneliness, and made her feel safe. Food was an inexpensive and accessible commodity. When nothing else was available, she ate three boxes of macaroni and cheese. Yolanda felt as if her body was the only thing she had left.

> I am here [in my body] because there is nowhere else for me to go. Where am I going to go? This is all I got. . . . That probably

contributes to putting on so much weight, 'cause staying in your body, in your home, in yourself, you don't go out. You aren't around other people. . . . You hide, and as long as you hide you don't have to face [others]. . . . Nobody can see you eat. You are safe.

When eating, Yolanda felt a momentary reprieve from worries. She binged not only because it was inexpensive and easy, but also because she had grown up amid positive messages about eating. In her family, eating was a celebratory and joyful act, so she turned to food to comfort herself and to numb pain when facing trauma as an adult. However, in adulthood, eating became a double-edged sword: While comforting her, it also led to weight gain. During the 3 years Yolanda was on welfare, she gained 70 pounds.

Yolanda's story captures how class inequalities shape women's eating problems. As a single mother, her financial constraints mirrored those of most female heads of households. The dual hazards of a race- and sex-stratified labor market further limited her options (Higginbotham, 1986). Yolanda said that she binged late at night rather than getting drunk because she could still get up in the morning, get her children ready for school, and attend college classes. By bingeing, women avoid the hangovers that result from drinking and can continue to care for their children, drive, cook, and study. Bingeing is also less expensive than drinking—a significant factor for many women.

Heterosexism

All of the women interviewed, both lesbian and heterosexual, were taught that heterosexuality was compulsory, although versions of this enforcement were shaped by race and class. Expectations were partly taught through messages about food and bodies. Some relatives fed boys more food than girls, because of their belief that girls must be thin to attract boys. As the girls approached puberty, many were told to stop being athletic, wear dresses, and watch their weight. Pressures to diet were accompanied by warnings that fat girls become old maids.

Women who linked heterosexism directly to their eating problems were those who knew that they were lesbians from an early age and who actively resisted heterosexual norms. This is not surprising. Their isolation, lack of knowledge of gay and lesbian communities, and economic and emotional dependence upon relatives who did not question compulsory heterosexuality all explain why "coming out" in youth is riskier than in adulthood.

One working-class Jewish woman, Martha, began eating compulsively when she was 11 years old—the same year she started getting clues about her lesbian identity. In junior high school, as many of her female peers began dating boys, Martha began fantasizing about girls. This made her feel utterly alone.

> My memories during that period of time have a whole lot to do with being very lonely and isolated. . . . At some point someone said, "Okay, now you have to be a girl. And that means you have to go to the Jewish community center on Sundays." I was not into that at all. I wanted to be riding my bike. I wanted to be out playing. I was not into boys from day one. I can remember going to the Jewish community center and hiding behind the coat rack for 4 hours until someone picked me up.

Confused and ashamed by her fantasies, Martha came home from school and binged: "It was the only thing I knew. I was looking for a comfort." Bingeing was also a way she felt touched that helped compensate for the lack of physical affection from people around her: ". . . I touched myself with food because you can't touch me because I am queer and I am not getting touched. It begins to be self-fulfilling." In her family, the daughters' access to food was restricted, and family meals were occasions for painful teasing about her weight. Bingeing became her method of exerting some control, of calming herself, and of rebelling against gender and cultural expectations that contradicted her emerging identity.

EXPANDING THE THEORETICAL FRAME

There is no monolithic "American" culture: the messages girls receive about body sizes and eating are shaped by ethnicity, nationality, class, race, and individual family members' personalities. In addition, intracultural variations also complicate notions of a single socialization process regarding eating and body size among African-Americans, Latinas, and white women. Among the African-American and Latina women I interviewed, the degree to which thinness was imposed on them as girls depended upon whether their families' class had changed, the families' geographical location, the schools the children attended, and nationality.

Although a few women of color experienced some protection from an emphasis on thinness, most were encouraged to diet and be thin. This casts doubt on the notion that women of color are protected from strictures about thinness. Recognizing eating problems as survival strategies in response to trauma suggests that the significance of the culture-of-thinness model needs to be considered in the context of various sexual, emotional, physical, economic, and/or racial injustices.

Among white women, religion, ethnicity, and nationality shaped socialization. All—with the exception of one Sephardic Jewish woman—were raised to fear fat. For some of the Jewish women and the Italian-American women, these fears were combined with worries about cultural exclusion. Sexual abuse across class and race also compromised many women's ability to feel safe and trusting of their bodies. How they used food to cope with sexual abuse was also shaped by their racial and ethnic identities.

One key distinction between the women of color, Jewish women, and Italian-American women on the one hand, and the white Protestant women on the other, is that many of the former said that being thin was not the *only* qualification for acceptance by classmates. For example, even if the Italian-American Catholic woman had been thin, her "loud, aggressive and emotional ways" did not fit in with Northern European ways. Had Joselyn been thin, she would still have been one of few African-American students at her school and church. Vera, a Puerto Rican woman, was still teased for speaking English with an accent. Ruthie, another Puerto Rican woman, was assaulted with racist comments by nuns who also ridiculed her skinny body. Being thin, or seeing themselves as thin, would not have changed these girls' outsider status.

Some of the African-American and Latina women who were encouraged to be thin cited their parents' aspirations to be middle-class. They were taught that middle-class standing depended upon upholding this aesthetic. None of the white women intimated this connection. Whereas some of the working-class Latino/Latina and black families experienced class mobility, all of the white women grew up in solidly working-, middle-, or upper-class families. The dual strain of racism and changing class expectations may explain why some of the women of color linked an emphasis on thinness to class notions while the white women did not. Class did not, by itself, determine whether or not women were exposed to an imperative toward thinness. The supposition that it does assumes, in a way that is both demeaning and inaccurate, that poor women—both women of color and white women—are somehow culturally "out of the loop." But changes in class did affect some women's understanding of eating and their bodies.

Clashes in cultural norms and the demands of assimilation intensified the emphasis on thinness. To understand why a girl's relatives want her to be thin, we need to know what forms of economic, racial, ethnic, or religious discrimination they have endured. Underlying an attempt to make a child thin are often unspoken assumptions by family members that while they may not be able to protect their children from racism or classism, having thin daughters may make life somewhat easier. Many people accept the notion that, given enough self-control and discipline, bodies can be sculpted. This ideology makes dieting appear to be a logical strategy.

Pressures that parents endure do not justify their attempts to mold their daughters' bodies. But understanding why women across race and class develop eating problems requires that we clarify what constitutes "culture" in the culture-of-thinness model. When caretakers accept an imperative toward thinness, some do so from the belief that they have more control over weight than over other, more complex and insidious forces.

TREATMENT AND PREVENTION

Understanding the intricacies of women's socialization and responses to oppression can tell us much about effective treatment of eating problems. Anorexic or bulimic women need access to treatment models that support positive racial and sexual identity development, since these are keys to self-esteem and empowerment. Women deserve multiracial and multicultural counseling in public and private agencies that employ women of color and lesbians at all levels. Building such therapeutic contexts depends upon the willingness of health professionals to, in the words of Maria Root, "take the initiative to be culturally literate with a diversity of cultural groups" (1990, p. 533).

Working effectively with women across class, race, religion, and ethnicity also hinges on understanding that there is more than one "emotional laundromat." Long-term healing is often born of counseling coupled with involvement in community, political, educational, and religious organizations. Therapists' ability to support a multifaceted approach to healing often depends upon their willingness to build multiracial, multicultural bridges, both personally and professionally. This commitment can greatly influence whether women of color and working-class women seek and benefit from treatment. This commitment can also change normative assumptions about the epidemiological portrait of eating problems—assumptions that hinder a comprehensive understanding of the causes and methods of healing from eating problems.

Prevention requires changing the social conditions that underlie eating problems. Beginning steps include ensuring that girls grow up without being sexually abused, that parents have adequate resources to raise their children, that children of color grow up free of racism, and that young lesbians have the chance to see their reflection in their teachers and community leaders. Ultimately, the prevention of eating problems depends upon women's access to economic, cultural, racial, political, social, and sexual justice.

ACKNOWLEDGMENTS

The research reported in this chapter was partially supported by a doctoral grant from the American Association of University Women Fellowship in Women's Studies. I am grateful to Patricia Fallon, Melanie Katzman, Gayle Pemberton, and Susan Wooley for their supportive comments on earlier versions of this chapter. I also want to thank the faculty of the African-American Studies Program at Princeton University and the Rockefeller Foundation for their generous support of this work.

NOTES

1. I use "eating problems" as an umbrella term for anorexia, bulimia, extensive dieting, and/or bingeing. I avoid using the term "disorder," since it categorizes the problems as individual pathologies, which deflects attention away from the social inequalities underlying them (Brown, 1985). By using the term "problem," however, I do not wish to imply blame. In fact, I argue throughout that the eating strategies women develop begin as logical solutions to problems, not as problems themselves.

2. For studies on African-American women, see Andersen and Hay (1985); Gray, Ford, and Kelly (1987); Hsu (1987); Pumariega, Edwards, and Mitchell (1984); Rand and Kuldau (1991); Robinson and Andersen (1985); Silber (1986); Thomas and James (1988); Thompson (1992); and White, Hudson, and Campbell (1985). For studies on Latinas, see Hiebert, Felice, Wingard, Munoz, and Ferguson (1988); Silber (1986); Smith and Krejci (1991); and Thompson (1992). For attention to Native American women, see Rosen et al. (1988) and Smith and Krejci (1991). Asian-American women are included in Nevo (1985) and Root (1990). See Root (1990) for attention to women of color. For a study on social class and anorexia, see Gowers and McMahon (1989). For a review of the literature cross-culturally, see Dolan (1991). For studies on lesbians, see Brown (1987); Striegel-Moore, Tucker, and Hsu, (1990); and Schoenfielder and Wieser (1983).

3. The fledgling research on women of color shows that bias in research has consequences for women of color. Tomas Silber (1986) asserts that many well-trained professionals have either misdiagnosed or delayed their diagnoses of eating problems among African-American and Latina women, as a result of stereotypical thinking that these problems are restricted to white women. As a consequence, when African-American women or Latinas are diagnosed, their eating problems tend to be more severe because of extended processes of starvation prior to intervention. In her autobiographical account, Retha Powers, an African-American woman, describes being told not to worry about her eating problems since "fat is more acceptable in the Black community" (1989, p. 78).

Stereotypical perceptions held by her peers and teachers of the "maternal Black woman" and the "persistent mammy–brickhouse Black woman image" made it difficult for Powers to find people who took her problems with food seriously (1989, p. 134).

4. I employed "snowball" sampling, a method in which potential respondents often first learn about the study from people who have already participated. Typically, I had much contact with the respondents prior to the interview; this was particularly important, given the secrecy associated with this topic (Russell, 1986; Silberstein, Striegel-Moore, & Rodin 1987), the need for women of color and lesbians to be discriminating about how their lives are studied, and the fact that I was conducting across-race research.

5. Among the women, 28% had been bulimic, 17% had been bulimic and anorexic, and 5% had been anorexic. All of the women who had been anorexic or bulimic also had a history of compulsive eating and extensive dieting. Of the women, half were compulsive eaters and/or dieters (39%) or compulsive eaters (11%), but had not been bulimic or anorexic.

6. For feminist theoretical discussions of these practices, see Baca Zinn, Cannon, Higginbotham, and Dill (1986); Comas-Diaz (1987); Combahee River Collective (1979); Lorde (1984); and Moraga and Anzaldúa (1983).

7. Iris Zavala Martinez (1986) explains that statistics and stereotypes often treat Puerto Rican women as if they were a homogeneous group. In her essay on the economic and "socioemotional" struggles of Puerto Rican women, Martinez writes that "such treatment fosters a myth that ignores class differences, racial variations, and differences in places of birth and cultural background, as well as in educational process or language preference" (p. 112). In response to this distorted picture, Martinez cautions that "only when the portrayals become richer, more sensitive to the multitude of such interacting characteristics, will the dynamic, complex and changing world of the Puerto Rican women come fully into view" (p. 112).

8. In this passage, the specific country referred to has been deleted and replaced with "North Africa." Although this change detracts from the cultural specificity of her experience, the change was necessary to protect her anonymity.

9. By "trauma" I mean a violating experience that has long-term, debilitating, emotional, physical, and/or spiritual consequences, which may occur immediately following the painful experience or have delayed effects. One reason why the term "trauma" is conceptually useful is its association with the diagnostic label "post-traumatic stress disorder" (PTSD; American Psychiatric Association, 1987). PTSD is one of the few clinical diagnostic categories that recognizes social problems (such as war or the Holocaust) as responsible for the symtoms identified (Trimble, 1985). The concept adapts well to the feminist assertion that a woman's individual symptoms cannot be understood as solely individual, considered outside of her social context, or prevented without significant changes in these social conditions.

10. Because of space constraints, I examine two traumas here—poverty and heterosexism. For a discussion of links between eating problems and sexual abuse, immigration and acculturation, and physical/emotional abuse, see Thompson (1991) and Thompson (in press).

REFERENCES

American Psychological Association. (1987). *Diagnostic and statistical manual of mental disorders* (3rd ed., rev.). Washington, DC: Author.

Andersen, A., & Hay, A. (1985). Racial and socioeconomic influences in anorexia nervosa and bulimia. *International Journal of Eating Disorders, 4,* 479–487.

Baca Zinn, M., Cannon, L. W., Higginbotham, E., & Dill, B. T. (1986). The costs of exclusionary practices in women's studies. *Signs: Journal of Women in Culture and Society, 11*(2), 290–303.

Boskind-Lodahl, M. (1976). Cinderella's stepsisters: A feminist perspective on anorexia nervosa and bulimia. *Signs: Journal of Women in Culture and Society, 2,* 342–356.

Boskind-White, M., and White, W. (1983). *Bulimarexia: The binge–purge cycle.* New York: Norton.

Brown, L. S. (1985). Women, weight and power: Feminist theoretical and therapeutic issues. *Women and Therapy, 4,* 61–71.

Brown, L. S. (1987). Lesbians, weight and eating: New analyses and perspectives. In Boston Lesbian Psychologies Collective (Ed.), *Lesbian psychologies* (pp. 294–309). Urbana: University of Illinois Press.

Bruch, H. (1973). *Eating disorders: Obesity, anorexia nervosa and the person within.* New York: Basic Books.

Chernin, K. (1981). *The obsession: Reflections on the tyranny of slenderness.* New York: Harper & Row.

Cole, J. B. (Ed.). (1986). *All American women: Lines that divide, ties that bind.* New York: Free Press.

Comas-Diaz, L. (1987). Feminist therapy with Hispanic/Latina women: Myth or reality? *Women and Therapy, 6*(4), 39–63.

Combahee River Collective. (1979). A black feminist statement. In Z. Eisenstein (Ed.), *Capitalist patriarchy and the case for socialist feminism* (pp. 362–373). New York: Monthly Review Press.

Dolan, B. (1991). Cross-cultural aspects of anorexia nervosa and bulimia: A review. *International Journal of Eating Disorders, 10*(1), 67–78.

Espin, O. (1986). Cultural and historical influences on sexuality in Hispanic/Latin women. In J. B. Cole (Ed.), *All American women: Lines that divide, ties that bind* (pp. 272–285). New York: Free Press.

Garner, D. M., Garfinkel, P. E., Schwartz, D., & Thompson, M. (1980). Cultural expectations of thinness. *Psychological Reports, 47,* 483–491.

Gowers, S., & McMahon, J. B. (1989). Social class and prognosis in anorexia nervosa. *International Journal of Eating Disorders, 8*(1), 105–109.

Gray, J., Ford, K., & Kelly, L. M. (1987). The prevalence of bulimia in a black college population. *International Journal of Eating Disorders, 6,* 733–740.

Hiebert, K. A., Felice, M. A., Wingard, D. L., Munoz, R., & Ferguson, J. M. (1988). Comparison of outcome in Hispanic and Caucasian patients with anorexia nervosa. *International Journal of Eating Disorders, 7,* 693–696.

Higginbotham, E. (1986). We were never on a pedestal: Women of color continue to struggle with poverty, racism and sexism. In R. Lefkowitz & A. Withorn (Eds.), *For crying out loud* (pp. 97–109). Boston: Pilgrim Press.

Hsu, G. (1987). Are eating disorders becoming more common in blacks? *International Journal of Eating Disorders, 6,* 113–124.

Lorde, A. (1984). *Sister outsider.* New York: Crossing Press.

Martinez, I. Z. (1986). *En la lucha:* Economic and socioemotional struggles of Puerto Rican women in the U.S. In R. Lefkowitz and A. Withorn (Eds.), *For crying out loud* (pp. 109–122). Boston: Pilgrim Press.

McAdoo, H. (1986). Societal stress: The black family. In J. B. Cole (Ed.), *All American women: Lines that divide, ties that bind* (pp. 187–198). New York: Free Press.

Millman, M. (1980). *Such a pretty face.* New York: Norton.

Moraga, C., & Anzaldúa, G. (1983). *This bridge called my back: Writing by radical women of color.* New York: Kitchen Table Women of Color Press.

Nevo, S. (1985). Bulimic symptoms: Prevalence and ethnic differences among college women. *International Journal of Eating Disorders, 4,* 151–168.

Orbach, S. (1985). Accepting the symptom: A feminist psychoanalytic treatment of anorexia nervosa. In D. M. Garner & P. E. Garfinkel (Eds.), *Handbook of psychotherapy for anorexia nervosa and bulimia* (pp. 83–104). New York: Guilford Press.

Polivy, J., & Herman, P. (1983). *Breaking the diet habit.* New York: Basic Books.

Powers, R. (1989, October). Fat is a black women's issue. *Essence,* pp. 75, 78, 134, 136.

Pumariega, A., Edwards, P., & Mitchell, C. (1984). Anorexia nervosa in black adolescents. *Journal of the American Academy of Child Psychiatry, 23,* 111–114.

Rand, C. S. W., & Kuldau, J. (1991). Restrained eating (weight concerns) in the general population. *International Journal of Eating Disorders, 10*(6), 699–708.

Rich, A. (1986). Compulsory heterosexuality and lesbian existence. In A. Rich, *Blood, bread, and poetry* (pp. 23–75). New York: Norton.

Robinson, P., & Andersen, A. (1985). Anorexia nervosa in American blacks. *Journal of Psychiatric Research, 19*(2–3), 183–188.

Rodin, J., Silberstein, L. R., & Striegel-Moore, R. H. (1985). Women and weight: A normative discontent. In T. B. Sonderegger (Ed.), *Nebraska Symposium on Motivation: Vol. 32, Psychology and gender* (pp. 267–307). Lincoln: University of Nebraska Press.

Root, M. P. P. (1990). Disordered eating in women of color. *Sex Roles, 22*(7–8), 525–536.

Root, M. P. P., Fallon, P., & Friedrich, W. N. (1986). *Bulimia: A systems approach to treatment.* New York: Norton.

Rosen, L., Shafer, C., Dummer, G., Cross, L., Deuman, G., & Malmberg, S. (1988). Prevalence of pathogenic weight-control behaviors among Native American women and girls. *International Journal of Eating Disorders, 7,* 807–811.

Russell, D. E. (1986). *The secret trauma: Incest in the lives of girls and women.* New York: Basic Books.

Schoenfielder, L., & Wieser, B. (Eds.). (1983). *Shadow on a tightrope: Writings by women about fat liberation.* Iowa City, IA: Aunt Lute Books.

Silber, T. (1986). Anorexia nervosa in blacks and Hispanics. *International Journal of Eating Disorders, 5,* 121–128.

Silberstein, L., Striegel-Moore, R. H., & Rodin, J. (1987). Feeling fat: A woman's shame. In H. B. Lewis (Ed.), *The role of shame in symptom formation* (pp. 89–108). Hillsdale, NJ: Erlbaum.

Smith, J. E., & Krejci, J. (1991). Minorities join the majority: Eating disturbances among Hispanic and Native American youth. *International Journal of Eating Disorders, 10*(2), 179–186.

Striegel-Moore, R. H., Tucker, N., & Hsu, J. (1990). Body image dissatisfaction and disordered eating in lesbian college students. *International Journal of Eating Disorders, 9*(5), 493–500.

Thomas, V., & James, M. (1988). Body image, dieting tendencies and sex role traits in urban black women. *Sex Roles, 18*(9–10), 523–529.

Thompson, B. W. (1991). *Raisins and smiles for me and my sister: A feminist theory of eating problems in women's lives.* Unpublished doctoral dissertation, Brandeis University.

Thompson, B. W. (1992). "A way outa no way": Eating problems among African-American, Latina and white women. *Gender and Society, 6*(4), 546–561.

Thompson, B. (in press). *A hunger so wide and so deep,* Minneapolis: University of Minnesota.

Trimble, M. (1985). Post-traumatic stress disorder: History of a concept. In C. R. Figley (Ed.), *Trauma and its wake: The study and treatment of post-traumatic stress disorder* (pp. 5–14). New York: Brunner/Mazel.

White, W. C., Hudson, L., & Campbell, S. N. (1985). Bulimarexia and black women: A brief report. *Psychotherapy, 22*(2S), 449–450.

V

POSSIBILITY

19

The Politics of Prevention

CATHERINE STEINER-ADAIR

IN MY EARLY YEARS as a therapist working with eating-disordered women, my feelings tended to swing from a strong belief in the process of therapy and its ability to heal, to the opposite feeling—that by practicing therapy I was in some way contributing to the problem, and that if I were to be truly effective, I should be involved in the political arena. It was clear to me that the disorder was in the culture, and that as women "eat" cultural values, images, and so-called "norms" about adult womanhood, they risk getting sick. But traditional therapy treats individuals and families apart from the culture that induces their sickness. Healing requires therapists to take a clear stand against the cultural norms and values that sicken women. This process challenges the assumptions of traditional, nonfeminist therapy that therapy is apolitical; it hints that, on the contrary, any therapy of adaptation risks being iatrogenic. There is a huge gap at present between what is taught in therapy and what is taught in the mass media and the culture at large.

Research from the Harvard Project on the Psychology of Women and Girls' Development (Gilligan, Lyons, & Hamner, 1990; Brown & Gilligan, 1992) shows that young teenagers encounter enormous conflicts when joining the cultural definitions of adult womanhood, in which they are forced to risk their authentic self in order to fit into androcentric norms, values, and images. For many girls, going underground begins with their bodies as they struggle to fit into culturally defined molds. Gilligan's research on the psychological development of girls describes adolescence as a time when "femininity seems on the line, a healthy resistance to disconnections turns into a political struggle and comes under pressure to turn into a psychological resistance—that is, a resistance to knowing what is happening and an impulse to cover the struggle" (Gilligan, 1992, p. 25).

This "crisis in connection" (Gilligan, 1992) is marked by girls' belief that they have to risk their personal safety (be thin, have sex, do drugs) in order to attain and maintain relationships. Furthermore, it is no longer safe to know what they know about unfairness, hurt, and abuse in relationships. Girls begin to experience a kind of duplicitous existence wherein there is a "me" who presents to the world her best approximation of what will be favorably received, and a "real me" who often does not fit the criteria that create the cultural molds of acceptability. At this juncture, girls begin to expend a lot of effort trying to guess what the externally defined "right" way to think or feel is—and simultaneously to hide the truth of their own perceptions, both from others and themselves. Girls are directed to remove their authentic selves from the process of creating relationships, a directive and dynamic doomed to fail in the establishment of healthy and real relationships.

From this perspective, we can understand eating disorders as a joining of the psychological and political drama in a literal enactment, and an unconscious conflict between women's bodies and the body politic (Steiner-Adair, 1986, 1988, 1989, 1992). The challenge of therapy is to transform what appears as psychological resistance (a reluctance to know what one knows) to a political resistance (a refusal not to know what one knows) (Steiner-Adair, 1992; Gilligan, 1990).

There is a curious parallel between the way in which therapists (the majority of whom are women) are silenced by their role, and the way girls and women are silenced in their families when they seek therapy to work on their history of abuse or other trauma. Both female patients and female therapists carry the secrets of their "families": the patients for their families of origin, the therapists for the family at large, the culture. Just as daughters are warned that naming their experience is disloyal and will destroy their families, we as female therapists are told not to speak outside our offices about what we do and what we know. Analysts could call us too emotional or criticize us for not having resolved our issues with authority. If we become political, we fear we will betray the good work that can be done in the sanctity of psychotherapy; in effect, we will be labeled troublemakers, like the adolescent girls who resist silencing themselves. I am not talking about betraying confidentiality, but rather about challenging the isolated position of psychotherapy in the culture and critiquing it from a systems perspective to see whose purpose the isolation serves.

What could happen if therapists and patients in our field joined together in naming the disorders in the culture and taking political action? This is not a simple or risk-free question. The resistance to therapists' taking action is enormous. In the *Frontline* documentary "My Doctor, My Lover" (Zaretsky, 1991), it was not the male psychiatrist who admitted to having sex with his female patient who lost his practice; rather, it was the woman psychiatrist who empowered her woman patient to take legal action. It was the woman psychiatrist who was forced to give up her home, her community of friends, her career. She was excluded from local hospitals and abandoned by her insurance company and professional alliances. She was forced to change her name, move her family, and start a new life and practice. However, the male psychiatrist kept his license, continued his admitting privileges at hospitals, and reports that his referral network remains strong. What does this teach us about empowering women to speak out? Perhaps the most positive outcomes of this drama were the patient's attribution of her recovery to her work with her female psychiatrist; her founding of a group for women who had been sexually abused by therapists; and her involvement in political action. We hear in her tale one woman's movement from psychological resistance to political resistance. But we also hear a tale of punishment.

ANALYZING THE RESISTANCE

To establish primary prevention programs, it is necessary to address powerfully embedded community values that support the problem. If eating disorders are the result of deeply held (although psychologically disabling) cultural values and norms about "ideal" female adulthood, then there is likely to be some resistance to challenging the disordered cultural values. Similarly, since women as patients support the mental health industry, there is a possible (albeit unconscious) investment in individualizing the pathology. This is a particularly thorny issue, since females make up the majority of mental health patients and 90% of the clinical population with eating disorders (Fairburn & Beglin, 1990). Furthermore, as Russo and Sobel (1981) have noted, mental health professionals are especially reluctant to treat women when the problem violates societal stereotypes about what problems females *should* have. If "you can never be too rich or too thin," then eating disorders and body shame are seen as normal and adaptive.

A poignant example of this is a story told to me by a graduate student with a history of anorexia nervosa in adolescence. Her professor, a senior faculty member, was working on a primary prevention manual for adolescents, and she suggested that he include eating disorders as a topic. His response was this: "Eating disorders—that's just a bunch of rich kids sticking their fingers down their throats." Those of us who work with eating disorders are acutely aware of the importance of sociocultural factors, and yet there appears to be both societal and professional resistance to the development of primary prevention programs.

The common arguments against primary prevention programs for eating disorders, outlined by Levine (1988), include (1) public and professional cynicism similar to that shown by the professor described above; (2) the belief that prevention programs create self-fulfilling prophecies (a risk I discuss later); (3) the culture's voyeuristic hysteria about and morbid fascination with celebrities such as Karen Carpenter, in which intrigue interferes with thinking about the average teenage girl; (4) the medicalization of eating disorders, in which one finds such paradoxical terms as "normal-weight bulimia" (which normalizes the bulimic syndrome if it is experienced without weight loss or gain); and (5) the psychologizing of eating disorders, so that the problems are seen as originating in individual and family pathology, not in the oppressive sociocultural context.

Two more patterns of resistance to primary prevention programs are (1) the debate over whether eating disorders are in fact epidemic (and if not, the feeling that there should be no investment in programs); and (2) what Forgays (1983) has called "the trite conventionalism that knowledge of the etiology of the psychological disorder is necessary before we can establish prevention programs" (p. 727). The latter opinion grows out of a medical model of eating disorders, as well as unconscious hostility toward women with eating disorders. As Levine (1988, 1989) states, we do not need to solve these complex riddles to know that eating disorders are serious and prevalent, and that chronic dieting and appearance anxiety cause related psychological problems. From the perspective of primary prevention, what is essential is our increased awareness of the devastating nature of anorexia and bulimia, and of how emotionally, physically, and financially exhausting they are to treat.

WEIGHTISM

One of the challenges of primary prevention is to take a metaposition to the culture, challenging values that promote psychopathology. We live in a "weightist" society with an insidious system of values about thin and fat people. Rigidly maintained and culturally reinforced assumptions about personality, intelligence, morality, level of success, relational life, and worth serve to idealize and overvalue thin people while devaluing and rejecting fat people. Weightism is a form of prejudice that negatively affects both thin and fat people, although in different ways.

Research reviewed by Wooley and Wooley (1979), Wooley,

Wooley, and Dyrenforth (1979), and Wooley and Garner (1991) has shown us that children as young as 3 years old attribute negative qualities to fat people (e.g., "cheating," "dirty," "mean," "lazy"), and that the same attributes seem to remain fairly constant and effective throughout adulthood, regardless of level of education. Significant relationships have been identified between weight and (1) teachers' evaluations of students; (2) mental health professionals' assessments of clients (more emotional problems are attributed to large people); (3) physicians' assessments of patients (doctors judge obese people to be weak-willed, as if their weight gain were strictly a matter of insufficient willpower); (4) admissions committees' assessments of candidates for higher education; (5) personnel decisions in hiring and promotion; and (6) landlords' decisions about rental candidates. All of these have a major impact on the quality of an individual's life.

The psychological effects of prejudice—in this case, weightism—force individuals to protect themselves with defenses that, no matter how sturdy, never provide an equal footing in the battles of everyday life. Identifying with the aggressors, they act out the roles expected of them according to their weight. Unfortunately, when people band together as mutual victims of oppression, it is often through shared self-hate rather than shared recognition (e.g., women over lunch may say, "Let's be *bad* and have dessert today"). Prejudice is defined by the failure to revise opinions when new knowledge is available. The failure of the medical and mental health professions to challenge commonly held misinformation about the etiology of obesity, and the portrayal of obesity as an illness for which there is a cure, have led large people to be seen as morally inferior. Weightism interferes with the healthy, normal psychosocial development of teenage girls, and directs girls to develop their self-image in terms of their body image. When maturational issues of loss and gain are reduced to bodily experiences of loss and gain, girls withdraw from the world around them into the private domain of the scale.

Weightism tells girls that to accept their natural bodies at puberty and menarche is "crazy"; subsequently, dieting is promoted as the primary tool for attaining success in love and work. Fear of fat, restrictive eating, bingeing and purging, and distorted body image are common among girls as young as 9 years old and increase with age. In a study of 494 middle-class girls between the ages of 9 and 10, Mellin, Scully, and Irwin (1986) found that 31% of 9-year-olds were afraid of being fat, increasing to 81% in 10-year-olds. Fifty-one percent of 9- and 10-year-old girls reported feeling better about themselves if they were on a diet. No less disturbing was the finding that 9% of the 9-year-old girls in this study reported some kind of purging behavior. Another study by Johnson, Tobiu, and Lipkin (1989) of 1268 adolescent females reported that 52% began dieting before the age of 14.

Since the "sexual revolution" of the 1960s, thinness has replaced virginity in its representation of goodness in women. Obesity is regarded with the scorn previously reserved for sexuality. Heads no longer turn in moral righteousness when a scantily dressed woman walks down the street, and we hear the same language of moral condemnation applied to the obese woman that used to be directed toward the sexually active woman: "She has no self-respect," "She's out of control," "How could she let herself go?", "She's destroyed herself," and so on.

There is a curious relationship between the onset of the current incidence of eating disorders and the struggle for equality. At a time when women are being encouraged to believe that they have an equal opportunity for achievement and success, weightism can be seen as an oppressive force to sabotage and undermine attainment of the available opportunities (Steiner-Adair, 1988; Faludi, 1991; Wolf, 1991). Telling a woman that she has the same chance for success as a man with comparable abilities, and then adding a between-the-lines requirement for an ideal body shape that is impossible for most women to obtain and maintain, constitute an extremely effective form of oppression and disempowerment. Anorexia initially appeared among white upper- and middle-class women—those best suited educationally and economically to compete for previously male-held positions of power and status.

If we look critically at the ideal image, we see a woman who lacks full female secondary sex characteristics and looks like a man. The cultural image of the female "superwoman"—a tall, thin, strong businesswoman who wears a man-tailored business suit and carries a briefcase—is familiar to us all. Equally familiar are the women stuck at home or in unfulfilling jobs, trying to look the part to convince employers that they are worthy applicants. Wooley and Wooley (1985) and Wooley and Kearney-Cooke (1986) define bulimia as a symbolic struggle with the rigid portrayal of womanhood as an endless experience of self-sacrifice and nurturing, and an attempt to escape these devalued traditional adult female role demands. We still enormously undervalue and underpay teaching, nursing, and child care. We repeatedly hear young women's disgust with their mothers' soft, round stomachs, symbolically representing the devalued position of nurturers within the family. We have no positive term to describe and value women who are working at home and raising children. We have no positive word to describe women with rounded female bodies. Boskind-Lodahl (1976) has suggested that bulimia is a woman's attempt to negotiate impossibly confused and unattainable sex role expectations to lead a dual life—a man (corporate executive) by day and a woman (sex object and mother) by night. Orbach (1978) has suggested that anorexia is a parody of women denying who they are in order to prove that they deserve to enter the world of social and political power long available to men. The girl with anorexia is often described as not wanting to grow up. In my own research (Steiner-Adair, 1986), I came to see her as dramatizing the life-threatening split between female and adult, as illustrated in the study by Broverman, Broverman, Vogel, Clarison, and Rosenkrantz (1972).

Jean Baker Miller (1976) has described the way in which women have carried for both sexes the activities of caring for those who are needy, dependent, and helpless, and have also carried in themselves the qualities of openness, fragility, and vulnerability—traits Miller considers signs of psychological strength. In "The Body Politic: Normal Female Adolescent Development and the Development of Eating Disorders" (Steiner-Adair, 1986, 1990), I have proposed that eating disorders dramatize the extent to which care and dependence have been doubly disparaged by their association with women and children, rather than seen as part of the human condition. More recently, O. Wayne Wooley (Chapter 2, this volume) discusses anorexic thinness as an adaptive retreat from a sexual body in a culture that condones sexual violence toward women. I have come to see weightism and its idealization of a thin female body as a symbolic statement about our culture's unhealthy infatuation with autonomy and independence, and its failure to value interdependence symbolically associated with the rounded female body.

PREVENTION

Prevention programs present options for change in the social context. The politics of primary prevention, as well as successful therapy and recovery, require that we challenge major assumptions and values of our culture, recognize the depth and variety of needs related to eating disorders, and promote an understanding of the problem. We must encourage the competencies that women need to gain control of their lives: skills such as those taught in feminist treatment programs (e.g., the Intensive Treatment Program at the University of Cincinnati or the Renfrew Center), and attitudes such as those encouraged by the National Association to Advance Fat Acceptance, Ample Opportunity, and Radiance (personal communication, William Davis, January 1993).

For prevention programs to succeed in creating change in the social context, weightism needs to be identified and named as a political problem and a real form of prejudice. Women and men need to locate the primary disorder in the culture, and must collectively resist the pressure to discount a political analysis of eating disorders. Just like African-Americans who have to resist internalized racism, Jewish people who have to resist internalized anti-Semitism, and gays and lesbians who have to resist internalized homophobia, individuals of all ethnic, racial, and class backgrounds need to be taught to resist internalized weightism. Like any form of prejudice, weightism needs to be presented within a political framework, in order to remove the shame and isolation that is so difficult to combat on an individual level.

Just as antiracism and antisexism are being taught to children in schools that are pedagogically committed to multicultural education, weightism needs to be included in curricula in very early years and throughout the duration of schooling. If girls and boys in first grade can be taught that it is hurtful and unjust to exclude someone because of skin color, religious background, or physical challenges, then children can be taught to see weightism as equally harmful. I believe that primary prevention will be most likely to succeed when eating disorders are addressed as a social justice issue, linked with other forms of prejudice. It is hard to scare teenagers out of eating disorders by teaching them the medical damages of dieting. As teenagers, they think, "It will never happen to me; I'll just use the technique to look better." On the other hand, it is possible to teach girls and boys that the ultrathin "superwoman" image is a devaluing image of female adulthood, and that the diet industry is exploitative. However, it is my impression from my experience in consulting with schools and colleges that by speaking to the sense of social justice in adolescents and children—capturing their passion, and providing critical and challenging perspectives—we can more successfully help them see the diet industry in a negative light. Children in grades 1–12 can be taught to identify and critique weightist thinking; in so doing, they may develop a healthier resistance to eating disorders.

Furthermore, there is a need to publicly challenge assumptions and myths that promote weightism. We need to offer broader definitions of normal weight, normal body size, and normal eating, incorporating what we have learned about nutrition, illness, and fitness. We must ask: In whose terms and for whose benefit are the norms prescribed? We need to teach females the difference between physical self-definition and self-acceptance on the one hand, and obsessive self-destruction and bodily preoccupation on the other. We need to recognize the value of relational skills and competence, and to include these in our psychological theory and our understanding of human nature. We need to recognize the value for both men and women of moral reasoning based on an ethic of care and connection (Gilligan, 1982) and maternal thinking (Ruddick, 1979). All of this needs to be approached in order to broaden and strengthen the roles of women in the family, the workplace, and the culture at large, so that women may occupy more space and men may occupy different space, each with more security.

As a culture, we need to challenge the notion that a woman's primary source of power is a reducing body, and recognize women as a natural resource that is currently undervalued, underused, and underpaid. We need to teach skills other than dieting, shopping, and elective surgery for dealing with the world. Programs in primary prevention must go beyond reducing problematic and symptomatic behavior to focus on teaching resistance to cultural values that diminish women's self-esteem. If young girls and adult women were less concerned with losing weight, they could act on deeper passions and "throw their weight around," challenging society to value equally the work, roles, and ethics that have traditionally been divided and devalued by gender.

SOME THOUGHTS ON STARVATION, EXTINCTION, AND TOXIC WASTE: A WAKE-UP CALL TO WHITE WOMEN OF PRIVILEGE (OR "WHAT IS THE MATTER?")

As a mother to two young children, I hear myself respond over and over to their crying: "What is the matter? Come have a hug, sweetie, and tell me what's the matter." As a therapist who has worked for well over a decade with girls and women—daughters, sisters, mothers, and grandmothers suffering deeply with what we call eating disorders—I ask myself and the women I work with over and over: "What is the matter?"

What is the matter? Why do so many women hate their bodies and reject their natural rounded female shape? Why is it that for 80% of women in America, being female means feeling too fat (Rodin, Silverstein, & Streigel-Moore, 1985)? What is the matter when 31% of 9-year-old girls are afraid of being fat? What is the matter when over 50% of 9- and 10-year-olds feel better about themselves when they are on a diet? (Mellin et al., 1986) What is the matter when, at any given moment, one out of three American white women is on a diet (Rodin et al., 1985)? What is the matter when women think they are better people if they don't eat? Why do we have a morality of orality?

As I have asked myself these simple words, "What is the matter?", I can no longer hear an individual woman's suffering in her body as separate from the suffering that is coming to collective consciousness in the body of the earth. As I listen more and more to girls' and women's struggles to honor their bodies, I hear echoes of the same struggle of honoring the body earth. If we teach ourselves to hear the same language when we talk about our struggles with our bodies and about ecological struggles, we hear parallel tales of starvation, extinction, toxic dumping, waste of natural resources, and rape of Mother Earth.

When psychiatry labeled the behaviors that we have come to call anorexia and bulimia, the naming process rendered invisible the meaningful aspects of these soulful struggles. "Anorexia" means "absence of hunger," "absence of appetite"; this is not an accurate description of the experience of anorexic girls and women, who are extremely hungry but willingly deny their bodily appetite in their drive to make their feminine matter extinct. What is missing from the psychiatric label is the power of the drive for starvation in order to make extinct the corporeal feminine form. In the naming of "bulimia," which means "oxen hunger," a significant aspect of the phenomenon is also obscured by the label: the problem of what to do with the excessive consumption and the problems of waste. Through the lens of bulimia, we see struggles with uncontrolled consumption, toxic waste, and waste disposal.

We have the same crises in women's relationships to their bodies as we do in our relationship to the body of the earth: issues of nurturance, starvation, and waste. And, interestingly, we have the same language of disrespect and violence applied to sexual abuse of women's bodies and the polluting of the body of the earth. For example, there are three meanings to the word "smut": "to affect a crop with smut"; "to stain or taint"; "to treat obscenely or feel foul." We are, in strip mining and the destruction of virgin rain forests, starving species to death at the rate of 1000 species per year. We "rape" the virgin forest in deforestation. In a global community with food enough to feed everyone, 10,000 people die each day of starvation.

We see the same dangers found in the idealization of nurturance in women as in the idealization of Mother Earth—as if she too can be all-giving; as if species and rain forests can grow back or be replaced with technology; as if oceans can detoxify themselves. The shadow of the idealization of nurturance in women is the violent aggression toward women that our culture condones. In the statistics of physical and sexual violence toward women and children, we again see parallels in the culture's relationship to the earth. We live in a culture where approximately one in four women are sexually abused, and one in three women are physically abused (Herman, 1992). These statistics challenge us to think about ways in which we devalue and damage the feminine spirit and the female body. On an unconscious level, the violent assault and abuse of women's bodies seem inseparable from the violence to the earth's body. Terms such as "the rape of the virgin rain forest" or "strip mine" have sadistically eroticized the language of domination and violation.

As in Thich Nat Hanh's words, "What we most need to do is hear within ourselves the sounds of the earth crying" (1987), I hear within myself a powerful connection between women's struggles within their bodies and the collective struggle with the body of the earth. As women, we are taught to hate our bodies and the values that are symbolically associated with them—the cyclical nature of life; the fundamental interdependence of life; the available and limited natural resources; the importance of caring and nurturing; the necessity of time for growth; the pain of giving life. If we separate ourselves from our bodies and it becomes hard to feel connected to nature . . . if men and women hate the rounded female body . . . then it is hard to identify compassionately with the needs of the body of the great Mother Earth. If we are told we are too sensitive, emotional, and angry about issues of justice, caring, and relationships in a social world, then it becomes hard to speak out about our love and our pain for all forms of life on earth, and the earth itself.

Perhaps the deepest level at which I see the connection between ecofeminism and eating disorders is in the struggle for recovery. It is my experience that women do not recover fully—cannot heal themselves and reinhabit their bodies, embody their psyches, or have passion and spirit—until they make a connection between their eating disorder and the oppression of women. The science of psychology as traditionally practiced is too narrow a framework from which to heal. Its theoretical fragmentation, or splitting off the psyche and soul, parallels a current struggle in the history of ideas: the split between technology and ecology. In both fields, if we practice a politic based on dominance, separation, and autonomy, then it is difficult to have a vision of the future in which we nourish and sustain the whole.

In this nuclear era of ecological and environmental atrocities, our disrespect for Mother Earth is paralleled in our disrespect for mothers on earth. And women with body image, weight, and eating problems are profoundly detached from their bodies as sources of wisdom, spirituality, and power. Weightism encourages women to dismember themselves—literally, through liposuction and other methods of bodily reduction, as well as through the obsessive internal dissection of their bodies.

We need to help men and women reclaim women's bodies as a source of connection to one another, to motherhood, to Mother Earth, and to collective creation and generativity. In "Psyche Embedded: A Place for Body, Relationships, and Culture in Personality Theory," Gilligan, Brown, and Rogers (1990) caution us:

> To take the fact of sex differences seriously and embed psyche in body means we must give up the Platonic legacy of one pure form (connote: or one ideal body image). At the same time, the embodiment of Psyche calls

our attention to vulnerability—to embed Psyche in relationships means to leave behind the image of perfection and the search for self-sufficiency and control. And finally, to embed Psyche in relationships and culture means to open psychology to moral scrutiny—to observe what voices are amplified and what voices are muted or silenced, as well as to identify values currently masquerading as psychological norms. (pp. 146–147)

Women risk becoming literally and metaphorically malnourished and psychologically destroyed when they ingest androcentric cultural norms, which project an ideal image of "she" who is just like "he" (thin, muscular, invulnerable, independent, autonomous, in control, highly competitive—an ideal image of adulthood that is also disabling to men). If primary prevention is to be successful, we need to deconstruct the social context to reveal underlying political forces that define and maintain eating disorders. We must empower women and men to challenge weightism and reclaim round female bodies as a source of real and symbolic power. Perhaps then women and men could address together their human hunger for a shared value system that nourishes and sustains ourselves and the earth as a whole.

ACKNOWLEDGMENT

Heartfelt thanks to Susan Wooley for her sustaining support and editorial help.

REFERENCES

Boskind-Lodahl, M. (1976). Cinderella's step-sisters: A feminist perspective on anorexia and bulimia. *Signs: Journal of Women in Culture and Society, 2,* 324–356.

Broverman, I., Broverman, P., Vogel, S. P., Clarkson, F. E., & Rosenkrantz, P. S. (1972). Sex role stereotypes: A current appraisal. *Journal of Social Issues, 28,* 56–78.

Brown, L., & Gilligan, C. (1992). *Meeting at the crossroads.* Cambridge, MA: Harvard University Press.

Fairburn, C., & Beglin, S. A. (1990). Studies of the epidemiology of bulimia nervosa. *American Journal of Psychiatry, 147,* 401–408.

Faludi, S. (1991). *Backlash: The undeclared war against American women.* New York: Crown.

Forgays, D. (1983). Primary prevention of psychopathology. In M. Hersen, A. Kazdin, & Bellack (Eds.), *Clinical psychology handbook* (pp. 701–733). Elmsford, NY: Pergamon Press.

Gilligan, C. (1982). *In a different voice: Psychological theory and women's development.* Cambridge, MA: Harvard University Press.

Gilligan, C. (1990). Teaching Shakespeare's sister: Notes from the underground of female adolescence. In C. Gilligan, N. Lyons, & T. Hamner (Eds.), *Making connections* (pp. 6–29). Cambridge, MA: Harvard University Press.

Gilligan, C. (1992). Women's psychological developments: Implications for psychotherapy. In C. Gilligan, A. Rogers, & D. Tolman (Eds.), *Women, girls, and psychotherapy: Reframing resistance* (pp. 5–31). New York: Haworth Press.

Gilligan, C., Brown, L. M., & Rogers, A. (1990). Psyche embedded: A place for body, relationships, and culture in personality theory. In A. I. Rabin, R. Zucker, R. Emons, & S. Frank (Eds.), *Studying persons and lives* (pp. 86–147). New York: Springer.

Gilligan, C., Lyons, N., & Hamner, T. (Eds.). (1990). *Making connections.* Cambridge, MA: Harvard University Press.

Hanh, T. N. (1987). *Being peace.* Berkeley: Parallax Press.

Herman, J. L. (1992). *Trauma and recovery.* New York: Basic Books.

Johnson, C. L., Tobiu, D. L., & Lipkin, J. (1989). Epidemiologic changes in bulimic behavior among female adolescents over a five-year period. *International Journal of Eating Disorders, 8,* 647–655.

Levine, M. P. (1988). *Eating disorders: Early intervention, prevention, and change.* Paper presented at the Anorexia Bulimia Care, Inc., Conference, Boston.

Levine, M. P. (1989). *Just demonstrate no!* Paper presented at the Eighth National Conference on Anorexia Nervosa and Bulimia Nervosa of the National Anorexic Aid Society, Columbus, OH.

Mellin, L. M., Scully, S., & Irwin, C. E. (1986). *Disordered eating characteristics in preadolescent girls.* Paper presented at the annual meeting of the American Dietetic Association, Las Vegas, NV.

Miller, J. B. (1976). *Toward a new psychology of women.* Boston: Beacon Press.

Orbach, S. (1978). *Fat is a feminist issue.* London: Paddington Press.

Rodin, J., Silverstein, L. R., & Streigel-Moore, R. H. (1985). Women and weight: A normative discontent. In T. B. Sonderegger (Ed.), *Nebraska Symposium on Motivation: Vol. 32. Psychology and gender* (pp. 267–307). Lincoln: University of Nebraska Press.

Ruddick, S. (1979). *Maternal thinking.* New York: Ballantine Books.

Russo, N. P., & Sobel, S. D. (1981). Sex preferences in the utilization of mental health facilities. *Professional Psychology, 12,* 7–19.

Steiner-Adair, C. (1986). The body politic: Normal female adolescent development and the development of eating disorders. *Journal of the American Academy of Psychoanalysis, 14*(1), 95–114.

Steiner-Adair, C. (1988). *Weightism: A new form of prejudice.* Keynote address at the Seventh National Conference on Eating Disorders, Columbus, OH.

Steiner-Adair, C. (1989). Developing the voice of the wise woman: College students and bulimia. *Journal of College Student Psychotherapy, 3*(2,3,4), 151–163.

Steiner-Adair, C. (1990). The body politic: Normal female adolescent development and the development of eating disorders. In C. Gilligan, N. Lyons, & T. Hamner (Eds.), *Making connections* (pp. 162–181). Cambridge, MA: Harvard University Press.

Steiner-Adair, C. (1992). When the body speaks: Girls, eating disorders, and psychotherapy. In C. Gilligan, A. Rogers, & D. Tolman (Eds.), *Women, girls, and psychotherapy: Reframing resistance* (pp. 253–266). New York: Haworth Press.

Wolf, N. (1991). *The beauty myth: How images of beauty are used against women.* New York: Morrow.

Wooley, O. W., Wooley, S. C., & Dyrenforth, S. (1979). Obesity and women II: A neglected feminist topic. *Women's Studies International Quarterly, 2,* 81–92.

Wooley, S. C., & Garner, D. M. (1991). Obesity treatment: The high cost of false hope. *Journal of the American Dietetic Association, 91*(10), 1248–1251.

Wooley, S. C., & Kearney-Cooke, S. (1986). Intensive treatment of bulimia and body image disturbance. In K. Brownell & J. Foreyt (Eds.), *Handbook of eating disorders: Physiology, psychology, and treatment of obesity, anorexia, and bulimia* (pp. 477–502). New York: Basic Books.

Wooley, S. C., & Wooley, O. W. (1985). Intensive residential and outpatient treatment of bulimia. In D. M. Garner & P. E. Garfinkel (Eds.), *Handbook of psychotherapy for anorexia nervosa and bulimia* (pp. 391–430). New York: Guilford Press.

Wooley, S. C., & Wooley, O. W. (1979). Obesity and women I: A closer look at the facts. *Women's Studies International Quarterly, 2,* 69–76.

Zaretsky (Producer). (1991, November 12). *My doctor, my love.* Boston: WGBH-TV.

20

Still Killing Us Softly: Advertising and the Obsession with Thinness

JEAN KILBOURNE

IN RECENT YEARS, advertising campaigns no longer simply interrupt the news; they have become the news. Community groups successfully halted the marketing of Uptown, a new cigarette that targeted inner-city African-Americans. People were (and still are) outraged by a cartoon camel called "Old Joe," who successfully sells Camel cigarettes to children. The Surgeon General and other public health activists called for restrictions on alcohol and cigarette advertising. The Swedish Bikini Team, featured in beer commercials, was also featured in a sexual harassment suit brought by female workers in the beer company.

More and more people are taking advertising seriously. They are realizing that the $130 billion advertising industry is a powerful educational force in America. The average American is exposed to over 1500 ads every day and will spend a year and a half of his or her life watching television commercials. Although the individual ads are often insipid and trivial, they have a serious cumulative impact (Ewen, 1976; Kilbourne, 1977; Williamson, 1978).

The current emphasis on excessive thinness for women is one of the clearest examples of advertising's power to influence cultural standards and consequent individual behavior. Body types, like clothing styles, go in and out of fashion, and are promoted by advertising (and by the women's magazines, whose editorial content is in many ways indistinguishable from advertising). The images in the mass media constantly reinforce the latest ideal—what is acceptable and what is out of date. Seid (Chapter 1, this volume) has elaborated on the many cultural, historical, and political reasons why certain fashions are popular at certain times, and I argue here that advertising and the media indoctrinate us in these ideals, to the detriment of most women. We need to be as outspoken about this issue as the prohealth activists are about alcohol and tobacco advertising.

IMPACT OF THE IDEAL

How do these images affect us as women? The tyranny of the ideal image makes almost all of us feel inferior. An internal voice rages at us: "You are fat. You are ugly. Your thighs are like jelly. You have cellulite. You have pimples. You have vaginal odor. Your hair is drab. Your skin is dry." We are taught to hate our bodies, and thus learn to hate our selves. This self-hatred takes an enormous toll. There is convincing evidence that negative body image leads to negative self-image, reflected by feelings of inferiority, anxiety, insecurity, and depression (Freedman, 1986; Wolf, 1991).

The ideal body type today (Figure 20.1) is unattainable by most women, even if they starve themselves. Only the thinnest 5% of women in a normal weight distribution approximate this ideal, which thus excludes 95% of American women. As Seid (Chapter 1, this volume) has said, "Societies have never been kind to deviants, but in America a statistical deviation has been normalized, leading millions of women to believe that they are abnormal" (p. 8). Television and the other media thus reflect a very small minority and not the general population. In fact, the majority of women on television are much thinner than they were in previous decades, as well as thinner than most women in the real world (Gordon, 1990).

As a result, more than half of the adult women in the United States are currently dieting, and over three-fourths of normal-weight American women think they are "too fat" (Sims, 1986). This mass delusion sells a lot of products. It also causes enormous suffering for women, involving them in false quests for power and control, while deflecting attention and energy from that which might really empower them. "A declaration of independence," proclaims the ad (Figure 21.1), but in fact the quest for a body as thin as the model's becomes a prison for many women.

The preoccupation with weight is beginning at ever-earlier ages for women. A 1986 study showed that nearly 80% of fourth-grade girls in the San Francisco Bay Area were watching their weight (cited in Stein, 1986). Rosen and Gross (1987), in a study of 3000 adolescents, found that

FIGURE 20.1. Lady Stetson perfume, April 1991.

most of the boys were trying to gain weight, but that at any given time, two-thirds of girls aged 13 to 18 were trying to lose weight. Boys, of course, are encouraged to be bigger and stronger, whereas girls are supposed to be thin and fragile.

Adolescents are especially vulnerable, given the ominous peer pressure on young people. Also, normal physiological changes during adolescence result in increased body fat for women. If these normal changes are considered undesirable by the culture (and by parents and peers), this can lead to chronic anxiety and concern about weight control in young women. "Is weight holding your daughter back?" asks an ad in *The New York Times* aimed at parents. At the same time, very little media attention is given to recent research indicating that girls get an inferior education in our schools (American Association of University Women, 1992). It isn't weight that is holding girls back; it is discrimination.

The stereotyping of little girls and boys in the media has perhaps never been worse. Television programs for children are filled with active boys and passive girls, brought to them by commercials for action products for boys and beauty products and dolls for girls. A print ad, headlined "Simply beautiful," features a little girl sitting at a vanity table, looking in the mirror. Imagine an ad like this featuring a boy: "Simply handsome," with a little boy looking into a mirror. Some people would recommend therapy, wouldn't they?

THE INFLUENCE OF ADVERTISING

Eating disorders have increased dramatically in recent years (Johnson & Connors, 1987). Estimates suggest that 4–15% of college women have serious problems with bulimia (Crandall, 1988). An amazing 49% of teenage girls responding to a recent survey by *Sassy* magazine reported using diet pills, while 13% of the magazine's young readers have tried laxatives or diuretics for weight loss (cited in *Drug Abuse Update*, 1991). These statistics are not lost on advertisers. The sixth most frequently prescribed drug in America is a diuretic. Many ads for laxatives that used to feature old people now use slim and attractive young women.

It would be simplistic, given the research on the biological, familial, and pyschological contributions to eating disorders, to hold advertising solely accountable for this recent increase. However, according to Garner and Garfinkel (1980), "the potential impact of the media in establishing identificatory role models cannot be overemphasized" [in the development of anorexia] (p. 652). At least one study of female college students suggests that this impact is indeed substantial: brief exposure to several ads showing highly attractive models resulted in decreased satisfaction with one's own appearance, in comparison to the satisfaction of students in a control group who saw ads without models (Richins, 1991).

Since advertising cashes in on women's unfortunately normative distortions, it sometimes deliberately promotes such distortion. A recent Virginia Slims campaign features an optically distorted, abnormally thin image of a woman (Figure 20.2). Apparently the tall, thin model isn't long and lean enough, because she has been "stretched" via a camera trick. An ad for Dannon Light yogurt (Figure 20.3) says, "How to go from seeing yourself like this . . . to seeing yourself like this," and portrays the "before" image with a pear. In fact, it is perfectly normal for a woman to be pear-shaped.

As Kim Chernin (1981) has so vividly stated,

> If we were admired for having fat around the neck, as women were in 1911, and were permitted to have large abdomens and well-padded hips, tens of thousands of women would not kneel down next to the toilet tonight and put our fingers down our throat, and vomit. (p. 87)

FIGURE 20.2. Virginia Slims Superslims cigarettes, May 1990.

The current obsession with weight is enormously profitable for many corporations and for the media in general. The diet industry has tripled in the last 10 years, increasing from a $10 billion to a $33 billion a year industry. It is expected to become a $50 billion industry in the next 5 years (Black, 1990). This industry includes diet drugs and other products, diet workshops and books, health spas, and more.

The magazines and other media also obviously prosper as a result of all the advertising. "Hey Coke," the *Ladies' Home Journal* proclaims to Coca-Cola in an ad placed in *Advertising Age*, "Want 17½ million very interested women to think Diet?" (Figure 20.4). *Ladies' Home Journal* and other such magazines gladly provide a climate in which ads for diet products will be looked at with interest, even with desperation.

In addition to all the psychic and physical damage the diet products do, they don't even fulfill their purpose—at least not for long. Ninety percent of those people who lose 25 or more pounds on a weight loss diet regain the weight lost within 2 years, and 98% regain the lost weight within 5 years (Black, 1990; Rothblum, Chapter 3, this volume). The experience of talk show host Oprah Winfrey provided a recent example

FIGURE 20.3. Dannon Light yogurt, March 1991.

of this phenomenon (Rosen et al., 1992). This information, if widely disseminated throughout the mass media, could be as damaging to corporate profits as is the information that cigarette smoking causes lung cancer. It is no surprise that in both cases, there is widespread distortion and suppression of such information.

DIET PRODUCTS AND THE FEAR OF FAT

Chronic dieting is damaging to one's health and upsets the body's natural metabolism. Many diet products are hazardous to health, and most diet pill consumers are women. At congressional hearings in 1990, scientists linked phenyl-propanolamine (PPA), a substance found in diet pills, to such problems as heart and kidney damage, hypertension, and stroke. At least 2 million Americans use diet pills (Snider, 1990).

Dangerous attitudes are often reflected and reinforced in advertising. An ad for Roxanne bathing suits proclaims, "You've earned it. Starving and suffering got you into shape. But it takes more than that to give you the figure you've strived for." Many young women are in fact

FIGURE 20.4. *Ladies' Home Journal* (advertising itself to Diet Coke), 1982.

starving themselves to death in their effort to achieve an image that is basically unattainable.

Some ads normalize and encourage women's fear of their own appetite. A recent ad for a diet product features a group of people from 30 or 40 years ago at a lunch counter and the following copy:

> Remember when your eyes really were bigger than your stomach? Before you worried about fat or counted calories? When the only thing between you and the food you loved was a shiny, speckled counter? Stouffer's Lean Cuisine takes you back. . . . Enjoy a second childhood. Without a second thought.

Sometimes the ads themselves acknowledge the dangers of dieting. As is typical of advertising, however, the solution is not to stop the dangerous practice; the solution is another product. One ad for yogurt features a very young and very thin woman, and the headline "A body like this could be missing out on a lot." The ad acknowledged that the dieting required to keep this teenager so thin is robbing her body of necessary minerals and vitamins. Similarly, another ad, for skin cream, reminds us that dieting damages skin tone. The solution, as always, is the product. Neither ad questions the practice of dieting.

Most ads for diets or dieting aids feature very thin women announcing their success at dieting (sometimes with "before" photographs). Occasionally, however, an ad features someone who is fat or who appears thin but has "cellulite." This strikes fear into the hearts of most women: "If you don't use this product, you too may look like this; you too may inspire this kind of revulsion." Women are conditioned to be *terrified* of fat.

Prejudice against fat people, especially against fat women, is one of the few remaining prejudices that are socially acceptable (Rothblum, Chapter 3, this volume). An episode of the popular (and usually fairly progressive) television show *L. A. Law,* broadcast on April 16, 1992, featured the wedding of a very successful, outgoing, and fat woman (a regular character on the show) to a very handsome man. The other characters, astonished, surmised that something other than love was the motive. Sure enough, it turned out that the man only wanted a "green card." Given the opportunity to sleep with the woman, he delicately declined. In a subsequent episode, the woman did succeed in seducing the man, although it seemed clear that they would never really have a relationship. Had this been a plot line featuring a woman with a disability, viewers across the country would have been outraged.

As we Americans become increasingly obsessed with being in control, it is no surprise that fat people become the scapegoats. We project onto them our own terror of being out of control. As the world becomes increasingly violent and unpredictable, and as we live with the increasing likelihood of environmental destruction, we feel increasingly powerless. One way to demonstrate our power and our control is to keep our own bodies in line. We may not be able to master our destinies, but we can master our bodies. "Oh what self-control," proclaims an ad for a fat-free yogurt (Figure 20.5). Seid (Chapter 1, this volume) argues powerfully that it is perhaps our idealization of technology that has led us to dehumanize the human form. We seek to distinguish ourselves from animals, not by the presence of a soul or conscience, but by suppressing animal fat.

Women today are particularly susceptible to this fear of loss of control. Women are exhorted to be superwomen. They are told by the media that it should be easy to combine careers with raising children, provided that they use the right products. Women are also told that they must be more like men in order to succeed in business. The primary message to men has always been "Be in control," and women are now encouraged to follow suit. However, ads and television shows rarely demonstrate women being in control in the same way men are. In the 1987–1988 television season, only 3 of 22 new prime-time dramas featured female leads. Sixty-six percent of the prime-time speaking char-

FIGURE 20.5. Light n' Lively Free yogurt, May 1992.

acters were male (Faludi, 1991). According to a 1993 study by the Screen Actors Guild and the American Federation of Television and Radio Artists, men under the age of 40 received 43% of the roles in films, while women under 40 received 23%, and women 40 years of age and older were cast in only 8% of the parts. The numbers were almost identical for television.

There is still tremendous fear in the culture of any kind of feminine power, as if it would be inherently destructive. Some argue that it is men's awareness of just how powerful women can be that has created the attempts to keep women small (O. W. Wooley, Chapter 2, this volume). No wonder there is such pressure on women today to be thin, to be like little girls—not to take up too much space, literally or figuratively (Greene, 1992; Kilbourne, 1986; Rothblum, Chapter 3, this volume). At the same time, there is pressure to succeed, to achieve, to "have it all." In other words, women can be successful as long as they stay "feminine" (i.e., powerless enough not to be truly threatening). One way to do this is to present an image of fragility, to look like a waif. This demonstrates that one is both in control and still very "feminine." The pursuit of thinness is also a way to compete without threatening men.

This is not to suggest that this is necessarily a conscious conspiracy. It is more likely the reflection of the shared fears, desires, and values of those in power. The magazines and the ads deliberately *create* and intensify anxiety about weight because it is so profitable. On a deeper level, however, they *reflect* cultural concerns and conflicts about women's power. Real freedom for women would change the very basis of our male-dominated society. It is not surprising that many men and women fear this. Fashion and advertising are just two aspects of the response of the dominant ideology to the threatening possibility of women's liberation. (Faludi, 1991; Wolf, 1991).

FITNESS

In recent years there has been an emphasis on physical fitness as well as thinness. The point, however, is to stay slim, lean, and hard, but not to develop muscles or strength. An ad for an exercise machine features a very muscular man and a slim woman, with the copy "Build Up, Slim Down, or Both." The whole idea of women using weight lifting to become strong is sometimes joked about in ads (Figure 20.6), which imply, as always, that all

FIGURE 20.6. L'Oreal makeup, April 1984.

they really need are the right products. Women's strength comes from their perfect image, not their healthy bodies.

The fitness craze co-opts the whole idea of power for women, reducing it to narcissism. A fit body may give the illusion of power, the illusion of change, but it does nothing to change the status of women in the society. An underpaid and undervalued woman who is physically fit is still underpaid and undervalued. A woman who lifts weights and becomes strong still has very little power and autonomy in the society.

Even worse, a woman who lifts weights and is also starving herself will have significantly decreased energy and power. Wolf argues that dieting leads to passivity, anxiety, and low self-esteem, and that "[i]t is *those traits, and not thinness for its own sake, that the dominant culture wants to create in the private sense of self of recently liberated women in order to cancel out the dangers of their liberation*" (1991, p. 188, emphasis in original). Thus, in the guise of offering health, fitness, and expanded opportunities to women, the culture restricts all of these things.

POWER AND FREEDOM

The current obsession with women's weight is an important part of an attempt to limit women's power and freedom (Rothblum, Chapter 3, this volume). At the same time that women's independence is being severely compromised, the advertisers offer women freedom through dieting. In a 1985 commercial for Weight Watchers, three thin young women danced and sang about the "taste of freedom." They were feeling free because they could now eat bread, thanks to Weight Watchers' low-calorie version. Similarly, a recent commercial for Wendy's fast-food chain features a very slim young woman who announces, "I have a license to eat." Wendy's salad bar and lighter fare have given her freedom to eat (as if eating for women were a privilege rather than a need).

Advertising often reduces the political to the personal. We are told that all we need to do is use the right products and get our own individual acts together, and all will be fine. We must constantly perfect and change ourselves, working for self-improvement rather than societal change. The wider world of discrimination, poverty, and oppression simply doesn't exist in advertising. There is never the slightest hint that people suffer because of a socioeconomic and political situation that could be changed. For example, if we are having difficulty with child care, the solution is to give our children sweets so they will love us, not to lobby for a national child care policy. If we are having trouble in our relationships with men, we can buy a book that will encourage us to make ourselves more agreeable to men, rather than joining a consciousness-raising group that might lead us in another direction. If we are unhappy, there is something wrong with us that can be solved by buying something. We can smoke a cigarette or have a drink or eat some ice cream. Or we can lose some weight.

Ads for many products promise to make us powerful. Cottage cheese is billed as "Snacks for the Power Hungry" (Figure 20.7). "Put on the power of Sheer Energy Control Top," proclaims another ad. An ad for gloves features the gloves surrounded with a halo, and this copy: "Get your hands on the newest source of energy. Take control! . . . And feel the power out to your fingertips." A 1991 ad in *TV Guide* for a candy bar called PayDay features the heading "Not satisfied with your payday? Try ours."

Thus the changing roles and greater opportunities for women promised by the women's movement are trivialized, reduced to the private search for the slimmest body. As Bennett and Gurin (1982) said,

> The central expression of the new, liberated woman was her thin body, which came to symbolize athleticism, nonreproductive sexuality, and a kind of androgynous independence. Almost immediately, however, this

FIGURE 20.7. Knudsen cottage cheese, 1985.

symbol of liberation itself became oppressive. As it was co-opted by fashion, the "bean-lean" body became, arbitrarily, a mark of status, sexual competitiveness, and self-mastery. By now, it is at least as oppressive to the majority of women, who are not naturally skinny, as were the extremes of Renaissance or Victorian high style. (p. 171)

We women are told today that we must be autonomous and independent in order to be successful. In addition to believing that a slender body will empower us, we may also fear that a curvaceous body would link us to the traditional powerless woman, and would thus symbolize weakness and dependence. Changing our bodies is the most visible way to reject the feminine stereotype.

The limited sense of power that most women have was strikingly revealed in a survey of middle-aged women who were asked what they would most like to change about their lives. One thinks immediately of low salaries, ill health, poverty, the environment. Over half of the women, however, said that what they would most like to change was their weight (cited in Pollitt, 1982). In another survey, 30 girls aged 11 to 17 were given three magic wishes for anything they wanted. The number one wish of most of them was "to lose weight and keep it off" (Surrey, 1984). This impoverishment of the imagination is perhaps even sadder than the impoverishment of the body.

MOTHERS AND DAUGHTERS

Young women are experiencing inevitable conflicts with their mothers today. Most of their mothers were brought up to be homemakers and then subsequently devalued. The new possibilities open to young women force them to reject their mothers' role, to surpass their achievements, perhaps even to achieve their suppressed dreams. This can lead to terrible guilt and anxiety. A serious eating disorder may be a way to postpone growing up and thus to postpone this betrayal of the mother (Steiner-Adair, 1986; Perlick & Silverstein, Chapter 4, this volume).

At the same time, a young woman knows that much good came from her mother—for example, closeness, intimacy, nurturance, and food itself. In a 1985 lecture at Radcliffe College, noted researcher Catherine Steiner-Adair suggested that the emaciated body of the anorexic is symbolic of a culture that does not support female development and that values the independent and not the interdependent (cited in Gilbert, 1985). The relationship with food may also be a substitute for the nourishment offered by the mother. The fixation on food and thinness thus allows a woman both to reject and to incorporate aspects of the mother.

However, women are also penalized for rejecting the "feminine" role of caretaker and nurturer. Women have always been closely identified with food—with its gathering, preparation, and serving. Women's bodies are identified with food ("peach," "tomato," "piece of meat," etc.) in a way that men's bodies never are. Women are socialized to value relationships, and usually feel terrible conflict between this value and the cultural value of autonomy. Women in ads are often serving others, especially by offering food to others. Sometimes it is implied that this food-giving demonstrates their love and ensures its requital. "Bake a Comstock pie. They'll love you for it," one ad says.

Not surprisingly, food is also often advertised as a way for a woman to demonstrate that she loves herself—as a way to pamper and reward herself. Very few ads feature women being given food by men or even by other women. A television commercial for Andy's Candies features a series of vignettes in which what a woman does for others (e.g., making a costume for her daughter) is ignored and unappreciated. At the end of each vignette, the woman pops a piece of candy in her mouth and says, "I thank me very much with Andy's Candies."

An especially insidious aspect of some recent advertisements is their portrayal of little girls as dieters in training. "I can always tell when Mom's on a diet," announces one little girl. "There's Unicap M on the table." This ad continues, "If you're a regular dieter—or even an occasional one . . . ," thus acknowledging the essential hopelessness of dieting. A television commercial for Fibre Trim, a diet product, features two little girls talking about how slender one of their mothers is, thanks to the product. For some inexplicable reason (perhaps simple pretentiousness), they speak in French and the commercial is subtitled. One of the little girls asks the other whether she is jealous of her mother's thinness. The other replies, "Not as long as she tells me her secrets."

Mothers do influence their daughters' attitude toward weight. One study (*American Family Practitioner*, 1988) found that half the girls who were dieting reported having been encouraged by their mothers to do so, compared to only 14% of the nondieting girls. As is usually the case, advertisers know what they are doing.

According to Kim Chernin (1985),

> [T]he problem with female identity that most troubles us, and that is most disguised by our preoccupation with eating and body size and clothes, has a great deal to do with being a daughter and knowing that one's life as a woman must inevitably reflect upon the life of one's mother. This is the anxiety that makes us yearn to wear male clothes, regardless of fit, and to work over and worry at and reshape these female bodies of ours so that they can help us pretend we have managed to escape being our mothers' daughters and have, in our appearance at least, become their sons. Our mothers' sons—those beings for whom self-development and the struggle for identity are entirely legitimate enterprises. (p. 37)

TEMPTATION AND SALVATION

A dominant issue in Western culture has been the fear of and subsequent control of women's bodies. Both men and women are conditioned and socialized to feel that women must be controlled, kept in their place. Women, of course, internalize these messages. Dieting is the modern self-purification ritual, today's mortification of the flesh. Ironically, what is considered sexy today is a look that almost totally suppresses female secondary sexual characteristics, such as large breasts and hips (Meadow & Weiss, 1992). Thinness is related to decreased fertility and sexuality in women.

Many ads for food play on a kind of self-indulgence and sensuality that is almost sexual. An ad for a frozen mousse dessert features Dr. Ruth Westheimer, America's sexual guru, digging in and advising the reader, "Achieving mutual satisfaction is easy. Just share some Mousse du Jour" (Figure 20.8). An ad for frozen yogurt features a closeup of a woman's face in what looks like sexual ecstasy and the copy "Vanilla so pure it sends chills down your spine and back up again." Another version of the ad shows the same ecstatic face and the copy "Your tastebuds cry out yes, yes, oh, yes" (Figure 20.9). Often the food is shot in extreme closeup and is very sensually inviting. A Weight Watchers ad features such a shot of a Boston cream pie, literally oozing its creamy filling, and the caption "Feel free to act on impulse." A Cool Whip ad shows a manicured hand plunging a strawberry into whipped cream and the caption "Go skinny dippin'." The caption for a Baker's Fudge-tastics ad

FIGURE 20.8. Mousse du Jour frozen dessert, December 1986.

FIGURE 20.9. Breyers ice cream and Breyers frozen yogurt, 1992.

featuring a closeup of a fudgsicle oozing its chocolate filling is "Introducing our deep, dark secret."

If the food is the temptation, the diet product is the salvation. Often this is expressed in religious terms. "Ask for a miracle," one ad for a diet product declares. In another, a rich chocolate sundae is labeled "Temptation" on one side of the page. On the other is the "Salvation," a low-calorie Alba shake (Figure 20.10). "40% Sin, 60% Forgiveness," proclaims an ad featuring a priest eating Land O Lakes Country Morning Blend of margarine and butter (Figure 20.11). An ad for Fibre Trim tells us that "Europeans know how to lead us into temptation" (with lots of wonderful pastries) "and help deliver us from it" (with the diet product). An ad for a low-calorie chocolate milk promises us "the ecstasy without the agony."

The "good girl" today is the thin girl, the one who keeps her appetite for food (and for power, sex, and equality) under control. That this is a character issue is both underscored and trivialized by an ad for a diet product that proclaims "How Fibre Trim gave new strength to the French resistance." A 1992 cover story in *People* magazine (January 13) featured Oprah Winfrey and the heading "Who's Winning, Who's Sinning? Diet Wars" (Rosen et al., 1992). "I'm a girl who just can't say no. I insist on dessert," proclaims a woman in an ad for Jell-O sugar-free gelatin (Figure 20.12). However, the dessert she can say "yes" to is colored, artificially sweetened gelatin and water, hardly the rich and delicious "goodies" that men get to indulge in. Also, she is very thin, so clearly she has nothing to fear; she is one of the "elect" (in the Calvinist

FIGURE 20.10. Alba Fit 'n Frosty shakes, July 1989.

sense). Imagine how different the ad would be if the model were even slightly "overweight"—or if it mentioned the difficulty many women have saying no to anything but food.

Guilt is another major theme in the diet ads. "Indulge without guilt," "Pizza without guilt," they tell us. Weight Watchers ads feature extreme closeups of rich foods and the slogan "Total indulgence. Zero guilt." What women are especially shamed for these days is eating. If a woman says she has been "bad," we assume that she broke her diet. The *menage à trois* a woman is made to feel guilty about is the one with Ben and Jerry (of ice cream fame). A 1989 study at Lafayette College (Basow & Kobrynowicz, 1990) found that both men and women judged women as more feminine and more likable when they ate less. The double standard for men and women is reflected in an ad for a low-fat pizza: "He eats a brownie . . . you eat a rice cake. He eats a juicy burger . . . you eat a low-fat entree. He eats pizza . . . **you** eat pizza. **Finally**, life is fair."

Sometimes the food itself is offered as a drug. "Enter the state of Häagen-Dazs" was once the slogan for this popular ice cream. Today the message is even more overt. A recent campaign features copy such as this:

FIGURE 20.11. Land O Lakes Country Morning Blend margarine, January 1989.

> Maybe I'm a bit of a perfectionist. My CD's are in alphabetical order. I can always find my keys. Yet everytime I have Häagen-Dazs I seem to lose control. Today it was Chocolate ice cream. I lost myself completely. Each creamy spoonful was a moment suspended in time. I would have stopped before I finished the whole pint. Only problem was, I couldn't find the lid.

Another ad in the same campaign says:

> I pride myself on my level-headed approach to life. I never stay in the sun too long. But all it takes is one smooth taste of Häagen-Dazs Strawberry ice cream and I find myself letting go. I savor every plump strawberry. I indulge myself in its creamy richness. I must do something about this Häagen-Dazs passion. Maybe I could organize it, structure it or control it . . . tomorrow.

The campaign slogan is "Tääste [*sic*] the Passion." What an invitation to binge this is—and what a message to someone who feels too controlled in her life, with too few avenues to real passion.

Food is also sometimes advertised as a way to alter one's mood, especially as a way to deal with disappointment with men. A Frusen

FIGURE 20.12. Jell-O sugarfree gelatin dessert, July 1989.

Glädjé ice cream ad features a beautiful young woman walking a dog and the copy, "He never called. So, Ben and I went out for a walk to pick up a pint of Frusen Glädjé. Ben's better looking anyway." The slogan for the product is *"It feels so good."*

THE MARKETING OF ADDICTIONS

In general, female adolescents take fewer drugs and take drugs less often than do males. The two exceptions are cigarettes and amphetamines, both of which are used by females to control their weight. Four percent more female than male adolescents smoke cigarettes and 10% more females than males take amphetamines (Bodinger-Deuriarte, 1991).

Cigarettes are directly marketed to women and girls as a way to control their weight. In 1928 Lucky Strike ads said, "To keep a slender figure, no one can deny . . . Reach for a Lucky instead of a sweet." Today advertisers use extremely thin models and copy that includes such words as "slim" and "slender." The Virginia Slims "Superslims" cigarette promises the smoker "more than just a sleek shape." Capri cigarettes use the slogan "The slimmest slim in town."

A 1991 ad for Michelob Light beer (Figure 20.13) that ran in many women's magazines also exploited anxiety about body image. The usual exhortations of the women's magazines—"Lose fat while you shop" and "Blast jiggly hips and thighs"—were juxtaposed with the message "Relax. You're OK. Improve your beer."

SOLUTIONS

What can we do? We must speak out forcefully about the dangers of the obsession with thinness. This is not a trivial issue; it cuts to the very heart of women's energy, power, and self-esteem. This is a major public health problem, one that endangers the lives of young girls and women. We can learn a great deal from the public policy advocates who have been battling the alcohol and nicotine industries for the past several years, with some striking success.

FIGURE 20.13. Michelob Light beer, 1991.

These activists have become very knowledgeable about media advocacy. They have used creative epidemiology to capture the attention of the media. For example, when Perrier withdrew its product from the shelves because some of it was tainted with benzene, the antismoking activists pointed out that it would take 33 bottles of tainted Perrier to equal the benzene in just one pack of cigarettes (Will, 1990). They held a press conference with the 33 bottles of Perrier lined up behind them. We need to be equally creative in dramatizing the damage that the obsession with thinness is doing to women and girls.

The norms for cigarette smoking have changed dramatically in the past 20 years. This is a result of many things, including warning labels on the packs, advertising restrictions, product liability suits, and increased health information. We can change the norms about dieting and thinness with many of the same measures.

There could and should be some restrictions on the advertising of diet programs and products, and on ads aimed at women's eating in general (not to mention a complete ban on ads for cigarettes). Again, we could learn from activists in the alcohol and nicotine fields. There has been a great deal of publicity in recent years about alcohol and cigarette campaigns that have targeted African-Americans (e.g. Uptown cigarettes and Powermaster malt liquor) and children (e.g., the current Camel campaign that features a cartoon camel). There should be similar widespread publicity about the diet ads and the ads featuring risky attitudes about eating. Individuals, as well as health and women's organizations, could protest ads for diet products and ads that feature very thin models. Perhaps there could be health warnings on the ads. We could also boycott these products.

Former U.S. Surgeons General Antonia Novello and C. Everett Koop have spoken out about alcohol and nicotine advertising. They have also spoken out about violence against women as a public health issue. We should encourage the current Surgeon General to become involved with the issue of thinness and eating disorders.

Congressional hearings on this issue were held in March and May 1990 by the House Committee on Small Business, Subcommittee on Regulation, Business Opportunity and Energy. The hearings included testimony from diet providers and medical experts. In 1992, the subcommittee concluded that the diet industry requires control, since dieting has been shown to have short-term positive effects but long-term failure.

A National Institutes of Health Technology Assessment Conference on Methods for Voluntary Weight Loss and Control was held in March 1992. The conference panel concluded that trying to achieve the ideal of thinness presented in the media is not an appropriate goal for most people; that weight loss strategies cause harm and do not work; and that many Americans who are not overweight are trying to lose weight, with significant psychological and physical health consequences (Berg, 1992). We should demand that Congress, the Federal Trade Commission, and the Food and Drug Administration take an active role in further investigating and regulating diet programs and products.

A growing number of women are joining an antidiet movement. According to *The New York Times,* "They are forming support groups and ceasing to diet with a resolve similar to that of secretaries who 20 years ago stopped getting coffee for their bosses" (O'Neill, 1992, p. 1). This movement focuses on wellness, not weight loss; it emphasizes feeling good about oneself, eating well in a natural and relaxed way, and being comfortably active. It is gaining momentum throughout North America (Berg, 1992).

The advertisers will never voluntarily change, because it is profitable for women to feel terrible about themselves. Thus, we need to educate everyone to be critical viewers of advertising and the mass media. This education should begin in kindergarten. Of course, we must also work in every way possible to eliminate gender bias in our society and to encourage women and girls who have been conditioned to feel powerless to develop authentic routes to power. As Simone de Beauvoir said, "It is in great part the anxiety of being a woman that devastates the feminine body."

REFERENCES

American Association of University Women. (AAUW). (1992). *How schools shortchange girls.* Washington, DC: AAUW Educational Foundation and National Education Association.

American Family Practitioner. (1988, October), 269–270.

Basow, S. A., & Kobrynowicz, D. (1990). *What is she eating? The effects of meal size on impressions of a female eater.* Paper presented at the annual meeting of the American Psychological Association, August 10–14, Boston.

Bennett, W., & Gurin, J. (1982). *The dieter's dilemma: Eating less and weighing more.* New York: Basic Books.

Berg, F. (1992, September–October). Nondiet movement gains strength. *Obesity and Health,* pp. 85–90.

Black, C. (1990, April 21). Diet fad fattens firms. *Boston Globe,* p. 1.

Bodinger-Deuriarte, C. (1991, September). Female adolescents use fewer drugs. *Western Center News* (Western Regional Center for Drug-Free Schools and Communities), 1.

Chernin, K. (1981). *The obsession: Reflections on the tyranny of slenderness.* New York: Harper & Row.

Chernin, K. (1985). *The hungry self: Daughters and mothers, eating and identity.* New York: Times Books.

Crandall, C. S. (1988). Social contagion of binge eating. *Journal of Personality and Social Psychology, 55*(4), 588–598.

Drug Abuse Update. (1991, Spring). Diet pills under scrutiny by Congress. pp. 10–11.

Ewen, S. (1976). *Captains of consciousness: Advertising and the social roots of the consumer culture.* New York: McGraw-Hill.

Faludi, S. (1991). *Backlash: The undeclared war against American women.* New York: Crown.

Freedman, R. (1986). *Beauty bound.* Lexington, MA: D.C. Heath.

Garner, D.M., & Garfinkel, P.E. (1980). Sociocultural factors in the development of anorexia nervosa. *Psychological Medicine, 10,* 647–656.

Gilbert, S. (1985, April). Eating disorders: The high price of independence and success. *Radcliffe College Second Century,* 14.

Gordon, R. (1990). *Anorexia and bulimia: Anatomy of a social epidemic.* Cambridge, MA: Basil Blackwell.

Greene, G. (1992, February 10). The empire strikes back. *The Nation,* pp. 166–170.

Hersh, A. (1993, June 18–24). Women, minorities still lagging in film and TV roles. *Back Stage: The Performing Arts Weekly,* pp. 1, 28.

House Committee on Small Business, Subcommittee on Regulation, Business Opportunities, and Energy. (1990). Congressional hearings chaired by Ron Wyden (Oregon), March 26, May 7, September 24, 1990.

Johnson, C. L., & Connors, M. (1987). *The etiology and treatment of bulimia nervosa.* New York: Basic Books.

Kilbourne, J. (1977). Images of women in TV commercials. In J. Fireman (Ed.), *TV book* (pp. 293–296). New York: Workman.

Kilbourne, J. (1986). The child as sex object: Images of children in the media. In M. Nelson & K. Clark (Eds.), *The educator's guide to preventing child sexual abuse* (pp. 40–46). Santa Cruz, CA: Network.

Meadow, R., & Weiss, L. (1992). *Women's conflicts about eating and sexuality.* Binghamton, NY: Harrington Park Press.

O'Neill, M. (1992, April 12). A growing movement fights diets instead of fat. *The New York Times,* pp. 1, 43.

Pollitt, K. (1982, May). The politically correct body. *Mother Jones,* p. 66.

Richins, M. L. (1991). Social comparison and the idealized images of advertising. *Journal of Consumer Research, 18,* 71–83.

Rosen, J. C., & Gross, J. (1987). Prevalence of weight reducing and weight gaining in adolescent girls and boys. *Health Psychology, 26,* 131–147.

Rosen, M., Gold, T., Stambler, L., McFarland, S., & Huzinec, M. (1992, January, 13). Hollywood takes it off. *People,* pp. 72–82.

Sims, S. (1986, May). Diet madness. *Vogue,* p. 73.

Snider, M. (1990, October 30). Diet drug ban just a start. *USA Today,* p. 1A.

Stein, J. (1986, October 29). Why girls as young as 9 fear fat and go on diets to lose weight. *Los Angeles Times,* pp. 1, 10.

Steiner-Adair, C. (1986). The body politic: Normal female adolescent development and the development of eating disorders. *Journal of the American Academy of Psychoanalysis, 14*(1), 95–114.

Surrey, J. (1984). *Eating patterns as a reflection of women's development* (No. 83-06). Wellesley, MA: Stone Center, Wellesley College.

Will, G. (1990, February 25). Tobacco's targets. *The Washington Post*, p. B7.

Williamson, J. (1978). *Decoding advertisements: Ideology and meaning in advertising.* London: Marion Boyars.

Wolf, N. (1991). *The beauty myth: How images of beauty are used against women.* New York: Morrow.

21

Toward a New Model for the Prevention of Eating Disorders

CATHERINE M. SHISSLAK
MARJORIE CRAGO

THE DEVELOPMENT OF ANY PREVENTION PROGRAM requires an understanding of the etiology of the targeted disorder. In the case of eating disorders, three general causes have been posited: individual (psychological and physiological), familial, and sociocultural (Garfinkel & Garner, 1982; Striegel-Moore, Silberstein, & Rodin, 1986). Some feminists maintain that focusing on the individual's psychological and physiological deficits as the cause of eating disorders, in effect, blames the victim and obscures the sociocultural origins of these disorders (Orbach, 1978; Szekely, 1988). Those who favor the sociocultural point of view, as we do, argue that this is the only model that can adequately explain the recent dramatic increase in eating disorders, since there is no evidence to suggest that mothering has become more inadequate, families more enmeshed, or biological and genetic factors more conducive to eating disorders in the past 25 years than previously (Brumberg, 1988; Schwartz, Thompson, & Johnson, 1982). There is, on the other hand, compelling evidence for the sociocultural hypothesis. For example, cross-cultural research suggests that eating disorders are culture-bound, since they are prevalent in Western cultures but virtually nonexistent in other cultures until they begin to adopt Western values and norms (McCarthy, 1990; Prince, 1985). Viewed from a cross-cultural perspective, eating disorders are simply extensions of normative and culturally acceptable modes of behavior (Nasser, 1988).

According to the sociocultural hypothesis, two major social pressures put women at increased risk for eating disorders. One is the emphasis on thinness as a requirement for attractiveness, and the other is the conflict between traditional and nontraditional roles. Women of today strive not only to be good wives and mothers, but to be successful in education and their careers. Although all women experience these social pressures to a greater or lesser degree, not all develop eating disorders. It has been proposed that women most likely to develop these disorders are those who have most deeply internalized and overadapted to the sociocultural mores for women (Mazur, 1986; Striegel-Moore et al., 1986). As Szekely (1988) and Striegel-Moore and her colleagues (1986) have emphasized, both the thinness and success ideals for women are unrealistic, since most women are unable to attain them. The attempt to achieve them can have detrimental effects on women's physical and mental health.

INEQUALITY AND EATING DISORDERS

Some feminists have suggested that eating disorders are a response to the unequal status of women in our society (e.g., Freedman, 1986; Orbach, 1978; Szekely, 1988; Wolf, 1991). Carmen, Russo, and Miller (1981) hold that women's unequal status contributes not just to eating disorders, but to other predominantly female disorders such as depression and phobias. They contend that any program to prevent mental disorders in women must have as a goal the eradication of sexism. If sexism is indeed the root cause of eating disorders, then preventive efforts must be aimed at social as well as individual change. It will not be easy, however, to change social institutions and attitudes that have been built up over thousands of years. Because the dominant group does not give up its power easily, Miller (1983) sees conflict as inevitable. There are indications that we are now in the midst of a violent backlash against the advances made by the women's movement over the past 25 years (Faludi, 1991; French, 1992; Wolf, 1991).

In developing prevention programs for eating disorders, we need to recognize that our current social order may have a vested interest in *promoting* rather than *preventing* these disorders. Wolf (1991), for example, maintains that the current emphasis on thinness is a "direct solution" to the dangers posed by the women's movement. Chronic dieting leads to passivity, anxiety, emotionality, and low self-esteem; these, Wolf (1991) contends, are traits that the dominant culture wants to create in women in order to cancel out opposite traits that the women's movement has begun to instill—traits such as courage, self-esteem, and a sense of effectiveness. The social changes required to prevent eating disorders are the same ones that feminists have sought for several decades—namely, changes that will promote the emotional, sexual, and economic freedom of women. It is important that women initiate and support legislation for equal pay, child care programs, reproductive freedom, and deterrents to sexual violence. These changes will be resisted, since, as Wolf (1991) argues, Western economies are dependent on the continued underpayment of women, and sexual crimes against individual women are intended to keep all women intimidated and submissive. Nevertheless, without social changes such as these, it may be impossible to prevent eating disorders and other mental and physical problems of women (Carmen et al., 1981).

DEVELOPING A FEMINIST EATING DISORDER PREVENTION PROGRAM

Challenging the Beauty Myth

If the beauty myth is indeed one of the most important factors in the recent increase in eating disorders, as various feminists have proposed, then changing current beauty standards is imperative. How can these standards be changed? One way is social action to improve the status of women, since an economically, emotionally, and sexually independent woman is less likely to rely on appearance as her primary source of power (Freedman, 1986). Women's success in school, work, and relationships is much more dependent on appearance than is men's (Striegel-Moore et al., 1986). According to Freedman (1986) and Wolf (1991), "looksism" controls women by keeping them so busy they do not have the time to fight discrimination against women.

Some benefits of challenging the beauty myth are (1) freedom from chronic appearance anxiety; (2) increased physical comfort and health; (3) gains in time, energy, and money; and (4) an increased sense of authenticity (Freedman, 1986). A feminist program for preventing eating disorders should explore ways in which current clothing and cosmetic fashions are psychologically restrictive or physically unhealthy. Because of the power of the mass media in promoting the beauty myth, prevention programs for eating disorders should include a segment on the images of women presented by the media and the effect of these images on women's physical and mental health.

Since most eating-disordered women have a negative body image, this is an area that needs to be targeted in preventive efforts. A number of techniques and exercises have been developed for the enhancement of body image in women (e.g., Freedman, 1990; Hutchinson, 1985; Miller,

1991; Weiss, Katzman, & Wolchik, 1985). Some of these, such as positive affirmations, imagery, mirror work, drawing or sculpting one's body, moving to music, and group feedback to help correct body image distortions, could be used to help women accept and live more comfortably in their bodies.

Sex Role Conflicts

Role destabilization resulting from the conflict between traditional and nontraditional female roles is another sociocultural factor that has been blamed for the recent increase in eating disorders. Some of the new freedoms for women won by the feminist movement evoke fear and anxiety, since there is inadequate support for women in nontraditional roles. Women who struggle to be successful in their work are paid less than men, are blocked from reaching higher-level positions, and are still expected to do most of the housework and child care. Because their success depends to a great extent on how they look, they are forced to spend much of their meager pay on their appearance (Freedman, 1986; Wolf, 1991).

For adolescent girls, there is often a conflict between achievement and popularity with boys, which many girls resolve by becoming underachievers (Conarton & Silverman, 1988; Gilligan, Ward, Taylor, & Bardige, 1988; Lawrence, 1984). Young women are often forced to choose between success in education and work or success in relationships. If they try to do both, they are faced with a dilemma, since each choice means denying many of their physical and interpersonal needs. If sex role conflicts are a primary cause of eating disorders, then minimizing such conflicts should be part of eating disorder prevention programs. How can the effects of these conflicts be lessened? The first step is to increase awareness of them.

Young girls must be taught to examine role prescriptions, and evaluate the possible negative consequences of trying to live up to them, critically. They must be helped to see that the perfect or ideal woman that they measure themselves against exists only on television or in the movies. The ways in which these images are harmful could be explored in discussion groups, beginning in junior high school or even earlier. Some of these groups could be facilitated by a range of older peer role models, in an attempt to bridge the gap between older and younger women created by the image of the ideal woman as young, thin, and beautiful.

Young-Eisendrath and Wiedemann (1987) and Murdock (1990) recommend greater androgyny or flexibility in sex roles, and believe that women should be encouraged to choose for themselves the mode of behavior—whether traditionally feminine or masculine—that is most authentic for them. This approach could be incorporated into eating disorder prevention programs by helping women explore ways of behaving in particular situations. On a broader social level, we need to modify socialization processes for women that emphasize ignoring personal needs and serving others, especially males. We must also undo the notion that women have to sacrifice relationships to pursue their own development through higher education or careers.

Empowering Women

The effects of the beauty myth and role destabilization can be ameliorated by helping women to acknowledge, accept, and feel comfortable with their power. Why are women so uncomfortable with or even fearful of their power? One reason is that any use of their power is likely to result in a negative reaction from men (Faludi, 1991; Miller, 1986; Wolf, 1991). Another reason is that women have been programmed to care for others and to believe that acting for themselves will deprive or hurt others (Miller, 1986). What can be done to empower women, and thereby perhaps to prevent some of these problems? One way is to help them come to see other women as allies rather than as competitors (Freedman, 1986; Szekely, 1988; Wolf, 1991).

According to Wolf (1991), only solidarity among women will give them what beauty promises—a sense of power, significance, and self-worth. Women need to develop the courage to speak in their own voice, a voice different from the male-dominant one of our culture (Gilligan, 1982). It is easier to do this when women support one another rather than give in to the patriarchal divide-and-conquer strategy, which makes them easier to manipulate and control. As Wolf (1991) and other feminists have pointed out, since women are not a minority group but comprise more than half of the human population, they could not have been dominated for so long without colluding in their own oppression. By working together, women not only empower themselves but have a better chance of affecting social change. And social action in itself is empowering.

A feminist prevention program for eating disorders could help to build solidarity among women in consciousness-raising or support groups, modeled on those developed in the 1960s and 1970s, in which young women could share the difficulties of growing up female. Developing a strong sense of female identity and power requires a lifetime of consciousness building. This process could be initiated and strengthened in schools through prevention programs for eating disorders based on some of the feminist principles discussed here. We have some preliminary data from one of our research projects involving the assessment of eating habits in girls from junior high school to senior year that support this premise (Shisslak & Nichter, 1992). In a recent interview with senior high school girls who participated in the project for 4 years, they unanimously reported the following:

1. Having the opportunity to meet together over this period of time and examine their behaviors and attitudes resulted in their being less accepting of a stereotypic body image for women. They felt more accepting of their less-than-perfect bodies and more interested in developing their inner selves.
2. They felt empowered by the fact that they could discuss these issues with other girls without having boys present.
3. They felt strongly that senior girls should be available to younger teens to be role models for healthy behavior.

This particular project was designed to monitor, not intervene in, eating behavior. The fact that these girls reported such a positive impact encourages the next stage of the research, which involves integrating these findings into a prevention program.

Women's Rituals and Spirituality

To help women reaffirm their feminine nature and bond with other women, many feminists have emphasized the importance of women's rituals and spirituality (e.g., Bolen, 1984; Murdock, 1990; Spretnak, 1981; Wolf, 1991). Chernin (1985, 1987) maintains that women need to develop rituals for themselves, in which they simultaneously leave behind the traditional roles in which their mothers were trapped and rediscover the sacredness and value of being female. To do this, Chernin contends, they may need to postulate the existence of the Divine Mother as a spiritual role model for women. Stone (1976) suggests that the suppression of women's *rites* has resulted in the suppression of women's *rights*. In a similar vein, Christ (1986) proposes that women's spiritual quest can provide the foundation for their social quest for equality, respect, and freedom. She sees the spiritual quest of women as integrally related to the telling of women's stories, because if women's stories are not told, the depth of women's souls will not be known. Christ and others who have written about women's spirituality emphasize the importance of forming support groups where women can share their stories and perhaps, in the process, can create new ways of living and an identity for women based on women's visions rather than men's images and myths.

SPECIAL SUBGROUPS

Eating disorders are more prevalent in groups that place great importance on low body weight and/or physical attractiveness, such as dancers, models, actresses, athletes, and gay men (Shisslak & Crago, 1992b; Striegel-Moore et al., 1986). There are also other subgroups, such as lesbians, in which eating disorders are thought to be lower (Brown, 1987). Since many lesbians reject patriarchal beauty standards and traditional sex roles for women, two of the most important sociocultural factors in the etiology of eating disorders, it has been hypothesized that they would be less likely to develop eating disorders. However, few empirical data are available on eating disorder rates among lesbians.

Bradford and Ryan (1987) conducted a national survey of lesbians and found that they were three times more likely to be binge eaters than dieters. In one of the few studies that has actually compared eating disorders in lesbians versus heterosexual women, Striegel-Moore, Tucker, and Hsu (1990) found no significant differences in eating disorder symptoms and body esteem in the two groups. They attributed this lack of difference between the groups, in part, to the relatively young age of their samples (mean age = 20); they speculated that older lesbians—many of whom were involved in the women's movement of the 1960s and 1970s—might be more self-accepting and therefore less likely to develop eating disorders. Another possible factor proposed by Striegel-Moore and her colleagues to explain the absence of a protective factor against eating disorders in the lesbian group was that the lesbian ideology was not strong enough to overcome the internalized cultural values.

Two other studies comparing lesbians and heterosexual women found that both groups were influenced by cultural pressures to be thin, but that lesbians tended to be more satisfied with their bodies and desired a somewhat higher ideal weight (Brand, Rothblum, & Solomon, 1992; Herzog, Newman, Yeh, & Warshaw, 1992). The results of these few studies suggest that lesbianism may provide some protection against eating disorders; lesbians do appear to be influenced by patriarchal beauty standards, but to a lesser extent than heterosexual women.

Another subgroup hypothesized to be protected against eating disorders is that of women with nontraditional sex role attitudes. A number of research studies have been conducted to investigate whether eating-disordered women are more or less likely to accept the traditional feminine role, but these studies have produced inconsistent findings (Striegel-Moore et al., 1986; Timko, Striegel-Moore, Silberstein, & Rodin, 1987). It is not possible to conclude on the basis of current research that women who endorse nontraditional sex role attitudes are less likely to develop eating disorders. One of the reasons for inconsistent findings in this area

may be that there are several types of women who endorse nontraditional sex role attitudes: those who reject the traditional passive/dependent
feminine role and who may be less likely to develop an eating disorder;
and those who are trying to fulfill aspects of both the feminine and
masculine sex roles (i.e., to be "superwomen") and who may be more,
rather than less, likely to develop an eating disorder. Obviously, including these two types of women in the same group cancels out the effects of
sex role attitudes on the development of eating disorders.

THE NEED FOR EATING DISORDER PREVENTION PROGRAMS

Prevention programs for eating disorders are still in the beginning stages.
Until a few years ago there were no prevention programs for these
disorders, although the need for such programs has been emphasized by
eating disorder theorists, researchers, and clinicians since the early 1980s
(American College of Physicians, 1986; Button & Whitehouse, 1981;
Crisp, 1979, 1988; McSherry, 1983; Piran, Hill, & Maine, 1992; Pratt,
1983; Shisslak, Crago, Neal, & Swain, 1987; Steiger, Leichner, &
Ghaadiria, 1987). Some of the reasons for this increased emphasis are the
dramatic increase in eating disorders over the past several decades
(Mitchell & Eckert, 1987), serious health consequences as eating disorders progress (Herzog & Copeland, 1985), low recovery rates (Keller,
Herzog, Lavori, Bradburn, & Mahoney, 1992), and higher mortality
rates than in any other psychiatric disorder (Herzog, Keller, & Lavori,
1988).

Whether eating disorders can actually be prevented has been a subject of controversy. Vandereycken and Meermann (1984), for example,
contend that we do not have sufficient knowledge of the etiology of these
disorders to develop prevention programs for them. They also question
whether it is possible to modify sociocultural factors such as the emphasis on thinness in women. Katz (1985) and Yager (1985), on the other
hand, consider sociocultural factors to be an important area to target in
preventive efforts.

Most suggestions for the prevention of eating disorders have emphasized the need for prevention programs in schools, beginning in
elementary school and extending through college (e.g., Clark, Levine, &
Kinney, 1989; Hotelling, 1989; Levine, 1987; Pratt, 1983; Shisslak et al.,
1987). Specific recommendations by these and other investigators include classes on eating disorders; workshops for at-risk groups such as
dance students, athletes, cheerleaders, and sorority women; in-service
training for residence hall personnel, teachers, coaches, and counselors;

groups for stress reduction and self-esteem enhancement; and changes in campus food services that will enable students to make healthier food choices. Community outreach programs, education of parents, and pressuring the mass media to stop promoting excessive thinness have also been suggested.

Chitty (1991) has outlined the role that nurses can play in preventing eating disorders by providing information about nutrition and normal eating patterns to parents, children, day care workers, and others. The importance of the child's early feeding relationship and the effect of this relationship on the development of eating disorders has been stressed by Bruch (1978) and Orbach (1978). The foundation for the development of an eating disorder is established before eating-disordered behaviors actually begin. Weight and body image concerns begin between the ages of 7 and 9 for girls in this country (Thelen, Powell, Lawrence, & Kuhnert, 1992).

EATING DISORDER PREVENTION PROGRAMS IN SCHOOLS

The most frequent suggestion for the prevention of eating disorders is to educate students about these disorders by developing eating disorder curricula to be used in schools. In response to this suggestion, several curricula have been developed and are currently in use. The National Eating Disorder Information Center (Kennedy, 1990) has developed a prevention resource kit for educators to use with children aged 9 through 12, and are developing a similar kit for high school use. The Center for the Study of Anorexia and Bulimia (1983) has published a curriculum guide for use in grades 7 through 12. This guide can be used by teachers to develop lesson plans covering all or some of the topics that are presented, such as the emotional uses of food and a sociocultural perspective on the relationship between body weight and beauty in women. The guide also includes questions for discussion and activities to facilitate the teaching of these topics.

Levine and Hill (1991) have published a 5-day lesson plan on eating disorders for grades 7 through 12, which emphasizes psychosocial rather than individual factors in the development of eating disorders. Some of the goals of their curriculum are (1) to heighten awareness of the processes by which thinness is idealized in our society and body fat is abhorred; (2) to provide students with information about fatness, such as the genetic determinants of body weight and set point theory; (3) to encourage respect for individual differences in body shape and weight; (4) to point out the negative consequences of dieting; (5) to describe the warning signs of eating disorders; and (6) to suggest ways in which eating disorders can be prevented, such as resisting media influences that encourage dissatisfaction with one's body shape or weight.

There have been, to our knowledge, only three studies in which the effectiveness of an eating disorder curriculum was evaluated. Moriarty, Shore, and Maxim (1990) evaluated a curriculum developed by Carney and Veilleux (1986), which included 16 lesson plans grouped into four sections: diet and eating disorders, male concerns with eating disorders, the sociocultural risk factors for eating disorders, and ways to forestall these sociocultural influences. The curriculum was evaluated by students and teachers in eight elementary and six Canadian high schools. The results of pre- and posttesting indicated that the students who received the curriculum showed a significant increase in knowledge about eating disorders and, according to Moriarty et al. (1990), had a more positive attitude toward eating disorders than students who were not exposed to the curriculum. The latter group showed a significant decrease in knowledge and a worsening of attitudes from pre- to posttesting. A qualitative evaluation of the curriculum indicated that teachers and students found the classes interesting, informative, and fun. A follow-up evaluation is planned.

We have designed and evaluated an eating disorder curriculum (Shisslak, Crago, & Neal, 1990). The curriculum was included in a high school health education class that met for 9 weeks. Fifty sophomore students attended. The topics covered included the symptoms, psychological and family characteristics, medical complications, and risk factors associated with eating disorders. The types of treatment available in the community were also discussed. In addition to the curriculum for students, presentations on eating disorders were made to faculty and staff members. A consultation component was included in the program. An eating disorder specialist was available for consultation with faculty, staff, and students for approximately 2 hours each week during the 9-week program. Four students initiated consultations, and two others were referred by parents or teachers. At the end of the 9-week period, a short questionnaire was administered to the students who had received the curriculum and to a control group. Analysis of the responses of both groups showed that those who had received the curriculum were significantly more knowledgeable about eating disorders than the control group of students.

The only long-term, controlled study evaluating the effectiveness of an eating disorder prevention curriculum was conducted by Killen and his associates (1993). A total of 995 sixth- and seventh-grade girls in four California middle schools were randomly assigned to receive either the prevention curriculum or no-treatment control classes. The curriculum consisted of 18 lessons divided into three principal components: (1) instruction on the harmful effects of unhealthy weight regulation; (2) promotion of healthy weight regulation through sound dietary principles and regular aerobic exercise; and (3) development of coping skills to resist sociocultural influences promoting thinness and dieting in women. The evaluation consisted of measures administered before the curriculum was begun and at four intervals during the 2 years following completion. The evaluation included self-report measures, anthropometric measures, and structured clinical interviews. Analysis of the results focused on changes in the scores of the intervention versus control groups and on changes in the scores of students who, during the pretesting phase, were determined to be at risk for the development of eating disorders.

Analysis of the results showed a significant increase in knowledge about eating disorders in the intervention group, but there were no significant differences between the intervention and control groups in eating attitudes, weight regulation practices, and body mass index (BMI) during the initial follow-up evaluation. Students from the intervention group who had been classified as high-risk also showed a significant gain in knowledge compared to high-risk girls in the control group. However, there were no significant differences at follow-up between the two high-risk groups in eating attitudes and weight regulation practices, and only a slight but statistically significant difference in BMI. Both groups showed increases in BMI from baseline to the first follow-up evaluation at 18 weeks, but the increase was somewhat less in the intervention group. Subsequent follow-up evaluations showed no significant differences between the intervention and control groups on any of the variables measured.

On the basis of these findings, Killen et al. (1993) concluded that the preventive intervention failed to achieve its hoped-for objectives. They attributed this failure, in part, to the relative stability of weight concerns and disordered eating behaviors in both the intervention and control groups during the 2-year follow-up period. They suggested that it might be more cost-effective to target only high-risk students for prevention efforts, or, alternatively, to imbed a more intensive intervention aimed at high-risk students within a curriculum providing information appropriate for all students. It was also possible that the full effect of the intervention might not be evidenced for another year or two. In addition, we wonder whether the "one-shot" intervention approach, as opposed to yearly interventions throughout junior high and high school, might not have decreased the effectiveness of the intervention.

There are only two published reports of eating disorder prevention programs implemented at the college level. One program for college students utilized peer educators to provide workshops on eating disorders to the campus community and individual informational sessions for students with concerns about eating disorders (Sesan, 1989a). The other was a three-level intervention program for female college athletes (Sesan, 1989b). The first level of intervention involved the education of athletic coaches about eating disorders; the second level consisted of an effort to assess and identify female athletes at risk for developing eating disorders and to provide them with referrals for individual or group counseling, nutrition education, or peer counseling on eating disorders; the third level consisted of workshops for athletic teams. There has been, to date, no published report on the effectiveness of either of these programs.

There are a number of similarities in the eating disorder curricula that have been reviewed here. For example, most of the curricula emphasize the dangers of dieting and the effects of oppressive beauty standards for women that encourage unhealthy weight regulation practices. However, none of the curricula stress the importance of conflicting role expectations for women, which Steiner-Adair (1989), Timko et al. (1987), and others have found to be an important factor in the development of eating disorders. Perhaps this is because this factor has more recently emerged and has been subjected to fewer research investigations, or perhaps because it reflects a feminist viewpoint.

POLITICS AND PREVENTION

There are a number of obstacles to undoing sexism and preventing eating disorders. Perhaps the most powerful are the political and economic structures that depend on cheap female labor and require passive and submissive women (Wolf, 1991). Both Wolf (1991) and Faludi (1991) have argued that the patriarchal power structure is threatened by advances of the women's movement and is engaged in a war to regain some power that its representatives feel has been lost.

Feminist fashion reformers are likely to meet resistance from both men and women. As Freedman (1986) has pointed out, women may cling to the beauty myth because they have much to gain—the pleasure of flattery, the security of a familiar image, a way to achieve without fear of success, the power of attracting and influencing others, and a rationalization for failure. Although beauty increases women's status, it also maintains women's subordination, which is why beauty reform has always been important in the feminist agenda (Freedman, 1986).

Trying to promote more flexibility or androgyny in sex roles is likely to evoke opposition from men, and from some women as well. Androgyny threatens men because they lose status if they adopt feminine traits or if women adopt masculine traits and begin to use power more directly. Women, on the other hand, are hesitant to adopt what have been considered masculine traits because they fear negative reactions from men.

Another major obstacle to prevention programs is the question of cost-effectiveness. Since eating disorders have a relatively low prevalence rate, it may not be cost-effective to intervene with all the students in a school, since only a few may be likely to develop an eating disorder. It would be more cost-effective to apply the most expensive program components only to those who are at high risk for developing these disorders, as has been done in school-based programs for cardiovascular risk reduction (Killen et al., 1988) and prevention of antisocial behaviors (Loeber, 1990).

A further obstacle is fear that a public education program may actually promote rather than prevent eating disorders. A number of women have reported learning their unhealthy weight control techniques from books, magazine articles, films, and television programs about eating disorders (e.g., Chiodo & Latimer, 1983; Murray, Touyz, & Beumont, 1990). This is an area of concern that needs to be addressed. Grodner (1991) contends that for an eating disorder program to be effective, it must help the participants realistically assess the benefits of reducing or eliminating eating-disordered behaviors in relation to the perceived benefits of continuing. For many participants, the perceived benefits create insurmountable barriers to behavioral change unless these barriers are demystified. Grodner (1991) has also pointed out that eating disorder prevention is different from traditional disease prevention. If an eating disorder prevention program fails and the targeted individuals "contract the disease," they may perceive these behaviors as having positive benefits, such as relief from sociocultural pressures to be thin. However, if a flu vaccination campaign is unsuccessful and the targeted individuals become ill, they are not likely to derive benefits from the illness.

Yet another obstacle to the development of prevention programs is that preventive efforts may threaten such specific economic interests (Albee, 1982) as the multibillion-dollar fashion, cosmetic, diet, and fitness industries (e.g., Freedman, 1986; Smead, 1985; Wolf, 1991). Fortunately, there are indications that women may be rebelling against the dictates of these industries. For example, there is a growing antidieting movement, which may help to alleviate some of the pressure women have felt to be so thin (e.g., Polivy & Herman, 1983, 1992). Women are also rebelling against the return of the "baby-doll" or "high-femininity" look with its miniskirts, flounces, and frills, which fashion designers have been trying to promote since 1987 (Faludi, 1991). Many working women do not want to adopt a look that emphasizes vulnerability rather than competence. Women's resistance to attempts to pressure them into a particular "look" may provide a more receptive climate for prevention programs, most of which stress the negative effects of dieting and obsessive concern with appearance.

SUMMARY AND CONCLUSIONS

Several curricula aimed at the prevention of eating disorders have now been developed and implemented at the junior high and high school levels. However, none of these curricula have been systematically evaluated, except the curriculum developed by Killen et al. (1993). In a very thorough and controlled study, they found that the curriculum did not achieve its objectives, despite being well designed and presented to capture the students' attention. Piran et al. (1992) have stressed that to succeed, a prevention program must involve the students in the program, rather than merely present information about eating disorders.

The negative findings of Killen et al. (1993) need to be tempered by the fact that eating disorder prevention programs in schools are relatively new, compared to school-based prevention programs for substance abuse, which began in the late 1960s. The early substance abuse prevention programs were effective primarily in increasing knowledge about substance abuse, but had little effect on attitudes or behaviors (Shisslak & Crago, 1992a). These programs continued to evolve, however, and are currently achieving more positive results than were obtained in the earlier programs (Shisslak & Crago, 1992a). The evaluations of these programs have also become increasingly systematic, complex, and refined. The development of eating disorder prevention programs may follow a similar process. Therefore, the negative results of early attempts to prevent eating disorders should not discourage researchers from further efforts to develop prevention programs for these disorders. We believe that it is critical to provide long-term opportunities for girls and young women to examine and challenge the attitudes and behaviors that lead to eating disorders, and to develop healthy attitudes and behaviors; we further believe that this can be done most effectively through school-based programs. We are currently in the process of advancing these goals by empirically testing, through pilot studies in schools, the following issues: (1) longitudinal versus one-time intervention effectiveness; (2) peer group and peer-led interventions versus teacher/trainer instruction; and (3) use of naturally formed peer groups (focus groups) versus artificially formed groups.

REFERENCES

Albee, G. W. (1982). Preventing psychopathology and promoting human potential. *American Psychologist, 37,* 1043–1050.

American College of Physicians. (1986). Eating disorders: Anorexia nervosa and bulimia. *Annals of Internal Medicine, 105,* 790–794.

Bolen, J. S. (1984). *Goddesses in every woman.* San Francisco: Harper & Row.

Bradford, J., & Ryan, C. (1987). *The National Lesbian Health Care Survey.* Washington, DC: National Lesbian and Gay Health Foundation.

Brand, P. A., Rothblum, E. D., & Solomon, L. J. (1992). A comparison of lesbians, gay men, and heterosexuals on weight and restrained eating. *International Journal of Eating Disorders, 11,* 253–259.

Brown, L. S. (1987). Lesbians, weight and eating: New analyses and perspectives. In Boston Lesbian Psychologies Collective (Ed.), *Lesbian psychologies* (pp. 294–309). Urbana: University of Illinois Press.

Bruch, H. (1978). *The golden cage: The enigma of anorexia nervosa.* Cambridge, MA: Harvard University Press.

Brumberg, J. J. (1988). *Fasting girls: The emergence of anorexia nervosa as a modern disease.* Cambridge, MA: Harvard University Press.

Button, E. J., & Whitehouse, A. (1981). Subclinical anorexia nervosa. *Psychological Medicine, 11,* 509–516.

Carmen, E., Russo, N. F., & Miller, J. B. (1981). Inequality and women's mental health: An overview. *American Journal of Psychiatry, 138,* 1319–1330.

Carney, B., & Veilleux, M. (1986). *A preventive curriculum for anorexia nervosa and bulimia.* Windsor, Ontario: Bulimia Anorexia Nervosa Association—Canadian American.

Center for the Study of Anorexia and Bulimia. (1983). *Teaching about eating disorders: Grades 7–12.* New York: Author.

Chernin, K. (1985). *The hungry self: Women, eating, and identity.* New York: HarperCollins.

Chernin, K. (1987). *Reinventing Eve: Modern woman in search of herself.* New York: HarperCollins.

Chiodo, J., & Latimer, P. R. (1983). Vomiting as a learned weight-control technique in bulimia. *Journal of Behavior Therapy and Experimental Psychiatry, 14,* 131–135.

Chitty, K. K. (1991). The primary prevention role of the nurse in eating disorders. *Nursing Clinics of North America, 26,* 789–800.

Christ, C. (1986). *Diving deep and surfacing: Women writers on spiritual quest* (rev. ed.). Boston: Beacon Press.

Clark, L. V., Levine, M. P., & Kinney, N. E. (1989). A multifaceted and integrated approach to the prevention, identification, and treatment of bulimia on college campuses. In L. C. Whitaker & W. N. Davis (Eds.), *The bulimic college student: Evaluation, treatment and prevention* (pp. 257–298). New York: Haworth Press.

Conarton, S., & Silverman, L. K. (1988). Feminine development through the life cycle. In M. A. Dutton-Douglas & L. E. Walker (Eds.), *Feminist psychotherapies: Integration of therapeutic and feminist systems* (pp. 37–67). Norwood, NJ: Ablex.

Crisp, A.H. (1979). Early recognition and prevention of anorexia nervosa. *Developmental Medicine and Child Neurology, 21,* 393–395.

Crisp, A. H. (1988). Some possible approaches to prevention of eating and body weight shape disorders with particular reference to anorexia nervosa. *International Journal of Eating Disorders, 7,* 1–17.

Faludi, S. (1991). *Backlash: The undeclared war against American women.* New York: Crown.

Freedman, R. (1986). *Beauty bound.* Lexington, MA: Lexington Books.

Freedman, R. (1990). *Bodylove: Learning to like our looks and ourselves.* New York: HarperCollins.

French, M. (1992). *The war against women.* New York: Summit Books.

Garfinkel, P. E., & Garner, D. M. (1982). *Anorexia nervosa: A multidimensional perspective.* New York: Brunner/Mazel.

Gilligan, C. (1982). *In a different voice.* Cambridge, MA: Harvard University Press.

Gilligan, C., Ward, J. V., Taylor, J. M., & Bardige, B. (Eds.). (1988). *Mapping the moral domain.* Cambridge, MA: Harvard University Press.

Grodner, M. (1991). Using the Health Belief Model for bulimia prevention. *Journal of American College Health, 40,* 107–112.

Herzog, D. B., & Copeland, P. M. (1985). Eating disorders. *New England Journal of Medicine, 313,* 295–303.

Herzog, D. B., Keller, M. B., & Lavori, P. W. (1988). Outcome in anorexia nervosa and bulimia nervosa: A review of the literature. *Journal of Nervous and Mental Disease, 176,* 131–143.

Herzog, D. B., Newman, K. L., Yeh, C. J., & Warshaw, M. (1992). Body image satisfaction in homosexual and heterosexual women. *International Journal of Eating Disorders, 11,* 391–396.

Hotelling, K. (1989). A model for addressing the problem of bulimia on college campuses. In L. C. Whitaker & W. N. Davis (Eds.), *The bulimic college student: Evaluation, treatment and prevention* (pp. 241–256). New York: Haworth Press.

Hutchinson, M. G. (1985). *Transforming body image: Learning to love the body you have.* New York: Crossing Press.

Katz, J. L. (1985). Some reflections on the nature of eating disorders: On the need for humility. *International Journal of Eating Disorders, 4,* 617–626.

Keller, M. B., Herzog, D. B., Lavori, P. W., Bradburn, I. S., & Mahoney, E. M. (1992). The naturalistic history of bulimia nervosa: Extraordinarily high rates of chronicity, relapse, recurrence, and psychosocial morbidity. *International Journal of Eating Disorders, 12,* 1–9.

Kennedy, S. H. (1990). A multifaceted program for preventing and treating eating disorders. *Hospital and Community Psychiatry, 41,* 1120–1123.

Killen, J. D., Taylor, C. B., Hammer, L. D., Litt, I., Wilson, D. M., Rich, T., Hayward, C., Simmonds, B., Kraemer, H., & Varady, A. (1993). An attempt to modify unhealthful eating attitudes and weight regulation practices of young adolescent girls. *International Journal of Eating Disorders, 13,* 369–384.

Killen, J. D., Telch, M. J., Robinson, T. N., Maccoby, N., Taylor, C. B., & Farquhar, J. W. (1988). Cardiovascular disease risk reduction in tenth graders: A multiple-factor school-based approach. *Journal of the American Medical Association, 260,* 1728–1733.

Lawrence, M. (1984). Education and identity: Thoughts on the social origins of anorexia. *Women's Studies International Forum, 1,* 201–209.

Levine, M. P. (1987). *How schools can help combat student eating disorders: Anorexia nervosa and bulimia.* Washington, DC: National Education Association.

Levine, M. P., & Hill, L. (1991). *A 5-day lesson plan book on eating disorders: Grades 7–12.* Columbus, OH: National Anorexia Society of Harding Hospital.

Loeber, R. (1990). Development and risk factors of juvenile antisocial behavior and delinquency. *Clinical Psychology Review, 10,* 1–41.

Mazur, A. (1986). U.S. trends in feminine beauty and overadaptation. *Journal of Sex Research, 22,* 281–303.

McCarthy, M. (1990). The thin ideal, depression and eating disorders in women. *Behaviour Research and Therapy, 28,* 205–215.

McSherry, J. A. (1983). Anorexia nervosa: A preventable illness? *Journal of the Royal Society of Health, 103,* 207–209.

Miller, J. B. (1983). The necessity of conflict. In J. H. Robbins & R. J. Siegel (Eds.), *Women changing therapy* (pp. 3–9). New York: Haworth Press.

Miller, J. B. (1986). *Toward a new psychology of women* (2nd ed.). Boston: Beacon Press.

Miller, K. D. (1991). Body-image therapy. *Nursing Clinics of North America, 26,* 727–736.

Mitchell, J., & Eckert, E. (1987). Scope and significance of eating disorders. *Journal of Consulting and Clinical Psychology, 55,* 628–634.

Moriarty, D., Shore, R., & Maxim, N. (1990). Evaluation of an eating disorder curriculum. *Evaluation and Program Planning, 13,* 407–413.

Murdock, M. (1990). *The heroine's journey.* Boston: Shambala.

Murray, S., Touyz, S., & Beumont, P. (1990). Knowledge about eating disorders in the community. *International Journal of Eating Disorders, 9,* 87–93.

Nasser, M. (1988). Culture and weight consciousness. *Journal of Psychosomatic Research, 32,* 573–577.

Orbach, S. (1978). *Fat is a feminist issue.* New York: Berkeley Books.

Piran, N., Hill, L., & Maine, M. (1992, April). *Prevention programs and eating disorders: What works, what doesn't work, and what we should do next.* Workshop presented at the Fifth International Conference on Eating Disorders, New York.

Polivy, J., & Herman, C. P. (1983). *Breaking the diet habit.* New York: Basic Books.

Polivy, J., & Herman, C. P. (1992). Undieting: A program to help people stop dieting. *International Journal of Eating Disorders, 11,* 261–268.

Pratt, J. (1983). Junior high and high school. In P. Neuman & P. Halvorson

(Eds.), *Anorexia nervosa and bulimia: A handbook for counselors and therapists* (pp. 165–185). New York: Van Nostrand Reinhold.

Prince, R. (1985). The concept of culture-bound syndromes: Anorexia nervosa and brain-fag. *Social Science and Medicine, 21,* 197–203.

Schwartz, D. M., Thompson, M. G., & Johnson, C. L. (1982). Anorexia nervosa and bulimia: The socio-cultural context. *International Journal of Eating Disorders, 1,* 20–36.

Sesan, R. (1989a). Peer education: A creative resource for the eating disordered college student. In L. C. Whitaker & W. N. Davis (Eds.), *The bulimic college student: Evaluation, treatment and prevention* (pp. 221–240). New York: Haworth Press.

Sesan, R. (1989b). Eating disorders and female athletes: A three-level intervention program. *Journal of College Student Development, 30,* 568–570.

Shisslak, C. M., & Crago, M. (1992a). Cigarette smoking. In E. R. McAnarney, R. E. Kreipe, D. P. Orr, & G. D. Comerci (Eds.), *Textbook of adolescent medicine* (pp. 263–265). Philadelphia: W. B. Saunders.

Shisslak, C. M., & Crago, M. (1992b). Eating disorders among athletes. In R. Lemberg (Ed.), *Controlling eating disorders with facts, advice, and resources* (pp. 29–36). Phoenix, AZ: Oryx Press.

Shisslak, C. M., Crago, M., & Neal, M. E. (1990). Prevention of eating disorders among adolescents. *American Journal of Health Promotion, 5,* 100–106.

Shisslak, C. M., Crago, M., Neal, M. E., & Swain, B. (1987). Primary prevention of eating disorders. *Journal of Consulting and Clinical Psychology, 55,* 660–667.

Shisslak, C. M., & Nichter, M. (1992). *Teen lifestyle project intervention.* Unpublished data, University of Arizona.

Smead, V. (1985). Considerations prior to establishing preventive interventions for eating disorders. *Ontario Psychologist, 17,* 12–17.

Spretnak, C. (Ed.). (1981). *The politics of women's spirituality: Essays on the rise of spiritual power within the feminist movement.* Garden City, NY: Doubleday.

Steiger, H., Leichner, P., & Ghaadiria, A. (1987). Perspectives on the prevention of anorexia nervosa and bulimia. *Canadian Family Physician, 33,* 145–149.

Steiner-Adair, C. (1989). Developing the voice of the wise woman: College students and bulimia. In L. C. Whitaker & W. N. Davis (Eds.), *The bulimic college student: Evaluation, treatment and prevention* (pp. 151–166). New York: Haworth Press.

Stone, M. (1976). *When God was a woman.* New York: Dial Press.

Striegel-Moore, R. H., Silberstein, L. R., & Rodin, J. (1986). Toward an understanding of risk factors in bulimia. *American Psychologist, 41,* 246–263.

Striegel-Moore, R. H., Tucker, N., & Hsu, J. (1990). Body image dissatisfaction and disordered eating in lesbian college students. *International Journal of Eating Disorders, 9,* 493–500.

Szekely, E. (1988). *Never too thin.* Toronto: Women's Press.

Thelen, M. H., Powell, A. L., Lawrence, C., & Kuhnert, M. E. (1992). Eating and body image concerns among children. *Journal of Clinical Child Psychology, 21,* 41–46.

Timko, C., Striegel-Moore, R. H., Silberstein, L. R., & Rodin, J. (1987). Femininity/masculinity and disordered eating in women: How are they related? *International Journal of Eating Disorders, 6,* 701–712.

Vandereycken, W., & Meermann, R. (1984). Anorexia nervosa: Is prevention possible? *International Journal of Psychiatry in Medicine, 14,* 191–205.

Weiss, L., Katzman, M. K., & Wolchik, S. A. (1985). *Treating bulimia: A psychoeducational approach.* Elmsford, NY: Pergamon Press.

Wolf, N. (1991). *The beauty myth: How images of beauty are used against women.* New York: Morrow.

Yager, J. (1985). Afterword. In R. Hales & A. Frances (Eds.), *Psychiatry update* (Vol. 4, pp. 516–521). Washington, DC: American Psychiatric Press.

Young-Eisendrath, P., & Wiedemann, F.L. (1987). *Female authority: Empowering women through psychotherapy.* New York: Guilford Press.

22

A Feminist Agenda for Psychological Research on Eating Disorders

RUTH H. STRIEGEL-MOORE

If feminism is the answer, what are the questions?
—Michelle Wittig (1983)

THIS CHAPTER REPRESENTS an effort to explore what it means to bring a feminist perspective to the psychological research of eating disorders—an area about which there is considerable confusion. Gender, sexism, feminism, and the psychology of women are issues that are often conflated. Being female is neither a necessary nor a sufficient qualification for feminism or expertise in the psychology of women. Not all who study the psychology of women are feminists or utilize feminist research methods. Although underrepresentation of women scientists at conferences is a feminist issue, it does not necessarily mean that feminism as a point of view, or the psychology of women as a body of knowledge, is underrepresented. Nor would the inclusion of more women necessarily address omissions in these areas. As we, as a field, struggle with the issues of including women, increasing our understanding of female psychology, identifying the role of sexism in the development of eating disorders, and evaluating the value of an explicitly feminist stance, we must pay close attention to these distinctions. This chapter defines and advocates feminist scholarship and its relevance to eating disorders.

FEMINIST SCHOLARSHIP

The term "feminism" has been used to describe both an ideology and a political movement. Peplau and Conrad (1989) write:

> As an *ideology,* feminism emphasizes the goal of gender equality, recognizes the traditional oppression of women and their historical exclusion from public life, and values the experiences of women as important and appropriate topics for scholarly inquiry. As a *political movement,* feminism strives for social changes . . . to bring about gender equality in all facets of society. (p. 381, emphasis added)

Although there is a wide range of opinions among feminist psychologists regarding the question of how much political activism should be a part of their work, they would agree that all scientific pursuits have political implications.

Feminist scholarship takes many forms; however, several basic commonalities have been identified. In addition to the fundamental goal of analyzing gender relations, these are as follows: a recognition of bias as an inherent aspect of any human inquiry, a stance of self-conscious reflexivity, and an emphasis on context as an essential factor in understanding behavior (Morawski, 1990).

There is a paradox inherent in trying to be both a psychologist and a feminist. The paradox arises because psychology as a science is rooted in experimentalism, a paradigm that views science as objective, value-free, and in pursuit of universal truths. In contrast, feminists recognize all scientific efforts as inherently biased and context-bound. As Harding (1986) notes, some feminists resolve this paradox by calling for a "successor science"—that is, the creation of a totally new science that would replace traditional science. Alternatively, others remain committed to systematic empirical research while advocating the reshaping of conventional scientific practices to serve feminist goals. (For a more extensive discussion of feminist epistemology and research methods, see Alcoff, 1987; Harding, 1986, 1987a, 1987b, 1991; Hubbard, 1988; Longino, 1987; Morawski & Steele, 1991; Parlee, 1975; Riger, 1992; Vaughter, 1976; Unger, 1983.)

Feminist scholarship has gained increasing recognition in psychology; its influence is reflected in the growing acknowledgment of women psychologists' contributions (e.g., O'Connell & Russo, 1991; Russo & Denmark, 1987; Scarborough & Furumoto, 1987), and in the proliferation of literature critiquing psychology's sexist biases in theoretical models of women's development (e.g., Crawford & Marecek, 1989;

Miller, 1976) and challenging the validity of research methods used to study women (e.g., McHugh, Koeske, & Frieze, 1986; Parlee, 1979; Sherif, 1987; Wallston, 1981). Furthermore, because of this influence, research programs have been initiated or expanded that are devoted to investigating experiences or problems that are particularly relevant to women. One such domain is, of course, eating disorders. Finally, the products of these scholarly efforts have been recognized through publication in prestigious and widely read psychology and psychiatry journals such as *American Psychologist* and *Psychological Bulletin* (e.g., Carlson, 1972; Cushman, 1990; Deaux & Major, 1987; Eagly, 1978; Eagly & Crowley, 1986; Eagly & Steffen, 1986; Hare-Mustin & Marecek, 1988; Hyde, 1986; Lerner, 1983; Lott, 1985; Marecek & Kravetz, 1977; Mednick, 1989; McHugh et al., 1986; Shields, 1975; Striegel-Moore, Silberstein, & Rodin, 1986; Unger, 1979; Worell, 1978).

EMERGENT FEMINIST RESEARCH CRITERIA

What, then, does it mean to apply a feminist perspective to research? Building on the very general common denominators of feminist scholarship described above, Michelle Fine (1985) and Judith Worell (in press) have each suggested more specific ways in which the feminist paradigm can be recognized in scholarly efforts. From her perspective as the editor of a feminist research journal, *Psychology of Women Quarterly,* Worell (in press) describes a set of emergent research criteria for evaluating a research project (see Table 22.1). In keeping with the "empiricist feminist" framework, these criteria are seen as *additions to* rather than *substitutes for* traditional standards of investigation. They are considered "emergent" because more criteria may be identified as we continue to struggle with the question of what it means to conduct feminist research. The four criteria to be considered in this chapter are as follows: affirmation of a positive view of women; adoption of a "contextual" approach; utilization of a broad spectrum of research methods; and consideration of the implications of research findings for social change. I discuss each one in turn, delineating ways to expand upon existing research or introduce new research efforts to meet the challenges each criterion represents, and considering how both might apply to the field of eating disorders.

Affirmation of a Positive View of Women

Affirmation of a positive view of women encompasses and goes beyond avoiding the use of negatively laden terms. It includes making a serious effort to "hear women's voices" and to study the entire range of experi-

TABLE 22.1. Emergent Feminist Research Criteria

1. Affirms a positive view of women
   a. Challenges traditional views of women; presents women in a range of roles
   b. Describes female experiences and female characteristics in nonderogatory terms
   c. Challenges the "deficit" model
   d. Includes a focus on women's strengths and contributions
2. Takes a "contextual" approach
   a. Studies the experiences of diverse groups of women
   b. Studies women's experience in natural settings
   c. Examines women's experience in the context of power imbalance and gender-related expectations
   d. Includes units of analysis larger than the individual
3. Utilizes a broad spectrum of research methods
   a. Expands the boundaries of accepted methodology to explore experiences
   b. Establishes a collaborative relationship with research participants
4. Considers the implications of research findings for social change
   a. Analyzes political, economic, and social conditions and how they influence women's experience
   b. Provides interpretations of findings that advance social change, rather than proposing solely individually based change strategies to mitigate gender inequalities

Note. Adapted from Worell (in press). Copyright by University of South Florida Press. Adapted by permission.

ences relevant to women's lives. This, at the most basic level, means studying girls or women *at all.* There is a lack of research on adolescent girls compared to research on adult women. Even though eating disorders develop during adolescence, the majority of empirical studies have focused on adult women. For example, of 199 studies on eating disorders published in 1988 and 1989 in the *International Journal of Eating Disorders,* only 14, or 7%, involved participants under the age of 18 years.

Eating disorders challenge us to gain an understanding of what it means to be female in this society at this time. To address this question, we need to take developmental issues into consideration. From our clinical work, we know that for patients of different ages, different factors contribute to the development and maintenance of the disorders (see, e.g., Bruch, 1985). This common-sense observation has received empirical support from Brooks-Gunn and her research team (e.g., Attie & Brooks-Gunn, 1989), who apply a developmental psychopathology perspective to the understanding of eating disorders (see also Gralen, Levine, Smolak, & Murnen, 1990).

The feminist challenge is not limited to studying previously unresearched or underresearched populations. Affirmation of a positive view of women also demands that serious attention be given to uncharted or insufficiently studied topics. Common themes in feminist theories of eating disorders, or in case reports written by feminists, include the mother–daughter relationship, competition between women, power imbalances between men and women (including the abusive consequences of incest and rape), and women's yearning to be nurtured by others, to name but a few (e.g., Boskind-Lodahl, 1976; Orbach, 1978, 1986; Chernin, 1981, 1985; Brown, 1985; Steiner-Adair, 1986; Root & Fallon, 1989; Wooley, Wooley, & Dyrenforth, 1979; Eichenbaum & Orbach, 1989).

In the area of body image research, for example, I believe that we need to go beyond the well-known facts that girls learn early the importance of beauty and thinness and that most women are dissatisfied with their weight and try to lose weight, thereby putting themselves at risk for disregulated eating (Rodin, Silberstein, & Striegel-Moore, 1985). We need to learn about the deeper psychological meanings of the female body and its shape. We need to go beyond the study of the body as an object of aesthetic evaluation by self and others, and to include bodily experiences arising from sexuality and reproductive functioning (e.g., see Tolman & Debold, Chapter 15, this volume). For example, is the trend toward engaging in sexual behaviors at an increasingly younger age somehow related to the increase in eating disorders? Based on clinical evidence, Crisp (1980) described anorexia nervosa as motivated in part by a fear of mature sexuality. Research by Beumont and his colleagues (Abraham & Beumont, 1982; Beumont, Abraham, & Simson, 1981) and by Leon and her colleagues (Leon, Lucas, Colligan, Ferdinande, & Kamp, 1985; Leon, Lucas, Ferdinande, Mangelsdorf, & Colligan, 1987) found that eating-disordered women experienced sexual difficulties such as lack of enjoyment of sexual activities. Since the publication of these early studies of female sexuality, the eating disorders literature has been almost silent on this important aspect of female experience. Whether anorexic or bulimic women's sexual problems are attributable primarily to poor body image, or whether they reflect other difficulties (e.g., fear of intimacy, moral conflict, or history of sexual abuse), deserves further exploration.

Another almost completely ignored female experience is that of pregnancy and motherhood. For example, how does fear of pregnancy figure into the development of body image disturbances or eating disorders? I believe that many young women, rather than fearing oral impregnation (as some psychoanalysts still argue), fear pregnancy and motherhood for their negative consequences—ranging from loss of control over one's body to loss of control over one's life. The few studies of the relationship between pregnancy and eating disorders have dealt with the more narrow question of how a pregnancy exacerbates or ameliorates symptoms of disordered eating (Brinch, Isager, & Tolstrup, 1988; Fahy & O'Donoghue, 1991; Lemberg & Phillips, 1989). The meanings of pregnancy and motherhood for female identity remain unexplored.

In my clinical work during my own pregnancies, I have been impressed with the range of emotions and expectations that patients have expressed. These varied from stunned disbelief that anyone would "let herself get fat" to profound envy that, while pregnant, the therapist is never alone and thus in a blissful state of relatedness. Katzman (Chapter 7, this volume) provides a comprehensive discussion of the wide array of issues that arise in response to a therapist's pregnancy. Her descriptions of eating-disordered clients' reactions to their therapist's pregnancy further support the need for a better understanding of the meaning of pregnancy to anorexic or bulimic women. Beyond investigation of these issues in eating-disordered women, we need to explore more thoroughly how the role of mother is constructed in our society and what symbolic meanings are expressed when legions of girls aspire to a body ideal that renders fertility unlikely.

Another topic central to understanding eating disorders is the impact of physical and/or sexual abuse on women's relationships to their bodies. The eating disorders field has been slow to investigate reports of disproportionately high rates of childhood sexual abuse in women suffering from eating disorders (e.g., Beckman & Burns, 1990; Kearney-Cooke, 1988; Oppenheimer, Howells, Palmer, & Chaloner, 1985; Root & Fallon, 1988, 1989; Steiner-Adair, 1992; see also S. C. Wooley, Chapter 9, this volume). Evidence is mounting that incest and other forms of childhood sexual abuse have profound and lasting negative effects on adult physical adjustment (e.g., Bifulco, Brown, & Adler, 1991). Root (1991) has conceptualized persistent disordered eating as a "gender-specific, post-traumatic stress response to sexual assault" (p. 100). A detailed description of the specific links between sexual abuse and symptoms of eating disorders has been offered by Root and Fallon (1989).

Given the unique problems inherent in trying to establish prevalence rates of sexual abuse, such as amnesia for the abusive events in some victims, perhaps the question of whether sexual abuse is a *specific* factor for the development of eating disorders can never be answered fully (for a more extensive discussion of methodological challenges, see Briere, 1992). However, sexual abuse undoubtedly has lasting effects on a woman's body image and her sense of self (Hall, Tice, Beresford, Wooley, & Hall, 1989; McClelland, Mynors-Wallis, Fahy, & Treasure, 1991; Sheldrick, 1991; Smolak, Levine, & Sullins, 1990). Ignoring sexual abuse interferes with the development of effective treatment strategies, and thus carries the risk of further victimization in the form of ineffective or inappropriate therapeutic interventions.

In sum, I believe that we need to move away from reductionist research efforts, such as experiments designed to develop the most accurate apparatus to measure body size distortion. Instead, we should focus our energies on exploring more fully how girls and women experience their bodies, and how this in turn affects female identity.

Taking a "Contextual" Approach

In gender research, two lines of inquiry into what constitutes gender differences have been intensely pursued (Hare-Mustin & Marecek, 1990). One line, referred to as "alpha bias," emphasizes gender differences by representing them as essential, universal, and enduring. The second line of gender research, a stance referred to as "beta bias," minimizes gender differences (e.g., Maccoby & Jacklin, 1974).

An advantage of the alpha bias and its exaggeration of differences is that it has allowed some theorists to assert the worth of certain "feminine" qualities, such as relatedness, and to question the worth of certain "masculine" qualities, such as self-interest and individualism (e.g., Gilligan, 1982). A potential cost of the alpha bias is ignoring the power inequities that have led to the observed gender differences. For example, research has shown that many well-established differences between men and women result from power differences, rather than from "male" versus "female" nature (Deaux & Major, 1987). Another cost is the disregard of within-group differences, such as differences among women of different racial or ethnic backgrounds, age, class, marital status, and sexual preference.

Most studies on eating disorders have involved white women (Dolan, 1991). Even when women of color are included in a study, they are often rendered invisible by poorly specified descriptions of the ethnic/racial composition of the study sample. For example, only 16% of all papers published in the *International Journal of Eating Disorders* (1988–1989) explicitly described the race or ethnicity of their samples. Even fewer (8%) provided information on social class. No study referred to sexual orientation as a potentially relevant variable. This problem is, of course, not unique to the *International Journal of Eating Disorders*. The annual report of *Psychology of Women Quarterly* indicates that in 67% of the papers submitted for review during 1991, ethnicity of the sample was not specified (Worell, 1991). To improve our understanding and treatment of eating disorders, studies are needed that include more heterogeneous samples and describe them in greater detail (see also Shaw &

Garfinkel, 1990). Lastly, the predictive value of demographic information should be studied, as exemplified in a study on race and treatment outcome (Hiebert, Felice, Wingard, Munoz, & Ferguson, 1988).

There have been significant gains from the beta bias, which has been used to justify greater access to educational and occupational opportunities for women. On the other hand, this perspective can detract attention from women's special needs, as well as from differences in power and resources between men and women. In family therapy, for example, "equal treatment" may overlook structural inequality between husband and wife (Fallon, 1990). This bias is also reflected in the high value placed on autonomy, assertiveness, and related personality traits. Efforts to increase a woman's autonomy or to improve her assertiveness are often initiated without acknowledgment of the gender-related differences in the social meaning and interpersonal consequences of assertive behavior. Autonomy may have a different meaning for, and thus may be experienced differently by, men and women. To many women, autonomy connotes loneliness—an emotional experience to be avoided (Gilligan, 1982). Furthermore, women's behavioral expressions of autonomy may meet with social disapproval and sanctions, whereas men are typically rewarded for autonomy.

Taking a "contextual" approach is, of course, a mandate voiced not only by feminist researchers. Psychology has long been criticized for being acontextual and ahistorical (for a review, see Cushman, 1990; see also Mishler, 1979; Morawski, 1986), and several respected research traditions in psychology study individuals in context (e.g., Moos, 1979). Despite evidence for the role of cultural factors in the development of eating disorders (Bordo, 1990; Brumberg, 1988), the unit of analysis in eating disorders research remains the individual. Studying larger units poses enormous methodological challenges—perhaps one reason why eating disorders research has not yet progressed very far on this issue. One promising study of the influence of contextual factors in the development of eating disorders was reported by Crandall (1988). His study of social groups on a university campus supports "the social contagion" of dieting and bingeing behaviors among college students. Primary prevention programs in which larger social systems (e.g., schools, university campuses), not individuals, are targets of intervention (e.g., Shisslak & Crago, Chapter 21, this volume) are sorely needed. In defense of eating disorder research, I want to point out that it is notoriously difficult to obtain research funding for such efforts. For instance, according to National Institutes of Health records for fiscal year 1990, none of the more than $2 million spent on eating disorders was allocated for prevention research.

Utilization of a Broad Spectrum of Research Methods

Although some feminist psychologists have proposed the wholesale rejection of quantitative data and have declared certain research methods such as experimentation incompatible with feminism (Graham & Rawlings, 1980; Mies, 1983), others have argued convincingly that all methods can be feminist methods (Peplau & Conrad, 1989). There is, however, an overreliance in psychology on "agentic" methods and an underutilization of "communal" methods used in scientific fields such as anthropology and astronomy. Agentic methods involve "separating, ordering, quantifying, manipulating [and] controlling," whereas communal methods involve "naturalistic observation, sensitivity to intrinsic structure and qualitative patterning of phenomena studied, and greater participation of the investigator" (Carlson, 1972, p. 20). As any textbook on methodology will point out, the potential costs of using a limited range of methods are diminished ecological validity and a narrowing of our vision. Methods determine to an extent the kinds of questions we can ask, and they limit the kinds of answers we may find.

"Feminist scholarship," according to Lott (1985), "rejects no careful, rigorous, intersubjective reputable method of inquiry" (p. 158). However, the simple assertion that all methods are potentially acceptable does not mean that we can settle back comfortably into business as usual. Rather, we need to take seriously the challenge to expand our repertoire of methods. Many of the early landmark research papers on eating disorders were based on *interview* data (see, e.g., Mitchell, Hatsukami, Eckert, & Pyle, 1985; Russell, 1979). Then, for a while, interviews played a very minor role in eating disorders research. I believe that the Eating Disorder Examination (Fairburn & Cooper, in press) represents a significant advance in research methodology. The interpersonal nature of the interview method permits a more collaborative relationship with the research participants, and facilitates exploration of the subjective meaning of the phenomena under investigation.

Considering the Implications of Research Findings for Social Change

To illustrate the importance of considering the implications of research for social change, I focus on treatment outcome studies. Fairburn (1990) has distinguished three different perspectives for interpreting the results of a controlled treatment study: the "clinical scientist perspectives," the "health care delivery perspective," and the "patient perspective." Interpretation of treatment outcome studies has far-reaching implications;

it informs decisions about the funding of subsequent research and about mental health policy and treatment practices. The clinical scientist perspective runs the risk of relying too heavily on quantitative methods without consideration of the context in which treatment is administered. Hence, a treatment that proves to be highly successful in a tightly controlled setting may prove unsuccessful in daily clinical practice. The health care delivery perspective emphasizes questions of cost-effectiveness and may ignore the individual client's needs. Not enough attention has been paid to the personal costs treatment failure may represent to a patient who is told that she is receiving an effective treatment, yet experiences no symptom relief. Having participated in unsuccessful treatment may mean more than not having improved; burdened with the experience of having tried but failed, the patient may be left to feel guilty and hopeless. Finally, the individual patient perspective suggests that we need to expand the design and methods of controlled treatment trials in order to include an assessment of prognostic factors; to study contextual variables that facilitate or impede treatment progress; and to study carefully the patient's experiences of the treatment. What types of interventions are acceptable to patients? Why are the dropout rates high for some treatments but not others? To what factors do patients attribute their treatment successes or failures? None of these three perspectives is inherently more scientific than the other two. Rather, each represents a particular bias, and the feminist challenge is to be honest with oneself and others about the vantage point one chooses.

RESISTANCES TO FEMINIST SCHOLARSHIP

The scholarly accomplishments of feminist researchers and the prominent display of their efforts in major scientific journals may lead us to assume that the feminist perspective has been well integrated into the various fields of psychology. However, studies examining the impact of feminism on psychological research suggest only modest effects (e.g., Fine, 1985; Fine & Gordon, 1989; Lykes & Stewart, 1986; Walsh, 1989). As is true for any work that challenges established scientific paradigms, most feminist papers are published in specialty journals—in this case, journals devoted to the dissemination of feminist scholarship. Some of these journals are well established, such as *Signs;* others are fairly new and not as well known, such as *Gender* or *Differences.* Some, such as *Signs,* are interdisciplinary, whereas others, such as *Psychology of Women Quarterly* or *Feminism and Psychology,* are directed primarily at psychologists. Feminist journals are read primarily by feminists, and they are likely to be unknown to or ignored by researchers in the "majority stance" or "mainstream stance." Lykes and Stewart (1986) have described the influence of feminism on social psychology as a "one-way street": Feminist researchers are familiar with both the mainstream literature and the feminist literature, whereas mainstream researchers read and cite only research published in mainstream journals.

The tremendously skewed gender distribution among contributors to feminist journals contributes further to this process of separation by domains of knowledge. For example, 88% of the articles submitted for review to *Psychology of Women Quarterly* in 1991 had a female first author, compared to 6% male first authors (and 6% first authors of unspecified sex) (Worell, 1991). Given the continued negative stereotype that women are "less scientific," the fact that most feminist scholars are female perpetuates the view that feminist scholarship is not scientifically rigorous.

When publishing in feminist journals, feminist researchers place themselves at a distinct disadvantage. Their papers are less likely to be read and cited by mainstream researchers; hence, their work has less impact on the field. Many academic departments consider feminist journals less prestigious than mainstream journals. As a result, work published in feminist journals is seen as less valuable—a stereotype that has a deleterious impact on decisions concerning research funding or tenure. Feminists face likely rejection of their work in mainstream journals, whereas they risk invisibility to mainstream researchers when publishing their research in feminist journals.

The continued resistance to feminist scholarship represents a significant source of work stress for feminist researchers. Many of my colleagues have described the powerful "pull" they feel toward clinical work, in order to escape the strain of doing research within a marginalized perspective. The withdrawal from research into the seemingly less "political" sphere of clinical practice is often experienced with a great personal sense of relief: Clinical practice permits a palpable sense of accomplishment that seems far less attainable in research activities. However, such a withdrawal represents a great loss to the field.

CONCLUSION

The feminist perspective mandates investigation of individuals and groups in their historical and cultural context, and encourages development of innovative research methods suitable for the aim of capturing the experiences of diverse populations. It permits us to generate previously neglected but potentially significant variables. Finally, it offers a language for thinking more clearly and constructively about the inherently political nature of research. These opportunities warrant attention to the feminist perspective, and a sensitivity to the ways in which it is resisted.

ACKNOWLEDGMENTS

An earlier draft of this chapter was presented at the International Conference on Eating Disorders. I am indebted to the many conference participants who continue to voice their concerns about adequate representation of women researchers and clinicians at the conference, and who insist upon including a feminist vision in conference presentations. "Popular demand" can make a difference. I am grateful to Jill Morawski for her feedback on this chapter. My thanks to Catherine Steiner-Adair, who continues courageously to accept what at times seem to be impossible challenges, and who, by her example, empowers others to find and use their own voices. With appreciation, I acknowledge Michael Neale's enthusiastic support of and constructive comments about this chapter.

REFERENCES

Abraham, S. F., & Beumont, P. J. (1982). How patients describe bulimia or binge eating. *Psychological Medicine, 12,* 625–635.

Alcoff, L. (1987). Justifying feminist social science. *Hypatia, 2,* 86–103.

Attie, I., & Brooks-Gunn, J. (1989). Development of eating problems in adolescent girls: A longitudinal study. *Developmental Psychology, 25,* 70–79.

Beckman, K. A., & Burns, G. L. (1990). Relation of sexual abuse and bulimia in college women. *International Journal of Eating Disorders, 9,* 487–492.

Bifulco, A., Brown, G. W., & Adler, Z. (1991). Early sexual abuse and clinical depression in adult life. *British Journal of Psychiatry, 159,* 115–122.

Bordo, S. (1990). Reading the slender body. In M. Jacobs, E. F. Keller, & S. Shuttleworth (Eds.), *Body politics: Women and the discourse of science* (pp. 83–112). New York: Routledge.

Boskind-Lodahl, M. (1976). Cinderella's stepsisters: A feminist perspective on anorexia nervosa and bulimia. *Signs: Journal of Women in Culture and Society, 2,* 342–356.

Briere, J. (1992). Methodological issues in the study of sexual abuse effects. *Journal of Consulting and Clinical Psychology, 60,* 196–203.

Brinch, M., Isager, T., & Tolstrup, K. (1988). Anorexia nervosa and motherhood: Reproduction pattern and mothering behavior of 50 women. *Acta Psychiatrica Scandinavica, 77,* 611–617.

Brown, L. S. (1985). Women, weight, and power: Feminist theoretical and therapeutic issues. *Women and Therapy, 4,* 61–72.

Bruch, H. (1985). Four decades of eating disorders. In D. M. Garner & P. E. Garfinkel (Eds.), *Handbook of psychotherapy for anorexia nervosa and bulimia* (pp. 7–18). New York: Guilford Press.

Brumberg, J. J. (1988). *Fasting girls.* Cambridge, MA: Harvard University Press.

Beumont, P. J., Abraham, S. F., & Simson, K. G. (1981). Psychosexual histories of adolescent girls and young women with anorexia nervosa. *Psychological Medicine, 11,* 131–140.

Carlson, R. (1972). Understanding women: Implications for personality theory and research. *Journal of Social Issues, 28,* 17–32.

Chernin, K. (1981). *The obsession: Reflections on the tyranny of slenderness.* New York: Harper & Row.

Chernin, K. (1985). *The hungry self: Women, eating and identity.* New York: Times Books.

Crandall, C. (1988). Social contagion of binge eating. *Journal of Personality and Social Psychology, 55,* 588–598.

Crawford, M., & Marecek, J. (1989). Psychology reconstructs the female. *Psychology of Women Quarterly, 13,* 147–165.

Crisp, A. H. (1980). *Anorexia nervosa: Let me be.* London: Academic Press.

Cushman, P. (1990). Why the self is empty: Toward a historically situated psychology. *American Psychologist, 45,* 599–611.

Deaux, K., & Major, B. (1987). Putting gender into context: An interactive model of gender-related behavior. *Psychological Review, 94,* 369–389.

Dolan, B. (1991). Cross-cultural aspects of anorexia nervosa and bulimia: A review. *International Journal of Eating Disorders, 10,* 67–80.

Eagly, A. H. (1978). Sex differences in influenceability. *Psychological Bulletin, 85,* 86–116.

Eagly, A. H., & Crowley, M. (1986). Gender and helping behavior: A meta-analytic review of the social psychological literature. *Psychological Bulletin, 100,* 283–308.

Eagly, A. H., & Steffen, V. J. (1986). Gender and aggressive behavior: A meta-analytic review of the social psychological literature. *Psychological Bulletin, 100,* 309–330.

Eichenbaum, L., & Orbach, S. (1988). *Between women: Love, envy and competition in women's friendships.* New York: Viking.

Fahy, T. A., & O'Donoghue, G. (1991). Eating disorders in pregnancy. *Psychological Medicine, 21,* 577–580.

Fairburn, C. (1990, April). *Treatment outcome studies.* Paper presented at the Fourth International Conference on Eating Disorders, New York.

Fairburn, C. G., & Cooper, Z. (in press). The Eating Disorder Examination. In C. G. Fairburn and Z. Cooper (Eds.), *Binge eating: Nature, assessment, and treatment.* New York: Guilford Press.

Fallon, P. (1990, April). *Psychology of women and the treatment of eating disorders.* Paper presented at the Fourth International Conference on Eating Disorders, New York.

Fine, M. (1985). Reflections on a feminist psychology of women: Paradoxes and prospects. *Psychology of Women Quarterly, 9,* 167–183.

Fine, M., & Gordon, S. M. (1989). Feminist transformations of/despite psychology. In M. Crawford & M. Gentry (Eds.), *Gender and thought: Psychological perspectives* (pp. 146–174). New York: Springer.

Gilligan, C. A. (1982). *In a different voice: Psychological theory and women's development.* Cambridge, MA: Harvard University Press.

Graham, D. L. R., & Rawlings, E. J. (1980). *Feminist research methodology: Comparisons, guidelines, and ethics.* Paper presented at the annual meeting of the American Psychological Association, Montreal.

Gralen, S. J., Levine, M. P., Smolak, L., & Murnen, S. K. (1990). Dieting and disordered eating during early and middle adolescence: Do the influences remain the same? *International Journal of Eating Disorders, 9,* 501–512.

Hall, R. C. W., Tice, L., Beresford, T., Wooley, B., & Hall, A. K. (1989). Sexual abuse in patients with anorexia nervosa and bulimia. *Psychosomatics, 30,* 73–79.

Harding, S. (1986). *The science question in feminism.* Ithaca, NY: Cornell University Press.

Harding, S. (1987a). Is there a feminist method? *Hypatia, 2,* 17–32.

Harding, S. (Ed.). (1987b). *Feminism and methodology: Social sciences issues.* Bloomington: Indiana University Press.

Harding, S. (1991). *Whose science? Whose knowledge?: Thinking from women's lives.* Ithaca, NY: Cornell University Press.

Hare-Mustin, R. T., & Marecek, J. (1988). The meaning of difference: Gender theory, postmodernism, and psychology. *American Psychologist, 43,* 455–464.

Hare-Mustin, R. T., & Marecek, J. (1990). Gender and the meaning of difference: Postmodernism and psychology. In R. T. Hare-Mustin & J. Marecek (Eds.), *Making a difference* (pp. 22–64). New Haven, CT: Yale University Press.

Hiebert, K. A., Felice, M. E., Wingard, D. L., Munoz, R., & Ferguson, J. M. (1988). Comparison of outcome in Hispanic and Caucasian patients with anorexia nervosa. *International Journal of Eating Disorders, 7,* 693–696.

Hubbard, R. (1988). Science, facts, and feminism. *Hypatia, 3,* 119–131.

Hyde, J. S. (1986). How large are cognitive gender differences? *American Psychologist, 36,* 892–901.

Kearney-Cooke, A. (1988). Group treatment of sexual abuse among women with eating disorders. *Women and Therapy, 7,* 5–21.

Lemberg, R., & Phillips, J. (1989). The impact of pregnancy on anorexia nervosa and bulimia. *International Journal of Eating Disorders, 8,* 285–295.

Leon, G. R., Lucas, A. R., Colligan, R. C., Ferdinande, R. J., & Kamp, J. (1985). Sexual, body-image, and personality attitudes in anorexia nervosa. *Journal of Abnormal Child Psychology, 13,* 245–258.

Leon, G. R., Lucas, A. R., Ferdinande, R. F., Mangelsdorf, C., & Colligan, R. C. (1987). Attitudes about sexuality and other psychological characteristics as predictors of follow-up status in anorexia nervosa. *International Journal of Eating Disorders, 6,* 477–484.

Lerner, H. E. (1983). Female dependency in context: Some theoretical and technical considerations. *American Journal of Orthopsychiatry, 53,* 697–705.

Longino, H. E. (1987). Can there be a feminist science? *Hypatia, 2,* 45–57.

Lott, B. (1985). The potential enrichment of social/personality psychology through feminist research and vice versa. *American Psychologist, 40,* 155–164.

Lykes, M., & Stewart, A. (1986). Evaluating the feminist challenge to research in personality and social psychology. *Psychology of Women Quarterly, 10,* 393–411.

Maccoby, E. E., & Jacklin, C. N. (1974). *The psychology of sex differences.* Stanford, CA: Stanford University Press.

Marecek, J., & Kravetz, D. F. (1977). Women and mental health: A review of feminist change efforts. *Psychiatry, 40,* 323–329.

McClelland, L., Mynors-Wallis, L., Fahy, T., & Treasure, J. (1991). Sexual abuse, disordered personality, and eating disorders. *British Journal of Psychiatry, 158*(Suppl. 10), 63–68.

McHugh, M., Koeske, R., & Frieze, I. H. (1986). Issues to consider in conducting nonsexist psychological research. *American Psychologist, 41,* 879–890.

Mednick, M. T. (1989). On the politics of psychological constructs: Stop the band wagon, I want to get off. *American Psychologist, 44,* 1118–1123.

Mies, M. (1983). Toward a methodology for feminist research. In G. Bowles & R. D. Klein (Eds.), *Theories of women's studies* (pp. 117–139). Boston: Routledge & Kegan Paul.

Miller, J. B. (1976). *Toward a new psychology of women.* Boston: Beacon Press.

Mishler, E. (1979). Meaning in context: Is there any other kind? *Harvard Educational Review, 49,* 1–19.

Mitchell, J. E., Hatsukami, D., Eckert, E. D., & Pyle, R. L. (1985). Characteristics of 275 patients with bulimia. *American Journal of Psychiatry, 142,* 482–485.

Moos, R. (1979). *Evaluating educational environments: Procedures, measures, findings, and policy implications.* San Francisco: Jossey-Bass.

Morawski, J. G. (1986). Contextual discipline: The unmaking and remaking of sociality. In R. Rosnow and M. Georgoudi (Eds.), *Contextualism and understanding in behavioral science* (pp. 47–66). New York: Praeger.

Morawski, J. G. (1990). Toward the unimagined: Feminism and epistemology in psychology. In R. T. Hare-Mustin & J. Marecek (Eds.), *Making a difference* (pp. 150–183). New Haven, CT: Yale University Press.

Morawski, J. G., & Steele, R. S. (1991). The one or the other? Textual analysis of masculine power and feminist empowerment. *Theory and Psychology, 1,* 107–131.

National Institutes of Health. (1990). [Complete listing of research grants funded by the National Institutes of Health from 1986–1990]. Unpublished raw data.

O'Connell, A. N., & Russo, N. F. (Eds.). (1991). Women's heritage in psychology: Origins, development, and future directions [Special issue]. *Psychology of Women Quarterly, 15.*

Oppenheimer, R., Howells, K., Palmer, R. L., & Chaloner, D. A. (1985). Adverse sexual experience in childhood and clinical eating disorders: A preliminary description. *Journal of Psychiatric Research, 19,* 357–361.

Orbach, S. (1978). *Fat is a feminist issue.* New York: Berkeley Books.

Orbach, S. (1986). *Hunger strike: The anorectic's struggle as a metaphor of our age.* New York: Norton.

Parlee, M. B. (1975). Review essay: Psychology. *Signs: Journal of Women in Culture and Society, 1,* 119–138.

Parlee, M. B. (1979). Psychology and women. *Signs: Journal of Women in Culture and Society, 5,* 121–133.

Peplau, L. A., & Conrad, E. (1989). Beyond nonsexist research: The perils of feminist methods in psychology. *Psychology of Women Quarterly, 13,* 379–400.

Riger, S. (1992). Epistemological debates, feminist voices. *American Psychologist, 47,* 730–740.

Rodin, J., Silberstein, L. R., & Striegel-Moore, R. M. (1985). Women and Weight: A mormative discontent. In T. B. Sonderegger (Ed.), *Nebraska Symposium on Motivation: Vol. 32. Psychology and gender* (pp. 267–308). Lincoln: University of Nebraska Press.

Root, M. P. P. (1991). Persistent, disordered eating as a gender-specific, post-traumatic stress response to sexual assault. *Psychotherapy: Theory, Research, and Practice, 28,* 96–102.

Root, M. P. P., & Fallon, P. (1988). The incidence of victimization experiences in a bulimic sample. *Journal of Interpersonal Violence, 3,* 161–173.

Root, M. P. P., & Fallon, P. (1989). Treating the victimized bulimic. *Journal of Interpersonal Violence, 4,* 90–100.

Russell, G. (1979). Bulimia nervosa: An ominous variant of anorexia nervosa. *Psychological Medicine, 9,* 429–448.

Russo, N. F., & Denmark, F. L. (1987). Contributions of women to psychology. *Annual Review of Psychology, 38,* 279–298.

Scarborough, E., & Furumoto, L. (1987). *Untold lives: The first generation of women psychologists.* New York: Columbia University Press.

Shaw, B. F., & Garfinkel, P. E. (1990). Research problems in the eating disorders. *International Journal of Eating Disorders, 9,* 545–557.

Sheldrick, C. (1991). Adult sequelae of child sexual abuse. *British Journal of Psychiatry, 158*(Suppl. 10), 55–62.

Sherif, C. W. (1987). Bias in psychology. In S. Harding (Ed.), *Feminism and methodology: Social science issues* (pp. 37–56). Bloomington: Indiana University Press.

Shields, S. A. (1975). Functionalism, Darwinism, and the psychology of women: A study in social myth. *American Psychologist, 30,* 739–754.

Smolak, L., Levine, M., & Sullins, E. (1990). Are child sexual experiences related to eating-disordered attitudes and behaviors in a college sample? *International Journal of Eating Disorders, 9,* 167–178.

Steiner-Adair, K. (1986). The body politic: Normal female adolescent development and the development of eating disorders. *Journal of the American Academy of Psychoanalysis, 14,* 95–114.

Steiner-Adair, K. (1992, April). *Treating the difficult client: Discussion and critique of a case presentation.* Paper presented at the Fifth International Conference on Eating Disorders, New York.

Striegel-Moore, R. H., Silberstein, L. R., & Rodin, J. (1986). Toward an understanding of risk factors for bulimia. *American Psychologist, 41,* 246–263.

Unger, R. K. (1979). Toward a redefinition of sex and gender. *American Psychologist, 34,* 1085–1094.

Unger, R. K. (1983). Through the looking glass: No wonderland yet! *Psychology of Women Quarterly, 8,* 9–32.

Vaughter, R. M. (1976). Psychology. *Signs: Journal of Women in Culture and Society, 2,* 1–23.

Wallston, B. (1981). What are the questions in psychology of women: A feminist approach to research. *Psychology of Women Quarterly, 5*(4), 597–617.

Walsh, R. T. (1989). Do research reports in mainstream feminist psychology journals reflect feminist value? *Psychology of Women Quarterly, 13,* 433–444.

Wittig, M. A. (1985). Metatheoretical dilemmas in the psychology of gender. *American Psychologist, 40,* 800–811.

Wooley, O. W., Wooley, S. C., & Dyrenforth, S. R. (1979). Obesity and women, II: A neglected feminist topic? *Women's Studies International Quarterly, 2,* 81–89.

Worell, J. (1978). Sex roles and psychological well-being: Perspectives on methodology. *Journal of Consulting and Clinical Psychology, 46,* 777–791.

Worell, J. (1991). Psychology of Women Quarterly: *1991 Annual Report to the executive committee of Division 35, American Psychological Association.* Unpublished manuscript.

Worell, J. (in press). Feminist journals: Academic empowerment or professional liability? In S. M. Deats and L. T. Lanker (Eds.), *Gender in academe: The future of our past.* Lanham, MD: University Press of America.

Index